THE SIR JOSEPH BANKS MEMORIAL

THE *ENDEAVOUR* JOURNAL
OF JOSEPH BANKS

IN TWO VOLUMES
VOLUME I

JOSEPH BANKS

from the painting by Sir Joshua Reynolds

THE *ENDEAVOUR* JOURNAL

OF

Joseph Banks

1768-1771

EDITED BY

J. C. BEAGLEHOLE

VOLUME I

THE TRUSTEES OF
THE PUBLIC LIBRARY OF NEW SOUTH WALES
IN ASSOCIATION WITH ANGUS AND ROBERTSON

First published in 1962

ANGUS & ROBERTSON LTD

89 Castlereagh Street, Sydney
54-58 Bartholomew Close, London
66 Elizabeth Street, Melbourne
168 Willis Street, Wellington

Set in Monotype Baskerville 11 point
Text printed on Burnie Mill Antique Wove
Illustrations printed by
L. Van Leer and Co., N.V., Amsterdam

PRINTED IN AUSTRALIA BY HALSTEAD PRESS, SYDNEY

FOREWORD

THE SIR JOSEPH BANKS MEMORIAL

THIS book is published by the Trustees of the Public Library of New South Wales as the first part of the State's memorial to Sir Joseph Banks. It contains the journal of the voyage with Captain James Cook in the *Endeavour*, which in April 1770 brought Banks to the eastern shores of Australia.

The Sir Joseph Banks Memorial had its origin in a public meeting held in Sydney on 25th May 1905, under the inspiration of J. H. Maiden, F.R.S. (1859-1925), one of Australia's foremost botanists. The appointment of an executive committee of ten with Sir Francis Suttor as president and Maiden as honorary secretary followed. A fund was subsequently raised, partly by public subscription but mainly by the sale of Maiden's book, *Sir Joseph Banks: The "Father of Australia"*, which was published in 1909.

The executive committee generally favoured a memorial in the form of a statue and in addition, if funds were sufficient, a university scholarship. However, in 1937 upon the death of Sir Daniel Levy, its last surviving member, the committee ceased to exist. Six years later, when the fund had increased to £1,089 15s 9d, the Parliament of New South Wales passed the *Sir Joseph Banks Memorial Fund Act*, 1943, which established a Trust to 'consider how the fund may be utilized for the purpose of providing a suitable and fitting memorial to perpetuate the memory and services of Sir Joseph Banks'. K. R. Cramp, O.B.E., was chairman of the Trust.

Upon the presentation of the Trust's report, including a minority report, a further Act was passed, the *Sir Joseph Banks Memorial Act*, 1945, which repealed the Act of 1943 and vested the fund in the Trustees of the Public Library of New South Wales, upon trust, 'to apply the same in or towards defraying the cost of editing, publishing and distributing the Banks Papers in a manner and form suitable and fitting to the memory and services of Sir Joseph Banks'. On 8th March, 1946, when the fund was transferred to the Trustees, it amounted to £3,941 14s 3d, including a Government grant of £2,000 and a gift of £500 by Mr E. J. L. (now Sir Edward) Hallstrom.

The Trustees immediately began their primary task of finding an editor with the necessary high qualifications. After a comprehensive survey of the relevant field of scholarship they invited Dr J. C. Beaglehole to assume the task, and he consented to make a beginning of it with an edition of this journal.

Arrangements were then made through the Prime Minister of New Zealand with the result that Victoria University College (now Victoria University of Wellington), generously permitted Dr Beaglehole, as Senior Research Fellow, to undertake the work as part of his normal duties. The Trustees here record their warm thanks to the Government of New Zealand, to the Council of Victoria University College, and to its Principal at that time, the late Sir Thomas Hunter, for their part in enabling Dr Beaglehole thus to act; and they particularly express their appreciation to Dr Beaglehole himself for his determination to make the memorial a worthy one.

The Trustees propose, as time and funds permit, to add to the Sir Joseph Banks Memorial by the publication of further volumes of the Banks Papers, many of which, like his original journal here reproduced, are in their possession.

H. V. EVATT
President of the Trustees

G. D. RICHARDSON
Principal Librarian and Secretary

PREFACE

THE aim of this volume is, primarily, to print the text of Banks's *Endeavour* journal as carefully edited and annotated as seems adequate to its importance. There is, however, supplementary material. From the great mass of Banks papers that exists in the Mitchell Library and other depositories in Australia and England, a number intimately connected with Banks's part in the voyage are important enough, it is thought, for inclusion as appendices. To these have been added certain other papers, relevant to Banks's refusal to sail on Cook's second voyage. Between about half and three quarters only of the journal has been printed before, and only a very few pages of the appendices; and what has been printed has appeared with various degrees of inaccuracy, whether of deliberate purpose or through carelessness.

An introduction, of some sort, to the journal seemed necessary, to give the reader his bearings. The precise form to be taken by it was not, however, immediately apparent; for the present editor had already dealt at length with the voyage of the *Endeavour* in an introduction to Cook's own journal;[1] and there was a quite vast amount of material that could be drawn on illustrative of Banks. As his figure bulks so largely in the scientific and social history of his time, it was concluded that a general essay on 'The Young Banks' might throw some light on the place of the journal in its writer's own development, as well as on his, and consequently on its, relation to that history.

The draft of such an essay, based on the usual secondary sources, although supplemented by the Mitchell Library papers, showed only too clearly the lacunae, the dubieties, and the lack of documentation in the brief biographies that are all that have been vouchsafed to Banks; and much work on manuscript and other material previously used, as well as on the unused, was necessary before any satisfactory story could be told. It is hoped that the essay now printed, tied down as firmly as possible to verifiable references, will not merely do what was first planned for it, but will provide the beginnings of a much-needed new approach to a biographical subject as complex as it is rich. The reader will find a good deal of quotation incorporated, both in the text and in the footnotes. If he

---

[1] *The Journals of Captain James Cook*, Vol. I, Cambridge University Press for the Hakluyt Society, 1955.

is already a student of Banks, some of the passages may seem to him familiar; but they are new, it is hoped, in being printed correctly. The majority of them, like so much else in the book, have not been printed before; and it is hoped, also, that they both illuminate the study in a way otherwise impossible and indicate the nature of the material. It would be too much to hope that the work is immaculate. The ground occupied by Banks in the eighteenth century has had too little attention from the historian, passionately as he has explored the politics and the literature and the scandal of the age, for one to feel more than provisionally satisfied with one's own results.

The papers to which I have had access, apart from the great collection in the Mitchell Library, are widely scattered. By gracious permission of Her Majesty the Queen, I have been enabled to use, and to quote from, the Georgian Papers preserved in the Royal Library at Windsor. I am deeply indebted to the owners of other collections, who so immediately and so generously gave me the freedom of them. For such freedom my thanks go to Viscount Hinchingbrooke, M.P.; Lord Brabourne; Sir David Hawley and Dr J. W. F. Hill of Lincoln; Mr Warren R. Dawson, F.R.S.E., F.S.A., of Bletchley, Buckinghamshire (who has helped me also in other ways); and Mr Kenneth A. Webster of London. I am indebted likewise to the librarians who have in their charge Banks and other MSS, and have allowed me to exploit their kindness: namely those of the Commonwealth National Library, Canberra; the Alexander Turnbull Library, Wellington; the Auckland Public Library; the Department of Manuscripts of the British Museum; the libraries of the British Museum (Natural History), the Herbarium at Kew, the Royal Society, the Society of Antiquaries, the National Maritime Museum, Greenwich; the Sheffield Public Libraries; and the McGill University Library, Montreal.

In the work of annotation I owe further debts. The principal of these, in fields quite beyond my competence—those of natural history—are due to Dr Averil M. Lysaght of London and Professor Joseph Ewan of Tulane University, New Orleans—scholars learned, the one in the zoology, the other in the botany, of the eighteenth century. Without their professional knowledge, and their close acquaintance with the scientific records of the *Endeavour* voyage, the proper presentation of the journal would have been out of the question. So far as this work is one of scientific interpretation, it is also one of large collaboration, and I am happy to make the fact clear. Dr Lysaght has also been good enough to co-ordinate a great number of suggestions from zoological specialists at the British

Museum (Natural History), who have my gratitude: the late Sir Norman Kinnear, Dr H. W. Parker (Keeper of Zoology), Dr G. O. Evans, Dr F. C. Fraser, Dr I. Gordon, Dr J. P. Harding, Mr N. B. Marshall, Dr T. C. S. Morrison-Scott, Mr A. K. Totton, the late Mr Guy L. Wilkins, Mr N. D. Riley (formerly Keeper of Entomology), Mr F. C. Sawyer, and Dr I. H. H. Yarrow. On the botanical side, Mr W. T. Stern and Miss M. R. J. Edwards have been very helpful. In England I owe thanks also to Dr W. R. P. Bourne of Hove. Among New Zealand scholars I am much indebted to the advice of Dr R. A. Falla and his colleagues of the Dominion Museum, Wellington, and to Mr I. L. Thomsen of the Carter Observatory, Wellington; in Australia to Miss Patricia Kott and Dr D. L. Serventy of the Commonwealth Scientific and Industrial Research Organization, to Mr A. Musgrave of the Australian Museum, Sydney, and to Mr R. H. Anderson, curator of the Botanic Gardens, Sydney. On a number of specific points (not only scientific ones) I have acknowledged help to other friends and informants in the relevant footnotes.

In the fields of linguistics, ethnology and history I have received assistance from Sir Richard Winstedt, F.B.A., Professor C. R. Boxer, of King's College, London, the late Mr J. Frank Stimson of Papeete, Dr Donald S. Marshall of the Peabody Museum of Salem; and in New Zealand, from Mr T. R. Smith, Mr J. M. McEwen, the late Mr Leslie G. Kelly, and the collections of the Dominion Museum. In naval and maritime affairs I have been helped by Mr G. P. B. Naish and Miss Katherine Lindsay-McDougall of the National Maritime Museum; in geographical and cartographical history as well as in other matters—and as always—by Mr R. A. Skelton of the British Museum. For assistance in the selection of illustrations I am obliged to Miss Janet D. Hine and Miss Heather Sherrie; for seemingly interminable typing and re-typing, over a period of years, to Mrs Rita Hollings and Miss Rona Arbuckle, at different times of my University, to Mrs Dorothy I. Croucher, of New Zealand House, London, and to Mrs Ilse Jacoby of Wellington. The index— no inconsiderable matter—is the work of Miss Sherrie. Though I leave to the last the name of Miss Phyllis Mander Jones, lately Mitchell Librarian and now Australian Joint Copying Project Officer in London, I do so but to emphasize my very real obligations, also, for her side of a long correspondence, her own explorations of the Banks papers and Parkinson drawings, and her patience at the ever-new demands I have made upon her energies.

The attention I have paid to the English sources—both in the introduction and in the body of the book—would have been impossible, at a time when it was very much needed, without the Carnegie Commonwealth Fellowship conferred upon me by the Institute of Commonwealth Studies of the University of London in 1955-56; and to the Institute, and to its then Director, Sir Keith Hancock, I tender my heartfelt thanks for the most friendly and generous way in which they allowed me to proceed unimpeded with my own work, dissimilar as it was in time and content from the subjects of seminars to which I might not unjustly have been expected to make some contribution.

Finally I must thank my own University. New Zealand universities are not so well-endowed financially that one of them can easily support a member of its staff whose time is almost entirely devoted to research and publication. I am very conscious of the episode in university history that led to this result in my case, and of my good fortune in my College—as it was for the greater part of the time I have worked on these volumes—and my colleagues. To say more could lead only to cumbrous explanation; to say less would be to do less than justice both to my academic home and to my sense of gratitude.

J. C. BEAGLEHOLE

VICTORIA UNIVERSITY OF WELLINGTON
October 1959

CONTENTS

LIST OF ILLUSTRATIONS

VOLUME I

Note

All the illustrations of the journal are taken from drawings—water colour, wash, pen or pencil—by Sydney Parkinson, unless otherwise specified. Most of the originals, when unsigned, can be attributed with a fair amount of confidence.

The topographical and ethnographical drawings are preserved in the British Museum, Department of Manuscripts, Add. MSS 9345, 15508, 23920 and 23921. The only ones not done on the spot during the voyage appear to be those which John Frederick Miller, one of the artists Banks maintained in London, made of the artifacts brought home. They are very carefully and precisely done.

The botanical and zoological drawings are in the British Museum (Natural History), South Kensington, bound up in volumes, 18 in the Botanical Library, 3 in the Zoological Library. Of the botanical volumes there are the following: Madeira 1, Brazil 1, Tierra del Fuego 1, Society Islands (including Tahiti) 3, New Zealand 4, Australia 7, Java 1. The Society Islands volumes are wrongly named on the spine as 'Friendly Islands'. The zoological volumes are (as named on the spine) 1 *Mammalia. Aves. Amphibia*, 2 *Pisces*, 3 *Insecta, Vermes*. But there are fish in the first volume. The birds have been fully described in Averil Lysaght's excellent *Some Eighteenth Century Bird Paintings in the Library of Sir Joseph Banks* (British Museum [Natural History] Bulletin, Hist. Series, Vol. I, No. 6, London 1959).

During the earlier part of the voyage Parkinson, by working extremely hard, was able to finish his coloured drawings of plants, though not of zoological subjects; and some of both sorts are quite exquisite. By the time the New Zealand collections came on board, however, he could not keep up, and on the Australian coast he was overwhelmed. He was, it must be remembered, acting also as topographical draughtsman, mainly in wash, and doing the best he could for the figure. Some of his figure drawings, of course, are appallingly amateurish, though they have considerable value outside the artistic; but he could also rise to his Maori heads. The plan he adopted with the plants was to make pencil outlines, add a little colour to indicate the key, and make notes on the back for his guidance in finishing the work later. An example of this is Pl. 16*a* in Vol. II, *Crepis novae-zelandiae*. He sometimes was able to make a second, finished drawing himself, but not often. In the end it was Banks's other botanical draughtsmen, Frederick Polydore Nodder, John Frederick

Miller, James Miller, and James Cleveley, who in England, over a long period of years, executed the finished water colour drawings, always sticking closely to Parkinson. The work of Nodder is particularly rich. On the back of the unfinished drawings, now bound up with the finished ones, Banks usually himself noted where the plant was found. As the actual plants in their hundreds are still preserved in the Banks herbarium at South Kensington, and Solander's careful descriptions still survive among the MSS there, we have thus a very complete record. It was from the finished drawings that the engravings were made for the great botanical work that Banks failed to publish. The engravings are bound up with the drawings, which they reverse. All the reproductions in the present volumes are from the finished water colours, unless otherwise indicated.

Captions to the plates, where the subjects are botanical or zoological, give the accepted modern scientific names, with the popular or native ones, when known. The other captions follow those of the originals; if it has been necessary to supply one, it has been placed within square brackets. The notes give the source of the individual plate, and whatever information about it seems useful or relevant. Apart from Parkinson and Banks, it is not always easy to identify the writers of notes on the back or the mounts of drawings, though with the differing botanical names one may certainly suspect both Robert Brown and, more recently, Britten, who edited the lithographed edition of the Australian engravings, 1900-5. The sizes given for the botanical and zoological drawings are those of the drawings themselves at their maximum extent; those for the topographical and miscellaneous drawings are the sizes of the sheets on which they are made as now bound up—where they are mounted, between the edges of the mount. Exceptions are noted.

The plates are arranged in roughly chronological order, except for the botanical ones, which form a sort of unity. Departures from either rule are made to avoid oddities in presentation.

The small drawings reproduced in the text, but not listed here, are from Banks's own illustrations in the manuscript.

The sketch-maps have been drawn by Miss Valerie Scott and Mr Bruce Irwin. By kind permission of the President and Council of the Hakluyt Society, they have been adapted from those in the Society's edition of the *Journals of Captain James Cook*.

COLOUR PLATES

I. Joseph Banks . . . . . . *frontispiece*

From a painting by Sir Joshua Reynolds. Oil on canvas, 50 x 40 in. The portrait was exhibited at the Royal Academy show of 1773. It is now in the possession of the Hon. Mrs Clive Pearson, of Parham Park, Sussex, by whose kind permission it is reproduced.

II. *Bougainvillea spectabilis* Willd. . . . *facing p.* 196

Brazil, 24. 36·5 x 23·5 cm. Titled 'Calyxis-ternaria' and signed 'Sydney Parkinson pinx^t 1768.' Banks has added the name 'Brasil' to the bottom right corner. Later inscriptions in pencil are 'Bougainvillea' and 'Buginvillea spectabilis Willd[enow]'.

III. *Berberis ilicifolia* Forst.f. . . . . *facing p.* 244

Tierra del Fuego 7. 37·1 x 23·5 cm. Titled 'Berberis-sempivirens' and signed 'Sydney Parkinson pinx^t 1769.' In a later hand 'sempivirens' has been lightly scored through in pencil and 'ilicifolia Forst.' substituted above.

IV. *Hibiscus abelmoschus* L. . . . . *facing p.* 260

Society Islands I, 15. 39·5 x 25·4 cm. Signed 'Sydney Parkinson pinx^t 1769.' In the bottom right corner the pencil note in Banks's hand 'Otahite'.

V. *Barringtonia speciosa* J. R. & G. Forst. . . *facing p.* 292

Society Islands I, 57. 41·1 x 20·3 cm. Unsigned. The name 'Barringtonia speciosa Willd.' is written in pencil in a later hand. The mount bears the title 'Agasta splendida Miers'. On the back are faint pencil notes, 'Mem the stamina are made rather too short', '56 Butonica splendida', and, in ink by Banks, 'Otahite'. There are also two unfinished pencil drawings, Nos. 56 and 58, with notes on the back: 56 'Butonica splendida', and 58, 'The fruit is bright grass green when dry dark brown'.

VI. *Spondias dulcis* Forst.f. Vi or Vi apple . . *facing p.* 308

Society Islands I, 30. 45·5 x 28·8 cm. (The height includes the inset drawing of inflorescence.) Signed 'Sydney Parkinson pinx^t 1769.'; pencilled note by Banks, 'Otaheite'.

[xv]

VII*a*. *Zebrasoma flavescens* Bennett?   .   .   .   *facing p.* 356

Zoological II, *Pisces* 22*a*. 7·4 x 8·3 cm. Unsigned. Name 'Chaetodon an militans' lower right, in Banks's (?) hand. On the back the pencil notes by Banks, 'No. 32. Zeus elevatus/ Erapepe'; by Parkinson, 'Taumatus, the same name with their [word illegible]'; and by Solander, in ink, 'Otahite'.

VII*b*. *Zanclus cornutus* (L.) Moorish Idol   .   .   *facing p.* 356

Zool. II, 29*a*. 14 x 9·6 cm. Unsigned, but Dryander has written in lower left, 'S. Parkinson'. Pencil notes: lower left, '+ ch. Cornutias'; by Parkinson lower right, 'Tátèhee' (apparently the island name of the fish), and above the fish, 'pale blue'. On the back, by Parkinson, 'there is of this fish as large again'; by Banks, 'N° 21 Chaetodon rostratus'; and by Solander, in ink, 'Otahite'.

VII*c*. *Rhinecanthus aculeatus* (L.)   .   .   .   .   *facing p.* 356

Zool. I, *Mammalia. Aves. Amphibia*, 59. 8·9 x 17·6 cm. Name 'S. Parkinson' in Dryander's hand lower left corner. Lower right, in pencil in Banks's hand, the name 'Balist aculeatus L.' and the further names, 'oidē / Oethi / Oiwe tea'. On the back the pencil note by Parkinson, 'The colours on the back soften'd in the Orange & purple bright'; by Banks, 'N° 50 Balistes ornatus'; and by Solander, in ink, 'Otahite'.

VIII*a*. *Anisochaetodon falcula* (Bloch) Butterfly-fish   .   *facing p.* 372

Zool. II, 22*b*. 7 x 10 cm. Name in Dryander's hand, 'S. Parkinson'. Title written later on recto, 'Ch.falcula (ulietensis, C.V.)'. On the back the pencil note, 'No. 67 The fish lost'; another note, on colours, some of which is erased and the rest illegible; and in ink, by Banks, 'Ulhietea'.

VIII*b*. *Anisochaetodon vagabundus* (L.) Butterfly-fish   .   *facing p.* 372

Zool. II, 30. 9·6 x 15·3 cm. Name in Dryander's hand, 'S. Parkinson'. Near the tail of the fish is a pencil note by Parkinson, 'dark chesnut', and on the lower right, 'Paraha'; elsewhere on the recto, by others, 'Ch. vagabundus', 'chaet. speciosus Mss/Paraharaha/[word illegible]'; on the back, by Banks, 'No. 48. Chaetodon aulicus', and by Solander, in ink, 'Otahite'.

VIII*c*. *Megaprotodon striangulus* (Gm.) ? Butterfly-fish   *facing p.* 372

Zool. II, 23*b*. 6·3 x 12 cm. Name in Dryander's hand, 'S. Parkinson'. The pencilled name, abbreviated on recto, 'Ch[aetodon] striangulus', is repeated on the back in full, with the note in ink by Banks, 'Otahite'.

ILLUSTRATIONS TO THE INTRODUCTION

B

side [of his paper], which look tolerably well. . . . If Miss Bank[s] will accept of a couple of Shadows done in the same [manner] as these I did for Miss Burnet I will do myself the honour of sending them'. The reproduction is from the letter. For some of Lind's activities with silhouettes see an article by F. Gordon Roe, 'A Forgotten Group of Profilists', in *Apollo*, XXII (1935), pp. 287-9.

From a painting by William Parry, A.R.A. (1742?-91). Oil on canvas, 59 x 59 in. Omai in a white robe, Banks in a grey suit, Solander in a red coat. Parry returned to England from Italy in 1775, and the picture must date from that year or the first half of 1776, before Omai left England with Cook. Reproduced by kind permission of Brigadier Charles Hilary Vaughan, D.S.O.

From the MS in the Mitchell Library, 23·2 x 18 cm.

PLATES AT THE END OF THE VOLUME

1*a*. *Munida gregaria* (Fabr.)

Zool. III, *Insecta Vermes* 9. 13·5 x 8·1 cm. Signed 'Sydney Parkinson pinx[t] 1769.', and with title 'Cancer gregarius.' Note by Banks in ink on back, 'Jan[ry] 2nd 1769 / Lat. 37.30.'

1*b*. *Glaucus atlanticus* (Forst.)

Zool. III, 23·9 x 17·5 cm. Signed 'Sydney Parkinson pinx[t] ad vivum 1768', and with title 'Mimus-Volutator'. Note by Banks in ink on back, 'Oct[r] 4.1768 / Lat. 11.00.N.'

2. *Motacilla flava* L.

Zool. I, *Mammalia. Aves. Amphibia* 38*a*. 15·7 x 20·4 cm. The title on the drawing is 'Motacilla-avida'. Signed 'Sydney Parkinson pinx[t] 1768'. Note by Banks in ink on back, 'Sep[tr] 28.1768 / Lat. 19.00 north.' The bird is a young one.

3. *Volatinia jacarina* (L.) Blue-black Grassquit

Zool. I, 37*b*. 24 x 19·5 cm. Entitled 'Loxia-nitens' and signed 'Sydney Parkinson pinx[t] ad vivum. 1768'. Note by Banks in lower right corner, 'Brasil'. Note by Banks in ink on back, 'of the coast of Brasil Nov[r] 8th 1768'.

are mounted is written 'Otaheite' and 'Sketches of Inhabitants'. The man is tying a sash round his *tapa* overgarment or *tiputa*, and is wearing what may be either a *pareu* or a *maro* underneath; the woman is wearing a *tiputa* over a *pareu*.

11*a*. [Making *Tapa*] Woman scraping bark

Add. MS 23921, f.50*a*. Pencil sketch by Parkinson, unsigned, 16·3 x 20·6 cm. Note at bottom right in Banks's hand, 'woman scraping bark to make cloth S[outh?] S[ea?]'.

11*b*. [Making *Tapa*] Woman beating cloth

Add. MS 23921, f.50*b*. Pencil sketch by Parkinson, unsigned, 20·1 x 23·1 cm. Note at bottom right in Banks's hand, 'women beating cloth'; and a note in ink on the mounting sheet, 'Girls beating out the Bark with their Cloth beaters'. Both these drawings are much foxed.

12. [Tahiti] Sketches of Dancing Girls

Add. MS 23921, f.38*b*. Pencil sketch by Parkinson, unsigned, 12·2 x 29·8 cm. In addition to the ceremonial *tapa* garments the girls are wearing head-dresses of *taamu*, or plaited hair.

13. [Tahiti] Distortions of the Mouth used in Dancing

Add. MS 23921, f.51*a* and *b*. Pencil sketches by Parkinson, unsigned, both 19 x 16·3 cm. On the back of 51*a* is a pencil sketch of tattoo-design on the buttocks.

14. A Tupapow in the Island of Otaheite

Add. MS 23921, f.31*a*. Wash drawing 23·7 x 37·4 cm., unsigned. On the back of the drawing is written in pencil 'Ewhatta no te tuobapaow' (spelling of last word conjectural)—i.e. *e fata no te tupapau*. A roofed platform with a fence round it; the corpse lies covered with *tapa*. In the foreground a 'chief mourner' in ceremonial dress; young coconuts planted out, a mature coconut with a boy climbing for the nuts, and a tree (Erythrina?) with a man sitting at its base.

15. [Tahiti] Dress of the Chief Mourner

Add. MS 23921, f.32. Pencil drawing 23·1 x 18·7 cm., unsigned, probably by Spöring. See p. 288.

16. A platform for supporting the offerings made to the Dead

Add. MS 23921, f.29*b*. Wash drawing 23·6 x 37 cm., unsigned. The platform is hung round with cloth, and on it rests a bunch of bananas. Banana trees left foreground and behind, and a coconut middle foreground with a yam vine climbing it.

17. View in Ulietea

Add. MS 23921, f.11. Wash drawing 23·6 x 37·3 cm., unsigned. A canoe-house with a large double canoe in it, in the foreground a man carrying coconuts on a stick over his shoulder, and two men in a small outrigger canoe. Various trees and plants, and hills in the background.

18. Canoe of Ulietea

Add. MS 23921, f.20. Wash drawing 30 x 48·1 cm., unsigned. A two-masted double canoe with sails raised; two shelters built on the deck, one shading a *tapa*-wrapped child; men dressed in the *maro* kneeling on ropes; other children, one holding a pig, another drinking from a coconut; a woman leaning on the forward shelter, fowls on the aft one. Other sailing canoes in the background. In lower right corner, three Reef Herons, *Demigretta sacra*.

19. Vessels of the Island of Otaha

Add. MS 23921, f.17. Wash drawing 30 x 47·8 cm., unsigned. Left foreground, men and women fishing, one woman nude, with topknot hair-dressing and tattooed buttocks. Right foreground, man paddling raft with coconuts. Middle, small outrigger canoe and large double sailing canoe, with *tapa*-dressed men and women, fruit, gourd containers, etc. Further canoes in background, hills, and atmospheric effect of sun shining through clouds. 'Otaha'=Tahaa.

20. Construction of Canoes

Add. MS 23921, f.23b. Pencil drawings of various details of canoe construction, 27·4 x 22·3 cm., unsigned. Hulls with cross-sections, 'deck-house', paddle, mast and rigging. Annotations in Banks's hand.

21. [Tahitian Tattoo-designs]

Add. MS 23921, f.51c *verso*, ink drawing 19·7 x 32·1 cm. The drawing shows the tattooing of the buttocks. See pp. 335-6.

22a. [Tahitian Weapons]

Add. MS 23921, f.57b. Wash drawing 20·4 x 16·5 cm. Signed 'J.F.Miller: del.'; drawn in England from artifacts brought home by Banks. (1) Sting of a ray, used for a spear-point; (2) bow (3) arrow (4) quiver of bamboo. The bow and arrow were not strictly speaking a weapon, but rather 'sporting equipment'.

22b. [South Sea Fish-hooks]

Add. MS 15508, f.25. Wash drawing 20·5 x 16·5 cm. Signed 'John Frederick Miller. del.' Underneath the drawing are pencil notes by Banks identifying the artifacts: '1. Decoy to Catch Cuttle fish from Otaheite 2. Hook of Nacre shell from D° 3. D° of mother of Pearl from D° 4. D° of Wood & bone from New Zeland.'

23*a*. [Tapa Beater and Adze]

Add. MS 15508, f.30. Wash drawing 20·5 x 16·6 cm. Unsigned. Under the drawing is a pencil note by Banks, 'Tools of the South Sea Isles / a instrument with which they beat out their cloth / b. Hatchet or axe'. A further note gives the size (height) of the beater as 1′ 3″ and of the adze as 1′ 11″.

23*b*. [South Sea Artifacts]

Add. MS 15508, f.31. Wash drawing 20·1 x 16·4 cm. Signed 'J.F.Miller. 1771'. A pencil note by Banks beneath the drawing lists the articles: 'Tools &c. from the South Sea Isles / a a flute / b Pestle of Stone to beat down their victuals into a soft paste which is looked upon by them as a delicacy / c small Hatchet the blade of which being taken off [serves *erased*] a chizzel / d Thatching needle / e Chizzel made of human bone'.

24. *Diospyros lotus* L.

Madeira 17. 25·8 x 20·2 cm. Signed 'Sydney Parkinson pinx^t 1768.' The word 'Linn.', added in ink to the title on the picture, appears to be in Banks's hand.

25. *Pereskia* sp.

Brazil 1. 18·3 x 30·3 cm. Titled 'Clusia-dodecapetala', and signed 'Sydney Parkinson pinx^t 1769.' On the back is the pencilled note, 'Mem the stamina to be done with Gamboge the stalks & Calix green'.

26. *Tillandsia stricta* Soland. ex Sims

Brazil 33. 27·9 x 19 cm. Signed 'Sydney Parkinson pinx^t 1769.'

27*a*. *Apium prostratum* Labill. Wild Celery

Tierra del Fuego 58. 41 x 26·2 cm. Signed 'Sydney Parkinson pinx^t 1769.' This is the *Apium antarcticum* of the Banks and Solander MSS.

27*b*. *Drimys winteri* J. R. & G. Forst. Winter's Bark

Tierra del Fuego 6. 33·3 x 21 cm. Titled 'Winterana-aromatica', and signed 'Sydney Parkinson pinx^t 1769.'

28. *Pernettya mucronata* Gaud.

Tierra del Fuego 100. 27 x 21·5 cm. Titled 'Arbutus, rigida' and signed 'Sydney Parkinson pinx^t 1769.' Above 'rigida' in the title has been written in pencil 'mucronata, Linn.fil.'

29. *Crataeva religiosa* Forst.f. Puaraau

Society Islands I, 5. 45·5 x 29 cm. (part of the drawing has been trimmed off). Titled 'Crataeva frondosa' and signed 'Sydney

Parkinson pinx^t 1769.' In the lower right-hand corner is a pencil note in Banks's hand, 'Otahite'; and on the back the following: 'The flowers that come last out are quite white gaining the purple colour by degrees. The underside of the leaves the same colour as the upper —The capsule is dark green being all cover'd with warts of dirty white'.

35. *Tacca leontopetaloides* (L.) O. Ktze.   Pia

Society Islands II, 206. 43·5 x 28·8 cm. Titled 'Chaitæa-Tacca' and signed 'Sydney Parkinson pinx^t 1769.'; a pencil note by Banks, 'Ulhietea'. The sheet has been trimmed at the top and sides. The wash drawing of the details of the capsule is on a separate piece of paper pasted down. The name of the plant usually accepted has been *Tacca pinnatifida* Forst.

36. *Piper methysticum* Forst.f.   Ava

Society Islands II, 139. 37·8 x 25 cm. Titled 'Piper-inebrians' and signed 'Sydney Parkinson pinx^t 1769.' Pencil note under title, 'Ulhietea'.

37. *Merremia peltata* (L.) Merr.

Society Islands II, 106. 43 x 27·7 cm. Titled 'Convolvulus peltatus' and signed 'Sydney Parkinson pinx^t 1769'; a pencil note by Banks, 'Ulhitea'.

38. *Cyanoramphus zealandicus* (Latham).   Red-rumped Parrot

Zool. I, 8. 17·6 x 17·5 cm. Ascribed by Dryander (no doubt correctly) to Parkinson. The right leg and claws and the branch on which the bird is perched are indicated only in pencil. A later pencil note at the bottom of the sheet gives the name as 'Psittacus pacificus'; and a note at the bottom right, by Parkinson, gives its island name as 'Aā' (*A'a*). The present specific name was given by Latham (1790), who erroneously thought New Zealand was the bird's habitat. It was confined to Tahiti, and was last collected in 1844, about which time presumably it became extinct. On the back are the notes in ink, (1) by Banks, 'No. 5. Green Peroquet', and (2) by Solander, 'Otahite'.

39. *Vini peruviana* (P.L.S.Müller).   Tahitian Blue Lory

Zool. I, 9. 11·9 x 15 cm. Unsigned pencil drawing, ascribed by Dryander to Parkinson. A pencil note by Parkinson on the front reads, 'Avinne'. On the back he has written, 'The face throat & breast white the rem/ & rec/. dirty grey turn^g blue towards the edge the feet & beak a bright Orange Claws black all the rest of the body— w^t dark Ultra-. shaded w^t P.B. like shining steell.'; and a note by Banks, 'N°3, Blue Perroquet / Otahite'.—In Parkinson's note 'rem/ & rec/.' = 'remiges & rectrices', i.e. flight feathers and tail feathers.

40a. *Acantherocybium solandri* (C.V.)

Zool. II, 87. 6 x 39·5 cm. Titled 'Scomber-lanceolatis' and signed 'Sydney Parkinson pinx^t 1769'. Below the signature is a note in pencil by Banks(?), 'Tatea', and below that Parkinson's note in ink, 'Mem.

one Pinulae spuriæ is wanting above & one below.' On the back is the pencil note by Banks, 'off thrum cap. Island'.

40*b*. *Plectorhinchus orientalis* (Bloch)

Zool. II, 77. 10·3 x 24 cm. Ascribed by Dryander to Parkinson. The name 'Tairhepha' (*Tairifa*) is pencilled below the drawing. On the back are the notes (1) by Banks (?), 'N° 45. Percoides pica'; (2) by Parkinson, 'The parts mark'd thus x are white inclining to gray especialy on the finns & on the face reddish. those marked w^t [a sign not possible to print] are black the scales edge'd w^t dirty white. the iris gold colour pupil black.'; (3) by Solander, 'Otahite'. The marks referred to by Parkinson are not visible on the drawing, and were presumably removed when it was coloured.

SKETCH MAPS

ABBREVIATIONS USED IN NOTES TO THE INTRODUCTION

ALS   Autograph letter signed (MS so classified in the Alexander Turnbull Library).

ATL   Alexander Turnbull Library, Wellington, New Zealand.

CAMERON   H. C. Cameron, *Sir Joseph Banks*. London, 1952.

D.T.C.   Dawson Turner Copies of Banks correspondence in the Botanical Library of the British Museum (Natural History), South Kensington, London.

Edward Smith   Edward Smith, *Life of Sir Joseph Banks*. London, 1911.

Hawkesworth   John Hawkesworth, *An Account of the Voyages undertaken by order of his present Majesty for making Discoveries in the Southern Hemisphere.* . . . London, 1773.
(Vols II and III are devoted to the voyage of the *Endeavour*.)

J.E.S.   Sir James Edward Smith (editor), *A Selection of the Correspondence of Linnaeus, and other Naturalists, from the Original Manuscripts*. 2 vols, London, 1821.

Kew B.C.   Manuscript Banks correspondence in the Library of the Herbarium, Kew.

ML   Mitchell Library.

S.S.B.   Sarah Sophia Banks.

'Voluntiers'   A Volume of Banks papers in the Mitchell Library, lettered 'Voluntiers, Instructions, Provision for 2d. Voyage'.

THE YOUNG BANKS

WHAT shall we call the eighteenth century? How often, and how vainly, has it been summarized in a phrase! — stuffed into a single garment, as it were, from which it bursts at every seam, its uncontrollable, magnificent, startling life forcing itself upon the eye of the beholder in lavish and indecent contradiction. It was an Age, there seems no doubt of that — the Age of the Despots, of Enlightenment, the Age of Reason, of Oratory, of Gin, the Mercantilist Age, the Age of the Augustans, the Age of Rococo, the Age of Johnson. There can be no harm, thinking of England, to which Johnson so immediately and forthrightly brings us, in conferring another name, no more nor less adequate: let us call those busy decades — or a sufficient selection of them — the Age of the Gentleman Amateur. For the century was, in so much of its activity, pre-professional. One must not say merely dilettante: that would be unjust. In the first place, the word has subtly changed its meaning; in the second, though the dilettante throve, never did he have a choicer field for his activity; never did dilettantism become, as with Horace Walpole, so exquisitely almost professional in itself. But no one would call dilettanti those men of profound scientific activity, Joseph Priestley and Henry Cavendish, any more than one would call this nonconformist minister and this recluse of a ducal family professional scientists. Was Lord Burlington merely dilettante in architecture, or Gibbon in history, or Gilbert White in natural history? Or Arthur Young in agriculture, or that equally assiduous traveller, Thomas Pennant, in zoology, or in the free field of general observation and antiquities? And for how many hundreds of the obscure do these large figures stand! — the country parsons devoted to local history, in at the birth, almost, of British archaeology; the scholars who had escaped from the common room and the port; the nobility who had no taste for gaming or politics — though was not politics itself, whatever its savagery and cupidity, its attraction

for men on the make, still one of the great preserves of the Gentleman Amateur?

Science, above all, apart from politics, it is that comes to the
aid of a generalization that may often seem to totter dangerously:
there is so much that rushes forth as contrary evidence in literature
and art and architecture, in theology and even in prize-fighting.
Science had not been organized, Science was not at all professional
and most imperfectly academic; Science, as we know it today, was
almost at the beginning of things; and yet Science was popular.
The educated classes of England, as of France, made it a cult;
that most unscientific figure Dr Johnson was throughout his life
given to 'chemical experiments'. True, in the mid-century it was
long since Sir Isaac Newton's *Principia* had begun to send its ceaseless
eddies through the European mind; true, by 1760 the Royal Society
had enjoyed a hundred years of irregularly scientific life; but even
the Royal Society was predominantly a society of Gentlemen, and
of amateurs. Science, indeed, as Priestley tinkered with his apparatus,
and Cavendish plumbed new depths of analytic thought, and
Western Civilization sailed in ships bearing the beneficent gifts
of Commerce and of War to the uttermost bounds of the earth,
saw empires expanding which had before been only a dream.
Empires were for conquest, arduous but exhilarating: to the
votaries of the descriptive, of geography, of zoology, of botany,
how fair the prospect! How almost intoxicating the scene on which
the natural historian could look forth, the young disciple of Linnaeus!
— for it is that light, famous, venerable, omnipresent, that shines
above our travellers, that presence that irradiates their farthest
wanderings; there in Uppsala is the centre and bosom of learning
from which, almost, all proceeds, to which all returns. To be the
pupil of Linnaeus, his friend, his correspondent, his informant — this
was to be sealed with the seal of a new virtue, this was to be enlisted
under a banner, to be one of a brotherhood, to have a master
and a father, and in Nature an intellectual home. Not even the
great Buffon ever stood in quite this relation with European science.
Should we, then, speak of the Age of Linnaeus? We might do
worse; but it does not really matter. What matters was that science
was both widening and deepening the scope of its command:
not always with true learning, sometimes almost accidentally —
led sometimes from old myth to new myth, undermining new as
well as old with new experience. And now rose up, indeed, within
Natural History, something new, something incomparably exciting,
Man in the state of nature: the Noble Savage entered the study

and the drawing-room of Europe in naked majesty, to shake the preconceptions of morals and of politics. He was not, it is true, universally admired, and behind him came illimitable files of savages something less than noble, insufficiently elegant, beings whose natural state caused the philosopher embarrassment. There were cultivated persons who, like Horace Walpole, were not entertained: scholars who, like Dr Johnson, refused to be instructed. But the science of ethnology was born.

So, on the scene of our scrutiny, into this busy age, steps the figure of Joseph Banks, the gifted, the fortunate youth: enthusiastic, curious, the voyager, the disciple of Linnaeus, the botanist and zoologist, the devotee of savages; not yet, as one examines his early career, a Public Figure, but certainly a Gentleman, certainly a figure typical of his age; and certainly as much as anyone, and more than most, the Gentleman Amateur of Science.

§

Joseph Banks came from that enviable class the landed gentry; close enough to the land to draw common sense from it, and with enough of it to draw from it also a handsome revenue; with brains enough, indeed, unlike some country gentry, to repay education, and with wealth more than enough to allow of a town as well as country existence, and of a standing in society which no mere rural squire could claim. The family was a Lincolnshire one; its seat was Revesby Abbey, not far from Boston; as the fens were drained its wealth increased, and intelligent management made its standing still greater.[1] Joseph's seventeenth century great-grandfather, another Joseph, was not merely wealthy, from his business as an attorney and from property transactions, but a member of parliament, for Grimsby and then for Totnes, and — we begin to see something of his descendant — an antiquary. His son, also Joseph, also an antiquary, also a member of parliament — for Peterborough — rebuilt Revesby church, served as sheriff of the county, and was a fellow of the Royal Society. This Joseph's son Joseph died in his twenties, unmarried, so that it was a William, a second son, who next came to the estate — member for Grampound, deputy-lieutenant of Lincolnshire, an agricultural improver, whose favourite pursuit, said his son, was drainage — i.e. drainage of the fens. William does not seem to have shone in antiquarian

---

[1] For the outline of Banks's ancestry here given, I have relied on his own notes, now in the possession of Mr Warren R. Dawson, Dawson MS 47. They are filled out in Dr J. W. F. Hill's excellent introduction to his edition of the *Letters and Papers of the Banks Family of Revesby Abbey 1704-1760*, Lincoln Record Society, Vol. 45 (Lincoln 1952).

or other intellectual pursuits, but we can see a sort of family pattern. It is a respectable pattern, of service to, as well as profit from, the land, of prominent public duties met in the conventional way, of intelligent interest in affairs, of some mild feeling for learning. The hereditary cell-structure which lay behind the disposition of this respectable pattern was perhaps given a slight twist by the marriage of William Banks to Sarah, eldest daughter of William Bate of Derbyshire, in 1741; for while we can see the same elements in the make-up of the next Joseph, who was born on 13 February 1743[1], in Argyle Street, Westminster, something has happened. With this new Joseph, everything is intensified, though the parliamentary tradition is broken: intelligence both deepens and widens, the affairs which claim his interest are practically everything except politics, interest becomes organization; the moderation of the polite antiquary is transformed into a consuming devotion to natural history, the travels from Lincolnshire to London become travels round the world, the county magnate becomes an international figure. One of the queer English excursions into individuality has happened. There has been also, it seems, a rise in the family's social fortunes: a sister of William Banks, Margaret, the delightful and radiant beauty Peggy Banks, for whom the Duke of Cumberland panted to give balls, married the Honourable Henry Grenville, and so came into a formidably aristocratic connection; her only child, Louisa, our Joseph's cousin, became the second wife of the third Earl Stanhope; and Sarah Banks's sister Hannah Sophia, Joseph's aunt on his maternal side, was the wife of the eighth Earl of Exeter. A child not himself born into ermine could hardly hope for more excellent connections. If he could have asked anything else of the gods, he might have asked for charm. He did not need to: that also they had given him. They gave him, to complete his felicity, in the year after that

[1] There has been a little confusion, to which Banks himself unwittingly contributed, over the date of his birth. In the latest life, Dr H. C. Cameron's *Sir Joseph Banks* (London 1952), p. 1, n., the date is given as 'February 2nd, 1743 O.S.' and Cameron adds, 'Lord Brougham, in giving the correct date and place, tells us that he has it "from a note in his own hand which lies before me"'. This note may possibly be one of the memoranda now in the possession of Mr Warren Dawson, which Dr Cameron quotes (p. 284) as 'Born 1743 Feb 2nd old style. . . .' But 'February 2nd, 1743 O.S.' would be 13 February 1744 New Style; and it is evident that Banks intended his 'old style' to apply merely to the day of the month, not to the year. This is borne out by a birth-certificate, now in the Public Library, Dunedin, New Zealand, copied from the register of the church of St James, Westminster, and dated 15 November 1753. This gives the date of birth as 2 February 1742—i.e. O.S. (the modern, or Gregorian, calendar was not adopted in Great Britain till 1752). Notes at the bottom of the document in Banks's hand begin 'Born Feb 13 1743' (i.e. N.S.), and go on to the dates of his entry to Harrow, Eton and Oxford, as given below.

of his own birth, a sister as individual as himself, Sarah Sophia; and their individualities did not clash. William and Sarah Banks had no further children; but they had not done badly by the eighteenth century.

We know little enough of the earliest years of Joseph. Presumably they were largely spent at Revesby, where fresh air, the open fields, and plentiful play laid the foundations of a remarkably tough constitution, and private tutoring gave him sufficient educational grounding to take him to Harrow, in April 1752, at the age of nine. Thence, either to get the best of both worlds, or because of invincible opposition to learning in the Harrovian atmosphere — for, to quote his later friend, Henry Brougham, 'Joe cared mighty little for his book' — he was in September 1756 removed to Eton. A pleasant good-tempered boy he continued to be, but it was with extreme satisfaction that his tutor found him one day, at the age of fourteen, reading and not sporting in his hours of leisure. He was not, however, we may judge, reading in the classics; Joseph always trod a perilous path in the learned languages — if in a rash moment he ventured into that country at all. Something more important had happened: he had undergone a sort of conversion. He gave his own account of this, late in his life, to Sir Everard Home the surgeon, who transmitted it to posterity.[1] Joseph, river-bathing with his friends one fine summer evening, had lingered beyond them in the water; when he came out they were all gone and he dawdled back to school by himself along a flowery lane. Solitude, the flowers, perhaps the evening light, had their effect: 'he stopped and looking round, involuntarily exclaimed, How beautiful! After some reflection, he said to himself, it is surely more natural that I should be taught to know all these productions of Nature, in preference to Greek or Latin; but the latter is my father's command and it is my duty to obey him; I will however make myself acquainted with all these different plants for my own pleasure and gratification. He began immediately to teach himself Botany', with the assistance of the women who gathered simples for the apothecaries' shops, paying sixpence for every valuable piece of information he got from them. Home for the holidays, he found in his mother's dressing-room an old and battered copy of Gerard's Herbal, with its woodcuts of the very plants he knew; he carried it back to school in triumph; 'and it was probably this very book that he was poring over when detected by his tutor,

---

[1] In his Hunterian oration, 1822; reprinted by Cameron, Appendix D, particularly pp. 297-8.

C

for the first time, in the act of reading'. One branch of natural history led to another (the dutiful sense of his father's command felt by Joseph, we may suppose, sat but lightly on the enthusiast), already he had a power of persuasion with his fellows; 'his whole time out of school was given up to hunting after plants and insects,' writes Lord Brougham, the son of one of his schoolmates, 'making a *hortus siccus* of the one, and forming a cabinet of the other. As often as Banks could induce [my father] to quit his task in reading or in verse-making, he would take him on his long rambles; and I suppose it was from this early taste that we had at Brougham so many butterflies, beetles, and other insects, as well as a cabinet of shells and fossils'.[1]

In 1760 he went home from school to be inoculated against smallpox. The time taken by this was so great that when he had recovered it was thought his next step might well be not back to Eton but forward to Oxford — which, though not, quite obviously, his spiritual home, was at least a home for gentlemen; and he was accordingly at the end of the year entered at Christ Church as a gentleman commoner.[2] There he rapidly made a reputation as one ignorant of Greek; equally rapidly he came to a determination that though he was shunned as a classicist he would be consulted as a natural historian. But where to turn for higher instruction in the science which he had so far pursued with cullers of simples and in the Elizabethan pages of Gerard? The academic months were passing by. Oxford had a professor of botany, but nothing was farther from the professorial chair than the idea that its occupant might give instruction in the subject that he professed. Humphrey Sibthorp is not to be blamed; the idea was foreign to every other person as well, and it may indeed be esteemed an excess of educational devotion that he did give one lecture in thirty-five years. To the odd situation which young Mr Banks forced upon him, and to his own character, we owe one of the most masterly statements of irony in the English language — unless, as is conceivable, Lord Brougham had no talent for irony, and was simply being sincere. For when, we are told, Banks 'applied to the learned doctor for leave to engage a lecturer, whose remuneration should be wholly defrayed by his pupil . . . it is highly creditable to the professor, and shows his love of the science, in which some of his family afterwards so greatly excelled, that he at once agreed to

[1] Brougham, *Lives of Men of Letters and Science in the Reign of George III*, II (London 1846), p. 340.
[2] He matriculated 16 December 1760.

the proposal'.[1] He did more than signify his agreement: since there
was no person eligible to teach botany in Oxford, he provided the
aspiring youth with a letter of introduction to Professor Martyn,
who occupied the chair at Cambridge — not to suggest that Professor Martyn might give lectures, but to inquire whether a teacher
could possibly be found in the other university or its town. Banks's
visit was triumphant: he found Israel Lyons, the son of a Jewish
silversmith and teacher of Hebrew, and a young man early distinguished both in botany and in astronomy, and brought him
back to be supported by the revenues of Revesby. Botany was
thereupon prosecuted in Oxford; the unorthodox undergraduate
grew in knowledge; and as it was the duty of the great to befriend
and patronize the lowly, in due course Banks was able to recommend
his tutor as astronomer on the Arctic voyage of 1773, on which
Captain Phipps, R.N., another friend, looked unavailingly for a
way to the North Pole.

Meanwhile — the Banksian chronology in these early years
is not very distinct, but here at least we have another certain
date — William Banks died unexpectedly, of 'the breaking of an
Imposthume in his Breast', and was buried at Revesby on 1 October
1761.[2] Mrs Banks thereupon moved to London, or rather to Chelsea,
with Sarah Sophia, to a pleasant house in Paradise Walk near the
Apothecaries' Garden that Sir Hans Sloane had founded not so
very many years before. It was an excellent situation for botanical
vacations. It had also the advantage of the neighbourhood of one
whose Huntingdonshire country seat was not far from Lincolnshire,
John Montagu, fourth Earl of Sandwich, a man who, though
twenty-five years older than Banks, became his fast friend. Sandwich
had for years already been deep in politics, his acquaintance with
the World was wide and his way of thinking — to blunt the point
of many accusations against him — liberal; to a talent for genial
foolery he united great intelligence, and, in spite of his rather peculiar deep-jawed face, an extreme personal charm — a charm,
indeed, even more winning and certainly more stable than that of
Banks. He was to be useful to Banks, and he was, it seems, to form a
pretty accurate estimate of some at least of the capacities of his
young friend. Sandwich was capable of sharing a botanical
expedition and both were passionate fishermen. Possibly it is to
their association of this period, possibly to some later year, that we
may refer a story that seems to have given the mature Banks a

[1] ibid., p. 341.
[2] Dawson MS 47, f.51.

great deal of pleasure (it is again to Brougham that we owe our account): 'So zealous were both these friends in the prosecution of this sport, that Sir Joseph used to tell of a project they had formed for suddenly draining the Serpentine by letting off the water; and he was wont to lament their scheme being discovered the night before it was to have been executed: their hope was to have thrown much light on the state and habits of the fish'.[1] The expectation for profitable research by this radical method is so tenuous that it is much more likely their hope was to have thrown confusion on London. The gentlemen, however, escaped trouble — into which Banks's other passion certainly brought him on a well known occasion. He had wandered out on the Hounslow road collecting plants and had crawled into a ditch. This was badly timed, for it was just after a traveller had been robbed by a footpad. The footpad decamped; search revealed Banks in his ditch — why did men hide in ditches? — and in spite of indignant denials and struggles he was hauled off to a magistrate. A turning out of pockets must have surprised investigating Justice: the young man was eccentric and not criminal; no doubt there were appropriate apologies. One should not arrest landed gentlemen; but at least this one got a second valued reminiscence for his old age.[2]

Banks entered into his inheritance in February 1764. To the expansion of mind consequent on that event we may perhaps attribute his summary way of reorganizing university teaching, for it was in July of that year that Lyons gave his Oxford course of lectures.[3] It was in that year also that Banks came down, with the world delightfully before him. A gentleman of means needed a London house; he bought one in New Burlington Street; and now, with town and country at his disposal, with Lincolnshire for shooting

[1] Brougham, II, p. 342.

[2] This story appears in the *General Evening Post*, 7 January 1772, in a rather different form, wherein the incident is said to have happened 'lately'—Banks having become a subject for gossip.

[3] According to the Christ Church battel books Banks was in regular residence from his matriculation date until the end of the Michaelmas quarter 1763; he then became irregular, but was still in residence, though with some breaks, for 21 weeks in 1764. He was charged for the last week of the term beginning Lady Day 1765—perhaps merely for college dues—and for four weeks of the Midsummer term 1765. His name remained on the battel books until 1766 but with no evidence that he was in residence after the single month in 1765. He never troubled to take a degree.—I am indebted for these particulars to the Deputy Librarian of Christ Church, Mr W. G. Hiscock. The dates cast a little light on the year of Israel Lyons's lectures, on which there is some conflict. Nichols, *Literary Anecdotes*, II (1812), p. 328, says he was brought to Oxford by Banks 'about 1762 or 1763, to read lectures, which he did with great applause, to at least sixty pupils', but in giving July 1764 I follow the definite statement of Cooper, *Annals of Cambridge*, iv (Cambridge 1852), p. 381. Banks was then a senior man and his own master.

and fishing and the exercise of a young squire's benevolence (while
Benjamin Stephenson, his father's steward, managed the estate),
with London for society and an elevated converse, he might indeed
be esteemed a happy young man. Towards his sister and his mother
he was warmly affectionate, while his circle of friends began steadily
to expand. They were excellent friends, curious about natural
history and antiquities, and they themselves had their friends. No
sooner was one in the philosophical circle, than it began to broaden
out illimitably. To date acquaintanceship seems impossible, but
to these years surely must belong something like intimacy with
Thomas Pennant, Banks's senior by seventeen years, the Flintshire
natural historian and traveller through Britain, the correspondent
of Linnaeus, the friend of Gilbert White (Pennant must even then
have been composing his folio *British Zoology* of 1766); and with
Daines Barrington, the lawyer and antiquary; and at least friendship
with Lightfoot the botanist; with Dr Morton, the librarian of the
British Museum; with Dr William Watson, distinguished in physics
and astronomy; with Professor John Hope, the botanist of Edinburgh. It was certainly about this time — we have his own word for
it[1] — that he first met Daniel Carl Solander, whose name was to be
so closely linked with his own, whose counsel henceforth was so
much part of his life. Our young man was, in fact, hard on the heels
of science, and we are not to be surprised that in April 1766 the
Bishop of Carlisle joined with Dr Morton and Dr Watson to nomin-
ate him for the fellowship of the Royal Society. He had made no
signal contribution to any department of learning whatsoever;
but that, at that time, was no disqualification whatsoever; he was
an excellent young man, energetic and interested, quite devoted to
botany; a landed gentleman with a really enviable income; it
would have been an insult to keep him out. The Royal Society
duly elected him, quite unwitting that it had taken the first step
towards an epoch in its own existence.

Even while it elected him, Joseph was at sea. Other men might
cross the Channel, and take by coach the well-worn road to Paris,
Lyons, Venice, Rome; other men might call on Voltaire or hobnob
with cardinals or collect medals and marbles and reputations as
virtuosi. But Banks was an original. He would go to Newfoundland
and inspect Esquimaux; he would collect plants. If this be regarded

---

[1] In a letter first published in Swedish (*Upfostrings-Salskapets Tidningar*, No. 14 [21
February 1785], pp. 105-10), and later in German ('Ueber Solander', *Berlinische Monats-
schrift*, 6 [1785], pp. 240-9). This letter gave Banks's recollections of Solander. I owe
my knowledge of it to Mr R. A. Rauschenberg, of the University of Illinois, who generously sent me a translation of the German version. I refer to it below as 'Ueber Solander'.

as an extraordinary, as well as unexpected, step for a young person of wealth and comfort in 1766, the comment is that Banks was an extraordinary young person. In that century an extraordinary person did not lack opportunity to show his nature. The opportunity was now provided by the economics of empire. On the coasts of Newfoundland, French and English fishermen had long contested desirable rights and harbours. The peace of 1763 had done something both to affirm and to delimit British claims. British fishermen themselves, however, had to be kept in order, and a web of standing custom to be reinforced and maintained by royal regulation and naval supervision. The ship detailed to cross the Atlantic on this duty for the summer of 1766 was H.M.S. *Niger*, Captain Sir Thomas Adams; and among her officers was Lieutenant Constantine John Phipps. Lieutenant Phipps was himself a rather unusual person: the heir to an Irish peerage and the nephew of an English earl, he had entered the royal navy from Oxford; not only was his career assured, as a man of 'interest', but he was able to help his friends and Banks was an Oxford friend. It is really in no way odd, therefore, to find our young naturalist leaving London on 7 April to join a naval vessel, and beginning the first of his many journals of travel.[1] Nor is it odd, after his arrival at Plymouth on the 9th, that he should spend the days before the departure of his ship in exploring the natural history of Plymouth, in taking a critical view of that seat of opulence Mount Edgecumbe, and in visiting Mr Cookworthy's shop to collect the details of the china manufacture in which Mr Cookworthy was engaged; for a gentleman of enquiring mind enquired into everything.[2]

[1] The original manuscript of the journal that Banks kept on this voyage is now in Adelaide, in the possession of the South Australian branch of the Royal Geographical Society. I have used a careful copy made by Sarah Sophia, in the library of the Botanical Department of the British Museum (Natural History), 121 pp. quarto; this is entitled 'Journal of a Voyage to Newfoundland & Labrador: commencing April yᵉ seventh, & ending November the 17th 1766', and is signed at the head, 'S: S: Banks 1772'. At the bottom of p. 2 she has a pencil note, 'mem: there are many References to Latin Names of Plants &c. which I shall leave out.' There is a second copy, which includes an additional section, 'Some Account of Lisbon, & the adjacent Country, & Customs of the Inhabitants'. This is one of a set of Banks's lesser journals copied out by her, now arranged in three volumes and in the possession of Sir David Hawley. Dr J. W. F. Hill has kindly lent me typescripts of these journals. The originals, apart from the Newfoundland and Iceland journals, have disappeared. I refer to the copies in footnotes hereunder as S.S.B., with the date.
[2] William Cookworthy (1705-80) was an interesting minor figure of the eighteenth century, a greatly respected Quaker, successful as a wholesale druggist, and with scientific leanings; the surviving examples of his chinaware are many of them delightful. Banks and Cook are said to have dined with him just before the *Endeavour* sailed from Plymouth (his grandson kept the dining table as a relic), but neither of them mentions such a meeting. Solander wrote to Ellis, 25 August 1768, 'When you see Dr. Fothergill give him my respects, and tell him that we here in Plymouth met with a friend of his, Mr.

The *Niger* sailed from Plymouth Sound on 22 April, and reached the harbour of St John's on the south-east coast of Newfoundland on 11 May. On the voyage Banks suffered and recovered from sea-sickness, netted and described jelly-fish, tried unsuccessfully to catch sea-birds with a hook and line, and saw a number of icebergs — the first 'an Island of Ice . . . like a Body of whitish light'. Gales were succeeded by mist and frost, and when he went on shore at St John's he found the spring very little advanced. But what a country for walking and botanizing, for fishing and shooting! Lobsters, crabs, starfish, 'great plenty of small trouts', 'Dog's violets both blew and white', 'water Bugs in abundance', mosses, shrubs and birds: all were there, and the amiable sailors brought in rocks and a tortoise shell for him. Snow was a very minor interruption. He inspected, here and elsewhere, the sites of passages of arms between the French and British, and made the military observations proper to a gentleman. On June 11, in pursuit of a roving commission, Sir Thomas Adams set sail for Croque harbour, inside the northern peninsula of the island, where a vegetable garden was started and Phipps set up a habitation called Crusoe Hall; there, said his friend, 'he works night and Day, and lets the Musquetos eat more of him, than he does of any kind of food, all through Eagerness'.[1] There was a white bear to look for, unsuccessfully. The weather became hot. Banks went out with the master in a shallop, examining the bays and harbours to the southward, botanizing where he could, sleeping in his clothes in 'the aft Cuddy'; and then on further expeditions of the same sort, unable to keep his journal properly because his shipmates were so curious to see what he wrote down in it. Then the blow fell: for the greater part of July he was confined to the ship by a fever, 'incapable of collecting Plants, at the very season of the year when they are the most plentifull'; indeed at one stage his life was despaired of. Weak and dispirited, he had to make do with what his servant[2] could bring in, and when he could get on shore again, he was 'baffled by every Butterfly who chose to fly away'. His strength soon returned, and he was out on another boat expedition, this time to the north, which gave him not only some valuable plants but also, at last, on Belle Isle, the sight of a wild bear. No sooner

Cookworthy, as worthy a man as can be, full of knowledge, and very communicative: we are very much obliged to him for his civilities'.—Sir James Edward Smith (ed.), *A Selection of the Correspondence of Linnaeus, and other Naturalists, from the Original Manuscripts* (London 1821), II, p. 11. I hereafter cite this work as J. E. S. For Cookworthy see D.N.B. and John Prideaux, *Relics of William Cookworthy* (London 1853).

[1] Journal, 16 June.
[2] Marginal note by S. S. B., Journal, p. 42, 'believe Peter Briscoe'.

was he on board ship again than she sailed for Chateau Bay on the coast of Labrador, inside Belle Isle, for a two months' visit. Although the passage was made in a strong gale, he found to his pleasure that he had mastered his sea-sickness. There were more boat expeditions, on one of which, on 2 September, he and his friend the master had the narrowest possible escape from sinking in a further, and terrific, gale;[1] for the blowing season had come on, and Sir Thomas was henceforth very careful of his boats. Banks preferred Chateau Bay to Croque: the country was more barren, but the absence of brushwood made him always sure of a good walk, and the abundance of partridge, teal, and curlews gave him good shooting. Croque on the other hand he thought intolerable in summer from its heat, its thick woods and its prodigious abundance not of game but of mosquitoes and gadflies; while field-mice ravaged the vegetable gardens and weasels the eggs of the ship's poultry kept on shore. Meanwhile he was busy at his journal again, over an account he had gathered of the Newfoundland Indians, not without a certain scepticism — 'if half of what I have wrote about them is true', he said, 'it is more than I expect'. They had their own method of taking a scalp, and a scalp he managed to get hold of. Then came accounts of the English and the French fisheries, and the habits of fishermen; followed by recipes for chowder, the soup made of salt pork, cod, and biscuit — which earned his great admiration — of spruce beer, and of the powerful variations which could be built upon it. The detail is very much Banks. He was in high spirits again; of which we may judge very well, not from his journal, but from the quite characteristic letter he wrote to Sarah Sophia from Chateau Bay, 11 August:

Dear Sister

I received yours two days ago with newspapers &c: &c: which I must thank you all for as I can assure you they were the greatest Comfort you can Conceive — we all sat round the Fire & hunted out all the deaths marriages &c: &c: as eagerly as a schoolboy does Plumbs out of a Pudding

How do you think I have spent my Leisure Time since I have been here Very Musically I can assure you I have learnt to Play upon a new Instrument as I have Forswore the Flute I have tried my hand upon strings what do you think it is now not a fiddle I can assure you but a Poor innocent Guittar which Lay in the Cabbin on which I can play Lady Coventries minuet & in Infancy &c: with Great success

---

[1] 'when mere accident preserved my Life', he wrote. Sarah Sophia preferred to think otherwise: 'Providence', she made her marginal annotation, p. 24.

Pray My Love to Coz Bate & tell her that she & I differ a little in opinion about Stamford races as I had rather be here Than at all the races in Europe — not but what I beleive she was at Least as happy there as I am here

I hope Mr Lee has been Very Civil & Given you Nosegays as often as you have been to him if not tell him he shall not have one of my Insects when I come home give my Comp^{ts} to him also & tell him that if I did not think it might Endanger Cracking some of Your Ladyships teeth I would Let him know by you some of the Hard names of the things I have got

So Miss Frederick is going to be married to our countryman a dangerous Experiment I think he killed his Last wife in a hurry I hope he may keep her alive a little Longer but maybe she intends to Revenge Miss Pit & kill him I know you women are Sad Husband killers in your hearts

I do not know what Else to say I am almost Exhausted thank you however for your ague receipt it has one merit however I think for if it would not Cure an ague I am sure it would kill a horse

We are here in daily Expectation of the Eskimaux Ladies here I wish with all my heart they were Come as I might have sent you a sealskin gown & Petticoat Perfumd with train oil which to them is as Sweet as Lavander water but more of them when I know them better at Present adieu only Beleive

Me Your very affectionate Brother

J BANKS

P: S: Pray My Comp^{ts} to all Freinds at Chelsea especialy our neighbours at the Garden I mean our Garden-ing uncle & aunt adieu[1]

This letter does not indicate very much of the adventures of a naturalist across the Atlantic; it is not very witty; but it does indicate the easy good humour of its writer's mind — when things were going well — and his excellent relations with this admiring and admirable sister.

He did not, alas, see the Eskimaux Ladies; and on 3 October the ship returned to Croque to fill water and pick up what vegetables and poultry had survived. Banks collected a few more plants, and gives us an account of the seal-fishery. On 10 October the ship sailed for St John's, the rendezvous for the whole Newfoundland squadron, where he notes his approval of a person who was later to receive in very full measure his disapproval: the commodore was 'Mr Palliser' of the *Guernsey*, 'whose civilities we ought to acknowledge, as he shewed us all we could expect'. And St John's?

---

[1] ML, Banks Papers, XVI, pp. 3ff. Some of the personal allusions in this letter escape me—'Miss Frederick', 'Miss Pit' and 'our countryman'. No doubt 'Coz Bate' was a relative on Banks's mother's side, and 'Mr Lee' was James Lee, the Hammersmith nurseryman.

'We all felt great pleasure in returning to Society, which we had so long been deprived of; St John's, tho' the most disagreable Town I ever met with was for some time perfectly agreable to us'. Our journalist deals faithfully with St John's, the very cows of which, he was assured, ate fish. The compensation was Coronation Day. To the celebration of this Commodore Palliser bent all his sense of style, while his guests had to smother what taste for social discriminations they possessed. The *Guernsey* was dressed for the occasion: 'after this we were all invited to a Ball, given by Mr Governor, where the want of Ladies was so great, that my Washer-woman and her Sister were there by formal Invitation; but what surprized me the most was, that after dancing we were conducted to a really elegant Supper, set out with all kinds of wine, and Italian Liqueurs, to the great emolument of the Ladies, who eat and drank to some purpose; dancing it seems agreed with them, by its getting them such excellent Stomachs'.[1] This gleam of light on social history — the poor ladies might well turn with enthusiasm from too much chowder and spruce beer to an elegant supper and Italian Liqueurs — is succeeded by an account of the sea-cow fishery; and that by the dimensions of a schooner, a remarkably good sea-boat; and that by a note on the absence of any distinct breed of Newfound-land dog; and that by further praise for Palliser as a governor. All was interesting, all was recorded; there was nothing that did not stimulate that rapid, that punctuation-free pen.

But the summer had come to an end, autumn drew on, fishing was over and the fishing-boats departed, the year was too far advanced for success in further plant-hunting; nevertheless, said the hunter, 'I have vanity enough to believe, that to the northward not many will be found to have escaped my observation'.[2] On 28 October the *Niger* left St John's for Lisbon, there to spend part of the winter. The Atlantic provided the gale that first impressed Banks with his very lively sense of the precautions necessary in the ocean carriage of plants — precautions which are underlined with more and more elaboration in his later correspondence; for on 5 November, off the Western Islands, the vessel shipped a sea which stove in the quarter, flooded the cabin, broke all its furniture in pieces and entirely demolished his collection of seeds and growing specimens. But the dried specimens survived, the larger number of his trophies, and into safe keeping they went at New Burlington Street: the foundation, on the foreign side, of the great Herbarium that was to be the pride of British botany and a

[1] *Journal*, pp. 105-6.   [2] *Journal*, p. 113.

lodestone for the scientific curiosity of all Europe.[1] The ship reached Lisbon on 17 November, the date on which the surviving journal ends, with its later-written descriptton of the harbour, the town, and the customs of the inhabitants. Portugal treated Banks kindly: although he never saw the inside of a Portuguese gentleman's house, he made friends in natural history,[2] added a good deal to his collections, and saw for the first time that rare substance, caoutchouc or indiarubber. Early in the new year the *Niger* duly returned to England, and Banks with her. He arrived in London on 30 January 1767.[3] There could by now be no doubt, even among the rare purists, that his election to the Royal Society was justified. Not only was he a man of substance, but he had travelled unconventionally; he had suffered the confinement of a naval vessel, storm, discomfort and fever, in the cause of science, and he had kept a journal with hard names that would endanger his sister's teeth. His journal, indeed, with the interest it displayed in everything, from fish to fortifications, and its treatment of human beings as essential parts of natural history, might be taken as a sort of trial run for the larger journal on which he was before long to embark. He had served his apprenticeship. He did not commit any of the journal to print, nor report on his adventures except in a social way. But he attended a meeting of the Royal Society for the first time on 15 February 1767; and there, no doubt, he bore himself with a proper dignity.

Meanwhile there were things to do in the metropolis, and beyond it. There was so much to raise the interest of an intelligent man. He went down into Kent on a little tour of universal enquiry — plants, shells, fossils, fortifications, the manufacture of vitriol, beer, and flints, dockyards, a fire ship and a court martial all claimed his attention — and then was again involved in London.[4] We have a letter to Thomas Pennant of 5 May 1767:[5]

I am ashamed I have not Long before wrote to you to tell you the truth

[1] It speaks highly of Banks's generosity that he was prepared to lend his herbarium to his friend John Sneyd, of Bishton, Derbyshire, for the period of his absence on the *Endeavour* voyage. See Sneyd to Banks, Kew B.C. I, 31, n.d., requesting the loan, and asking him also to buy textiles for Sneyd's wife in China and Japan if he should visit those countries; and ibid., 30, 9 January 1773, thanking him for the loan.

[2] There are, for instance, in Kew B.C. I, several letters from Gerard De Vismes, of Lisbon, beginning with 2 June 1767; the second announces the gift of a hogshead of 'that choice Calcavellas', with instructions for its treatment.

[3] There is a marginal note to this effect at the beginning of the description of Lisbon in the second copy of the journal by S. S. B. The *Niger* arrived at Plymouth on 20 January 1767.

[4] Journal of an Excursion to Chatham, Rochester, Sheerness, Sheppey, &c. began Feb^ry 21st 1767 Ended March 4th 1767.—S.S.B. 1772.

[5] Alexander Turnbull Library (hereafter referred to as ATL), ALS 269.

my Idleness is only to be excusd by alledging a still greater as a palliative Circumstance which is that I have not yet got your Beaver [i.e. a print of the animal] Colourd to tell you the truth I have been so hurried Ever since you left town by furnishing my house that I have scarcely had time to think of anything Else.

Mᴿ White called upon me today in your name & left some Specimens of Birds . . . . I intend tomorrow to call upon him at Horaces head and hold Ornithological Converse tho I can assure you it does not go on with the spirit it used to do when you was with us.

[A paragraph follows on the colouring of plates.] I want you of all things to visit a new Branch of trade I have lately discoverd which I think may be of Service to us the Horners a set of people who live by selling the Horns of all sorts of animals unworked up to those who work them into Knife Hafts &c. the People sell what they Call Buffaloes horns every day & must Certainly have many of animals unknown to us.

adieu Floreat Res Zoologica says

Your affectionate J BANKS

Another to the same correspondent, of 14 May,[1] touches on journeys:

I am Just upon the wing setting out for Dorsetshire . . . I mean to be out about a fortnight in which time I shall visit Bristol & the other side of the Channell I am much obligd to you (for an obligation you are not perhaps at present apprizd of) I mean an acquaintance with Mᴿ White who mentiond your name & promises to send divers & various discoveries to town. . . . Instead of remaining Idle as I intended till I should set out for Flint I find I am to be well employd for I must set out for Lincolnshire as soon as I return from my present expedition. . . .

The 'Dorsetshire' visit was more in the line of the ordinary cultivated county tour of the day than was that sudden leap across the Atlantic, and it lasted longer than a fortnight. It was in fact a leisurely progress from 15 May, on which day Banks descended upon his aunt Mrs Grenville at Eastbury, to 20 June, when he returned to New Burlington Street. Between those dates he went through Dorset and Somerset to Bristol, Chepstow — so that he did, as he planned, get across to 'the other side of the Channell' — Wells, Glastonbury and Taunton. There were country houses to inspect, starting with his aunt's — 'exceedingly large and possibly one of the heaviest piles of stone Sᴿ Jⁿᵒ Vanbrugh ever erected'; Pearcefield, 'the finest place I ever saw'; Burton Pynsent, where Lord Chatham had in two years done a great deal to the house:

[1] ibid.

'He has built several rooms, some very good ones, but has shewn that his Buildings in Brick are not more durable than his Administrations, as he has already found it necessary to pull down and alter what he himself set up' — an isolated political observation in all Banks's mass of papers. There was Chepstow Castle to admire; there was Tintern Abbey — 'a most noble Ruin, by far the Lightest Pi[e]ce of Gothick architecture I ever saw'; the cathedral at Wells (where he went with his antiquarian friend the Rev. Richard Kaye), 'Rather Good'; the abbey at Glastonbury, where he was 'almost bit to death' by gnats; there were pictures and coins and birds and the Cheddar gorge and fire engines, Roman circumvallations and barrows for archaeological speculation, the fossilized bones of 'an Elephant found bedded in Ocre on the Mendip hills'; there were riding and walking and a great amount of botanizing; and there was at Bristol 'a very singular curiosity which was a woman who had for reasons not yet well known been confined since August Last in a deal Box which I myself measurd and found the dimensions to be Lengh 2 feet 6 inches, Breadth and Depth each one foot 4'. Finally on the way back to London, between Silbury and Marlborough, there were the great boulders of sarsen scattered about Fyfield Down, the 'Grey Wethers' of the local inhabitants, who were breaking them up to build their walls; so that the botanist and man of taste could geologize as well, take some pieces home, and find them to be 'a very hard and fine graind Sand Stone'.[1] It is all very completely Banks, this tour, and this sample being given, we need not quote him on his other English, or rather British, journeys.[2]

Presumably this tour was followed by the visit to Lincolnshire, for Banks kept a close eye on his estate. There was also the anticipated journey to Flintshire and his friend Pennant. But was not something possible of nobler note?

I am Just Returnd to London From my Excursion [he wrote to Pennant] & as I prophesied in my Last found two of yours which your kindness had sent to me in my absence

What will you say to me if I should be prevented from paying my respects to you & N: Wales this year tho I so fully intended it nothing but your Looking upon it with the Eye of an unprejudiced nat: Historian

[1] 'Grey Wethers'—not 'weathers', as spelt by Banks—from their resemblance at a distance to a flock of sheep. The stone circle at Avebury, a mile and a half away, is believed to have been built with sarsens from this site, which was declared a nature reserve in 1956.

[2] His little journal of this tour exists in a copy by S.S.B., Hawley coll. It was admirably edited by Spencer George Perceval, and printed in the *Proceedings of the Bristol Naturalists' Society*, New Series IX, 1899, pp. 6-37.

can bring any excuse to be heard with Patience Look then with Zoologick
Eyes & tell me if you could Blame me if I Sacraficed every Consideration
to an opportunity of Paying a visit to our Master Linnaeus & Profiting
by his Lectures before he dies who is now so old that he cannot Long
Last

I know you cannot Blame me & you will not when I tell you that
nothing shall hinder my attendance in Flintshire but such an
expedition. . . .[1]

An expedition to Uppsala would certainly not have been an impossible one, and it could hardly have failed to have been beneficial
to Banks — if his capacity to assimilate lectures in Latin were
sufficient — as well as gratifying to Linnaeus, who loved his foreign
pupils, though he could speak no language of theirs. There would
have been distinction, too, in such close contact with the Master.
Nor was his demise so imminent at this time as Banks seems to
have thought: he had just passed his sixtieth year, and though his
most energetic days of open-air teaching were gone, he was still
a vigorous and lively presence, in lecture room or botanic garden.
Banks did inevitably come under his notice, in due course, but
only at second hand. For to Flintshire, not to Sweden, in this late
summer of 1767 did our young man go, with companions of whom
the most eminent, botanically, was the sociable apothecary William
Hudson — whose *Flora Anglica*, with its Linnaean classification,
had been the fundamental work on its subject since its first publication in 1762. It was a journey not only to Flintshire, but through
Wales from south to north, on to Cheshire and Derbyshire, and
south home again through Warwickshire, Oxfordshire and Berk-
shire. It was the longest of all Banks's British journeys, and it lasted
from the middle of August 1767 to the end of January 1768.[2]
He had not, however, abandoned thought of a pilgrimage to the
Master's feet. More than that, he would tread in the Master's
feet themselves, he would go to Lapland; Pennant, writing in

[1] This letter has no date or address, but it is with other letters addressed to Pennant,
ATL, ALS 269. It must be after 20 June; though Kew B.C. I, 7, a letter from Pennant,
10 June 1767, at first sight appears to be an answer to it: 'I sincerely wish y^r tour may
answer; but, not being greatly smitten with the charms of Linnaeus, must be doubtfull
till I hear from you'. Banks may have mentioned his plan to Pennant earlier. Pennant
thought Linnaeus was deficient in ornithology, 'madripology', and fossils: 'his fort is
Botany'. By 'madripology', a word not in the dictionaries, I take it he meant the study of
corals—from 'madrepore', generally applied in his day to any perforate coral. Again,
ibid., 8, 3 July 1767, 'I have no very high opinion of Linnaeus's zoologick merits'. In
another letter, 26 July 1767, D.T.C. I, p.13, he wishes Banks luck on the journey.

[2] 13 August 1767-29 January 1768. Banks kept a journal on this tour, the copy
of which by S.S.B. runs to 159 pp., illustrated with sketches and diagrams. It is now in
the National Library of Wales, MS 147. He kept also a memorandum book of very
characteristic 'Observations & facts relating to Nat. Hist. Commerce &c. Learnt from
different people'; Dawson MS 44.

January, is solicitous about the return from Chester to London, 'thro all the perils of snow and ice, a good foretaste of your Lapland Journey';[1] and in the following month Thomas Falconer, the classical scholar and learned antiquarian of Chester, wrote of his pleasure at the expected tour, for which he gave a good deal of advice to the tourist.[2] We do not know exactly when there flashed upon his mind the vision of a greater journey — an idea, if only it could be realized in fact, of a quite stupendously satisfying nature. This was the idea of a journey round the world and across the Pacific Ocean, where no natural historian had ever been before. It took on elaboration, it gathered weight, it was favourably received by the philosophical. And in this same season, it appears, of hope and speculative excitement, Joseph Banks fell in love.

§

Among the branches of science in which Banks was not interested, two, astronomy and geography, ranked pre-eminent. Yet the voyage on which he had fastened his mind was a voyage which had for its objects the increase of knowledge of precisely these two; and it was the result of impulses, from the Royal Society and the British Government, with which he had had nothing to do. It was a voyage, in short, for the observation of the transit of the planet Venus across the disc of the sun, and for the investigation of the great continent which was alleged by a number of theoretical geographers to exist in the more southern and western parts of the Pacific, and probably in high latitudes of the Atlantic as well — the *Terra australis incognita* of long tradition. The two men who in the eighteenth century most enthusiastically elaborated upon this theory were the French geographer Philippe Buache (1700-73) in whose *Considérations géographiques et physiques sur les nouvelles découvertes de la grande mer* (Paris, 1753) were what the author regarded as '*hypothèses déraisonnables*' on the outlines and formation of the continent; and the Scotsman Alexander Dalrymple, whose *Account of the Discoveries made in the South Pacifick Ocean, Previous to 1764* (London, 1769), displayed an immense and dogmatic confidence in its existence — founded, like the theories of Buache, on arguments both physical and historico-geographical. But indeed,

---

[1] Pennant to Banks, 15 January 1768; D.T.C. I, p. 16.

[2] 'I am extremely glad to find you are projecting a Northern Journey this summer for the benefit of Natural History. You intend, I hear, to visit if possible the great Lapland fair. . . .'—15 February 1768; Kew B.C. I, 17. Falconer, a generous recluse, was called by the enthusiastic Miss Seward 'the Maecenas of Chester'. Pennant was his kinsman by marriage. His letters to Banks are always very long, deferential, and full of advice on matters which call for scientific investigation.

most people accepted the general hypothesis with the simple faith that they gave to the existence of a south pole.

The Transit of Venus was a different matter. There could be no argument about it whatever. It was not a phenomenon that could be inspected every day. It had been first observed by the young, brilliant, and short-lived Jeremiah Horrocks in the year 1639, in his parsonage at Hoole in Lancashire; it had been last observed, with no great advantage to philosophy,[1] in 1761; it was due to occur again in 1769; and then more than a century would elapse till in 1874 it would give the astronomers another chance. Good observations would make it possible to calculate with some accuracy the distance of the earth from the sun, a pre-requisite to other important calculations in astronomy. In the event of 3 June 1769 therefore the Royal Society took a very lively interest; for undeniably, in 1761 British science — through no fault of its own — had not shone. The Rev. Nevil Maskelyne had been sent to St Helena, where a cloudy day had been sufficient reason for failure; and Messrs Mason and Dixon to Sumatra, which they had never reached — and, deposited by the exigencies of war at the Cape of Good Hope, they had found that by no means an ideal place for their operations. The Society was determined that no shortcoming on its part would inhibit a happier outcome on the next occasion, whatever the scientists of other nations might do, and as early as a meeting in June 1766 it resolved to despatch observers to 'several parts of the world'. Discussion did not become close, however, till towards the end of the following year, when it was decided that the British effort should be devoted to three widely separated places of observation — the first, Fort Churchill in Hudson Bay, the second the North Cape, and the third some suitable island in the Pacific Ocean. But what island? Mr Maskelyne, now Astronomer Royal, suggested the group called the Marquesas, or alternatively Rotterdam or Amsterdam, in the archipelago we know as Tonga; and there were other suggestions made, such as the Solomon Islands. The difficulty about any of these was that before a telescope could be stood upon it, it would have to be rediscovered; for the Solomons

---

[1] I am writing of the eighteenth century, and I here deliberately use this word with its eighteenth century meaning of 'science'. Physics in some universities is still 'natural philosophy'. Johnson's *Dictionary* defines 'Philosopher' as 'A man deep in knowledge, either moral or natural'—we should say for the latter 'scientist'; and 'Philosophy' as (1) 'Knowledge natural or moral'; (2) 'Hypothesis or system upon which natural effects are explained'; (4) 'The course of sciences read in the schools'. At the same time I admit that I am not consistent in this usage, and that 'philosopher' and 'philosophize' occur below in much more modern connotations—my hope being that the reader will be neither confused nor irritated.

had not been seen since their discovery by Mendaña in 1568, or the Marquesas since their discovery, also by Mendaña, in 1595, or Amsterdam and Rotterdam since their discovery by Tasman in 1643. Assuming that the island could be rediscovered, how was it to be rediscovered? Again, astronomers themselves would need transit, and while the Hudson Bay Company would no doubt take observers to Fort Churchill, and they might go to the North Cape on the annual naval vessel for fisheries protection, the Pacific Ocean was a different matter. The Royal Society had no money with which to charter a ship; like other learned societies without funds, therefore, it decided to appeal to government. The Council submitted a memorial to the king requesting a grant of four thousand pounds and the necessary ship; observers it had in mind for the Pacific were Mr Dalrymple the geographer and Mr Green, late of the Royal Observatory at Greenwich. Mr Dalrymple, it may be noted, found it necessary to observe that he had no thoughts of making the voyage as a passenger, or in any other capacity than that of 'having the total management of the ship intended to be sent'. As Mr Dalrymple, though neither 'bred to the navy' nor a professional seaman, had had some experience of command in the East Indies, this did not seem to the Society unreasonable; and the king having expressed his willingness to provide the money, the Admiralty was directed to provide a ship. The official investigations into this matter began early in March 1768, and by the end of that month the 'cat-built bark' *Earl of Pembroke*, soon to be given the more famous name *Endeavour*, had been brought into the navy.

Meanwhile there had been discussion of the command of the vessel. The Admiralty, quite unmoved by the claims of Mr Dalrymple, settled on Mr James Cook. This was somewhat surprising, because Mr Cook was not even a commissioned officer, and he did not have that 'interest' with government that was so useful as a means to promotion. He had, however, made his own interest by solid merit, more particularly by his distinguished career as a marine surveyor in Newfoundland, where, at the time of Banks's visit, he had been working on the south coast and had observed an eclipse of the sun from the Burgeo islands.[1] He was

---

[1] It was in the Newfoundland and not Pacific context that Banks first heard of Cook. Captain Wilkinson of the *Niger*, 18 December 1767 (Kew B. C. I, 15) writes to him, 'Sir, As my meeting with the Indians was very uncertain, The Cask of things you left on board of the Niger for Truck with 'em Mr Palliser took on board the Guernsey to Chatteaux, & I believe he has procure'd you some of their dresses &c. I'd got a Canoe for you which I sent home in the Grenville as she came to Deptford, but she Unluckily run on shore & it was wash'd over board & lost as I am told, tho I have not been able to see Mr Cook to ask him about it, nor I am afraid shan't as I am going into the Country but if you'll

D

very well known to influential men like Captain Palliser, now of
the Navy Board, and Philip Stephens the Admiralty secretary, and,
though promotion came late to him, they had no doubt of his
ability to command. The decision reduced Mr Dalrymple to fury;
attending the Council of the Society in person, he reaffirmed his
determination not to go on the voyage at all. There was nothing
the Society could do but find another observer. Here it was in
luck: Mr Cook appeared a proper person, and Mr Cook was
appointed, with Mr Green as his astronomical colleague. Just
at this point another naval vessel completed a voyage round the
world by arriving in England: it was the *Dolphin*, Captain Samuel
Wallis, and it reported the discovery of an island and harbour
quite admirably fitted for the Society's purpose of observation.
Furthermore, the position of this island had been accurately fixed;
no time need be occupied in rediscovery. It was King George the
Third's Island, and its harbour was Port Royal — or as we have
learnt to call them, Tahiti and Matavai Bay. Early in June the
Society informed the Admiralty of its wish to have the observers
conveyed there; and simultaneously brought forward something new:

Joseph Banks Esqʳ Fellow of this Society, [wrote the secretary] a Gentleman of large fortune, who is well versed in natural history, being
Desirous of undertaking the same voyage the Council very earnestly
request their Lordships, that in regard to Mʳ Banks's great personal
merit, and for the Advancement of useful knowledge, He also, together
with his Suite, being seven persons more, that is, eight persons in all,
together with their baggage, be received on board of the Ship, under
the Command of Captain Cook.[1]

This was something new, however, only in the formal correspondence; for though we do not know, unfortunately, when Banks
first had his brilliant idea, the time was certainly long before,
and there had certainly been a great deal of talk — and, quite
obviously, of preparation, because we have the suite already
precisely numbered. The Council of the Royal Society had directed
the sending of its letter last quoted on 9 June; and 9 June was the
date on which Banks himself received a farewell letter from a

please to send to him he will let you know whether there are any hopes of getting it by
Advertising which I thought off as it was drove ashore on the Essex coast I believe. . . .
Mʳ Cook lives I am told some where about Mile end, but the Vessel I believe is got up
to Deptford [so] that I fancy it will be best to send to enquire on board her'.—The
Grenville was Cook's surveying schooner; in heavy weather off the Nore, 11 November
1767, she dragged her anchor and went on shore, but was refloated next day with very
little damage.
  [1] I quote from the letter as it is entered in the Minutes of the Council of the Royal
Society, 9 June 1768.

friend: 'I have for some time been in Doubt whether you was [in] England or on the Seas; last Night's Papers acquainted me that a North Country Cat was fitting out at Deptford for the South Seas, and was to take on board some Gentlemen of Fortune Students in Botany'.[1] But this was already late in the day: as early as 10 April Pennant was writing with advice on umbrellas, 'both the thin silk french kinds and the strong oil skin ones; also oil skin coats to guard against the torrents of rain you may expect to meet'.[2] It is clear that Banks's friends caught some of his excitement — excitement summarized in his traditional reply to one more conservative, who expostulated over the hare-brained project, and advised the conventional Grand Tour instead: 'Every blockhead does that; my Grand Tour shall be one round the whole globe'.[3]

Now on 10 April, when Pennant was writing about umbrellas, the ship had been bought, and the mode of her fitting-out determined, and it seems clear that her master had been selected. But it does not seem likely that the Admiralty had by then agreed to accommodate Mr Banks, or even been asked to do so. Mr Banks, however, had had his idea, and clearly assumed that it would be acceptable to all others concerned. His assumption is characteristic: it is characteristic both of the young Banks and of the eighteenth century. A gentleman of large fortune who had had his own way since early youth, who had chosen his own subjects of study and provided the means himself, who went where he wished and took his place in any society he wished, whose friends were scientific, and naval, and ministerial — we must not forget the Earl of Sandwich — hardly needed to hesitate. What he was proposing to do was to plant himself, a train of dependants and a mass of impedimenta on a small and already overcrowded vessel, commanded by a man he did not know, for purposes not at all envisaged by government, in a fashion that would undoubtedly entail further expense on government and inconvenience on other people; and he was proposing it in the sure, certain, and unhesitating conviction that he had a right to be obliged, and would be made welcome. This it was that was so highly characteristic of the English gentleman of fortune of that age, so effortlessly superior, so candidly appropriative of privilege, upon his Grand Tour; this it was that was so completely the Banksian attitude to life. The extraordinary thing is, to a later age, that he brought it off. There were no

[1] Richard Kaye to Banks, 26 June 1768; Kew B.C. I, 27.
[2] Pennant to Banks, 10 April 1768; Kew B.C. I, 21.
[3] Edward Smith, *Life of Sir Joseph Banks* (London 1911), pp. 15-16.

difficulties raised. He simply, we may say, walked on board the *Endeavour*, elbowed her officers out of the way, and was made welcome. The touring Englishman expected a welcome, and generally got one, at his inn; but it was a professional welcome, he paid for it. There was no doubt about the welcome that met Banks; for there was no doubt about the Banksian charm. It was not a deliberate or calculated charm. Banks was not, like so many of his contemporaries on their travels, the *grand seigneur*. Indeed the *grand seigneur* could not by any stretch of the imagination have chosen the mode of travel that Mr Banks chose. There were times when Banks could act the spoilt child, and other times when he could put on style; but ordinarily it was the directness of the child, or the youth, that he displayed, mingled with his belief in his own privilege. As things turned out on this voyage, there were no seriously unpleasant consequences; and there were, in the presence and talents of Mr Banks, certain positive advantages. For once he had had his great idea, nothing, as we have seen, could stop him, and on 22 July Cook was directed by the Admiralty secretary to receive not only 'Mr Charles Green and his Servant and Baggage', but also 'Joseph Banks Esq. and his Suite consisting of eight Persons with their Baggage, bearing them as Supernumeraries for Victuals only, and Victualling them as the Barks Company during their Continuance on board'.[1] (There were also a couple of dogs, but no doubt they were included with the baggage.) That is, once these persons were on board, they were to get no special treatment they did not pay for themselves, or that Mr Banks did not pay for. The Admiralty would give them food and cabin or hammock space — and not much of that — and they must make the best of it.

Who were these eight persons that Banks so blithely added to the eighty-six others already thrust on board the small ship under the newly created Lieutenant Cook's command? Their number, it will be noted, had risen by one since the Royal Society communicated with the Admiralty in June. They were, in some sort of order of social and scientific rank, Dr Daniel Carl Solander, Herman Didrich Spöring, Sydney Parkinson, Alexander Buchan, Peter Briscoe, James Roberts, Thomas Richmond and George Dorlton. Dr Solander already was a man of mark. He was a Swede, born at Pitea in the northern part of his country, in 1733. His medical studies were but his avenue into natural history. After the brilliant and beloved Petrus Löfling the ablest of the Uppsala pupils of Linnaeus, he contributed plants from his own province

[1] Cook I, p. 620.

to the Linnaean herbarium, and earned golden opinions from the Academic Consistory of the University as well as from the Master himself. When the ardent London natural historians, Peter Collinson and John Ellis, both correspondents of Linnaeus, urged him to send a pupil to England to spread the gospel, the choice fell on Solander, and he was not unwilling. He bade farewell to Linnaeus at the beginning of April 1759, but, falling sick in the south of Sweden, did not arrive in England till July 1760.[1] Ellis took him in charge, with what Linnaeus called 'paternal affection', and before long he was widely known for both his extreme good humour and the acuteness of his learning. From as far as Charleston, South Carolina — ' a horrid country, where there is not a living soul who knows the least *iota* of Natural History' — a naturalist friend of Ellis, Dr Alexander Garden, wrote with some despair, 'I confess I often envy you the sweet hours of converse on this subject with your friends in and about London. How must you enjoy Solander! O my God!'[2] This was in 1761. By 1762 Solander was attending the meetings of the Royal Society;[3] and Collinson testifies to his impact on English science and natural historians in a letter to Linnaeus of 2 September in that year: 'My dear Linnaeus cannot easily conceive the pleasure of this afternoon. There was our beloved Solander seated in my Musaeum, surrounded with tables covered with an infinite variety of sea-plants, the accumulation of many years. He was digesting and methodizing them into order, and for his pains he shall be rewarded with a collection of them, which no doubt you will see. Afterwards at supper we remembered my dear Linnaeus, and my other Swedish friends, over a cheerful glass of wine. . . . Solander is very industrious in making all manner of observations to enrich himself and his country with knowledge in every branch of natural history'.[4] A man so able was marked for learned preferment, and in 1762 the Petersburg Academy of

[1] Cf. the letter from Linnaeus to Ellis, 6 November 1759, J.E.S. I, p. 125. Linnaeus had already written with undue optimism to Ellis as early as 30 May 1759, 'No doubt my much-loved pupil Solander has, ere this, found a tranquil asylum in your friendship. I have recommended him to your protection, as I would my own son. . . .'—ibid., pp. 123-4.

[2] J.E.S. I, p. 502.

[3] He heard some surprising things at the Royal Society; e.g. his letter to Ellis, 5 March 1762 (J.E.S. II, p. 8). 'Last night I was at the Royal Society. It was a long meeting, but very few things of consequence. One Rev. Dr. Foster had sent two letters; in one he will prove, against Mr. Collinson, that swallows really, during winter, immerse themselves in water. . . . likewise mention is made of frogs in winter, during a hard frost, being found frozen, apparently dead, being hard and brittle like flint, so that they break with a blow. But if taken into a warm room, they come to life again.'—Linnaeus seems to have believed the story about the swallows.—Collinson to Linnaeus, 15 September 1763 (a rather sceptical letter, suggesting some practical experiments), J.E.S. I, pp. 59-62.

[4] J.E.S. I, pp. 56-7.

Sciences was anxious, on the recommendation of Linnaeus, to appoint him its professor of botany. London was in despair: could not someone less eminent teach science to Russian bears?[1] But Solander himself refused to go to Russia; he liked his new friends, and they were diligently looking out for his advantage. It is now Ellis who writes to Linnaeus, in December 1762, about the delightful person: 'He is exceedingly sober, well behaved, and very diligent, no way expensive; so that I hope he will do very well. I can assure you, the more he is known, the more he is liked; and now peace is near settled, he has a greater probability of succeeding, than when we were engaged in the hurry of a troublesome, though victorious war'.[2] Solander had one defect, it must be admitted, of which Linnaeus had had experience, and which most of his friends were to remark: he was reluctant to answer letters. This was unfortunate, and we feel the misfortune even today, because when he conquered his reluctance he was an excellent letter-writer. Short and plump men are not infrequently bustling: it is clear that Solander, though short and to become plump, never bustled. Meanwhile his reputation as a natural historian of the widest interests and knowledge continued to grow, and at last in 1764 he obtained an assistantship in the British Museum; in this year too he was elected F.R.S. He was busy making catalogues; he surveyed the fabulous collection of the Duchess of Portland.[3] Mr Banks, who in 1764 entered upon his independency and his career in London, could hardly have been unaware of the existence of this brilliant and amiable man, and when they met, they quickly formed a firm and mutual regard. It was at Lady Anne Monson's, at dinner, that Solander, fired with the conversation about the forthcoming voyage, leapt to his feet and proposed himself as a travelling-companion. Banks was enraptured; and next day he talked the Admiralty into acquiescence.[4] Solander had placed himself in a great line; for there was a Linnaean tradition of travel, and from the study of the man who had tramped through Lapland his 'apostles' went north, south, east and west, to the Arctic, North America, Guiana, Arabia Felix, the Cape, to the Atlas mountains and Palestine, to the East Indies, China and Japan. They were

---

[1] Collinson to Linnaeus, 16 November 1762; ibid., pp. 57-8.
[2] Ellis to Linnaeus, 21 December 1762; ibid., p. 160.
[3] Collinson to Linnaeus, 1 May 1765; J.E.S. I, p. 65. This was the greatest private collection of the time. It was dispersed in 1786. Horace Walpole wrote on 8 April 1786 to his nephew Thomas, 'The catalogue of the Duchess of Portland's collection is come out. The auction begins on the 24th. Out of thirty-eight days there are but eight that exhibit anything but shells, ores, fossils, birds' eggs, and natural history'.—*Letters* (ed. Toynbee), XIII, p. 376.   [4] 'Ueber Solander', pp. 244-5.

victims of pirates and plague, hunger, thirst and poverty, and some of them died far from home; but, by so great sacrifices, the harvest of knowledge was enormous. It was one of the heroic ages of science, and it was only by extreme good luck that Solander was not one of the apostles who died.

Of Spöring we know a great deal less. His father was a professor of medicine at the University of Åbo in Finland, and, like so many of the learned, a correspondent of Linnaeus. The son was born about 1730: he was a student at Åbo from 1748 to 1753, going afterwards to Stockholm for a course in surgery. He must have sought his fortune in London and become known there, and he must have become an able naturalist, as did other men trained in medicine. Banks seems to have engaged him as a sort of secretary.[1] 'A grave thinking man', as he was later called by his employer, he was also a good draughtsman, and clever with his fingers in the mechanical way: amid all the miscellaneous collections of appliances on board the *Endeavour*, the set of watchmaker's tools was taken by him. Sydney Parkinson, the botanical or natural history draughtsman, was born about 1745, the younger son of a Quaker brewer, Joel Parkinson of Edinburgh. This was one brewer who did not in that century amass wealth: his sons, on his death, having to fend for themselves, Sydney was apprenticed to a woollen-draper. His talent for drawing, however, would out; he came to London, where his flowers and fruits attracted the attention of botanists and other connoisseurs of natural history — among whom was Banks. It was to Parkinson that Banks in 1767 committed the task of copying on vellum a collection of drawings brought back from Ceylon by Governor Loten,[2] while he worked busily also on living specimens from Kew and from Mr Lee the Hammersmith nurseryman. His talent was such indeed that he was an obvious choice for draughtsman on a journey in which natural history would, according to Banks's calculations, bulk so large; and Banks had intended him for the northern journey now abandoned.[3] But his talent did not

[1] James Roberts, in his 'journal' (see p. 28, n. below) lists 'Armon Dedrich Sporing' as Banks's 'svt [servant] writer'; and Parkinson refers to 'Mr. David [*sic*] Sporing, clerk to Mr. Banks'.

[2] 'our Freind Governor V [?] Loten is fixd in N Bur'ington Street so we shall with ease get the Rest of his Drawin[g]s'.—Banks to Pennant, 14 May 1767.—He has got hold of Governor Loten's drawings and is getting them copied as fast as possible—he will not let Parkinson do anything else.—To Pennant, n.d. ATL, MS Folder 269. Cf. Pennant to Banks, 27 June 1767: 'My dear fellow Labourer, avoid procrastination: we may lose our opportunity: Loten is old and his wife is young; and the odds are against his life'.—D.T.C. I, p. 10.

[3] 'I am extremely glad you take Parkinson with you & doubt not you will gain treasures from the several collections of drawings you will find.'—Pennant to Banks, 4 August 1767; Kew B.C. I, 12.

stop with the pencil or the brush — he was in every way highly intelligent, both sensible and sensitive, eager to learn as well as extremely hard-working, with interests that expanded to every new thing he saw or heard; guided by his Quaker conscience, and not averse from moral judgments; to pronounce from the stiffly-drawn portrait by James Newton prefixed to his published journal, a slightly-built dark wisp of a young man, long-nosed and with long thin fingers and a rather prim little mouth; obviously a very serious young man indeed. His fellow-artist, Buchan, has left much less of an impression on the history of the voyage. Presumably he was a Scot. We know that he was epileptic; but whether Banks was acquainted with that unhappy fact when he engaged him, as 'an ingenious and good young man', for landscape and figure drawing, we do not know. His early death was to throw a very large load of work on Sydney Parkinson, helped out a little by Spöring; and while the landscape remained to posterity, and could be drawn at any time (a fact not very consoling to Banks), we miss extremely a really good and full record of the personal appearance of the oceanic peoples at this critical moment of impact of a new culture upon them. The remaining four men were Banks's personal servants, and they hardly come alive for us. Peter Briscoe and James Roberts, a boy of sixteen, were from Lincolnshire, apparently from the Revesby estate; Briscoe, who had been on the Newfoundland expedition, had sharp eyes, and both were interested enough to copy someone else's journal;[1] they had enough capacity for survival to die long years afterwards in their native country. Richmond and Dorlton, on the other hand, negroes (it was the fashion to have negroes in one's service in contemporary London), were doomed to but a short lease of life; they appear, and their master's journal records them almost only to describe their cold and melancholy end.

So much for the companions and adherents of our adventurer, as he prepared to set out on a very remarkable voyage. We may note something else that he had with him. This was a copy of Dalrymple's pamphlet on Pacific discoveries, with its interesting and inaccurate map, which the author had given him. The map

---

[1] I regret that the journals written by Roberts and Briscoe escaped listing with the other civilian journals in Cook I, pp. ccxxxix-xlii. Roberts's is now in the Mitchell Library; Briscoe's in the Dixson Library. They have however no particular value as journals, their first few entries being copied from the ship's log—perhaps at some removes—and the rest from Pickersgill. They do, however, include useful lists of the ship's company, with the 'qualities' in which individuals sailed: the 'quality' of Roberts and Briscoe being 'Footman'. The Briscoe volume has the unusual and pious title-page, 'A Journal of His Majesties Bark Endeavour By Gods Permishon Bound to the South Seas. . .'.

was interesting because it showed a passage north of Australia with a ship's track marked through it — the track of Torres in 1606. Banks's mind, so far as we can see, was not much stirred by this, but Cook's was. Cook had a geographical mind; Banks had not. And the map was to play its part in the remarkable voyage.[1] The voyage would have been remarkable in English history, apart from its extraordinary geographical importance, apart even from the success that was to attend it in the realm of natural history, as the first voyage of discovery which went equipped with a scientific staff. Its primary purpose, to observe the Transit of Venus, was of course scientific, and for this purpose Cook and Green were the staff. With all the careful preparations of the Royal Society, with all the expense incurred by the Admiralty, and with all the conviction of the observers that their efforts had been rewarded with success, the end was failure. Although no astronomer was, or could be, aware of the fact, it was impossible to make accurate observations of Venus in the way intended. The triumph therefore was in the descriptive sciences of zoology and botany and in ethnology, and it was a triumph which installed in British voyages of discovery the tradition of scientific work over a wide ambit. It was not indeed the first voyage of discovery on which a naturalist had sailed; the honour implied therein belonged to the French. Bougainville, with whom was Philibert Commerson,[2] eminent in botany, was at the moment of the *Endeavour*'s departure making his painful way towards the Moluccas, after an able passage of the Pacific by way of Tahiti, the New Hebrides and the Solomon Islands. The achievement of French men of science was thereafter very great. Nor must we forget what we have noted already, the travels of the pupils of Linnaeus. But these devoted men had no official standing, they picked up a passage where they could, and, wherever their wanderings by land took them, by sea they followed a conventional trade route. Banks created the habit of officially recognized and supported science on the British voyages, simply by breaking in at his own expense. What this voyage cost him it is impossible to say. The well-known estimate given by Solander seems to mean merely that the gentleman of fortune was free with his wealth; and after all, Banks did not buy the ship. The estimate comes in a letter from Ellis to Linnaeus of 19 August 1768, a week before the *Endeavour* sailed from Plymouth — a letter that contains more than one inaccuracy:

[1] For its significance see Cook I, pp. clvii-xiv.
[2] See p. 287, n. 6 below.

I must now inform you, that Joseph Banks, Esq. a gentleman of £6000 per annum estate, has prevailed on your pupil, Dr. Solander, to accompany him in the ship that carries the english astronomers to the new discovered country in the South sea, Lat. about 20° South, and Long. between 130° and 150° West from London, where they are to collect all the natural curiosities of the place, and, after the astronomers have finished their observations on the transit of Venus, they are to proceed under the direction of Mr. Banks, by order of the Lords of the Admiralty, on further discoveries of the great Southern continent, and from thence proceed to England by the Cape of good Hope. . . . No people ever went to sea better fitted out for the purpose of Natural History, nor more elegantly. They have got a fine library of Natural History; they have all sorts of machines for catching and preserving insects; all kinds of nets, trawls, drags and hooks for coral fishing; they have even a curious contrivance of a telescope, by which, put into the water, you can see the bottom to a great depth, where it is clear. They have many cases of bottles with ground stoppers, of several sizes, to preserve animals in spirits. They have the several sorts of salts to surround the seeds; and wax, both beeswax and that of the *Myrica*; besides there are many people whose sole business it is to attend them for this very purpose. They have two painters and draughtsmen, several volunteers who have a tolerable notion of Natural History; in short Solander assured me this expedition would cost Mr. Banks ten thousand pounds. All this is owing to you and your writings.

About three days ago I took my leave of Solander, when he assured me he would write to you and to all his family, and acquaint them with the particulars of this expedition. I must observe to you, that his places are secured to him, and he has promises from persons in power of much better preferment on his return.

Everybody here parted from him with reluctance; for no man was ever more beloved, and in so great esteem with the public from his affable and polite behaviour.[1]

§

And Banks had fallen in love. He was twenty-five, and his journal indicates that the flame was easily kindled in him. Unfortunately the circumstances of this particular kindling, like so much other detail of his earlier life, are unknown to us; but for the fact we have excellent testimony. In 1768 Horace Benedict de Saussure, a young Swiss — three years older than Banks — of ample means and scientific interests, visited England with his wife on his own Grand Tour. He was later to attain fame as a physicist and geologist, and one of the first conquerors of Mont Blanc. On Friday, 15 August, in

[1] J.E.S. I, pp. 230-2.

London, de Saussure went to the opera to hear *La Buona Figliuola*.[1]
The performance had its merits and demerits: what de Saussure
enlarged on in his journal was not, however, these, but a more
interesting matter.

Saw for the first time [he writes] Miss Harriet Blosset, with Mr Banks,
her betrothed. Returned on foot from the opera with them and supped
together. The eldest daughter, tall, decided, agreeable, a great musician,
splendid voice, fond of society, polished. The second Miss Harriet,
desperately in love with Mr Banks, from whom she was to part next
day — hitherto a prudent coquette, but now only intent on pleasing
her lover, and resolved to spend in the country all the time he is away.
The youngest, a Methodist dévote, delighted to pass two or three years
in the country with her sister and live out of the world. The mother,
a good-natured little woman, talking politics. As Banks cannot speak a
word of French, I could not judge of his abilities. He seems to have a
prodigious zest for natural history. I supped there with him and Dr
Solander, who is also starting with him for Isle St George. They will
work on natural history. They have an astronomer for the passage of
Venus, a draughtsman, all the instruments, books, and appliances
possible; after observing the passage they will endeavour to make
discoveries in the Southern Ocean and return by the East Indies. Miss
Blosset, not knowing that he was to start next day, was quite gay. Banks
drank freely to hide his feelings. He promised to come and see me at
Geneva and bring me some curios. We were charmed to have made
acquaintance with this family, and I particularly to have seen before
his departure a remarkable man.[2]

Thus this very agreeable supper. Banks must already have bade
farewell to his mother and sister, and next day he was gone. M.
de Saussure however continued to see something of the interesting
family while he remained in London; for on that next day he dined
on a fine piece of venison sent by Mrs Blosset, and afterwards
accompanied Miss Blosset to Ranelagh; on the following day again
called on the Misses Blosset, 'arranged for the theatre and ball,
dined with Turton and the Misses Blosset and left my wife to dine
alone and dress her hair at our lodgings. . . . Fine theatre. Thence
to supper with Mrs Blosset and to the ball at the Redout with
the eldest Miss Blosset. . . .'[3] But we are not to think that M. de

---

[1] This was an *opera buffa* by Nicola Piccini (1728-1800), its text arranged by Goldoni
from Richardson's *Pamela*. It was so popular that it ran in Rome two years without
interruption, and in London, says Horace Walpole in 1766, it was 'crowded every time;
the King and Queen scarce ever miss it'.—*Letters* (ed. Toynbee), VII, p. 77.
[2] Douglas W. Freshfield, *Life of Horace Benedict de Saussure* (London 1920), pp. 105-6.
I have tried in vain to discover the origin of the family that de Saussure found
so interesting. There appear to have been Blossets about this period both in Dublin
and in Middlesex. From what is said later about 'the country', a Middlesex home is
not unlikely.   [3] ibid., pp. 106-7.

Saussure, swept with admiration for the tall, decided, splendid-voiced Miss Blosset (a person perhaps rather too formidable to make conquest of Joseph Banks) was immune to the charms of Miss Harriet Blosset — who, midway between the magnificent creature her elder, and the creature of piety, her younger sister, seems to have provided the right balance in female character for a young man who was himself neither a great musician (in spite of the flute and the guitar) nor particularly *dévot*. On 19 August the de Saussures and their friend Turton went once again to break-fast with the charming ladies. Afterwards the Swiss gentleman took Miss Harriet in his carriage 'to see the garden and the rosaries of Lyse,[1] a gardener patronised by Mr Banks, on the road to Richmond, walked about with her, collected many plants. . . . Thence, still with Miss Blosset, to see the insects of Mr Banks, a superb collection beautifully arranged, insects pinned with the names underneath each, English and foreign, in drawers covered with glass and framed in cedarwood. Took tea with Mrs Blosset, Miss Harriet, and her younger sister, the eldest had gone with my wife to the opera. I had a serious conversation with Miss Harriet. Her deep melancholy, her persuasion she should die, her firm resolve to live in the country to show her true love, make her very interesting'.[2] So the romantic Miss Harriet Blosset, luxuriating in grief, while her betrothed is still on his way to Plymouth, passes for the time being out of history.

§

The betrothed young gentleman joined his ship, was sea-sick and recovered, looked overboard at the denizens of the deep, and began to write his journal. It was a journal that was to assume large proportions, and to be composed with unflagging interest, and often excitement, but it exhibits one regrettable defect. Banks's eye was always outward — always, except for one brief glimpse of the great cabin[3] — and nowhere does he give an adequate picture, or any picture at all, of his shipmates. We have an isolated phrase or two; we can tell that he came to admire some of them extremely; from other sources we can tell that this one or that one earned his regard, and that the regard was returned: but what would we not give for a full-length study of the captain of that ship, and of some of his officers, from the pen that devoted so much

[1] Presumably 'Lee's'.
[2] Freshfield, p. 108.
[3] See p. 396 below.

space — quite justly — to marine zoology and the inhabitants of New Zealand or Batavia! He could have done it: he was a good observer, hard up against the subject of observation, he was ready with words; but we look in vain. In one way, no doubt, it was as well; there is plenty of evidence that on board the *Endeavour* journals were not exactly private documents. None the less there are ways round such embarrassments, and as posterity we mourn the missed chance.

In any case it seems clear that Banks and his philosophical companions fitted well enough, not only into the narrow physical space provided for them but into the psychological environment. The eighteenth century sailor was used to narrow quarters; the eighteenth century gentleman simply had to knuckle down to them. Banks knew what to expect after his Newfoundland journey, and no doubt Solander had been warned. Solander's status seems to have been that of a guest and co-scholar; it was those two who were referred to in the other journals as 'the gentlemen', in distinction from those who were technically 'the officers' and 'the people' — i.e. these last, the crew. Parkinson, Buchan and Spöring were employees, and having accepted engagement, could nourish no legitimate feelings about physical conditions. The servants were servants, and while on shipboard the indications are that they were mustered into the watches with the crew, and took up what space and hammocks they could. With all Banks's virtues, however — his tolerance and high spirits and sense of adventure — one three years' voyage on a ship of this type was enough for him; the gentleman and philosopher revolted against narrow quarters, pined after the greater elegance due to six thousand a year, and, as we shall see, made his later desires known with some force. Solander's feelings are unknown to us: we are perhaps not wrong in fancying that he liked the creature comforts, but he was an uncommonly even-tempered man, and committed no opinions of any sort, as he committed nothing else, to a journal. He was otherwise employed. Banks later testified to his industry and astuteness. There were differences enough between them, but no heat and no bitterness. At sea they were to develop a sort of regimen: 'We had a suitable stock of books relating to the natural history of the Indies with us; and seldom was there a storm strong enough to break up our normal study time, which lasted daily from nearly 8 o'clock in the morning till 2 in the afternoon. From 4 or 5, when the cabin had lost the odour of food [dinner was at midday], we sat till dark by the great table with our draughtsman opposite and showed him in what way to make his drawings, and ourselves made rapid descriptions of all the details of natural history while our specimens were still fresh.'[1] Then the descriptions were fair-copied by a 'writer' (one supposes Spöring) and the plants were pressed; and so the work went on. Persons so happily employed could have few discontents to visit on their shipmates, and we know that by their shipmates the gentlemen were much liked. The evidence is not so much in the records of this voyage as in later letters. It is very clear that warm personal friendship sprang up between them both and Cook, as well as with such men as Gore the practical third lieutenant[2] and Charles Clerke the master's mate, a farmer's son of cheerful eye and amusing talk. The relation with Cook was of course the critical one, and it belongs as much to a study of Cook as to a study of Banks.

The relation could hardly have been better between the seaman, at the beginning of the voyage nearing forty, the child of rural poverty and the professional product of native genius and a determined self-education, and the young gentleman, six months past twenty-five, the child of fortune whose inheritance was the land and not service to the land. Nothing could have been more violently disparate than their upbringing, yet they had this in common, that Banks, though by no means a genius, was yet strongly an individual, and — in all that counted for him — also self-educated. They were both used to the exercise of authority — Cook, the disciplined authority of experience, as one who had himself been, and was even now, under orders; Banks, the authority of his birth and breeding, as one who by nature gave, and did not take, orders. They both had a full measure of common sense — in Cook perhaps rather austere, a part of his genius for planning a campaign of discovery, but also a fundamental in that elasticity of mind that made him always equal to the unexpected; in Banks an endowment that gave him some appreciation at least of the extraordinary quality of the man he had to deal with, and that kept him—almost invariably —in his place as a passenger. Almost invariably!—we know that once, off the New Zealand coast, Banks was extremely anxious for a landing to be made, in blithe disregard of the prevailing wind and of the responsibilities of a captain, and we know that he could never really forgive Cook's refusal to oblige him; but what is once in three years? We know of criticisms made, or implied, of 'the

---

[1] 'Ueber Solander', pp. 245-6; and see also p. 396 below.
[2] It may be pointed out here that the rank of Cook, always referred to on the ship as 'Captain Cook' or 'the Captain', was that of first lieutenant. He was 'captain' conventionally, like other persons in charge of a ship. The second lieutenant was Zachary or Zachariah Hicks, the third John Gore. See Cook I, pp. cxxviii ff.

sailors', but what are they beyond the passing reaction to moments when any man's mind might be unsettled by danger or alarm? We know also that when there was extreme danger, and something that the gentleman could do to meet it, Banks took the handle of a pump and worked it till he was as exhausted as any seaman. The two men, again, could learn from each other. It is hard to say in so many words precisely what Banks learnt from Cook, because he does not give a list of acquirements, and close scrutiny of his holograph journal is not as rewarding in the internal evidence it yields as is a corresponding scrutiny of Cook's. Yet he had the example of that immense patience, that immense technical competence, that immense capacity for dealing with men, before him for three years, and he was not unaffected by the spectacle of greatness. Banks was to live for half a century after the *Endeavour*'s voyage, but he never met a greater man than Cook. Cook himself learnt things more easily discernible. He learnt a little bit of grammar. Each man's journal was open to the other, and while Banks found it worth while to make an abstract of Cook's, with all the names that had been conferred on geographical features and the co-ordinates of latitude and longitude — things that hardly entered into his own composition at all — Cook learnt from Banks how to describe people and things. He unashamedly cribbed on a large scale,[1] he unashamedly went back on his own drafts and rewrote them to incorporate some of the language of Banks. He regarded himself as an uneducated man, he may even have had the verbally uneducated man's awe of words in the mass; and here, beside him, he had an educated man who could pour them out in large quantities to some purpose. We can have no doubt that Banks was glad to help. But once Cook had learnt how to proceed, we do not get plagiarism on the grand scale again. The description of Tahiti is Banks's; except for phrases, occasional echoes, bits of natural history information, words that would strike an unlearned man as 'good', there are two separate accounts of New Zealand and New South Wales. In the end we have in the two journals, as it were, a vast diptych of Pacific exploration; a little of the design is the same, a few brush-strokes in one are modelled on those in the other; they contain corresponding figures and action; but the pictures are complementary, not identical. Banks, or rather Banks and Solander together, were the agents of a more general change in Cook's mind also. At the beginning of the voyage he was a seaman, a marine

[1] I have printed parallel passages from both journals in Cook I, pp. ccv-viii; cf. pp. ccxiii-iv.

surveyor, a little of an astronomer, a man with a passion for exactitude in limited fields of enquiry. At its end he had become not, certainly, a natural historian, but a man whose intelligence had widened considerably to an understanding of the importance of all knowledge. The two men his companions had thus an importance beyond the importance of natural historians, considerable as that was.

It is time to return to our philosopher as, 'in excellent health and spirits perfectly prepard . . . to undergo with chearfullness any fatigues or dangers' he might encounter, he was borne with no great speed southwards upon the Atlantic bosom. In excellent spirits he was; the deep was full of wonder; other men might be irritated at a calm, but he and Solander had 'easy contented countenances' as they fished away and referred their catch to the Linnaean pages. They were honeymoon weeks, those early ones; the sailors too began to be interested; and when an African latitude was reached, and leave was taken of Europe, 'perhaps for ever', it was possible to spare one sigh but not two, for friends left behind — 'friends', it is to be assumed, including both sexes, Miss Harriet Blosset as well as Thomas Pennant. There was the brief stay at Madeira, lighted up by the agreeable Dr Heberden, *il Doctore docto*, philosophy in a wilderness of ignorance; there were the plants to be collected, the scenery and the people to be observed, the Franciscan monastery to be visited, and the convent where the sisters were so naively and delightfully confident in the visitors' mastery of the secrets of nature; the governor to be shocked with the electrical machine. (Meanwhile the captain was acquiring wine and fresh water and onions.) Banks was far too busy to write letters home, but Solander got one away to Ellis. Then the routine of the sea again till early November, though a routine part of which was excitement: the glimpse of the Peak of Teneriffe raised above the sea, the ceremony at the crossing of the Line, so vividly described, the birds, the fish, the lunar rainbow, the catching of sharks, the expeditions in the small boat during calms, the sighting at last of the coast of Brazil. Down in the cabin, when activity on deck was impossible, Banks examined his specimens, Solander described, Parkinson drew, grabbing at his paints as the table tilted. Then the harbour of Rio de Janeiro, after eight weeks at sea; and the first blow at cheerfulness.

Cook called at Rio after due thought. He did not, strictly speaking, need to, though his instructions allowed him to do so if he wished, as they allowed him to call at Port Egmont in the Falkland Islands.

Solander

He was well enough provided to make Port Egmont quite easily. But he was a careful man, and thus early he had developed his passion for getting fresh water and fresh food on every possible occasion — the onions at Madeira were another example, which had later to be explained to the accountants — and for seeing that they were consumed in place of stale water and salt meat. Also he wanted to heel his ship and look at the sides. The Portuguese had been spoken of very highly as hosts by Lord Anson, after his experience at St Catherine's island, and Commodore Byron (whose journal Cook had with him) had met with an excellent reception at Rio itself. The reception given by a new viceroy to the *Endeavour* was the reverse of excellent. The reasons that he made explicit seemed to Cook totally inadequate. They may be summarized as his orders from the Portuguese court for dealing with foreign vessels in general, his difficulty in believing that the *Endeavour* belonged to His Britannic Majesty's navy (she certainly did not look as if she did), and his suspicion that her real errand was not the observation of the Transit of Venus — a matter which he did not understand — but smuggling. There may have been complications in Portuguese foreign policy that he was not at liberty to explain. Nothing Cook could say or do could alter the determination of the Conde de Azambuja to take no risks. Cook said a good deal, and he adopted a high tone, and his paper war with the viceroy is one of the curiosities of the voyage;[1] whether a lower tone would have made any difference is a matter for conjecture, but it does not seem probable. It is certain that in the production of the 'memorials' with which he bombarded the viceroy Banks took some part. Among the MSS in the Commonwealth National Library are four draft folio pages, written in a rapid indignant hand, the paragraphs much deleted, smudged and altered: it is the hand of Banks, and the draft is that of Cook's communication of 19 November 1768. Possibly this indicates that Banks did a good deal of drafting for Cook, for the papers are much of a style, and the crisis was not the sort of thing that Cook had dealt with before. An English gentleman, however, esteemed himself the equal of any viceroy, and this was a very furious English gentleman indeed. It is true nevertheless he managed to make his own memorials scrupulously polite.[2] Banks's fury can be well understood, for his predicament seemed both ridiculous and gratuitous. He wanted to get ashore. The remarks of his journal are adequately condensed in his letter of 1 December to the Earl of Morton:

[1] See Cook I, Appendix I, pp. 481 ff.   [2] See below, II, pp. 315-20.

Your lordship Can more easily imagine our Situation than I can describe it all that we so ardently wishd to examine was in our sight we could almost but not quite touch them never before had I an adequate Idea of Tantalus's punishment but I have sufferd it with all possible aggravations three weeks have I staid aboard the ship regardless of every inconvenience of her being heeld down &c &c. which on any other occasion would have been no Small hardship but small evils are totaly swallowd up in the Larger bodily pain bears no comparison to pure in short the torments of the Damnd must be very severe indeed as doubtless my present ones Cannot nearly Equal them.[1]

Solander was more moderate, writing to Ellis: at Madeira, he recalled, they had met with a very good reception, 'which is more than I can say of this place, where the viceroy has been so infernally cross and ill-natured, as to forbid us to set our feet upon dry land. How mortifying that must be to me and Mr. Banks, you best can feel. . . . We have, nevertheless, by fair means and foul, got about 300 species of plants, among them several new, and an infinite number of new fish. . . '.[2] By fair means and foul — though nothing very foul; outraged Science had to do its best through what it could pick up casually, or through innocent bribery, or by sur- reptitious and unhappily confined visits, while a continent stretched before it. South America, indeed, was inimical to natural historians: they went to the Dutch possessions and died there of tropical fevers, or the state of international politics turned them, in the admin- istrative mind, into spies. Banks took what private revenge he could, in his journal; the Portuguese in Madeira might be ignorant, but here they were slaves, their rulers were not merely stupid and prejudiced but tyrannical. Considering his virtual imprisonment on board the ship, the account he gives of Rio de Janeiro is sur- prisingly full; but no doubt we owe a great deal, if not to his observation, to the information of Mr Burrish, the Englishman who served in the customs, of Lieutenant Forster, the other English- man, of the Portuguese Estermoz regiment, who suffered badly in fortune for befriending his compatriots,[3] and of the Spanish naval officers, whose liberties were so much greater than those of the English, and who proved so conversable.

The *Endeavour* got away from 'these illiterate impolite gentry' on 2 December, and stood south. With all inconveniences, Cook had got a sufficient refreshment for his men at Rio, and decided not to call at Port Egmont — a disappointment for Banks, who

---

[1] See Appendix, II, pp. 313-5 below.
[2] For the full text of this letter, see II, pp. 308-10 below.
[3] See Lieutenant Forster's letter to Banks, 5 November 1771, II, pp. 321-3 below.

feared he would have no chance to collect in this southern part of the world. His fear was needless: the Bay of Good Success, on the coast of Tierra del Fuego, gave him a great deal of collecting, a view of the most primitive people he had ever seen, and a thoroughly bad scare into the bargain. His remarks on the people were, and remain, valuable, for no thorough study has been made even yet of this Ona tribe; his passion for collecting seems to have puzzled Cook, who just then looked at plants with a severely practical eye: could they be eaten? — were they anti-scorbutic? These plants, alas! were 'most of them unknown in Europe and in that alone consisted their whole value'.[1] His scare was the result of bad luck and lack of acquaintance with an unpredictable summer climate. The young Darwin of the *Beagle* and the young Hooker of the *Erebus* in after years followed Banks and his party up the Tierra del Fuegian hills, and experienced some of the same embarrassments underfoot; but they were luckier with the weather, and did not have to stay out all night — nor did they expend a great deal of their energy walking round in a circle. Banks was probably not in such danger as he apprehended, and he certainly made too much of the deprivation of food for some hours, and of the low temperature itself. The real cause of the party's unhappiness was, it seems likely, too much exertion too lightly undertaken after being cooped up on shipboard for four months, so that the effect of snow and cold was greater than it would otherwise have been. Buchan complicated the whole matter by his epileptic fit, and the two unfortunate negroes had paralysed their powers of resistance by the rum they had drunk. Banks's greyhound lay out with them in the snow without ill effect. And though the members of the party after regaining the ship were put into warm beds Banks was excepted: he went at once in a boat to haul the seine. We may conclude that the adventure, though unpleasant, and though it saw the end of poor Richmond and Dorlton, does not rank amongst the great crises of the voyage.

On 21 January 1769 the ship sailed from the Bay of Good Success and out of the Strait of le Maire to make the Horn passage, and then north-west. On 4 April Peter Briscoe, in the second watch, snatched from the sailors the honour of first sighting land — it was Lagoon Island, or Vahitahi, one of the Tuamotus — and on 13 April they were at anchor in Port Royal, in King George the Third's Island. A few more days, and they would be familiarly calling it Otaheite. The intervening weeks had been for Banks a

[1] Cook I, p. 44.

continued excitement of sea-birds. Now we see a change in the character of his journal. At Madeira and Rio de Janeiro he had been both natural historian and any intelligent man. He had made lists of the plants and fishes of Madeira, of Brazilian plants, and stuck the lists in the journal, as he stuck in the letter from Dr Hulme about the use of inspissated lemon juice as a cure for scurvy. At Tierra del Fuego he met his first savages, and was highly delighted, and he still made a list of plants. Crossing the Pacific, there were the birds and fishes to be seen, captured, noted. From the arrival in Tahiti, all this took second place. The natural historian becomes the natural historian of man. The collecting still goes on, riches are piled up beyond the dreams of botanists and zoologists, in the islands, in New Zealand, in Australia; the really extraordinary phenomena get their sentence or paragraph; but all this has become the peculiar province of Solander, and of Spöring, and of Sydney Parkinson, busily, interminably, drawing and fighting the flies. Mr Buchan has succumbed to his fits — the loss of an ingenious and good young man, certainly, but what a loss to — we must seize on a word not yet invented — ethnography! For Mr Buchan was employed for the figure as well as the 'landskip'. Banks would do his best in words. We have, in all the journals of this voyage, a pretty full description of the appearance and material culture of Tahiti, one not quite so good of New Zealand, one as good as possible of the eastern Australian coast; but it is Banks who gives us most. He even shows a capacity for going beyond the merely material. He has, in his excitement, his capacity for throwing himself into native ceremonial, his greed for recording everything, become the founder of Pacific ethnology. It may be pointed out that Tahitian was the only language not his own that Banks ever succeeded in learning.

It was at Tahiti that Banks's contribution to the success of the voyage was greatest. Telescopes and drying-books were important, it was immensely important that Spöring should be able to mend the stolen and damaged astronomical quadrant; but a capacity for dealing with people was fundamental. Cook had it, but perhaps he was a little formal, he was feeling his way: with Banks, on the other hand, all was ease and spontaneity. No one so able as he to manage the ship's trade; no one so confident and generous in his proffered friendship, or — in the main — so naturally tactful. He had advantages: he was young and personable yet authoritative, good-humoured, interested and unabashed, equally prepared to denounce Tahitian wrongdoing and to apologize for his own misjudgments, attractive to men and women, old and young, chief and commoner alike. Who other than Banks would have thought of stripping and blackening himself to take part as a subordinate in a mourning ceremony — or so hugely enjoyed himself in the process? — he of 'the white jacket and waistcoat, with silver frogs', as described by Parkinson. And who would have measured with such diligence everything capable of being measured, or followed with such careful attention the process of beating out and dyeing tapa cloth, or of tattooing a young girl's buttocks, or have noted so exactly the amount of food consumed by one chiefly person at one meal? Banks, naturally, must be himself tattooed — though on the arm, it appears, and nowhere else.[1] All things conspired to favour him — the cast of his mind, his gift for observation and rapid description, his cheerfulness, his ability to ingratiate himself without trying. We read (not in his own journal) of only one quarrel in which he was involved, and it is significant that this was with another young man, Monkhouse the surgeon, and over women. Most attractive to women Banks most certainly was, and — with equal certainty — he carried in his own bosom a susceptible though discriminating heart. It was on his second day only in Tahiti that he turned from the exalted lady he referred to as Tomio — 'ugly enough in conscience' — to that 'very pretty girl with a fire in her eyes' he had 'espied among the common crowd'. Was this pretty one identical with 'Otheatea' — 'my flame'? It does not seem so, because Otheatea was attached to that eminent figure, Purea, who came later on the scene: well, was Otheatea one of the three charming celebrants of the ceremony of May 11? No, that is evidently not so; but they turn up at every point, these delightful young persons, from one end of the island to the other, and when once Banks notes, as a reason for his discourtesy to the eminent, that he was 'otherwise engag'd,' it was not, we must regretfully conclude, of Miss Harriet Blosset that he was thinking.[2] Very pleasant all this was for Joseph Banks: we have forgotten entirely the gentleman of liberal fortune; New Burlington Street, Revesby Abbey have faded into an unremembered mist; we have merely an enthusiastic investigator deep in experience. Then we are

[1] So, at least, I gather from a letter from Charles Davy, of Hensted, Suffolk, 5 June 1773 (D.T.C. I, p. 54): 'If it is not giving you too much trouble, I should be much obliged to you for an exact copy of the characters stain'd upon your arm. . . '. Davy was the author of an essay on alphabetic writing, and was much interested to know whether the 'characters' represented amulets, things, or sounds. But it is odd that Banks does not mention this personal experience in his journal, if it did indeed take place.

[2] Considering this episode (see p. 279 below), the later intimate linking of Banks's name with that of Purea (p. 101) has its light irony.

brought up with a round turn, we do have a touch of *grand seigneur*. There was the question of Tupaia the priest and expert navigator: should he be taken on the *Endeavour* or not? The captain thought not, the captain was not a romantic, he knew something of officialdom; 'I therefore', announces Banks to his journal, 'have resolvd to take him. Thank heaven I have a sufficiency and I do not know why I may not keep him as a curiosity, as well as some of my neighbours do lions and tygers at a larger expence than he will ever probably put me to; the amusement I shall have in his future conversation and the benefit he will be of to this ship, as well as what he may be if another should be sent into these seas, will I think fully repay me'. It was the age of private zoos; but Tupaia would be better than a zoo. If Banks had only known it, a Tahitian was already the rage in Paris, with abbés writing poetry about him and fashionable ladies gazing at him desperately at the opera.

There were the Society Islands to visit, and then a new voyage south, with prodigious quantities of sea-birds, and whales, and porpoises — but no Southern Continent — before Cook set his course for what he knew must exist, the eastern coast of New Zealand, up the western side of which Tasman had sailed in December 1642 and January 1643. Tasman had sprung to the conclusion that this must indeed be the coast of a continent, which stretched away eastward somehow to join with 'Staten Land' — i.e. Staten Island, on the eastern side of Le Maire Strait. The latter part of this assumption had been shattered by the Dutch in the same year 1643, by the simple process of sailing round Staten Island, and now Cook was to shatter the first part also, by sailing right round New Zealand, in a sort of *tour de force* of navigation and survey which left very little to the fancy of speculative geographers. Banks had accepted the speculations — had, it appears, like most other people, taken a southern continent for granted — and he hung on to his belief that New Zealand must be a part of it with a comic persistence which he annotates very well himself, until the ship turned the southern point 'to the total demolition of our aerial fabrick calld continent'. He was not, that is, as experimental, as sceptical, in his geographical approach as was Cook. His general reasonings on the subject, entered in his journal after the decision was taken to make for the east coast of 'New Holland' (and added to, as we can see, from the later references to the facilities at the Cape), show clear traces of discussion with Cook and the others in the great cabin of the *Endeavour*: here, we may be pretty certain, the plan for another and conclusive voyage is a Cook and not a Banks plan. Cook, in his own journal, made it plain that he was guided by experience and would wait on fresh experience. Banks is rather more sentimental. To stand to the westward for New Holland might mean discoveries interesting to trade, but it would mean the abandonment of

our first great object, the Southern Continent: this for my own part I confess I could not do without much regret. — That a Southern Continent really exists, I firmly beleive; but if ask'd why I beleive so, I confess my reasons are weak; yet I have a preposession in favour of the fact which I find it dificult to account for. . . . it must be prodigiously smaller in extent than the theoretical continent makers have supposd it to be. . . . we have taken from them their firmest Ground work, in Proving New Zealand to be an Island, which I beleive was lookd upon even by the most thinking people, to be in all probability at least a part of some Vast Countrey. . . . As for their reasoning about the Balancing of the two poles, which always appeard to me to be a most childish argument, we have already shorn off so much of their supposd counterbalancing land that by their own account the South pole would already be too light, unless what we have left should be made of very ponderous materials. As much fault as I find with these gentlemen will however probably recoil on myself, when I on so slight grounds as those I have mentiond again declare it to be my opinion that a Southern Continent exists, an opinion in favour of which I am strongly preposesd; but foolish and weak as all prepossesions must be thought I would not but declare myself so, least I might be supposd to have stronger reasons which I conceald.[1]

Perhaps we may regard this as in fact highly judicious; for there was, surely enough, a southern continent — though what we know as Antarctica, all that remained after a great deal more had been shorn off than was the result of the *Endeavour*'s operations, proved to be violently different from the construction of the theoretical continent makers.

We are departing, however, from Banks's real rôle as that of an observer of natural phenomena; and in both New Zealand and Australia we find him at his best. New Zealand may in one way be judged his real triumph; for at no place there did he have a long stay, such as in Tahiti or even during the enforced weeks at the Endeavour river — weeks which were so fruitful in collecting and then became so dull. On the botanical side, the brief days in New Zealand harbours were highly productive; the description Banks gives of the people is — to speak moderately — extremely good. He even noticed dialectal differences in the pronunciation of the

[1] II, pp. 38-40 below.

language. If we had the whole of William Brougham Monkhouse's journal, and if it kept on as it began for this New Zealand visit, we should clearly have something as good; and in the descriptions that have survived from the French visits of Surville and Marion du Fresne to Doubtless Bay and the Bay of Islands in 1770 and 1772 we have a great deal more detail on certain matters.[1] In one or two respects, Banks went wrong: he gave a general judgment on the scantiest acquaintance with land birds, and he was all too eager to build that peculiar chief 'Teratu' into an 'Indian King';[2] but with all defects, he gives us a masterly sketch. In more than one way, also, he casts some light on his own character: as when he records his melancholy over what seemed either the enforced or the needless slaying of Maoris at Poverty Bay; or his enchantment at the singing of the bell-birds at Queen Charlotte Sound; or his determination, also at Queen Charlotte Sound, to get hold of positive material proofs of Maori cannibalism. On cannibalism he would philosophize, just as, beginning with his New Zealand and South Seas vocabularies and going on to whatever else he could pick up, he would, like a good eighteenth century philosopher (language exerted its charm on many men) reason historically on his findings in comparative philology. Indeed, bring all his scattered observations on this particular subject together, and one finds him not merely a collector of word-lists (there are, after all, longer lists in Parkinson) but the discoverer of the underlying linguistic unity that leads the modern philologist to talk of an 'Austronesian' language group. A little philosophizing there is too in the description of New South Wales: 'Thus live these I had almost said happy people, content with little nay almost nothing, far enough removd from the anxieties attending upon riches', and so on; this, in that day and age, was almost irresistible, but Banks does not go very far; Cook (of all people) is far sillier. Banks does not on the whole shine in general reflection; his strength, it becomes ever more clear as one proceeds with his journal, was description — often detailed, as in his account of the Australian ants; generally vivid, as when he writes of the harrowing twenty-three hours spent on the reef, or the shorter, but even more harrowing, period of tension outside the reef on August 16. 'The Fear of Death is Bitter', he says, and he leaves no doubt in our minds that there was ample opportunity to fear it, and that he knew the bitterness. He was an honest man. Cook, who found Banks

[1] See, e.g. *Historical Records of New Zealand*, II (Wellington 1914), pp. 230 ff.
[2] See Cook I, clii-iii.

(to use the old phrase) so 'damned good to steal from', and whose own statement is habitually one of moderation, does not seem to have found him ever immoderate. So it was with a very large cargo not only of dried plants and other specimens, but of immediately remembered tribulation that the ship turned the northern point of Australia into the Endeavour Channel of Torres Strait. It is curious how lightly Banks takes this significant moment in geographical history. 'We observd both last night and this morn that the main lookd very narrow so we began to look out for the Passage we expected to find between new Holland and New Guinea. At noon one was seen very narrow but appearing to widen: we resolv'd to try it so stood in'. To a student of the cartographical history of the Pacific there is a slight sense of anti-climax about this. The problem was not, evidently, a problem Banks worried about. He had Dalrymple's map. The geography was incidental to the botany.

There was indeed a passage, and with the ship safely through it the exploratory part of the voyage may be said to have ended, whatever Cook found out about the sandbanks of New Guinea. It may be said to have ended, if we need a precise date, on 23 August 1770, when he and Banks came away from Booby Island, where now is the lighthouse marking the western entrance to the strait — the island on which Banks, instead of shooting boobies, 'botanizd and found some plants which I had not before seen'. But his explorations were not at an end. The 'people' were becoming bored with the voyage. They were not starved, they were well looked after, their health, at the end of two years out from home, was excellent; not one man had died of sickness — an astonishing feat for any captain. What they wanted, however, was not the consolation of good health or reflections on the excellence of their commander's administration, but a known port, the sight of European faces, and a great deal of fresh food of the kind that was recognized by Europeans as food. After that they wanted a conventional voyage across known seas homeward. They were suffering, Banks concluded, from 'nostalgia' — a word the doctors were beginning to use. Not so himself and the captain: their minds were busily occupied as usual. Banks's mind was to be busily occupied to the very end. He could not find anything new, strictly speaking, in plants at Savu, or Batavia, or the Cape; was not everything East Indian in Rumphius, known from the great folios in Europe? Had not Linnaeus a generation earlier got the very *Musa*, the banana, noblest of plants, to flower and fruit in the glass-house of Georg Clifford, East India Company director, at Hartecamp near Leyden? But he could find plenty of plants and fruit new to him that were a joy to identify and describe; and there was still man in his infinite variety of appearance and behaviour and mentality to enquire into. What happened when one raja succeeded another in Savu, how the Dutch collected tribute, the domestic architecture, markets, sanitation, economics, government and currency of Batavia, Javanese folk-lore, the position of the Chinese under Dutch rule, specimens of language, the aspect of Cape Town, Hottentot physiology, South African settlement and animals, the charms of South African young women, Bougainville's voyage — all, whether observed or enquired into in conversation, were assiduously noted down and recorded. And there was still St Helena. Banks was omnivorous. There were excellent precedents. Had not Linnaeus, the Master, been omnivorous in exactly the same way on his famous Lapland journey? Was not the highest peak of public interest always reached at his appearance in Lapland suit, with drum? And was not Batavia as much unknown to the English as Lapland, or the South Seas? It seemed well worth an editor's while, when the official volumes on the voyage were in preparation, to give as many pages to that town and its people, drawn from Banks, as to the general account of New Zealand.

Meanwhile, of course, the most dreadful part of the whole great three years' voyage had come to pass, the onset of malaria, and fearfully worse, dysentery, at Batavia and on the passage between Prince's Island and the Cape. The achievement had been masterly; the luck, after coming off the reef with a paper-thin bottom and a hole plugged with coral, stupendous: and there is something cruelly gratuitous in the fatal sickness that then struck practically the entire ship's company, and that neither Cook, nor Banks, nor anyone else could avert by whatever thought beforehand, or action in its presence. The Batavian sailors, noted Banks, 'were almost as spectres'; so that the *Endeavour*'s people, 'who truly might be calld rosy and plump' — after all those months! — 'Jeerd and flouted much at their brother sea men's white faces'. It was too soon to jeer and flout. Too many men were to die; and Banks's own physical agonies were of a sort he had not taken into account when writing so glibly from Rio to Morton of the comparison between the pains of the body and of the mind. Of Banks's own people Solander narrowly escaped with his life, to gossip as cheerily as ever to a sympathetic and wondering London; but poor Tupaia (if we may make him belong to Banks, like a lion or tiger) and his servant-boy died; Parkinson died; Spöring died. Their virtues deserved a better fate; they were both men to whom the historian of the voyage owes much. By the time the ship left the Cape, where three more men died (a fourth, Molyneux the master, succumbed shortly after she sailed), the sickness was virtually over; Lieutenant Hicks died on the passage home, but he had begun the voyage with consumption, and was a doomed man. Nothing further happened to Banks. The ship picked up the East India fleet at St Helena and sailed with it for a while, until outpaced; she sighted England on 10 July 1771, and two days later the adventurer closed his journal and landed at Deal.

§

The question arises for general consideration, as he steps on shore, how really good is this journal? Various portions of it have been praised in the foregoing pages, but can one summarize simply, by rendering additional praise, and leaving it at that? Or must one make modifications? Does Banks give us an adequate account of the voyage? Is he invariably accurate? In particular — though we have called him a good observer — was he a really good observer?

We may answer, first of all, by stressing again some of the journal's virtues. It is full, it contains a large amount of invaluable detail, it has unending vivacity, it is obviously the work of an exceedingly quick and lively mind. The mind is that of a young man. To read the original, with its quite astounding lack of punctuation, is to get the feeling of almost breathless excitement, as the impressions crowded and the words tumbled on to the paper. That in itself is good, in a record of discovery, as long as the record remains coherent, and we cannot say that Banks lacks coherency. We may say certainly that his journal is essential to an understanding of the voyage and its results: without it we should be disastrously worse off in our knowledge. When Cook's journal was turned over to Dr Hawkesworth for editing, with the journals of the voyages of Byron and Wallis and Carteret, Banks, on the suggestion of Sandwich,[1] handed over his journal also. Hawkesworth was delighted; he was a general practitioner in literature, not a seaman or a geographer; he had not the remotest interest in the southern continent or the behaviour of Venus; but he knew what would go

---

[1] So I infer from Hawkesworth's words: 'I am happy in your Lordship's powerfull Influence with Mr Banks for the use of his Journall. I flatter myself that I shall be able to prevent ill humour, and satisfy the utmost Delicacy of a Gentleman to whom I shall be so much obliged'.—Hawkesworth to Sandwich, 19 November 1771; Sandwich Papers, Hinchingbrooke.

down with the public; he knew — if the vulgarism be allowed —
when he was on to a good thing. He knew what to accentuate,
and when 'Joseph Banks Esquire, a Gentleman possessed of considerable landed property in Lincolnshire', gave his permission
to an editor to take out of the gentleman's journal whatever the
editor thought would 'improve or embellish' a narrative, that editor
hastened to improve and to embellish. 'I knew the advantage
would be great', wrote Hawkesworth in his introduction,[1] 'for
few philosophers have furnished materials for accounts of voyages
undertaken to discover new countries. The adventurers in such
expeditions have generally looked only upon the great outline of
Nature, without attending to the variety of shades within, which give
life and beauty to the piece. . . . It is indeed fortunate for mankind,
when wealth and science, and a strong inclination to exert the
powers of both for purposes of public benefit, unite in the same
person. . . '. This is just, though it could have been said less respect-
fully, and in fewer words. And Hawkesworth's text is, in the end,
at least as much Banks as Cook.[2] Yet he could not drop Cook —
if for no other reason, because Cook gave him the voyage as a piece
of navigation, as an exercise in geographical discovery; which,
after all, apart from the observation of the Transit, was its purpose.
This Banks did not give him. The practical seaman, pushing into
the Pacific, with some island landfall before him over the horizon,
and a lively feeling about coral reefs, would take Cook's journal
rather than Banks's, if both were offered him. The observations
he wanted were precise ones, in the nautical sense, not those of the
natural historian or of the 'human geographer' — though it was
surprising how many of those he would find in Cook too.

But this is, strictly speaking, irrelevant. Banks kept a journal,
not 'of' the voyage, but 'on' the voyage. We may be surprised at
some of his omissions. It would have been interesting to get his
view of the situation surrounding the cropping of Mr Orton's
ears, that night of drunken frolic on the Australian coast that
aroused Cook's anger so; one would have expected him to notice,
if barely, the death of poor Hicks, whose rôle as second in command

---

[1] Hawkesworth, I, pp. xiii-xv.

[2] 'But in the papers which were communicated to me by Mr. Banks, I found a great
variety of incidents which had not come under the notice of Captain Cook, with
descriptions of countries and people, their productions, manners, customs, religion,
policy, and language, much more full and particular than were expected from a Gentleman whose station and office naturally turned his principal attention to other objects;
for these particulars, therefore, besides many practical observations, the Public is indebted to Mr. Banks. To Mr. Banks also the Public is indebted for the designs of the
engravings which illustrate and adorn the account of this voyage. . . .'—Hawkesworth.
II, p. xiv.

had been not unimportant. But though we should have liked him to give us even more than he does give us, that again is not the point. We are not to ask him — it would be absurd to ask him — for everything. He makes a large contribution to the material for the history of the voyage, and the voyage is to be understood in its totality only from study of all the material — his own journal, Cook's journal, the logs and journals of the rest of the ship's company, the other documentation, the scientific results printed by the Royal Society and the observations critically examined later by William Wales, later geographical and hydrographic knowledge, Solander's great series of botanical and zoological notes and descriptions, the natural history specimens brought back, the drawings, the artifacts. As the list lengthens, we realize how very little we have in fact known about this familiar piece of history. The question therefore is, is Banks accurate as well as interesting in what he writes? The answer is, on the whole and so far as he can be checked by the words of his shipmates or of later observers, yes, admirably so. We should be lucky indeed to have corresponding journals for certain other great voyages of discovery. What makes us hesitate is some of his remarks about St Helena, which, in their Hawkesworthian guise as part of Cook's journal, got Cook into trouble on his homeward passage in 1775. They were damning paragraphs. Wanton cruelty to slaves? No carriages or wheelbarrows? No porter's knots? Ill-built houses? The inhabitants were outraged. Cook was mortified. 'How these things came to be thus missrepresented, I can not say, as they came not from me. . . . I am not a little obliged to some people in the isle for the obligeing manner they pointed out these Mistakes'.[1] Banks should certainly have been more careful about his generalizations after so short a visit, one day of which was devoted to 'Botanizing on the Ridge' and climbing around the hills, and we may need to be cautious about his hearsay evidence. These particular remarks, however, are an extremely small part of a large journal. If we go further back, to Tahiti, we find a little misapprehension about the class of persons known as the *teuteu*, the hereditary retainers of the chiefly class or *arii*; the *teuteu*, concluded Banks, were 'upon almost the same footing as the Slaves in the East India Islands'. They were not slaves, and he had no direct knowledge of slaves anywhere; but class-structure is a difficult thing to gauge, even in three months, and the mistake was pardonable. In New Zealand, with preconceived notions in his head about 'kings', and inadequate acquaintance with the

[1]Cook II, p. 662. Cf. Cook I, pp. ccxlv-lvii. See also II, p. 267, n. below.

Polynesian language, he made the large mistake about 'Teratu';
but that too is very pardonable. His account of the construction
of the Maori canoe is quite inaccurate,[1] and compares badly with
his description of ship-building in the Society Islands. In giving
his general account of New South Wales he denied too definitely
the existence of fresh water: true, it had not been found conveniently
all along the coast, and Cook's name, 'Thirsty Sound', indicates
decided disappointment. Cook nevertheless is the more judicious:
the country, he reports, 'is indefferently well watered, even in the
dry Seasons, with small Brooks and streams. . . . It was only in
Thirsty Sound where we could find no fresh water'. 'Indifferently'
means moderately, tolerably; Banks, we may take it, wanted a
large river. If he had been Dampier (to whom he refers more than
once in other connections), digging unsuccessfully in the sand,
he might have had more reason for his remark. Off the east coast
of Africa he registers a much greater alarm at what he regards as
the ship's dangerous predicament than does anyone else. Is this
to be taken as an error, merely a landsman's excited judgment, or
the Voice of Truth which the seamen were willing to smother?
Between Batavia and the Cape, he is more than once demonstrably
wrong over his dates; he is wrong again at the Cape, for which
indeed he refers to 'my irregular journal',[2] and he is wrong in
the Atlantic after leaving St Helena. What then, taking such matters
into consideration, are we to conclude? The mere fact that we
pick them out so is enlightening. Banks was a good observer. His
record is a trustworthy as well as lively one. It is also, one may
reflect as one turns its rich pages, apart altogether from its reporting
of the varied strange and new, a not inadequate introduction to
the natural history, and to the classic authors of the natural history,
of the eighteenth century.

§

He stepped ashore into an agreeable aura of public attention.
Cook reported to the Admiralty, and went home to Mrs Cook and
his modest house in the unfashionable village of Mile End. But
above New Burlington Street, we may assume, the sky was radiant
with glory, as Mr Banks gazed once more on papered walls and
curtained windows, and Peter Briscoe and James Roberts began
to unpack the pressed plants and bottles of animals in spirits, the
island curios, the *tapa* cloth and New Zealand cloaks, the fisgigs

---

[1] '. . . built of very thin planks sewd together'.—See II, p. 22 below.
[2] It had been irregular before, at Batavia, but certainly no blame attaches for that,
or for the absence of any specific entry at all between 14 and 24 November 1770.

and throwing sticks from New Holland, the shells and the drawings. The newspaper offices buzzed with paragraphs. The voyage had been protracted beyond its estimated length; there had been anxious weeks at the Admiralty, and fears that the ship was lost. The newspapers had opined that it had been sent to the bottom 'by order of a jealous Court' — oh dire atrocious Spain! — with Mr Banks and 'the famous Dr Solander' as well as its less distinguished company. In October 1770 Sarah Sophia Banks, steadfast in faith, had assured Thomas Pennant that there was not the least foundation for these very alarming reports — 'we begin to fear we shall not see them till spring, upon account of their having missed the Trade Wind, but that is a very different situation to what the papers represented'.[1] Now all was joy, and soon she would be settling down to copy her brother's journal for him. Poetry was not slow to celebrate the voyagers.

> The muse, O BANKS, with great respect attends,
> To hail thee welcome to desponding friends,
> Who long with pungent sorrows were assail'd,
> Whilst thoughts uncertain of thy life prevail'd: . . .

The muse[2] contrasted him with the generality of modern youths, greatly to their disadvantage, and contemplated his attributes with the highest approval. The newspapers became positively reverential: they were all Mr Banks, or Mr Banks and Dr Solander — or sometimes Dr Solander and Mr Banks; it was Mr Banks's voyage, Mr Banks's and Dr Solander's discoveries; the nobility were calling at Mr Banks's house to see his curiosities; there was a more specialized excitement over the Tahitian seeds now germinating in Mr Lee's Hammersmith soil;[3] Mr Banks had brought back 'no less than seventeen thousand plants, of a kind never before seen in this kingdom'; Mr Banks was introduced to His Majesty at St James's Palace by Lord Beauchamp, and received very graciously; Dr Solander and Mr Banks had the honour of another interview at Richmond, 'when they presented' the monarch 'with a coronet of gold, set around with feathers, which was given them by a chief on the coast of Chili'; the peak was reached with the information that 'Mr. Banks is to have two ships from government to pursue his discoveries in the South Seas, and will sail upon his second voyage

[1] S.S.B. to Pennant, 6 October 1770; ATL, ALS 269.
[2] It was a Quaker muse. The lines quoted are from an effusion by Mrs Jane Gomeldon, the cousin of Sydney Parkinson; they were written on receiving a letter from Sydney at Batavia, which announced the expedition's safety, and are prefixed to some copies o Parkinson's *Journal*. See Cook I, p. 627.
[3] *Letters and Journals of Lady Mary Coke*, III (Edinburgh 1892), p. 443.

next March'. The peak was left with a flight into the pure empyrean
when it was announced that 'the celebrated Mr Banks' would
shortly make another voyage to St George's Islands, with three
ships, men, arms and provisions, in order to plant a colony there.[1]
Dr Solander and Mr Banks even attended a private meeting of the
Board of Admiralty, to receive instructions for this intended voyage;
and now they were to have one ship of fifty guns, two frigates, and
three smaller sail. They were particularly charged, not with coloniza-
tion, but with making discoveries on the coasts of New Holland and
New Zealand, 'which are at present almost entirely unknown'.[2]
It was more than a nine days' wonder; and everybody wanted to
hang on the heroes' lips. Lady Mary Coke, after recording the
gossip for Friday, 9 August, remarked 'But the people who are most
talk'd of at present are Mr Banks and Doctor Solander: I saw them
at Court and afterwards at L[ad]y Hertford's, but did not hear them
give any account of their Voyage round the world, which I am told
is very amusing'.[3] They must have talked a great deal at one time
or another.[4] They dined with Dr Johnson and Boswell, and Johnson, at Banks's request, wrote the celebrated distich in honour of
the ship's goat, now browsing in distinguished superannuation.[5]
They dined with the Royal Society Club. In November they went
to Oxford to receive honorary doctorates.[6] They went to stay with

[1] For these quotations in their contexts see Cook I, pp. 642 ff., except that on the
'coronet of gold', which I take from the *Annual Register*, 1771, Chronicle p. 150, for 23
September.

[2] *Gent. Mag.*, XLI (1771), p. 567.

[3] *Letters and Journals*, III, p. 435.

[4] One person who got no satisfaction from the conversation, though we do not know
when it took place (perhaps it was on Banks's passage through Scotland late in 1772),
was Lord Monboddo. 'We travelled towards Aberdeen, another University, and in the
way dined at Lord Monbodo's, the Scotch Judge who has lately written a strange book
about the origin of Language, in which he traces Monkeys up to Men, and says that in
some countries the human species have tails like other beasts. He enquired for these
longtailed Men of Banks, and was not well pleased, that they had not been found in
all his peregrination'.—Johnson to Mrs Thrale, 25 August 1773, *Letters* (ed. R. W.
Chapman, Oxford 1952), I, p. 321.

[5] Johnson to Banks, 27 February 1772, *Letters*, I, p. 272. Boswell himself did not run
down the gentlemen till later, as we learn from his London Journal, 22 March 1772.
On that date he visited Sir John Pringle, the President of the Royal Society. 'He
had with him Lord Lyttelton and several more Gentlemen, in particular the famous
Mr. Banks and Dr. Solander, whom I had a great curiosity to see. Mr. Banks was a
genteel young man, very black [i.e. dark], and of an agreable countenance, easy and
communicative, without any affectation or appearance of assuming. Dr. Solander, though
a Swede, spoke english with more fluency and propriety than most natives.'—*Private
Papers of James Boswell*, 9 (New Haven 1930), p. 28. Much (in fact years) later, Johnson
remarked to Mrs Thrale, 'You may remember, I thought Banks had not gained much by
circumnavigating the world'; but what precisely he meant by this, or when he first said
it, or how he could judge, we do not know. He wrote on 16 October 1780, *Letters*, II,
p. 406.

[6] They were both created D.C.L. on 21 November 1771.—Foster, *Alumni Oxonienses*,
I (London 1887), p. 57. This was the only academic degree Banks ever attained.

Sydney Parkinson

Sandwich, who had become First Lord of the Admiralty, at Hinchingbrooke. When the Royal Society measured the height of St Paul's, in its researches into atmospheric weight at different elevations, the names of Dr Solander and Mr Banks were particularly noticed.[1]

Of course Ellis wrote to Linnaeus very early, indeed first on 10 May, the day after the newspapers heard from the India House the definite news of the ship's arrival at Batavia; the learned and curious in England felt universal joy. Solander would be introduced to the Royal Family as soon as he was returned, and then probably his merits would be rewarded. The travellers did return; they were 'laden with spoils, particularly of the vegetable world, some few rare ones of the animal kingdom; but I do not hear much of the mineral kingdom. . . . Dr. Solander has been very ill, but is now very well. . . . They have sufficient for one thousand folio plates. . . . They are so very busy getting their things on shore, and seeing their friends, after an absence of three years, that they have scarce time to tell us of any thing but the many narrow escapes they have had from imminent danger. . . . Be so good to inform Dr. Solander's friends of the success he has had in returning safe after so many perils, laden with the greatest treasure of Natural History that ever was brought into any country at one time by two persons. . . . I hope Dr. Solander will write to you soon himself; I shall beg of him not to defer it'.[2] Solander did defer it. The old man, feverish with excitement at the prospect of seeing new plants from 'Banksia, or Terra australis',[3] wrote at once both to Banks and to Solander; to the 'immortal Banks', the glory of England and the whole world, to whom botanists should raise a statue more enduring than the Pyramids;[4] but, said Ellis, 'they have been so hurried with company that they have very little time' to write back.[5] The hurry of company was quite enough also to keep them from sending the Master specimens of their discoveries, and when he read in the English newspapers of an intended new voyage, he was almost sleepless with worry.[6]

The hurry of company might deter Banks from writing to the man whose correspondence, three years before, he would have regarded as a sublime honour; but it could not save him from

[1] *Annual Register*, 1771, Chronicle, p. 154, for 12 November.
[2] Ellis to Linnaeus, 10 May, 16 July 1771; J.E.S. I, pp. 259-60, 263-4.
[3] The phrase is in a later letter from Linnaeus to Ellis, 20 December 1771; ibid., p. 123.
[4] 8 August 1771; B. M. Add. MS 8094.33. The letter is in Latin.
[5] Ellis to Linnaeus, 19 November 1771; J.E.S.I, pp. 271-2.
[6] Linnaeus to Ellis, 22 October 1771; ibid., I, p. 267. See p. 70-1 below.

F

embarrassments. The first of these arose from Miss Harriet Blosset; who, it appears, at the intoxicating tidings of the arrival of the *Endeavour*, did not hurry up at once to town, but, with proper delicacy, waited a few days in the country for her impassioned lover to make some advance to her. Now Banks may well be pardoned if, during an absence of three years, of much stimulation to his mind and some to his heart, the vision of Miss Blosset grew dim. What home thoughts from abroad he entrusted to his journal do not embrace that young woman, and one of his remarks upon the Cape would have been singularly discouraging to her, could she have read it. He admired the Cape ladies: 'In general they are handsome with clear skins and high Complexions and when married (no reflextions upon my country women) are the best housekeepers imaginable and great childbearers; had I been inclind for a wife I think this is the place of all others I have seen where I could best have suited myself'. One would guess at this stage that not merely had the vision of Miss Blosset grown dim; she must have been entirely blotted from his mind. Return, however, revived the awkward memory; our young man found he had not the slightest interest in Miss Blosset, but what was he to do? He shelved the problem in the hurry of company; he did nothing. His friends, whose memories had been more lively, were distressed; in the end they were appalled. It became plain that Mr Banks was not acting like a gentleman. Gossip was lively: we have Lady Mary Coke again, as early as 14 August. 'I saw Mr. Morrice this morning. . . . He was excessively drole according to custom, and said he hoped Mr Banks, who since his return has desired Miss Blosset will excuse his marrying her, will pay her for the materials of all the work'd waistcoats She made for him during the time he was sailing round the World. Everybody agrees that She passed those three years in retirement, but whether She imploy'd herself in working waistcoats for Mr Banks I can't tell you, but if She loved him I pity her disappointment'.[1] Miss Blosset was indeed in the most unenviable situation. At least she managed to keep her head rather better than did Mr Banks, if we may rely on the circumstantial information supplied by one friend of Banks, the good Daines Barrington, to another, Thomas Pennant, in the following letters.[2]

[1] *Letters and Journals*, III, p. 437.
[2] Both in ATL, ALS 269. They appear to have come to the library with other fragments of Pennant's papers, some already quoted. The second is merely the portion of a letter, with no date or address, but in the same writing as the first, to which it almost certainly refers.

(i)

Carnarvon Augt 24 1771

Dear S^r

The account I have receivd of Mr Banks's infidelity is the following & I believe you may depend upon every circumstance of it.

Upon his arrival in England he took no sort of notice of Miss Blosset for the first week or nearly so at the same time that he went about London & visited other friends & acquaintance.

On this Miss Blosset set out for London & wrote him a letter desiring an interview of explanation.

To this Mr Bankes answer'd by a letter of 2 or 3 sheets professing love &c but that he found he was of too volatile a temper to marry.

The answer as you may suppose rather astonished & some how or other after this there was an interview when Miss Bl: swoon'd &c & Mr Bankes was so affected that Marriage was again concluded upon. Notwithstanding this however a short time afterwards he writes a second letter to the same purport with the former, & leaves poor Miss Bl: in the most distressing as well as ridiculous situation imaginable.

Mr Bankes's behaviour seems therefore to me to be totally without excuse as he admits he gave Miss Bl: the strongest reason to expect he would return her husband.

Supposing him however to have discovere'd in a three year voyage (during which by the way he would scarcely have seen any other woman) that he should not prove a good husband.

Should he not have immediately dispatch'd a Messenger on his landing with the best reasons he could muster for declining what he had so thoroughly settled? Should he not also have immediately plac'd in the Stocks & in Miss Blossets name a most noble satisfaction (as far as money could repair it) for this injury. And when he had done both these things could the satisfaction be otherwise than highly inadequate?

To prove however beyond a doubt how very shamefull his behaviour hath been to this poor girl Mrs Bankes his mother who always disapprov'd of the match blames him as much as anyone.

The Blossets also as you may imagine resent the injury to such a degree that upon some ones intimating that Mr Banks could not do otherwise than make a most large pecuniary satisfaction they declare that the offer of his whole estate would be consider'd as the highest insult & that the only consolation they can ever receive is that Miss Blosset will not now become the wife of a man who hath behav'd so infamously.

I find this account runs to such a length that I must deferr my Welsh Anecdotes to the next place — Dolgelly.

Ever Yrs

D: B:

P: S: The Blossets complain of Solander as I am told but I have not heard any particulars of what they lay to his charge.

(ii)

I have receiv'd at this place a most particular account from a Lady
of what hath pass'd between Mr Banks & Miss Blosset who strongly
confirms that the former made the most explicit declaration.

What think you of the following facts?

Mr Banks had an interview with her in London which lasted from
ten O'clock at Night to ten the next Morning during which he said he
was ready to marry her immediately.

Miss Blosset however would not catch at this proposal but told him
if he was of the same mind a fortnight hence, she would gladly attend
him to church Three or four days after which he wrote her a letter
desiring to be off.

Mr Tunstall writes me word that Mr Banks and Dr Solander mean to
fall plump from the Cape of Good Hope upon 70 Deg^s of Southern
Latitude

Ever Yrs

D: B:

P.S. Mr Banks in this conversation said he had acted by *the advice of a
friend* & hence the Blossets blame Solander as I before inform'd you.[1]

Whether Solander's common sense made him urge Banks to get
out of the false situation at any cost to his dignity, or whether
Banks's imagination conjured up 'the advice of a friend' to help
him out, we do not know. Solander himself was a confirmed bachelor,
and knowing Banks by this time pretty well, he may have judged
that the young man was no husband for Miss Blosset. There, it
seems, the afflicting matter must be left.

Miss Blosset was not the only embarrassment that afflicted the
returned traveller in the midst of his glory. There was also Stanfield
Parkinson. From the difficulties hereby created we see Banks
emerge with more credit. These difficulties lasted some months,
and involved a number of people, but it is convenient to deal with
the whole rather tangled story here. After the death of the unfortunate Joel Parkinson, brewer, of Edinburgh, it appears that not
only Sydney but his mother, Elizabeth, his elder brother Stanfield,
and his sister Britannia, had migrated to London. Sydney, accom-
plished and amiable, had been engaged by Banks as his botanical
draughtsman for the voyage at a salary of £80 a year. On his
departure from England he left his will with his sister Britannia.

---

[1] The other side of the page on which the foregoing is written has for some reason
been crossed through, but contains, *inter alia*, the following remarks which probably
refer to Bougainville's account of his voyage, published in 1771: 'I do not conceive that
Bougainville or Commercons observations will be as accurate as Solanders, however
I think you must allow that the Voyage is very entertaining & interesting. I wish the
French would learn of the Northern Naturalists to *describe* & that the Swedes would
learn of them to think'.

He had worked exceedingly hard at his drawings,[1] and in what spare time he could make had not only collected shells and other curiosities but had put down many notes and drafts for a journal, a fair copy of which was generally thought to have been written by him; what he wrote as well as what he drew was in any case highly admired by his shipmates. He died on 26 January 1771. Before he died, he asked Solander to see that his friend James Lee the nursery-man had the perusal of his papers; and he seems to have given Banks a copy of his will. Banks handed this copy to the executors, Elizabeth the mother, and Stanfield, who found it contained no alterations; and as Elizabeth withdrew from all administration in favour of her son, Stanfield entered upon the execution of the will. There are three factors on the Banks side to be noted at this moment: Banks was in all the hurry of company, his mind fully engaged with his own concerns, which included the distraction and confusion of his relations with Miss Blosset; he was a gentleman, who did not like his word to be doubted; he intended well by the Parkinsons. On the Parkinson side, it must be noted that Stanfield, though carrying on trade as an upholsterer, was an illiterate man, and though a Quaker, highly suspicious. It is possible also that he was already affected by the mental instability which increased until, not long afterwards, he died insane; but whether or not that is true, his suspicions were raised enormously by Banks's dilatoriness. Banks, undoubtedly, should have acted much more promptly than he did. In London, it may be surmised, he was a less tactful man than Banks in Tahiti; the matter was for him a quite subordinate one, and Stanfield, after the first contacts, merely an impertinent tradesman; with Stanfield, on the other hand, suspicion became an obsession. There were not wanting other people, admirers of Sydney among the ship's company, and friends of his own, to build up an entirely false picture of the literary and other remains of poor Sydney, and of his own rights.

When the ship arrived in England, Banks wrote to Stanfield, who immediately called on him, to receive an assurance of Banks's interest, and his intention of rendering an account of all Sydney's belongings. Banks also immediately gave him work, and continued to do so throughout the misunderstandings that now followed.[2]

---

[1] Cf. Banks's entry for 12 May 1770, II, p. 62 below: 'In 14 days just, one draughtsman has made 94 sketch drawings, so quick a hand has he acquird by use'. This could be no one but Sydney.

[2] Stanfield's receipts, preserved in the 'Voluntiers' volume cited below, p. 68, n. 2, are for goods supplied or work done for Banks, sometimes at New Burlington Street, from 20 July 1771 to 24 February 1772, a total of £89 8s 6d.

Shortly afterwards Stanfield was told by somebody else (hearsay begins to play its part) that James Lee had been informed by Banks that Sydney had bequeathed his journal to Lee, together with other papers that had been lost. This at once put him on fire; he questioned Banks, who confirmed the information, but said he could not find the journal: as soon as his goods arrived from the ship, he added, Stanfield would receive Sydney's, among which there were some curiosities he would like to buy. Several weeks passed during which Banks made no sign, and the fire continued to burn. Stanfield then called on Banks, who arranged to send him some, at least, of Sydney's property. This came; it did not correspond with the inventory, said Stanfield; people talked to him again, and he began to ask further questions. Five weeks later Banks sent for him, to complain about these enquiries; in answer to which Stanfield complained that Banks was wrongfully keeping Sydney's journal and drawings. At these two last meetings, it seems, one or the other, or both, men had difficulty in preserving moderation of speech. Banks, referring the question to Solander, found that he had been mistaken over the alleged bequest to Lee; Stanfield saw a small bundle of papers in Sydney's handwriting. He went away to brood for another considerable time, hearing no more from Banks; and then began to call for assistance on Dr John Fothergill, a fellow Quaker of his own Westminster connection, a physician famous alike for his professional skill, scientific leanings, and benevolence,[1] who had known Joel Parkinson in Edinburgh, and in London had given his patronage to both the sons. Fothergill, against Stanfield's expressed intention of going to law, counselled patience and reliance on the generosity of 'a gentleman of J. Banks's character'; but at last, badgered beyond endurance, consented to approach the gentleman, a perfect stranger,[2] in the hope of bringing the absurd difference to an end; he also had some talk with Solander, an old friend, to whom he suggested the payment of a suitable sum by Banks in quittance of the whole business. Banks was by now anxious to be quit of it, and the essential para-

[1] John Fothergill, M.D., F.R.S. (1712-80), was eminent also as a botanist. He had a fine botanical garden at Upton, near Stratford, and, like Banks later, employed a number of draughtsmen. Banks greatly admired his collections. His *Works* were published by John Coakley Lettsom, his pupil and successor in medical practice, in 1783-4. Benjamin Franklin's judgment was, 'I can hardly conceive that a better man has ever existed'.

[2] At least, Fothergill himself says (Parkinson's *Journal*, 'Explanatory Remarks', p. 3), 'I wrote to J. Banks, to whom I was then personally a stranger'. But then how do we account for the present of 'the North American apples which Dr Fothergill gave me', made into a pie on 23 September 1769 (p. 393 below)? Perhaps they came through an intermediary.

graphs of his letter to Fothergill may be quoted, both as his justification and as a garland on the memory of Sydney:

On leaving England, I agreed to give eighty pounds a year to S. Parkinson, besides his living of all kinds, as my draughtsman, to make drawings for me: of this agreement, £151. 8s. 1d is now due to his executors, besides some small sum for such cloths, &c. of his, as I could dispose of, or make use of in the ship, which I chose rather to do, than bring them home liable to be damaged, as those which came home were in some degree.

Curiosities of all kinds I gave up to them, and such of his papers as I had, excepting only some loose sheets of a journal, which seemed to be only foul copies of a fair journal that I never found, and which is now the chief object of their enquiry; these foul papers, as all the journal I had, was to be given to Mr. Lee, for his reading, by S. Parkinson's own desire, expressed to Dr. Solander just before he died: the curiosities I offered to purchase at the time I delivered them, at such price as the executors should put upon them, but was refused.

Now as S. Parkinson certainly behaved to me, during the whole of his long voyage, uncommonly well, and with unbounded industry made for me a much larger number of drawings than I ever expected, I always did and still do intend to shew to his relations the same gratitude for his good services as I should have done to himself; the execution of this my intention was only delayed by the fear of being involved in a vexatious law-suit after all.

Now you, sir, in conversation with Dr. Solander, have been so good as to suggest a mode of pleasing all parties, which I confess I very much approve of; the only thing that now remains is, that, as a friend to both, you think of a certain sum to be paid by me to them, as an acknowledgement of S. Parkinson's good services, taking or not the curiosities, &c. just as may seem to you most proper: in this, if you are good enough to undertake it, I beg leave to hint, that I do not at all mean to be sparing in my acknowledgment; but to err rather on the other side, that any one who may hear the transaction may rather say I have been generous than otherwise.[1]

The worthy Fothergill therefore took into consideration the whole circumstances, and thought of £500. 'J. Banks', he says, 'very readily fell in with the proposal, and settled at the same time a pension upon a black woman, the wife of a faithful black servant who went out with him, and perished by the cold of Terra del Fuego'. The Parkinsons also agreed; Stanfield and Britannia met Banks (it was now the end of January 1772), and, with Fothergill as witness, signed a receipt.

But the tedious business was not yet over. Fothergill had not

[1] Parkinson's *Journal*, 'Explanatory Remarks', pp. 4-5.

made himself entirely clear. Among the 'curiosities' temporarily
in Stanfield's possession the doctor had selected for himself a few
shells. He had also made it a condition of the settlement that all
these curiosities, including those he had selected, should be sent
to Banks, for him to retain whatever was needed to complete the
general collection made on the voyage. Banks, acting under a
misunderstanding, retained all except those which Fothergill
wanted. Fothergill paid Stanfield twice the amount he considered
the market-price for these shells, warning the man that that was so,
and that he must not look for such prices elsewhere. Again, it had
been agreed in the general settlement that Banks should have all
Sydney's manuscripts (the bundle that Stanfield had once seen)
as well as the drawings that were admittedly Banks's own property.
Stanfield wished to borrow the manuscripts to read; Banks hesitated,
but on Fothergill's pledging himself that they would be put to no
improper use, made the loan. Stanfield immediately had them
copied; and then, smarting under the persuasion that Banks had
cheated him of the value of the shells, determined to make a profit
by publishing them. By the middle of 1772 he was certainly beginning to take leave of his senses; for it was then, hearing that
Banks was proposing a journey to Iceland, that he advertised in the
newspapers offering a reward of a hundred guineas for information
as to where Sydney's journal and drawings, 'pretended to have
been lost', were secreted; with the insolent note added, 'It is
supposed that they are not many Miles from New Burlington
Street'. He certainly did not draw the advertisement himself. He
did, it appears, manage to come by a few drawings from Sydney's
shipmates — or he may have come by them during his transactions
with Banks. He had too many friends; there was natural public
eagerness to see anything in print about the great voyage; the
booksellers were anxious to lay their hands on anything to get in
ahead of the official narrative entrusted to Hawkesworth. Banks
and Solander had already had to disclaim connection with one
anonymous much-trumpeted account which had invoked their
names,[1] and Banks, in his anxiety to maintain the proprieties,

[1] This was the *Journal of a Voyage round the World* published by T. Becket and P. A. de
Hondt, London 1771; see Cook I, pp. cclvi ff; Holmes, *Captain Cook: A Bibliographical
Excursion* (London 1952), pp. 20-1. Cf. a letter from Banks's naval friend Captain Bentinck
of the *Centaur*, Spithead, 10 October 1771: 'As to Mr Becket, and his Catch-penny, the
subject is so interesting that there is no putting the book down, at the same time that the
inaccuracy with which it is wrote makes it most tiresome and indeed the most provoking
reading I ever met with'.—D.T.C. I, p. 27. There is further reference, not highly
accurate, to the subject by Mrs Delany, writing to Mrs Port of Ilam, 19 November
1771: 'I believe I wrote you word that the book published of George's Land (or Otahitee)

had had to buy up and destroy the whole impression of a printed version of a private letter he had written to his friend the Comte de Lauraguais describing the voyage.[1] It was easy for Stanfield to find a hack who would take the copies of the 'foul papers' and knock them into publishable shape. This was James Kenrick, a notorious Grub Street practitioner and literary libeller of the day. Fothergill got to hear what was afoot: he was horrified beyond measure — had he not pledged his honour to Banks that no improper use would be made of the papers? — and in vain tried to restrain the unhappy Stanfield, by argument, proffered indemnification, and the good offices of still a third Friend. What he could not do, Hawkesworth did for a period by applying to Chancery for an injunction, which was not taken off till after Hawkesworth's own volumes had appeared in 1773. The Quaker connection finding, when Stanfield's book was at last published, a serious attack on one member of the Society by another — for Kenrick had been only too pleased to add a skilfully composed preface traducing both Banks and Fothergill — was compelled to treat with Stanfield over his breach of discipline. 'After much labour', he was brought to acknowledge this; but while a written document was being drawn up, 'such evident marks of insanity appeared, as to render it of no consequence to proceed with him any further'.[2] By that time Banks had long freed his mind of the matter. It was not likely that an attack from Kenrick would do a man any harm in the polite world.[3] And there were other adventures to envisage.

was not by Mr. Banks and Dr. Solander's direction, but they are preparing an account of their voyage; but the Natural History will be a work by itself, entirely at the expense of Mr. Banks, for which he has laid by ten thousand pound. He has already the drawings of everything (birds, beasts, plants, and views) that were remarkable; the work to be set in order, that is, the history written, by Mr. Hawkesworth, under the inspection of Mr. Banks and Dr. Solander; it will hardly come out in my time, as it will consist of at least fourteen volumes in folio. As this was *private* talk, perhaps it should not be mentioned in general'.—*Autobiography and Correspondence of . . . Mrs Delany* (2nd series, 1862), I, pp. 371-2.

[1] Louis Léon Félicité Lauraguais, Comte de Lauraguais and later Duc de Brancas (1733-1824), was interested in letters and science, a member of the *Académie des Sciences*, a liberal in politics and social life, a supporter of inoculation, and a wit whose life was said to combine '*bons mots et bonnes actions*'. He had been prepared to print together Banks's letter to him and a letter of his own to D'Alembert enlarging on the subject. He argued that all the facts were already public property, and that he little deserved reproaches; but he had had some difficulties, 'For the Printer (whom I do not know) is so eager to sell them that he does little care for correction', as he naively told Banks in a letter headed Brompton 17th [February?] 1772.—D.T.C. I, p. 31.

[2] Parkinson's *Journal*, 'Explanatory Remarks', p. 16.

[3] Stanfield Parkinson's affairs, as well as his mind, were disordered; his wife died shortly before he became quite insane, and the Friends undertook the maintenance of his children. Fothergill, their friend as he had been their father's and grandfather's, bought up the unsold remainder of Sydney's *Journal*, about four hundred copies. This was reissued in 1784, with eighteen pages of 'Explanatory Remarks' by Fothergill on Kenrick's preface. The foregoing account is founded on these remarks and on what seems credible in the preface. No fair copy of Sydney's journal was ever found.

§

We may at this point with some profit scrutinize the portraits of Banks. We may omit the early one, the charming boy with the long hair and the lace and the book of botanical pictures.[1] Returning from such a voyage he must, quite obviously, have his portrait painted. He had it painted twice. Reynolds, naturally; but he found it worth his while also to patronise the rising star of British art, Benjamin West. Reynolds gave the gentleman an air; West, removing his attention from the death of General Wolfe, produced something at once more prosaic and more romantic. With Reynolds we have a three-quarter length, seated, with, of course, easy grace — a grace that, nevertheless, does not destroy the figure's lively energy; the right hand grips firmly the leather arm of a chair; the left, lightly clenched, rests equally firmly upon a sheaf of papers — can they be part of the Journal? — on a table otherwise adorned with an inkstand, a few books, and — equally of course — a terrestrial globe. Through a window behind the table one's eye is carried to an expanse of sea and sky. The young man's coat is lavish, fur-trimmed, the waistcoat is heavily embroidered, the neck-cloth is laced. It is a comely face, the oval rendered by drawing and shadow rather narrower at the chin, rather more stylish, than seems actually to have been so; a face to which the disposal of the hair across the forehead gives almost the conventional outline of a heart. The brow is wide, the eyes large, the eyebrows, the nose and the mouth very definite. The shadow beneath the lower lip suggests a certain size and mobility; there is the possibility of a quite charming smile. It is a face that, as one gazes into it, ceases to be entirely handsome; the chin, the nose, the eyebrows, accentuate themselves; authority is not yet carved on the brow, as in Phillips's picture of the President of the Royal Society in his last years, the Roman emperor upon the rostrum, but there is in that nose and that jaw the promise of heaviness; there is a latent obstinacy; there is even — revolt as we may from making the charge, for which the journal, too, read between the lines, once or twice proffers a basis — a hint of sulkiness.[2] Turn now to West: it is of course a stiffer performance,

[1] The artist is unknown. The picture is reproduced in Cameron, pl.1.

[2] This is not, it may be said, a characteristic that has struck previous critics, who have been writing about Reynolds and not Banks. The portrait is certainly one of Reynolds's best, and has called forth great enthusiasm from the artist's biographers. 'Sir Joshua's portrait of Banks, painted at this time, is an excellent illustration of the importance of intelligent and intimate relations between painter and sitter. The painter has thoroughly understood his subject. . . . The burning eyes are focussed by the will that knits the brow, and gives their tension to the hands. . . . The energy of the man seems to be lifting him out of the seat by an irrepressible force. The globe at his side, the wide stretch of sea

inelegant by the side of Sir Joshua, thoroughly conventional in spite of the exotic properties the subject has brought into it. He is standing as if his progress forward had been just arrested; behind him is the heroic classical column with drawn-back curtain which signifies perhaps Western civilization, perhaps merely something the artist did not know how to do without; the hands and the ruffles look as if they had been drawn not from Banks but from Vandyck. Round the shoulders and enveloping most of the body is a Maori cloak, undoubtedly a fine one, with dog's hair fringe; to his right lean upwards a Maori *taiaha*, or carved fighting-staff, a canoe paddle, and other ethnographical specimens; before him, on the other side, is a large Polynesian adze and some rather crumpled folio pages — this time not a journal but, one guesses, a section of a book for pressing plants. And the head? Though the hair, or wig, is severer than that of Sir Joshua's painting, the face has a softer curve; the large eyes, the distinct eyebrows, nose and mouth are there, but compared with Reynolds, they have lost in character; it is altogether a more feminine face — could this be, the sudden absurd fancy strikes one, Sarah Sophia dressed up? No, it is Joseph; a Joseph this time of rather ingratiating charm; it is not a stubborn face, but a face — again the half-hidden shade — that holds the possibility of petulance; and petulance, alas! is half-sister to sulkiness, it too may lead to obstinacy.

The two portraits, so dissimilar, thus unite in giving us a Banks who is not quite all gallant adventurer, not quite all modesty, not quite necessarily all generous charm. We have presented, in fact, the wherewithal of a less admirable Banks, a Banks who in conceivable circumstances might be a very great fool. The difficulty with Miss Blosset may have been inevitable. The trouble with Stanfield Parkinson could very likely have been avoided, if Banks had acted sooner, and kept his temper even if he had to give away a little dignity; but once the trouble had come to a head he acted like a man of honour and reputation. In the matter that now arose he acted not like a man of honour but like a man of consequence, and of consequence that had gone to his brain. 'Joseph Banks Esquire, a Gentleman possessed of considerable landed property in Lincolnshire', had ceased to be a simple gentleman; Joseph Banks the student of natural history, who would have knelt before

visible from the window, are significant of voyages past and to come. No painter could have so expressed the "hungry heart" of a man smitten with the passion of exploring and inquiring, unless he had felt a deep and intelligent sympathy with his sitter.'—C. R. Leslie and Tom Taylor, *Life and Times of Sir Joshua Reynolds* (London 1865), I, pp. 428-9. This seems to the present writer somewhat overdone.

the chair of Linnaeus as at a throne, had, almost, enthroned himself; Joseph Banks, whose three years' voyaging should, one would have thought, have given him an enlarged appreciation of other men and of their rôle in the scheme of things, had lost all sense of proportion where he and other men were concerned. Joseph Banks — the conclusion is ineluctable — had a swelled head. It showed itself with disastrous amplitude during the preparations which began, towards the end of 1771, for another adventure into the unknown. We may return to Sir Joshua's picture. The sheaf of papers surmounted by our young man's energetic hand is surmounted by something else, calculated to convey the right ardency of enthusiasm: it is the Horatian tag, *Cras ingens iterabimus aequor* — 'Tomorrow we set out once more upon the boundless main'. Mr Banks had no doubt of his destiny.

Another adventure there certainly had to be. Cook, in a postscript to his journal, had laid down its essential lines; and doubtless it had been discussed on board the *Endeavour*, for Banks adumbrates its course in his own pages. The Admiralty, agreeing with Cook over its necessity, and properly appreciative of his merit, had no doubt who should conduct it. Sandwich asked Banks if he too would care to make a second voyage. It was to be a voyage far to the south. Banks did not hesitate: both he and Solander would go. 'O how Glorious would it be to set my heel upon the Pole! and turn myself round 360 degrees in a second', he wrote to his French friend Lauraguais.[1] Before August was out the newspapers had got hold of the rumour. Nobody could doubt from those newspapers that Mr Banks and Dr Solander had triumphantly conducted the previous voyage, and that Mr Banks was now the presiding genius of exploration; and for the next few months letters descended upon New Burlington Street as if it were a department of government. They were communications of all kinds, long and short, in English, French and even Latin, not merely from London and the English counties, but from France and Holland, Switzerland and Germany; they were learned and illiterate, models of calligraphy and almost illegible, graceful and awkward, enthusiastic, respectful, extravagant, argumentative, incoherent. They tendered congratulations on a safe return and proffered advice on assaying and mineralogy, on salting cabbage, painting flowers, preserving animals — Mr Hunter, the eminent surgeon, hoped the expedition might secure the essential parts of a whale — on chronometers, catharpings and triangular courses and harpoons; they asked for

[1] Banks to Lauraguais, December 1771. ML MSS.

the command of a ship or they recommended young persons of unimpeachable character on the recommendation of someone else. There was a memorandum about the Spanish visit to Easter Island, brought back by Mr Harris from his Embassy at Madrid. There were thoughts on geography, and highly speculative considerations on the prehistoric movements of the peoples of Ireland, Mexico, and Tahiti — even the Norse gods came into it; there were suggested subjects of enquiry: on the saltness of water, chemistry, mineral waters, the diet and diseases of native peoples — 'What Burning Mountains are there in New Zealand. . . . What Shell-fish are *characteristick* of *particular* Climates?' What Globe or Map of the Earth did Mr Banks think best, and where was it to be got? Should not Mr Banks apply to the courts of Madrid and Lisbon, that instructions might be sent to their governors abroad to render the expedition all possible assistance? Should not every ship carry a small vessel which would take to pieces, strong enough to bear a sea in a good gale of wind? Dr Watson of Trinity College, who wanted a quart or two of sea water corked up for him in different latitudes, and a few short vocabularies, is 'sorry to be so troublesome, but he hath a particular conjecture to be established or destroyed'. Dr Priestley would be pleased at any time to explain his method of sweetening water by fixed air. 'Worthy Cosmopolites and My dear Freinds Mr Bancke and Dr Solander', exclaimed one gentleman with an indecipherable signature, and went on to describe at intolerable length the workings of his newly invented cooking-stove. 'You will undoubtedly discover the great Southern continent, the existence of which I think admits of no dispute', another gentleman assured them, dilating on how to find islands, and the advisability of leaving animals and birds to breed on islands when found.

But the greater number of correspondents were those who — to put it briefly — wanted to go too. More at length, William Cawthorne suggests that the 'national and general Advantage' of the voyage would be more fully served 'by including in your Suite a person appointed by the Board of Trade under the Character of COMMERCIAL INTELLIGENCER, whose province should be (leaving you to pursue your philosophical Disquisitions) to consider and digest the Errors and Deficiencies in the System of Commerce now subsisting between this Country and the various places and Nations you will necessarily visit. . . . To Gentlemen of your exalted understandings, the Wisdom and Utility of this appointment will instantly appear' — an appointment for which, granting the remarkable

abilities required, Mr Cawthorne modestly offers himself. 'A person
of a liberal Education (a Surgeon by Profession)' wants to travel
for a few years. 'I Understand the Theorical as well as the Practical
Part of Most Mathermatical Learning Particularly Navigation',
writes William Cooke, whose letter was neglected; and again,
'I Longed for An Answer But Never had the Hapiness to Get
one. . . . I have a Very Ernest Desire to Go Along with You in
Your most Honourable Employment in Circulating the Teraquous
Globe (if I may be Allowed the Express'on of A Geographer) I
flatter my Self that you will not Doney My Imperause Desire. . . .'
'I am a young Man of about 22; have had a liberal Education
and, if I am not flattered by my Friends, have a tolerable Genius':
thus Thomas Davies, in the service of Lord Weymouth. Mr Davies
kept accounts, could survey land, was remarkably fond of botany,
and 'P.S. Could I not supply the place of one of your Domestics?
I care not how Servile the Station if I could be near you; tho' I
shall purchase it, at the Expence of a good Place'. A turkey and a
chine followed, to compensate Mr Banks for the trouble caused
him. Stephen Elgin, from the East Riding, fond of botany, now in
London in a shop, is 'a young person Who hath for a long time had
the greatest Noetion of going Abrod'. James Farquharson, a watch
and clock maker, is similarly situated. John Davidson, a house
carpenter and joiner, 'through Variegated and unforseen misfortunes Should now be glad to embrace the oppertunity of Satisfying
(what I believe is an innate desire) of Seeing the Wonders of Nature
and providence'. 'In the utmost Anxiety of Hope I have presumed
to address you, Sir', says J. Fletcher, 'I ask no Recompence but the
Permission to serve you' in ever so humble a capacity — 'I would
even assist in navigating the ship. . . . Even a recommendation
to Capt. Cooke, if I cannot go with you, would be a Favour'.
'Curiosity is natural to the Soul of Man' announces Mr Hatherley
of Bideford, though he asks Dr Solander and Mr Banks not to
inform his connections in London of his ambition, as if it were
unsuccessful it might affect his prospects in the law. John Hyacinth
de Magalhaens — a serious scientific name at last — of distinguished
historical connection and some skill with scientific instruments,
wants, if possible, to 'preform as much in the Service of England,
as the brother of my fifth grandfather did in ye Service of Spain'.
Joseph Scothern and William Wortley, joint applicants, understand
navigation, can play a large variety of musical instruments, and are
prepared to learn themselves the French horn. Matthew Rouviere,
an usher, 'being informd by a Gentleman that you want several

Young Men skill^d in Arts and Sciences', provides ten lines of accomplishments, from languages to fortification. William Pearce can spell with justice and accuracy. John Frazier has great usefulness in going under water. One Prescott, who is 'extreamly anxious of seeing more of the World, than has hitherto fallen to my lot', adds with unusual reserve, 'Perhaps it may be pertinent to remark, that I am no Seaman'. Signor Pilati is suspected by the Pope and clergy of having written certain books: he did write them; and as he understands and speaks Portuguese, and admires a grandeur of soul such as Mr Banks's, offers his services. Fathers write on behalf of sons, the Vice-Chancellor of Oxford on behalf of a young graduate who has 'a very curious Turn'. Mr John Smith, an unsuccessful wholesale hosier of the Isle of Wight, understands Dr Solander to be the principal manager in an enterprise to settle the Falkland Islands; if Dr Solander will take Mr Smith, his wife, three small children, and sister, 'in all probability you will save a sinking Family from ruin'. With a great excess of optimism Mr Smith informs Dr Solander that an immediate answer will be esteemed, and is under the consequent necessity of writing two further letters before he gives up. Dr Solander and Mr Banks have indeed a great responsibility upon them: for Edward Williams, a youth well brought up, of a liberal education, 'if not soon protected by some kind hand, ruin must ensue, and even non existance follow. . . .'

It is curious that not merely do such persons 'have the notion of going abroad', and 'pant' to go with Banks, but even seamen in the royal navy apply to him as a patron. Edward Turrell of the *Barfleur*, on 'January ye 8' pens a cry from the heart:

sir I shall be very Glad if your honnour Will be Pleasd to grant me this small Request and I hope your honnour will Exques me for making so bold as to wri[t]e to your Honnor but that I hear your honnour and mr sillander is a going out upon Descovers and shold be very glad of having the Pleasure of going with your honnour for I am on Board of the Barfleur. I was a going out In the Endeavour But was taken sick and was sent on shore to the hospitall But thank the almighty god I heave got the Better of my Eleness sir I shall Take it as great favour and shall be Bound to Pray for your honnour all the Days of my life so No More at Present from your humble servent to Command.

William Packover had been an A.B. on the *Endeavour*: 'I ham now Emboldend to solicit Your Goodness to have me appointed Supernumery Midshipman in one of the Ships newly Commissioned for the South Seas'. Henry Walker, who had been in the *Niger* on the Newfoundland voyage, is now a midshipman, and wants to sail with Banks as a junior lieutenant. Most curious of all perhaps, in some ways, is the long letter from George Robertson, who had been the master of the *Dolphin* under Wallis, on the voyage that discovered Tahiti; for Robertson was a man of ability, and must have known very well to whom the success of the *Endeavour*'s voyage was due.

At present [he writes] I am on half pay, but Lord Sandwich has promised me the Comm^d of the first Cutter that becomes Vacent, but if you are going another Voyage on Descoverys as the publick peapers Informs us I should much rather take the Command of a small Vessel on that Expedition, as my Curiosity is not yet fully satisfied. If it be true that you are going on that Voyage, as I cannot rely on the publick peapers, I shall take it as a Singular favour if you will advise me in Course, that I may apply in time. . . . Were my Circumstances as good as they have been, I could willingly come and see you without any other errand, as I am certain your descoverys must have been very great, as I well know one of your Noble turn of mind would not stick at every trifleing Danger, where there was the least probability of making any kind of Descoverys, that could be of the least use to your King and Country, or to Mankind in General, you Appear to me to be a Gentleman born to Serve Mankind in General and this Nation in Particular, and I am tould kind providence has blest you with the means to cary on your Plan, I sincerely wish you Success in all your publick and privet undertakings, and may your Name be handed down in the Brittish Annals, with the greatest Honour, is the Earnest wishes of him who thinks near as you do, but wants the means. . . .[1]

On that latest theme of the Brittish Annals, we may return to a civilian voice, the voice of Mr Sheffield, a natural historian who was soon to become keeper of the university museum at Oxford: 'Yr first Voyage and Discoveries will transmit yr Fames to posterity, a second, attended with equal, and perhaps greater Success, will render you Immortal!'[2] Immortal? Linnaeus had used the word already.

Banks thought all these letters, and more, worth keeping, though their writers, with uniform consistency, failed to attain the object of their desire. There was a single exception, that of the young Dutchman Sigismund BacStrom ('Backstrom' was good enough for Banks). He was a person of unexceptionably elevated sentiments,

---

[1] Possibly Banks, in due course, was able to do something for Robertson. A paragraph in a letter from Solander to Banks, three years later, runs, 'Mr Robertson (now Lieut^t of the Phoenix, formerly Master of the Dolphin under Wallis) desires his best Compl^ts to You—He supposes You have spoke in his behalf to Ld Sandwich, and is much obliged to You'.—22 August 1775; Webster coll.

[2] I make all these quotations from the correspondence in the volume of Banks's papers in ML, lettered 'Voluntiers, Instructions, Provision for 2d. Voyage'.

Mr. Joseph Banks

from the mezzotint after the portrait by Benjamin West

he had already been rescued from some distress by his patron, 'and as to returning to Holland', he asserted, 'where I have lived in a decent and respectable manner, in my present dejected State, the Very thought is worse than Death'. He had no mercenary views; the allowance of a common seaman would be enough, with 'the Consideration of the honour I Should acquire, if I should ever return after having been so extraordinary and curious a voyage, and in Company with so celebrated and respectable personages'; also he was expert in taking birds alive, and possessed of a curious process of preserving them, when dead, in the most lively and natural manner; and for one reason or another Banks agreed to engage him as a secretary. To quote at such length this romantic person, and other adulatory young men, would not be right except for one thing, that they surrounded Banks with an atmosphere; and when two or three experienced seamen, of whatever rank, began to seek his patronage, his common sense was tried too severely. He was not immune to incense; and this incense was very strong. At the same time he was extremely busy himself, and plunged in the most extensive preparations. A man of system, he kept all his bills, duly receipted,[1] and we have in them not only an extraordinary list of what Banks deemed necessary for his life on shipboard and of what would be advantageous for trade or gifts in the South Sea, but also a vivid picture of 'running around'. Leather bottles, screw-drivers, magnifying glasses and microscopes, gross upon gross of variegated beads, gross upon gross of combs, dog chains, fish-hooks and harpoons, drugs, pistols, guns and bayonets, 'a Cross Bowe', mirrors, wire catchers for insects and birds, drawing-tables, sealing wax, Windsor soap, casks of nails, rat traps, 'a Round Tent, like a Bell Tent', a silver hanger with a steel waistband, a copy of *Tristram Shandy*, a large quantity of black and red feathers, forty iron 'Patapatoes for New Zealand in imitation of their stone weapons', coloured silk handkerchiefs, 'A travelling kist with drawers and petitions', a large collection of sea charts, Dutch almanacs, artist's colours, '1 Equatorial Instrument Complete', a magic lantern, 2000 'platina' or brass medals (with two of gold and 142 of silver), sextants, two French horns, '2 rods to try the Electricity of ye foggs', and (thoroughly baffling) '1 Grean God' — the list might go on indefinitely; and the barrels, the boxes, the casks, the kegs, the bundles, were a formidable quantity to go on any ship. There was no fancy, it seems, that did not take concrete form — even down to the barrels of dried hips and cherries, the

[1] See again the MS volume 'Voluntiers'.

G

keg of juniper syrup, the bundle of salted cod and the half ton of stockfish specially procured from Copenhagen and Amsterdam at the request of Dr Solander. Banks, as he told Thomas Falconer, had a multiplicity of employments to occupy him during his short stay in his native country: 'to collect together all the nescessaries for so long a voyage to enlist artists, to prepare myself & answer the Calls of an acquaintance from my present circumstances swelld to a preposterous size is a large undertaking'; and there was the overseeing of the publication of the *Endeavour*'s voyage as well.[1] But there is no sign that he did not enjoy the bustle.

Meanwhile the world of natural history was impatiently awaiting accurate information on the collections brought back by the *Endeavour*. The insects, it is true, had been handed over to the young Fabricius — still another pupil of Linnaeus — for description.[2] Fabricius had been delighted to help Banks and Solander get ready for the voyage, and now he was delighted to labour on part of their harvest. The insects were not a large part — two hundred and twelve from New Holland and those from elsewhere were not much to set beside the botanical glories:[3] nevertheless they were something, and they were duly described in the *Systema Entomologiae* of 1775. That, for the Banksian collections, was quick work. But when was Banks going to publish his account? Was Solander at work on a catalogue? The news of an immediate second voyage was bound to cause consternation. Poor Linnaeus, longing in vain for a letter from Solander, was driven nearly frantic. 'I have just read, in some foreign newspapers,' he wrote to Ellis in a remarkable letter of excitement and anxiety, 'that our friend Solander intends to revisit those new countries, discovered by Mr. Banks and himself, in the ensuing spring. This report has affected me so much as almost entirely to deprive me of sleep. How vain are the hopes of man! Whilst the whole botanical world, like myself, has been looking for the most transcendent benefits to our science, from the unrivalled exertions of your countrymen, all their matchless and truly astonishing collection, such as has never been seen before, nor may ever be seen again, is to be put aside untouched, to be

---

[1] Banks to Falconer, 7 January 1772, Hawley coll.

[2] Johann Christian Fabricius (1745-1810), a Dane, whose *Systema Entomologiae* (Leipzig 1775) was a considerable advance on Linnaeus.

[3] Johnson again: Boswell had brought up the subject of 'Hawkesworth's Book'. '*Johnson*. "Sir, if you talk of it as a subject of commerce, 'twill be gainful. If as a Book, that is to increase human knowledge, not much of that. Hawkesworth can tell only what Banks tells him, and he has not found much. But one Animal." *Boswell*. "Many insects." *Johnson*. "Ray reckons of british Insects 20,000 species. Banks might have staid at home and discovered enough in that way".'—Boswell, *Private Papers*, 6, p. 133.

thrust into some corner, to become perhaps the prey of insects and of destruction. . . . By all that is great and good, I entreat you, who know so well the value of science, to do all that in you lies for the publication of these new acquisitions, that the learned world may not be deprived of them. . . . Do but consider, my friend, if these treasures are kept back, what may happen to them. They may be devoured by vermin of all kinds. The house where they are lodged may be burnt. Those destined to describe them may die. . . . I therefore once more beg, nay I earnestly beseech you, to urge the publication of these new discoveries. I confess it to be my most ardent wish to see this done before I die'.[1] The botanical account was all ready, wrote Ellis in return: he would do what he could to urge its printing. 'I assure you it greatly distresses me to think of losing Solander for ever, for I cannot expect to see him more, should he return; but I fear he never will return alive'.[2] These were sombre reflections; but, though vermin did not devour, nor Solander sink beneath Antarctic seas, neither of these worried correspondents was ever to turn over the longed-for pages. The reason, however, was not the immediate departure of Solander with Banks on a southern voyage.

Before the end of 1771 the Admiralty had bought two further ships into the navy for the new expedition, both Whitby-built like the *Endeavour*, and of the same type. Cook chose them himself, and the larger of them, the *Resolution*, was to prove perhaps the most wonderful vessel ever engaged on an exploratory purpose. There was the usual official reticence, to which Banks paid a little tribute in a letter to Falconer:

The A[d]miralty have thought fit to be Mysterious about us so that I myself cannot Positively say where we are going and when I tell you that it is my opinion we are for the South Seas I must beg the favour of you not to mention it again for those parts however we are pretty certainly design'd and if we proceed to make discoveries on the Terra Australis Incognita I shall probably have a finer opportunity for the Excercise of my Poor Abilities than ever man before had as there seems to be a strong Probability from the Scarce Intelligible accounts of Travelers That almost every Production of Nature is here very different from what we see at this end of the Globe.[3]

---

[1] Linnaeus to Ellis, 22 October 1771; J.E.S. I, pp. 267-70.
[2] Ellis to Linnaeus, 19 November 1771; ibid., p. 272.
[3] Undated, probably late January 1772. This was all the more ridiculous as Banks had already told Falconer the plan of the voyage in his letter of 7 January 1772 quoted above, and even asked him for 'hints relative to Observations which you might wish me to make'. Falconer's letter of 4 February 1772, 'Voluntiers', seems to be in answer to both these letters. On the destination of the voyage, cf. Daines Barrington's letter to Pennant of late August or early September 1771, 'Mr Tunstall writes me word' etc., p. 56 above.

This was concealment so obvious that it was never noticed, and the fitting out of the ships was carried briskly and lavishly forward. On 2 May Banks gave an entertainment on board the *Resolution* to Sandwich, the French Ambassador, and 'several other persons of distinction'. Sandwich came more than once to inspect the work, 'not', as Cook wrote, 'out of Idle curiosity as many of all ranks did, Ladies as well as gentlemen, for scarce a day past on which she was not crowded with strangers who came on board for no other purpose but to see the Ship in which Mr Banks was to sail round the world'.[1] Banks's scientific plans widened in scope: he asked Dr Priestley to go with him, apparently as an astronomer, and on the appointment of the Board of Longitude. He had to draw back, for Priestley, still a Unitarian minister at Leeds, was obviously unsound on matters of faith.[2] The Board, however, appointed two astronomers, William Wales and William Bayly. And then Parliament agreed, on Banks's nomination, to make a special grant of £4000 to engage Dr James Lind, of Edinburgh, another astronomer and physician, to go — 'but what the discoveries were the Parliament meant he was to make and for which they made so liberal a Vote will hardly ever come to the knowlidge of the publick much less to me as an individual', remarked Cook later.[3] Banks and Solander were overjoyed at this scientific

[1] B.M. Add. MS 27888, f. 4,4v.

[2] Priestley's letter to Banks will bear quoting: 'You now tell me that, as the different professors of Oxford and Cambridge will have the naming of the person, and they are all clergymen, they may possibly have some scruples on the head of religion, and that on this account, you do not think you could get me nominated at any rate, much less on the terms which were first mentioned to me. Now what I am, and what they are, with respect to religion, might easily have been known before the thing was proposed to me at all. Besides, I thought that this had been a business of *Philosophy*, not of *Divinity*. If, however, this be the case, I shall hold the board of longitude in extreme contempt, and make no scruple of speaking of them accordingly; taking it for granted, that you have just ground for your suspicions'.—1 December 1771, 'Voluntiers', pp. 597-8. See also Priestley's *Memoirs* (Birmingham 1810), p. 50, where he remarks, 'I was much better employed at home, even with respect to my philosophical pursuits.' The professors were no doubt the professors of astronomy and geometry at Oxford, and astronomy and mathematics at Cambridge, all *ex officio* members of the Board. But they did not by themselves have the nomination. See Cook II, Appendix III, pp. 719 ff. Banks in any case was taking too much on himself.

[3] B.M. Add. MS 27888, f. 3. Lind was elsewhere highly thought of, however. Hume wrote to Benjamin Franklin, on 17 March 1771, 'Brother Lin expects to see you soon, before he takes his little Trip round the World. You have heard, no doubt, of that Project: The Circumstances of the Affair coud not be more honourable for him, nor coud the Honour be conferred on one who deserves it more'.—Raymond Klibansky and Ernest C. Mossner, *New Letters of David Hume* (Oxford 1954), pp. 193-4. James Lind (1736-1812), a Scotsman, visited China as surgeon on an East Indiaman in 1766. M.D. Edinburgh 1768. In 1769 he observed the transit of Venus at Hawkhill near Edinburgh; by this and other observations he made some reputation as an astronomer, though it is difficult to see why Banks should have so particularly thought him worth £4000. In 1777 he was elected F.R.S. and settled at Windsor as physician to the royal household. His sweetness of disposition was well known, and in his last years he befriended the young Shelley.

acquisition, and they do not seem to have wasted tears over the dissenter Priestley. But their trial was about to come. By May 1772 Banks had worked up a train of fourteen persons besides Solander, beginning with the painter Zoffany, whom he had engaged at £1000 for the voyage. What this master of the theatrical and domestic conversation piece would have made of icebergs and Tahitians it is hard to say. There were also three draughtsmen, two secretaries, six servants (including the seasoned Peter Briscoe and James Roberts) and two horn-players. Twelve of these, with Banks and Solander, and no doubt the desirable Dr Lind, were to sail in the *Resolution*; two, a draughtsman and the ardent Bacstrom, in the other ship, the *Adventure*.[1] The precise details of what happened may even yet not have been ascertained, because no doubt they included much discussion and many impatient words that did not go on to paper. But we have enough. The main events are quite clear, and we can now understand the psychological background. When Banks first saw the *Resolution*, on her purchase, he did not approve of her. He did not regard her as roomy enough, because he had already determined to take more people with him than he had taken in the *Endeavour* (whether he had by then determined to take a private band we do not know). Sandwich was First Lord, and the Admiralty was prepared to make alterations, even if in doing so it had to override the opinion of the Navy Board and Captain Palliser, the Comptroller. These alterations entailed raising the ship's upper works about a foot and laying a new deck from the quarter-deck to the forecastle, and — as Cook was to be turned out of the great cabin to leave it for Banks — building a 'round house' for the captain on top. Banks did not like the alterations. Nor did Cook;[2] for they made the ship top-heavy, to which the staggering amount of baggage in 'the Gentlemen's apartments' also contributed. Early in May she was ordered from Long Reach, where she had taken in her guns, round to the Downs, and it was apparent she would not do. At the Nore she was reported dangerously 'crank', or liable to capsize; and beyond the Nore the pilot refused to take her lest he should ruin his professional

---

[1] A note in Banks's hand in 'Voluntiers', p. 431, specifies the names and wages of these persons: '*Resolution*: Zoffany, J. F. Miller and James Miller (draughtsmen) £100 a year each; Walden (secretary) £100; Peter Briscoe (servant) £40; James Roberts, John Asquith, Peter Sidserf, Nicholas Young (servants) £20: Sander (servant) £10; John Marchant and Robert Holbrooke (horns) £40. *Adventure*: John Clevely (draughtsman) £100, S. Backstrom (secretary) £100. Sander was the man whom Banks engaged at Batavia.

[2] Though he seems to have been hopeful at first. Cf. Sandwich, II, p. 350 below: 'Captain Cooke (who had so high an idea of the ship that he thought she could bear all this superstructure) gave it as his opinion that it would not be too much. . .' .

reputation. The high-spirited Charles Clerke, who was on board as second lieutenant, thereupon wrote to Banks: 'Hope you know me too well, to impute my giving this intelligence to any ridiculous apprehensions for myself, by God I'll go to Sea in a Grog Tub if desir'd, or in the Resolution as soon as you please; but must say, I do think her by far the most unsafe Ship, I ever saw or heard of: however if you think proper to embark for the South Pole in a Ship, which a Pilot, (who I think is, by no means a timorous man) will not undertake to carry down the River; all I can say, is, you shall be most chearfully attended, so long as we can keep her above Water, by' Charles Clerke.[1] Cook, who would not go to sea in a grog-tub, gave it as his opinion that the ship must be returned to her original state; the Navy Board agreed; the work was put immediately in hand, and Banks was offered all possible accommodation. So — he sprang furiously to the conclusion — he had been the victim of a plot; the Navy Board had never wanted him; the alterations had been deliberately made so heavy as to render the *Resolution* unsafe, so that they would have to be undone, and the work of himself and his party would be impossible. He would not tolerate such conditions, they were quite beyond bearing; his rage burst all bounds;[2] he would not go on the voyage at all; and he ordered everybody and everything of his off the ship. He was the second gentleman to retire from a great voyage in a bad temper. Did he ever think of Dalrymple?

He drafted long memoranda to Sandwich, hitherto his close friend. One, dated 30 May, he unfortunately sent. It is a very revealing document; and it is — to use an adjective quite inescapable — a very foolish document. To present the First Lord with a lecture on naval construction was bad enough; to provide such witness to his own unbounded conceit was unwise in the extreme. For the Admiralty was still strongly under the impression that the expedition it was fitting out was an expedition of geographical discovery, and that the commander it had appointed was Cook. There is the melancholy duty of quoting Banks. He had made pledges, he said, to Sandwich and to all Europe: 'The navy Board was in consequence order'd to purchase two ships and to fit them up in a proper manner for our reception that we might be enabled

---

[1] 15 May 1772, ML Banks Papers, II (1), 28.
[2] 'Mr Banks came to Sheerness and when he saw the Ship, He *swore* & *stamp'd* upon the *Warfe*, like a Mad Man.'—John Elliott, a midshipman in the *Resolution*, who later wrote his memoirs.—B.M. Add. MS 42714, f.10v. Probably Elliott gave the ship's opinion generally, when he wrote, 'a more proud, haught[y] man could not be, and all his plans seem'd directed to show his own greatness'.—ibid., f. 11.

to exert our utmost endeavours to serve the publick wheresoever
the course of our discoveries might induce us to proceed. . . . we
have pledgd ourselves my lord to your Lordship & this nation to
undertake what no navigator before us has even suggested to be
practicable; . . . Shall I then my lord who have engagd to leave
all that can make life agreable in my own country & throw on
one side all the Pleasures to be reapd from three of the best years
of my life[1] merely to compass this undertaking pregnant enough
with dangers and difficulties in its own nature after having been
promisd every security and convenience that the art of man could
contrive without which promise no man in my situation would
ever [have] undertaken the voyage be sent off at last in a doubtfull
ship with accommodations rather worse than those which I at
first absolutely refusd after spending above £5000 of my own
fortune on the equipment upon the credit of those accommodations
which I saw actually built for me.[2] will the publick be so un-
generous as to expect me to go out in a ship in which my people
have not the room necessary for performing the different duties
of their professions, a ship apparently unhealthy and probably
unsafe merely in conformity to the official opinion of the navy
board who purchasd her without ever consulting me and now
in no degree consider the part which I have taken in the voyage

[1] In an earlier paragraph he has remarked that when Sandwich first asked him to go,
'I Joyfully embracd a proposal of all others the best suited to my disposition and pursuits'.
[2] This '£5000' has been repeated a good deal, and J. H. Maiden, in his *Sir Joseph
Banks* (Sydney 1909), p. 45, actually says he has seen 'receipts for money paid by Banks,
amounting to over £5000, for scientific stores and appliances, presents for the natives,
and so forth, for this voyage. These documents are now in the Mitchell Library'. Now
the only documents of this sort in the Mitchell Library are in the 'Voluntiers' volume
already referred to. A careful addition of all the sums receipted in this volume comes to
a great deal less than £5000. Some of them have nothing to do with the *Resolution* expenses
at all—for example, the costs of chartering the ship for Banks's Iceland voyage are
included, and a payment of £89 8s 6d to Stanfield Parkinson for miscellaneous work
at New Burlington Street: 'To Makin a sett of Curtians of blew Check for the Garret
bed Head a Sett of Lathes with hooks and spicks and putin up', £3 3s; 'Menden two
Mohogney french Chairs', 3s 6d, and so on; there is 'Od Jobes in the House & Door
Way in the Londerrey', £5 3s 7d, with other similar items. Whether 'a Globular Silver
Punch Bowl', £24 18s, was for use on the ship or at home we need not enquire; but 'an
Enamelled Gold Watch', 35 guineas, does not seem to have any necessary nautical
significance. Nor does the item 'To lighting the Lamp from 25 March 1772 to 1st
June 1772', 7s 4d. But 'A Poket Time Keeper', £100, bought like the gold watch of
John Arnold, may possibly have been a chronometer, and so of considerable scientific
interest. Banks seems to have collected all his bills for a certain period and bound them
up together with his second voyage 'in-letters'. After throwing out a small number of
obvious interlopers among these bills, though leaving others it would have been tedious
to extract, I have made the total spent £2317 4s 6½d. Of course as a round sum this
is not as good as £5000. No doubt there were other expenses not noted in these papers.—
I owe Banks an apology for giving his estimate in Cook I, p. cxxxvii as £10,000. We
do not know his income at this time, but Weld, *History of the Royal Society*, II, p. 116,
gives it later as above £30,000 a year, so he was in no danger of reducing himself to
beggary in the cause of science.

or the alterations which on my remonstrance they concured with me in thinking necessary but have now taken away or should I embark could anything material be done by people under circumstances so highly discouraging. . . .' Other considerations followed; and then came what, with its side-blow at Cook, after all that experience of the *Endeavour*, was possibly the least generous remark Banks uttered in his life. Give him the ship he wanted, he said, and he would gladly embark; for he well knew 'that there are many commanders in his majesties service of undoubted abilities and experience who would willingly undertake to proceed with her on the intended expedition ambitious of shewing the world that the success of such an undertaking depends more upon the Prudence and Perseverance of the Commander than upon any particular built of the ship that may be employd'.[1]

To all this the Navy Board — when Sandwich, according to what Banks called scornfully 'Forms of office', referred it for comment — made the obvious, the simple, the crushing reply; after which it was hard for Mr Banks to rise again. 'As to the proper kind of Ship and her fitness and sufficiency for the Voyage, his opinion was never asked nor could have been asked with propriety, he being in no degree qualified to form a right Judgement in such a matter; and for the same reason his opinion now thereon is not to be attended to. . . . Mr Banks seems throughout to consider the Ships as fitted out wholly for his use; the whole undertaking to depend on him and his People; and himself as the Director and Conductor of the whole. . . .' Even now matters had been so contrived as to take away from him only six feet of the length of the great cabin (presumably to give Cook somewhere to sleep), and from his attendants only one small cabin. For a man who had begun by saying nothing but that the fore part of the cabin was an inch or two too low, and then had kept on adding to his 'suite' and his demands in complete disregard of the ship, the Board thought it had not done badly.[2] It did not suggest, what in retrospect one might tentatively suggest, that Mr Banks could have cut down his suite a little to fit the ship. Indeed such a suggestion, at that stage, would have been quite useless. It would have been worse than useless; it would have been the last insult. The last

---

[1] There are a number of copies of this letter: in the 'Voluntiers' volume; in S.S.B.'s copy of the Iceland journal; among Sandwich's papers at Hinchingbrooke (endorsed No. 93); among George III's papers at Windsor, Georgian Papers, No. 1322. It was first printed by Fortescue, *Correspondence of King George the Third*, II (1927), pp. 343-7. I have used the autograph draft of the 'Voluntiers' volume.

[2] 3 June 1772; Sandwich papers, Hinchingbrooke (endorsed No. 95); Georgian Papers, Windsor, No. 1323*; Fortescue II, pp. 350-2.

insult? No; because Mr Banks could have been insulted by a little more of the truth, and that little more might have come from a source of veracity quite unimpeachable. Lord Sandwich was by this time a much tried, a much irritated man, and he had for his friend a rod in pickle, a blast in reserve. He had already written Banks a letter which implies that before receiving the young man's lucubration he had seen it in draft, and had listened to the threat that it might be published; and he now gave some advice:

I am sorry that the alteration you proposed to make in the said letter has not taken place, as it will probably make it necessary that some answer should be given if your letter is made public; for it is a heavy charge against this Board to suppose that they mean to send a number of men to sea in an unhealthy ship. In this point, and in most of the reasoning of the above-mentioned letter, I differ greatly with you in opinion, and shall therefore be sorry if anything is printed on either side; but I am sure if you will give yourself time to think coolly, you will at once see the impropriety of publishing to the world an opinion of your own, that one of the King's ships is unfit for a voyage she is going to be employed in, and that her crew will be in danger of losing their lives if they go to sea in her. . . . I am positive. . . . we shall be able to bring the fullest proof to the contrary; that paragraph being in your letter should in my humble opinion induce you not to print it.[1]

But the possibility had to be met; and if we examine the papers at Hinchingbrooke, we find the rod in pickle, the highly destructive countermine. We find also a revealing backward light. The Forms of Office had brought Sandwich the Navy Board's comments upon Banks's letter, and from Palliser himself a very moderately phrased paper entitled 'Thoughts upon the Kind of Ships proper to be employed on Discoveries in distant Parts of the Globe';[2] and he had his own knowledge of what had passed. There was one Great Person who was deeply interested in the whole matter. On 20 June Sandwich sent to the king 'a sketch of a letter in answer to that written to him by Mr Banks, which may possibly be proper to be printed in case the other is made publick. Your Majesty will observe that it is under a fictitious name, which for many reasons is most adviseable'.[3] It is this 'sketch' or draft, though

[1] Sandwich to Banks, 2 June 1772; Sandwich Papers, Hinchingbrooke. This is a modern copy of the letter.
[2] Sandwich Papers, Hinchingbrooke; n.d.; endorsed No. 98.
[3] Georgian Papers, Windsor, No. 1342; Fortescue II, p. 361. There is no doubt of the king's deep interest in the voyages, though the lavishness of Hawkesworth's dedication of his volumes brought some public criticism: "it exceeds the licence of dedicatory compliment', held the *Annual Register* for 1773 in its review of the volumes after the writer's death, pp. 266-73. Hawkesworth's principle seems to have been that if you are using butter, you may as well use plenty of it.

without the 'fictitious name', that has lain unscrutinized at Hinchingbrooke;[1] for Banks did not print, and the rejoinder was deemed
uncalled for.

'As it is very possible that his Lordship may not have leisure
or inclination to enter into a paper war upon this occasion', remarked Sandwich at the beginning of his twenty folio pages, and
as his fictitious other self had 'had opportunities of knowing allmost
every circumstance that passed relative to the equipment of the
Resolution Sloop of War, on board of which you was to have been
recieved as a passenger', he would deal with the charges made.
Banks had never complained about want of room on the *Endeavour*.
When the time came to select a new ship, it was 'agreed on all
hands, that the opinion of the very great and able Sea officer who
lately presided at the admiralty[2] was well founded; namely
that the only ship that was fit for a voyage of this kind was a vessel
built for the coal trade. . . . in this arrangement you readily
acquiesced professing yourself not a competent judge what ship
was the fittest for the service, tho' you intimated an opinion of
your own that a West Indiaman would be more proper. . . .' The
idea was, not to enlarge the ship to the quantity of Banks's attendants,
but to adapt their number to the size of the ship. Cook had been
directed to go all over the Pool of London, and choose the ships he
wanted; the ships he wanted were bought. Banks looked at the
one that was to become the *Resolution*, and now showed discontent:
'she was not fit for a gentleman to embark in'; if considerable
alterations were not made 'you would not proceed upon the voyage'.
(Alas! Banks had begun to make his threat too soon, and he made
it too often.) There was a clash of opinion. Cook thought the ship
would bear the alterations — a bad misjudgment, though Sandwich
did not say this; the Navy Board and the shipwrights did not, and
Sandwich overruled them; and then 'several other demands
were made by you in which the constant burthen of your song
was, that their being complied with or not, should be the decision
whither you should or should not proceed on the voyage'. These
demands about the ship had been followed by demands about
the conduct of the voyage, which if complied with would have been
tantamount to 'giving you the absolute command of the expedition':
Cook was to be ordered to follow Banks's directions; the officers
were to be ordered to look to Banks for promotion. Banks had
worried about the health of the crew: which showed his humanity

---

[1] It is in Sandwich's handwriting, undated, and is endorsed No. 94.
[2] Sir Edward Hawke (Lord Hawke 1776).

but not his experience. And what about the officers? 'I percieve that your attention extends only to the common seamen, for when conveniences were made for all your suite the officers were stowed as close as herrings in a barrel, and yet you never took their distress into your humane consideration'. Point by point the unfortunate arguments are reduced to nullity (Sandwich made skilful use of the papers supplied to him); the proper tribute is paid to learning, public spirit, and refusal to baulk at expense; Banks had been received with open arms by the Admiralty, it was not their fault that he was not now embarked; but — the controversialist could not refrain from expressing the 'distant idea' — did he really want to go on the voyage? Had he not already begun to tire of it? There was a final amiable piece of advice: 'Upon the whole I hope that for the advantage of the curious part of Mankind, your zeal for distant voyages will not yet cease, I heartily wish you success in all your undertakings, but I would advise you in order to insure that success to fit out a ship yourself; that and only that can give you the absolute command of the whole expedition; and as I have a sincere regard for your welfare and consequently for your preser- vation, I earnestly entreat that that ship may not be an old Man of War or an old Indiaman but a New Collier'.

There is no reason to doubt the underlying goodwill of this last broadside. Whatever Banks's aberrations, and however exasperating he might be, Sandwich, and others, still had a sincere regard for his welfare and his preservation. In the cause of human friendship, we may be glad there was no public paper war; Banks knew Sandwich well enough not to be deceived about his castigator, and the breach between the two, which could not but be inevitable, might have been deep and lasting. In the meanwhile there was nothing useful to be done to mend a breach. A brief passage in Parliament was met by the usual ministerial silence;[1] behind the scenes Lord North, who had had some idea that Banks might change his mind again, was persuaded to the contrary by Sandwich;[2] and Banks himself wrote to Burke on the inutility of further parliamentary action.[3] Mr Banks would not go on the

---

[1] There was evidently a little campaign. The *General Evening Post*, 4 June 1772, reports, 'Yesterday Mr D-mpst-r moved for an inquiry into the motives for laying aside the prosecution of our discoveries towards the South Pole. The speakers referred him to the Treasury Bench, but Lord N—th and all his colleagues were as still as night, and there the affair dropped.' The paper recurred to the subject on 6 June.

[2] Sandwich to North, 8 June 1772; Sandwich Papers, Hinchingbrooke.

[3] 'Mr Banks presents his Compts to Mr Burke & heartily thanks him for the Interest he has been so kind as to take in his business throughout the whole prosecution of it. Several of Mr Banks's freinds met this morn at the Speakers where on finding that the present Equipment had proceeded too far to be either alterd or stoppd they resolvd

voyage; Dr Lind therefore would not go; and when the *Resolution* sailed from Plymouth on 13 July it carried not the fifteen scientific gentlemen, artists, and servants, collected by Banks, but simply one astronomer — and the disastrous John Reinhold Forster and his son, to whom Dr Lind's £4000 had been diverted.

So far was Banks from any suspicion that his suite might be too large, that there is evidence that he contemplated enlarging it still further. When Cook got to Madeira he met with an odd story, which is reported by more than one member of his company. His own account has come to rest among the papers of George III, though it could hardly have been addressed to that august personage.[1] He speaks well of the *Resolution*, and goes on, 'Three days before we arrived a person left the Island who went by the name of Burnett he had been waiting for M⟨r⟩ Banks arrival about three months, at first he said he came here for the recovery of his health, but afterwards said his intention was to go out with M⟨r⟩ Banks, to some he said he was unknown to this Gentleman, to others he said it was by his appointment he came here as he could not be receiv'd on board in England, at last when he heard that M⟨r⟩ Banks did not go, he took the very first opportunity to get of the Island, he was about 30 Years of age and rather ordinary than otherwise and employ'd his time in Botanizing &c⟨a⟩ — Every part of M⟨r⟩ Burnetts behaviour and every action tended to prove that he was a Woman, I have not met with a person that entertains a doubt of a contrary nature, he brought letters of recommendation to an English House where he was accomodated during his stay, It must be observed that M⟨rs⟩ Burnett must have left London about the time we were first ready to sail'. Now there is nothing inherently improbable about this story, fantastic as it may appear. We have seen that Banks was susceptible to women, and not entirely master of his mind where they were concerned. Had he taken a hint from the tale of that other naturalist, Commerson, and his valet, who on Bougainville's voyage so remarkably concealed her sex till

to put off meeting on tuesday & hope that some other expedition might be set on foot which they conceivd great hopes might be effected in a much more agreable way than this ever was in. M⟨r⟩ Banks returns a thousand thanks for M⟨r⟩ Burkes Caveat which he understands has in Conjunction with the Speak[e]r stoppd totaly what M⟨r⟩ Banks so much dreaded that he should be lookd upon as usefull to the voyage only in catching butterflies & the publick be contented if that matter was done by any one else whether well or ill.'—This undated note is among the Wentworth Woodhouse papers in the Sheffield Public Library, Bk 2/219, and I am grateful to Earl Fitzwilliam and the Trustees of the Fitzwilliam Settled Estates for allowing me to print it.

[1] Cook to—, 1 August 1772; Windsor Castle, Georgian Papers, No. 1359. The letter, which is a copy, simply begins 'Sir', and does not have the addressee's name subscribed. It was very probably sent to Philip Stephens, the Secretary to the Admiralty. Fortescue prints it, II, pp. 372-3.

the keen-witted Tahitians discovered her to be not Jean but Jeanne?
He might have had difficulty in getting her on the ship at Madeira
under Cook's sharp eye; but the chance, he might have thought,
was worth taking. The *Endeavour* had carried hands beyond those
on the muster-roll, so why not the *Resolution*? 'The time we were
first ready to sail' was the time immediately before it was found
the ship could not sail. Mrs, or Miss, Burnett, a victim of circumstance, left London just too soon. Even if the scheme broke down,
nothing much would have been lost; the lady, obviously, was
used to looking after herself. It did break down, though for a more
remote cause; and the lady did look after herself.

§

To moralize further on any part of the whole unhappy matter is
hardly necessary. There was a little coolness between Banks and
Cook, whose sentiments on the ship were perfectly well known, but
no real estrangement; and Cook wrote from Sheerness, immediately
after the break, 'I Pray my best respects to the D^r & sence I am
not to have your Company in the Resolution I most sin[c]erely
wish you success in all your exploring undertakens'.[1] He wrote
again, with equal generosity, from the Cape. Banks let Clerke
have a 'Cagg of Nails' for trade: '. . . . flatter myself', said Clerke,
'with the hopes of making an addition to the Burlington Street
collection. . . . Must again express my unhappiness that I cannot
have the pleasure of attending you. . . . the Gentlemen of the Gun-
room intreat your acceptance of their respects and Compliments'.[2]
Here was nothing but friendship. There was estrangement, though
temporarily, from Sandwich. The Navy Board, and Palliser, Banks
never forgave. The public prints had a due amount of speculation
and scandal — the Court of Spain was again freely blamed[3] — and
Banks himself, who maintained a proper public dignity, drafted a
long letter of attack, and self-justification, to the *Gazetteer*, signed
with the pseudonym 'Antarcticus'. Luckily he thought better of
sending it in. He still, he announced, in this abortive effusion,
'keeps his companions together at a large expence, and labours
earnestly to prevail upon the publick to put it in his power to make
the same voyage as he has been disapointed of; declaring to all
his freinds that when disapointed of every hope from the publick,
he will undertake at his own expence, such a voyage as his circum-

---

[1] 2 June 1772, ML MS.
[2] ML Banks Papers, II, f. 3.
[3] *General Evening Post*, 27 June 1772.

stances will allow him to bear the charge of; tho he is conscious,
that without publick assistance he can do little; yet will he exert
himself to the utmost, not at all doubting that if he meets with
success, the publick [will] on his return be inclind to indulge him
in the execution of his favourite plan'.[1] Although he could not,
indeed, have placed very much reliance on 'the publick', he did
at this time entertain some hope that the East India Company
would support him in a southern voyage — a hope that certainly
misapprehended the nature of the East India Company. The
Comte de Lauraguais had a little to say on that subject, not without
irony: the shareholders were getting only 12½ per cent, he told
Buffon, the Company would discover that it was too poor to bear
the expense. Lauraguais was writing to Buffon and to D'Alembert,
the secretary of the French Academy — no doubt as representatives
of the Europe to which Banks had given pledges — about the
'manifeste littéraire' which Banks had sent them — perhaps copies
of his abortive letter to the *Gazetteer*. Banks and Bougainville (who
also wanted to go on another voyage, to the North Pole), he said,
must not lament; they must recall the history of Columbus and of
Cortes. If the French government wished the fame of its navy to
outshine the strength of England's, let it give a ship to the dissatisfied
ones, 'et le globe serait découvert et connu'. Mr Banks would bear
the natural history expenses.[2] Mr Banks was not to get a ship
from any government. He was not long, however, without a
destination. He already had had some thoughts of a northern
voyage,[3] and now they revived. He would take his suite to Iceland,
and include in it the unfortunate Lind, who, not having received
the £4000, was much out of pocket over his preparations for the
southern journey. Lind as a friend was begged to command his

[1] 'Voluntiers', p. 23 ff. Banks was stimulated by a letter in the *Gazetteer and New
Daily Advertiser*, 11 June 1772, signed by 'A Briton', which said, *inter alia*, 'From what
I can see, Mr. Banks, Dr. Solander, Dr. Lind, and Mr. Zoffani, are likely to be excluded
from a voyage which, from their sharing it, did honour to the nation; and in
all probability, the noblest expedition ever fitted out will dwindle to nothing, and disgrace
this country'. A gentleman without a signature answered this on 16 June: 'The whole
of the matter is, Mr. B. did not chuse to go the voyage, unless he could ride the waves
triumphantly, in all the pomp and splendour of an Eastern Monarch'. There were other
letters, on 17 June from 'An Englishman' (anti-Banks), and on 23 June from 'Detector'
(pro-Banks).

[2] Copies of these two letters are in 'Voluntiers', pp. 391-3. That to D'Alembert is
dated 12 July 1772. Banks had apparently himself composed a letter to D'Alembert
in a French over which Lauraguais shakes his head. The letter to Buffon has no date in
the copy, but must have been sent at the same time.

[3] In the letter to Falconer already quoted from (p. 71 above) he remarks, 'The
Very Intelligent observations which I meet with in your last about the Northern Countreys
make me almost regret the having given up my Northern plan in which they would
have been so usefull I shall however lay it by as a treasure I may sometime make use
of. . . '.

share of Banks's estate. He was not prepared to reimburse himself thus, but henceforth he maintained an extreme admiration for the man to whom, he held, he owed so much.[1] As for Zoffany, he went to Florence, and some at least of his friends congratulated him. 'This . . . is better than his going to draw naked savages and be scalped with that wild man Banks', wrote Horace Walpole.[2] He, in his turn, had agreed to return to Banks's service on a fort-night's notice.[3]

Why Iceland? Iceland was coming into fashion, but it was a literary fashion, the fashion of Runic inscriptions, of the sagas that were so engaging to scholars of philology and the Northern past, of an epic that could hardly fail to impinge upon the mind cultivated in romance. Iceland had its antiquities. It could not rival Greece and Rome, nor did it shine with the imperial visions of the South Sea; but it was in the air. Dr Johnson, who dealt so summarily with Boswell's circumnavigatory leaning, himself idly thought of a voyage to Iceland. The age was fond of volcanoes, and Iceland had a volcano. For Banks indeed the suggestion may have come from Solander, indirectly inspired by that other Linnaean pupil Johann Gerhard König, who had collected plants there in 1764-5, and spoke highly of the country; it may have gathered force from a young Swede whom Banks met in London at the time, Uno von Troil, later archbishop of Uppsala, a person devoted to

[1] Lind to Maskelyne, 30 January 1775; D.T.C. I, pp. 82-3. Presumably Maskelyne passed on to the Admiralty this letter, so much more complimentary to Banks than to the British government. Maskelyne had been sounding Lind on his willingness to go on a northern Pacific voyage.

[2] Walpole to Sir Horace Mann, 20 September 1772, *Letters* (ed. Toynbee), VIII, p. 207.

[3] Iceland Journal, p.6. Here another letter to Banks, not in the Voluntiers volume, may be quoted. It seems to indicate that he had already, early in June, announced publicly his intention of going on a voyage of his own. The writer, Richard Rollett, was a Lincolnshire man, who seems to have had some objection to the *Resolution*, or to Cook.— 'Resolution Sheerness June 9th 1772. Most Honoured Sir—I not having an oppertunity of waiting on you in person have made bold to make this Letter the Messinger of my Nessessitys, Which is to do me the Honour of a birth in your Service, in the Capacity of Mastr Sail maker, Which I now am On board the Resolution I am very desirous to proceed on the Voyage, but in the ship with Which you & Dr Solander goes, I should have gone with the Adventure, if you had not been going in the Resolution when I first shipd myself.—It is the Desire of my friends, I should go this voyage, which If I Do not, the Disadvantage will be very great to me as it Lyes in there power to do very genteel for me at My Return, Which I must & will suffer Reather than go in this Ship, altho I am so Desirous of Proceeding the Voyage, therefore I hope you'll be pleas'd to Favour me with my Desire which will make me Intirely happy, & till such time as I Know your pleasure Remain your Honours most Obedient & Most Devoted Servt Richd Rollett— I hope you please to let me know your pleasure Which I Impatiently wait for & hope it will be a profound Secret to Captn Cook for if it Dont sute you & he heres of it my time will be Very Miserible to me'.—ATL, *Miscellaneous material relating to Cook's voyages*. Rollett however duly sailed on the *Resolution*.

every aspect of Scandinavian history. Or he may simply, as a man of his time, have thought of it for himself. Botany, zoology, volcanoes called; and he was ready for a Runic inscription. Certainly he had no doubt that Iceland merited a visit. The reasons that seemed valid to him (however unjust to König) may be given in his own words. The East India Company, he persuaded himself, had made overtures and seemed inclined to send him on a voyage to the South Sea in the spring of 1773. Meanwhile, though Zoffany had gone to Italy, the rest of his following were left upon his hands, 'and as they were a considerable running expence I thought it prudent to employ them in some way or other to the advancement of Science, a voyage of some kind or other I wishd to undertake and saw no place at all within the compass of my time so likely to furnish me with an opportunity as Iceland, a countrey which from its being in some measure the property of a danish trading company has been visited but seldom and never at all by any good naturalist to my knowledge; the whole face of the countrey new to the Botanist and Zoologist as well as the many Volcanoes with which it is said to abound made it very desirable to explore it and tho the season was far advanced yet something might be done, at least hints might be gatherd which might promote the farther examination of it by some others'.[1] He would thus both keep his people together and keep them busy pending the greater voyage. The Danish embassy in London readily granted a passport, and Banks chartered a brig of 190 tons, the *Sir Lawrence*, Captain Hunter and a crew of twelve, 'to proceed according to my directions at the Rate of 100 pounds a month for four Months Certain'.[2] At last he had a ship under his own orders. He proceeded to open a new journal.

It is a journal interesting, like nearly everything Banks wrote, but as an Iceland journal not wholly satisfactory, for it breaks off soon after the writer reached Iceland; and what other information we have on the visit is satisfactory only to the extent that it mentions a date or two, a few places, some isolated incidents. A biographer is too much tantalized. The first eight pages of the journal are indeed spent on an obsessional reworking of Banks's case against the Admiralty, pages which could well have been given to his travels; while the *Letters on Iceland* which von Troil published at

[1] Iceland Journal, pp. 6-7.
[2] The brig was in the end under charter for five months, from 11 July to 4 December, as we see from the account in the 'Voluntiers' papers

Banks and Solander

from 'shadows' by James Lind

Uppsala in 1777 touch on those travels only incidentally.[1] The obsession could certainly not go farther without our worrying about the balance of our young man's mind: he cannot resist recording a little scandal about the artist who finally went with Cook; Solander, whose pre-eminence in his own branches of science was acknowledged and admired on all hands, is 'now well known in the learned world as my assistant in nat[ural] Hist[ory]'; while as for the voyage of the *Resolution*, Banks had been offered by the Admiralty 'the alternative to go or let it alone, with a great deal of Coolness however, for I now had inadvertently opend to them Every Idea of discovery which my last voyage had suggested to me and these they thought themselves able to follow without my assistance now they had once got possession of them'. But for his 'people' he maintained his charm, as well as his importance as a source of livelihood. He took with him, independent of the captain and crew of the *Sir Lawrence*, twenty-one persons in all: he had added a cook and a gardener to the original company, and there were three more newcomers — von Troil, who wished to make observations upon the Icelandic language; 'Mr Riddel, a young gentleman intended for the Sea', who wanted also to go south with Banks if the East India Company provided a ship;[2] and Gore of the *Endeavour*,

[1] Banks's MS does not seem to have been previously utilized by any student. It is now in the McGill University Library, and I am greatly indebted to the generosity of the Librarian of McGill in providing me with a microfilm copy. The MS has 8 pp. of introduction, followed by 88 pp. of journal, 12 July–6 September 1772, and an appendix giving the text of the passport. Of the 88 journal pages, 60 are devoted to the Scottish islands, and 14 to Iceland. In the introduction Banks says he will include his long letter to Sandwich of 30 May in an appendix, but does not do so. It is possible that he wrote more journal than is extant, but if so, why has the passport appendix survived and not the rest of the journal? A copy of the journal by S.S.B. survives (Hawley coll.); this breaks off at 5 September, but does include the letter to Sandwich. Banks did write more, though it may not have been in journal form, because he lent some notes to W. J. Hooker to aid the latter in his own tour of Iceland in 1809, and Hooker quotes Banks's account of the ascent of Mount Hecla (see p. 92 below). Lord Brabourne, also, has a small notebook with a few details attributable to September and October (I have not seen this and owe my knowledge of it to Miss Janet D. Hine). And there are two long and interesting letters to Falconer, quoted below. Von Troil's book appeared in 1778 in a German edition, from which J. R. Forster made the English version, London 1780: *Letters on Iceland, made during a Voyage undertaken in the year 1772, By Joseph Banks Esq., F.R.S. and Dr. Solander, F.R.S., Dr. Lind, F.R.S., Dr. Uno von Troil, D.D., and several other Literary and ingenious Gentlemen*—to give the gist of its intolerably verbose title-page.— All the evidence available a generation ago on the visit, from Icelandic as well as English sources, was brought together in the valuable monograph by Halldór Hermannsson, *Sir Joseph Banks and Iceland* (Ithaca, N.Y., 1928), pp. 4-20. Hermannsson unfortunately did not have the journal or the Falconer letters. He reproduced 24 of the 75 drawings made by the Millers and Cleveley, now in the British Museum, Add. MSS 15511 and 15512.

[2] This is presumably the person of whom Hume wrote (to Lind?), 24 February 1772: 'There is a young Gentleman of the Name of Riddal, Grandson of Sir Walter Riddal, who goes with you in your nautical & philosophical Expedition in the Station of a Midshipman: I am much connected with his Friends who desire to have him recommended to you'.—Klibanksy and Mossner, *New Letters of David Hume*, p. 195. Young

H

who 'out of mere freindship chose to take the trip'. Gore, we may
note, had now been three times round the world, with hardly
a rest in between, and might well feel that he had earned a little
leave and — if he could not keep away from the sea — a period
as passenger.

The adventurers sailed from Gravesend on the night of 12 July,
carrying Count Lauraguais as far as Dover, and arranging there
for the transport to Calais of a bird that Banks was sending to
Buffon. There was a historic brass cannon to inspect at the castle,
and a little botanizing to do. The wind turned contrary and blew
fresh, and for several days Banks was too sick to write. By 20 July
they were at the Isle of Wight — 'a little paradise', thought von
Troil, though Banks was more measured in his description. Going
ashore early at Cowes to buy butter and eggs, they had to walk
about till the shops opened. Cowes was a pleasant town; the small
and ill-built Yarmouth, where they 'landed with French Horns
to the no small surprise of the people who little expected to see
such a motley crew issue from so small a vessel', less so, its people
'much less humanisd' than those of Cowes, less used to strangers:
'the children followd us about the streets begging for halfpence'.
It was not quite like landing on a South Sea island, but at least the
French horns had had their effect. Three more days brought them
to Plymouth, to find that Arnold, the instrument-maker, had
carried Banks's chronometer back to London. Once more Mount
Edgcumbe was inspected, with regrets that its noble owner was
not more a man of refined taste, who could have added some
touches of art to the magnificent inadequacies of nature; but the
docks called forth unqualified enthusiasm. Then by ship again,
with the wind still west, and more and worse sea-sickness from day
to day. A bout of fishing yielded only four dogfish, 'in whose fins
were however a new species of Oniscus'; and when, a few miles off
the Cornish coast, a flag was hoisted to attract fishing-vessels,
a legion of small boats shot out to see what smuggled goods the
Sir Lawrence had on board. Such was the eighteenth century. At
last, on 28 August, near Land's End, with a south-west sea growing,
it was decided to sail up the Irish Channel; the wind turned
favourable, and the morning of the 31st showed the Mull of
Kintyre.

Riddell may have been 'intended for the Sea', but he does not appear to have been
appointed to either of Cook's ships. He was a relative of the wife of Hume's elder brother
John, a niece of Sir Walter Riddell of Riddell, who was the head of 'an ancient and
honourable family' in Roxburghshire. His presence, like Lind's, illustrates how Banks's
relations were extending over the kingdom.

There followed a fortnight among the Hebridean islands — a longer time than Banks had meant to spend, but a fortnight that gave full scope to his romantic, sporting, observing mind, and to his recording pen. Neither rain, nor fog, nor foul winds blurred his enthusiasm. On Saturday, 1 August, the ship anchored in Lochindale, to find an immense crowd gathered together for the single communion of the year next day. Banks had to have tents pitched for shelter, while the Sunday was deemed so sacred by the inhabitants that he could not even walk out botanizing — though certainly that pleasure would have been marred by the immoderate rain. On Monday he could at least go for a walk, to Killam, a small town at the head of the bay, where he found the ruins of a religious foundation, and set his artists to drawing tombstones; there were lead-mines also, originally worked by the Danes. On Tuesday more rain, and another walk to see a cave of which he had received 'a very pompous account', but it turned out to be 'a dirty nasty hollow in a rock'; on Wednesday still more rain, and the decision to move to the other side of the island. Banks rode overland, with an eye on the country and its farms. On 6 August the rain broke; the travellers crossed to the isle of Jura with a barometer to measure the height of the stony hills; the following day they fixed the latitude of Freeport, and the day after that arrived dripping wet on Oronsay to inspect its ancient monastic remains. Once again the artists were set to work. On the 9th they left the Sound of Islay: Banks wanted to sail straight to 'Y Columb Kill' — Icolmkill or the isle of Iona, but his pilot insisted on going through the Sound of Mull. (Cook was not the only sailor to prefer his own professional judgment to Banks's.) At least this gave him some fishing and shooting; he shot gulls, 'as all our gentlemen think these excellent meat', including the first Arctic Gull he had ever seen. There was an old fort, miserably broken down but picturesque, for the artists. And there was full liberty to the soul. It was 11 August; the ship was passing between Mull and Morven when Mr Banks's emotions, in the literary way, came to the top: he gazed on the fabulous shore entranced.

Morven the Land of Heroes once the seat of the Exploits of Fingal the mother of romantick scenery of Ossian I could not even sail past it without a touch of Enthusiasm sweet affection of the mind which can gather pleasures from the Empty Elements and realise substantial pleasure which three fourths of mankind are ignorant of I lamented the busy bustle of the ship and had I dard to venture the Censure of my Companions would certainly have brought her to an anchor to have read ten pages of Ossian under the shades of those woods would have been Luxury above the reach of Kings.[1]

Soon after came the anti-climax; for passing the mouth of a beautiful inlet 'the cruel pilot' would not let the enthusiast land, declaring it a bar harbour. They had to anchor, 'as fate directed in as ugly a spot as we could have chose along the whole coast, sufficiently so I think to have destroyed the enthusiasm of even an Ossian'. Yet even here, once ashore, the enquiring mind found food: he could observe the burning of kelp, of which we get a full description.

More was at hand than kelp-burners. Banks met an English gentleman, a Mr Leach, who told him that on an island about nine leagues off were pillars like those of the Giants' Causeway. The Giants' Causeway was a phenomenon that only lack of time had kept him from visiting earlier. Here was a chance to make up for the omission. He had two days' provision and his tent loaded into a boat, sent the ship round to wait in Tobermory harbour, took eight of his people and was rowed over to Staffa — a tedious eight hours' passage without a breath of wind. It was night when they landed; the tent was too small, so four volunteers, led by Solander, braved the smoke and suspected lice of a nearby fisherman's hut. In the morning — it was 13 August and a great day in Banks's life — enthusiasm once more rushed to the surface. On the south-west side of the island 'we were struck with a scene which exceeded our Expectations'. This was the great range of natural pillars for which Staffa has since then been pre-eminently known. Banks made a rhetorical flight which perhaps compensates for his discontent with the unaided nature of Mount Edgcumbe.

Compard to this what are the Cathedrals or the palaces built by man mere models or playthings imitations as diminutive as his works will always be when compard to those of nature where is now the boast of the architect regularity the only part in which he fancied himself to exceed his mistress nature is here found in her possession & here it has been for ages uncounted, is not this the school where the art was originaly studied & what had been added to this by the whole grecian school a Capital to ornament the Column of nature of which they could execute only a model & for that very capital they were obligd to a bush of acanthus.

how amply does nature repay those who study her wonderfull works.

With his mind full of such reflections was Mr Banks guided over the new giants' causeway. But there was still more to come —

[1] Iceland Journal, pp. 34-5. The contrast between the emotions of Banks in the Hebrides in 1772, and of Johnson in 1773, is really comic.

there was the magnificent, the stupendous cave of 'Ouwa Eehn', 'Fiuhn Mac Coul whoom the translator of Ossians works has calld Fingal' — Fingal's Cave, in fact; 'how fortunate that in this cave we should meet with the remembrance of that cheif whose existence as well as that of the whole Epick poem is almost doubted in England'. Dubious the reception of James McPherson's misty eloquence by the critics of Britain might be; but certainly Mr McPherson could have no reason for complaint about this particular reader. — 'Enough for the beauties of Staffa', continues Banks, science regaining its command of his mind, 'I shall now proceed to describe it and its productions more Philosophicaly'. He, Dr Solander, Dr Lind and the rest had had a most exhausting day, climbing up and down with ropes and measuring rod and pencils and paper; but by four o'clock all was done, drawings and measurements, and we have the precise details in the journal. By that time too the lice had made their presence felt, at which the affected gentlemen complained to the woman of the house 'with some peevishness'. Her husband was regrettably unmoved: lice being unknown on Staffa before, he reasoned, obviously they must have come with the gentlemen.

The gentlemen crossed over to the sacred ground of Iona, where for the first time in the Highlands they were asked how much they would give for their board and lodging. Nevertheless board and lodging they soon got — an empty house, clean straw, sour curds and cream, and a fire they had to put out for lack of a chimney — preparation for another day of rain and ruins, with a good deal of unlikely story thrown in by their guide.[1] That night they reached the ship, 'in Tobir more, a prodigious fine harbour', and after an unsuccessful day hunting roebuck on Oronsay again set sail, northwards between Skye and the Outer Hebrides. Banks had liked the 'scotch nation', deplored their housing, admired their education; disliked their home-distilled whisky, which drove him to drink milk; regretted that he could say nothing about their language, called 'Galick'. Now he was anxious to visit St Kilda; but dirty weather both made a landing impossible and plunged everybody in the usual sickness. It fell calm: he went out in the boat, shot sea-birds and picked up three Portuguese men-of-war,

[1] Banks elsewhere tells a pleasant story about the visit to Iona: 'in each of the 4 sides of this Island which answer the 4 Cardinal points is a stone in which seamen place great faith beleiving that if they cleen carefully any one of them a wind will arise from its respective quarter. When we were there the Stone on the North side was nicely swept & a northerly wind arising fannd us gently away to our ship where we arrivd at night'.— Banks to Falconer, 12 January 1773, Hawley coll.

unusual in those latitudes; a fair wind blew and raised all spirits; it blew strong, and all spirits were depressed. At last, on 25 August, rocks were seen. They were the rocks of Iceland.

It took three days to come in with the land, and by the time the flat shore and scattered houses were visible, long ridges of hills behind, there were fishing-boats all round. The fishermen were unexpectedly shy; as Banks learnt later, some dispute was in train between Denmark and England, and they suspected the ship to be the forerunner of a conquering fleet.[1] At last a few were enticed on board, fishy, and 'lousy to admiration'; Solander found that his Scandinavian tongues made conversation easy; they ate, drank, and gained such happy confidence from learning that the English were Christian that one of them agreed to pilot the ship into Hafnafiord, an important trading point, in the south-west corner of the island. Next day, 29 August, accordingly, they anchored near Bessastad, the residence of the governor, a place famous in the sagas; Solander got permission to land; the governor received them politely; and the famous visit could begin. They could have the vacant warehouses of the Danish merchants to stay in, but must not take possession until after the following day, Sunday. To acquire virtue in Icelandic eyes, therefore, the English put on their best clothes, went to church, and rigidly eschewed all sign of work or amusement, 'which as there were above 30 just landed in a new countrey was rather extrordinary'. The early days were spent in building up good relations and trade, much as if the visitors were on a South Sea island; ribbons and tobacco were given away; Dr Lind had 'a great Levy' dispensing medicines and electrical shocks from Banks's electrical machine;[2] and there was fishing, botanizing, and the first exploration of lava beds. Another Sunday came, when Banks entertained the governor, one of his subordinates, and their families to dinner — the ladies in Icelandic dress duly described; everything was a great success, 'but most of all the French horns which playd to them at their desire they having explaind

---

[1] Von Troil, on the other hand, merely says there was a severe penalty for piloting a strange ship into harbour without official permission, as a measure against smugglers—which does not contradict Banks, any more than Banks contradicts him. Shyness of smugglers would argue a radical difference between the Icelanders and the Cornishmen. Foreign trade with Iceland was in fact forbidden. It is said also that the Icelanders remembered an Algerian pirate-raid in the previous century, and feared another.—Hermannsson, p. 9.

[2] Cf. pp. 158, II, 276-9 below. This use of the 'electrical machine', for purposes of amusement, is very typical of the age. Unhappily there were no 'humorous effects': of the poor Icelanders, thus surprised in the clinical routine, 'every one looked as a fool who had received an unexpected slap on the face nothing lively appeared no good prognostick of Bright parts in our new freinds'.—Iceland Journal, 3 September.

to us that musick was a laudable occupation even on a sunday'.[1]
Then they galloped away on their little horses over the rough
lava — and Banks's journal, so rich in endearing detail, so much
the reflection of his lively mind, comes to an end.

We are compelled to fall back upon our other sources. There
must have been a week more of local exploration of the volcanic,
treeless country, with its vast lava-beds, its small farms and vegetable
gardens, till the party set out on the grand expedition, to climb
Mount Hecla: this was a twelve days' journey, and they climbed
to the top, von Troil tells us, on 24 September. We have an itinerary
noted down by Solander.[2] From Hafnafiord they first made their
way to Heitharbaer, a farm on the north-west shore of Lake Thing-
valla. Next day they visited the meeting place of that venerable
institution the Althing, or Icelandic parliament, and went on to
Lake Laugarvatn with its neighbouring hot springs and geysers;
in one of the springs they had the happiness of boiling a piece of
mutton, some trout, and a ptarmigan ('which was almost boiled
to pieces in six minutes, and tasted excellently');[3] and so on to
Muli to spend the night. Then came the great day with geysers at
Haukadal, where they stayed from 6 in the morning till 7 at night,
enchanted with forty or fifty boiling and spouting springs, and
especially with Geysir, which has given its name to all such
phenomena; Lind set up his quadrant and measured the 92 feet
of its greatest rise. This was on 21 September. There followed a
day of literary interest; for they were received at Skalholt not
merely with kindness from Bishop Finnur Jonsson, the learned
historian of the Icelandic church, but with a Latin and Icelandic
ode composed by the headmaster of the cathedral school in honour
of Banks. The leader of the expedition made return of suitable
gifts; and the expedition passed on to more hot springs at Laugaras,
was ferried across the two rivers Hvita and Thiorsa, and reached
the parsonage of Skarth to spend another night. They were almost
at their goal. On 23 September they reached Grafell, a mountain
in the lava field west of Hecla, pitched a tent for a short night,
and at one o'clock next morning started on the ascent. It took
them thirteen hours.

They scrambled up — for they had to leave their horses — in
intense cold, with a violent wind blowing against them — so violent
that sometimes they were forced to lie down to save themselves

[1] Iceland Journal, 6 September.
[2] *Plantae Islandicae et Notulae itinerariae*; B.M.(N.H.), Botany Library.
[3] Von Troil, p. 10.

from being hurled over the precipices. They were 'covered with ice in such a manner that our clothes resembled buckram. . . . The water we had with us was all frozen. Dr Lind filled his wind machine with warm water: it rose to 1..6 and then froze into spiculae, so that we could not make observations any longer'.[1] Mount Hecla has more than one peak: they seemed to have reached the top, when, in the manner of mountains, the top presented itself still farther beyond. Solander gave up and stayed with an Icelander in the intermediate hollow — did he have unpleasing memories of the snows, the fatal hills, of Tierra del Fuego? — but the rest persevered into triumph. Hecla is 5000 feet above the sea. They were the first, they were convinced, who had stood upon its height. They had all wished to see a burning mountain. The drawback was, that the mountain would not burn — at least visibly: there were patches on the sides where underlying heat had melted the snow, and on the top was a small space whence, said Banks, 'there proceeded so much heat and steam that we could not bear to sit down upon it';[2] and at least that was satisfactory. Hecla had last erupted in 1766, devastating the country with its lava-flow, and flamed a few weeks before the climb: how seldom does Nature oblige the desires of the human heart! Nor was this ascent the first: the mountain had been climbed twenty-two years before. Yet it was a gratifying achievement. A three days' journey brought the adventurers back to Hafnafiord — first along Langafell and to Skarth, over the Thiorsa river and to Hraungerthi parsonage; then the river Olvesa, and a ride along Ingolfsgall to Reykir, where they could study another group of boiling springs; then over Hellisheithi safe to their warehouse-headquarters.

Where else Banks went in Iceland we cannot say with precision. The names given by von Troil argue another tour of hot springs, westwards and north-west to the North Cape, and then perhaps east and south round the island; and we may infer the inspection of 'Remains of Antiquity', or, as our age has it, ancient monuments, from his mention of their existence. We judge that there was a lively British-Icelandic social life: there was for example the country parson who was entertained with singing and the music of some unknown instrument;[3] there was the dinner given by the surgeon-general, Bjarni Palsson — at Banks's request, an Icelandic dinner —

---

[1] Banks, as quoted by W. J. Hooker, *Journal of a Tour in Iceland* (London 1813), II, pp. 116-7.

[2] ibid.

[3] An occasion described in the *Autobiography* of Jon Steingrimsson, quoted by Hermannsson, p. 10.

where spirits, dried fish, and sour butter proved tolerable, but not the dessert of whale and shark, looking very much like rusty bacon. Presents were exchanged; minerals and other natural objects, antiquities, and books came to Banks in abundance. Of printed books he purchased whatever he could: manuscripts, alas, there were exceedingly few, for Scandinavian scholars had scraped the country almost bare. We read of no social contretemps — it is evident that Banks was again at his heart-winning best; the governor, Olafur Stephensen, became his life-long friend. It was a serious people, records von Troil; they rarely laughed, and in their leisure hours they either recited the sagas or played cards. But — there is no doubt — they were amiable. The draughtsmen drew assiduously: their sketches and water colours present an invaluable picture of the Icelandic life of that period. In this pleasant atmosphere of goodwill the visit ended. Some time in the latter part of October the ship was ballasted with lava, loaded with the extraordinary variety of articles that Banks had managed to collect, and stood southwards for Scotland again by way of the Orkney Islands. In Scotland Banks spent a further period, we do not know how, till on 19 November he departed with Solander and Lind from Edinburgh for London.[1] The journey, although it had not embraced the globe, had been a rewarding one. Its trophies, at one time or another, were dedicated to the public advantage: the lava ballast went to Kew to form the 'moss garden', and to the rockeries of the Apothecaries' Garden at Chelsea; the printed books and manuscripts, with others that Olafur Stephensen sent later, were to be the foundation of the British Museum's Icelandic collection; the description of Staffa, with the drawings of Cleveley and the Millers, went into the *Tour in Scotland* that Thomas Pennant published in 1774.[2] Solander's *Flora Islandica* and the greater

[1] One of the Iceland drawings is dated 15 October; so, as Hermannsson points out, the ship must have left Iceland after that date. The note-book in Lord Brabourne's possession has the final entries, '21 [October?] Idle. 22 Idle too resolve to go away fair or foul'. If October is the month referred to then the departure could not have been earlier than the 23rd. In a letter to Falconer of 12 January 1773, Banks remarks, 'the course I steerd was through the western Islands to Iceland from whence after having remaind 8 weeks I returnd by the orkneys to Edinburgh & from thence by land to London'; but in another, 2 April 1773, he says 'we were only 6 weeks ashore on it'— i.e. Iceland.—Hawley coll. Smith, p. 34, apparently following *Gent. Mag.* xlii, p. 540, says Banks left Edinburgh on 19 November, after spending some time there and in the Highlands, but gives no authority for the statement. *Gent. Mag.* merely gives the date. The *General Evening Post*, 24 November 1772, announces that 'Joseph Banks Esq., Dr Solander and Dr Lind, are on their return to London from Scotland. . .'.

[2] *Tour in Scotland and Voyage to the Hebrides.* Banks's description, which appeared in Vol. I (Chester, 1774), pp. 261-9, stuck closely to the words of his journal. Vol. II was published in London, 1776. The work was dedicated to Banks.—'. . . Staffa, so lately raised to renown by Mr Banks.'—Johnson, *Journey to the Western Islands of Scotland*

part of the drawings were never published. Mr Banks had a new visiting card made, a map of Iceland engraved upon it, with Mount Hecla prominent and the Arctic circle carefully dotted in. Nobody could say — even the Navy Board could not say — that he had not added lustre to his name.

§

But he still felt restless. It is plain — we have touched on the point already — that, though Joseph Banks might be called a philosopher in the eighteenth century sense, without placing any strain at all on the word, in the sense of the twentieth century no man was less a philosopher than he. Nor was it that, like Dr Johnson's friend, he tried to be a philosopher but cheerfulness kept breaking in. He would have seen no conflict between philosophy and cheerfulness, and he was generally cheerful. He knew there was an Order of Nature, and as a general idea, a rational explanation of the universe, that was enough for him.[1] A voyager he esteemed himself, but he was never a voyager through strange seas of thought, alone. His devotion to natural history was an open-air devotion. However vast his herbarium, he was not a man of the study; his instinct was never to sit quiet. The collation of results, the fundamental brain-work, could be left to Solander. Banks, more even than Solander, needed people; he needed something to do. There was something to see in London that he had failed to see in Newfoundland — a visiting party of 'Esquimaux Indians', lodged in Leicester Street. Nevertheless this was small beer. Within a few weeks he was off again — not on a grand voyage, with newspaper paragraphs and a scientific staff, but simply to Holland by ordinary packet, in company with the Hon. Charles Greville, a son of the Earl of Warwick and Brooke — a *savio*, as Horace Walpole called him, a charming companion, but no very romantic or striking figure. On 15 February 1773, late at night, we have the traveller sitting down at the Hague to write to his sister: that morning he had landed at Helvoetsluys, walked 'seven long miles' to the Brill, and completed the journey in waggons and a thick fog, through country

(1775). Banks's connection with Staffa could have been even closer: Lind suggested he should buy it. 'Talking of the Highlands I beg to acquaint you, that the Island of Staffa is to be sold this Spring; the annual rent of it is about £10, and it is supposed £200 will buy it. If you choose to purchas it, you'll please to let me know, and I shall get some friend to bid for it at the Sale, as it will not be proper for you or any of your friends to appear in it, lest it should enhance it[s] value.'—Lind to Banks, 2 March 1775, Webster coll.

[1] On the 'Chain of Creation', or the 'Chain of Being', and Banks's references to it in his Journal, see II, p. 20, n. 1 below.

that (so far as he could see it) reminded him strongly of his native Lincolnshire.[1] At the Hague, 'a most beautiful town', he stayed a week, calling on the Prince of Orange, examining the Prince's menagerie, the chief cabinets of shells and other curiosities of natural history, pictures and people, and attending a concert, 'the Musick intolerably indifferent, and stunningly loud'.[2] On the 25th he was at Amsterdam, 'conveyd by a Track Skoot a most easy cheap and pleasant conveyance which has determined me to follow your advice and keep a Journal for as in that we have a Cabbin and table I can employ all the time we are traveling a saving of time which realy ought to be esteemd as a great benefit and must be so by those who can employ themselves'.[3] He had passed through Leyden and Haarlem, greatly impressed by the organ at the latter and by the sluices between the Haarlemer meer and the sea, 'a fine work ten times larger and more magnificent than our Grand Sluice in Lincolnshire and yet the Dutch think little of it'. At Amsterdam he went to the opera, a 'singular performance with a second act an hour and three-quarters long'.[4] There were more cabinets here and at Utrecht; at Utrecht he went to church with the Moravians, and was much edified; but by 5 March he had reached Rotterdam, where next day he and Greville were inducted into a Society of Literature, lately established for the discussion of Hydrostatics. This was above Banks's head, and he got away with relief to the study of strange birds and to sauntering round the town; perhaps he was glad to return to the Hague. Here, on 10 March, he 'had a Levee of Greenland Captains, who had been sent for from Rotterdam, in order to give me such information as they might be able, which might forward Cap^{tn} Phipps's plan of sailing towards the Pole'[5] — the voyage stimulated by one of Banks's friends, Daines Barrington, through the Royal Society, and to be commanded by his other friend Phipps; a voyage for which the two 'bombs' *Racehorse* and *Carcass* were then being prepared. Banks himself nourished some hopes of going on this voyage,[6] and he

[1] ML Banks Papers, XVI, 9-10.

[2] Journal, p. 8 (18 February); cf. following note.

[3] 'Journal of a trip to Holland beginning with the time of leaving London (Feb^{ry} 12. 1773) & ending with the day of returning thence again (March 22. 1773)'.—S.S.B. 1773.

[4] Letter of 24 February 1773, ML Banks Papers, XVI, pp. 5-8.

[5] Journal, pp. 69-70.

[6] Cf. the postscript of his letter to Falconer, 2 April 1773: 'we are employd in fitting out an expedition in order to penetrate as near to the North Pole as Possible it consists of two Boom Ketches chose as the strongest species of Ships therefore the best to Cope with the Ice they will sail before the middle of the next month commanded by a good Freind of mine Cap^{tn} Phipps your opinion of the Frigid Zone cannot but be useful to him & very agreable to me at this Juncture'. Banks's known interest in this voyage and his

listened eagerly to talk of ice and currents. There was another visit to court, and a ridotto, and more curiosities; there were many friends; and Joseph, writing again to Sophia, found himself 'tolerably well pleasd with this fenny muddy country as the inhabitants of it have been civiler to me than I deservd'.[1] Did he perhaps, amid those calm and fertile flats, as he gazed at the willows or the fields, or lifted his pen from the address 'To Miss Banks near the Physick Garden Chelsea', pause and think with a pang of the *Resolution*? The Low Countries were very well, but they were not adventure; the Hague, though agreeable, was not Tahiti. He passed again through Rotterdam to Helvoetsluys, to embark in the tedious and 'stinking Pacquet'; before the end of March he was home in New Burlington Street; and Cook, after the gales and ice-fields of the far south, was in Dusky Sound, on that coast of New Zealand where, three years before, Banks had so much wished to land.

Of friends and admirers there was no lack. It was in 1773 that Sir Joshua Reynolds began to present Banks with copies of his *Discourses* to the students of the Royal Academy.[2] The great Dr Robertson of the College of Edinburgh had accepted the Banksian case against Government at its face value. 'I look with impatience into every News Paper to learn something about your future motions', he wrote. 'What a shame it is that the first literary and commercial nation in the world should hesitate a moment about encouraging the only voyage which in modern times has no other object but the advancement of science. I am afraid we are neither so learned, so intelligent, nor so public spirited as we pretend to be'.[3] Perhaps there was balm in this. Perhaps there was balm in reflecting on the corresponding membership of the French Academy of Sciences, conferred in the previous March,[4] when every prospect was still fair; or in the appointment of both Banks and Solander that now came, to the Royal Academy of Sciences at Ulrichstadt.[5] The learned Falconer was once more

meeting with the men of learning at Rotterdam, confused with his 'Levee of Greenland Captains' at the Hague, was perhaps the basis of the report in the *Annual Register*, 1773, p. 82, that he and Greville assisted at a session of the Batavian Society at Rotterdam, whereat he communicated his design of undertaking the voyage, asked for information of Dutch discoveries up to 84° north latitude, and promised in return to report all the discoveries he might make. Banks's journal mentions no such meeting.

[1] n.d. ML Banks Papers, XVI, p. 11.

[2] See F. W. Hilles, *The Literary Career of Sir Joshua Reynolds* (1936), bibliographical appendix.

[3] Robertson to Banks, 18 February 1773; D.T.C. I, pp. 47-8.

[4] He was 'nommé correspondant de La Lande, le 11 mars 1772'.—*Index Biographique des membres et correspondants de l'Académie des Sciences de 1666 à 1939* (Paris 1939). Banks had further steps in the hierarchy of French honour in 1787 and 1801.

[5] *Annual Register*, 1773, p. 106.

full of encouragement: he had heard 'with great pleasure' that Banks had had 'some views of undertaking a Mediterranean Voyage. There would be a noble field for a Naturalist'.[1] In the summer there was a trip not to the North Pole, nor to the hardly less noble Mediterranean, but to Wales, with Solander, the botanist Lightfoot, and a new friend, Dr Charles Blagden, a physician from Edinburgh, a delightful person who rapidly became one of the most intimate of Banks's friends, and a copious and unwearied correspondent. Another companion, it seems likely, was Paul Sandby the artist, whose works Banks approved and bought.[2] It was a seven weeks' botanical tour, repeating on the way the earlier journey to Bristol, Chepstow and Tintern, and then proceeding along the Glamorgan coast — new ground for botanists — with a dash into Breconshire and westward to the coast of Pembrokeshire. Alas! there are too many choices in life; the party stayed so long here, and so engrossed, that it had to ignore one of its more northern objectives, Cader Idris; for it seemed essential to work back across southern Wales into England, and then turn west to Anglesey and the ascent of Snowdon. Banks was in London by the middle of August; he had a load of rare plants, he had helped to solve some botanical problems, he had climbed the highest English mountain; certainly he could feel that life was pleasant.[3] When September brought Phipps back from the impenetrable ice north of Spitzbergen, Joseph could write to Sophia without envy: 'one of the Ships from the North is returnd without success so I am glad I was not of the Party'.[4] If he had been of the party, indeed, he might have gone hunting bears with the young Horatio Nelson.

But the year 1773 was remarkable not so much for travels — travels which had now become no more than excursions — as for Banks's inauguration as an Adviser. The capital letter is justified.

[1] Falconer to Banks, undated, but with a pencil note at the top, 'May 17, 1773'; D.T.C. I, p. 52.

[2] The memoir of Sandby by his son remarks, 'He also travelled with Sir Joseph Banks, the late Dr Solander, and Mr Lightfoot, upon a tour of the Principality'—a journey he remembered with delight.—*Monthly Magazine*, 1 June 1811, p. 437; the memoir was reprinted by A. P. Oppé in the *Burlington Magazine*, LXXX (1946), pp. 143-7. The 1773 tour seems to be the only one that fits. I owe my references in this matter to Dr Bernard Smith.

[3] What we know of this journey comes from a 'Journal of a Botanical Excursion in Wales', kept by Lightfoot, and letters from him to Banks, edited by the Rev. H. J. Riddelsdell, and printed in the *Journal of Botany*, 43 (1905), pp. 290-307. I do not know of any journal by Banks. Lightfoot afterwards wrote to Banks, 'I never became a Party in any Scheme which afforded me more Satisfaction or sincere Delight. . . . I believe it may without vanity be said, that few, if any Botanical Excursions in Great Britain have exceeded our Collection, either in Number or Rarity of Plants or Places'.—24 August 1773, loc. cit., p. 292.

[4] 21 September 1773, ML Banks Papers, XVI, p. 21.

On his early life, as he advanced into his thirties, a career was being superimposed that was to make him one of the most considerable figures in English life, outside politics and mere society. Obviously he had regained firm ground, after his sudden ballooning into the air of self-consequence: 'the inhabitants . . . have been civiler to me than I deservd', though a sentence of rather conventional sentiment, is not quite conventional when addressed to a sister who knew him. Its moderation is very different from the high tone he had adopted about the Navy Board. The importance which now began to be attached to the name of Joseph Banks was not importance attached by himself, nor adventitious, it did not arise simply from the supreme good luck of having been taken round the world by Lieutenant Cook, or even from the contribution which, before the end of the year, he was seen to have made to the history of that voyage. It was rooted in a capacity which he undoubtedly had, to advise, but to advise with discrimination, and with tact, on matters in which he was competent. He could still, for decades to come, be enthusiastic, persistent, strong-willed, even dogmatic; he could still therefore make enemies; but he was never again gratuitously foolish. He had a sense of the possible. His authority became formidable — partly, no doubt, because he cared to exert it; but also because it was both conceded and earned. It was many-sided; but that was because it arose from a real as well as many-sided interest. It was not earned in a day; and when at last all Europe looked to him, he made a good deal less play with 'all Europe' than he had done in that fatal month of May 1772. In the meanwhile he was just beginning; and he gave advice, wise enough, to Dr Hawkesworth over the preparation of his *Voyages* and his relations to Stanfield Parkinson.[1] He had become interested in a matter that never ceased to be interesting to him, the transference of useful plants from one part of the world to another, and he advised on that.[2] Nothing else, however, equalled in importance the influence he began to wield as a sort of scientific overseer to the royal gardens at Kew.

For a hundred years already the gardens at Kew had had an honourable history, and they became royal when in 1730 Frederick Prince of Wales got a long lease of Kew House from the family

[1] 'I long for the month of April when we are to be entertained and instructed', wrote Robertson, in the letter already quoted, no doubt in anticipation of the appearance of the *Voyages*.

[2] Banks to S.S.B.: 'My Dear Sister, I send you Mʳˢ Boones paper relative to the bringing vegetable [s] to Antigua [from the East Indies]. . . .' n.d. Endorsed by S.S.B. '26 April sent to Mrs. Boone 27. 1773'. ML Banks Papers, XVI, pp. 13-14, with the directions carefully copied out by Sophia, pp. 15-18.

of the founder, Sir Henry Capel. To Kew in 1751 the Dowager
Princess went to live, and forthwith expanded her domain to take
in the adjoining derelict estate of Richmond Lodge. She set out to
garden on the grand scale, with an excellent adviser. Lord Bute
had the misfortune to have a political career, which has tended to
blind posterity to his merits; though it is true that history at no
time has paid great attention to horticulture. Wherever he lived
he made a garden — on the island of Bute, at Luton Hoo in Bed-
fordshire, a third in Hampshire; and it was with Bute that botany
at Kew became a scientific subject. He himself planted a number of
the noble trees still there surviving; and he appointed the young
man William Aiton in 1759 as royal gardener, the position Aiton
occupied until his death in 1793, with the *Hortus Kewensis* as his
literary monument. His monument otherwise Banks helped to
raise; it was the gardens. Both men owed something to another
great gardener, Philip Miller of the Apothecaries' Garden at
Chelsea. Aiton had been his pupil; the youthful Banks had haunted
the Chelsea walks, made a friend of the old man, and after his
death bought his herbarium. Miller had gathered in rare plants
from all over the world; Bute had directed Aiton to lay out a 'physic
garden' at Kew on the Chelsea model; and when the Princess
Dowager died in 1772 and Bute departed from the royal scene,
the way was open to another man, animated by the same passion
but with rather different ideas, to take command. The destiny
that brought Banks and George III together therefore was important. The king was only five years older than Banks; as a country
gentleman devoted to farming and gardening he could have lived
a very successful life — he was not called 'Farmer George' for
nothing — and when he came to town he could have had his fill
of concerts; Banks, introduced to him so soon after the return of the
Endeavour, could talk about a subject and show him things that
roused his lively interest; Banks was quite non-political; Banks,
while full of information and devoted to a Cause, nourished no
sentiment whatsoever that could possibly disturb the Established
Order. The Cause of the botanical exploration of the world, the
experimental cultivation of the world's plants in one great centre,
the extension of horticultural curiosity into scientific study, was a
Cause the king could make his own. Once Banks had been in the
royal presence, he was asked to come again; it is clear that the
friendship between the two men rapidly ripened; and clear that
there was only one candidate for the unofficial directorship of
what Banks was to call His Majesty's Botanic Garden. The king

was to have a life-long interest and refreshment — he bought
Kew House outright; Banks was to have the pleasing advantage
of pursuing his own hobby with resources very much greater
even than his own. The beginning of all this in 1773[1] was a matter
of the utmost importance not only to the two men, but to British
botanical development; it was significant to the empire, not only
of Britain, but of science.

As the months moved on into 1774 the social web became more
complex. There were new friends — James Bruce, the African
traveller, the botanical Suffolk parson Sir John Cullum, Dr Alexander
Hunter, who was editing Evelyn's *Sylva*. If social lustre were to be
acquired competitively, Banks would have lost that year and Bruce
would have won. Africa, wrote Horace Walpole, was coming into
fashion. 'There is just returned a Mr. Bruce, who has lived three
years in the court of Abyssinia, and breakfasted every morning
with the Maids of Honour on live oxen. Otaheite and Mr. Banks
are quite forgotten'.[2] Banks, however, was in full career, and
had more staying power than Bruce. He was elected to the Society
of Dilettanti, whose interests were allegedly in art, but more particularly social.[3] The Society of Arts, or to give it its full title, the
Society for the Encouragement of Arts, Manufactures and Commerce, with its strong technological leaning, was a body to which
of course he already belonged, having been accepted as early as
1761, in his first year at Oxford;[4] but perhaps the Society of Arts
lacked conviviality. He was elected to the Council of the Royal
Society. He had his autumns at Revesby — he was a systematic
estate manager — and there was the shooting and fishing; one might
say that Joseph Banks was settling down. He was also dragged into

[1] The precise date when Banks began to advise on Kew is obscure. It may possibly
have been towards the end of 1772, after his return from Scotland, but 1773 seems the
safer guess.

[2] Walpole to Sir Horace Mann, 10 July 1774; *Letters* (ed. Toynbee), IX, p. 16. Banks's
first introduction to Bruce may have come through a letter from the African traveller (11
January 1774, D.T.C. I., pp. 67-8), forwarded by Zoffany in Florence, seeking his help in
getting Bruce's drawings through the Customs. Zoffany adds, 'Your book of the last voyage
[i.e. Hawkesworth] goes off here amazingly, and I hear it is to be translated'.—W. T.
Whitley, *Artists and their Friends in England, 1700-1799* (London 1928), I, p. 296.

[3] He was proposed by 'Athenian' Stuart, who comes into the Banks-Cook story otherwise in one or two minor ways.—Cook II, pp. xli and 609, n. 3. He was certainly among
friends. It is recorded that on 6 December 1778—he had just become President of the
Royal Society—'Lᵈ Sandwich & Mr Banks having called this respectable Society by the
disrespectful name of Club were fined a bumper each which they drank with all proper
humility. Lord Mulgrave do. do.'—Cust, *History of the Society of Dilettanti* (London 1898),
p. 35.

[4] The precise date was 21 October 1761 (the Curator-Librarian of the Royal Society
of Arts, Mr D. G. C. Allan, has kindly informed me), three weeks after the death of his
father. His application to this Society may therefore have been one of his first serious
independent acts.

the public view for the purpose of buffoonery in a manner more appropriate to the eighteenth century than to our own. Hawkesworth's three guinea three volume account of the recent voyages had appeared midway through 1773. The improper poets had been a little slow to get up steam, but by the beginning of 1774[1] they had gone into production, stimulated by what one of them called 'Doctor Hawkesworth's very luscious descriptions'. Banks of course was an obvious butt: a shilling would buy Major John Scott's *Epistle from Oberea, Queen of Otaheite to Joseph Banks, Esq. Translated by T.Q.Z. Esq. Professor of the Otaheite Language in Dublin, and of all the Languages of the undiscovered Islands in the South Sea; And enriched with Historical & Explanatory Notes*. It was announced in the introduction that to facilitate the labours of those curious to study the Tahitian language, the professor would shortly be publishing a complete grammar and dictionary, which would 'be printed on the same Paper, and with the same Letter as Doctor Hawkesworth's celebrated Voyages, and will be ready to be delivered next Spring for the *moderate* Price of Three Guineas'. So much for Hawkesworth. Banks was taken at more length. It was the sort of thing that might be expected — even as fugitive verse not of a very high standard, though aimed accurately enough at the public taste:

> Read, or oh! say, does some more amorous fair
> Prevent *Opano*, and engage his care?
> I *Oberea*, from the southern main
> Of slighted vows, of injur'd faith complain.

> *   *   *

> Ah! I remember on the river's side,
> Whose bubbling waters 'twixt the mountains glide,
> A bread-tree stands, on which with sharpen'd stone,
> To thy dear name I deign'd unite my own.
> Grow, bread-tree, grow, nor envious hand remove
> The sculptur'd symbols of my constant love.

There was a large mass of footnotes, mainly from Hawkesworth and Ovid. Ovid was still fashionable, and the *Amores* seemed *à propos*. Carried away by his own wit, or in response to an irresistible

---

[1] There is a quite minor—a minimal—bibliographical point to be raised here. The dates of the squibs quoted below are all given on the title-pages as 1774, and Sir Maurice Holmes's Cook bibliography follows this. But a copy of the third edition of the *Epistle from Oberea*, the first of them, in the ATL has on the title-page also the inscription 'Spilsby Society, Decr 29th 73' (Spilsby is a village in the eastern part of Lincolnshire). The Introduction is dated Sept. 20th, 1773, and the Introduction to the *Epistle from Mr. Banks*, which followed it, Dec. 20, 1773; so it is possible that in printing they were post-dated.

I

demand (for this squib ran into a fourth edition), Major Scott then penned *An Epistle from Mr. Banks, Voyager, Monster-Hunter, & Amoroso*:

> Carv'd is thy name upon the bread-tree's rind?
> Thy face, thy soul, are carv'd upon my mind;
> And, well I ween, blest produce of thy charms,
> My image lives and prattles in thy arms.

And followed that still with *A Second Letter from Oberea*:

> The children grow in stature and in grace,
> While all the father blooms in either face. . . .
> And when I weep I almost hear them say
> Why, cruel, went our Father far away;
>
> *　　　　　*　　　　　*
>
> Yet think at least my copious tears you see,
> And spare one thought from Botany for me. . . .
> Think on the raptures which we once have known,
> And waft one sigh to *Otaheite's* throne.

The samples are enough. Delicacy was not the Major's strong point, and if he had read Banks's journal he would not have been misled on the relations between his hero and heroine: that did not matter, but he became very repetitive and excessively tedious. He does not figure in the grand procession of English poetry; he does nevertheless witness to the fact that Banks was a prominent enough figure to take rewarding liberties with.

Then came the Event, the vast excitement, of 1774. In July (to offset Abyssinian Bruce) returned from the South Sea Captain Tobias Furneaux, Cook's second in command, with the *Adventure*, with news from Tahiti — everybody had been enquiring after Banks — and with that best ethnological specimen of all, a veritable Tahitian, the simple and sweet-tempered Omai. What to do with Omai? The extent to which Banks had regained his ground with Sandwich we may now see: Omai was handed over to him. This was magnificent; at last he had something which none of the menagerie-keepers among his neighbours could hope to match: something to take the place of poor Tupaia. Like the rarest of exotic plants, Omai was borne off for the inspection of the king: 'How do, King Tosh!' he exclaimed upon his introduction, with true courtesy. The king made the sensible suggestion that he should be inoculated against smallpox. It was done; he recovered, was lodged near Banks, and became the darling of social London. Even Solander was excited enough to write a letter about him, with a few odd phrases. Omai, he said, had been living 'as a private Gentleman of a small fortune' on Huaheine; he had parted from his own country in high spirits; he was aged 21 or 22. 'When he saw Mr Banks who happen'd to have no powdre in his hair he knew him instantly. . . . It has been very pleasing to us, to him and many others, that both Mr Banks, myself, and Mr Banks's servant James have not forgot our South Sea Language. So we all can keep up a Conversation with him. . . . Omai is [a] sensible communicative Man, so he is a valuable acquisition. . . . Omai don't yet speak any english, but I think he will soon learn it, as he has got several words and begins to pronounce S tolerably well. . . . He is well behaved, easy in his Manners, and remarkably complaisant to the Ladies'.[1] Lord Sandwich and Mr Banks, he added, were now quite cordial again. As Omai's visit extended, and his English improved, it became apparent that he was not very sensible; but his manners passed from ease to elegance; he visited the House of Lords and managed like any gentleman the sword the king had given him; he dined with the great, he dined with Dr Burney and Dr Johnson; he went to stay with Lord Sandwich at Hinchingbrooke; Miss Burney put him into her diary, Mrs Thrale put him into *Thraliana*, Cowper put him into *The Task*; Reynolds painted his portrait; the muse descended upon Major Scott again, with quite colossally tedious results. Omai in fact was to London all that Bougainville's Ahutoru had been to Paris five years before. Perhaps the Romantic Movement got more from Ahutoru than from Omai; the 'noble savage' was, after all, more diligently cultivated in France than in England.

Kew, the library and herbarium at New Burlington Street, the meetings of the Royal Society and its Council, the dinners of the Royal Society Club, the Dilettanti, the management of Omai, the superintendence, even at a distance, of the Revesby estate, the ordinary demands of the season and of society — here was enough to keep busy a person who was not content merely to be a landed proprietor living in London. It was an extremely agreeable life, and the summer excursions still kept on. We have a record of one in Yorkshire, in the reminiscences of George Colman the younger, who at the age of thirteen was taken by his father on a journey full of the ingredients of joy. The elder George Colman was a popular playwright and a successful theatrical manager, well-off and highly regarded in society. It was in the early summer[2]

---

[1] To an unnamed correspondent, 19 August 1774, ATL *Holograph Letters and Documents of and relative to Captain James Cook.*

[2] Or possibly late spring. Colman says midsummer, but Banks spent June and July on two (so it would appear) yachting parties with Sandwich. See the following pages.

of 1775 that the two Colmans, Constantine Phipps and his young
brother Augustus, Omai and Banks all piled into Banks's enormous
travelling coach with a vast amount of nautical luggage belonging
to Phipps, who was transporting it to the family seat at Mulgrave,
and still more, not nautical, which belonged to Banks, large boxes
included for anything he might collect on the way. Other encum-
brances mentioned by Colman indicate the close touch with applied
science that was maintained by the proprietor. 'In particular
there was a remarkably heavy *safety-chain*, — a drag chain upon
a newly constructed principle, to obviate the possibility of danger
in going down a hill; — it snapp'd short, however, in our very
first descent; whereby the carriage ran over the post-boy, who
drove the wheelers, and the *chain of safety* very nearly crush'd him
to death. — It boasted, also, an internal piece of machinery with a
hard name — a *hippopedometer*, or some such Greek coinage, — by
which a traveller might ascertain the precise rate at which he was
going, in the moment of his consulting it: this also broke, in the
first ten miles of our journey; whereat the philosopher to whom
it belong'd was the only person who lost his philosophy. . . . Our
progress, under all its cumbrous circumstances, was still further
retarded by Sir Joseph's indefatigable botany: — we never saw a
tree with an unusual branch, or a strange weed, or anything singular
in the vegetable world, but a halt was immediately order'd; — out
jump'd Sir Joseph; out jump'd the two boys, (Augustus and myself,) after him; and out jump'd Omai, after us all'.[1] At Scar-
borough Omai took George for an early morning bathe, carrying
him seaward on his back; between Whitby and Mulgrave the
heavy coach got on the sands in the dusk, with a rising wind and a
roaring sea, and then behind frightened horses into the surf, whence
the postilions with great difficulty rescued it and its inmates; at
Mulgrave the whole party stayed awhile. Omai shot grouse and
barn yard fowl with equal enthusiasm, but mainly the latter; Banks
lectured the boys nightly on the Linnaean system, cutting up
a cauliflower for illustration, and sent them out in the morning
for plants. The researches of the elders were devoted to opening
ancient barrows, a particular hobby with Phipps. This employment
entailed all-day expeditions into the fields, and open-air cooking;
Banks shone at making stews, 'in a tin machine', Omai at baking
in an earth-oven after the Tahitian mode, with buttered paper
for plantain leaves and potatoes for yams. Everything was admirably

[1] Colman, *Random Records* (London 1830), I, pp. 157-9.

good-humoured. From Mulgrave they moved on to Skelton Castle,[1] where the Colmans left their cheerful companions.

Banks was in London again only a few days before going off on two further expeditions. The first was a six weeks' trip, in June and July, from Deptford to Plymouth and back with Sandwich in the Admiralty yacht *Augusta*, on the First Lord's visitation of the royal dockyards.[2] Sandwich's labours, and Banks's amusements, were touched with a different excitement which could not fail to have, for Banks, a double edge. Letters had arrived from the *Resolution*, letters sent from the Cape. Solander wrote to his friend:

. . . . As a Copy of Capt Cooks Letter was sent down to Ld Sandwich, I take it for granted you know all concerning his Voyage. . . . Mr Penneck has sent Mr Forsters Letter to Mr Dr Barrington and made the following Abstract: 260 new Plants, 200 new animals — 71° 10' farthest Sth — no continent — Many Islands, some 80 Leagues long — The Bola Bola savage an [in] corrigible Blockhead — Glorious Voyage — No man lost by sickness.[3]

Glorious voyage indeed! — for those who had made it, and for those who could think of it with an unentangled mind. How long would it be till the ship herself reached home? The waiting time was filled by a second yachting trip down Channel, with Sandwich, his virtual wife the beautiful and charming Martha Ray, Phipps, Augustus Phipps and Omai — a trip broken up by the tremendous news. Cook was back. Solander again sent the unofficial tidings.

Two oClock Monday — This Moment Capt Cook is arrived. I have not yet had an opertunity of conversing with him, as he is still in the board-room [i.e. of the Admiralty] — giving an account of himself & Co. He looks as well as ever. By and by, I shall be able to say a little more — Give my Compl^{ts} to Miss Ray and tell her I have made a Visitation to her Birds and found them all well.

Captn Cook desires his best Compl^{ts} to You, he expressed himself in the most friendly manner towards you, that could be; he said: nothing could have added to the satisfaction he has had, in making this tour but having had your company. He has some Birds, in Sp.[irits of] V. [inum] for you &c &c that he would have wrote to you himself about,

[1] Near Skelton Castle was the village of Kirkleathem, where Colman mentions that the party met a venerable old man of distinguished deportment, the father of Captain Cook. It is doubtful whether James Cook the elder ever lived at Kirkleathem, but the village was not far from Redcar, where it is understood he did live, with his married daughter Margaret Fleck. He died in 1778, at the age of 84.

[2] Banks kept a semi-facetious journal of this trip, 2 June-14 July 1775, now at Hinchingbrooke among the Sandwich papers.

[3] Solander to Banks, 28 June 1775; ML Banks Papers, J 1-4. This has a pencilled endorsement in a hand unknown to me, 'Sir J B on road from Portsmouth to Plymouth?', which does not fit the known chronology.

if he had not been kept too long at the Admiralty and at the same time wishing to see his wife. He rather looks better than when he left England. Mr Hodges came up in his chaise, I saw him and his Drawings. He has great many portraits — some very good — He has two of my friend Tayoa. Otu is well looking man — Orithi whom they call Ohiriri was really a handsome man according to his pictures.

Fo[r]ster Senr and Junr are also come up, but I have not seen them, they did not call at the Admiralty.

Hodges says the Ladies of Otaheite & Society Isl^ds are the more hansomer they have seen. But the Man of the Marquesas seem[s] to carry the prize. Hodges seems to be a very well behaved young man. All our friends are well

Inclosed You will find a Letter from Ch' Clark. . . .[1]

He added a few remarks on Cook's maps, which he had seen, and on some of the islands he had heard about.

Then there was Clerke's letter, written on board the *Resolution*, 'Sunday Morn: 5 o'clock':

We're now past Portland, with a fine fresh NW Gale and a young flood Tide, so that in a very few Hours we shall anchor at Spithead from our Continent hunting expedition. I will not now set about relating any of the particulars of our Voyage, as I hope very soon to have the Honour and happiness of paying my personal respects, when I can give you a much clearer idea of any matters you think worth inquiring after, than its possible to do at this distance.

I hope I need not assure you that it is utterly out of the power of length of time, or distance of space, to eradicate or in the least alleviate the gratitude your friendly offices to me has created. I assure you I've devoted some days to your service in very distant parts of the Globe; the result of which I hope will give you some satisfaction; at least it will convince you of my intentions and endeavours in that particular. I shall send this away by our civil Gentry, who will fly to Town with all the sail they can possibly make. God bless you send me one Line just to tell me you're alive and well, if that is the case, for I'm as great a stranger to all matters in England as tho' I had been these 3 Years underground — so if I recieve no intelligence from you I shall draw bad conclusions and clap on my suit of black; but you know I never despair, but always look for the best, therefore hope and flatter myself this will find you alive and happy, which that it may, is the sincerest Hope and Wish of, Dear Sir, Your Gratefully Oblig'd & most H'ble Servt Chas Cler^ke.

Excuse the Paper, its gilt I assure you, but the Cockroaches have piss'd upon it. — We're terribly busy — you know a Man of War. My respects and every social wish to the good Doctor. I'll write him as soon

---

[1] ML Banks Papers, L 1-4. The letter is undated, but the Monday on which it was written must have been 1 August.

as possible — here's too much damning of Eyes & Limbs to do any
thing now.[1]

These were greetings such as any man might have been proud
and glad to have. His friends nourished none but the warmest
thoughts of him: Cook wished he had been on the voyage. Sandwich and Miss Ray hurried up to London; Banks, with every
inducement of friendship and curiosity, remained where he was,
and remained for a month.[2] We have not his answers to these
letters; he may have felt under some obligation to Phipps and
Omai, but it is much more likely that his principal sensation was
embarrassment. When he had been embarrassed about Miss Harriet
Blosset, he did nothing; and now he did nothing. The conviction
must have forced itself upon him that he had been a fool. He had
made one of the great refusals; he had missed one of the most
remarkable voyages in the history of the world; and Cook and
Clerke brought him back not reproaches but specimens for his
natural history collection. Solander's next letter could not have
added to his self-satisfaction:

Our Expedition down to the Resolution, made yesterday quite a feast
to all who were concerned. We set out early from the Tower, review'd
some of the Transports; Visited Deptford yard; went on board the
Experiment, afterwards to Wolwich, where we took on board Miss
Ray & Co, and then proceeded to the Galleon's where we were wellcomed
on board of the Resolution — and Lord Sandwich made many of them
quite happy.

Providentially old Capt[n] Clements died 2 or 3 days ago, by which a
Captain's place of Greenwich was made Vacant. This was given to
Capt Cook, and a promise of Employ whenever he should ask for it.
M[r] Cooper[3] was made Master and Commander. M[r] Clerke was prom-
ised the command of the Resolution to carry M[r] Omai home. . . .

All our friends look as well as if they had been all the while in clover.
All inquired after You. In fact we had a glorious day and long'd for
nothing but You & M[r] Omai. M[r] Edgcomb & his Marines made a
fine appearance. — L[d] Sandwich asked the Officers afterwards to dine
with us at Woolwich.

Most of our time, yesterday on board, was taken up in ceremonies,
so I had not much time to see their curious collections. M[r] Clerke shew'd
me some drawings of Birds, made by a Midshipman, not bad, which I

[1] ML Banks Papers, II, f.4. The Sunday of Clerke's writing was 31 July.
[2] Unless the yachting was continued with Phipps and Omai. But he certainly remained
away from London: Solander's next letter is dated 14 August, and endorsed by Banks
as received on the 20th and answered on the 25th. One would give much for his answers.
A third letter from Solander, 22 August, includes the greeting, 'My best Compl[ts] to
Capt Phipps, M[r] Augustus, M[r] Omai. . . .'—Webster coll.
[3] First lieutenant of the *Resolution*.

believe he intends for you. I was told that Mr Anderson one of the Surgeons Mates, has made a good Botanical Collection, but I did not see him. There were on board 3 live Otaheite Dogs, the ugliest & most stupid of all the Canine tribe. Forster had on board the following Live Stock: a Springe Bock from the Cape, a Surikate, two Eagles, & several small Birds, all from the Cape. I believe he intends these for the Queen. If I except Cooper & 2 of the new made Lieutenants I believe the whole Ship's Company will go out again. Pickersgill made the Ladies sick by shewing them the New Zealand head of which 2 or 3 slices were broiled and eat on board of the Ship. It is preserved in Spirit and I propose to get it for Hunter, who goes down with me to morrow on purpose, when we expect the Ship will be at Deptford. . . .[1]

Apart from all the enticements touched on by Solander, Banks could not stay away forever. People wanted to see him; he had duties. If he felt foolish, he simply had to master the feeling, and it is clear that the friendliest and most unforced relations were immediately re-established on both sides between himself and his old shipmates. Cook went at his invitation more than once to dine with the Royal Society Club. And the position of authority he had by now come to occupy was important. It was real authority; he could now be as tactful in London as he had been in Tahiti; and he was consulted accordingly. He began to assume — it is a curious development — the functions of a sort of superintending elder brother in relation to some of the concerns of Cook. He became, as it were, a point of reference, a master of the disinterested judgment. This involved him in the awkwardness over the publication of the history of the voyage, which arose from the character of the elder Forster, and in even worse later irritations over this man. Forster was a person of total incapacity in money matters, and of no great scrupulousness either in money matters or in others. He was also a master of the unjustified assumption, the wielder in writing of a fluent but overblown English style, and a harbourer of grudges. He suffered under a continual and plaintive sense of injustice, and did not hesitate to make a tool, in either unscrupulousness or complaint, of his rather more attractive son George. Undoubtedly he had a good deal of learning, unmixed with any sense of proportion whatever. He had been a difficult companion on shipboard,

---

[1] London, 14 August 1775. ML Banks Papers, M 1-4. 'Hunter' was the famous surgeon and anatomist. Cf. another letter from Solander, 22 August 1775: '. . . Several of the Resolutions Men have called at Your house, to offer you their curiosities:—Tyrrell was here this Morning. . . . Capt Cook has sent all his curiosities to my apartments at the Museum—All his Shells is to go to Lord Bristol—4 Casks have your name on them and I understand they contain Birds & fish, &c the Box D° with Plants from the Cape. . . .' —Webster coll.

officious and censorious. He now alleged that at £4000 he had been quite inadequately paid; that Sandwich had promised him that he should both write the history of the voyage and monopolise the profit therefrom; and that he should subsequently receive employment for life. Granted that the man had a family to provide for, this was hardly the way to provide for it. Certainly the possibility of his being an official historian had been entertained, at a somewhat smaller reward than he fancied his due;[1] and certainly after due consideration it had been rejected — a decision for which we may be extremely grateful. Cook preferred to do his own writing, with a moderate amount of revision from Canon Douglas of Windsor. Forster was furious with Cook, with Sandwich, with printers and engravers: at last — how could it have been avoided? — with Banks.[2] Nevertheless, in letter upon letter, then and thereafter, he made Banks the recipient of his outraged and injured feelings: he would appeal to the public; he would expose the infamy of Cook — who would 'be proved to have forfeited the Appelations and the Characters of a Gentleman' — and of Sandwich, who had 'endeavoured to ruin me by the weight of His power and opulence'.[3]

[1] Solander probably had the matter right, so far as Sandwich was concerned, when he wrote to Banks, 5 September 1775, 'Lord Sandwich has desired him to, by way of specimen, send in some Sheets, containing an account of what happened in Dusky Bay, New Zealand. If approv'd of, he is to write the account of the Voyage; and he is to have ½ the profits & ⅓ to Captain Cook'.—D.T.C. I, p. 99. In the same letter Solander remarks, 'Mr Forster overwhelms me with civilities upon your account. He is of all men I know either the most open or the greatest fool'. It looks from a letter from George Forster to Banks, 4 January 1778, as if Forster had erected a cloud castle on some vague, hypothetical but hopeful words of Barrington's before the voyage.—ibid., p. 163. There is an immense letter from J. R. Forster to Banks, undated but probably early 1778, traversing the whole story from his point of view, and in elevated terms, which lends colour to this supposition.—ibid., pp. 171-81. See also George Forster's *Letter to the . . . Earl of Sandwich* referred to below.

[2] Daines Barrington wrote to Sandwich, 5 June 1776, 'Dr Forster hath just now call'd upon me in excellent humour both with your Lordship & Capt Cooke the poor man having now transferr'd his jealousy to Mr Banks, who he conceives to have done him ill offices with your Lordship. . . .'—Sandwich Papers, Hinchingbrooke.

[3] The letter from which these last words are taken is very typical of Forster, and may be here given in full: 'Dear Sir, Your unexpected absence out of town threw my Son and me into the disagreeable circumstance to sell for 350£ what even to booksellers would have been worth £750. Thus at the loss of £400 I have extricated myself out of the most pressing difficulties. But necessity has no Law. Since You decline, for good reasons to intercede in my favour, I shall be obliged to appeal to the public & lay before this impartial Judge, an infamous Transaction of a Man, who has endeavoured to ruin me by the weight of His power & opulence & I hope 5000 Copies shall inform all England of this dark iniquitous transaction & perhaps do more, than all my hitherto passive conduct could operate: for not one of the circumstances shall be omitted in it which have served to bring about such a consummate Scheme of bad actions. My son is gone for a few weeks to Paris, on some private business; as soon as he comes back, he shall wait on You with my whole Collection, which is not yet searched, & You may have whatever You shall want of it. Being convinced of Yr friendship and generosity I shall never forget Yr benevolence, and ever shall be Yr most obliged affectionate humble Servt J. R. Forster'.—Endorsed by Banks as received 7 October 1777. ML Banks Papers, R 1-3.

To Sandwich himself George Forster was later, with an excess of effrontery, impelled to write a public letter, attributing the betrayal at bottom to the influence of Miss Ray.[1]

For this fury and this insolence both Banks and Sandwich, it seems, were willing to make allowances. Forster was a foreigner and a natural historian, and his threats were empty enough. Within the community of science Banks was bound to act as his patron, so far as that was possible. He was allowed the rights to German and French translations of Cook's book and to use a number of the engravings; and, to aid him in the compilation of his own scientific *Observations*,[2] he was supplied with proof-sheets of Cook's account. He had kept a journal; and from this George, who was not included in the agreement his father had made, was set to compose a Forster book which would beat the official one to the public — which it did by about six weeks. While all this was going on both the Forsters were given the run of Banks's library and collections, together with the full use of his premises while they laboured over the description and publication of their own gatherings. Their first production was found to be largely the work of Anders Sparrman, the Swedish naturalist whom Forster had engaged as an assistant at the Cape; their later ones owed a great deal to the plundering of Solander's manuscripts from the first voyage.[3] Banks had to forbid them the house. But he still came rather reluctantly to the rescue when the cries of despair were too heart-rending. In August 1776 he paid four hundred guineas for George's drawings made on the voyage — a sum which was accepted 'with pleasure', wrote Forster.[4] Eighteen months later there was another letter: 'Though You have declined it before to assist me, I come however to implore Y^r friendly assistance. My affairs are at this moment in a Situation that makes me shudder, for it is only the distress of the moment; could I but gain time, I should certainly be able to extricate myself. My litterary productions and the sale of my artificial and natural Curiosities, for which I am entered into a negotiation with a powerful Sovereign abroad, are more than sufficient to give me relief. Be therefore exorable Dear Sir and lend me a helping hand, and You shall experience not to have bestowed Your friendly assistance to an ungrateful man'.[5] And so on. In September 1778 he was trying to

---

[1] *A Letter to the right honourable the Earl of Sandwich, First Lord Commissioner of the Board of Admiralty, &c. From George Forster, F.R.S.* London 1778.

[2] *Observations made during a Voyage Round the World, on Physical Geography, Natural History, and Ethic Philosophy.* London, 1778.

[3] Elmer Drew Merrill, *The Botany of Cook's Voyages* (Waltham, Mass. 1954), pp. 186, 201 ff.

[4] J. R. Forster to Banks, 9 August 1776, D.T.C. I, p. 132.

[5] Forster to Banks, 7 February 1778, ML Banks Papers, S 1-2.

sell Banks his shells; he was putting up some scheme about timber for masts to Stephens, the Admiralty secretary ('But I'll advise my Correspondents to conclude a bargain rather with France than with the ungrateful English Admiralty'); he had proposed to Lord North a plan for funding two millions sterling without taxing the public ('I begged only Secrecy in case my plan were rejected and I stipulated a Sum and an Annuity if it were adopted. . . . But I have some Notion, that Ld North will not be long at the head of the Treasury and I shall reserve my plan for his Successor. To whom I can likewise offer 10,000 from a foreign Prince. . . . I could serve the Public, if Ld Sandwich had not given me a bad character, which prevents me from being employed in the Service of this Kingdom'.)[1] Banks lent the near-lunatic £250, apparently about this time, and the long-suffering George having been able to secure a professorship for him at Halle, he fortunately left the country.[2] What chances George Forster might have had of a useful career in England had been ruined by his father. 'I have only the satisfaction of recollecting', he was later to write, 'that whilst I acted under his direction and by his positive order, the offence I might give, was involuntary, for which, if I now suffer, I stand acquitted in my own mind'.[3] It is not so easy for others to acquit George of all blame. He held chairs both at Cassel and at Vilna, a place he disliked extremely, and died rather prematurely, a nervously-exhausted revolutionary leader, before his father, in 1794.

§

The trouble caused by Forster, tedious, preposterous, exasperating, was still in its early stages when Cook left England for his third voyage, on 11 July 1776. With Banks the personal situation was

[1] 26 September 1778; endorsed by Banks 'saw him'. ML Banks Papers, T 1-4.

[2] This £250 had a later history. Banks did not expect to get it back, but when he found that the Duke of Brunswick had been induced to come to Forster's rescue, and that Forster had omitted it from his list of debts, he thought it was time to demand some security, both from the father and the son. His letter to Forster on the subject, 20 May 1782 (ML Banks Papers, A 1-2) is a model of moderation and good-humoured expostulation. George wrote a long letter from Vilna to Pennant in 1787, explaining with absurd indignation that he 'declined entering into this obligation, which, as it would have put me entirely in his power, might have ruined me, without satisfying him, and for ever rendered me incapable of acquiring the means of acquitting my father's debt, which my inclination, more strongly sollicits me to do, than any bond or paper security'. (To Pennant, 5 March 1787, ibid., Z 1-11). Banks's annoyance was added to by Forster's allegations in the *Göttingen Magazin* that he and not Cook deserved the credit for the prevention of scurvy on the *Resolution*, and that he should have had the Copley Medal that the Royal Society had awarded to Cook; and by his ill-natured attack on Solander after the latter's death. Banks instructed a Hamburg solicitor to take legal action for the payment of the debt, quite unsuccessfully; and after Forster's death, in 1798, let it lapse in favour of the widow.

[3] George Forster to Pennant, 5 March 1787; ML Banks Papers, Z 1-11.

very different from that in July 1772. Cook had something to say about descriptions of plants that Banks had offered to supply for the journal of the second voyage, now in the press, concluding his letter, 'Sʳ Jnᵒ Pringle writes me that the Council of the Royal Society have decreed me the Prize Medal of this year. I am obliged to you and my other good friends for this unmerited honour'.[1] Gore, the companion of the first voyage and the expedition to Iceland, was sailing as Cook's first lieutenant. During his time on shore he had acquired a wife and a child, and he too wrote to Banks, as to the centre of his reliance: 'The Young one whom you was so kind As to promise an attention To in Case of my Death, is under the Care of the Reverend Mʳ Firebrass of Braintree In Essex, him I have refer'd to you. Inclosed you have my will, and that with a Good will'.[2] Gore was not to die, he was to return as commander of the expedition, after the death of Cook and Clerke — the merry Clerke, who was 'in prosperity or adversity' Banks's 'Gratefully Obliged and Devoted Servant' (no mere form of words), and whose last letter, dictated off the coast of Kamchatka, is perhaps the most moving document in the whole history of Cook's voyages. It was a letter to Banks.[3] To Banks the Admiralty and the secretary of state were to send the despatches as they came in after many months, from Cook, from Clerke, from the British ambassador at St Petersburg; to Banks went copies of the messages from the East India Company; it was Banks who would draft the memorial asking for a pension for Elizabeth Cook, Banks who would supervise the publication of the history of the voyage, be consulted by the Admiralty (his crony Sandwich no longer First Lord,[4] but Keppel the political admiral, the enemy of the detested Palliser), be reported to by artist and bookseller; Banks who would see that there was a proper distribution of profits. It is the completion of the process which began after the second voyage; Banks has almost, so to speak, taken over Cook. Even that statement is inadequate. James King, to whom was given the task of completing the account of the third voyage, writes — not without a sad break in his grammar — to the man he esteems his true patron: 'it is with real pleasure and satisfaction that I look up to you as the common center of we discoverers'.[5] Allowing for a certain licence in the sentiments

---

[1] Cook to Banks, 10 July 1776. ML MSS.
[2] 12 July 1776, ATL *Miscellaneous material relating to Cook's voyages.*
[3] 10 August 1779, dictated to King but signed by Clerke; ML Banks Papers, II, f.11.
[4] Though it was Sandwich who made the first move before going out of office: 'Your advice will be of great use to me in the conduct of this matter'.—Sandwich to Banks, 10 October 1780; D.T.C. I, p. 300.
[5] King to Banks, 'Thursday Evening' [late 1780], D.T.C. I, p. 304.

of a man who is pleased, we may agree that Banks has become a common centre.

But these, in 1776, were things for the future. Meanwhile we are not to consider Mr Banks as exclusively occupied in advising George III on gardening, or sighing over the correspondence of the deplorable Forster. The moments of relaxation were still not few. We come upon our man unexpectedly, as we peruse the memoirs and letters of the time: the dying David Hume, for example, whose interests lay in quite different directions, adds light to the record. Journeying to Bath this year he stopped at an inn near Newbury, in Hampshire; at the inn was Lord Denbigh, an acquaintance of Hume's fellow-traveller, whom he informed 'that he, Lord Sandwich, Lord Mulgrave, Mr Banks, and two or three Ladies of Pleasure had pass'd five or six Days there, and intended to pass all this Week and the next in the same Place; that their chief object was to enjoy the trouting Season; that they had been very successful; that Lord Sandwich in particular had caught Trouts near twenty inches long, which gave him incredible Satisfaction. . . .' Hume proceeded to meditate upon the spectacle of the First Lord of the Admiralty, at a time when the British Empire was in revolt, finding 'so much Leizure, Tranquillity, Presence of Mind and Magnanimity, as to have Amusement in trouting', far from his place of business, for three weeks during the most critical season of the year. 'What an Ornament would it be in a future History to open the glorious Events of the ensuing Year with the Narrative of so singular an incident'.[1] The events of the ensuing year were not glorious; indeed one week before Cook sailed from Plymouth the rebellious colonies agreed upon their Declaration of Independence. This was not a thing in which Mr Banks took much interest, though no doubt he regretted inglorious events when they came to pass. America, for him, was not the land of Jefferson and Washington and John Adams; his American names are such as Clayton and Young and Bartram, Turner and Kalm — collectors whose trophies went into the great herbarium. The American whom he knew personally was Benjamin Franklin, and the mark this one made was not political. Banks, Solander and Blagden were Franklin's companions when he went to Portsmouth in October 1773, to experiment with the effect of oil on a breaking surf; Franklin was of course a Fellow of the Royal Society, much senior to them,

[1] Hume to William Strahan, 10 May 1776; *Letters* (ed. J. Y. T. Greig, Oxford 1932), II, pp. 318-19. Lord Mulgrave was Constantine Phipps, who had succeeded to his barony in 1775.

and in 1773 a member of its Council. It was Banks who wrote to
Franklin in 1784, sending him the Cook commemorative medal.[1]

Neglecting events of glory, or their reverse, passing beyond
the joys of the trouting party, and Ladies of Pleasure, and the
farewell to friends bound for the arctic ice-fields, we may choose,
as undoubtedly the most important event for Banks of the year
1776, his move from New Burlington Street to No. 32 Soho Square.
This was a large house, at the south-west corner of the square,
its back extending to Dean Street. The last few sad remains of
eighteenth century Soho Square have still some dignity; in Banks's
day, though not indeed the most fashionable part of the town, it was
airy and sweet with gardens, and fashionable enough for him and
a Venetian Resident; the house itself took after Adam, its elegant
drawing-room designed by the remarkable Robert Adam himself.[2]
Some people thought meanly of it — there was one person who
thought meanly of Banks, his town house and his country house
all together: the Hon. John Byng, on tour through England, con-
fided to his diary his disgust at Revesby Abbey, adding, 'but when
a man sets himself up for a wild eccentric character, and (having
a great estate, with the comforts of England, at command) can
voyage it to Otaheite, and can reside in a corner house in Soho-
Square, of course his country seat will be a filthy neglected spot'.[3]
Mr Byng's information about the wild eccentric character was
rather out of date: although it is regrettably true that Banks had not
pulled down his inherited mansion and rebuilt it in the Palladian
style, with a portico and an orangery, yet his estate was one of
the best-managed in the country; and the corner-house in Soho
Square rapidly came to acquire an international fame. For there
went the library and the herbarium, ever expanding from east
and west and south, from India and China and Malaya and Asia
Minor, from Jamaica and Dominica and South Carolina, from

[1] Carl van Doren, *Benjamin Franklin* (London 1939), pp. 434-5, 719. It is perhaps
surprising that one comes on no trace in Banks's papers of Jefferson, whose *Notes on
Virginia* would have been the ideal book to him. Apart from politics, there was probably
no one on the other side of the Atlantic more akin to Banks in range of interest. But
Jefferson never lived in England, nor even visited it.

[2] Its demolition in 1937, says Sir John Summerson (*Georgian London*, 1945, p. 127),
was a national scandal.

[3] *The Torrington Diaries* (1935), II, p. 376. He went on to aim some other ill-natured
remarks at people of learning, which illuminate his own character more than Banks's.
None the less, 'We left our cards for Sr J.B.'.—Soho Square, it may be remarked, was
a good enough address for all but the most particular, though its supremely aristocratic
days, when it was much patronised by ambassadors and the nobility, were rather earlier.
Members of the nobility, and persons otherwise distinguished, continued to live there
in Banks's time. See, e.g., John Thomas Smith, *Nollekens and his Times* (ed. W. Whitten,
London 1920) I, pp. 37-8.

Polynesia and Australia and Madagascar, from Switzerland, from Hammersmith and Kew. By 1783 he could afford not to buy the Linnaean collection, which he had been eager to acquire when the Master died in 1778. To Soho Square went also Solander, dividing his time between that centre of learning and the British Museum. There went also Sarah Sophia, an individual in her own right — rapidly becoming indeed a formidable one — to live with her brother and direct the domestic establishment. Mrs Banks, it seems, preferred still to live at Chelsea.[1] To Soho Square, as time went on, came everybody of scientific note, everybody immersed in scientific studies, to ask advice, to report on work done, to seek patronage, to share in the famous Thursday breakfasts, to listen to Solander while Solander lived, to consult Dryander or Brown, his successors, over the library or the herbarium; thither came explorers like Flinders and Mungo Park, botanical collectors like Masson and Menzies, thither men with a cause at heart, purveyors of curiosities, the deserving and the undeserving, the social and the anti-social, English, Frenchmen, Germans, Swedes. All this, like Banks's accumulating authority, did not come to pass at once; but the foundation was laid in 1776. The library, the herbarium, the personality of the owner, the personality of Solander, were like a fourfold powerful magnet. Nobody came for the Banksian small talk — there was none; the conversation might not go very deep at times, but at least it was informed, the conversation of able and often really scientific minds. Sunday evenings were for a more general society, ladies were present; they were informed and entertained alike by Dr Solander, whom all loved, and freely abused when he forgot his appointments, as he freely did. 'My father has very exactly named him in calling him a philosophical gossip', wrote Miss Burney.[2]

So, very agreeably for those who did not worry about the crash of empires, life proceeded. No doubt there was occasional speculation about Cook, no doubt the conversation, or the gossip, reverted

---

[1] She died at Soho Square, however, on 27 August 1804.—B.M. Add. MS 33982, f. 111; also Add. MS 6673, p. 107. She was 84 when she died.

[2] *Diary and Letters of Madame d'Arblay*, I (1904), p. 318. It is from 1796, long after Solander's death, that we get a curious note on Banks's social abilities. He was by then unquestioned master of the scientific scene; and Farington wrote, 'Malone observed how difficult it would be to establish a plan for collecting select Society in the way Sir Joshua Reynolds carried his on. [Reynolds had died in 1792.] Malone only knows three persons who could undertake it; and each is unfit in many respects. Sir Joseph Banks, as President of the Royal Society, and possessing a large fortune, might undertake it; but his knowledge and attention is very much confined to one study, Botany; and his manners are rather coarse and heavy'. The other two persons were Burke and Windham.—*Farington Diary*, I (London 1922), p. 136.

now and again to the old days in the *Endeavour*, when a botanist
drew out a dried specimen from the herbarium, or a lady exclaimed
over a Tahitian fly-whisk or some carved curio from New Zealand.
Beyond the walls of Soho Square the town, as well as the country,
had its diversions, and these too were agreeable. Banks and Solander
went together to a popular haunt for the unbuttoned hours of
science and art, Young Slaughter's Coffee House in St Martin's
Lane;[1] Solander, the treasurer of the 'Mitre Society of Royal Philosophers', had the happiness to inform Banks of his election to membership of that august body;[2] Banks himself was elevated by the
convivial Dilettanti to their offices of High Steward and secretary,
which he was to retain for many years.[3] But life was not yet full
enough. Dignity and power, in addition to authority, lay just ahead
for Joseph Banks. In August 1778 Sir John Pringle made up his
mind to resign the presidency of the Royal Society. Who should
succeed him? The Society was by no means exclusively a body of
scientists — less than a third of its membership, indeed, could be so
described; it included a large proportion of the rich and the great,
of noblemen who did not disdain to be considered in some sort
philosophers, as well as country parsons with an interest in their
local archaeology and plants and rocks, and physicians with an
interest which went beyond their fees. Of the twenty-one members
of Council only eight were men of science.[4] A person of high rank
therefore might be thought indicated as Pringle's successor — more
particularly as the Royal Society, under Pringle, had fallen out with
royalty. It was about lightning-conductors, and Sir John had been
tactless enough to inform the king, modestly but firmly, that the
President of the Royal Society could not reverse the laws of nature.[5]
Little consideration however was given to persons of high rank. As
soon as Pringle announced his intention there was talk, and Solander
sent a note to Banks: 'It is true that [Sir John] has given hints about
Mr Aubert, but all look to you. Dr Pitcairne and others have
desired me to tell you that'.[6] Again, 'Sʳ John Pringle has certainly can-

[1] Whitley, *Artists and their Friends*, I, p. 296.
[2] Solander to Banks, 1 August 1777, ML Banks Papers, O1. This must have been one of
the innumerable dining clubs of London.
[3] He was elected High Steward, or treasurer, on 1 February 1778, and secretary in
March of that year. He remained treasurer till 1794, and secretary till February 1797.—
Cust, *History*, pp. 28-9, 114. As secretary, he kept the Society's marbles in his house till
1784, when some of them, if not all, were presented to the British Museum. The contents
of Banks's house were extremely varied.
[4] Sir Henry Lyons, *The Royal Society* (Cambridge 1944), p. 197.
[5] George III ardently supported knobs on top of lightning conductors, against points
as invented by the American Benjamin Franklin, and requested Pringle to do the same.—
Weld, *History of the Royal Society* (1848), II, pp. 92-102.
[6] 11 August [1778]; D.T.C. I, p. 198.

Omai, Banks and Solander

from the painting by William Parry

vass'd for Mr Aubert, at which every one who I have seen is displeased. . . . If you cannot find out a man of high Rank who will accept of the Chair, you must listen to the voice of the People. All talk of you'.[1] Mr Aubert was an excellent man, and would not have disgraced the chair; he was a wealthy London merchant, and also a very good astronomer who had built himself three different observatories. The contest, therefore, if there was to be one, was to be between two commoners, both with some real pretensions to science. Though Dr Pitcairn and his friends were premature in assuring Banks that all looked to him, it is a little curious that none besides these two was seriously considered. But they were both rich, both non-political, and neither was connected with lightning-conductors. As time went on from August into November feeling rose, and Banks, who was not at all averse to his elevation, thought it wise to do some polite canvassing. 'Dear Sir', he wrote to Thomas Astle the antiquary and keeper of the State Papers, on 22 November, 'as I have venturd to declare myself a Candidate for the vacant Chair of President of the Royal Society I take the liberty to address you in strong [hopes?] that I shall have your Friendly assistance in the prosecution of that undertaking in which if my Freinds of the Antiquarian Society will support me I have not the least doubt of succeeding in a very creditable manner. as Yet no other Candidate has Started Ld Hillsborough has been wrote by a few Members but as the letter has now been absent a long while and as the people who wrote it were but few and had not a very great Weight in the Soc I am inclind to think his Lordship will decline. I shall attempt to see our Freind S^r Jo^s today whose decision in my Favor would be indeed very flattering and surely very decisive — Your very affect Servant Jos: Banks'.[2] This of course was not impeccably true; for Banks knew very well that Aubert had a great deal more support than that unimpressive politician Hillsborough; but it is possible that Aubert had not yet gone out asking for votes. At the end of November the Council met to make its recommendation. If keeping in with the king was important, then Banks was important; and a memorial to the king had been judged the in-

---

[1] 17 August [1778]; ibid., p. 199.

[2] ML Banks Correspondence, C 181, pp. 5-7. It appears from Banks's letter that he was anxious to get on to his side those gentlemen, like Astle, who were both F.S.A. and F.R.S. 'Sir Jo^s', in the last sentence of this letter, is I think Sir Joshua Reynolds, F.R.S. 1761. Reynolds, however, was not at this time F.S.A. He had been elected in 1772, but not paying his dues, was removed by the Council, and was not re-elected till 1784. There is another, shorter note to Richard Gough, F.R.S., the director of the Society of Antiquaries from 1775 to 1795. I have seen, in private hands, a number of replies to Banks's letters to other persons.

K

dispensable first step towards both the observation of Venus in 1769 and Phipps's polar voyage in 1773. The candidate had other virtues, of course. Nineteen of the twenty-one members of the Council took part in its deliberations; it decided on Banks; at the Anniversary Meeting that followed, 30 November, he was elected, 'unanimously to appearance by 220 votes'. The subsequent formal dinner was delayed by the lateness of the new president, who waited for the election of a new secretary: he 'came in a great hurry, quite out of breath, and sitting down. . . . said with good humour, but with rather too little dignity 'I believe never did a President of the Royal Society run so fast before'.[1] He was amply to compensate for that temporary lack of dignity; and the gout-smitten time was to come when those active legs would totally fail him.

Banks was about to receive another signal honour: to be deemed worthy to sit with Burke and Reynolds and Johnson, and to be elected to the Literary Club. 'The Club is to meet with the Parliament;' wrote Johnson to Boswell, 'we talk of electing Banks, the traveller; he will be a reputable member'.[2] It was Sir Joshua Reynolds himself who, on 11 December, announced to the candidate that 'he was *this Evening* elected a member of the Club at the Turks head Gerard Street';[3] and it was not every man who could say

[1] The quotations are from a letter of Banks's friend Sir John Cullum to the Rev. Michael Tyson, 7 December 1778, given in Edward Smith, p. 57.

[2] 21 November 1778; *Letters of Samuel Johnson* (ed. Chapman), II, p. 272. An earlier letter from Johnson to Bennet Langton, 31 October, had already mentioned the new candidature: 'Mr Banks desires to be admitted; he will be a very honourable accession'.—ibid., p. 264. Banks's qualifications were certainly not literary. We know very little of his intellectual tastes, if he had any, outside science and light music and plays. Boswell gives us one gleam of light, discussing Johnson's famous passage on Iona ('That man is little to be envied, whose patriotism would not gain force upon the plain of Marathon, or whose piety would not grow warmer among the ruins of Iona', etc.)—'Sir Joseph Banks, the present respectable President of the Royal Society, told me, he was so much struck on reading it, that he clasped his hands together, and remained for some time in an attitude of silent admiration'.—*Tour to the Hebrides*, 19 October 1773. As for art, 'Accuracy of drawing seems to be a principal recommendation to Sir Joseph'.—*Farington Diary*, I, p. 27. This is not surprising in the patron of Sydney Parkinson and the other botanical draughtsmen. Cf. the following passage: 'Indeed Sir Joseph Banks used to say that Mrs. Delany's representations of flowers "were the *only* imitations of nature that he had ever seen, from which he could *venture* to describe botanically any plant without the least fear of committing an error" '.—*Autobiography and Correspondence of . . . Mrs Delany*, (2nd series, 1862), III, p. 95. Again, some lines from the journal of the tour in Holland, 18 February 1773, describing how he went to see 'the Princes Cabinet, where were several Pictures, which the Connoisseurs seemed to admire: one of Oxen & a Shepherd painted by Potter, pleased me much: immensely high finished, but absolute nature'. Banks's patronage of that charming topographical draughtsman Paul Sandby has already been mentioned, and can be understood. See A. P. Oppé, *The Drawings of Paul and Thomas Sandby . . . at Windsor Castle* (London and Oxford 1947), *passim*.

[3] Reynolds to Banks, 11 December 1778. The owner of this letter, Mr Richard Border of Pulborough, Sussex, has kindly allowed me to use it. It has been printed, though not from the original, by F. W. Hilles, *Letters of Sir Joshua Reynolds* (Cambridge 1929), p. 67.

that he had been proposed by Reynolds and seconded by Johnson.[1]
Not for very much longer could he be intelligibly identified as
'Banks, the traveller'; and within a few months more he had taken
the final step, without romantic gesture, or alarm to his friends,
into a settled stability. On 23 March 1779, at St Andrew's, Holborn,
he married Dorothea Hugessen, the daughter of William Western
Hugessen of Provender in the parish of Norton, Kent, 'a comely
and modest Young Lady' almost sixteen years his junior.[2] He
was thirty-six; his youth was over.

§

It had been a youth fortunate, interesting, exciting; crowned, one
supposes, in a social way, with success. Banks had done whatever
he really wanted to do, with one notable exception. He had not
gone on Cook's second voyage. But, we are compelled to ask, if
he wanted to go only with that large entourage of his own, did he
really want to go? Was his refusal a tribute paid to science, or a
tribute paid to Joseph Banks? He had had plenty of time to think
over his decision. Psychological springs go deep, and one hesitates
to give an assured answer, a hundred and eighty years later, to
such a query. There must have been times when he was bitten by
regret, when he made hypothetical statements to himself as well
as to his friends, but to say that is not to answer yes or no. To the
end of his life, through all the multifarious and distracting and
benevolent activities in which he was engaged, he maintained his
position; we have the absurd statement passed on to Robert
Brown, the last of his librarians, some time before he died;[3]
we have the bitter attack on Palliser, obviously directly derived,
in Brougham's book of 1846.[4] This is self-justification; we need
have no doubt that Banks had persuaded himself that every word
he uttered on the subject was literally true; but we have no need

---

[1] Leslie and Taylor, *Reynolds*, II, p. 268.

[2] The phrase quoted is Sir John Cullum's; Edward Smith, p. 62, n. 1. The young
lady was born on 8 November 1758.—Dawson MS 47, f.58.

[3] Of this statement Dr Cameron says (*Sir Joseph Banks*, p. 51), 'In Banks's old age,
at the request of his friend Robert Brown, the botanist, he dictated his recollections of his
disappointment and the dispute'; and Dr Cameron prints it in his Appendix C, pp.
294-6. The statement is certainly in Brown's handwriting, and is bound up with his
manuscript correspondence in the Botanical Library of the British Museum (Natural
History), I, 17. It is undated, but probably was written in the last decade of Banks's
life, as Brown did not succeed Dryander as his librarian till 1810. There is nothing to
show that Banks dictated it to Brown, or that Brown asked for it: it is in fact a copy
of the introduction to Banks's Iceland journal (see p. 84 above). Possibly, even, it was
copied after Banks's death, as he willed all his books and papers to Brown for the latter's
life; but with this reserve I let my statement in the text stand.

[4] *Lives of Men of Letters and Science*, II, pp. 360-1.

to believe him. The significant thing is that throughout his forty later years the subject remained alive to him, in the same way that the voyage that he did go on remained alive. And this voyage, the three years in the *Endeavour*, remained also one of the things that gave his life a value to himself. It was a positive good; it was his, but he could contemplate it almost with a disinterested satisfaction, as a service rendered to mankind. 'I may flatter myself', he wrote in 1782, 'that being the first man of scientific education who undertook a voyage of discovery and that voyage of discovery being the first which turned out satisfactorily in this enlightened age, I was in some measure the first who gave that turn to such voyages'.[1] He ignores the element of luck, he might have remembered that Bougainville had been accompanied by Commerson, but he does not much overpraise himself. If the remembrance were to be forced upon him, he would no doubt have argued that Commerson's collections lay unpublished and neglected, and that he might just as well never have made the voyage. The answer to that no doubt would be that nothing scientific that Banks did was published either.

To that he would have a rejoinder: at least he would have a rejoinder in 1782. He gave it in the letter just quoted, shortly before Solander's death: 'Botany has been my favourite Science since my childhood; and the reason I have not published the account of my travels is that the first, from want of time necessarily brought on by the many preparations to be made for my second voyage, was intrusted to the care of Dr Hawkesworth; and since that I have been engag'd in a Botanical work which I hope soon to publish, as I have now near 700 folio plates prepar'd: it is to give an account of all the new plants discovered in my voyage round the world, somewhat above 800'.[2] Solander died of a stroke, amid general grief, on 16 May 1782. The work subsequently stopped. Why should it have stopped? There were the plates, prepared at great expense to Banks, and there were Solander's MS volumes, fair-copied, containing the descriptive text for the whole voyage. As late as 1785, Banks was writing to a Swedish correspondent,

The botanical work with which I am at present occupied is nearing its conclusion. Solander's name will appear next to mine on the title-

---

[1] Banks to Edward Hasted, D.T.C. II, p. 97 (evidently copied from a draft). This was in answer to a letter of 25 February 1782 asking for information for a county history (of Kent, into which Banks came through his marriage). Banks goes on, interestingly though somewhat indecipherably in the original, 'or rather to their Commander Capt Cook, as guided and directed those which came after, as well as [word illegible] which was personally concern'd'.   [2] ibid., p. 99.

page because everything has been brought together through our common industry. There is hardly a single clause written in it, while he lived, in which he did not have a part. Since all the descriptions were made while the plants were fresh there is nothing left to do beyond completing those drawings which are not yet finished, and entering the synonyms in the books which we did not have with us or have just come out. All that remains to do is so little that it can be completed in two months if only the engraver can be brought to put the finishing touches to it.[1]

Yet the great work was never published. It is ridiculous to blame Solander — as he has often been blamed — for sloth. His part was done. If Banks lacked time himself, there were men perfectly capable of seeing a large folio through the press. Jonas Dryander, who succeeded Solander as Banks's librarian, was one. As for the journal, it was true that Banks had handed it over to Hawkesworth to use as he thought fit; but if Banks had wished to put it into shape and publish it as a separate entity, there was nothing to stop him. There was ample material in his Newfoundland and Iceland journals as well to interest a large public, as he must have been told by those to whom he showed them. Why then did he print nothing, all his life? Or rather, strictly speaking, why were his publications confined to a few articles of a few pages, of which the best known was the 'Short Account of the Cause of the Disease in Corn, called by Farmers the Blight, the Mildew, and the Rust'? One of his biographers sees in him a certain lack of self-confidence,[2] and some words written much later in his life argue in favour of the supposition: 'I am scarce able to write my own Language with Correctness, & never presumd to attempt Elegant Composition, Either in Verse or in Prose in that or in any other Tongue'.[3] True, that was in answer to an invitation to join a Society for Belles Lettres, where the demand on elegance might have been deemed stringent. But it is equally true that the scientific mind has sometimes been frightened of the medium of prose, performed with in public. There were indeed critics who thought the President of the Royal Society was mostly façade. Examples have not been unknown, again, of men thoroughly competent, and quite convinced of their competence, on the practical side of life, who have manifested a curious shrinking from any overt display of their

[1] 'Ueber Solander', pp. 247-8.
[2] Cameron, p. 74, and note from the *Farington Diary*, I, p. 61: 'Some think Sir Joseph does not choose to encounter the opinion of the world on the merits of [his work], and, indeed, it is probable ill disposed criticks wd. not be wanting'. But this refers to the botanical work from the *Endeavour* voyage, Solander's work as well as Banks's, on which Banks could well snap his fingers at the criticks, however ill disposed.
[3] Banks to Henry Greville [June 1807], B.M. Add. MS 33981, f. 256v.

minds. There was certainly no reason why Banks should print his journals, if he did not wish to; presumably he wrote them for himself and his friends; and just as there was a class of educated men in eighteenth century England, like Pennant, who loved authorship and print, so there was another class who, if they could not refrain from writing, regarded print in their own cases as being not quite gentlemanly. To this class Banks possibly, though not probably, belonged. The truth seems to be simply that he did not have a literary mind. He shared with such men, however, one characteristic. They could be generous with information. They would make 'communications'. He handed his *Endeavour* manuscript entire to Hawkesworth, who was getting £6000 out of his editing of sailors' journals; he communicated his observations on the island of Staffa to Pennant to incorporate in the *Tour in Scotland*. He did give a reason for that. Pennant, he argued to Falconer, the friend of both, had as a traveller a prior right to the Western Islands: 'I while in that Countrey Lookd for him with assiduity conceiving myself as no more than a poacher who might get leave of the Lord to shoot upon the mannor but in return owd at least the offer of whatever he might Kill'.[1] His scientific papers are mostly little communications, such as any polite dabbler might produce, to the *Transactions* of the Linnean Society and the Horticultural Society.

The question still remains why the scientific work of the great voyage was not completed; for completion meant publication. Banks might possibly have another answer: that he did not need to publish, because anyone competent to profit from the collections or from Solander's work could come and use the herbarium and the library. What serious student had he ever turned away? Was not 32 Soho Square a sort of Mecca to which every pilgrim was welcomed — and where, on Thursdays, he would get breakfast as well? This would have been an inadequate answer, because it is only the minority of men who can go on pilgrimages, and there were a great many natural historians all over Europe to whom Soho Square was as unattainable as Mecca itself. One is compelled, rather to one's surprise, rather against one's will, to the conviction

---

[1] Banks to Falconer, 2 April 1773, Hawley coll. Pennant, in his dedicatory epistle to Banks, was equally polite: 'You took from me all temptation of envying your superior good fortune, by the liberal declaration you made that the Hebrides were my ground, and yourself, as you pleasantly expressed it, but an interloper. May I meet with such, in all my adventures!' After such courtesies, the modern student derives a minor but undeniable pleasure from the use, in the British Museum, of Banks's own copy of the work, with Pennant's fly-leaf inscription 'From the Author', and Banks's name-stamp, the facsimile of his signature.

that Banks did not publish because he had lost interest. He had lost interest because of the very nature of his mind; and his mind was never, in relation to science, truly 'professional'. He was a Gentleman, and an Amateur. With all his collecting journeys and all his collections, all his patronage of men of science,[1] all his final vast prestige, he remained (in the eighteenth century sense) a dilettante. One might almost unsay some of the things already said, and hold that he had never been educated. One implies here, it is true, that education entails a real discipline of the mind, a devotion to 'professional' as exalted from 'amateur' standards of intellectual activity. Banks — it was the logic of his birth and wealth, his perfect ability to dispose of himself as he liked, the logic even of his time in history as well as of his place in society — remained the gentleman-amateur. If he had had the mind of Priestley, if he had been a first-rate genius like Cavendish, if he had had the singleness of character of Linnaeus, he would have been a greater man — although a much less representative man. But of course, at running the Royal Society — again at that time in history, when no violent reform in constitution or administration was called for — he was to be superb. His talent was a managing talent. We can see exactly why Sir Humphry Davy summed up his predecessor in the chair as he did: 'He was a good-humoured and liberal man, free and various in conversational power, a tolerable botanist, and generally acquainted with natural history. He had not much reading,[2] and no profound information. He was always ready to promote the objects of men of science; but he required to be regarded as a patron, and readily swallowed gross flattery. When he gave anecdotes of his voyages he was very entertaining and unaffected. A courtier in character, he was a warm friend to a good King. In his relations to the Royal Society he was too personal, and made his house a circle too like a court'. For Davy came from a quite different stratum of society, Davy was all con-

[1] We get a hitherto unnoted illustration of this, just as Banks was moving into his maturity, in a letter from Anders Sparrman, who had been employed by the elder Forster as an assistant on Cook's second voyage, to George Forster, 25 July 1777: 'As for Mr. Banks and Dr. Solander please to remember me to them in the best terms; I am very much obliged to the Former for his kind offer of 60L. a year, but it is too small a salary for me to subsist on in England, besides I do not know all that I should have to do. Please to excuse me in the best terms.'—*Johann Georg Forsters Briefwechsel* . . . (Leipzig 1829), II, p. 705.
[2] Why, then, the great Banks library, Dryander's catalogue alone of which ran to five octavo volumes and 2464 pages? Simply because it was a scientific library exclusively, a *Bibliotheca historico-naturalis*. The catalogue appeared between 1796 and 1800.—Banks had certainly read Ossian, as we have seen, and Johnson's *Tour to the Hebrides*.

centration, a laboratory man, Davy belonged to — was the maker of — a new age.[1]

Banks, we may conclude, had not the instinct of thoroughness. It was one matter to keep a journal, and to dash down in it at high speed the glowing, the exciting, the intoxicating things that happened. To punctuate it was another matter. It would have been another thing altogether to brood over the shape of sentences and the sound of words, to make them answer exactly to the least nuance of experience and thought. But, one might plead, on board the *Endeavour*, or on the beach at Matavai Bay, experience was not taken in nuances; and when Banks does set out to punctuate one wishes he had not. Are we to make our criterion a literary one? It may be argued that at times he was thorough, more thorough than Cook, as when he raced about measuring canoes, or sketched a pattern of Polynesian weaving, or — even — collected together so many artists and servants for the second voyage that no plant would be undrawn, no stone remain ungathered. In the South Seas, however, from the very nature of voyaging, he was limited, there was little choice of activities; his services and his notes were so valuable because they could not wander. We may contrast him with Cook, whom he so admirably complemented. Cook was a dedicated man. Banks was — one searches for a phrase — a rich and extremely intelligent young man let loose on life. Once again it is the contrast between the professional and the amateur. The pages of our journal therefore are a by-product, which is the secret of their unforced, unlaboured charm. Let the devoted Sarah Sophia then make a fair copy, leaving out the hard Latin names; by all means let Phipps have another copy. But do not revise. But do not think of them as an end in themselves. It is their spontaneity that is so captivating for the unprofessional reader. The professional reader, the ethnologist, the natural historian,

---

[1] Davy's remarks are in the *Memoirs of the Life of Sir Humphry Davy, Bart.*, by his brother, John Davy (1836), II, pp. 126-7. Banks was defended against some of them by his warm admirer Sir John Barrow, who thought that the phrases, 'a tolerable botanist', 'a lover of gross flattery', 'a house like a court' were 'unfounded and unjust'.—*Sketches of the Royal Society and the Royal Society Club* (1849), p. 40. No one can go through the Banks correspondence without seeing that he was subjected to gross flattery, and apparently had no difficulty in swallowing it; but whether it made any difference to his constitution, in his later life, is a different matter. He certainly preferred to be addressed with due respect and could adopt a lofty tone, but with certain of his difficult and complaining correspondents—e.g. Caley—he exhibited a remarkable forbearance. He was never affected again, so far as one can see, as he had been after the return of the *Endeavour*. James Britten, after careful study, thought it was clear that Banks 'had much more botanical knowledge than was at one time supposed'.—Introduction to *Illustrations of the Botany of Captain Cook's Voyage round the World*, Part III, 1904, last page (this introduction is unpaginated).

drinks greedily, and deplores the fate that defrauded him of more, of Banks's second voyage. Enough has been said perhaps on that subject to render otiose any further discussion on its relevance to thoroughness of mind. French horns could not have found a southern continent, or contributed appreciably to the natural history of Polynesia.

For Banks, indeed, there was so much that he could do, so much that he wanted to do. We may study his later life in the light of his early life, but the reverse process is also useful. He was able, he was interested, he was active, he was not introspective; he was cheerful, he was generous; his activities are so very difficult to summarize, his life so difficult to write, simply because of the extraordinary number of things he found to do, or that were found for him to do. There were the botanical tours, the objects of archaeological curiosity, the fishing-parties with the Ladies of Pleasure. There were the 'Plays, Operas, Concerts, masquerades &c.' to which he was so ardently devoted, 'till prevented by infirmities';[1] we may indeed perhaps picture him, a member of that tuneful circle that had its surprising moments, in attendance on some of those Christmas oratorios at Hinchingbrooke when Miss Ray sang and Sandwich played the kettle-drums.[2] There was Soho Square, there was Revesby Abbey, there was soon a third house, Spring Grove at Heston, and later a fourth, Overton in Derbyshire, inherited from Joseph's uncle, Robert Banks Hodgkinson. There were the natural historians, the Royal Society, the dining clubs, there were the British Museum and the Board of Longitude, the draining of the fens, the service as Recorder of Lincoln and sheriff of the county, the crumbling fabric of Lincoln Cathedral, the Royal Mint and the colonial coinage, the King's merino sheep, the botanical collectors, the transference of the bread-fruit to the West Indies — the list is by no means complete; there was Kew, there was the foundation of the settlement of New South Wales; there was Flinders; there were the tribulations of Governor Bligh, and Mr Caley's dog and the Rev. Samuel Marsden's rabbits. Lady Banks (the baronetcy came in 1781) was a little old china mad: that had to be attended to. There were foreign scientific societies. There were scientists and scientific collections to be looked after during the war. There were the misfortunes of Iceland. There were Cook's surviving relatives in Yorkshire — his sister Mrs Fleck

[1] The quoted phrases are from Banks's letter to Henry Greville [June 1807], B.M. Add. MS 33981, already quoted, p. 121 above.
[2] Joseph Cradock, *Literary and Miscellaneous Memoirs* (1828), I, p. 117.

who was addicted to inebriety, and her son James who was reduced through misfortune to selling his trading vessel. There was more than enough for an able and interested and generous man to attend to. Under the impact of all this, a man whose sole devotion was science, a man whose life was lonely thought, would have gone insane. Joseph Banks did not go insane. He showed now and again that he was displeased, never that he was disturbed. He had found his multifarious calling, and he pursued it, on the whole, with triumphant success. His rôle was to be not an original genius, but a sort of director of scientific and industrial research. In a later day he would have been, in that department, a magnificent civil servant. Was he then born too soon? Clearly, no; for the management of men, the organization of useful enterprises, does not belong exclusively to one age. We may add yet again to the characterizations of his century; we may speak of the Age of Banks. Or, simply, we may reflect that in his character, in his activities, in his good fortune, in his shortcomings, in his accomplishments, Joseph Banks was eminently of his age.

TEXTUAL INTRODUCTION

THE editor of Banks's *Endeavour* journal is confronted with few textual problems. The history of the original manuscript,[1] however, and of the MS copies — of which there are five — is interesting. It has also been much misunderstood. It is bound up with the history of Banks's will, or rather of the testamentary dispositions which he made thereby, not very many months before he died. He died childless, 20 June 1820. His will, dated 7 January 1820, was necessarily long and complicated.[2] The bulk of his property, real estate, was left to his wife for life, and thereafter to three principal legatees, who were also executors; of these the most important in our history was Sir Edward Knatchbull (1781-1849), the nephew of Lady Banks, whose sister Mary had married Sir Edward Knatchbull, Bart., of Mersham Hatch, Kent. It is not the main will that is important to us, however, but the codicils, of which there were two. The first of these, dated 21 January 1820, made provision for Robert Brown (1773-1858), the great botanist and the last of Banks's librarians, and for other persons, and secured certain financial arrangements. Brown, 'my indefatigable and intelligent librarian', was left an annuity of £200. The codicil went on,

I also give to the said Robert Brown the use and enjoyment during his life of my library herbarium manuscripts drawings copperplates engraved and every thing else that is contained in my collections usually kept in the back buildings of my house in . . . Soho Square . . . and after his decease then I give and bequeath the same to the Trustees for the time being of the British Museum;

[1] In the brief history of the Banks papers that follows, I owe a good deal to a typescript memorandum on the 'History of the Papers of Sir Joseph Banks' prepared by Miss Phyllis Mander Jones, when Mitchell Librarian; to an interesting paper by Mr Warren R. Dawson, on 'Sir Joseph Hooker and Dawson Turner', in the *Journal of the Society for the Bibliography of Natural History*, II, pt. 6 (1950), pp. 218-22; and to an interchange of information and opinions with Mr Dawson, most valuable to me. The preface to Sir Joseph Hooker's edition of Banks's journal is not very useful, except as a stimulant to contradiction and further research; as Mr Dawson has shown, Hooker's own statements are exceedingly unreliable. I have made new investigations, and the interpretations and conclusions finally adopted are my own. For permission to use and quote from correspondence in the records of the Department of Manuscripts of the British Museum I am deeply indebted to the Department; and for help in exploring those records, to Mr T. J. Brown.

[2] P.C.C. 510 Kent.

but if the Trustees wished and Brown consented these collections might be removed to the Museum during Brown's life-time, satisfactory access to them being allowed for him and his friends. Certain agreeable duties were laid down for Brown in return, entailing the continuance of his life of scientific scholarship. The Soho Square house itself was left to Lady Banks for life or as long as she required it, with provision for Brown's residence, and there-after to Brown under the same conditions of duty fulfilled. Lady Banks preferred to reside in Portland Place, where she died in 1828. Brown, therefore, a bachelor, had the whole of No. 32, Soho Square to himself: a problem which he solved by letting the front portion to the Linnean Society in 1821, keeping the 'back buildings', fronting on Dean Street, for his own residence and working purposes.

In 1827 Brown became the first keeper of the Botanical Department of the British Museum, officially entitled Keeper of the Banksian Botanical Collections. This was possible because he and the Trustees had agreed on the application of the alternative clause of the codicil to Banks's will, whereby the library, the herbarium, the drawings, the copperplates, and certain manuscripts — those manuscripts actually in the library — went to the Museum during Brown's life-time. This was admirable. Did it ensure the safety of the *Endeavour* journal? No; because the *Endeavour* journal, like the bulk of the MSS in Banks's possession when he died, was not actually in the library, and did not come directly under the provisions of that part of the will at all. It would have been a great deal better if they had done so; but Banks, with the best intentions in the world, had taken a false step. His papers were multifarious, and he had concluded that further provision was necessary for them; but he had made a ruinously bad choice of a person to execute his wishes. Attempts to understand the history of the journal, among other MSS, in the light of the codicil of 21 January, have been baffled because it can be understood only in the light of the second codicil, of 7 March 1820. This second, and vital, codicil began by bequeathing the botanical drawings of Banks's draughtsman Francis Bauer to the king, in the hope that Bauer would be taken on to the staff at Kew as the first holder of a permanent position there, failing which his annuity under Codicil I was to be maintained. That clause is typical Banks, though for our purposes it is irrelevant. The relevant portion is as follows:

And it is my will and desire that my dear relative Sir Edward Knatchbull Baronet be requested to look over all my boxes of papers and other things deposited in my room and the passage room next to it in my house in Soho Square and that he do burn all papers in my hand writing except such as have reference to any part of my estate or to the County of Lincoln and that he do deliver all such other written or printed papers as shall be found in any of them to the persons to whom he thinks they will be most acceptable the papers respecting the Royal Society and the affairs thereof to the Royal Society those respecting the Mint or Coinage to the Mint and that all papers and letters relative to the County of Lincoln be sent to Revesby Abbey and be deposited in the evidence room there my foreign correspondence bound and unbound to be sent to the British Museum and all the other things in the said rooms to be disposed of as the said Sir Edward Knatchbull shall think best.

Now Codicil I had made over to Robert Brown everything in the 'collections usually kept in the back buildings' of the house. Banks's 'room and the passage room next to it' were, it seems certain, part of these 'back buildings', much more closely allied to the library and the herbarium than to the rooms on the Soho Square side where he had his famous philosophical breakfasts and evening parties. The two codicils therefore cut across each other, and one can imagine a pretty set of legal arguments if there had ever been a lawsuit; unless, as in the case of legislation, the particular — i.e. Codicil II — took precedence of the general — i.e. Codicil I. One would have thought, indeed, that a good executor, faced with the will as a whole, would have considered its general as well as particular provisions, and that having duly burnt and distributed according to the desire of Codicil II he might in due course have made over the residuum of the 'boxes of papers and other things' as part of the 'collections', if not to Brown — who could hardly have cared about them — then to the British Museum; for the Museum was an institution with which Banks, an able and highly regarded Trustee,[1] had been long and intimately associated, and as we have seen, he had already designated it as his ultimate legatee.

Sir Edward Knatchbull, so far as this second codicil was concerned, was not a good executor. He was a ruinously bad choice because he was negligent; and not negligent in any ordinary degree, but to the point of complete irresponsibility. What he burnt we do not know; perhaps we should be thankful that he did not burn much. Perhaps he burnt nothing; for large items, as well as very many inconsiderable scraps in Banks's handwriting, have by devious routes come down to us, and now lie in widely disparate repositories.

[1] His portrait by Lawrence still hangs in the Trustees' Room, the only portrait of a Trustee which does.

He delivered to the Royal Society practically nothing, to the Mint nothing at all. He did, in 1828, hand over to the Museum the bound, but not the unbound foreign correspondence — a burst of activity it is hard to account for, unless his memory was somehow jogged by the arrangement between Brown and the Trustees in 1827, or possibly by Lady Banks's death in 1828. But the total effect was that the person to whom he thought (if he thought at all) the great bulk of the papers would be most acceptable was Sir Edward Knatchbull. If he thought at all: for though the boxes certainly went to his house, he may hardly even have looked at them. We have to make the assumption that though the provisions of the will and its codicils were public property (for their gist had appeared in the newspapers)[1] no public body concerned thought fit to make any claim, and that there was general content that the ownership of all those boxes of papers should rest with Knatchbull.

Where then was the *Endeavour* journal? Let us repeat: if it had been in the library it must surely have come to the British Museum with the library in 1827. The library came under Codicil I. But, it has already been said, the *Endeavour* journal did not come under that codicil: the hypothesis, that is, is irresistible that it was in one of the boxes in Banks's room or 'the passage room next to it'. As it was in Banks's handwriting, should it then have been burnt? Apparently so — absurd as the conclusion may seem; but like so much else, it survived. We know it was in Knatchbull's possession, together with a copy of it made by Sarah Sophia Banks, which is still in the possession of Knatchbull's family; because when it first comes into our view, after its use by Dr John Hawkesworth in 1771 and 1772, it is in connection with the biography of Banks that a number of his admirers were anxious to have written.

It had been hoped that Robert Brown would write Banks's life. Brown, however, was a scientific man, without the slightest interest in the writing of biographies; nor, even had he been interested, would he have been particularly fitted for the task. In 1830 Brown himself proposed to Dawson Turner, the Yarmouth banker, botanist, and collector of books and MSS, that Turner should carry it out. An able man, a practised writer, Turner had a mind that ranged widely; he already had, as a collector, transcripts of Banks's minor journals; Knatchbull agreed to make all the papers in his possession available; and in 1832 Turner consented. A great heap of correspondence, mainly letters of all kinds to Banks, was at once sent to him;

---

[1] e.g., in the unnamed newspaper a cutting from which is included in B.M. Add. MS 6673 (Derbyshire Collections), p. 106a.

he set to work sorting and arranging them, and set his daughters
and clerks to work making copies. As sorting and arrangement was
necessary, the papers must have included other material besides
the letters carefully classified and numbered by Banks himself
or under his direction — unless the Turner arrangement was —
as it seems it may have been — exclusively chronological; or unless
Knatchbull did indeed 'look over' the contents of the boxes, and
bring confusion into them. Turner needed the journal; he got it
from Knatchbull in the latter part of 1834 and had that copied
also. In 1839 he informed Brown that he intended to spend a
month in London to obtain the materials he still needed to complete
the task. But the life of Banks was not to be written thus, and after
having the papers in his hands for twelve years, spending £200
and a good deal of his leisure on them, Turner gave in; in 1844
or 1845 he returned everything to Knatchbull, originals together
with twenty-three indexed and bound volumes of copies, starting
with the journal. Knatchbull died in 1849, in which year the eldest
son of his second marriage, still another Edward (1829-93),
assumed the additional surname of Hugessen.

Edward Knatchbull-Hugessen's main distinction, except for
one thing, was that Jane Austen was his great-aunt. The exception
was his dealings with the Banks papers. From 1857 to 1880 he was a
politician, holding minor office under both Palmerston and Glad-
stone; in 1880, however, he was given a peerage instead of another
undersecretaryship, and changed his political views. As Lord
Brabourne, a man of letters, he pursued a new career, writing a
series of fairy-stories for children that had some success. Like his
father, he did not, it appears, have much sense of responsibility
towards historical records, although it is true that he collected books
on county history. In the context of that sentence, one further
observation may be made, preliminary to the rest of our story. It
has been a habit of those who have mourned over the fate of Banks's
collections to bestow blame unequivocally upon Brabourne; and
with blame a vast amount of indignation. It is now, however,
clear that, whatever disapproval is levelled at Brabourne, the blame
and indignation must be more widely spread. He did not play a
very happy part; but at least it may be said for him that the part
he did play was rendered less unnatural by the antecedent behaviour
of Sir Edward Knatchbull. When the crisis came, furthermore,
there was no very laudable behaviour elsewhere.

After Knatchbull's death the commonly recognized owner of
the papers was Lady Knatchbull, his widow. There were still hopes

of somehow obtaining a biographer, and a series of gentlemen glanced at the material and recoiled. While the search was going on, recourse was again had to the British Museum, and our next definite point is a memorandum dated 25 June 1861 and signed by Joseph Ball, among the records of the Department of Manuscripts: 'The papers contained in this box and in a smaller case kept herewith were this day received by me from Thomas Bell Esq[r] late President of the Linnean Society who had received them from the Dowager Lady Knatchbull. It is her wish that after the papers and correspondence of Sir Joseph Banks leave my hands they should be deposited in the British Museum'.[1] According to William Carruthers, later Keeper of the Botanical Department, they were on Lady Knatchbull's death to become the property of the Trustees. Carruthers is our only authority for this, but the story is at least not improbable. The papers went from Ball to Carruthers in the Botanical Department, for in October 1873 Carruthers was instructed to place them in the Department of Manuscripts; then at the beginning of 1876 he was allowed to take away again the twenty-three volumes of the Dawson Turner transcripts for the use of yet another potential biographer, the young Daydon Jackson.[2] These, owing to some fortunate lapse in administration, were not returned, and are still in the library of the Botanical Department.

Lady Knatchbull died, in her ninetieth year, at the end of 1882, and it might seem that the safety of the papers would now be assured, in an agreed and permanent resting-place. This was not so, because by 1882 they were not in the Museum at all, but at Lord Brabourne's house in Queen Anne's Gate. How did Brabourne come to have them? It has been freely stated[3] that he demanded the papers from the Librarian of the British Museum as his personal property, was met by expostulation, replied with insistence, and carried off everything in a 'box' to put it up for auction: that, to put it brutally, he was guilty of a sort of large-scale bare-faced daylight robbery. The truth is more complicated. We are impeded in our search for it by the fact that the Department of Manuscripts did not keep copies of outgoing correspondence. The Keeper's incoming letters were, however, preserved; and from these a part, at least, of the story emerges with some definiteness. They do not

---

[1] B.M. Dept. of MSS, Miscellaneous Letters and Papers. Joseph Ball, F.R.S. and Thomas Bell, F.R.S. were both looked on as possible biographers.

[2] Carruthers's statements, some of them highly inaccurate, were made to Sir Joseph Hooker, in a letter of 14 July 1893, printed in Hooker's edition of the Journal, pp. x-xi.

[3] e.g., by Carruthers, ibid., p. xi. Carruthers, writing in 1893, puts the incidents 'Some seven or eight years ago'.

25 After having waited in this place ten days; the
ship, & every thing belonging to me, being all that
time in perfect readyness to sail at a moments
warning; we at last got a fair wind, & this day
at 3 OClock in the even weigh'd anchor, & set
sail, all in Excellent health & spirits,
perfectly prepar'd (in mind at least) to undergo
with Cheerfullness any fatigues or dangers that
may occur in our intended Voyage.

6 Wind still fair, but very light breezes, saw
this even a shoal of those fish which are
particularly calld Porpoises by the seamen,
probably the Delphinus Phocæna of Linnæus, as
their noses are very blunt.

7 Wind fair & a fine Breeze; found the ship to be
but a heavy sailer, indeed Probably the
we could not expect her to be any other from
her built, so are oblig'd to set down with this
Inconvenience, as a necessary consequence
of her form; which is much more calculated
for stowage, than for sailing.

8 little wind today, in some sea water which
was taken on board to season a cask, observed
a very minute sea Insect, which Dr Solander
described by the name of Podura marina.
In the Evening very calm, with the smell

show the Librarian — i.e. the Principal Librarian, E. A. (later Sir Edward) Bond — to have been engaged at all, though discussions by word of mouth may have been carried on; nor is there any record at all of the Trustees having been consulted. The Museum official concerned was the Keeper of the Department of Manuscripts, E. (later Sir Edward) Maunde Thompson; and Maunde Thompson, a celebrated palaeographer, was certainly less interested in memorials of the eighteenth and early nineteenth centuries than we in our day are. Nor, it seems, could he have been acquainted with the terms of Banks's will. Sixty years after Banks's death, indeed, nobody seems to have been acquainted with the terms of his will. In May 1880 Edward (later Lord) Stanhope, another possible biographer, wished to search the papers, and Maunde Thompson must have consulted the man he regarded as their owner; for a letter from Knatchbull-Hugessen (he did not complete his peerage formalities till later on in the year) signifies his agreement: 'I have seen Mr Stanhope to-day and shall be quite willing that the MSS of Sir Joseph Banks shall be entrusted to his custody until he has been able to make such search amongst them as he desires. Probably the result of Mr Stanhope's examination may determine the future destination of these papers, with the exact nature of which I am at present unacquainted'.[1] Stanhope gave a receipt for four parcels of papers on 22 May, which he subsequently endorsed, 2 July 1880, as 'Transferred to Lord Brabourne, 3 Queen Anne's Gate'. He took another '14 Boxes of Miscellaneous Papers' on 7 July.[2] These fourteen boxes he also transferred to Brabourne, adding to his note giving this information the postcript, 'I have ventured to recommend to Lord Brabourne handing over at once to the Museum all the scientific correspondence. Some of the more private correspondence and his journals appear to be rather for his relatives'.[3]

There for eighteen months the matter rested,[4] until in February 1884 Brabourne took it up again, as if it were something entirely new. 'I have here', he wrote to Maunde Thompson, 'a quantity of papers and letters inherited from the late Sir Joseph Banks — he and my grandfather having married sisters. Amongst them are Sir Joseph's journal of his voyage to Newfoundland &c and many

---

[1] Knatchbull-Hugessen to Maunde Thompson, 21 May 1880; Dept. of MSS. Misc. Letters and Papers.
[2] ibid.
[3] Stanhope to Maunde Thompson, 12 July [1880], ibid.
[4] Though Brabourne had a sale of books, drawings, and MSS relating to Lincolnshire at Sotheby's as early as 15 June 1880.

L

letters from scientific people and other papers of interest. I had an
idea of putting these up to auction but after a conversation with
Mr Stanhope who has looked through them all, I have come to the
conclusion that it would be right in the first instance to offer them
to the British Museum, which has already many papers and other
things from Sir Joseph Banks'. He invited the Keeper therefore
to come and inspect the papers, and judge the advisability of
purchasing them.[1] Stanhope's recommendation of 1880 had not,
evidently, met with favour. The next letter, in March, argues that
Maunde Thompson had seen Brabourne, and got the papers back
to the Museum for examination. Brabourne regrets he cannot
himself examine them (he had been ordered abroad to convalesce
from bronchitis). 'This, however, is of the less consequence, as I
have not the remotest notion of the value of such things — whether
they are worth £100 or £1000 or £2000. All I know is that there
are *some* of them which would fetch money at Sotheby's or elsewhere
as Mss of Sir J. Banks, and some which might be acceptable perhaps
to certain colonies or to India. There are I think several volumes
of the Journal. . . .' Perhaps indeed Brabourne's friend Mr A. H.
Todd of the Temple could go through the papers with the Keeper,
and either settle the matter or 'put it in a train of speedy settlement'.[2]
Mr Todd duly called at the Museum, and now a fresh possibility
was raised. Mr Bentley the publisher was considering the desirability
of publishing some of the journals, and that would affect the price
to be paid.[3] Mr Todd then gave his opinion. Acknowledging a
letter from the Keeper, he put the value of the papers at 'between
£250 and £300, to be reduced or increased by the permission or the
refusal of the purchaser to allow publication of the journals and
narratives. There is a certain amount of interesting matter that
might be turned to advantage in the latter documents, among
the letters there are a great number of interest and value'.[4] This
was not to show an excess of enthusiasm, but indeed no great
enthusiasm was being shown anywhere. At least one can say for
Lord Brabourne that he knew what he wanted. He wanted £250.
So far as the concrete evidence takes us, there is nothing to show
that either he or Maunde Thompson was aware that they were
negotiating for the purchase by the Museum of what was — it
can be reasonably argued — already the Museum's property.

[1] Brabourne to Maunde Thompson, 22 February 1884, ibid.
[2] Brabourne to Maunde Thompson, 10 March 1884; Papers Relating to the Purchase
and Acquisition of Manuscripts.
[3] Brabourne to Maunde Thompson, 14 March 1884, ibid.
[4] Todd to Maunde Thompson, 24 March 1884, ibid.

The Keeper seems to have made an offer. Our last letter is again from Todd. 'I have heard from Lord Brabourne', he writes on 18 April. 'He desires me to say that as Sir Joseph, Lady and Miss Banks gave papers coins medals and curiosities of very great value and interest to the British Museum, and as the papers you have now under consideration will complete that collection, he does not consider that £250 is a large sum for him to ask as the price of such of the papers as you may require. He is anxious however not to enter into any correspondence or to bargain about the matter, and therefore if the British Museum authorities decline to give that sum, he will be much obliged to you if you could return all the books and documents to Queen Anne's Gate in order that they may be sold by auction or dispersed among Local and Colonial Museums or otherwise disposed of, as his Lordship may deem advisable. He desires me further to ask that you will kindly decide as soon as possible as to the course you will take'.[1] Lord Brabourne was a little peremptory, and it did not do to be peremptory with Maunde Thompson. The communication is endorsed, 'Declined Papers sent back 22 Apr 84'. Thus did the British Museum, for the time being, relinquish interest in one of the greatest of its benefactors and Trustees.

The plundering process now began. It was 'the colonies' that were to have first turn. Before the fatal year 1884 was out Sir Saul Samuel, the agent in London for New South Wales, acting on behalf of his Government, bought from Brabourne for £375 a large and miscellaneous collection of papers relating mainly to Australia. They were, wrote Samuel later to Sir Joseph Hooker, bought 'on the understanding, in writing, that if [Lord Brabourne] discovered any more papers relating to the same subject he would send them to me, for the colony, without further payment'.[2] The *Endeavour* journal was not included in the purchase, which did at least put a great number of important papers into responsible ownership (they are now in the Mitchell Library, bound in twenty-two volumes as the 'Brabourne Papers'). Encouraged, Brabourne proceeded to put up a further section of the papers for auction at Sotheby's on 11 March 1886, and then a very large collection on the following 14 April. Samuel was sent a catalogue of this last sale — 'amongst which', he continued in his letter to Hooker, 'were papers relating to New South Wales, which I considered were

[1] Todd to Maunde Thompson, 18 April 1884; Papers Relating to the Purchase and Acquisition of Manuscripts.

[2] Samuel to Sir Joseph Hooker, n.d., published by Hooker in the *Athenaeum*, 24 April 1897, pp. 547-8.

included in my purchase. I thereupon wrote to Lord Brabourne, requesting him to cause the documents to be withdrawn from sale and handed over to me for my Government. Receiving no reply, I subsequently wrote to Messrs Sotheby, Wilkinson and Co. protesting against the sale of the papers, and claiming them as the property of the Government of New South Wales. The papers were withdrawn at the time.' But they were not handed over. 'What became of them I never heard, except that when I was in Auckland, New Zealand, in 1888, I visited the Public Library in that city, and saw a number of the papers which I believe had been withdrawn from the sale to which I have referred. I was informed that these papers had been presented to the Auckland Library by Sir George Grey, by whose agent they had been purchased in London'. There is here, however, evidence of poor memory on the part of his informant, or of misinformation: the Auckland or Grey MSS had not been bought by Grey's agent in London, nor had they been withdrawn from the sale; they were bought there with other papers (perhaps by the dealer John Waller, who bought largely), sold to J. D. Enys of Canterbury,[1] and sold by him to Grey, apparently in 1888. They were bought at the sale at a very low price; for the weakness in Brabourne's plan for continued profit now appeared. People had ceased to be interested in Sir Joseph Banks, his doings, and his friends. The 207 lots put up realized a derisory sum — various attempts at addition were made, £178 5s, £180 5s, £182 19s; twenty-six lots went at 2s each, fourteen at 1s. The Museum acquired a few important ones: for example, the Blagden correspondence and the letters to Sir William Hamilton; but it let go all too much.[2] A few collectors got bargains. Large bundles were taken by autograph dealers, to be broken up and re-sold where signatures were well-known and fashionable; where they were not, to be destroyed or lie around collecting dust in the back rooms or cellars of shops. Individual letters and bundles of letters, stray memoranda and notes, drifted about the market for years — a few are still drifting — sometimes acquired by pious botanists from dealers for whom they were simply a deadweight, and added to the papers at Kew;

[1] Canterbury province in New Zealand, where Enys was a well-known sheep-farmer. He retired in 1890 to the family seat in Cornwall, whence other Banks papers have lately come. Cf. p. 145 below.

[2] 'In 1891 I presented to the British Museum, *nine hundred and sixty eight* letters, a portion *only* of a large mass of the Banks Correspondence which I purchased of John Waller the Auto: Dealer for the sum of £10. 10s. !!! '—Spencer G. Perceval to James Britten, 28 May 1899, a letter attached inside a copy of Perceval's printing of Banks's journal of his Bristol journey, in the Botanical Library, B.M. (N.H.). 'The whole transaction was an outrage on the memory of Banks!' Perceval remarks in another note to Britten, 30 May 1899, ibid.

sometimes, as the years went on, sold at prices that would have lifted the heart of the first Lord Brabourne, could he have been the recipient. It was not the whole that was sacrificed in 1886. By 1928, when another large amount came on the market, the returns were much more satisfactory. Thus was one of the greatest collections of records for the history of science and the social life of the intellect ever assembled, a collection fundamental for our knowledge of certain aspects of the eighteenth century, flung away and dissipated all over the earth. What was utterly destroyed in the process it is impossible to say. But the student of Banks and of Banks's time who wishes to master his subject will find the Dawson Turner transcripts at South Kensington only a beginning; his material now lies in private hands and public collections, uncoordinated and largely uncatalogued, in London and a dozen other parts of England, in Sydney, in Adelaide, in Canberra, in Auckland, in Wellington, in New Haven, in San Francisco, in Toronto — we do not know where else. It is a melancholy end to Banks's sixty years of systematic preservation and classification. Certainly it would be a great deal more melancholy if such an enormous mass of material did not in fact exist, wide-spread as it is.[1]

Among the few lots at the Brabourne sale which fetched a sum reckoned in pounds and not shillings was Lot 176. This was described as 'Banks's (Sir Joseph) Journal of a Voyage to the Sandwich Islands and New Zealand from March 1769 to July 1771, in the autograph of Banks'. Waller gave £7 2s 6d for it. The description was a fantastic one, whatever the journal was. The dates do not correspond with those of any MS of Banks we now have, or that ever, so far as we know, existed. The original journal runs from 25 August 1768 to 12 July 1771. A fragmentary 'journal' in Banks's handwriting (Grey MSS 51-2: see below p. 146) runs from 7 October 1769 to 10 October 1770, and from 26 October 1770 to 9 July 1771. Carruthers told Hooker that Waller did not specially remember the purchase. If Waller had bought the two bound volumes of the original he could not but remember it: they were a solid fact which would stick in a dealer's memory even if he had sold them next day. Let us assume, however, that part of the Grey MSS, the so-called 'journal', was correctly described so far as its beginning date was concerned (for the gap between 10 October and 26 October

<hr />

[1] I do not go into detail on the dispersal of the Banks papers, apart from the *Endeavour* journal. The interested person may turn to Mr Warren Dawson's list of sources in his calendar of *The Banks Letters*, published by the British Museum (Natural History) in 1958. This calendar includes only those letters in collections in Great Britain—something over 7000. Mr Dawson estimates the total as 50,000, or even more.

1770, the early days at Batavia, is of no significance, as will be seen from the note on the MSS below). Then it would be quite possible that Waller, when going over his heap of purchases, mislaid and destroyed the early pages of a MS that may even have been imperfect before. What he sold a little later, then, would be not quite what he had bought. This, at any rate, we may adopt as a provisional hypothesis, and we may conclude that the original journal did not come up at the sale, but that the Grey MSS did, and were there sold.

What then of the original? We know that Sir Edward Knatchbull had it, that he lent it to Dawson Turner in 1834, that Dawson Turner gave it back, at latest, in 1845. It then sinks from sight till we find it in the early nineties in the hands of [Sir] J. Henniker Heaton, M.P. In a letter from Francis Edwards the bookseller, to Alfred Lee the Australian collector, 4 May 1894,[1] Edwards says, 'I have just been told in confidence that it is the original, in Banks's handwriting, with information as to its history and former possessors'. Why there should be any necessity for confidence it is hard to guess. Brabourne had died in 1893, but there may have been someone concerned in some anterior transaction who had a sense of shame. We are left to infer that Henniker Heaton bought the journal from Brabourne privately — we do not know when — or from somebody else who had acquired it from Brabourne. The story after this point becomes plain. From Henniker Heaton it passed in 1894 to Alfred Lee, and from Lee, with the rest of his collection (including other invaluable Banks material) in 1906 to David Scott Mitchell. In the Mitchell Library it remains. Inside the front cover of the first volume is an MS note by Sir Edward Knatchbull that it was 'lent to Mr. Brown, March 26 1833' (the two final figures are not however very clear). A similar note in the second volume is defective through trimming of the paper. Each volume contains Alfred Lee's bookplate. Apart from such external evidence, there is no doubt about this being the original MS, composed on board the *Endeavour*. It is in the handwriting of Banks as a young man, and every page bears the idiosyncrasies of his written expression. The deletions and substitutions, the characteristic and consistent misspellings, the experiments with the renderings of Polynesian names, the alteration of present tenses to past, the mis-numbering of pages, the incorporation of separate lists and memoranda, not always as a part of the composition, but bound into the volumes at a convenient place — all these are obvious and overwhelming arguments, if

[1] Mitchell MS 1808.

argument is necessary, for the authenticity of this journal as Banks's original work. This it is that is here edited and printed.

§

The journal is contained in two leather-bound quarto volumes, of page-size $9\frac{1}{8}$ x $7\frac{1}{4}$ in. (23.2 x 18 cm.). Apparently Banks made up the pages himself by taking larger sheets, folding them in half, and then folding them again transversely, so producing a set of four leaves. He then sometimes placed other leaves inside these, giving himself sections of from four to sixteen leaves. So at least the volumes as bound seem to imply, with watermarks often occurring on four or more consecutive leaves, or with a succession of leaves lacking any watermark at all. He then gave himself a guide to both inner and outer margins by further folding.[1] Volume I comprises the period 25 August 1768-14 August 1769, pp. 1-332, followed by the description of 'Manners and Customs of the South Sea Islands', pp. 333-437, with three blank leaves at the end. Banks occasionally slipped in his numbering: p. 33 is repeated; 220 is numbered 120; pp. 242-366 were first numbered 142-266 and then corrected, while there is no 391 or 393 at all; and so on. After writing a number of pages — how many it is impossible to say — he added 'running-heads', generally of geographical names, which he very rarely mentioned in his text, or some like indication of the ship's position, together with the month and the year. His 'Manners and Customs' pages have a general running head. Bound in between the two pp. 33 is a one page list of Madeira fish and a list of Madeira plants, pp. 1-13; between pp. 62 and 63 is his memorandum on electrical experiments, pp. 1-13; between pp. 131 and 132 a list of Plantae Brasilienses, 11 pp. unnumbered; between pp. 176 and 177 a list of plants of Tierra del Fuego, pp. 1-6; and between pp. 214 and 215 Dr Nathaniel Hulme's letter on the use of citrus juices. All these are printed in Appendix I of the present work, Vol. II, pp. 276 ff.

Volume II comprises the period 15 August 1769-12 July 1771 The pages are numbered 1-603, which latter figure should be 703, as p. 301 is followed by 202. In the second series of 200's p. 243 is followed immediately by 246 on the verso side of the same leaf; pp. 10, 568, and 574 are blanks. Banks follows the same plan of writing as in his first volume. Whether he thought in terms of volumes is uncertain: the blank leaves at the end of Volume I may perhaps argue that he did, though it is much more likely that they are accounted for by the fact that while he was writing

---

[1] I owe these details to Miss Phyllis Mander Jones, lately Mitchell Librarian.

his general account of the South Sea Islands he was also keeping
the journal up to date with current happenings. Volume division
came later when he had the journal bound, and the matter has
no particular importance. For the reader the plan followed has
what some may deem the disadvantage of a certain amount of
repetition; for the strictly chronological entries on what happened
are followed in turn by 'Some Account of New Zealand', 'Some
Account of New Holland', and of Batavia, and the Cape, and
of St Helena. In these accounts, as in that of the islands, Banks
tends, bringing together all his impressions, to say over again a
good deal of what he has said before, though he adds a good deal
also. It cannot be denied, however, that the summaries he thus
produces are very useful. He certainly made them part of his
technique of journal-writing.

The early part of the journal, for something like 150 pages, is
written in a big rather untidy hand, as if the journal-keeper is
hastening on in breakneck excitement; the writing then becomes
smaller, with more lines to the page, perhaps from some prudential
motive of ensuring a sufficient supply of paper; then towards the
end of Volume II it becomes bigger again, as if a new excitement,
that of being turned homewards, had asserted itself. Excitement
cannot be the cause of Banks's lack of punctuation, because it was
his nature not to punctuate, as is clear not merely from this journal
but from his MSS in general. If, now and again, he is visited by a
conviction that he ought to punctuate, whether because of a feeling
that he is advancing on some grand set piece or for some other
reason, he is likely to carry the eighteenth century conventions
to so absurd a point that one can hardly get on for the commas.
Fortunately these schoolboyish outbursts are very rare, and one
can make one's way without deliberate obstruction from the writer.
Like many of his contemporaries, in cursive writing he was prone
to begin a sentence, or even a paragraph, without a capital letter;
but he makes up for this by overdoing capitals elsewhere —
particularly E C L J K S M. On the other hand, not all these may
be capitals to Banks: he appears, for example, to have known only
one form of K; his S's and C's come in all sizes; he uses a Greek
E in all varieties of size, as well as the ordinary written e, for
adjectives, adverbs and verbs as well as for nouns; his L is sometimes
clearly an intended capital, sometimes emerges merely as a sort of
habitual slip of the pen equivalent to l; capital J seems to be used
at random, like C and S — but not for the reason that, like them, it
frequently falls from the pen, in rapid writing, in a size larger

than the rest of a word. M is very frequently dubious; Banks never makes an elaborately formal capital, as he sometimes does with N. Inconsistency is perhaps most complete with the names of countries and peoples, even in successive lines; so that we have England, england, english, India, india, North america, new Holland, Dutch or Duch, duch, Spain, spain, spanish, and so on. Even personal names are sometimes deprived of a capital. All this is liable to cause irritation to those who go by rule — e.g. printers.

Banks's manuscript text has a few peculiarities in spelling. He is not good on final th — he always writes, e.g. *lengh*, *strengh*, for *length*, *strength*. He generally, but not always, writes his past participle -ed without either an e or an apostrophe — e.g. *inclind*, *lookd*, *seemd* — unless the previous syllable contained a t or d — e.g. *existed*, *provided*. It is frequently impossible to tell whether he is spelling with a c or an s — e.g. *immence* or *immense*. With the possessive case he rarely uses an apostrophe before his s. With the word *notwithstanding* he seems to have peculiar trouble, as if its succession of letters were altogether too long and too complicated to get right, except by extreme chance. *Of* generally represents *off*. He rarely writes out *and* in full, preferring the ampersand, and preferring *&c* to *etc*. With underlinings of personal or scientific names he is inconsistent. Occasionally a word necessary to the sense is omitted, and he makes the small slips common to everybody in short words — *ad* for *as*, *if* for *is*; but here we move away from peculiarities. It does not seem necessary to provide further detail.

THE TRANSCRIPTS

The five MS copies of the journals are two of them contemporary, one was made in the early nineteenth century, one in the mid-1830's, and one towards the end of that century. The first two are useful in annotating the original.

(1) A careful copy made by Sarah Sophia Banks, in the possession of the present Lord Brabourne; referred to in footnotes as S. Two volumes quarto, pp. 435, 703. The copying took a long time, as it must have been begun soon after the return of the ship, and went on into 1775. In 1772 Sarah Sophia was busy also copying Banks's other journals, long and short — so that as a sister she was more than dutiful. Different sections have different title pages, as follows: (i) 'Copy of Journal from Plymouth to Terra del Fuego. Including an Account of Terra del Fuego'. Signed at the top, 'S:S:Banks 1771'; pp. 1-177. (ii) 'Copy of Journal from Cape Horn to the

Islands in The Pacifick Ocean. Including an Account of the Islands in the Pacifick Ocean'. Signed at the top, 'S:S:Banks 1771 to page 217. From thence (beginning with page 217. and ending with page 435.) 1772'. (iii) 'Copy of Journal from the Islands in the Pacifick Ocean to New Zealand. Including an Account of New Zealand'. Signed at the top 'S S Banks 1772 to page 49. From thence (beginning with page 49, & ending with page 228.) 1773'. (iv) 'Copy of Journal from New Zealand to the Islands of Savu. Including an Account of Savu'. Signed at top, 'S:S:Banks 1773'. This part finishes on p. 486. (v) 'Copy of Journal from Savu to the Cape of Good Hope. Including an account of the Cape of Good Hope'. Signed at the top, 'S:S:Banks 1773 to page 501. From thence (beginning with page 501, & ending with page 666.) 1774. From thence (beginning with page 667, and ending with page 674.) January 4th 1775'. (vi) 'Copy of Journal from the Cape of Good Hope Home'. Signed at top, 'S:S:Banks 1775. Began this part in January. Finished February ye 13. 1775'. The last page has again a note of the date when it was finished.

This copy is important because of a number of additional notes, referred to on the title page of (iv): 'mem: the loose bits of paper pasted in different places are not copied from the Journal, but are only occasional memorandums & observations'. These memorandums & observations' are in the main obviously supplied by Banks himself, it would appear in answer to questions from Sarah Sophia, but at least in one place to add a further observation of his own on 'betel-chewing' (see II, p. 166, n. below). A few others seem to be notes by Sarah Sophia, commenting on statements made: e.g. the arithmetical correction on II, p. 238, n. Sarah Sophia, even less of a classical scholar than her brother, declined transcribing a large amount of scientific terminology, and very soon has her own note, frequently repeated, 'For the future shall omit copying the Latin names & instead of them only put a serpentine dash 〰 to avoid numberless mistakes'; and omits the catalogues of plants altogether. Her copy therefore is of only secondary use to the natural historian. On the other hand it re-spells and punctuates, its readings are welcome in some cases of dubious legibility in the original; while it supplies several words omitted in Banks's MS, and thus does away with the need for conjectural emendation. The delicacy of Sarah Sophia's mind is witnessed by her inability to bring herself to copy out certain words in full, and by the dashes (not serpentine) she accordingly adopts: 'the detestable vice of S——y' (p. 461 below); 'the B——ks which in the Islands was the principal seat of this ornament' — i.e. of tattooing (II, p. 14 below). In the account of the Cape the passage about the 'Grand Quaere' (II, p. 260) is entirely omitted and the paragraph in which it occurs finishes at the words 'part of their Food'.

(2) A copy made for Banks's friend Constantine Phipps (1744-92), in the hand of a professional clerk, and now in the Alexander Turnbull Library, Wellington; referred to in footnotes as P. It is entitled 'Journal kept by Joseph Banks Esqr From August 25th 1768 To July 12th 1771'; two volumes quarto, pp. 375, 593. The second volume begins with 15 August 1769. Both volumes bear the book-plate of the 'Honble Constantine John Phipps'; and as Phipps succeeded to his Irish peerage as the 2nd Baron Mulgrave in 1775, the assumption is that the copy was made before that date. Not merely was Phipps a close friend of Banks, but he collected 'a library the most perfect in England as to all works of naval science, with many unpublished charts and notes of soundings',[1] so that his eagerness to possess the journal may be understood. This copy is the work of a good writer, who regularizes Banks's eccentricities, and leaves spaces, where he cannot read a word, to be filled in later; some of these appear to have been filled by Banks himself, so that the copy has some claim to be regarded as authoritative. Presumably it came on the market with the breaking up of Phipps's library; it was bought by Alexander Horsburgh Turnbull in 1892 from Henry Sotheran and Co.[2]

(3) A copy belonging to Lord Stanley of Alderley, now on loan to the National Maritime Museum, Greenwich. It seems likely that this copy was made for Sir John Stanley (1766-1850) of Alderley Park in Cheshire, F.R.S. 1790, Baron Stanley of Alderley 1839, who had followed Banks's example in visiting Iceland, and had published an *Account of the Hot Spring* at Edinburgh in 1791. Unlike the copies previously described, this was written in uniform large quarto blank volumes, already bound: Vol. I runs from 25 August 1768 to 31 July 1770, 494 pp.; Vol. II from 1 August 1770 to 12 July 1771, 237 pp., the remainder blank. The date of the copy is uncertain, but the paper of the first volume is watermarked 1804, that of the second 1807,[3] so that it is probable it was made before or about 1810. This was within Banks's lifetime, but he could not

---

[1] *Gent. Mag.*, lxii, p. 965.

[2] A. H. Turnbull to William Carruthers, 26 May 1898—a letter preserved inside the front cover of the Dawson Turner copy in the Botanical Library of the British Museum (Natural History).

[3] The information given to me, and printed in Cook I, pp. ccxxxix, that the watermark of the whole MS is Whatman 1809, is erroneous.

have taken any interest in it. It is done in a rather ungainly hand, with not a few misreadings: e.g. 3 June 1769, 'Pandenus Lectinus' for Pandanus Tectorius; 6 June 1769, 'Oritta' for Orette; among other proper names, 'Terutu' for Teratu; in the discussion of the New Zealand language, the particle 'the', writes Banks, 'was generaly He, or Ko' — which becomes 'was generally He, or She'; and so on. This copy, therefore, while it has the interest of relative antiquity, has not much other interest, and is of no importance textually.

(4) The copy made for Dawson Turner, c. 1834-5; two volumes fol., pp. 351 (+8 on electrical experiments), 461; now in the Botanical Library of the British Museum (Natural History), South Kensington, with the other Dawson Turner transcripts. It was carefully done.

(5) A copy in the library of the Herbarium, Royal Botanic Gardens, Kew; three volumes fol. About 1893 Sir Joseph Dalton Hooker turned his attention towards editing and publishing the journal, for which purpose he was anxious to borrow the original from the then owner, Henniker Heaton.[1] It was in 1894 that Heaton sold the MS to Alfred Lee; and with it safely out of reach Hooker seems to have temporarily given up his plan. He found, however, that he could get a transcript of the Dawson Turner copy, and on the three volumes of this transcript, those now in the Herbarium Library, he proceeded to operate. The end result was his *Journal of the Right Hon. Sir Joseph Banks, Bart., K.B., P.R.S. during Captain Cook's first voyage in H.M.S. Endeavour* in 1768-71 . . . (London 1896). Nothing can dim the botanical fame of Hooker, but at this time he was in his late seventies (he was born in 1817 and died in 1911) and his long and remarkable scientific career had never embraced any training in the treatment of historical documents. He was at a stage indeed when an eminent Victorian acted with vigour and entire lack of remorse. It is consequently difficult to forgive him for what he did. In his preface he remarks, 'I have largely exercised my duties as editor in respect of curtailments'.[2] He exercised his duties with red ink. These volumes are not a journal, they are a scene of carnage: a sort of battlefield, where stricken battalions lie inanimate and bleeding, and mutilated captives, dragged from

---

[1] Letter from Francis Edwards to Alfred Lee, 16 November 1894; Mitchell MS 1808.
[2] p. xii. 'The omitted portions are chiefly observations on the wind and weather; extracts from the ship's log, which find their proper place in Cook's Journal; innumerable notices of birds and marine animals that were of constant recurrence; and lists of plants and animals, many with MS. names that have been since superseded.'—Banks never, so far as I can tell, makes 'extracts from the ship's log': it is hard to understand why a scientist should be so summary with the other matters Hooker mentions.

massacre, are forced beneath the triumphant general's yoke. Whole paragraphs, whole pages are scored through: what was left, Hooker did not hesitate to rewrite. It was an editor's duty to secure proper grammatical observance, proper spelling,[1] a proper regard to the decencies. Certainly one may read Hooker's edition without a blush, for either Banks's syntax or his morals. Certainly in Banks's MS there is some repetition, as has been already pointed out; and certainly, in an editor of Hooker's period, one could forgive a moderate amount of tactful and judicious curtailment. But Hooker, in his 457 pages, reduces a text of something like 260,000 words to about 175,000. Certainly the book could not fail to be interesting. But it had ceased to be Banks's journal. It was something to do with a baronet, a Knight of the Bath, a President of the Royal Society. The three volumes at Kew remain an awful witness to a large conception of duty.

SUPPLEMENTARY PAPERS

(1) *The Grey MSS.* In the Auckland City Public Library is a small group of MSS in Banks's hand, relating to Captain Cook, known as *Grey MSS* 47-75 — part of the miscellaneous and valuable collection bequeathed to the Library by Sir George Grey. Grey had acquired them about 1888, as already remarked, from J. D. Enys, a settler in the New Zealand province of Canterbury, who later retired to his native Cornwall; and Enys, writing to Grey, 7 April 1888, in a letter preserved with the collection, had informed him that they 'were bought and sent to me from the sale of the MSS. of Sir Joseph Banks sold by his great nephew Lord Brabourne'. As we can see from the enumeration of the leaves, most of them were from Banks's bound volumes of papers. Those bearing on the *Endeavour* voyage are the following:

(i) *Grey MS* 48. Four pp. folio, of which the last page contains only one line; this is a description of Tahiti, possibly a draft outline produced while Banks was still making up his mind what form his journal entries should take, or perhaps a supplementary note.

(ii) *Grey MS* 49. Three ff. small quarto: notes on the position and size of the Society Islands and a number of the Tuamotu islands that had been sighted, with some other unimportant

---

[1] '... the grammar and orthography are in the original very loose, and I have therefore corrected the language to accord with modern requirements. ...'—ibid.

particulars. On Tahiti there is a reference, 'see the account on a full sheet', which may refer to No. 48.

(iii) *Grey MS* 51. Forty ff. small quarto, portion of a journal, running from 9 October 1769 to 10 October 1770. It has been thought that this, and not the Mitchell Library original, may have been the Lot 176 sold at Sotheby's for £7 2s 6d; but this, no more than the original, answers the description given in the catalogue of the sale — whatever that fact may be worth. This 'journal', though it was written out by Banks, is in no real sense a journal at all; it is simply an abstract of parts of Cook's journal, made as a summary of the ship's movements and of the geographical features encountered — details which Banks almost entirely excluded from his own journal as mere matters of latitude and longitude. Shore happenings are, correspondingly, excluded from this version, and thus for many days there are no entries at all. The language is all Cook's, except that for Cook's first person Banks substitutes 'the Capt', and makes a number of other adaptations. There is also evidence of individual curiosity in the addition to the geographical names conferred by Cook of a number of native names collected by Banks himself, and of blank spaces left for other native names in Queen Charlotte Sound. Very oddly, where Cook had given the Maori names for the main islands of New Zealand, Banks omits these, and writes in pencil (the hand seems to be his) 'the Northern Island' and 'the Southern Island'. The abstracting from Cook seems to have been done before Cook made his own corrections and re-drafts: see Cook I, p. ccxli.

(iv) *Grey MS* 52. Six ff. small quarto; apparently a continuation of No. 51, 26 December 1770 to 9 July 1771; it is a bare record of the daily positions of the ship, with a few notes on landfalls and other observations.

(2) 'Mr B's Circuit round Otaheite June 1769'. This is a fragment of 8 pp. quarto in the Alexander Turnbull Library, in a folder entitled 'Miscellaneous material relating to Cook's voyages'. It is in a quite small and very neat hand, to which can be attributed an even smaller fragment of a journal (possibly the midshipman Jonathan Monkhouse's?), also in the Alexander Turnbull Library in the same folder, and the surviving portion of that of William Brougham Monkhouse, the surgeon, now in the British Museum (see

Cook I, pp. ccxxxi-ii, ccxxxvii, 549-51, 564-87). It has one or two corrections by Banks himself. In spite of its character it did not come from Banks's collection, but from a source closely connected with Cook, and it was sold with Cook's own journal and other important Cook material at auction by Messrs Puttick and Simpson on 11 March 1868; it was bought by the dealer Waller who acquired so many of Banks's papers at Sotheby's in 1886. What happened to it between 1868 and its purchase by Mr Turnbull, and when he purchased it, is unknown, owing to the loss of a large portion of Turnbull's correspondence. Precisely how to account for its existence, or for its provenance with the Cook MSS, is difficult: I have suggested in the Textual Introduction to Cook I, p. ccxxxix, that it is a fair copy of an earlier form of Banks's account of his expedition with Cook round the island. This suggestion was a tentative one, founded on the feeling that Banks may have made other drafts of the nature of Grey MS 48. Closer study leaves little doubt: and a comparison with Cook's account of the expedition (Cook I, pp. 105-14) shows that it was after reading this that Cook discarded his own earlier version (ibid., pp. 531-4) for a new one founded closely on Banks, just as he utilized other portions of Banks's Tahitian descriptions. But in this case Banks himself wrote a new version; preserving the first, which must then have been transcribed for some special purpose. In the absence of evidence fruitful speculation is impossible on the relation of these few pages with the other MSS in the same hand. These ones are printed as Appendix II, Vol. II, pp. 302-7 below.

PRINTING AND ANNOTATION

If Banks is to be read with any comfort, then something must be done to his text in printing it. On the other hand, not too much must be done, or something of the flavour of his rapid-running mind and pen departs. Something — though it may be merely superficial — is bound to depart in print anyhow: the problem is to conserve all that can be conserved. I have therefore adopted the following rules. (1) I have maintained Banks's own spelling and abbreviations; the exception here is his ampersand, which so often repeated would have been a needless offence to the eye, and is therefore consistently expanded. (2) Obvious slips and repetitions of small words have been silently corrected, but where it has seemed necessary letters or words supplied have been enclosed in square brackets. Such words are generally vouched for by the texts of S or P, or both; where this is not so the word supplied is followed by a query. (3) After a good deal of hesitation, I have capitalized normally the names of persons, people and countries, whether used as nouns or as adjectives, not merely to avoid up-setting too much the reader's established expectations — which may not after all matter — but to get rid of the problem of Banks's own frequent indeterminate forms. Apart from this, I have retained capitals for nouns when Banks clearly intends them, and otherwise when they do not clutter up the page: this is arbitrary and perhaps illogical, but at least does keep some of the 'feeling' of the MS. I have imposed them at the beginnings of sentences. (4) I have, so far as possible in type, followed Banks's accents. (5) I have punctu-ated — enough, I hope, to render the sense easily intelligible, but without entering into refinements. (6) As Banks is highly inconsistent in his underlinings — e.g. of his scientific binomials — I have regularized this in type, and italicized according to modern practice, though retaining his capitals.

To give the reader who may be interested a certain number of specimens of Banks unadulterated, I have, however, in the intro-duction, printed quotations from his letters and other journals as nearly as possible as he wrote them.

In so long a text the question of division inevitably arises. I have retained Banks's paragraphing, but that does not answer the question. When faced by this mass of words, the reader may legitimately demand some relief for the eye. I have therefore divided the text, not into 'chapters', which might give a fundamentally false idea of what is, after all, one continuous piece of description, but into six parts, corresponding with the main divisions of the voyage: the passage to Tahiti; the sojourn there and the period in the Society Islands; New Zealand; New South Wales; New Guinea and the East Indies; and the passage from Batavia home. Inside these divisions I have broken the text only by cross-headings giving the month and the year — as an aid, as it were, to the reader's navigation. I have followed the original MS in placing the month at the head of the page. I have removed the memorandum on electrical experiments and Hulme's letter to Banks to an appendix, as I have done with his lists of fishes and plants.

The annotation has presented a number of general problems, as well as innumerable particular ones. The aim has been, first, to make the journal intelligible in relation to the voyage as a whole, and secondly, to make the references in it intelligible in themselves.

This implies a body of annotation geographical, historical, and personal, ethnological, linguistic, botanical and zoological. I have tried not to exceed due bounds in this, but a good deal of explaining is sometimes necessary. The non-scientific reader may perhaps regard the botanical and zoological annotation in particular as being more than is called for. But to Banks the voyage was one of scientific enquiry, and his journal was a record not of navigation nor even, primarily, of geographical discovery, but of discovery in the field of natural history — however much his definition of natural history had in practice to be expanded. With the MSS of Solander and the drawings of Parkinson we have a precise and invaluable commentary on this side of the journal, and it would be a poor tribute to Banks and his companions that did not make the fullest possible use of these aids to comprehension. Indeed, in the Banksian Herbarium and other collections in the British Museum (Natural History), and in the Mitchell Library, we have very many of the actual specimens they brought back.[1] The overt use made in footnotes of these MSS, drawings, and specimens will be found to vary, as will the detail of reference to them. Some of the botanical material, for example, has been well worked over by such men as James Britten, who used it for the three volumes of reproductions of the Australian plant engravings published in 1900-05. It has been assimilated into the corpus of botanical knowledge. At the same time, Banks's own lists in the journal of the plants collected at Madeira, at Rio de Janeiro, and in Tierra del Fuego, have not been thus worked over, and it is clear that proper scientific attention to these lists would mean a body of annotation valuable, certainly, as a contribution to botanical history, but tending on the whole to overweight the appendixes in one particular direction. The lists are printed, therefore, in Appendix I as a basis for desirable study; but that study is left to the interested expert.

Banks's birds and fishes have not hitherto been adequately treated: with these, precise references are made to the sources and means of identification. When the location of an MS source is not given it is to be taken as belonging to the British Museum (Natural

---

[1] In the botanical notes, for instance, the reader will find more than one reference to the 'Pocket Book'. This is a name bestowed by Dr Ramsbottom, late of the British Museum (Natural History) on a bound elephant folio of 147 ff. of which 146 bear small mounted vouchers of the larger specimens from the voyage, prepared for Banks's herbarium and now incorporated in the BMNH Herbarium. This bound series begins with Madeira and includes New Zealand, and there are a very few specimens which may represent Australia. These vouchers assume critical importance for certain monocotyledons where the principal specimen was damaged or lost during World War II.

History) collections — e.g. Solander Z4 is a Solander zoological
MS thus classified;[1] Parkinson I [II, III] refers to volumes of
Parkinson's drawings of birds and fish now in the Zoological Library
of that museum. When no note at all is given on any phenomenon
mentioned by Banks, either zoological or botanical, it may be
taken that in the absence of detail it is not safely identifiable; or
that, a scientific name having been given in the journal, that name
remains unaltered.

For the general human background in the Pacific, I may perhaps
refer the reader to the 'Note on Polynesian History', printed in
The Journals of Captain James Cook, I, pp. clxxii-cxcii. One particular
problem which arose in connection with the ethnological side of the
voyage was how to treat the vocabularies and the comparative
philological data upon which Banks was so fond of dilating. After
considerable thought and experiment I concluded that what was
really called for was some general notes on the processes by which
Banks arrived at his lists, and that no particular end would be
served by giving equivalents in present-day conventional orthography. The non-philologist would be no further forward, and the
philologist, having the primary material put before him, would
prefer to make his own deductions in a field which is still open to
scrutiny and discussion. With individual names and expressions,
on the other hand, wherever there is little possibility of error —
where, indeed, the point is really one of historical fact — I have
given transliterations.

A small number of notes will be found repeated, where Banks
repeats statements already made. This repetition is not consistent,
and is aimed mainly at refreshing the reader's mind without too
much recourse to cross-reference. A little cross-reference seems
essential.

'Cook I', frequently cited, refers to *The Journals of Captain James
Cook*, Volume I, *The Voyage of the* Endeavour (Cambridge University
Press for the Hakluyt Society, 1955); 'Cook II' to the second volume
of that edition, *The Voyage of the* Resolution *and* Adventure (1961).
Where no number is given, the first volume is to be understood.

---

[1] It consists of 512 pp. folio of descriptions in Latin of animals, vertebrate and inverte-
brate, collected on the voyage. It is carefully compiled, with notes on localities, some
vernacular names, references to earlier descriptions, etc. The whole is a fair copy, not in
Solander's hand; the original has disappeared.—Solander Z1 is an MS in Solander's
hand: it consists of five sections now bound in one volume but paginated separately and
irregularly. The sections are *Pisces Australiae; Pisces etc. Novae Hollandiae; Pisces etc. Anim.
caetera Oceani Pacifici; Animalia Javanensia & Capensia; Pisces Islandici.*—Solander Z2 is a
fair copy, not quite complete, of Z1.

THE *ENDEAVOUR* JOURNAL

OF JOSEPH BANKS

THE *ENDEAVOUR* JOURNAL
OF JOSEPH BANKS

I

25. After having waited in this place ten days, the ship, and every-thing belonging to me, being all that time in perfect readyness to sail at a moments warning,[1] we at last got a fair wind, and this day at 3 O'Clock in the even weigd anchor, and set sail, all in excellent health and spirits perfectly prepard (in Mind at least) to undergo with Chearfullness any fatigues or dangers that may occur in our intended Voyage.

26. Wind still fair, but very light breezes; saw this Even a shoal of those fish which are particularly calld *Porpoises* by the seamen, probably the *Delphinus Phocæna* of Linnæus,[2] as their noses are very blunt.

27. Wind fair and a fine Breeze; found the ship to be but a heavy sailer, indeed we could not Expect her to be any other from her built, so are obligd to set down with this Inconvenience, as a nescessary consequence of her form; which is much more calculated for stowage, than for sailing.

28. Little wind today; in some sea water, which was taken on board to season a cask, observed a very minute sea Insect, which Dr Solander describd by the name of *Podura marina*.[3] In the Evening

---

[1] Banks begins with a rather extravagant statement. The *Endeavour* had been at Plymouth since 14 August, on which day Cook 'Dispatched an express to London for Mr Banks and Dr Solander to join the ship, their Servants and baggage being already on board'; but on the night of the 15th Banks was at the opera with Miss Harriet Blosset. H. B. de Saussure met them there, walked home with them and had supper. 'Miss Blosset', he says 'not knowing that he was to start next day, was quite gay. Banks drank freely to hide his feelings. He promised to come and see me at Geneva and bring me some curios'. (See p. 31 above.) Presumably therefore he left London on the 16th and posted down to Plymouth. He and Solander did not go on board finally until the ship sailed. The ship was taking stores on board till the 19th; and it is not till the 21st that Cook records 'The Shipwrights having finished their work, intended to have sail'd, instead of which was oblig'd to let go another anchor', owing to gales and thick weather. Ship-wrights and joiners had been employed refitting 'the Gentlemens Cabbins' and making a platform over the tiller to facilitate their promenades.

[2] *Phocaena phocaena* (Linn.), the Common Porpoise.

[3] *Podura* is an insect genus: Solander (MS Z4, p. 279) described a tiny shrimp which has not been identified.

very calm; with the small casting net took several specimens of *Medusa Pelagica*,[1] whose different motions in swimming amus'd us very much: among the appendages to this animal we found also a new species of *oniscus*.[2] We took also another animal, quite different from any we had Ever seen; it was of an angular figure, about 3 inches long and one thick, with a hollow passing quite through it. On one end was a Brown spot, which might be the stomach of the animal.

Four of these, the whole number that we took, adherd together when taken by their sides; so that at first we imagind them to be one animal, but upon being put into a glass of water they very soon separated and swam briskly about the water.[3]

29. Wind foul: Morning employd in finishing the Drawings of the animals taken yesterday till the ship got so much motion that Mr Parkinson could not set to his Pencil; in the Evening wind still Fresher so much as to make the night very uncomfortable.

30. Wind still Foul, ship in violent motion, but towards Evening much more quiet: Now for the first time my Sea sickness left me, and I was sufficiently well to write.

31. Wind Freshend again this morn; observ'd about the Ship several of the Birds calld by the seamen Mother Careys chickens, *Procellaria Pelagica* Linn.[4] which were thought by them to be a sure presage of a storm, as indeed it provd, for before night it blew so hard as to bring us under our Courses,[5] and make me very sea sick again.

---

[1] A species of *Pelagia* of which Parkinson made five charming paintings, III, pl. 54, and which was described in detail by Solander, p. 471.

[2] Possibly '*O. Macropthalmos*', or '*Onidium*' of 7 Sept. (p. 158); Parkinson's drawing of *Onidium quadricorne* (III, pl. 18) dated 28 Aug. 1768 was identified by Stebbing in 1888 as the amphipod *Hyperia medusarum* (O. F. Müller). *Challenger Repts.*, Zoology, xxix, 1617.

[3] The cluster (angular figure), was the aggregate form of *Pegea confoederata* Forskål, a salp. Solander described it as *Dagysa saccata*, p. 489; Parkinson III, pl. 27, lower figs.

[4] Mother Carey's Chickens: either the Common Storm Petrel *Hydrobates pelagicus* or the Madeiran Storm Petrel *Oceanodroma castro* (Harcourt); they are not easily distinguished in flight.—Mother Carey: a name derived from *Madre Caria*; sailors believed that the Virgin Mary sent the storm petrels to warn them of approaching tempests. S, at a later stage (after copying Banks's description of Tierra del Fuego, pp. 224-9 below) includes a separate page on this subject: 'Mother Careys Chickens [footnote: 'The right Mother Careys Chicken, is much like a Blackbird'] or other Birds called Mother Careys: are those that live 8 or 10 Months at Sea, without going upon Land: therefore when Seamen see them, they are not sure of being near Land, as they are when they see other Birds. The Tradition of their being called by that name, was, that some years ago one Mother Carey lived in New York, and was reputed by the Sailors a Witch: and they were afraid of her. The Family of the Careys (are said) now to live at New York. Mother Careys Successors'.

[5] The lowest sails on the fore and main masts—i.e. the foresail and the mainsail. Cook, who was not concerned with his passengers' sea-sickness, records that the gale 'Washed over board a small boat belonging to the Boatswain and drown'd between 3 and 4 Dozn of our Poultry which was worst of all'.

SEPTEMBER 1768

1. Still Blew, Mother Careys chickens had not yet left us, but towards night wind slackened so that we were again tolerably easy; by our reckoning we must make some part of the coast of Spain before Morning.

2. This Morn about 7 saw the coast of Gallicia between Cape Ortegal and Finisterre; weather tolerably fine, so that we could use the casting net, which brought up two kinds of Animals, different from any before taken; they came up in Clusters, both sorts indifferen[t]ly in each Cluster, tho much fewer of the Horned ones than of the others. They seem to [be] two species of one genus, but are not at all reducible to any genus hitherto describd.

3. Blew fresh this morn. We were employd all day in describing the animals taken yesterday; found them to be of a new genus and of the same with that taken on the 28 of August Calld the genus *Dagysa* from the likeness of one Species to a Gem.[1] Towards Even wind fair Settled tolerably fine.

4. Calm today; we were employd in fishing with the casting net and were fortunate in taking several specimens of *Dagysa saccata*[2] adhering together, sometimes to the Lengh of a yard or more, and shining in the water with very beautifull Colours; but another insect which we took today was possest of more beautiful Colouring than any thing in nature I have ever seen, hardly excepting gemms. He is of a new genus and calld   of which we took another species who had no beauty to boast, but this which we called *opalinum* shone in the water with all the splendor and variety of colours that we observe in a real opal; he livd in the Glass of salt water in which he was put for examination several hours; darting about with great agility, and at every motion shewing an almost infinite variety of changeable colours.[3] Towards the Evening of this day a new phænomenon appeard, the sea was almost coverd with a small species of Crabbs *Cancer depurator* of Linnæus,[4]

[1] A salp, *Thalia democratica* Forskål. *Dagysa* is Greek for a gem. The aggregate form was described by Solander both as *Dagysa gemma* and *D. serena*, and the solitary one as *D. cornuta* (pp. 485, 507 and 497). Parkinson's drawings are in III, pls. 27 (upper figure), 35, and 31 (upper figure), respectively.
[2] Now known as *Pegea confoederata* Forskål. See 28 August above.
[3] *Carcinium opalinum*, a copepod belonging to the genus *Sapphirina*: Parkinson III, pl. 21, top figure, and Solander, p. 353.
[4] *Polybius henslowi* (Leach). See Parkinson III, pl. 8, and Solander, p. 327. The unsigned painting of this little crab is bound with Parkinson's work but is in fact by Buchan; this is confirmed in Dryander's MS catalogue of the zoological drawings in Banks's library.

floating upon the surface of the water, and moving themselves with tolerable agility, as if the surface of the water and not the bottom was their Proper station. Here again as usual our casting net was of great service, we took with it as many as were wanted, and went to bed well contented with the Produce of the day.

5. I Forgot to mention yesterday that two birds were caught in the rigging, who probably had come from Spain, as we were not then distant above 5 or 6 Leagues,[1] this morning another was caught, and brought to me, but so weak that it dyed in my hand almost immediately; they were all three of the same species, and not describd by Linnæus, we calld them *Motacilla velificans*, as they must be sailors who would venture themselves aboard a ship which is going round the world.[2] But to make some balance to our good fortune now become too prevalent, a misfortune happned this morn, equaling almost the worst which our enemies could have wishd; the morn was calm and Richmond employd in searching for what should appear on the surface of the water, a shoal of dagysa's were observd and he Eagar to take some of them threw the cast-net fastned to nothing but his wrist, the string slippd from him and the net at once sunk into the profound never more to torment its inhabitants but Leaving us for some time intirely without a resource, plenty of animals coming past the ship, and no netts but in the hold, stowd under so many things that it was impossible even to hope for their being got out today at least, however an old hoop net was fastned to a fishing rod, and with it one new speces of Dagysa was caught and calld *Lobata*.[3]

6. Fine and calm this morn, immence numbers of *Dagysa Lobata* floated by, and were taken by our new contrivance, some of them in clusters as many as 14 together, united by a Lobe on the underside. Towards the Middle of the day the sea was almost coverd with dagysa's of different kinds among which two intirely new ones were taken, *rostrata* and *strumosa*,[4] but neither of these were observd hanging in clusters as most of the other Species had been, indeed whether from the badness of the new machine or their scarcity I cannot say; only one of *rostrata* and two of *strumosa* were taken.

[1] At noon, says Cook, Cape Finisterre was south by east distant 4 leagues.
[2] These were *Oenanthe oenanthe*, European Wheatears, on migration to their winter quarters in Africa. There is a signed and dated drawing of one of them by Parkinson, I, pl. 38b.
[3] A salp, *Cyclosalpa pinnata* Forskål. Parkinson III, pl. 30, and Solander p. 495.
[4] *Dagysa rostrata* was the MS name given by Solander, p. 503, to the aggregate form of the salp *Thetys vagina* Tilesius; his *Dagysa strumosa*, p. 505, is the solitary form of the same species. Both were painted by Parkinson, III, pls. 33, 34.

It is now time to give some account of the genus of Dagysa, of which there are already six species taken, all agreeing in many particulars vastly well but cheifly in this very singular one, that they have a hole at each end, which holes Communicate by a tube, often as large as the body of the animal, by the help of which they swim with some degree of activity when seperated from each other, for several sorts are seen most generaly Joind together, *gemma*[1] more particularly which adhere in clusters of some hundreds irregularly shap'd; in the midst of these were generaly found a few specimens of *cornuta*, from which circamstance we may Judge that they are very nearly allied.

It seems singular that no naturalist before this time should have taken notice of thise animals as they abound so much where the ship now is, not twenty Leagues from the coast of Spain; from hence however great hopes may be formd, that the inhabitants of the deep have been but little examind, and as Dr Solander and my self shall have probably greater opportunity in the course of this voyage than any one has had before us, it is a very incouraging circumstance to hope that so large a feild of natural history has remaind almost untrod, even till this time, and that we may be able from this circumstance alone (almost unthought of when we embarkd in the undertaking) to add considerable Light to the science which we so eagerly Pursue.

This Evening a large quantity of the *Carcinium opalinum* which may be calld opal insect came under the ships stern, making the very sea appear with uncommon bea[u]ty, their colours appearing with vast brightness even at the depth of two or three fathoms, tho they are not more than three lines[2] long and one broad.

7. On examining the Dagysa's which were taken yesterday, several small animals were found Lodgd in the hollow parts of their bodys, and some in the very substance of the flesh, which seems to be their food, as many of the dagysas were full of scars which had undoubtedly been the Lodgment of these animals some time before; upon a minute inspection they provd to be animals not to be class'd under any of Linnæus's genera tho nearly related to *Oniscus*, from which Circumstance the name of *Onidium* was given to the new genus,[3] and to them was added an animal taken the 28th of

---

[1] i.e. 'buds'.

[2] 'Line' as a unit of measurement, one-twelfth of an inch. The axiom that twelve lines make one inch is still proclaimed in Australian school-tables.

[3] These small crustacean parasites were hyperiid amphipods. Parkinson's drawings of them (III, pl. 18) were discussed by Stebbing (Amphipoda, *Challenger Repts.*, 1888, Zoology, xxix, p. 1617). He did not know of Solander's MS notes, pp. 357-68, on them.

August and mentiond in the second Page by the name of *Oniscus Macropthalmos*.[1]

In one circumstance these insects differ from any hitherto describd, and in that they all three agree, viz the having two Eyes joind together under one common membrane, without the least distinction or division between them, which circumstance alone seems a sufficient reason for constituting a new genus.

The wind was now fair and we went very pleasantly on towards our destind port, tho rather too fast for any natural Enquiries, for my own part I could well dispence with[2] a much slower pace, but I fancy few in the ship, D[r] Solander excepted, are of the same opinion, tho I beleive Every body envyed our easy contented countenances during the last Calm, which brought so much food to our pursuits.

8. Blew fresh today, but the wind was very fair so nobody complaind, nor would they was the wind much stronger, so impatient has the Calms and foul wind made every body; by the reckoning we were off Cape S[t] Vincent so shall soon bid adieu to Europe for some time.

10. Since the northerly wind began to blow it has not varied a point, the Sea is now down and we go pleasantly on at the rate of about 6 Knotts; could any contrivance be found by the help of which new subjects of natural history could be taken D[r] Solander and myself would be Quite happy, we are forc'd to be content; three days are now passd since any thing has been taken or indeed seen, except a stray turtle who swam by the ship about noon, but was left far behind before any instrument by which he might have been taken could possibly have been got to hand.

Today for the first time we dind in Africa,[3] and took our leave of Europe for heaven alone knows how long, perhaps for Ever; that thought demands a sigh as a tribute due to the memory of freinds left behind and they have it; but two cannot be spard, twold give more pain to the sigher, than pleasure to those sighd for. Tis Enough that they are rememberd, they would not wish to be too much thought of by one so long to be seperated from them and left alone to the Mercy of winds and waves.

---

[1] No description of *O. macropthalmus* is known; it may be Parkinson's *Onidium quadricorne* (p. 154, n. 2). Amphipods have a pair of compound eyes but in most copepods there is a single median eye. See also October 7 with reference to *Cystisoma spinosum* in which the very large compound eyes are separated only by a thin membrane which is very difficult to detect. The 'second Page' is of course the second page of his journal.

[2] *dispence with* in its now obsolete sense of 'put up with'.

[3] He appears to mean they were in an African latitude: Cook gives the noon position as lat. 35° 20′N, long. 13° 28′W.

11. Wind fair but rather slackend upon us, nothing however was observ'd, we expected to have made Porto Santo[1] tonight but did not.

12. This morn Porto Santo and Madeira were in full veiw, they were seen at day break, indeed we had a little overshot them; as the wind was rather scanty we had however no doubt of fetching in at night. Accordingly at ten tonight came to an anchor in Fonchiale[2] bay.

13. This morn about 11 the product[3] boat (as it is calld by English Sailors) which is the boat from the oficers of health who must give leave before any ships crew can land, came on board, and we immediately went on shore in the town of Fonchiale, the Capital of the Island, situate in Latitude 32:40 North, calld so from the Fennel which grows in plenty upon the rocks in its neighbourhood and which is calld Funcho in the Portugese Language. Here we immediately went to the house of the English Consul Mr Cheap, one of the first merchants in the place, where we were receivd with uncommon marks of civility; he insisted upon our taking possession of his house and living intirely with him during our stay which we did and were by him furnishd with every accomodation that we could wish. Leave was procurd by him for us to search the Island for whatever natural productions we might find worth taking notice of, people were also employd to procure for us fish and shells which we could not have spard time to have collected ourselves, horses and Guides were also got for Dr Solander and myself to carry us to any part of the Island which we might chuse to visit. But our very short stay which was only five Days inclusive made it impossible to go to any distance, so we contented ourselves with collecting as much as we could in the neighbourhood of the town, never going above three miles from it during our whole stay.

The season of the year was undoubtedly the worst for both plants and insects, being the hight of the vintage, when nothing is green in the countrey but just on the verge of small brooks, by which these vines are waterd; we made shift however to collect specimens of several plants, &c: of which a catalogue follows[4] as it is not worth while to mix them in the Journal, where they would take up much room.

[1] The small island north-east of Madeira.
[2] i.e. Funchal.
[3] 'Pratique'.
[4] See Appendix I, Vol. II, pp. 281-9 below.

The five days which we remained upon the Island were spent so exactly in the same manner, that it is by no means nescessary to divide them, I shall therefore only say, that in general we got up in the Morn, went out on our researches, retur[n]d to dine, and went out again in the Evening; one day however we had a visit from the Governor, of which we had notice before and were obligd to stay at home, so that unsought honour lost us very near the whole day, a very material part of the short time we were allowd to stay upon the Island: we however contrivd to revenge ourselves upon his excellency, by an Electrical machine which we had on board; upon his expressing a desire to see it we sent for it ashore, and shockd him full as much as he chose.[1]

While at this place we were much indebted to Dr Heberden, the cheif Physitian of the Island, and brother to the Physitian of that name at London; he had for many years been an inhabitant of the Canaries and this Island, and had made several observations cheifly philosophical, some however were Botanical, describing the trees of the Island: of these he immediately gave us a copy, together with such specimens as he had in his possession, and indeed spard no pains to get for us such living specimens of such as could be procurd in flower.[2]

We tryed here to learn what Species of wood it is which has been imported into England, and is now known to Cabinet makers by the name of Madeira mahogeny, but without much success, as we could not learn that any wood had been exported out of the Island by that name; the wood however of the tree calld here Vigniatico, *Laurus indicus* Linn.[3] bidds fair to be the thing, it being

---

[1] The particulars Banks gives of his electrical machine, 'made by Ramsden' (see Appendix I,), inform us that he was quite up-to-date with his apparatus. It was in this same year 1768 that Jesse Ramsden (1735-1800), one of the celebrated instrument-makers of the time, first constructed his plate electrical machine, an assemblage of glass plate rotated by a winch, leather rubbers, insulated metal forks and an insulated conductor. Electrical experiments were very popular among the philosophical at this period, and it was only two years since Priestley, in 1766, had discovered his fundamental Law of Inverse Squares. Banks seems never to have got beyond the experiments he refers to here and the use of his machine for practical jokes upon unsuspecting persons.

[2] Thomas Heberden (1703-69) practised both at Teneriffe and at Funchal. He was elected F.R.S. in 1761. Between 1756 and 1769 he communicated to the Royal Society's *Philosophical Transactions* a number of papers on his observations in Madeira, mainly geological and meteorological—Banks's 'chiefly philosophical'; he was the first of a number of Heberdens who distinguished themselves in meteorology. His description of trees does not seem to have been a Royal Society paper; perhaps he gave his visitors an MS copy.—See Solander's praise of him to Ellis, II, p. 309 below. It was to commemorate him that Banks and Solander conferred the name *Heberdenia*, now a synonym of *Ardisia*. His London brother was William Heberden (1710-1801), famous for learning and benevolence as well as for his professional skill—Cowper's 'Virtuous and faithful Heberden' and Johnson's 'ultimus Romanorum'.

[3] *Persea indica* (L.) Spr. 'Vinhatico'.

of a fine grain and brown like mahogeny, from which it is dificult
to distinguish it, which is well shewn at Dr Heberdens house where
in a bookcase vigniatico and mahogeny were placd close by each
other, and were only to be known asunder by the first being not
quite so dark colourd as the other.

As much of the Island as we saw shewd evidently the signs of a
volcano having some time or other possibly produced the whole;
as we saw no one peice of stone which did not evidently shew signs
of having been burnt, some very much, especialy the sand which
was absolutely cinders. Indeed we did not see much of the countrey,
but we were told that the whole was like the specimen we saw of it.

When you first aproach it from seaward it has a very beautifull
appearance, the sides of the hills being intirely coverd with vine-
yards almost as high as the eye can distinguish, which make a
constant appearance of verdure tho at this time nothing but the
vines remaind green, the grass and herbs being intirely burnt up
except near the sides of the rills of water by which the vines are
waterd, and under the shade of the vines themselves; tho these
very few Species of plants were in perfection the greater part being
burnt up.

The people here in general seem to be as idle, or rather unin-
formd a set as I ever yet saw; all their instruments, even those
with which their wine, the only article of trade in the Island is made,
are perfectly simple and unimprovd. Their method is this: the
Grapes are put into a square wooden vessel, of dimensions according
to the size of the vineyard to which it belongs, into which the
servants get (having taken off their stockins and Jackets) and with
their feet and Elbows squeeze out as much of the Juice as they
can; the stalks &c are then collected, tyed together with a rope
and put under a square peice of wood which is pressd down by
a Leaver, to the other end of which is fastned a stone that may be
raisd up at pleasure by a screw; by this way and this only they
make their wine, and by this way probably Noah made his when
he had newly planted the first vineyard after the general destruction
of mankind and their arts; tho it is not impossible that he might
have used a better, if he rememberd the ways he had seen us'd
before the flood.

It was with great dificulty that some (and not as yet all) of them
were persuaded not long ago to graft their vines and by this means
bring all the fruit of a vineyard to be of one sort, tho before the
vine which it producd had been spoild by different sorts of bad
ones which were nevertheless sufferd to grow, and taken as much

care of as the best, because they added to the quantity of the wine.
Yet were they perfectly acquainted with the use of grafting, and
constantly practisd it on their chestnut trees, by which means they
were brought to bear sooner much than they would have done had
they been allowd to remain unimprovd.

Wheel carriages I saw none in the Island of any sort or kind,
indeed their roads are so intolerably bad that if they had them
they could scarcely make use of them: they have however some
horses and mules, wonderfully clever in traveling upon them,
notwithstanding which they bring to town every drop of wine
they make upon mens heads, in vessells made of goat skins. The
only imitation of a carriage they have, is a board a little hollowd
out in the middle, to one end of which a pole is tyed by a strap
of whitleather,[1] the whole machine comeing about as near the
perfection of a European cart as an Indian canoe does to a boat
with this they move the pipes of wine about the town. Indeed
I suppose they would never have made use even of this had not
the English introd[u]ced vessels to put their wine in which were
rather too large to be carried by hand, as they used to do every
thing else.

A speech of their late governeur is recorded here, which shews
in what light they are lookd upon even by the Portugese, (themselves I beleive far behind all the rest of Europe, except possibly
the Spaniards): it was very fortunate said he that this Island was
not Eden in which Adam and Eve dwelt before the fall, for had it
been so the inhabitants here would never have been induc'd to
put on Cloaths; so much are they resolvd in every particular to
follow exactly the paths of their forefathers.

Indeed were the people here only tolerably industrious, there
is scarcely any Luxury which might [not] be produc'd that either
Europe or the Indies afford, owing to the great difference of Climate
observable in ascending the hills; this we experien[c]d in a visit to
Dr Heberden, who lives about two miles from the town, we left
the Thermometer when we set out at 74 and found it there at 66.
Indeed the hills produce almost spontaneously vast plenty of Wall-
nutts, chestnutts, and apples, but in the town you find some few
plants natives of both the Indies, whose flourishing state put it out
of all doubt that were they taken any care of they might have any
quantity of them. Of these I mention some: the Banana tree,
(*Musa sapientum* Linn.) in great abundance; the guava (*Psidium*

---

[1] 'Leather of a white or light colour and soft pliant consistence, prepared by dressing
with alum and salt, so as to retain the natural colour.'—O.E.D.

pyriferum Linn.)[1] not uncommon; the pine apple, *Bromelia ananas*
Linn.[2] of this I saw some very healthy plants in the provadores[3]
Garden; Mango, *Mangifera indica* Linn. one plant also of this in
the same garden Bearing fruit every year; Cinnamon, *Laurus
cinnamomum* Linn. very healthy plants of this I saw on the top of
D[r] Heberdens house at Fonchiale, which had stood there through
the winter without any kind of Care having been taken of them.
These without mentioning any more seem very sufficient to shew
that the tenderest plants might be cultivated here without any
trouble; yet the indolence of the inhabitants is so great, that even
that is too much for them; indeed the policy of the English here
is to hinder them as much as possible from growing any thing
themselves except what they find their account in taking in exchange
for Corn, tho the people might with much Less trouble and expence
grow the corn themselves. What corn grows here, which indeed is
not much, is of a most excellent quality, Large graind, and
very fine; their meat also is very good, mutton, pork, and beef
more especialy, of which what we had on board the ship was
agreed by all of us to be very little inferior to our own; tho *we
Englishmen* value ourselves not a little on our peculiar excellence
in that production. The fat of this was white like the fat of mutton,
yet the meat Brown, and coarse graind as ours, tho much smaller.

The town of Fonchiale is situated at the Bottom of the Bay,
very ill Built, tho larger than the size of the Island seems to deserve.
The houses of the bettermost people are in general large but those
of the poorer sort very small, and the streets very narrow and
uncommonly ill pavd. The Churches here have abundance of
ornaments, cheifly bad pictures and figures of their favourite saints
in lac'd cloaths; the Convent of the Franciscans indeed which we
went to See had very little ornament; but the neatness with which
those fathers kept everything was well worthy of commendation,
especialy their infirmary, the contrivance of which deserves to
be taken particular notice of; it was a long room, on one side of
which were windows, and an altar for the convenience of admin-
istering the sacrament to the sick; on the other were the wards,
each just capable of containing a bed, and lind with white duch[4]
tiles; to every one of these was a door communicating with a gallery
which ran paralel to the great room, so that any of the sick might

---

[1] *Psidium guajava* L., probably introduced from Brazil by the Portuguese.
[2] Now known as *Ananas comosus* (L.) Merr.
[3] *Provadore* or *provedore, provedor*, purveyor or contractor; probably he means the agent
who supplied the ship.
[4] i.e. Dutch.

be supplied with whatever they wanted without disturbing their neighbours.

In this Convent was a curiosity of a very singular nature; a small chapel whose whole lining, wainscote, and ceiling, was intirely compos'd of human bones, two large thigh bones across, and a  skull in each of the openings. Among these was a very singular anatomical curiosity, a skull in which one side of the Lower jaw was perfectly and very firmly fastned to the upper by an ossification, so that the man whoever he was must have livd some time without being able to open his mouth, indeed it was plain on the other side that a hole had been made by beating out his teeth, and in some measure damaging his Jaw bone, by which alone he must have receivd his nourishment.

I must not leave these good fathers without mentioning a thing which does great credit to their civility, and at the same time shews that they are not bigots to their religion: we visited them on Thursday Even just before their supper time; they made many apologies that they could not ask us to sup, not being prepard; but said they, if you will come tomorrow, notwishstanding it is fast with us, we will have a turkey roasted for you.

There are here, beside friarys, 3 or 4 houses of nunns. To one of these (Sa'nta Clara) we went, and indeed the ladies did us the honour to express great pleasure in seeing us there; they had heard that we were great Philosophers, and expected much from us, one of the first questions that they askd was, when it would thunder; they then desird to know if we could put them in a way of finding water in their convent, which it seems they were in want of; but notwishstanding our answers to these questions were not quite so much to the purpose as they expected, they did not at all cease their civilities, for while we stayd, which was about half an hour, I am sure there was not the fraction of a second in which their tongues did not go at an uncommonly nimble rate.

It remains now that I should say something of the Island in general, and then take my leave of Madeira till some other opportunity offers of visiting it again, for the climate is so fine that any man might wish it was in his power to live here under the benefits of English laws and liberty.

The hills here are very high, much higher than any one would imagine, Pico Ruevo the highest is 5068 f[t1] which is much higher than any land that has been measured in Great Britain; indeed

[1] The height of Pico Ruivo is 6056 feet.

as I hinted before the whole Island has probably been the production of a Volcano, notwishstanding which its fertility is amazing, all the sides of the hills are coverd with vines to a certain hight, above which are woods of chestnut and pine of immense extent; and above them forests of wild timber of kinds not known in Europe, which amply supply the inhabitants with whatever they may want. Among these some there were whose flowers we were not able to procure and consequently could not settle their Genera, particularly those calld by the Portugese *Mirmulano*[1] and *Pao branco*,[2] both which, and especialy the first, from the Beauty of their leaves promise to be a great ornament to our European gardens.

The inhabitants here are supposd to be about 80,000; and from the town of Fonchiale (its custom house I mean) the King of Portugal receives 20000 pounds a year, after having paid the Governor and all expences of every kind, which may serve to shew in some degree the consequence which this little Island is of to the crown of Portugal; was it in the hands of any other people in the world its value might easily be doubled, from the excellence of its climate capable of bearing any kind of crop, a circumstance which the Portugese do not make the least advantage of.

The Coin current here is intirely Spanish, for the Balance of trade with Lisbon being in disfavour of this Island all the Portugese money naturaly goes there, to prevent which Spanish money is allowd to pass: it is of three denominations, Pistereens, Bitts, and ½ bitts; the first worth about 1 shilling, the 2nd 6 pence, the third 3 pence; they have also Portugese money of Copper, but so scarce that I did not in my stay there see a single peice.

18. This Evening every thing being ready for sea, we went on board, and at 8 o'Clock got under way with a very light breeze.

19. Light Breezes all day, without any event worth writing about.

20. Still almost calm, which gave us an opportunity of taking with the casting nett a most beautifull species of Medusa, of a colour equaling if not exceeding the finest ultramarine; it was describd and calld *Medusa azurea*.[3]

---

[1] *Apollonias canariensis* Nees.

[2] *Oreodaphne foeteus* (Ait.) Nees <JDH>; now *Ocotea foeteus* (Ait.) Webb and Berthel. Specimens of both this and *Apollonias canariensis* survive from the voyage. Here and elsewhere <JDH> signifies an identification made by Hooker in his edition of Banks's journal.

[3] *Porpita porpita*. There are two sets of paintings of this animal by Parkinson, III, pls. 44, 45, and a description by Solander, pp. 447-8, who assigned it to the correct Linnean species.

21. This morn wind foul, saw however some rocks call'd in the old charts Salvages[1] which lay to the northward of the Canarys.

22. No land in sight this morn, towards noon almost calm, many fish were about the ship, but our fishermen could not contrive to catch any of them.

23. This morn we were calld up very early to see the pike of Teneriffe, which now for the first time appeard at a vast distance much above the clouds (I mean those which form a bank near the Horizon); the hill itself was so faint, that no man who was not used to the appearance of land at a great distance could tell it from a cloud, it soon however appeard something clearer and a sketch was made of it.

While we were engagd in looking at the hill a fish was taken which was describ'd and called *Scomber serpens*;[2] the seamen said they had never seen such a one before except the first lieutenant, who rememberd to have taken one before just about these Islands; S[r] Hans Sloane in his Passage out to Jamaica also took one of these fish which he gives a figure of, Vol.1,T.1, f.2.[3]

The Pike continued in sight almost all day, tho sometimes obscurd by the clouds; at sunset however its appearance was most truely elegant, the rays of the sun remaining upon it sometime after it was set and the other land quite Black, and giving it a warmth of colour not to be express'd by painting.

---

[1] A small group of islets and rocks south of Madeira, and just north of the 30th parallel.

[2] *Gempylus serpens* Cuv. The first of these rather rare oceanic fishes known to science was the specimen belonging to Sir Hans Sloane, to which Banks refers. This second one was described by Solander, pp. 269-70; it was 37 inches long. The only specimen now in the British Museum is but an inch or so long and was brought back from one of the cruises of the *Discovery*. Another of these fishes was taken by the *Kon-Tiki*.—S gives the name of the fish as 'Hember Serpens', and appends a note, 'For the future shall omit copying the Latin names and instead of them only put a serpentine dash [an illustrative wavy line follows] to avoid numberless mistakes'. This note is repeated from time to time in her manuscript, but will not be repeated in the following pages.

[3] Sir Hans Sloane (1660-1753) the physician, naturalist and collector. Banks's reference is to his *Voyage to the Islands Madera, Barbadoes, Nieves, St Christopher's and Jamaica, with the Natural History . . . of the last . . .* (2 vols. folio, London 1707, 1725). Sloane, an Irishman, studied medicine at Paris and Montpellier, and botany at the latter, and became a Fellow of the Royal Society in 1685. In 1687 he went to the West Indies as physician to the Duke of Albemarle, the governor of Jamaica, and for fifteen months made observations and collections of natural history. He brought 800 specimens of plants back to London, the foundation of his *Catalogus Plantarum quae in Insula Jamaica sponte proveniunt, vel vulgo coluntur* (1696). He was secretary of the Royal Society 1693-1712; and on Newton's death in 1727 elected its president, remaining so till 1741. The first volume of his *Voyage* brought him European fame as a scientist, while his eminence in medicine gave him a large practice, which included the persons of Queen Anne and George II. Generous throughout his life, he bequeathed his noble collections of natural history, manuscripts and books, which had cost him £50,000, to the nation, on condition that £20,000 was paid to his family. This was done, and Sloane thus became virtually the founder of the British Museum.—'T.1, f.2': Tabula 1, figura 2.

24. This Morn the Pike appeard very plain and immensely above the clouds, as may well be imagin'd by its hight which Dr Heberden of Madeira who has been himself upon it communicated to us, 15,396 feet.[1] The D^r also says that tho there is no eruption of visible fire from it, yet heat issues from the chinks near the top so strongly that a person who putts his hand upon these is scalded; from him we receivd among many other favours some salt which he supposes to be the true natron or nitrum of the ancients, and some native sulphur exceedingly pure, both which he collected himself on the top of the mountain, where large quantities, especialy of the salt, are found on the surface of the Earth.[2]

25. Wind continued to blow much as it had done so we were sure we were well in the trade; now for the first time we saw plenty of flying fish, whose bea[u]ty especialy when seen from the cabbin windows is beyond imagination, their sides shining like burnishd silver; when seen from the Deck they do not appear to such advantage as their backs are then presented to the view, which are dark colourd.

26. Went as usual and as we expect to go these next two months; flying fish are in great plenty about the ship. About one today we crossd the tropick,[3] the night most intolerably hot, the Thermometer standing all night at 78 in the cabbin tho every window was open.

27. About one this morn a flying fish was brought into the cabbin, the first that had been taken; it flew aboard, I suppose chasd by some other fish, or maybe merely because he did not see the ship; at breakfast another was brought, which had flown into Mr Green the Astronomers Cabbin. This whole day we saild at the rate of 7 knotts, sometimes a fathom or two more the wind being rather stronger than it usualy is in the trade.

28. Wind rather slackend; three birds were today about the ship, a swallow,[4] to all appearance the same as our European one, and two motacillas, about night fall one of the latter was taken; about 11 a shoal of Porpoises came about the ship, and the fisgig was soon thrown into one of them but would not hold.

---

[1] Its highest point is 12,200 feet.

[2] The sulphur is understandable, but not the other substance, under Heberden's denomination. Natron is an obsolete word for saltpetre or potassium nitrate; this is a salt which would dissolve in rain on top of the mountain. My colleague Professor A. D. Monro suggests that what Heberden collected was the mineral alunite, a whitish-looking basic alum, which would not so dissolve, and might be expected under the conditions.

[3] i.e. the Tropic of Cancer. Cook gives the noon position for September 26 as lat. 23° 43′ N, long. 19° 23′ W.

[4] Probably the common swallow on migration.

29. This morn calm; employd in drawing and describing the bird taken yesterday, calld it *Motacilla avida*;[1] while the drawing was in hand it became very familiar, so much so that we had a brace made for it in hope to keep it alive; as flies were in amazing abundance onboard the ship we had no fear of plentiful supply of provision.

About noon a young shark was seen from the Cabbin windows following the ship, who immediately took a bait and was caught on board; he provd to be the *Squalus Charcharias* of Linn[æus][2] and assisted us in clearing up much confusion which almost all authors had made about that species; with him came on board 4 sucking fish, *echineis remora* Linn.[3] who were preserved in spirit. Notwistanding it was twelve O'Clock before the shark was taken, we made shift to have a part of him stewd for dinner, and very good meat he was, at least in the opinion of Dr Solander and myself, tho some of the Seamen did not seem to be fond of him, probably from some prejudice founded on the species sometimes feeding on human flesh.

30. This Morn at day break made the Island of Bonavista, one of the Cape Verde Islands: Mr Buchan employd in taking views of the land; Mr Parkinson busy in finishing the sketches made of the shark yesterday.

This Evening the other *Motacilla avida* was brought to us, it differd scarce at all from the first taken, except that it was something larger; his head however gave us some good, by supplying us with near twenty specimens of ticks, which differd but little from the *acarus vicinus* Linn; it was however described and calld *Motacilla*.[4]

OCTOBER 1768

1. This Morn Bonetos were in great plenty about the ship, we were calld up early to see one that had been struck, found it to be the *Scomber Pelamys* Linn.,[5] had a drawing made of it; I confess however that I was a good deal disapointd, expecting to find the

---

[1] A young Yellow Wagtail; Parkinson I, pl. 38a; Solander p. 121. See Pl. 2.

[2] Probably *Carcharodon carcharias*, the Great White Shark; this is one of the largest of all sharks and is found throughout temperate and tropical seas. There are two drawings from this voyage labelled *Squalus carcharias*, both ascribed by Dryander to Parkinson, though only one is signed, I, pls. 51, 54.

[3] *Remora remora*, Sucking-fish.

[4] Wagtails are parasitized by several kinds of ticks; from Solander's notes, p. 289, it appears that this one was an *Ixodes*, but the description is not sufficiently detailed to allow of specific identification. S, substituting a 'serpentine dash' for the name of the bird, adds the note, 'those referred to was what became so familiar ye 29th while drawing and describing. page 38'.

[5] The Bonito, *Euthynnus pelamis*. See Parkinson II, pl. 92; this is an unfinished and unsigned painting and may not be Parkinson's work.

animal much more bea[u]tifull than it provd, tho its colours were extreemly lively, especialy the blue lines on the Back (which equald at least any ultramarine); yet the name, and accounts I had heard from all who had seen them, made me expect an animal of a much greater variety of colour, this consisting of no other than blue lines on the back crossing each other, a gold and purple changeable on the sides, and white with black lines on the bottom of the sides and belly.

After having examind and drawn the animal we proceeded to disect him, and in the course of the operation were much pleasd by the infinite strenght we observd in every part of him, specialy the stomack, the coats of which were uncommonly strong especialy about the sp[h]incter, or extremity by which the digested meat is discharged; this I suppose is intended to crush and render usefull the scales and bones of fishes which this animal must continualy swalow without seperating them from the flesh.

From the inside of its scales we took a small animal who seemd to be a louse (if I may so call it) as it certainly stuck to him and preyd upon the Juices which it extra[c]ted by sucktion, probably much to his disquiet; it provd to be *monoculus piscinus* Linn.[1] which Baster has given a figure of in his *Opera subcessive*,[2] but has by some unlucky accident mistaken the head to be the tail, and the tail the head, and the ovaria for antennae.

In the inside of the fish were also found two animals which preyd upon him, one in his very flesh tho near the membrane which covers the intestines, *Fasciola Pelamines* Mss,[3] the other in the stomach *sipunculus piscium* Mss.[4]

2. This morn two swallows were about the ship, tho we must now be 60 Leagues at least from any land, at night one of them is taken and proved to be *Hirundo domestica* Linn.[5]

3. This morn the other swallow was found dead upon the deck; now for the first time we have lost the trade, and expected calm and squally weather till we shall cross the line.

[1] *Caligulus* sp., a parasitic copepod. See Parkinson III, pl. 17, and Solander, pp. 347-9.
[2] Job Baster (1711-75), a Dutch physician, who published many works on natural history. The one Banks refers to is the *Opuscula subseciva*, a series of miscellaneous observations on animals and plants—to give its more extended title, *observationes miscellaneæ, de animalculis et plantis quibusdam marinis, eorumque ovariis et seminibus, continentia* (Haarlem, 2 vols., 1759-65).
[3] A larval tetrarhynchid, one of the tapeworms. See Solander, p. 421. Mss: manuscript, i.e. no description had been published. In his botanical and zoological lists Banks uses similarly the abbreviation Mscr.
[4] A trematode, probably *Hirundinella clavata* (Menzies). See Solander, p. 419.
[5] *Hirundo rustica* was the name given by Linnaeus to the European Swallow.

The trade had now lasted us pretty free from squalls or calms these days it has been in general between   [1] but ever since we have been in it the air has been uncommonly damp, every thing more than usualy liable to mould, and all Iron work to rust, the air has seldom been Clear, but a haize in it which was even perceiveable to the human frame.

4. Today quite calm, I went out in a boat and took *dagysa strumosa*,[2] *medusa porpita*,[3] the same which we before calld azurea, *mimus volutator*,[4] and *cimex*   [5] who runns upon the water here in the same manner as *C. Lacustris* does on our ponds in England. Towards even two small fish were taken under the stern, they were following a shirt which was towing and showd not the least signs of fear, so that they were taken with a landing net without the least difficulty. *Balistes monoceros* Linn.[6]

5. Weather pretty good, at night a squall with Lightning and rain, another swallow came to the ship today and was taken with the snippers as soon as he went to roost.

6. Blew fresh this morn with heavy rain; towards noon five swallows came on board and were taken at roosting time, and provd like all we have taken before to be *H. domestica* Linn.

7. This morn calm; went out in the boat and took what is calld by the Seamen a Portugese man of war, *Holothuria Physalis* Linn;[7] also *Medusa velella* L.[8] *onidium spinosum* Mss,[9] *Diodon Erinaceus* Mss,[10]

---

[1] Cook records a 'fresh' or 'steady' breeze from 24 September, when he remarks, 'I take this to be the NE Trade we have now got into'. There was a switch to variable winds with calms on his 3 October, and then to southerlies for some time.

[2] Solitary form of *Thetys vagina*; cf. 6 September above.

[3] *Porpita porpita*; cf. 30 September above.

[4] *Glaucus atlanticus*, a beautiful and remarkable little nudibranch mollusc described by Forster and painted by Parkinson, III, pl. 23. See Pl. 1*b*.

[5] *Cimex* was a name used by Linnaeus for a number of hemipterous insects, but now marks the genus to which the common European bedbug belongs. Banks was probably referring to the British Pond Skaters which belong to the same order; *Halobates* and its allies are related apterous forms which occur far out to sea in the tropical and sub-tropical oceans.

[6] *Monacanthus* sp. Parkinson I, pl. 64; Solander, p. 191.

[7] *Physalia physalis*. There are five plates (37-41) of this siphonophore in Parkinson III; two are signed and finished while the others are in various stages of completion. Solander described them under three specific names, *Holothuria physalis*, *H. obtusata* and *H. angustata* (pp. 393-7).

[8] *Velella velella*. There is a series of paintings signed by Parkinson, III, pl. 56, of this siphonophore which was described by Solander who, as was his usual practice, listed the various localities where it was taken, p. 475.

[9] *Cystisoma spinosum* (Fabr.). There are several pencil and pen and ink studies of this hyperiid amphipod by Parkinson, III, pls. 19, 20, and a long description by Solander, pp. 365-6. It is an interesting animal, generally considered to be a deep-sea form, but since it was captured in excellent condition—this is clear from the drawings—it would appear that it sometimes comes into the upper oceanic layers.

[10] *Diodon* sp. Parkinson made two paintings of this curious little fish, I, pl. 68, which was also described by Solander, p. 193.

dagysa vitrea Mss,[1] *Helix Janthina* Linn,[2]—*violacea* Mss[3] and *procellaria Oceanica* Mss.[4] The Holothuria proved to be one of the most bea[u]tifull sights I had ever seen, it consisted of a small bladder in shape much like the air bladder of fishes, from the bottom of which descended a number of strings of bright blue and red, some three or four feet in lengh which if touchd stung the person who touchd them in the same manner as nettles, only much stronger: on the top of this Bladder was a membrane which he turnd either one way or the other as the wind blew to receive it, this was veind with pink in an uncommonly beautifull manner, in short the whole together was one of the most beautifull sights I have seen among the mollusca, tho many of them are beautifull.

The floating shells *H. Janthina* and *violacea* from their particularity deserve also to be mentiond, they are found floating on the top of the water by means of a small cluster of Bubbles filld with air, which are composd of a tenacious slimey substance, not easily parting with its contents; these keep him suspended on the surface of the water and serve as a hiding for his Eggs, and it is probable that he never goes down to the bottom, or willingly comes near any shore, as his shell is of so brittle a construction that few fresh water snails are so thin.

Every shell contains within it about a teaspoonfull of Liquid, which it easily discharges on being touched, this is of a most beautifull red purple colour and easily dies linnen clothes; it may be well worth inquiry whether or not this is the *purpura* of the ancients as the shell is certainly found in the Mediterranean. We have not yet taken a sufficient quantity of the shells to try the experiment, probably we shall do soon.[5]

Procellaria oceanica differs very little from *P. pelagica* Linn,[6] but from his place of abode so far south and some small difference in plumage it is more than likely that he is different in species.

[1] A nectophore of *Diphyes dispar* Chamisso and Eysenhardt. Very little was known in the eighteenth century about the complex structure of the Siphonophora, a group to which the Portuguese Man-of-war also belongs, and it is not surprising that Solander confused this nectophore with the much more highly organized salps, to which it has some slight superficial resemblance. Parkinson III, pls. 31 (lower figure) and 32; Solander p. 501.

[2] *Janthina janthina*. There is a painting of these marine snails by Buchan (see Parkinson, III, pl. 72). The colouring of *Janthina* shells is very variable. See also Solander p. 417.

[3] *Helix violacea: Janthina globosa* Swainson. See Buchan's painting in Parkinson III, pl. 71.

[4] Wilson's Petrel, *Oceanites oceanicus* (Kuhl). Solander gave an MS description of this bird, p. 55, but Parkinson did not draw a specimen until 22 December; on that occasion Banks did not record the specimen.

[5] The usual source of the famous Tyrian purple was *Murex trunculus*, an abundant littoral species in the Mediterranean. It is unlikely that *Janthina* was used for this purpose, since its appearance in that sea is only sporadic.

[6] See 31 August above.

8. A fine Breze today; employd in figuring &c. what was taken yesterday.

9. This morn a shark calld us out of our bedds, and was soon hookd, but as soon broke his hold and went off: at noon went out in the boat but found nothing on the surface of the water; on returning home however found on the stern of the ship two new species of *Lepas vittata* and *midas*,[1] they were both sticking to the bottom in company with the *anatifera*,[2] of which there was great abundance. After dinner calld upon deck by another shark, who had been lately wounded by a harpoon, but he was two cunning after his misfortune to bite at our baits, which we much Lamented as he had sucking fish upon him that were quite white, probably a species not yet describd.

10. Went out in the boat today, took plenty of *Helix Janthina* and some few of *violacea*, shot the black toed gull of *Penn.* *Zool*.[3] It had not yet been describd according to Linnæus's system, so calld it *Larus crepidatus*; its food here seems to be cheifly Helixes which appeard probable at least, on account of its dung being of a lively red colour, much like that which was procurd from the shells.[4]

I was drove home from this excursion by a very heavy squall of rain, which intirely wetted me through long before it was possible to return to the ship, however I receivd no other harm from the ducking than the present inconvenience of being so thoroughly wet. The remainder of today was very squally, with much rain; indeed it has been so ever since we lost the trade, and the people who have been here before say that it is generaly so in these latitudes; I can liken it to nothing so much as April in England, when it is very showery, the weather is never certain for two hours, or indeed

---

[1] *Lepas vittata*: the Striped Stalked Barnacle, *Conchoderma virgatum* Spengler. See the drawing by Buchan, Parkinson III, pl. 68, and notes by Solander, p. 385. *Lepas midas*: the Eared Stalked Barnacle, *Conchoderma auritum*. Parkinson signed his painting of this animal, III, pl. 67; see also Solander, p. 387.

[2] *Lepas anatifera*, the Goose Barnacle, so-called on account of the mediaeval belief that Barnacle Geese did not procreate in the usual way but sprang from these organisms. For this reason these birds were regarded as a class apart from other animals, and could be eaten on fast days.

[3] *The British Zoology* (1766) of Thomas Pennant (1726-98). Pennant, a landed gentleman of Flintshire, a naturalist and antiquary, and a correspondent of both Linnaeus and Banks, was best known at this time for this book, though later on for the journals of his travels in England, Scotland and Wales. He was a most voluminous author. Johnson thought him a Whig and a sad dog, adding (of his *Tour in Scotland*, 1771) 'But he's the best traveller I ever read'. White's *Selborne* was written in the form of letters to Pennant and to Daines Barrington, another friend of Banks (cf. Introduction, above, *passim*).

[4] *Stercorarius parasiticus*, the Arctic Skua. This seems to have been the immature bird described by Solander, p. 39, as although his account is not dated he refers to its feeding on *Janthina janthina*.

half the time, tho calms spend[1] much the greatest part of our time in idleness.

11. Today much like yesterday, very squally; saw a dolphin, and admired the infinite beauty of his colour as he swam in the water, but in vain, he would not give us even a chance of taking him.

12. A shark, *squalus carcharias* Linn.[2] taken this morn, and with him two pilot fish; at noon calm, I went out in the boat and took several Blubbers. The pilot fish *Gasterosteus ductor* Linn.[3] is certainly as bea[u]tyfull a fish as can be imagind: it is of a light blue with cross streaks of darker colour; it is wonderful to see them about a Shark, swimming round him without expressing the least signs of fear; what their motive for doing so is I cannot guess as I cannot find that they get any provision by it, or any other emolument, except possibly the company of the shark keeps them free from the attacks of Dolphins or other large fish of prey, who would otherwise devour them.

The blubbers[4] taken today were *Beroe Labiata*[5] and *Marsupialis* Mss,[6] the first of which made a pretty appearance in the water, by reason of its swimmers, which line its sides like fringes, and are of a change-able fire colour; *Callirhoe bivia* Mss,[7] the most lifeless lump of Jelly I have seen, it scarcely seems to be possessd of life but for one or two motions we saw it make.

13. Calm this Morn; a shark was taken, but not one pilot fish attended him, which is rather uncommon as they seldom are without a shoal of from ten to twenty. At noon I went in the boat, and took the Sallee man *Phyllodoce velella* Linn.[8] who is a Sailor tho inferior in size to the Portugese man of war, yet not without its beauty, cheifly from the charming blue of its bottom; its sail is transparent

[1] 'Spend' in the obsolete eighteenth century sense of 'waste'.

[2] *Squalus carcharias*, probably *Carcharodon carcharias*; cf. 29 September above.

[3] *Naucrates ductor*, the Pilot-fish. See Parkinson II, pl. 86. 'Naucrates' is derived from a Greek word meaning 'ruler of the ships'. There is an interesting discussion of the relationship between the Pilot-fish and their sharks in J. R. Norman and F. C. Fraser's *Giant Fishes, Whales and Dolphins* (1948).

[4] Blubbers was a name commonly applied by sailors to jellyfish and some other trans-parent pelagic animals.

[5] *Beroe labiata*: there are eight small paintings of this unidentified ctenophore by Parkinson III, pl. 58, lower series, and a description by Solander, p. 431, who however used the MS name of *bilabiata* for it.

[6] *Beroe marsupialis*: this too is an unidentified ctenophore; Solander thought that it was perhaps only a variety of his *B. bilabiata* (p. 435); Parkinson's painting, III, pl. 58, upper figure, suggests that it was a paler specimen. Both he and Solander used the MS name of *marsupium*, not *marsupialis*, for it.

[7] A ctenophore belonging to the group Lobatae, possibly a species of *Deiopeia*. See Parkinson's painting, III, pl. 42, and Solander, p. 401.

[8] *Velella velella*; cf. 7 October above. 'Sallee-man', originally a Moorish pirate vessel from the port of Sallee.

but not moveable, so it trusts itself to the mercy of the winds without being able to turn to windward as the Portugese man of war may-be can? We saw several of the latter today, and observd many small fish under their tentacula who seemd to shelter there as if with its stings it could defend them from large enemies.[1]

14. Calm today but so squally and rainy that I dar'd not venture out with the boat.

15. Ventur'd out today, but found the surface of the water so ruffled that nothing at all floated upon it, I had the good fortune however to see a bird of the shearwater kind which I shot, and it provd to be not describd; it was about as large as the common but differd from it in being whiter, especialy about the face: calld it *Procellaria crepidata*, as its feet were like the gulls shot last week, black without but white near the leggs.[2]

A large shoal of fish were all this day under the shipp's stern, playing about, but refusing to take bait; we however contrivd to take one of them with a fish gigg, which provd not describd; it was in make and appearance like a Carp, weighing near two pounds, its sides were ornamented with narrow yellow lines and its finns almost intirely coverd with scales: calld it *Chætodon cyprinaceus*.[3]

16. A fine breeze of wind started up last night which held us all day, so I found it impossible to go out in the boat; tonight however to make these 24 hours not intirely unprofitable I had the opportunity of seeing a Phenomenon I had never before met with, a lunar rainbow which appeard about ten O'Clock very faint and almost or quite without colour, so that it could be tracd by little More than an appearance which lookd like shade on a cloud.

17. This morn went out in the boat but caught no one thing, I had never been before so unfortunate. In the Evening a breeze of wind sprung up from SE by S which makes us hope we had got the S.E. trade.

---

[1] If the fish sheltering under the tentacula of the Portuguese Man-of-war were *Nomeus gronovii* (Gm.), as seems most probable, this was the first time that their commensalism with the siphonophore was noted; an account of this now well-known relationship was first published by G. C. Wallich in 1863. Young Pilot-fishes also behave like this.

[2] *Pterodroma mollis feae* (Salvadori), the Soft-plumaged Petrel. In his *Hand List* of 1871, (pt. III, p. 107), Gray considered that Solander's *Procellaria crepidata* (p. 87, undated) was probably equivalent to Gould's *mollis*. Solander also calls it Mother Carey's Pullet and refers to a figure by Parkinson, long mislaid—since for some inexplicable reason it was not bound with the other plates from Cook's voyages but is in the Print Room, British Museum (199* B1, pl. 52).

[3] *Kyphosus sectatrix*. Parkinson II, pl. 32.

18. Wind continued to blow fresh so we had little doubt of the reality of yesterdays hopes. This evening trying as I have often (foolishly no doubt) done to exercise myself by playing tricks with two ropes in the Cabbin I got a fall which hurt me a good deal and alarmd me more, as the blow was on my head, and two hours after it I was taken with sickness at my stomack which made me fear some ill consequence.[1]

19. Today thank God I was much better and easd of all apprehensions, the wind continuing fair and I had given over all thoughts of boat expeditions for some time at least.

20. Quite well today, employd in describing[2] and attending the Draughtsmen.

21. Trade continues. Today the cat killd our bird *M. Avida* who had lived with us ever since the 29th of Septr intirely on the flies which he caught for himself; he was hearty and in high health so that probably he might have livd a great while longer had fate been more kind.

22. Trade had got more to the Southward that it usualy had been, which was unlucky for me as I proposd to the Captain to touch for part of a day at least at the Island of Ferdinand Norronha, which he had no objection to if we could fetch it: that however seemd very uncertain. This Evening we saw 6 or 7 large fish of the whale kind which the Seamen calld Grampuses tho I think they were very different from the fish commonly so calld; they were however Certainly of the whale kind and blew throug[h] two? pipes on the top of their heads. They had heads smaller and rounder than those fish in general have and very low back finns and very small tails; thus much was all that I could see as they never came within two cables lengh of the ship.[3]

23. Trade today was still more to the Southward, almost due South, so that we tackd and stood to the eastward lest we should fall in with the coast of Brazil to the Northward of Cape Frio.

24. Wind today as fair as we could wish, ship layd up so well[4] that it renewd our hopes of touching at the Island.

[1] One would like to know what exercises Banks was able to improvise with two ropes in a cabin 6′ x 6′ x 7′.

[2] i.e. writing descriptions of his zoological specimens.

[3] These were possibly Pilot Whales (*Globicephala* sp.) which have rounded heads and low dorsal fins in comparison with those of the Killer.

[4] 'Layd up so well': she sailed into the prevailing south-easterly winds so satisfactorily. . . .

About noon today we experiencd what the Seamen call a white squall, that is a gust of wind which came upon us quite unawares, unattended with a cloud as squalls in general are and therefore took us quite unprepard; it was however very slight so no ill consequence ensued except Mr Parkinson and his potts[1] going to leward, which diverted us more than it hurt him.

25. This morn about 8 O'Clock crossed the Æquinoctial line in about 33 degrees West Longitude from Greenwich, at the rate of four knotts which our seamen said was an uncommonly good breeze, the Thermometer standing at 29. (The Thermometers used in this voyage are two of Mr Birds making[2] after Farenheights scale, which seldom differ above a degree from each other and that not till they are as high as 80, in which case the medium between the two instruments is set down.) This Evening the ceremony of ducking the ships company was performd as always customary on crossing the line, when those who have crossd it before Claim a right of ducking all that have not, the whole of the ceremony I shall describe.

About dinner time a list was brought into the cabbin containing the names of every body and thing aboard the ship, in which the dogs and catts were not forgot; to this was affixd a petition, sign'd 'the ships company,' desiring leave to examine every body in that List that it might be know[n] whether or not they had crossd the line before. This was immediately granted; every body was then calld upon the quarter deck and examind by one of the lieutenants who had crossd,[3] he markd every name either to be duckd or let off according as their qualifications directed. Capt[n] Cooke and Doctor Solander were on the Black list, as were my self my servants and doggs, which I was oblig'd to compound for by giving the Duckers a certain quantity of Brandy for which they willingly excusd us the ceremony.

Many of the Men however chose to be duckd rather than give up 4 days allowance of wine which was the price fixd upon, and

---

[1] i.e. his paint pots.

[2] John Bird (1709-76), mathematical instrument maker, had a very great reputation for accurate division, founded particularly on his astronomical quadrants. In early life a cloth-weaver at Durham, he became interested in engraving dial-plates for clocks, and went on to become himself one of the great instruments of eighteenth century science. He was closely associated with John Bradley, the astronomer royal, but also supplied many continental observatories with accurate instruments. He wrote on his methods of division. It is not known, apart from this reference, that he actually 'made' thermometers: perhaps he graduated their glasses. He certainly sold them. Cook received '2 Thermometers [bespoke] of Mr Bird' for use on the voyage.—See Cook I, pp. cxliii, 87.

[3] Probably Gore, who had been round the world twice already, with Byron and with Wallis on the *Dolphin*.

as for the boys they are always duckd of course; so that about 21 underwent the ceremony which was performd thus:

A block was made fast to the end of the Main Yard and a long line reved through it, to which three Cross peices of wood were fastned, one of which was put between the leggs of the man who was to be duckd and to this he was tyed very fast, another was for him to hold in his hands and the third was over his head least the rope should be hoisted too near the block and by that means the man be hurt. When he was fas[t]ned upon this machine the Boatswain gave the command by his whistle and the man was hoisted up as high as the cross peice over his head would allow, when another signal was made and immediately the rope was let go and his own weight carried him down, he was then immediately hoisted up again and three times served in this manner which was every mans allowance. Thus ended the diversion of the day, for the ducking lasted till almost night, and sufficiently diverting it certainly was to see the different faces that were made on this occasion, some grinning and exulting in their hardiness whilst others were almost suffocated and came up ready enough to have compounded after the first or second duck, had such proceeding been allowable.[1]

It is now time that I should say something of the climate and degree of heat since crossing the tropick, as we have been for some time within the bounds which were supposd by the ancients to be uninhabitable on account of their heat.

Almost immediately on crossing the tropick the air became sensibly much damper than usual, tho not materialy hotter, the

---

[1] This is one of the best accounts we have of the (or of one) method by which this 'Ancient Custom of the Sea' was carried out—'the Ceremony . . . practised by all Nations', to quote Cook's words. In essentials it was a sort of 'baptism', combining propitiation of the sea-god with present benefit (in the form of strong drink) shared out among the old hands. The ceremony varied according to the nationality of the actors: the English seem to have copied the Dutch, to judge from an account given in the first chapter of Esquemeling's *Buccaneers of America* (Amsterdam 1678, English translation 1684). Esquemeling writes, 'He, therefore, that is to be baptized is fastened, and hoisted up three times at the mainyard's end, as if he were a criminal. If he be hoisted the fourth time, in the name of the Prince of Orange or of the captain of the vessel, his honour is more than ordinary. Thus they are dipped, every one, several times into the main ocean. But he that is the first dipped has the honour of being saluted with a gun. Such as are not willing to fall are bound to pay twelve pence for their ransom; if he be an officer in the ship, two shillings; and, if a passenger, according to his pleasure. . . . All the profit which accrues by this ceremony is kept by the master's mate, who, after reaching their port, doth usually lay it out in wine, which is drunk amongst the ancient seamen. Some will say this ceremony was instituted by the Emperor Charles the Fifth; howsoever, it is not found amongst his Laws'. Mr G. P. B. Naish writes that the same ceremony was frequently performed at the entrance to the Baltic, the Straits of Gibraltar, and crossing the Tropics; and that Neptune started coming on board English ships just before 1790.

thermometer then in general stood from 80 to 82. The nearer we approachd to the calms still the damper every thing grew, this was perceivable even to the human body and very much so, but more remarkably upon all kinds of furniture: every thing made of Iron rusted so fast that the knives in peoples pockets became almost useless and the razors in cases not free. All kinds of Leather became mouldy, Portfolios and truncks coverd with black leather were almost white, soon after this mould adheerd to almost every thing, all the books in my Library became mouldy[1] so that they were obligd to be wiped to preserve them. About this time we came into the calms which we met with earlier than usual; the thermometer was then at 83 and we sufferd from the heat and damp together. Bathing however kept me in perfect health, tho many of the ship[s] company were ill of bilious complaints which however were but of short duration.

This continued till we got the S.E. trade, when or a little before the glass fell to 88 and soon to 78 and 79, but the dampness continued yet; to that I cheifly attribute the ill success of the Electrical experiments of which I have wrote an account on separate papers that the different experiments may appear at one view.[2]

The air during the whole time sin[c]e we crossed the tropick and indeed sometime before has been nearly of the same temperature throughout the 24 hours, the Thermometer seldom rising above a degree during the time the sun is above the horizon. The windows of the cabbin have been open without once being shut ever since we left Madeira.

26. Last night and today the weather has been squally, wind rather fresh but keeping very much to the Southward; great plenty of flying fish have been about the ship few or none of which have been seen since we left the N.E. trade.

27. Fine weather but Wind rather too much to the Southward.

---

[1] There is a marginal note here, 'Piso p. 5', and the reader will find further references to Piso below. Willem Piso, a Dutch naturalist and doctor of the early seventeenth century, went as physician to Prince Maurice of Nassau on a voyage to Brazil in 1636, when part of the country was occupied by the Dutch. He took with him a young German physician and scholar, George Marggraf (Marggrav, Marcgrav), and their discoveries were later published in a folio *Historia naturalis Brasiliae* (1648). Piso's part of this was the *De Medicina Brasiliensi libri quatuor*, the first of which treats of the climate and the nature of the country in general, while the others deal with endemic diseases, poisons, and the virtues of plants. Piso was a rather diffuse writer, given to taking over popular stories: he himself admitted that he had done his work somewhat precipitately, but revised it with care for a subsequent volume *De Indiae utriusque re naturali et medica* (Amsterdam 1658). In spite of its defects the joint work of Piso and Marcgrav remained for a long time the most complete thing available on the country of their exploration. Their other gift to Europe was the drug ipecacuanha.

[2] See Appendix I.

We are today nearly in the latitude of the Island of Fernand de Norhona, so that I am not without hopes of making it if rightly laid down; night however put an end to our hopes for the present at least, and left us in no very agreable situation as shoals and foul ground is laid down all round the Islands.[1]

28. Fine breeze today, our hopes of seeing the Island were again renewd but without success, so at night we judge ourselves to be past it and that the longitude is wrong laid down.

29. Wind East very pleasant, we now gave up all thoughts of the Island. This Evening the sea appeard uncommonly bea[u]tifull, flashes of light coming from it perfectly resembling small flashes of lightning, and these so frequent that sometimes 8 or ten were visible at the same moment; the seamen were divided in their acco[u]nts some assuring us that it proceeded from fish who made the light by agitating the salt water, as they calld it, in their darting at their prey, while others said that they had often seen them and knew them to be nothing but blubbers (*Medusas*). This made us very Eager to procure some of them, which at last we did one by the help of the landing net. They prov'd to be a species of Medusa which when brought on board appeard like metal violently heated, emitting a white light; on the surface of this animal a small *Lepas* was fixd exactly the colour of it, which was almost transparent not unlike thin starch in which a small quantity of blue is disolv'd. In taking these animals three or 4 species of Crabbs were taken also but very small, one of which gave light full as much as a glow-worm in England tho the Creature was not so large by $\frac{10}{9}$ths;[2] indeed the sea this night seemd to abound with light in an uncommon manner, as if every inhabitant of it furnishd its share, which might have been the case tho none kept that property after being brought out of the water except these two.

[1] The ship was now approaching the coast of Brazil. Cook writes (October 28), 'This day at Noon being nearly in the Lat^d of the Island Ferdinand Noronha to the westward of it by some charts and to the Eastward by others, was in expectation of seeing it or some of those shoals that are laid down in most charts between it and the main, but we saw neither one nor a nother. We certainly pass'd to the Eastward of the Island, and as to the shoals I do not think they exhist grounding this my opinion on the Journal of some East India Ships I have seen, who were detained some days by contrary winds between this Island and the main and being 5 or Six Ships in compney, doubtless must have seen some of them did they lay as marked in the charts'. This indicates both the current state of hydrographical knowledge and Cook's wide-ranging mind where hydrography was concerned. A dangerous reef, the As Rocas, does in fact lie 80 miles west of Fernando Noronha. The *Endeavour* passed 60 miles east of the island.

[2] This, odd as it may seem, is what Banks wrote, over something else, smudged, which appears to have been $\frac{9}{10}$ths; and I think that 'nine-tenths' was probably what he meant, though his symbol is unknown to mathematicians.

30. This Morn employd in Examining the things caught last night, which being taken by the light of our lamps (for the wind which blows in at the windows always open will not suffer us to burn candles) we could hardly then distinguish into genera, much less into species, had the good fortune to find that they were all quite new. Calld them *Medusa pellucens*,[1] *Lepas pellucens*,[2] ,[3] *Clio* ,[4] *Cancer fulgens and Cancer amplectens*,[5] but we had the misfortune to loose two more species of Crabbs overboard by the tumbling of a glass overboard in which they were containd.

In the Evening the Sea was lighted in the same manner as it was last night only not near so strongly; we renewd however our endeavours to take some of the light carriers, not without success as two new species of Crabbs were taken one of which was very singular.

31. Nothing to be done today, found however that the crabbs taken yesterday were both new, calld them *vitreus*[6] and *Crassicornis*.[7]

NOVEMBER 1768

1. A shoal of small fish were today under our stern who attended the ship for some time; she had however too much way through the water for our instruments so we could not take any of them.

2. This day was quite void of Events, the wind however was very fair and we now approachd the place where we were next to refresh ourselves apace.

3. This morn the sun was immediately over our heads notwiths[t]anding which the Thermometer was no higher than 77. Since we left the calms under the line the weather has grown cooler by gradual degrees, now we reckon it quite moderate after having felt the heat of 83 so lately.

[1] *Phacellophora* sp. There is a signed sepia painting of this animal by Parkinson, III, pl. 53; see also Solander p. 467.

[2] This barnacle has not been identified; Parkinson's figures are small, III, pl. 68, upper figure. Solander, p. 383, compared its structure with that of *Conchoderma virgatum* (see 9 October above).

[3] There is a blank here in the MS never filled in by Banks.

[4] This may have been one of the pteropods of the genus *Clio* described by Linnaeus. There appears to be no drawing or description of it.

[5] *Cancer fulgens* and *C. amplectens*: the first of these may have been a young euphausiid, the second is a larval form with some likeness to that of the hermit crabs. There is not sufficient detail for identification in Parkinson's drawings, III, pls. 13, 10, or in Solander's descriptions, pp. 309-13.

[6] A stomatopod larva, Alima stage. Parkinson III, pls. 15, 16; Solander, pp. 337-9.

[7] An amphipod, *Scina* sp. Parkinson III, pl. 14, and Solander, pp. 317-20.

This Even I for the first time (for other people had seen them much before) observd two Light spots in the heavens apearing much like the milky way, one the largest and brightest Bore S. by E. the other about South.[1]

4. Still as we got more to the westward the wind became more favourable, today it was almost aft and has been all along creeping to the northward.

5. The thermometer kept still gradualy falling as the wind got more to the northward, which appears odd as the North wind should now be the warm wind; we were not yet however enough to the Southward to find much alteration. Wind this morn was North-east, at noon North by west, between this place and mid channel it has changd from South by East. The Trade being to the Northward upon this coast has been observd long ago, tho I question whether our navigators are sufficiently apprisd of it. *Piso* in his Natural history of the Brasils[2] says that the winds along shore are constantly to the Northward from October to March and to the southward from March to October. Dampier also who certainly had as much experience as most men says the same thing,[3] advising ships outward bound to keep to the westward where they are almost certain to find the Trade more Eastward than in mid channel, where it sometimes is due South or within ½ a point of it as we ourselves experienced.

6. Today light winds and very pleasant weather, the Thermometer was never above 76. Towards evening the colour of the water was observd to change upon which we sounded and found ground at 32 fathom; the lead was cast three times between 6 and 10 without finding a foot difference in the depth or quality of the bottom, which was incrusted with coral; we supposd this to be the tail of a great shoal laid down in all our charts by the name of Albrolhos, on which Ld Anson struck soundings in his outward bound passage.[4]

---

[1] These must have been the Magellanic Clouds, two cloud-like condensations of stars in the southern constellation of Mensa, with a remarkable resemblance to the stars of the Milky Way, though entirely detached from it. They would be visible from the ship's latitude (15°-16° S) in clear weather.

[2] See p. 178, n. 1 above.

[3] In his *Discourse of Winds* (1700), Chapter III, 'Of the Coasting Trade-Winds that shift'.—*Dampier's Voyages*, ed. Masefield (London 1906), II, pp. 243 ff.

[4] Cook spells the name of the shoal 'Abrollos': more properly 'Abrolhos', from the Portuguese *abre os olhos*, literally 'open your eyes', hence 'look out, take care'. The Dutch conferred the same name on a reef on the western coast of Australia, 'Houtman's Abrolhos'. The reference to Anson is to his famous voyage round the world, 1741-4. The account of the voyage by his chaplain, Richard Walter (1748) was evidently on board the *Endeavour*, as Cook also refers to it. Anson struck soundings in lat. 20° S, long. 36° 30′ W; Cook in lat. 19° 46′ S, long. 36° 54′ W. This is in a region of coral banks, the nearest of which, in modern reckonings, are the Montague Bank and the Sylvia Bank.

o

7. This morn at four no ground with 100 Fathoms of Line. About noon long ranges of a yellowish colour appeard upon the sea, many of them very large, one (the largest) might be a mile in lengh and 3 or 400 yards wide. The seamen in general affirmd roundly that they were the spawn of fishes and that they had often seen the same appearance before; upon taking up some of the water so coloured we found it to be causd by innumerable small atoms, each pointed at the end and of a yellowish colour, none of them above a quarter of a line in lengh; in the microscope they appeard to be fasciculi of small fibres interwove one within the other, not unlike the nidi of some Phryganeas which we call caddices. What they were or for what purposes designd we could not even guess, nor so much as distinguish whether their substance was animal or vegetable.[1]

8. At day break today we made the Land which Provd to be the Continent of S. America in Lat. 21.16; about ten we saw a fishing boat who told us that the countrey we saw belongd to the Captainship of Espirito Santo.

Doctor Solander and myself went on board this boat in which were 11 men (9 of whom were blacks) who all fishd with lines. We bought of them the cheif part of their cargo consisting of Dolphins,[2] two kinds of large Pelagick Scombers,[3] Sea Bream[4] and the fish calld in the West Indies Welshman,[5] for which they made us pay 19 shillings and Sixpence. We had taken Spanish silver with us which we imagind was the currency of the Continent, we were therefore not a little surprizd that they askd us for English shillings and preferrd two which we by accident had to the Pistereens, tho they after some words took them also. The Business of these people seemd to be going a good distance from land and catching large fish, which they salted in bulk in a place in the middle of their boat made for that purpose; in this place was about 2 Quintals of fish laid in salt which they offerd to sale for 16 shillings, and would doubtless have taken half the money had we been inclind to buy them, but fresh provisions was all we wanted and the fresh fish they had which we bought servd the whole ships company.

---

[1] Dr W. R. Taylor writes, 'the reference here is almost certainly to *Trichodesmium thiebautii* Gomont'. Banks refers to these 'small particles' again off Rio de Janeiro, 9-10 December 1768, pp. 205-6 below.

[2] In the eighteenth century and earlier the term dolphin usually denoted a small cetacean, but it was also applied, as here (p. 183 below), to the fish *Coryphaena hippuris*, identified by Solander, p. 209.

[3] See below, p. 183, n. 6.

[4] Probably Banks's *Sparus pagrus*, see below, p. 183, n. 8.

[5] *Holocentrus ascensionis* (Osbeck); cf. p. 183, n. 9.

Their provision for the Sea consisted of a cask of water and a bag of the flour of Cassada¹ which they call Farinha de Pao or wooden flour, a very proper name for it which indeed tastes more like powderd chipps than any thing else.

Their method of drinking out of their cask of water was truely primitive and pleasd me much. The cask was large, as broad as the boat and exactly fitted a place in the Ballast made for it, they consequently could not get at the bottom of it to put in a tap by which the water might be drawn out. To remedy this dificulty they made use of a cane about three feet long hollow and open at each end; this the man who wanted to drink desired his neighbour to fill for him, which he did by putting it into the cask, and laying the palm of his hand over the uppermost hole hinderd the water from running out of the other, to which the drinker applyd his mouth and the other taking off his hand lett the liquor run into the drinkers mouth till he was satisfied.

Soon after we came on board a Sphynx² was taken which provd to be quite a new one, and a small bird also who was the *Tanagra Jacarini* of Linn; it seemd however from Linnæus description as well as Edwards's³ and Brissons⁴ that neither of them had seen the Bird which was in reality a *Loxia nitens*.⁵

The fish Brought on board provd to be *Scomber anxia* and *Falcatus*,⁶ *Coryphæna Hipparis**⁷ *Sparus pagrus*⁸ and *Sciæna rubens*;⁹ the second and last not being before describd we calld them by these names.

¹ Cassada or Cassava, or Manioc (*Manihot utilissima*); from its fleshy tuberous roots was obtained the flour, a sort of nutritious starch. There is another species, *M. aipi*, the sweet cassava.

² A Hawkmoth, one of the Sphingidae.

³ George Edwards (1694-1773), naturalist. Of humble origin, he got a good education, and after travelling some time in Holland, Norway, and France he attained some note for his coloured drawings of animals, and in 1733 was appointed on Sir Hans Sloane's recommendation librarian to the Royal College of Physicians; F.R.S. 1757. He was the author of *A Natural History of Birds* (4 vols., 1743-51), which brought him the gold medal of the Royal Society in 1750. It was lavishly illustrated with engravings, and is singular, at a time when fashionable patrons were much sought after, in being dedicated to God.

⁴ Mathurin Jacques Brisson (1723-1806), French naturalist and physicist, and in his day an extremely eminent scholar. In his youth he was attached to Réaumur, 'the Pliny of the eighteenth century', whose collection was the basis of his great *Ornithologie, ou Méthode contenant la division des oiseaux en ordres, sections, genres, espèces, et leur variétés* (6 vols., Paris 1760). It is to this book (III, p. 28), the major work on birds before Buffon's *Histoire naturelle des oiseaux*, that Banks refers. Brisson wrote other works on zoology, and on physics and chemistry.

⁵ *Volatinia jacarina*: Parkinson I, pl. 37*b*; Solander, p. 119.

⁶ *Scomber amia*: now *Seriola lalandi* Cuv. and Val., Amber Jack. Parkinson II, pl. 99; Solander, p. 275. *Scomber falcatus* now *Caranx amblyrhynchus* Cuv. and Val. Parkinson II, pl. 94; Solander, pp. 271-2.

⁷ See p. 182, n. 2 above.

⁸ Now *Pagrus pagrus*; reported by Solander, p. 231, right across the Atlantic.

⁹ Now *Holocentrus ascensionis* (Osbeck), known both as the Welshman and Squirrel-fish. Parkinson II, pl. 63, upper figure; Solander, pp. 249-50.

Afternoon the wind came about South and South by East and it soon came on to blow fresh which we were not at all accustomd to, so we Boarded it[1] along shore wihout gaining much.

9. This morn wind continued South and South by west but is more moderate, but still more sea than we should chuse were we directors of the winds and waves.

We however stood in with the land till we found ourselves in a large bay the shores of which were very flat; in the middle of this bay were some large hills which lay far inland and made the prospect very remarkable, as expressd in the view.[2] At this time we were by guess within five miles of the shore and our water had decreasd gradualy till we had less than five fathom; it was about four in the Evening so our Captain thought proper to put about and stand off to sea; in the Evening the wind freshend a little but was not near so troublesome as last night.

10. Wind more moderate this morn; we stood in with the land and made it nearly in the same place as we left it last night, our soundings being from 15 to 10 fathoms.

After dinner the wind came more to the Eastward and freshend, and little peices of Seaweed now came floating by the ship which we took and it provd to be Sargaso *fucus natans*,[3] which is generaly supposd to increase upon the surface of the sea in the same manner as duck weed *Lemna* does on fresh water without having any root; this however plainly shewd that it had been rooted in the Coral rock on the bottom, as two specimens particularly had large lumps of the coral still adhering to their bottoms. Among the weed we got were some few animals but scarcely worth mentioning, one *Balistes*[4] but quite a fry so young that it was impossible to referr it to its species; a worm also was in it which provd to be *Neireis pelagica*.[5]

In the course of this night we ran over a small bank on which the water suddenly shoald to 7 fathom and kept thereabouts for some time, it however deepend gradualy.

11. Light breezes to day, the wind much more fair than it has been so that we began to get to the Southward. The Thermometer today

[1] 'Boarded it': tacked off and on.
[2] Views or 'coastal profiles' were drawn in abundance on the voyage, by Buchan and others—Cook did a great many—but this particular one, if it has survived, seems unidentifiable.
[3] Genus *Sargassum* (from Spanish *sargazo*, seaweed, a name given by mariners to floating seaweeds). The botanist Kjellman recognized about 150 spp.
[4] Possibly a *Monacanthus* sp.
[5] *Nereis pelagica*: a Linnean species of polychaete worm which still bears that name.

was no more than 72, so that we felt cold or cool at least, tho we could [not] prevail on ourselves to shut the cabbin windows as we are soon to come into much warmer weather.

Just before dark the Land was seen ahead which we supposed to be an Island off Cape Frio so we hoped to be the lengh of Cape Frio by tomorrow morn.

12. This morn we were abreast of the land which proved as we thought last night to be the Island just without Cape Frio, which is calld in some maps the Isle of Frio;[1] the wind was fair and we passd it with a pleasant Breeze hoping tomorrow to get into the harbour. About noon we saw the hill calld Sugar Loaf[2] which is just by the harbours mouth, but it was a long way off yet so there were no hopes of reaching it this night.

The shore from Cape Frio to this place has been one uninterruptd beach of the whitest Colour I ever saw which they tell me is a white sand.

This Evening wind still continued fair but very little, we now saw the Sugar Loaf very plain but could not tonight reach it, so shortend sail; we had seen for some time a small vessel under the land which seemd to steer into the harbour as well as we.

The Land all along this Coast has been exceedingly high inland except in the bay mentiond on the 7th:[3] the mountains seen now about Rio Janeiro were immensely high so that some of our people compared them with the Pike of Tenerife, tho I do not myself think they deserve a comparison so much higher is the Pike. Notwithstanding the hills are high and begin to rise near the shore the beach is sandy and appears to be of a firm sand.

In the Course of this Evening we aproachd very near the Land and found it very cold, to our feelings at least; the Thermometer at ten O'Clock stood at 68¼ which gave us hopes that the countrey would be cooler than we should expect from the accounts of travellers, especially Mr Biron[4] who says that no business is done here from 10 till 2 on account of the intense heat.

---

[1] If one goes by modern nomenclature, one may feel a little confusion here. Cape Frio (lat. 23° 01′ S, long. 42° 00′ W) is itself the south-east extremity both of Cape Frio Island and of the coast of Brazil, where it turns west to Rio de Janeiro. But a mile north-east of the Cape there is a small islet close to the shore. This perhaps is the island referred to at the end of Banks's previous entry, and was what was 'called in some maps the Isle of Frio'.

[2] In modern nomenclature Pão de Açuçar, 1294 feet.

[3] sic, but he means the 9th.

[4] The reference is to C. Biron, *Curiositez de la nature et de l'art, aportées dans deux voyages, l'un aux Indes d'Occident en 1698 & 1699, et l'autre aux Indes d'Orient en 1701 & 1702. Avec une relation abregée de ces deux voyages.* Paris 1703. Biron is an obscure figure, who comes into none of the biographical dictionaries; even his Christian name seems to be unknown.

13. This Morn the Harbour of Rio Janeiro was right ahead about
2 leagues off but it being quite Calm we made our aproaches very
slowly. The sea was inconceveably full of small vermes[1] which
we took without the least dificulty; they were almost all new except
Beroe labiata,[2] *Medusa radiata*,[3] *fimbriata*[4] and *Chrystallina*,[5] *Dagysa*
.[6] Soon after that a fishing boat Came a board and
sold us three Scombers which proved to be new and were calld
Salmoneus;[7] his baites were *Clupea Chinensis*[8] of which we also procurd
specimens.

As soon as we came well into the River the Capt[n] sent M[r] Hicks
his first Leutenant with a midshipman to get a pilot and stood
up the river expecting him down very soon. He did not nor did
the boat till we were on the point of dropping an anchor just under
the town; the boat then came without either of our officers, in
exchange for whom came a Subaltern Portugese who seemd to
have no kind of Business with us; the Cockswain brought word
from the Leutenant that he was detaind on shore till the Captain
should go off. Soon after we came to an anchor a ten Oard boat
came alongside the ship with 12 or 14 soldiers in it who rowed
round us without taking any notice of us or saying a word; a quarter
of an hour after came a boat in which was a Disembargador[9] and
a Colonel of a Portugese rejument who askd us many questions
which at first seemd to discourage our stay, as telling us that the
Governor would furnish us with any quantity of water in two days.
In the conclusion however he was immensely civil telling us that the
Governor would give us every assistance in his power; that the
Leutenant had not been confind but on account of the Practica
had not been allowd to go on shore, he should now however be
sent on board immediately; that the Captain was welcome to

---

[1] Vermes, a term applied to many invertebrates besides worms from the time of
Aristotle until the nineteenth century.

[2] See p. 173, n. 5 above.

[3] *Aequorea forskalia* Péron and Lesueur. Parkinson III, pl. 48, and Solander, p. 455.

[4] Perhaps a variety of *A. forskalia*? Parkinson III, pl. 49; Solander, p. 459.

[5] *Liriope* sp. Parkinson III, pl. 50, and Solander, p. 461.

[6] This is perhaps the '*Dagysa costata*' of Parkinson III, pl. 36 lower fig., as this is marked
'Rio Janeiro': it has not been possible to identify it.

[7] *Pomatomus saltatrix*, Bluefish or Skipjack. Parkinson III, pl. 90; Solander, p. 277.

[8] *Clupea sinensis* Linn. has not been identified by later workers.

[9] There is no precise equivalent in English for the word *Desembargador*, and older
English writers at various times used 'judge', 'magistrate', 'overseer' and 'assessor'.
The *desembargador* was a crown lawyer whose legal functions included both judicial
and administrative work; and the *desembargadores* of the council or tribunal *da Fazenda*
acted as overseers of customs houses. Though they were not primarily customs officials,
it was no doubt in his customs capacity that Banks's *desembargador* rowed round the
ship.—I am indebted to Professor C. R. Boxer for generous instruction on this point.

go on shore now but he wishd the rest of the crew might remain on board till the Paper they drew up had been delivered.[1]

14. This morn Cap^tn Cooke went ashore, Dr Solander and myself impatiently waiting for his return which he promisd should be the moment he had spoke with the viceroy, who would no doubt tell him that the practica paper had been deliverd and we were all at liberty to come ashore when we pleasd. About twelve he came on board with a Portugese officer in his boat who had been put there by order of the viceroy, out of a compliment as he termd it, and an English gentleman Mr Forster by name a Leutenant in the Portugese service. The Cap^tn told us that we could not be allowd to have a house or sleep ashore, so the Viceroy had told him, but Mr Forster told us that he had given orders that no person but the Cap^tn and such common sailors as were requird to be upon duty should be permitted to go ashore, and that we the passengers were probably particularly objected to. We however in the Evening dress'd ourselves and attempted to go ashore under pretence of a visit to the Viceroy, but were stopd by the Guard boat whose officer told us that he had particular orders, which he could not transgress, to Lett no officer or Passenger except the Captain pass the boat; after much conversation to no purpose we were obligd to return on board and the Cap^tn went ashore to remonstrate to the viceroy about it, but could get no answer but that it was the King of Portugals orders and consequently must be.

15. This morn the Cap^tn went again ashore and told the viceroy that it was nescessary to give the ship a heel, in which case it would be almost impossible for the gentlemen who were passengers to

---

[1] I have discussed the episode of the *Endeavour* at Rio de Janeiro in the Introduction to Cook I, pp. cxxxviii-xl, and in notes to the text of Cook's Journal, and have given the epistolary exchange between Cook and the Viceroy in Appendix I to that volume. There is no essential difference between Cook's account and Banks's, though Banks adds one or two details, in particular on his own movements. The Viceroy, Don Antonio Rolim de Moura (1709-82), had had a distinguished career in the Portuguese imperial service, but seems hardly by nature to have been fitted to cope with scientific reasoning. It also seems very probable that he was acting under recent orders, which made it difficult for him to give the same sort of good reception to an English vessel which Anson had had at the Brazilian island of St Catherine's in 1741 and Byron at Rio in 1764. The Portuguese also were nervous about spies under the guise of scientists, and their treatment of Bougainville in 1767 led to official complaints by the French government. It was certainly true that the *Endeavour* looked most unlike a naval vessel, and the English had a bad reputation both as smugglers on the South American coast and as forgers of documents—though, as Cook pointed out, in one of his exchanges with the Viceroy, it would have been difficult to forge officers' and marines' uniforms. Gore reports in his journal (18 November) that 'one suspicion of us among many Others is that our Ship is a Trading Spy and that Mr Banks and the Doctor are both Supercargoes and Engineers and not naturalists for the Business of such being so very abstruse and unprofitable That They cannot believe Gentlemen would come so far as Brazil on that Account only'.

stay on board her; the viceroy as I suppose misunderstood him, and supposing that he wanted to have the ship hove down said that if the ship was reported by one of his carpenters (who should be sent on board) to want such repairs he would give her all nescessaries for so doing; in that case the Gentlemen should have a house ashore, but gave him to understand that a centinel would be put at the door with orders not to let us stir out or any one come in on any pretence whatever.

16. The Cap^tn went ashore again and remonstrated particularly against the Centinel that was put in his boat whenever he landed or came aboard, which he was told was a compliment but now found to be a guard. He received no satisfactory answers or rather none at all but that it is the King of Portugals orders.

17. Tird with waiting and remonstrating only in words, both the Cap^tn and myself sent ashore written memorials (of which mine is subjoind as well as another with the answers)[1] which complain of his excellency the viceroys behaviour to us as a Kings ship as almost a breach of treaty.

18. Answers to our memorials came on board in which the Cap^tn is told that he has no reason to complain, as such usage as he has receivd has been constantly the custom of the Ports of Brasil and that the Viceroy himself servd an English ship just in the same manner at Bahia; as for me I am told that as I have not brought proper credentials from the Court of Lisbon it is impossible that I can be permitted to land.

19. Both the Cap^tn and myself sent answers to his excellencys memorials this morn by the Leutenant, who had orders not to suffer a guard to be put into his boat but if the Guard boat insisted upon it to return on board. The boat let him pass, but the viceroy as soon as he heard that he had come ashore without a guard orderd Centinels to be put into the boat, and on the Leutenant refusing to go on board unless the Centinels are taken out, orderd the boats crew to be taken into custody, the boat detain and the leutenant to be sent on board in a guard boat under care of an officer. When he came on board he reported what he has seen, that the men in our pinnace made not the least resistance, not-

---

[1] Banks's memorials are not with his journal, but they are extant both in his drafts now in the Commonwealth National Library, Canberra, and with the copy of his letter to the Earl of Morton, 1 December 1768, B.M., Add. MS 34744 (West Papers, XVIII). See Appendix III, Vol. II, pp. 315-20 below. The original letter has been separated from the copies sent with it: the letter is now in the Nan Kivell collection; the copies of the memorials in the Yale University Library.

withstanding which the soldiers who took them into custody behavd with great indecency, striking them many times and thrusting them out of the boat. The same guard boat also brought back the letters unopend.

This Evening it blew very hard at about South, Puffs coming off about three minutes distant from each other, which seldom lasted above half a minute but in that time were as violent as I ever saw.

At this time Our long boat came on board with 4 cask of rum in her, she with difficulty fetchd the ship and soon after by some mismanagemen[t] which I cannot account for[1] broke adrift, carrying with her my small boat which was made fast to her; we had now no boat on board but a small 4 oard yawl, which was immediately sent after her and took her in tow, but notwithstanding all that could be done by the people who rowd in the long boat and those who towd in the yawl she was very soon out of sight, and we were under the greatest uneasiness well knowing that she drove directly upon a reef of Rocks which Runns out from the point of Ilhoa das Ferreiras, just to Leward of where we lay. After remaining in this situation till two in the morning our people cam[e] onboard and told us that the Long boat was sunk, but that they had left her riding to her grapling tho full of water; as for my boat they had in returning to the ship faln in with a reef of rocks, in which dangerous situation they had been obligd to cut her adrift: this was poor comfort tho we were glad to find the people safe, yet the Loss of our long boat which we much feard was perhaps the greatest misfortune that could happen to people who were going as we were upon discoverys.

I should have mentiond that on the detainder of our boats crew a petty officer was sent ashore with the memorials and a letter from the Cap[tn] demanding the Boat and men, who was sufferd quietly to go ashore on taking a soldier out of the guard boat; the only answer he got was verbal that the affair could not be settled as yet.

20. This morn the yawl, now the only boat we had, was sent ashore to ask assistance: they returnd about nine and brought with her our boat and crew that had been detaind, as well as another of the Viceroys which had orders to assist us in searching for our boats.

The people who came in the Pinnace declard that they never made the least resistance but said that the soldiers struck them

---

[1] Cook mentions no mismanagement. This is not the last time that Banks the landsman casts a sharp critical eye on the sailors.

often, that they were confind in a loathsome dungeon where their companions were cheifly Blacks who were chaind, but the Cockswain purchasd a better apartment for seven petacks (about as many shilling English).

Our situation this whole day was better imagind than describd: the Shore boat came onboard at noon that the people might have their victuals but brought no news of the Longboat. Tird with expectation I confess I had almost given over all hopes of ever seeing her again, when Just at dark night the pinnace came bringing with her both the boats and all their contents: we now immediately passd from our disagreable though[t]s to a situation as truly happy, and concluded with defying the Viceroy and all that he could do to us.

21. Letters came from the Viceroy to both the Cap^{tn} and myself, in which he told me very politely that it is not in his power to permit to go ashore; in the cap^{tns} he raises some doubts of our ship being a Kings ship, so I who could ground my pretensions to going ashore on no other Foundation thought it best to drop them, hoping that by and by when things were more quiet I might have an opportunity of smugling myself ashore.

22. This morn I sent my servants ashore at day break who stayd till dark night and brought off many plants and insects.

23. The viceroys answer to the Cap^{tns} last memorial came on board in which the Captn is accusd of smugling, which made us all angry but our venting our spleen against the Viceroy will be of very little service to us.

24. My servants went ashore again and brought off many plants &c.

25. This morn Dr Solander went into the town as surgeon of the Ship, to visit a friar who had desird that the surgeon might be sent to him; he receivd civilities from the people rather more than he could expect.[1]

26. I myself went ashore this morn before day break and stayd till dark night; while I was ashore I met several of the inhabitants who were very civil to me, taking me to their houses where I bought of them stock for the ship tolerably cheap, a porker midlingly fat for 11 shill, a muscovy duck something under two shil^s &c.

---

[1] Solander does not mention this episode in his letter to Ellis, but gives a rather different account of his day as 'surgeon's mate'. See below, II, pp. 308-9. Monkhouse, the surgeon, was on shore every day to buy provisions.

The countrey where I saw it abounded with vast variety of Plants and animals, mostly such as have not been describd by our naturalists as so few have had an opportunity of coming here;[1] indeed no one that I know of even tolerably curious has been here since Marcgrave[2] and Piso about the year 1640, so it is easy to guess the state in which the nat hist of such a countrey must be.

To give a Cataloge of what I found would be a trouble very little to the purpose, as every particular is mentiond in the general catalogues of this place.[3] I cannot however help mentioning some which struck me the most and consequently gave me particular pleasure: these were cheifly the parasitick plants especialy renealmias,[4] for I was not fortunate enough to see one epidendron, and the different species of Bromelia,[5] many not before describd had I been fortunate enough to see fructifications which I did of very Few. *B. Karratas* I saw here growing on the decayd trunk of a tree 50 feet high at least, which it had so intirely coverd that the whole seemd to be a tree of Karratas.[6] The growth of the [7] also pleasd me much tho I had before got a very good Idea of it from Rumphius,[8] who has a very good figure of

[1] The Pocket Book contains 245 specimens collected on this brief encounter with the Brazilian flora.

[2] 'George Marcgrave' (1610-44) was the German physician and traveller, who with Piso accompanied the Prince of Nassau on his expedition to Brazil in 1636 (cf. p. 178, n. 1 above). He travelled in the country for six years, from Rio Grande to Pernambuco, making observations on geography, astronomy and natural history. These were edited after his death in Guinea in 1644 and published with Piso's in the *Historia Naturalis Brasiliae* (1648) as *Georgii Marggravii historiae rerum naturalium Brasiliae libri octo.* The first three books are devoted to plants, the others to fish, birds, quadrupeds and serpents, insects, and an imperfect sketch of the country and its inhabitants.

[3] See Appendix I, Vol. II, pp. 289-96 below.

[4] Dr L. B. Smith suggests these were *Tillandsia recurvata* and *T. usneoides,* formerly classified as Renealmiae.

[5] Both 'epidendron' and 'Bromelia' are here used in the general sense, as the terms orchids and bromeliads are today.

[6] *Neoregelia,* most likely *N. cruenta* (Graham) L. B. Smith, would probably be the first bromeliads encountered on making a beachhead (*teste* L. B. Smith).

[7] Banks here writes 'Rizophane' or 'Rizophanes', but deletes the word without substitution.

[8] George Eberhard Rumpf or Rumphius (1626-93) was a German physician and botanist who went to the East Indies, made his way in 1654 to the Sunda Islands, and entering the service of the Dutch East India Company, became their consul and principal merchant at Amboina. He was a good servant to the Company, but a still better naturalist, and his travels in the islands enabled him to make remarkable collections. In 1669 he was on the point of returning home when he was smitten with total blindness, apparently the result of overwork in an unfavourable climate. This misfortune was followed by the death of his wife and two of his children in an earthquake in 1674. He remained, nevertheless, for the rest of his life at Amboina, and with the help of secretaries and his son produced his classic *Herbarium Amboinense* (7 vols. folio, Amsterdam 1741-55); this, together with its supplement or *Auctuarium,* presented students with a Dutch and Latin text and 695 plates (before his blindness Rumphius was a fine draughtsman). A less important work is the *D'Amboinsche Rariteitkamer* (1705), a folio volume mainly devoted to shells and crustaceans. Banks, it will be seen, refers to Rumphius more than once.

the tree in his *Herb:Amboin*. Tab: Add to these the whole
Contrey Coverd with the Beatifull blossom of *Malpigias, Bannis-
terias, Pasifloras*, not to Forget *Poinciana*[1] and *Mimosa sensitiva*[2] and a
beatifull species of *Clutia*[3] of which I saw great plenty, in short the
wildest Spotts here were varied with a greater quantity of Flowers
as well as more beatifull ones than our best devisd gardens, a
sight infinitely pleasing to the Eye for a short time tho no doubt
it would soon tire with the continuance of it.

The birds of many species especialy the smaller ones sat in great
abundance on the bough's, many of them coverd with most Elegant
plumage. I shot *Loxia Brasiliensis*[4] and saw several specimens of
them. In sects also were here in great abundance, many species
very fine but much more Nimble than our Europæans especialy
the Butterflies, which almost all flew near the topps of the trees
and were very difficult to come at except when the sea breeze
blew fresh, which kept them low down among the trees where
they might be taken. Humming birds I also saw of one species
but could not shoot them.

The banks of the Sea and more remarkably all the Edges of
small brooks were coverd with innumerable quantities of small
Crabbs, *cancer vocans* Linn,[5] one hand of which is very large. Among
these were many both whose hands were remarkably small and
of equal size: these my black servant told me were females of the
others, and indeed all I examind, which were many, provd to be
females tho whether realy of the same species with *vocans* I cannot
determine on so short an acquaintance.

I saw but little cu[l]tivation and that seemd to be taken but
little pains with; grass land was the cheif on which were many
Lean cattle feeding and lean they might well be, for almost all
the species of grass which I observd here were creepers, and consequently so close to the ground that tho there might be upon them
a sufficient bite for horses or sheep yet how horned cattle could
live at all was all that appeard extraordinary to me.

I also saw their gardens or small patches in which they cultivate
many sorts of European garden stuff as Cabbage, peas, beans,

---

[1] *Poinciana pulcherrima*, as shown by the existing herbarium collection.

[2] A general term for several species of sensitive-leaved *Acacias* and related genera.

[3] Possibly the plant they called *Clusia dodecapetala* (*Pereskia* sp.), but the pertinent coll.
has not been located—none was preserved in the Pocket Book. See Pl. 25.

[4] Possibly *Ramphocoelus brasilius* (Linn.); see pl. 36*a* of Parkinson I, on the front of
which is written in Banks's hand '*Loxia mexicana*'.

[5] *Uca vocans*, one of the fiddler crabs in which the sexes differ as Banks describes. They
are noted for the briefly resplendent colours assumed during courtship by the male,
who then uses his greatly enlarged claw for beckoning to the female.

kidney beans, turnips, white raddishes, pumkins, &c. but all much inferior to ours except perhaps the last; here also they grow water melons and pine apples the only Fruits which I have seen them cultivate. The water melons are very good but the Pines much inferior to those I have tasted in Europe; hardly one I have yet had could have been reckond among the midling sort, many were worse than I have seen sent from table in England where nobody would Eat them, tho in general they are very sweet they have not the least flavour; but more of their Fruits by and by.

In these gardens grow also Yamms and Mandihoca or Cassada which supplys the place of Bread here, for as our Europæan bread corn will not grow here all the Flour they have is brought from Portugal at a large expence, too great for even the midling people to purchase much more the inferior ones.

27. This morn when the Boats returnd from watering they brought word that they heard it said in the town that people were sent out in search of some of our people who were ashore without leave: this we concluded meant either Dr Solander or myself which made it nescessary for us to go no more ashore while we stayd.

28. These three days nothing material hapned, Every thing went
29. on as usual only we if possible increasd our haste to be gone
30. from this place.

DECEMBER 1768

1. This Morn our boat returning from shore brought us the very disagreable news that Mr Forster, who I before mentiond, was taken into custody chargd with having smuggled things ashore from our ship: this charge tho totaly without foundation was lookd upon as a sufficient reason for his being put into prison, but we beleive the real cause to be his having shewn some countenance to his Countrey men, as we heard at the same time that five or six Englishmen residing in the town and a poor Portugese who used to assist our people in buying things were all put into prison also without any reason being given.[1]

2. This Morn thank god we have got all we want from these illiterate impolite gentry, so we got up our anchor and saild to the point of Ilhoa dos cobras, where we were to lay and wait for a fair wind which shoud come every night from the Land. We were fortunate in the arrival of a Spanish Brig comeing from Buenos

---

[1] For further information about the unfortunate Thomas Forster, see his letter to Banks of 5 November 1771, printed in the Appendix, II, pp. 321-3 below.

Ayres with Letters for Spain which arrivd about a week ago; her officers were receivd ashore with all possible politeness and allowd to take a house without the least hesitation. The Captⁿ Don Antonio de Monte Negro y Velasco with all possible politeness offerd to take our letters to Europe which we accepted of as a very Fortunate circumstance and sent them on board this morn.[1]

3.
4. } We remain without any Sea breeze.

5. This Morn early a dead calm, we attemptd to tow down with our boats and came near abreast of Sta Cruz their cheif Fortification, when to our great surprize the Fort fird two shot at us one of which went just over our Mast: we immediately brought to and sent ashore to enquire the reason, were told that no order had come down to allow us to pass without which no ship was ever sufferd to go below that fort. We were now obligd to send to town to know the reason of such extraordinary behavior, the Answer came back about 11 that it was a mistake, for the Brigadier had forgot to send the letter which had been wrote some days: it was however sent by the boat and we had leave to proceed. We now began to weigh our anchor which had been droppd in foul ground when we were fird at, but it was hung so fast in a rock that it could not be got out while the Land breeze blew, which today continued almost till four in the Even; as soon as the Sea breeze came we filld our sails and carrying the ship over the anchor tripd it but were obligd to sail back almost as far as we had towd the ship in the Morn.

This day and yesterday the air was crowded in an uncommon manner with Butterflies cheifly of one sort, of which we took as many as we pleasd on board the ship, their quantity was so large that at some times I may say many thousands were in view at once in almost any direction you could look, the greatest part of them much above our mast heads.

6. No land breeze today so we are confind in our disagreable situation without a possibility of moving: many curses were this day expended on his excellence.

7. This morn weighd and stood out to sea. As soon as we came to Sta Cruz the pilot desired to be dischargd and with him our enemy

[1] These letters included a very full and indignant report by Cook to the Admiralty on his controversy with the Viceroy, and a letter from Banks to the President of the Royal Society.—See II, pp. 313 ff. below. Cook also left a packet of his correspondence with the Viceroy with that official for forwarding to Lisbon, and thence to London.

the guard boat went off, so we were left our own masters and immediately resolved to go ashore on one of the Islands in the mouth of the harbour: their ran a great swell but we made shift to land on one calld Raza,[1] on which we gatherd many species of Plants and some insects. *Alstromeria salsilla*[2] was here in tolerable plenty and *Amarillis mexicana*,[3] they were the most specious[4] plants; we stayd till about 4 oClock and then came aboard the ship heartily tired, for the desire of doing as much as we could in a short time had made us all exert ourselves in a particular manner tho exposd to the hottest rays of the sun just at noonday.

Now we are got fairly to Sea and have intirely got rid of these troublesome people I cannot help spending some time in describing them tho I was not myself once in their town, yet my intelligence coming from D[r] Solander who was, and our Surgeon M[r] Monkhouse a very sensible man who was ashore every day to buy our provisions, I think cannot err much from truth.

The town of Rio de Janiero the capital of the Portugese dominions in America situate on the banks of the River of that name, both are call'd I apprehend from the Roman saint Januarius accord[in]g to the Spanish and Portugese custom of naming their discoveries from the Saint on whose feast they are made.[5]

It is regular and well built after the fashion of Portugal, every house having before its windows a Lattice of wood behind which is a little balcony. For size it is much larger than I could have thought, probably little inferior to any of our Countrey towns

[1] '. . . sent a Boat to one of the Islands laying before the Bay to cut Brooms a thing we were not permitted to do while we lay in the Harbour'.—Cook I, p. 29.

[2] *Bomarea edulis* Herb., but the Banks and Solander specimen is immature and identification uncertain. All the Brazilian specimens collected have tickets with two slits for slipping over the stem; those from Madeira lack this feature.

[3] Probably *Hippeastrum reginae* Herb.—*Amaryllis reginae* of the Banks-Solander MS. Catalogue, p. 12—but the pertinent coll. has not been located. According to Spix and Martius, Banks on this occasion secured one very lovely prize, the irid *Neomarica northiana*, referred to by them under a different name: 'it was upon an island . . . which lies before the mouth of the bay, and is called Ilha raza, that Sir Joseph Banks, when he touched at Rio de Janeiro in the company of Captain Cook, discovered the beautiful *Moraea northiana*, which has since then become the ornament of European gardens'. *Travels in Brazil, in the years 1817-1820* (London 1824), I, p. 226. If this is so, it is curious that Banks does not mention collecting the very distinctive plant; nor can any name used by him for it be perceived in the Catalogue. We may note another very beautiful plant that he did collect, *Bougainvillea spectabilis*, Willd.—the *Calyxis ternaria* Mscr. of the Pocket Book, p. 21.

[4] *Specious*: used apparently in its obsolete sense of beautiful, pleasing to the sight. Sir Thomas Browne, quoted in O.E.D., refers to 'fair and specious Plants'.

[5] Banks's apprehension was wrong. Rio de Janeiro is not situated on a river but on a bay, the discovery of which is generally attributed by Portuguese historians to André Gonçalves, on 1 January 1502. Gonçalves however thought he had found the mouth of a great river—hence its name, the River of January.

in England Bristol or Liverpool not excepted;[1] the streets are all straight intersecting each other at Right angles and have this peculiar Convenience, that much the greater number lay in one direction and are commanded by the Gunns of their citadel calld S[t] Sebastian which is situate on the top of a hill over looking the town.

It is supplyd with water by an aqueduct which brings it from the neighbouring hills upon two stories of arches, said in some places to be very high; the water that this brings is conveyd into a fountain in the great square immediately opposite the Governors palace, which[2] is guarded by a sentry who has sufficient work to keep regularity and order among so many as are always in waiting at this place; there is also water laid into some other part of the town but how it is brought there I could not hear, only that it was better than the fountain which is exceedingly indifferent, so much so as not to be likd by us tho we had been two months at sea in which time our water was almost continualy bad.[3]

The Churches here are very fine dressd out with more ornaments even than those in Europe, and all parts of their religion is carried on with more shew; their processions in particular are very extrordinary, every day one or other of the parishes go in solemn order with all the insignia of their church, altar, host &c through their parish, begging for what they can get and praying in all form at every Corner of a street.

While we were there one of the largest churches in the town was rebuilding and for that reason the parish belonging to it had leave to walk through the whole City, which they did once a week and collected much money for the carrying on of their Edifice: at this ceremony all boys under a certain age were obligd to attend nor were the gentlemens sons ever excusd. Each of these were dressd in a Black cassock with a short red Cloak reaching half way down their shoulders, and carried in his hand a Lanthorn hung on the End of a pole about 6 or 7 feet long, the light caused by this (for there were always at least 200 Lights) is greater than can be imagind; I myself who saw it out of the cabbin windows

---

[1] Cook: 'This City and adjacent parts about the Bay are said to contain one hundred thousand Souls, but not much above a twentieth part are Whites the rest are blacks many of whom are free and seem to live in tolerable circumstances'.—I, p. 33.

[2] i.e. the fountain, not the palace.

[3] This is a revealing comment; for it summarizes one of the great problems of nautical administration at the time, and explains Cook's determination to lose no opportunity of supplying his ships with fresh water. If Cook could not keep water sweet, who could? There was no solution to the problem till the discovery in the nineteenth century that wooden casks were unsuitable containers, and the substitution of metal.

Calyxes ternaria.

Sydney Parkinson pinx.t 1768.

Pl. II. *Bougainvillea spectabilis*

Brazil

call[d] together my mess mates and shewd it to them imagining that the town was on fire.

Besides this traveling[1] religion a man who walks the streets has opportunity enough to shew his attachment to any saint in the Calendar, for every corner and almost every house has before it a little cupboard in which some Saint or other keeps his Residence, and least he should not see his votaries in the night he is furnishd with a small lamp which hangs before his little glass window: to these it is very customary to pray and sing hymns with all the vociferation imaginable, as may be imagind when I say that I and every one Else in the Ship heard it very distinctly every night tho we lay at least half a mile from the town.

The Goverment of this place Seems to me to be much more despotick even than that of Portugal tho many precautions have been taken to render it otherwise. The Cheif Magistrates are the Viceroy, the Governour of the town and a Council whose number I could not Learn, but only that the Viceroy had in this the casting vote: without the consent of this Council nothing material should be done, yet every day shews that the Viceroy and Governour at least if not all the rest do the most unjust things without consulting any one. Puting a man into prison without giving him a hearing and keeping him there till he is glad at any rate to get out without asking why he was put in, or at best sending him to Lisbon to be tried there without letting his family here know where he is gone to, is very common. This we experien[c]d while here, for every one who had interpreted for our people, and some who had only assisted in buying provisions for them, were put into Jail merely I suppose to shew us their power. I should however except from this one John Burrish an officer in their customs, a man who has been here 13 years and is so compleatly become a Portugese that he is known by no other name than Don John: he was of service to our people, tho what he did was so clogd with a suspicious fear of offending the Portugese as renderd it disgustfull. It is nescessary that any one who should Come here should know his Character, which is mercenary tho contented with a little as the present given to him demonstrated, which consisted of 1 doz^n of beer 10 gall^s of Brandy 10 peices of ships beef and as many of Pork: this was what he himself askd for, and sent on board the Cagg for the spirit and with this he was more than satisfied.[2]

---

[1] *traveling* substituted for the more accurate *walking*, no doubt because of the phrase *who walks* immediately after.

[2] Burrish does not come into either Cook's Journal or his account of the Rio de Janeiro affair written to the Admiralty, but in his draft of that account, now in the Mitchell

P

They have a very extrordinary method of keeping people from traveling — to hinder them I suppose from going into any districk where gold or diamonds may be found, as there are more of such than they can possibly guard, which is this: there are certain bounds beyond which no man must go, these vary every month at the discretion of the Vic[e]roy, sometimes they are a few sometimes many Leagues Round the City: Every man must in consequence of this come to town to know where the Bounds are, for if he is taken by the guards who constantly patrole on their edges he is infallibly put in prison, even if he is within them, unless he can tell where they are.

The inhabitants here are very numerous, they consist of Portugese, negroes, and Indians aborigines of the countrey. The township of Rio, whose extent I could not learn but was only told that it was but a small part of the Capitanea or province, is said to contain 37,000 whites and about 17 negroes to each white, which makes their numbers 629,000 and the number of inhabitants in all 666,000. As for the Indians they do not live in this neighbourhood tho many of them are always here doing the Kings work, which they are obligd to do by turns for small pay for which purpose they come from their habitations at a distance. I saw many of them as the guard boat was constantly rowd by them, they are of a light copper colour with long lank black hair; as to their policy or manner of living when at home I could not learn any thing about it.

The military here consist of 12 regiments of Regulars, 6 Portugese and 6 Creolians and as many of Provincial militia who may be assembled upon occasion. To the regulars the inhabitants shew great deference, for as Mr Forster an English Gentleman in their service told me, if any of the people were not to pull off their hatts when they meet an officer he would immediately knock them down, which custom renders the people remarkably Civil to strangers who have at all a gentlemanlike appearance. All the officers of these regiments are expected three times a day to attend at the

Library, is a passage omitted from his final version: [referring to his memorial to the Viceroy of 17 November] 'a Copy of which to gether with the answer I the next day receved I have here inclosed, with his Excellencys answer came on board Mr Burrish an English Gentlemen who resides here, to translate it, this gentlemen offer'd to accommodate me with directions for sailing in to the southern parts on this coast and in some measure advised me to gon [*sic*] on shore and by force oppose a Soldier being put into my Boat, this advice of his surprised me as he had upon all occation before been very shy of giving his advice, but when he did it, it was to bear patiently any restrictions they laid upon me'. Burrish's signature to a receipt for an account paid by Cook, transmitted to the Victualling Board, 30 November, appears on the documents now in the Public Library. Auckland. No doubt as an agent the man was in a difficult position—particularly if, as Banks says, he was a customs officer.

Sala or Viceroys levee, where they formaly ask for commands, where their constant answer is there is nothing new: this policy is Intended as I have been told to prevent them from going into the countrey which it most effectualy does.

This town as well as all others in South America belonging either to Spanyards or Portugese has long been infamous for the unchastity of its women; the people who we talkd with here confirmd the accounts declaring, especialy Mr Forster, that he did not beleive there was one modest woman in the township, which I must own appeard to me a most wonderfull assertion but I must take it for granted as I had not even the least opportunity to go among them. Dr Solander who was ashore declares however that as soon as it was night the windows were every one furnishd with one or more women, who as he walkd along with two more gentlemen gave nosegays to which ever of them each preferrd, which Complement the gentlemen returnd in kind, notwithstanding which each of them threw away whole hatfulls of flowers in their walk tho it was not a long one.

Assassinations are I fancy more frequent here than in Lisbon as the churches still take upon them to give protection to criminals: one accident of the kind happned in the sight of S. Evans our Cockswain, a man who I can depend upon, who told me he saw two people talking together to all appearance in a freindly manner, when one on a sudden drew a knife and stabbd the other twice and ran away pursued by some negroes who saw the fact likewise, but what the farther Event of this was I could not learn.

Thus much for the town and its inhabitants. I shall now speak of the countrey which I know rather more of than of the other as I was ashore one whole day: in that time I saw much Cleard ground but cheifly of an indifferent quality, tho doubtless there is such as is very good as the sugar and tobacco which is sent to Europe from hence plainly testifies; but all that I saw was employd in Breeding cattle of which they have great plenty, tho their pastures are the worst I ever saw on account of the shortness of the grass, and consequently the beef sold in the market tho it is tolerably cheap is so lean that an Englishman can hardly Eat it.[1] I likewise saw great plantations of *Iatropha manikot*,[2] which is calld in the West Indies Cassada and here Farina de Pao i.e. wooden meal, a very proper name, for the cakes they make with it taste as if

---

[1] Cook: 'Fresh Beef (tho bad) is to be had in plenty, at about 2¼d a pound and Jerke'd [dried] Beef about the same price'.—Cook I, p. 33.

[2] Banks seems to write 'manikot' rather than 'manihot', perhaps with 'manioc', the alternative name for cassava, in his mind. See p. 183, n. 1 above.

they were made of Sawdust and yet it is the only bread which is Eat here—for European bread is sold at nearly the rate of a shilling a pound, and is also exceeding bad on account of the flour which is generaly heated in its passage from Europe.

The Countrey produces many more articles but as I did not see them or hear them mentiond I shall not set them down, tho doubtless it is capable of bringing[1] any thing that our West India Islands do, notwithstanding this they have neither Coffee or chocolate but import both from Lisbon.

Their fruits however I must not pass over in Silence, they have several I shall particularly mention those that were in season while we were there, which were Pine apples, Melons, water melons, oranges, Limes, Lemons, sweet Lemons, citrons, Plantanes, Bananes, Mangos, Mamme apples,[2] acajou apples and nutts,[3] Jamboira,[4] another sort which bears a small black fruit,[5] Coco nutts, Palm nuts of two kinds,[6] Palm berries.[7] Of these I must seperately give my opinion, as no doubt it will seem strange to some that I should assert that I have eat many of them and especialy pine apples better in England than any I have met with here. Begin then with the pines as the Fruit from which I expected the most, they being I beleive natives of this countrey, tho I cannot say I have seen or even heard of their being at this time wild any where in this neighbourhood: they are cultivated much as we do cabbages in Europe or rather with less care, the plants being set between bedds of any kind of garden stuff and sufferd to take their chance, the price of them in the Market is seldom above and generaly under a vintain which is 3 halfpence. All that D[r] Solander and myself tasted we agreed were much inferior to those we had eat in England; tho in general they were more Juicy and sweet yet they had no flavour but were like sugar melted in water. Their Melins are still worse from the Specimen we had, for we got but one, which was perfectly mealy and insipid; their water melons

---

[1] Apparently in the obsolete sense of 'bringing forth'.

[2] The Mamey, or Mammee Apple, *Mammea americana* L., has a large fruit with a yellow pulp of taste generally esteemed pleasant; but for Banks's opinion see p. 201 below.

[3] *Anacardium occidentale* L.; acajou generally corrupted in English to 'cashew'. The 'apple' is a fleshy pear-shaped receptacle—not the fruit—which bears the nut on its end. As will be seen, Banks ate the wrong thing, and formed an unfavourable opinion.

[4] Jambosa, *Eugenia jambos* L. The early spread of Eugenias is indicated by Philip Miller's account (*Gard. Dict.* ed. 8, 1768), where there is mention of Dr Heberden's sending him plants of *E. malaccensis* received from Brazil.

[5] Jaboticaba, *Myrciaria cauliflora*, which Banks probably saw detached, otherwise he would surely have remarked on the cauliflorous habit.

[6] He seems here to be referring to the fruit of the pandanus.

[7] 'Palm berries': the allusion is doubtless to soft-fruited palms such as genus *Butia*.

however are very good for they have some little flavour or at least a degree of acid which ours have not. Oranges are large and very juicy, we thought them good, doubtless better than any we had tasted at home, but probably Italy and Portugal produce as good had we been there in the time of their being in perfection. Lemons and limes are like ours, Sweet Lemons are sweetish and without flavour, Citrons have a sickly faint taste otherwise are like them. Mangos were not in perfection but promisd to be a very fine fruit, they are about the size of a peach, full of a melting yellow pulp not unlike that of a summer peach which has a very gratefull flavour, but in all we had it was spoild by a taste of turpentine which I am told is not found in the ripe ones. Bananas are in shape and size like a small thick sausage, coverd with a thick yellow rind, which is peeld off and the fruit within is of a consistence which might be expected from a mixture of Butter and flour but a little Slimey, its taste is sweet with a little perfume. Plantanes differ from these in being longer and thinner and having less lusciousness in their taste: both these fruits were disagreable to most of our people but after some use I became tolerably fond of them. Acajou or casshou is shapd like an apple but larger, he taste very disagreab[l]e sourish and bitter, the nut grows at the top of them.[1] Mamme apples are bigger than a Codlin in England, Coverd with a deep yellow skin, the pulp on the inside is very insipid or rather disagreable to the taste, and full of small round seeds coverd with a thick mucilage which continualy Cloy your mouth. Jamboira is the same as I saw at Madeira, a fruit calculated more to please the smell than the taste; the other sort are small and black and resemble much the taste of our English bilberries. Coco nutts are so well known in England that I need only say I have tasted as good there as any I met with here. Palm nutts of two sorts, one long and shapd like dates the other round, both these are rosted before their kernels are Eatable and Even then they are not so good a[s] Coco nuts. Palm berries appear much like Black grapes, they are the fruit of *Bactris minor*,[2] but for Eating have scarce any pulp covering a very large stone and what there is has nothing but a light acid to recommend it. Here are also the

---

[1] Cashew nuts contain a poisonous juice in the shell which is driven off by roasting. The kernel contains an irritant oil painful to the lips and tongue when eaten raw.

[2] *Bactris minor* is of difficult identity. Perhaps Banks refers to Jacquin's *B. minor*. Gaertner based his name on a Banks collection but not of Banks's own gathering; it was evidently of Jamaican origin. *Index Kewensis* identifies this as *Acrocomia lasiospatha*?; Dahlgren (1936), as *A. aculeata*.

202]   BANKS'S *Endeavour* JOURNAL   [*December*

fruits of several species of prickle pears[1] which are very insipid. Of Europæan Fruits I saw apples but very mealy and insipid and one peach which was also a very bad one.

Tho this Countrey should produce many and very valuable druggs we could not find any in the apothecarys shops but *Pareira Brava* and *Balsam Copivi*,[2] of both which we bought at excessive cheap prices and had very good of the sort. I fancy the drug trade is cheifly carried on to the northward as is that of the Dying woods, at least we could hear nothing of them here.

For manufactures I know of none carried on here except that of Cotton hammocks, which are usd for people to be carried about in as we do Sedan chairs, these are made cheifly by the Indians. But the cheif riches of the countrey comes from the mines, which are situated far up in the countrey, indeed no one could tell me how far, for even the situation of them is as carefully as possible conceald and Troops are continualy employd in guarding the Roads that lead to them, so that it is next to impossible for any man to get a sight of them except those who are employd there; at least no man would attempt it from mere curiosity for every body who is found on the road without being able to give a good account of himself is hangd immediately.

From these mines a great quantity of gold certainly comes but it is purchasd at a vast expence of lives; 40,000 negroes are annualy imported on the Kings accompt for this purpose, and notwithstanding that the year before last they dyed so fast that 20,000 more were obligd to be draughted from the town of Rio.

Pretious stones are also found here in very large quantities, so large that they do not allow more than a certain quantity to be collected in a year, which is done thus: a troop of people are sent into the Countrey where they are found and orderd to return when they have collected a certain quantity, which they sometimes do in a month more or less, then they return and after that it is

---

[1] Fleshy fruit of the cactus *Opuntia ficus-indica*, a cultigen of ancient and uncertain derivation. Though the genus is most probably of American origin, Theophrastus asserted that it grew about Opuntium, hence the generic name. Cf. Philip Miller (*Gard. Dict.* ed. 8, 1768) for early notes.

[2] *Pareira brava* in Linnaeus's time referred to *Cissampelos pareira*, 'Velvet-leaf'; but the name was later given to the related plants, *Chondrodendron tomentosum* R. and P. or *C. ovatum*—the former Peruvian, the latter Brazilian. The root was much esteemed for urinary complaints, and seems to have been an important export from Brazil in the late eighteenth century and through most of the nineteenth. 'Balsam Copivi' is a seldom used name for the drug extracted from the widely known Copaiba or Copaiva, *Copaifera lansdorfii* Desv. (properly *langsdorfii*)—'Copaiva Balsam'. Burton has an interesting note on the tree, to which he refers as a 'leguminous celebrity', and calls *Pau de Oleo*, 'Oil-wood': he describes the Indian mode of gathering the oil and its uses.—*Explorations of the Highlands of the Brazil* (London 1869), II, p. 84.

death for any one to be found in the Countrey on any pretence whatever till the next year.

Diamonds Topazes of several different qualities and amethysts are the stones that are cheifly found. Of the first I did not see any but was told that the viceroy had by him large quantities and would sell them on the King of Portugals account, but in that case they would not be at all cheaper than those in Europe. Topazes and amethysts I bought a few of for specimens; the former were divided into three sorts of very different value, Calld here pinga dogua Qualidade premeiro and segondo, and chrystallos ormerilles; they were sold large and small good and bad together by octavos or the eighth part of an ounce, the first sort 4^{sh}:9^{d}; 2[nd sort] 4:0; 3[rd sort]   . Amethysts   . But it was smugling in the highest degree to have any thing to do with them formerly there were Jewelers here who wo[r]kd stones, but about 14 months ago orders came from the Court of Portugal that no more stones should be wrought here except on his account; the Jewellers were immediately orderd to bring all their tools to the Viceroy which they were obligd to do, and from that time to this have not been sufferd to do any thing for their support. Here are however a number of slaves who work stones for the King of Portugal.

The Coin current here is either that of Portugal especialy 36 shill peices, or Coin made here which is much debasd, especialy the silver which are calld petacks, of which there are two sorts one of less value than the other, easily distinguishable by the number of rees markd on the outside, but they are little used; they also have Copper coin like that in Portugal, 5 and 10 rey peices, two of the latter are worth 3 halfpence, 40 petacks are worth 36 shillings.

The harbour of Rio de Janeiro is certainly a very good one: the Entrance is not wide but the Sea breeze which blows every morning makes it easy for any ship to go in before the wind, and when you get abreast the town it increases in breadth prodigiously so that almost any number of ships might lay in 5 or 6 fathom water oozey bottom. It is defended by many works, especialy the entrance where it is narrow, there is their strongest fortification calld Sta Cruz and another opposite it; there is also a platform mounting about 22 gunns without that just under the Sugar Loaf on the sea side, but that seems intirely calculated to hinder the Landing of an Enemy in a sandy bay from whence there is a passage to the back part of the town, which is intirely void of Defence except that the whole town is open to the Gunns of the Citadel St Sebastian as I said before. Between Sta Cruz and the town are several small batteries of 5 to 10 gunns and one pretty large one calld Berga Leon. Immediately before the town is Ilhoa dos Cobras, an Island fortified all round, which seems incapable of doing much mischeif from its immense size, at least it would take more men to defend it even tolerably in case of an attack than could Possibly be spard from a town totaly without Lines or any defence round itself. As for Sta Cruz, their cheif fortification on which they most rely seems very incaple of making any great resistance if smartly attackd by shipping: it is a stone fort which mounts many gunns indeed, but they lie tier above tier and are consequently very open to the atack of a ship which may come within 2 cable lengh's or less of them. Besides they have no supply of water there but what they have from a cistern in which they catch rain, or in times of Drouth are supplyd from the adjacent countrey; this they have been obligd to build above ground Least the water should taint by the heat of the climate, which a free access of air prevents; a shot consequently which fortunately should break that cistern would reduce the defenders to the utmost nescessity.

I was told by a person who certainly knew and I beleive meant to inform me right, that a little to the southward just without the South head of the harbour was a bay in which boats might land with all facility without an obstruction, as there is no kind of work there, and from this bay it is not above three hours march to the town, which you aproach on the Back part where it is as defenceless as the Landing place; but this seems incredible yet I am inclind to beleive it of these people whose cheif policy consists in hindering people from looking about them as much as possible. It may therefore be as my informer said that the existence of such a bay is but lately found out, indeed was it not for that policy I could beleive any thing of their stupidity and ignorance, when the Governor of the town Brigadier General Don Pedro de Mendoza y Furtado ask'd the Captain of our ship whether the transit of Venus which we were going to observe was not the passing of the North star to the South pole, which he said he always understood it to be.[1]

---

[1] Banks has the name of the governor wrong: it should be (in full) Antonio Carlos Vicente Xavier Furtado de Castro do Rio e Mendonça; in 1767 he was appointed a colonel of the Regiment of Elvas stationed at Rio de Janeiro. The peculiar idea of the Transit of Venus also appears to be wrongly fathered on him. Cook attributes this to the Viceroy in his conversation of 14 November, and Cook is much more likely to be right than Banks: 'he could form no other idea of that Phenomenon (after I had explained it to him) than the North Star passing thro the South Pole (these were his own words)'. Cook does not seem to have had any contact with the governor. But Banks in his letter to Lord Morton, 1 December 1768, also attributes the remark to the Viceroy (see II, p. 315 below).

The river and indeed the whole coast abounds with greater variety of Fish than I have ever seen;[1] seldom a day passd in which we had not one or more new species brought to us, indeed the bay is the most convenient place for fishing I have ever seen for it abounds with Islands between which there is shallow water and proper beaches for drawing the Seine. The sea also without the bay is full of Dolphins and large mackrell of several sorts who very readily bite at hooks which the inhabitants tow after their boats for that purpose, in short the Countrey is Capable with a very little industry of producing infinite plenty both of nesscessaries and luxuries: was it in the hands of Englishmen we should soon see its consequence, as things are tolerably plentifull even under the direction of the Portugese, who I take to be without exception the laziest as well as the most ignorant race in the whole world.

The Climate here is I fancy very good, the Countrey certainly is very wholesome, during our whole stay the Thermometer was never above 83. We had however a good deal of Rain and once it blew very hard. I am rather inclind to think that this countrey has rather more rain than those in the same northern Latitude are observd to have, not only from what happend during our short stay but from Marcgrave who gives us metereological obser-vations on this Climate for 3 years: you may observe that it raind here in those years almost every other Day throughout the year, but more especialy in May and June in which months it raind along without Ceasing.

8. This morn at day break a dolphin was taken and soon after a shark appeard who took the bait very readily, and during the time that we were playing him under the cabbin window it cast something out of his mouth that either was or appeard very like its stomack, this it threw out and drew in again many times. I have often heard from seamen that they can do it but never before saw anything like it before.[2] (this circumstance which by mistake is attributed to this shark belongs to one taken the 11th).

9. A very heavy swell last night and this morn: we Judge that it has blown very hard to the Southward and in this particular think ourselves obligd to the viceroy of Brasil who by his dilatoryness in supplying us kept us out of it, the swell however carried away

---

[1] There are twenty-two paintings and drawings of Brazilian fishes in the Parkinson collection; a list of these will be published in the fourth volume of the edition of Cook's voyages now in preparation by the Hakluyt Society.

[2] Dr D. L. Serventy states (personal communication) that this symptom of extreme distress in sharks is well known to fishermen in Australasian waters.

our fore top galant mast. The sea is today coulord with infin[it]e[1] small Particles the same as those seen Nov[r] 7[th] and laying like them in broad streaks.

10. Today also we see large quantities of the same small particles.

11. This morn took a shark who cast up his stomack when hookd or at least appears so to do, it proves to be a female and on being opend 6 young ones were taken out of her, five of which were alive and swam briskly in a tub of water, the 6th was dead and seemd to have been so for some time.

12. Wind fair today, no events.

13. Fair wind today likewise, at night a squall with thunder and lightning which made us hoist the Lightning chain.

14. Wind Foul, blew fresh all day, in the evening saw a sail standing to the northward.

15. Less wind but a great swell.

16. Wind fair.

17. Wind foul, blew rather fresh, so the ship heeld much which made our affairs go on rather uncomfortably.

18. Calm at night, wind to the northward; we began to feel ourselves rather cool tho the thermometer was at 76 and shut two of the Cabbin windows, all which have been open ever since we left Madeira.

19. Charming fair wind and fine weather; the people were employd in preparing a new suit of sails for the bad weather we are to expect. Therm 70.

20. Fair wind today and rather warmer than it has been. During the course of last night we had a very heavy squall which tho it did not last above 10 minutes yet in that time blew as hard as it has done since we have been on board the ship.

21. Foul wind and little of it.

22. This morn quite calm. A very large shoal of Porpoises came close to the ship, they were of a kind different from any I have seen but so large that I dared not throw the gig into any of them, some were 4 yards long, their heads quite round but their hinder parts compressd, they had one fin upon their backs like a porpoise and white lines over their eyes also a spot of white behind the fin;[2]

---

[1] The MS reads *infine*, in which it is followed by P and S, but the emendation seems necessary.

[2] These were *Globicephala edwardii* (Smith), the Southern Pilot Whale.

they stayd above ½ an hour about the ship. When they were gone Dr Solander and myself went out in the boat and shot one species of Mother Careys chickens and two shearwaters, both provd new, *Procellaria Gigantea* and *sandaliata*.[1] The Carey was one but ill describd by Linnæus, *Procellaria fregata*.[2] While we were out the people were employed in bending the new set of sails for Cape Horn.

23. This morn calm again: went out shooting, killd another new procellaria, *æquorea*,[3] and many of the sorts we had seen yesterday; caught *Holothuria angustata*,[4] a species of floating helix much smaller than those under the line,[5] *Phyllodoce velella* very small, sometimes not so large as a silver penny ye: I beleive the common species;[6] in the evening went out again, killd an albatross *Diomedæa exulans*, who measurd 9 f^t 1 ^{inch} between the tipps of his wings,[7] and struck one turtle *testudo caretta*.[8]

24. Fair wind and steady tho but little of it.

25. Christmas day; all good Christians that is to say all hands get abominably drunk so that at night there was scarce a sober man in the ship, wind thank god very moderate or the lord knows what would have become of us.[9]

26. Blows fresh today. A vast many birds are about the ship cheifly procellarias, all that we shot last week and one more who is quite

[1] *Procellaria gigantea*, now the Giant Petrel, *Macronectes giganteus* (Gm.). Parkinson I, pls. 17, 18; Solander, pp. 73, 75. *Procellaria sandaliata*: currently *Pterodroma incerta* (Schlegel), Schlegel's Petrel. Parkinson I, pl. 20, Solander, p. 89.

[2] The White-bellied Storm Petrel, *Fregetta grallaria* (Vieill.). Parkinson I, pl. 14. Only the first part of Solander's note (p. 51) on *P. fregata* applies to *F. grallaria*; the rest concerns *Fregetta tropica* (Gould), the Black-bellied Storm Petrel.

[3] The White-faced Storm Petrel, *Pelagodroma marina* (Lath.). Latham actually described the species from Parkinson's drawing, I, pl. 13, which is therefore the type (*General Synopsis of Birds* 1785, p. 410, *Index Ornithologicus* 1790, p. 826). See also Solander, p. 57. Wilson's Petrel was also taken on this day.

[4] The Portuguese Man-of-war. Cf. 7 October 1768. This particular specimen was the subject of several pencil studies by Parkinson, and one painting, III, pls. 39, 40.

[5] This helix is unidentifiable.

[6] *Velella velella*. See 7 October above.

[7] The Wandering Albatross. Parkinson's dated painting (I, pl. 25) shows that this bird was apparently in second-year plumage; this is confirmed by Solander's account, p. 3. (Cf. Fleming's fig. 2, D, C, *Emu*, 49, 1950, p. 174).

[8] There is a description by Solander, p. 127, and dated drawings by Parkinson, I, pls. 41-3, of this loggerhead. These suggest that it was probably not *Caretta caretta* (Linn.) but more probably *Lepidochelys kempi* (Garman). The figures show four infra-marginal plates, a number which is normal in *Lepidochelys* but unusual in the other loggerhead genus *Caretta*; the description of the colour, 'Testa nigrofusca, absque ullis maculis. . . ' is also more compatible with the former, which is dark grey to olive green, whereas *Caretta* is reddish brown.

[9] Cook puts it more mildly: 'Yesterday being Christmas day the People, [i.e. the crew] were none of the Soberest'. Cook I, p. 37.

Black without spot or speck that can be seen as he flies [1] Towards even many beds of seaweed came past the ship which the seamen call rockweed, but none near enough to the ship for us to catch them tho we were constantly prepard.

27. Blows strong this evning, at night came to under a balancd mizzen[2] till day light when it grows more moderate. The water has been discoulerd all day 50 fathom. All this day I have smelt a singular smell from windward tho the people in the ship did not take notice of it, it was like rotten seaweed and at some times very strong.

During the whole of this gale we had many procellarias about the ship, at some times immense numbers, who seemd perfectly unconcernd at the badness of the weather or the hight of the sea but continued often flapping near the surface of the water as if fishing.

28. Less wind, the sea soon falls; the water both yesterday and today has been a good deal discolourd. Sound and find 48 fathom.

29. Fair wind, water very white, sounded 46 fathom, about 4 in the Even 44. We observd now some feathers and peices of reed to float by the ship which made us get up the hoave net to see what they were; soon after some drowned Carabi[3] and Phalænæ[4] came past which we took and employd the hoave till dark night taking many specimens. Lat. 41:48. This morn a large sphinx came off probably from the land and was taken.

30. This morn fine weather, water whiter than ever almost of a clay colour; sounded 47 fathom. Plenty of insects passd by this morn, many especialy of the carabi, alive, some grylli[5] and one Phalæna. I stayd in the main chains from 8 till 12 dipping for them with the hoave and took vast numbers. In the evening Many Phalenæ and two papilios[6] came flying about the ship, of the first took about 20 but the last would not come near enough to be taken and at last flew away; they appeard Large. We have

---

[1] Either the Cape Hen, *Procellaria aequinoctialis*, or the Sooty Shearwater, *Puffinus griseus* (Gm.). The former species constantly follows ships in the southern hemisphere, but Sooty Shearwaters are indifferent to them. The Cape Hen is particularly abundant in the vicinity of the Cape of Good Hope—hence its popular name.

[2] A balanced mizen was a mizen sail reduced to as small an area as possible by a reef-band that crossed it diagonally, so that the ship was put under the minimum sail to hold her steady when brought to. But Banks may have been too technical: Cook merely says 'At 8 pm it blew a Storm of wind with rain which brought us under our Main sail with her head to the westward'.—Cook I, p. 37.

[3] *Carabus*, a genus of beetles.

[4] *Phalaena*: a name used by Linnaeus to include many different kinds of moths.

[5] Linnaeus used *Gryllus* for a variety of orthopterous insects.

[6] Linnaeus placed all the butterflies known to him in the genus *Papilio*.

also both yesterday and today taken several Ichneumons[1] flying about the rigging. All the seamen say that we cannot be less than 20 leagues from the land,[2] but I doubt Grylli especialy coming so far alive as they must float all the way upon the water. They ground their opinion cheifly on the sounding[s] which have been all along sand of different colours, which had we been nearer the land would have been intermixd with shells; their experience on this coast must however be but slight.

This whole day the evening especialy has been a series of calms and squalls, towards night a thunderstorm in which the lightning was remarkably bright, and rangd in long streaks sometimes horizontal and sometimes perpendicular, the thunder was not loud but continued an immence while with a noise in some claps so like the flapping of sails that had I not been upon dcek I should not have beleivd it to be thunder. Just before the storm we had an appearance of land to the westward which all who had not been in these latitudes before imagind to be real; it made like a long extent of lowish land and two Islands to the Northward of it, the South end was buried in the clouds; this lasted about ½ an hour and then rose gradualy up and disapeard.

Lat. 42:31. A sea lion was enterd in the log book of today as being seen but I did not see him.[3] I saw however a whale coverd with barnacles as the seamen told me, he appeard of a reddish colour[4] except his tail which was black like those to the Northward.

31. No insects seen today; the water changd to a little better colour. On looking over those taken yesterday find 31 species of land insects all so like in size and shape to those of England &c. that they are scarcely distinguishable, probably some will turn out identicaly the same. We ran among them 160 miles by the log without reckoning any part of last night, tho they were seen till dark, and most of this southing. Our latitude made us nearly opposite Baye Sans Fond near which place Mr Dalrymple supposes

[1] These ichneumons do not appear to have been sketched by Parkinson, nor does there appear to be any specific reference to them in Morley's paper on the Banksian Ichneumonidae (*The Entomologist*, 42, 1909, pp. 131-7).—'For several evenings, swarms of butterflies, moths, and other insects, flew about the rigging, which we apprehended had been blown to us from the shore. Thousands of them settled upon the vessel; Mr. Banks ordered the men to gather them up; and, after selecting such as he thought proper, the rest were thrown overboard; and he gave the men some bottles of rum for their trouble.'—Parkinson, *Journal*, p. 6.
[2] Cook: 'yet at this time we could not be less than 30 Leagues from land'.—p. 38. His position for November 30 puts him roughly 150 miles east of the Valdés Peninsula, the nearest land
[3] Probably the Southern Sea Lion, *Otaria byronia* (Blainville).
[4] The whale is unidentifiable: its red colour would be caused not by barnacles but by lice, *Cyamidae*.

there to be a passage quite through the Continent of America.[1] It should seem by what we have seen that there should be at least a very large river, and that probably at this time much flooded: if even that could have so great an effect as (supposing us to be 20 leagues from the land) discolouring the water to almost a clay Colour and bringing of insects who never fly 20 yards such as grylli and one aranea.[2]

I lament much not having tasted the water at the time which never occurrd to me, but probably the difference of saltness would have been hardly perceptible to the taste and my Hydrostatick balance being broke I had no other method of trying it.

JANUARY 1769

1. New years day today made us pass many Comp[ts] and talk much of our hopes for success in the year 69. Many whales were about the ship today and much sea weed in large lumps but none near enough to be caught.

In the Evening rather squally; the true sea green colour upon the surface of the water was often to be seen now between the squalls, or rather under the black clouds when they were about half a mile from the ship. I had often heard of it before but never seen it in any such perfection, indeed most of the seamen said the same, it was very bright and perfectly like the stone calld aqua-marine.

2. Fresh breezes today. In the Evening, Lat. about 45:30, met with some small shoals of the red lobsters which have been seen by almost every one who has pass'd these seas. They were however so far from couloring the sea red as Dampier and Cowley say that I may affirm that we never saw more than a few hundreds of them at a time, we took however several in the Casting and hoave netts and describd them by the name of *Cancer Gregarius*.[3]

---

[1] The bay seems to be the 'Baye Sinfondo' of the French charts, on the South Atlantic coast of America, c. 42° S. The name *baia sin fondo* was given to the Gulf of San Mathias either by Magellan or Loaysa, but whether because it could not be sounded or because its limits could not be seen we do not know. Dalrymple, both on his 'Chart of the South Pacifick Ocean' (1767) and his 'Chart of the Ocean between S. America and Africa' (1769) simply continued the bay through America as a strait emerging on the Pacific ocean opposite Chiloe island. I know of no printed reference by him apart from this.

[2] A spider; no painting or description of it is known.

[3] They were Lobster Krill, *Munida gregaria* (Fabr.). Parkinson has a drawing, III, pl. 9. There is some conflict of testimony as to how many were seen. Wilkinson the master's mate says 'a great Quantity'. Bootie the midshipman, perhaps talking in the tradition, says 'a great Quantity of red shrimps insomuch that you could not tell the Colour of the water they was so thick'. Hicks refers to shoals. Cook merely says 'saw some Whales and Porposes, and small red Crawfish some of which we caught'. Dampier's

3. Lat: 47:17, all hands looking out for Pepys's Island;[2] about observing time[2] an appearance was seen to the westward so like an Island that we bear away after it almost assurd that it is Land as the midshipman at the mast head declard; for half an hour, which time he had steadily lookd at it, it did not alter its appearance at all, however about 4 we were convincd that we were in chace of Cape fly away as the seamen call it, no signs of Island or any thing else appearing where it ought to have been.

This Evening many large bunches of sea weed came by the ship; we caught some of it with hooks, it was of an immense size every leaf 4 feet long and the stalk about twelve, the footstalk of each leaf was swelld into a long air vessel. M[r] Gore tells me that he has seen this weed grow quite to the top of the water in 12 fathom, if so the swelld footstalks are probably the trumpet grass or weed of the Cape of Good Hope; we describd it however as it appeard and calld it *Fucus Giganteus*.[3] Here were also this Evening large quantities of a small bird somewhat like Mother Careys chickens but rather larger and grey on the back,[4] and plenty of Albatrosses indeed we have seen more or less of them every day for some time.

4. Blew fresh today and night: the officer of the watch told me that in the night the sea was very much illuminated in patches of many Yards wide which appeard of a pale light colour.

5. Fair wind: the sea very light at night more so than ever I had seen it, so that the ships course and every curl of a wave was of a light colour, but none of the light patches seen last night were now observd, which were cheifly remarkable as the animals there must have shone without being agitated. In some of the water taken up observd a small insect of a conical figure, very nimble, who movd himself with a kind of whorl of legs or tentacula round

reference is in his *New Voyage round the World* (*Voyages*, ed. Masefield, I, p. 109): 'great shoals of small Lobsters, which coloured the Sea red in spots, for a mile in compass. . . .' Captain Ambrose Cowley, the buccaneer and colleague of Dampier, in the abstract of his journal printed by Captain William Hacke, *A Collection of Original Voyages* (1699), p. 5, writes, 'steer'd away [from the coast of Brazil] S.W. finding the Sea as red as Blood about the lat. of 40 deg. South, which was occasioned by great Shoals of Shrimps, which lay upon the water in great patches for many Leagues together'. See pl. 1a.

[1] Pepys Island was the name given by Captain William Hacke, the editor of Cowley's journal, to land sighted by Cowley in January 1684. Hacke placed it on his chart too far north. Both Cowley and Dampier agreed that what had been sighted was one of the Falkland Islands, but the separate identity bestowed by Hacke held the field—or the chart—for many years. One of the objects of Byron's voyage in 1764 was specifically to verify and identify Pepys Island. For further discussion, see General Introduction to Cook I, pp. lxxi, lxxxvi.

[2] i.e. noon, the time for determining by observation the position of the ship.

[3] *Macrocystis pyrifera* (L.) Ag. <JDH> or less likely, *Lessonia flavicans* Bory.

[4] Probably some kind of prion, *Pachyptila* sp.

the base of the cone; we could not find any nereides or indeed any other insect than this in the water but were not able to prove that he causes the light so deferrd our observations on him till the morning.[1]

6. Blew fresh foul wind, forcd to throw away the insects taken last night from the ship having so much motion. The Southeast wind now became very cold, to us at least so lately come from the Torrid Zone. Therm at noon 48. All hands bend their Magellan Jackets (made of a thick woolen stuff allowd them by the goverment calld fearnought) and myself put on flannel Jacket and waistcoat and thick trousers. In the Evening blew strong, at night a hard gale, ship brought too under a mainsail; during the course of this my Bureau was overset and most of the books were about the Cabbin floor, so that with the noise of the ship working, the books &c. running about, and the strokes our cotts or swinging beds gave against the top and sides of the Cabbin we spent a very disagreable night. We this morn expected to have made Falklands Islands where we intended to put in for a small time,[2] so the missing of them which we much fear was a great disapointment to me, as I fear I shall not now have a single oppertunity of observing the produce of this part of the world.

7. Blew strong, yet the ship still Laying too, now for the first time saw some of the Birds calld Penguins by the southern navigators; they seem much of the size and not unlike *alca pica*[3] but are easily known by streaks upon their faces and their remarkably shrill cry different from any sea bird I am acquainted with.[4] We saw also several seals but much smaller than those which I have seen in Newfoundland and black, they generaly appeard in lively action

---

[1] Banks's description could apply to *Noctiluca*, one of the largest of the Protozoa, which occurs at times in countless numbers and is the cause of many of the startling displays of phosphorescence familiar to voyagers. *Nereides*: polychaete worms.

[2] Cook does not mention this intention, and he passed well to the west of the Falklands. His instructions had left him free to call at Port Egmont, the English settlement in these islands, or somewhere on the coast of Brazil, or at both places, for refreshment, but, as he records, he had chosen Rio de Janeiro because of the certainty of finding supplies there, and had abandoned thoughts of Port Egmont. If he had wished to call at the Falklands he would have had no difficulty in finding them. We shall more than once see evidence of a conflict in purpose between Cook, who naturally put first his instructions as commander of a voyage with a specific scientific purpose, and afterwards of geographical discovery, and Banks, who would have liked to get off the ship everywhere in pursuit of objects of natural history.

[3] A synonym for the Razorbill, *Alca torda*.

[4] A number of penguins have 'streaks upon their faces'. The most likely candidate in these seas would be *Spheniscus magellanicus*, with the broad white semicircular stripe upon the side of its head and its bray like that of a 'ackass; but identification cannot safely be made.

leaping out of the water like porpoises, so much so that some of our people were deceivd by them mistaking them for fish.[1]

About noon weather much more moderate; set the lower sails; before night sea quite down tho the wind still stood at south east. The sea rises and falls quicker in these latitudes than it does about England, which we have observd Ever since we came into variable winds way to the South of the tropicks. During this whole gale we observed vast plenty of birds about us, Procellarias of all the kinds we have before mentiond, the grey ones of the 3ᵈ of this month and a kind? all black, *procell. aquinoctialis*? Linn.[2] but could not discern whether or not their beaks were yellow, and plenty of Albatrosses; indeed I have generaly observd a much greater quantity of birds upon wing in gales of wind than in moderate weather, owing perhaps to the tossing of the waves which must render swimming very uneasy; in this situation they must be oftener seen than when they set on the water.

The ship during this gale has shewn her excellence in laying too remarkably well, shipping scarce any water tho it blew at times vastly strong; the seamen in general say that they never knew a ship lay too so well as this does, so lively and at the same time so easy.

8. Smooth water and fair wind: many Seals and Penguins about the ship, the latter leaping out of the water and diving instantly so that a person unusd to them might easily be deceivd and take them for fish; plenty also of Albatrosses and whales blowing very near the ship. We were now too sure that we had missd Fauklands Islands and probably were to the Westward of them.

The ship has been observd to go much better since her shaking in the last gale of wind, the seamen say that it is a general observation that ships go better for being what they call Loosnen in their Joints, so much so that in chase it is often customary to knock down Stantions &c. and make the ship as loose as possible.

9. Clouds to the westward appear so like land this morn that even our first Lieutenant who prided himself on His judgement in this particular was deceivd. Wind vereable and calmer, many seals and some Albatrosses but none of those whitish birds which we saw in the gale of wind.

10. Fine weather: Seals plentifully today and a kind of birds different from any we have before seen, they were black and a

---

[1] They were probably the Southern Fur Seal, *Arctocephalus australis* (Zimmermann).

[2] *Procellaria aequinoctialis* was the Cape Hen. See 26 December 1768. These might equally well have been Sooty Shearwaters, *Puffinus griseus* (Gm.).

Q

little larger than pidgeons, plump like them and easily known by their flapping their wings quick as they fly contrary to the custom of sea birds in general.[1] This evening a shoal of Porpoises swam by the ship different from any I have seen, spotted with large dabbs of white and white under the belly, in other respects as swimming &c. like common porpoises only they leap rather more nimbly, sometimes lifting their whole bodys out of the water.[2]

11. This morn at day break saw the land of Terra del Fuego, by 8 O'Clock we were well in with it, the weather exceedingly moderate. Its appearance was not near so barren as the writer of Ld Ansons voyage has represented it, the weather exceedingly moderate so we stood along shore about 2 Leagues off, we could see trees distinctly through our glasses and observe several smokes made probably by the natives as a signal to us. The captain now resolved to put in here if he can find a conv[en]ient harbour and give us an opportunity of searching a countrey so intirely new.

The hills within land seemd to be high and on them were many patches of snow, but the sea coast appeard fertile especialy the trees of a bright verdure, except in places exposd to SW wind which were distinguishable by their brown appearance; the shore itself sometimes beach and sometimes rock. At 4 in the evening wind came on shore so stood off.

12. This morn make the land again soon after which it dropd calm, in which time we took *Beroe incrassata*,[3] *Medusa limpidissima*[4] and *plicata*[5] and *obliquata*,[6] *Alcyonium anguillare*, probably the thing that Shelvocke mentions in his Voyage round the world page 60, *Alcyonium frustrum*.[7] After dinner a small breeze sprung up and to

---

[1] Diving Petrels, which have a rapid flight. Two species occur here, *Pelecanoides magellani* (Matthew) and *P. urinatrix* (Gm.).

[2] Probably Commerson's Dolphin, *Cephalorhynchus commersoni* (Lacépède). It has the alternative common names of Piebald Porpoise and Le Jacobite, which last was Commerson's own name for it.

[3] *Beroe incrassata*: Parkinson's plate, III, 59, of this date, bears this name and appears to represent *Beroe ovata* Chamisso and Eysenhardt. Solander, p. 437, noted its occurrence in October 1769, when they were approaching New Zealand from the east.

[4] Possibly an *Aglaura* sp. See Parkinson III, pl. 51; Solander, p. 463.

[5] *Medusa plicata*: the animal with this name in Parkinson III, pl. 47, is too worn to be identifiable, and Solander's description, p. 453, is of the same specimen.

[6] *Medusa obliquata*: unidentifiable; Parkinson III, pl. 52, Solander, p. 465.

[7] *Alcyonium*: neither of the species mentioned can be identified either from the drawing by Parkinson, III, pl. 74, of *A. anguillare*, or from the descriptions by Solander, pp. 477, 479. George Shelvocke (fl. 1690-1728), a privateer, commanded a fraudulent and semi-piratical but exciting voyage from England to Formosa, and wrote a not very honest book about it, *A Voyage round the World, by the Way of the Great South Sea, performed in the years 1719, 20, 21, 22. . . .* (London 1726). The book enjoyed some fame, and not only Banks, but Coleridge, found it useful: Shelvocke's account of the killing of an albatross provided the seed of the *Ancient Mariner*. The thing that he mentions on page 60, he mentions thus: sailing south beyond the River Plate, 'we had on the surface of the water

our great Joy we discoverd an opening into the land and stood in for it in great hopes of finding a harbour; however after having ran within a mile of the shore were obliged to stand off again as there was no appearance of shelter and the wind was on shore.[1]

When we were nearest in we could plainly discover with our glasses spots in which the colour of white and yellow were predominant which we judg'd to be flowers, the white were in large clusters almost every where, the yellow in small spots or patches on the side of a hill coverd with a beautifull verdure;[2] the trees could now be distinguishd very plainly and seemd to be 30 or 40 feet high with flat bushy tops, their trunks in many places were bare and resembled rocks a good deal till the glasses cleard up the deception.

Among the things taken today observd *ulva intestinalis*[3] and *corrallina officin[alis]*.[4] The wind very vereable all day, at nine this even the Three Brothers and Sugar Loaf[5] were in sight and we stood gently along shore in hopes to be at the streights mouth by the Morning.

About 6 this even the gentlemen upon deck observd the Sugar Loaf coverd with a cloud for a short time which left it intirely white, they judgd it to have been a fall of snow upon the hill but as I did not myself see it I cannot give my opinion.

13. This morn at day break we were at the streights mouth and stood in a little way, but the tide turning against us soon set us out again; at ½ past 8 tide again turnd in our favour but soon after wind came foul so were forcd to turn to windward; the wind soon

abundance of things appearing like white snakes. We took some of them up, but cou'd not perceive there was any life in them, nor were they form'd into any shape resembling any kind of animal, they being only a long cylinder of a white sort of a jelly, and may probably be the spawn of some of the larger sort of fish'.

[1] The ship was near the entrance to the Strait of le Maire, through which Cook intended to pass.

[2] 'The trees all belong to one kind, the Fagus betuloides; for the number of the other species of Fagus and of the Winter's Bark, is quite inconsiderable. This beech keeps its leaves throughout the year; but its foliage is of a peculiar brownish-green colour, with a tinge of yellow. As the whole landscape is thus coloured, it has a sombre, dull appearance; nor is it often enlivened by the rays of the sun.'—Darwin, *Naturalist's Voyage round the World* (ed. 1888), p. 210. It is possible that Banks's yellow colour was thus accounted for. But see also p. 226, n. 2 below, on the fungus of *Nothofagus antarctica*.

[3] This name may refer to *Enteromorpha intestinalis* (L.), 'since it is more or less cosmopolitan in temperate and cold seas' (W. R. Taylor).

[4] *Corallina officinalis* (L.) may be accepted with a query. Both *Corallina officinalis* and *C. chilensis* occur in the area, and though abundantly distinct, early travellers would not distinguish between them; cf. L. Gain, *La Flore algologique . . . Deux. Expéd. Antarct. Française (1908-1910) commandées par le Dr. Jean Charcot* (Paris, 1912).

[5] Prominent landscape features on the coast of Tierra del Fuego. The Three Brothers have still the same name—Tres Hermanos; the Sugar Loaf seems to have been the remarkable table-topped hill called Meseta de Orozco.

freshning made us pitch most violently, so much that our Gib netting[1] was quite under water. At 12 today Lat: 54:42. Staten land is much more craggy than Terra del Fuego tho the view of it in Ld Ansons Voyage is exaggerated. About 4 it blew very hard and the tide turning against us quickly drove us out of the streights the second time. At night less wind tho still South West, stood into the Streights the third time and had another violent pitching bout, the tide turnd against us before we are half through so in the morning

14. we found ourselves the third time drove out, wind SSW, Short sea and ship pitching most violently. The Captn stood into a bay just without Cape St Vincent[2] and while the ship plyd off and on Dr Solander and myself went ashore in the boat and found many plants, about 100, tho we were not ashore above 4 hours; of these I may say every one was new and intirely different from what either of us had before seen. The countrey about this bay was in general flat, here is however good wood and water and vast plenty of fowl and in the cod[3] of the bay a flat coverd with grass where much hay might be made. The bay itself is bad affording but little shelter for shipping and in many Parts of it the bottom rocky and foul. This however may be always known in these Countreys by the beds of Fucus Giganteus which constantly grow upon the rock and are not seen on sand or owse; they are of an immence lengh, we sounded upon them and had 14 fathom water; as they seem to make a very acute angle with the bottom in their situation on the water it is difficult to guess how long they may be, but probably they are not less than one half longer than the depth of the water, which gives their lengh to be 126 feet, a wonderfull lengh for a stalk not thicker than a mans thumb.

Among other things the bay affords there is plenty of winters bark,[4] easy to be known by its broad leaf like a laurel of a light green colour and blueish underneath, the bark is easily stripd off with a bone or stick as ours are barkd in England; its virtues are so well known that I shall say little except that it may be us'd as

---

[1] The netting stretched as a safety measure under the jib-boom, the spar run out from the bowsprit, to which the lower corner, or foot, of the jib was secured.

[2] Which he called Vincent's Bay; now Thetis Bay.

[3] The bottom extremity.

[4] *Drimys winteri* Forst., named for Captain John Winter, who was with Drake in the Straits of Magellan in 1578, and there successfully used it to combat scurvy. The bark was first described by de l'Ecluse in 1582, and later by Dalechamps (1586) and Clusius (1605), etc., under the name *Winteranus cortex*. It was much valued as an antiscorbutic. Although extensively used in Europe for over two centuries it finds a place today only in local domestic medicine. *Drimys* is a primitive bihemispheric and presumably paleo-antarctic genus, 'only very remotely related to the Magnoliaceae proper' (cf. A. C. Smith, *Jour. Arnold Arbor.* 26: 48-59. 1945). See Pl. 27*b*.

a spice even in culinary matters and is found to be very wholesome. Here is also plenty of wild celery *apium antescorbuticum*,[1] scurvy grass *cardamine antescorbutica*,[2] both which are as pleasant to the taste as any herbs of the kind found in Europe and I beleive possess as much virtue in curing the scurvy.

The trees here are cheifly of one sort, a Kind of Birch *Betula antarctica*[3] with very small leaves, it is a light white wood and cleaves very straight; sometimes the trees are 2 or 3 feet in diameter and run 30 or 40 feet in the bole; possibly they might in cases of nescessity supply topmasts. Here are also great plenty of cranberries both white and red, *Arbutus rigida*.[4] Inhabitants I saw none but found their hutts in two places, once in a thick wood and again close by the beach; they are most unartificialy made, Conical but open on one side where was marks of fire so that probably the fire servd them instead of a door.

15. Stopd tide this morn in a bay on the Terra del Fuego side of the water, probably Prince Maurice's Bay, which servd our purpose very well; at 10 tide turnd and we stood out and by dinner came to an anchor in the Bay of Good Success. Several Indians were in sight near the Shore.

After dinner went ashore on the starboard side of the bay near some rocks which make smooth water and good landing. Before we had walkd 100 yards many Indians made their appearance on the other side of the bay, at the End of a sandy beach which makes the bottom of the bay, but on seeing our numbers to be ten or twelve they retreated. Dr Solander and myself then walkd forward 100 yards before the rest and two of the Indians advanc'd also and set themselves down about 50 yards from their companions. As soon as we came up they rose and each of them threw a stick he had in his hand away from him and us, a token no doubt of peace, they then walkd briskly towards the other party and wavd to us to follow, which we did and were receivd with many uncouth

---

[1] *Apium prostratum* Thouin <JDH>, as validated by a specimen bearing Solander's MS name. See pl. 27a.

[2] *Cardamine glacialis* DC. 'Scurvy grass' was a loose term applied to many unrelated plants sharing antiscorbutic properties: *Cardamine nasturtioides*, as well as *C. glacialis*; *Oxalis enneaphylla* of the Falkland Islands; *Amaranthus* spp. *Brassica juncea*, *Portulaca oleracea*, *Sesuvium portulacastrum*, collectively called 'verdura' by the Spanish navigators, were all used in the Pacific Islands.

[3] Banks's 'birch', as determined by an examination of his coll., was *Nothofagus antarctica* (Forst.) Oerst., a southern hemisphere counterpart of the beech.

[4] *Pernettya mucronata* Gaud. <JDH> validated by a Banks collection. Pernety's original specimen, the basis of the illustration in his account of his voyage with Bougainville, *Histoire d'un Voyage aux îles Malouines fait en 1763 & 1764* (Berlin 1770), was collected in the Falklands. Skottsberg, *Wilds of Patagonia* (London 1911), p. 56, remarks on the use of *chaura* (the native name) berries as emergency rations.

signs of freindship. We distributed among them a number of Beads and ribbands which we had brought ashore for that purpose at which they seem'd mightily pleasd, so much so that when we embarkd again aboard our boat three of them came with us and went aboard the ship. Of these one seemd to be a Preist or conjuror or at least we thought him to be one by the noises he made, possibly exorcising every part of the ship he came into, for when any thing new caught his attention he shouted as loud as he could for some minutes without directing his speech either to us or to any one of his countreymen.

They eat bread and beef which we gave them tho not heartily but carried the largest part away with them, they would not drink either wine or spirits but returnd the glass, tho not before they had put it to their mouths and tasted a drop; we conducted them through the greatest part of the ship and they lookd at every thing without any marks of extrordinary admiration, unless the noise which our conjurer did not fail to repeat at every new thing he saw might be reckond as such.

After having been aboard about 2 hours they expressd a desire of going ashore and a boat was orderd to carry them. I went with them and landed them among their countreymen, but I can not say that I observd either the one party curious to ask questions or the other to relate what they had seen or what usage they had met with, so after having stayd ashore about ½ an hour I returnd to the ship and the Indians immediately marchd off from the shore.

16. This morn very early Dr Solander and myself with our servants and two Seamen to assist in carrying baggage, accompanied by M^{srs} Monkhouse and Green, set out from the ship to try to penetrate into the countrey as far as we could, and if possible gain the tops of the hills where alone we saw places not overgrown with trees.[1] We began to enter the woods at a small sandy beach a little to the westward of the watering place and continued pressing through pathless thickets, always going up hill, till 3 o'Clock before

[1] The next naturalist to come to the Bay of Good Success was Darwin, on the voyage of the *Beagle*, in December 1832. 'One side of the harbour', he writes, 'is formed by a hill about 1500 feet high, which Captain FitzRoy has called after Sir J. Banks, in commemoration of his disastrous excursion, which proved fatal to two men of his party, and nearly so to Dr. Solander. . . . I was anxious to reach the summit of this mountain to collect alpine plants; for flowers of any kind in the lower parts are few in number. A ridge connected this hill with another, distant some miles, and more lofty, so that patches of snow were lying on it. As the day was not far advanced, I determined to walk there and collect plants along the road'.—*Naturalist's Voyage*, pp. 210-11. See also Nora Barlow (ed.), *Charles Darwin's Diary of the Voyage of H.M.S. 'Beagle'* (Cambridge, 1933), pp. 122-3.

we gaind even a near view of the places we intended to go to.
The weather had all this time been vastly fine much like a sun-
shiny day in May, so that neither heat nor cold was troublesome
to us nor were there any insects to molest us, which made me think
the traveling much better than what I had before met with in
Newfoundland.

Soon after we saw the plains we arrivd at them, but found to
our great disapointment that what we took for swathe[1] was no
better than low bushes of birch about reaching a mans middle;
these were so stubborn that they could not be bent out of the way,
but at every step the leg must be lifted over them and on being
plac'd again on the ground was almost sure to sink above the anckles
in bog.[2] No traveling could possibly be worse than this which
seemd to last about a mile, beyond which we expected to meet
with bare rock, for such we had seen from the tops of lower hills
as we came: this I particularly was infinitely eager to arrive at
expecting there to find the alpine plants of a countrey so curious.
Our people tho rather fatigued were yet in good spirits so we pushd on
intending to rest ourselves as soon as we should arrive at plain ground.

We proceeded two thirds of the way without the least difficulty
and I confess I thought for my own part that all difficulties were
surmounted when Mr Buchan fell into a fit.[3] A fire was immediately
lit for him and with him all those who were most tird remaind
behind, while Dr Solander Mr Green Mr Monkhouse and myself
advancd for the alp which we reachd almost immediately, and
found according to expectation plants which answerd to those we
had found before as alpine ones in Europe do to those which we find
in the plains.

The air was here very cold and we had frequent snow blasts.
I had now intirely given over all thoughts of reaching the ship
that night and though[t] of nothing but getting into the thick of
the wood and making a fire, which as our road lay all down hill
seemd very easy to accomplish, so Msrs Green and Monkhouse

---

[1] Banks is here using a bit of Lincolnshire dialect; 'swathe' in his native tongue meant
to him a measure of grass-land in open pasture; or in this case it might have been his
spelling of 'swarth'—sward, the surface of the ground.—Wright's *English Dialect Dictionary*.

[2] Cf. Darwin again: 'We followed the same watercourse as on the previous day, till
it dwindled away, and we were then compelled to crawl blindly among the trees. These,
from the effects of the elevation and of the impetuous winds, were low, thick, and crooked.
At length we reached that which from a distance appeared like a carpet of fine green
turf, but which, to our vexation, turned out to be a compact mass of little beech-trees
about four or five feet high. They were as thick together as box in the border of a garden,
and we were obliged to struggle over the flat but treacherous surface'.—*Naturalist's
Voyage*, p. 210.

[3] Buchan was unfortunately for the expedition an epileptic.

returnd to the people and appointed a hill for our general rendevous from whence we should proceed and build our wigwam. The cold now increasd apace, it might be near 8 O'Clock tho yet exceedingly good daylight so we proceeded for the nearest valley, where the short Birch, the only thing we now dreaded, could not be ½ a mile over. Our people seemd well tho cold and Mr Buchan was stronger than we could have expected. I undertook to bring up the rear and se[e] that no one was left behind. We passd about half way very well when the cold seemd to have at once an effect infinitely beyond what I have ever experiencd. Dr Solander was the first who felt it, he said he could not go any fa[r]ther but must lay down, tho the ground was coverd with snow, and down he laid notwisthstanding all I could say to the contrary. Richmond a black Servant now began also to lag and was much in the same way as the d^r: at this Juncture I dispatchd 5 forwards of whom Mr Buchan was one to make ready a fire at the very first convenient place they could find, while myself with 4 more staid behind to persuade if possible the d^r and Richmond to come on. With much persuasion and intreaty we got through much the largest part of the Birch when they both gave out; Richmond said that he could not go any further and when told that if he did not he must be Froze to death only answerd that there he would lay and dye; the D^r on the contrary said that he must sleep a little before he could go on and actualy did full a quarter of an hour, at which time we had the welcome news of a fire being lit about a quarter of a mile ahead. I then undertook to make the Dr Proceed to it; finding it impossible to make Richmond stir left two hands with him who seemd the least affected with Cold, promising to send two to releive them as soon as I should reach the fire. With much difficulty I got the D^r to it and as soon as two people were sufficiently warmd sent them out in hopes that they would bring Richmond and the rest; after staying about half an hour they returnd bringing word that they had been all round the place shouting and hallowing but could not get any answer. We now guess'd the cause of the mischeif, a bottle of rum the whole of our stock was missing, and we soon concluded that it was in one of their Knapsacks and that the two who were left in health had drank immoderately of it and had slept like the other.

For two hours now it had snowd almost incessantly so we had little hopes of seeing any of the three alive: about 12 however to our great Joy we heard a shouting, on which myself and 4 more went out immediately and found it to be the Seaman who had wakd almost starvd to death and come a little way from where he lay. Him I sent back to the fire and proceeded by his direction to find the other two, Richmond was upon his leggs but not able to walk the other lay on the ground as insensible as a stone. We immediately calld all hands from the fire and attempted by all the means we could contrive to bring them down but finding it absolutely impossible, the road was so bad and the night so dark that we could scarcely ourselves get on nor did we without many Falls. We would then have lit a fire upon the spot but the snow on the ground as well as that which continualy fell renderd that as impracticable as the other, and to bring fire from the other place was also impossible from the quantity of snow which fell every moment from the branches of the trees; so we were forc'd to content ourselves with laying out our unfortunate companions upon a bed of boughs and covering them over with boughs also as thick as we were able, and thus we left them hopeless of ever seeing them again alive which indeed we never did.

In these employments we had spent an hour and a half expos'd to the most penetrating cold I ever felt as well as continual snow. Peter Briscoe, another servant of mine, began now to complain and before we came to the fire became very ill but got there at last almost dead with cold.

Now might our situation truely be calld terrible: of twelve our original number 2 were already past all hopes, one more was so ill that tho he was with us I had little hopes of his being able to walk in the morning, and another very likely to relapse into his fitts either before we set out or in the course of our journey: we were distant from the ship we did not know how far, we knew only that we had been the greatest part of a day in walking it through pathless woods: provision we had none but one vulture which had been shot while we were out, and at the shortest allowance could not furnish half a meal: and to compleat our misfortunes we were caught in a snow storm in a climate we were utterly unaquainted with but which we had reason to beleive was as inhospitable as any in the world, not only from all the accounts we had heard or read but from the Quantity of snow which we saw falling, tho it was very little after midsummer: a circumstance unheard of in Europe for even in Norway or Lapland snow is never known to fall in the summer.

17. The Morning now dawnd and shewd us the earth coverd with snow as well as all the tops of the trees, nor were the snow squalls

at all less Frequent for seldom many minutes were fair together; we had no hopes now but of staying here as long as the snow lasted and how long that would be God alone knew.

About 6 O'Clock the sun came out a little and we immediately thought of sending to see whether the poor wretches we had been so anzious about last night were yet alive, three of our people went but soon returnd with the melancholy news of their being both dead. The snow continued to fall tho not quite so thick as it had done; about 8 a small breeze of wind sprung up and with the additional power of the sun began (to our great Joy) to clear the air, and soon after we saw the snow begin to fall from the tops of the trees, a sure sign of an aproaching thaw. Peter continued very ill but said he thought himself able to walk. Mr Buchan thank god was much better than I could have expected, so we agreed to dress our vulture and prepare ourselves to set out for the ship as soon as the snow should be a little more gone off: so he was skinnd and cut into ten equal shares, every man cooking his own share which furnishd about 3 mouthfulls of hot meat, all the refreshment we had had since our cold dinner yesterday and all we were to expect till we should come to the ship.

About ten we set out and after a march of about 3 hours arrivd at the beach, fortunate in having met with much better roads in our return than we did in going out, as well as in being nearer to the ship than we had any reason to hope; for on reviewing our track as well as we could from the ship we found that we had made a half circle round the hills, instead of penetrating as we thought we had done into the inner part of the cuntrey. With what pleasure then did we congratulate each other on our safety no one can tell who has not been in such circumstances.[1]

[1] We owe to the journal of Molyneux the master a side-light upon the quenchless enthusiasm of Banks. As soon, he says, as the travellers 'came on Board & Refresh'd they were put into warm Beds, Mr Banks excepted who considering our short Stay & the Uncertainty of the weather, Apply'd for a Boat to Haul the Sane which was done without Success the foul Ground & depth of water rendering the Sane useless. However he had the Satisfaction in his late Excursion to make a Valuable Collection of Alpine & other Plants Hitherto unknown in Natural History'. Banks apparently, though he had not expected to be out all night, had relied too much on the fact of summer. Sir Joseph Hooker, who, when a young man, went with Ross to the Antarctic in the *Erebus* (1839-43) made some relevant comments. He and his companions, he said, had frequently been overtaken by heavy snowstorms on their expeditions on the Tierra del Fuegan hills. 'Nothing, however, but personal weakness, or too sudden a change, would have made Sir J. Banks feel their effects so much, for we thought nothing of it, and were it necessary, even without a fire, a shelter might be made which with the warmth of two or three persons close together, might have defied death by cold'.—Hooker to his Mother, 6 December 1842, quoted in Leonard Huxley, *Life and Letters of Sir J. D. Hooker*, I, p. 138. Again, 'This part of the world (Fuegia) has always borne the character of being eminently rigorous and inhospitable,—very much because poor Sir Joseph Banks and Dr Solander, after being accustomed to tropical heat and that hottest of

18. Peter was very ill today and Mr Buchan not at all well, the rest of us thank god in good health tho not yet recoverd from our fatigue.

It blew fresh without and made such a heaving swell in the bay that no one could go ashore and even the ship was very uncumfortable, rolling so much that one could scarcely stand without holding.

19. The swell still continued and we were again hinderd from going ashore tho the loss of two days out of the short time we had to stay here made the D^r and myself ready to venture any risk. The officer who was sent to attempt landing returnd bringing word that it was absolutely impossible without great danger of staving the boat, if even that would do. Both yesterday and today a good deal of snow fell in squalls.

20. Last night the weather began to moderate And this morn was very fine, so much so that we landed without any difficulty in the bottom of the bay and spent our time very much to our satisfaction in collecting shells and plants. Of the former we found some very scarce and fine particularly limpits of several species: of these we observd as well as the shortness of our time would permit that the limpit with a longish hole at the top of his shell is inhabited by an animal very different from those which have no such holes.[1] Here were also some fine whelks, one particularly with a long tooth,[2] and infinite variety of *Lepades, Sertularias, Onisci*[3] &c &c &c much greater variety than I have any where seen, but the shortness of our time would not allow us to examine them so we were obligd to content ourselves with taking specimens of as many of them as we could in so short a time scrape together.

harbours, Rio Janeiro, were rather suddenly cooled down here in the height of summer. The climate in winter is, however, as mild in proportion as the summers are chilly; the annual temperature is assuredly low, but the averages of that of each season are remarkably close'.—To Mrs Boott, 28 November 1842, ibid., pp. 138-9. Hooker overdoes the element of sudden change, for Banks and the others had had plenty of time to get used to lower temperatures than that of the tropics. Richmond and Dorlton would have survived if it had not been for the rum. It was not the snowstorm, or lack of food for a few hours, that was the danger, but for Buchan his epilepsy, and for Solander— one guesses—the effect of too much exercise after too little. Naturally Banks could not help painting the most horrific picture in his journal.

[1] *Fissurella picta* Lamarck. One of Banks's specimens of this shell is still at the British Museum.

[2] *Acanthina calcar* (Martyn). One of these too is in the Banksian collection at the British Museum. Other molluscs collected at that time are listed by Wilkins in his Catalogue account of Banks's shell collection published in 1955 (*Bull, B.M. (N.H.) Historical Series*, I, No. 3).

[3] *Lepades, Sertularias, Onisci*: there are no dated descriptions or drawings by which these animals (barnacles, hydroids, crustaceans) can be identified.

We returnd on board to dinner and afterwards went into the Countrey about two miles to see an Indian town which some of our people had given us intelligence of; we arrivd at it in about an hour walking through a path which I suppose was their common road tho it was sometimes up to our knees in mud. The town itself was situate upon a dry Knowl among the trees, which were not at all cleard away, it consisted of not more than twelve or fourteen huts or wigwams of the most unartificial construction imaginable, indeed no thing bearing the name of a hut could possibly be built with less trouble. They consisted of a few poles set up and meeting together at the top in a conical figure, these were coverd on the weather side with a few boughs and a little grass, on the lee side about one eighth part of the circle was left open and against this opening was a fire made. Furniture I may justly say they had none: a little, very little, dry grass laid round the edges of the circle furnishd both beds and chairs, and for dressing their shell Fish (the only provision I saw them make use of) they had no one contrivance but broiling them upon the Coals. For drinking indeed I saw in a corner of one of their hutts a bladder of some beast full of water: in one side of this near the top was a hole through which they drank by elevating a little the bottom which made the water spring up into their mouths.

In these few hutts and with this small share or rather none at all of what we call the nescessaries and conveniences of life livd about 50 men women and children, to all appearance contented with what they had nor wishing for any thing we could give them except beads; of these they were very fond preferring ornamental things to those which might be of real use and giving more in exchange for a string of Beids than they would for a knife or a hatchet.[1]

As this is to be the last time of our going ashore on this Island I take this opportunity to give an account of such things the shortness of my stay allowd me to observe.

Notwithstanding almost all writers who have mentiond this Island have imputed to it a want of wood, soon after we first saw it even at the distance of some leagues, we plainly distinguish'd that the largest part of the countrey particularly near the sea coast was coverd with wood, which observation was verified in both the bays we put into, in either of which firing might have been

---

[1] Cook does not mention the visit to this 'town', but other traces of it, and of the 'Indians' of the vicinity, are found in Buchan's drawings, four in number, in B.M. Add. MS 23920, ff. 11 (?), 12, 16, 17, and in one by Parkinson, f. 13. Buchan, much 'improved' by Cipriani, will be found as pl. I in the second volume of Hawkesworth. See Pl. 5.

got close by the beach in any quantity, and some trees which to all appearance might be fit for repairing a vessel or even in case of nescessity to make masts.

The hills are high tho not to be calld mountains, the tops of these however are quite bare and on them frequent patches of snow were to be seen, tho the time of the year when we were there answerd to the beginning of July in England. In the valleys between these the Soil has much the appearance of Fruitfullness and is in some places of a considerable depth; at the bottom of almost every one of these runs a brook the water of which in general has a reddish Cast like that which runs through turf bogs in England but is very well tasted.

Quadrupeds I saw none in the Island, exept the Seals and Sea lions[1] which we often saw swimming about in the bay might be calld such, but Dr Solander and myself when we were on the top of the highest hill we were upon observ'd the footsteps of a large beast imprinted on the surface of a bog, but could not with any probability guess of what kind it might be.[2]

Land birds there are very Few. I saw none larger than an English blackbird except hawks and a vulture,[3] but water fowl are much more plentyfull; in the first bay we were in I might have shot any quantity of ducks or geese but would not spare the time from gathering plants. In the other we shot some but probably the Indians in the neighbourhood had made them shy as well as much less plentiful, at least so we found them.

Fish we saw few nor could with our hooks take any fit to eat. Shell fish however are in the greatest abundance, limpits, muscles, Clams &c. none of them delicate yet such as they were we did not despise them.[4]

Insects there are very few and not one species either hurtfull or troublesome; all the time we have been here we have seen neither gnat nor musqueto a circumstance which few if any uncleard countrey but this can boast of.

Of Plants here are many species and those truly the most extrordinary I can imagine, in stature and appearance they agree

[1] The Southern Sea Lion, *Otaria byronia*, and the Southern Fur Seal, *Arctocephalus australis*.

[2] The beast was no doubt the Guanaco, *Auchenia huanaco*, one of the two species of South American llamas, the other being the Vicuña, which is sometimes used as a beast of burden. Cf. p. 227 below.

[3] The only bird of prey from Tierra del Fuego figured on this voyage was the Chimango Caracara, *Milvago chimango* (Vieill.); Parkinson I, pl. 7.

[4] These are discussed by Wilkins (op. cit.), who shows that one of the principal clams they used was the large *Marcia exalbida* (Dillwyn). See 20 January 1769.

a good deal with the Europæan ones only in general are less specious, white flowers being much more common among them than any other colours. But to speak of them botanicaly, probably No botanist has ever enjoyd more pleasure in the contemplation of his Favourite pursuit than Dr Solander and myself among these plants; we have not yet examind many of them, but what we have have turnd out in general so intirely different from any before describd that we are never tird with wondering at the infinite variety of Creation, and admiring the infinite care with which providence has multiplied his productions suiting them no doubt to the various climates for which they were designd. Trees here are very Few, Birch *Betula antarctica*,[1] Beach *Fagus antarcticus*,[2] winters bark *Winterana aromatica*,[3] the two first for timber the other for its excellent aromatick bark so much valued by Physicians are all worth mentioning; and of Plants we could not ascertain the virtues not being able to converse with the Indians who may have experiencd them, but the Scurvy grass *Cardamine antescorbutica* and wild Celery *Apium antarcticum* may easily be known to contain antescorbutick virtues capable of being of great service to ships who may in futurity touch here. Of these two therefore I shall give a short description. *Scurvy grass* is found plentifully in damp places near springs, in general every where near the beach especialy at the watering place in the Bay of Good Success; when young and in its greatest perfection it lays flat on the ground, having many bright green leaves standing in pairs opposite each other with an odd one at the end which makes in general the 5th on a footstalk; after this it shoots up in stalks sometimes 2 feet high at the top of which are small white blosoms which are succeeded by long podds. The whole plant much resembles that that is calld Ladys Smock or Cuckold flower in England only that the flowers are much smaller. *Wild Celery* resembles much the Celery in our gardens only that the leaves are of a deeper green, the flowers like it stand in small tufts at the tops of the Branches and are white; it grows plentifully near the Beach, generaly in the first soil which is above spring tides, and is not easily mistaken as the taste resembles Celery or parsley or rather is between. Both these herbs we us'd plentifully while we stayd here putting them in our soup &c, and found the benefit from them which

---

[1] *Nothofagus betuloides*, the Guindo, whose more accessible stands are now nearing extinction, though some timber is sawed at local mills.

[2] *Nothofagus antarctica*, known as Mire, is host to an orange-yellow fungus (*Cyttaria*), as is also *N. cunninghami* of Tasmania. 'The fact that species of *Nothofagus*, widely separated geographically, have unusual similarities extending even to the parasites, lends support to the theory of the former continuity of the antarctic continents.' (Record and Hess).

[3] *Drimys winteri*; cf. 216, n. 4 above.

seamen in general find from vegetable diet after having been long deprivd of it.

The inhabitants we saw here seemd to be one small tribe of Indians consisting of not more than 50 of all ages and sexes. They are of a reddish Colour nearly resembling that of rusty iron mixd with oil: the men large built but very clumsey, their hight from 5 ft 8 to 5 ft 10 nearly and all very much of the same size, the women much less seldom exceeding 5 ft. Their Cloaths are no more than a kind of cloak of Guanicoe[1] or seal skin thrown loose over their shoulders and reaching down nearly to their knees; under this they have nothing at all nor any thing to cover their feet, except a few of them had shoes of raw seal hide drawn loosely round their instep like a purse. In this dress there is no distinction between men and women, except that the latter have their cloak tied round their middle with a kind of belt or thong and a small flap of leather hanging like Eve's fig leaf over those parts which nature teaches them to hide; which precept tho she has taught to them she seems intirely to have omitted with the men, for they continualy expose those parts to the view of strangers with a carelessness which thoroughly proves them to have no regard to that kind of decency.

Their ornaments of which they are extreemly fond consist of necklaces or rather Solitaires of shells and braceletts which the women wear both on their wrists and legs, the men only on their wrists, but to compensate for the want of the other they have a kind of wreath of brown worsted which they wear over their Foreheads so that in reality they are more ornamented than the women.

They paint their faces generaly in horizontal lines just under their eyes and sometimes make the whole region of their eyes white, but these marks are so much varied that no two we saw were alike: whether as marks of distinction or mere ornaments I could not at all make out.

They seem also to paint themselves with something like a mixture of grease and soot for particular occasions, as when we went to their town there came two out to meet us who were dawb'd with black lines all manner of ways so as to form the most diabolical countenance imaginable, and these two seemd to exorcise us or at least made a loud and long harangue which did not seem to be address'd either to us or any of their countreymen.

Their language is guttural especialy in some particular words which they seem to express much as an Englishman when he hawks

[1] Guanaco, *Auchenia huanaco*, one of the two South American llamas; cf. p. 225, n. 2.

to clear his throat, but they have many words that sound soft enough. During our stay among them I could learn but two of their words, *Nalleca* which signified beads, at least so they always said when they wanted them instead of the ribbands or other trifles which I offerd them, and *oouda* which signified water, or so they said when we took them ashore from the ship and by signs ask'd where water was: oouda was their answer, making the sign of drinking and pointing to our casks as well as to the place where we put them ashore and found plenty of water.

Of Civil goverment I saw no signs, no one seemd to be more respected than another nor did I ever see the least appearance of Quarreling or words between any two of them. Religion also they seemd to be without, unless those people who made strange noises that I have mentiond before were preists or exorcisers which opinion is merely conjectural.

Their food at least what we saw them make use of was either Seals or shell fish. How they took the former we never saw but the latter were collected by the women, whose business it seemd to be to attend at low water with a basket in one hand, a stick with a point and barb in the other, and a satchel on their backs which they filld with shell fish, loosning the limpits with the stick and putting them into the basket which when full was emty'd into the satchel.

Their arms consisted of Bows and arrows, the former neatly enough made the latter neater than any I have seen, polishd to the highest degree and headed either with glass or flint very neatly; but this was the only neat thing they had and the only thing they seemd to take any pains about. Their houses which I have describd before are the most miserable ones imaginable and furniture they have none.

That these people have before had intercourse with Europæans was very plain from many instances: first from the Europæan Commodities of which we saw Sail Cloth, Brown woolen Cloth, Beads, nails, Glass &c, and of them especialy the last (which they used for pointing their arrows) a considerable quantity; from the confidence they immediately put in us at our first meeting tho well acquainted with our superiority; and from the knowledge they had of the use of our guns which they very soon shewd, making signs to me to shoot a seal who was following us in the boat which carried them ashore from the ship. They probably travel and stay but a short time at a place, so at least it should seem from the badness of their houses which seem intirely built to stand but for a short time; from their having no kind of household furniture but what has a handle adapted to it either to be carried in the hand or on the back; from the thinness of their Cloathing which seems little calculated even to bear the summers of this countrey much less the winters; from their food of shell fish which must soon be exhausted at any one place; and from the deserted huts we saw in the first bay we came to where people had plainly been but a short time before, probably this spring.

Boats they had none with them but as they were not sea sick or particularly affected when they came onboard our ship, possibly they might be left at some bay or inlet which passes partly but not all the way through this Island from the Streights of Magellan, from which place I should be much inclind to beleive these people have come as so few ships before us have anchord upon any part of Terra del Fuego.

Their dogs which I forgot to mention before seem also to indicate a commerce had some time or other with Europæans, they being all of the kind that bark, contrary to what has been observd of (I beleive) all dogs natives of America.[1]

The weather here has been very uncertain tho in general extreemly bad: every day since the first more or less snow has fallen and yet the glass has never been below 38: unseasonable as this weather seems to be in the middle of summer I am inclind to think it is generaly so here, for none of the plants appear at all affected by it, and the insects who hide themselves during the time a snow blast lasts are the instant it is fair again as lively and nimble as the finest weather could make them.

21. Saild this morn, the wind Foul, but our keeping boxes being full of new plants we little regarded any wind provided it was but moderate enough to let the draughtsmen work, who to do them justice are now so used to the sea that it must blow a gale of wind before they leave off.

22. Weather pleasant but a little cold wind came to the Northward and we get a little westing.

23. At day break this morn there was land almost all round us,

[1] Banks gives us here the best early description of the Ona people of the main island of Tierra del Fuego, a people of obscure origin who were, as he rightly surmised, nomadic hunters, living in small groups bound together by family ties, and without 'civil government'. They were remarkable as an insular people who did not use boats. Their diet, besides the seals and shell fish that Banks saw them use, was guanaco, and tussock roots and wild celery; their distaste for strong drink was noticed by more than one journalkeeper on English ships. Their numbers have declined. E. Lucas Bridges, in his *Uttermost Part of the Earth* (London 1948), has some interesting remarks.

R

which we judged to be Terra del Fuego not far from the streights and attributed the little way we had made to the streng[t]h of the current setting us to the Eastward. Our old Freind the Sugar Loaf was now in sight who seemd to have followd us, for he was certainly much nearer to us now than he was when we saw him last on the other side of the streights.

24. Many Islands about us today: weather very moderate: one of the Islands was surrounded by small pointed rocks standing out of the water like the Needles.[1]

Ever since we left the streights the albatrosses that have flown about the ship have either been or appeard much larger than those seen before we enterd them, but the weather has never been moderate enough to give us an opportunity of getting out a boat to shoot any of them.

25. Wind today Northwest: stood in with some Islands which were large, we could not tell for certain whether we saw any part of the main. The little Island mentiond yesterday was in view, and beyond that the land made in a bluf head, within which another appeard tho but faintly which was farther to the Southward; possibly that might be Cape Horn, but a fog which overcast it almost immediately after we saw it hinderd our making any material observations upon it, so all we can say is that it was the Southermost land that we saw and does not ill answer to the description [of] Cape Horn given by the French, who place it upon an Island and say that it is composd of two bluff headlands: v. *Navigat aux terres australes tom 1. pag. 356.*[2]

26. Weather vastly moderate today, wind foul so we were sorry that we had ran away from the land last night.

[1] Cook: 'this I take to be the Island of Evouts, it is about one League in circuit and of a moderate height and lies 4 League from the Main, near the south point of it are some peeked Rocks pretty high above water'.—I, p. 48.

[2] See Cook's discussion of Cape Horn, I, p. 49. The French volumes were those of de Brosses, *Navigations aux terres australes* (1756). Charles de Brosses (1709-77), lawyer and magistrate, classical scholar, *philosophe*, was the author of the first published account of the excavations at Herculaneum (1750), which was translated into Italian and English, of a great edition of Sallust (1777), and of works on fetish-worship, etymology and grammar, musical theory, etc. A number of his MSS were destroyed in the Revolution. He had a considerable correspondence with savants and men of letters, but had the misfortune to make an enemy of Voltaire (see the diverting paper by Lytton Strachey in *Portraits in Miniature*). For the story of Cook and Banks, de Brosses's two volumes on South Sea discoveries, imperfectly arranged and discursive as they are, are his important work. I have touched on his place in eighteenth century geographical thought in my Introduction to Cook I, pp. lxxviii ff. See also A. Rainaud, *Le Continent Austral* (Paris 1893), pp. 413-22; and Alan C. Taylor, *Le Président de Brosses et l'Australie* (Paris 1938).

27. Wind came to the northward and we got some little westing, possibly today we were to the westward of the cape, at least a great swell from the NWt makes it certain that we were to the Southward of it. Many large albatrosses *d. exulans* were about the ship whose backs were very white;[1] at noon a shag *Pelecanus antarcticus*[2] came on board the ship and was taken. Soon after dinner saw an Island to the northward possibly Diego Ramires.[3]

28. Pleasant breezes but a heavy swell from NNW continued and made it likely that we were past the Cape, tho we had made but little westing.

29. Wind still Foul and swell continued; today at noon lat. 59.00.

30. At noon today Lat 60.04: near calm: almost all navigators have met with Easterly winds in this Lat. so we were in hopes to do the same: towards Even wind got to the Southward.

31. Wind SE: stood to the westward with very fine weather.

FEBRUARY 1769

1. Calm this morn: went out in the boat and Killd *Diomedea antarctica*,[4] *Procellaria antarctica*[5] and *turtur.*[6] *Diomedæa antarctica* the Black billd albatross is much like the common but differs from him in being scarce half as large and having a bill intirely black. *Procellaria lugens* the Southern shear water differs from the common one in being less and darker colourd on the back, but is easily

---

[1] These were possibly not the Wandering but the Royal Albatross, *Diomedea epomophora* Lesson. Murphy considers it probable that many of the sight records of large white albatrosses in the southern waters of South America refer to the latter species (*Oceanic Birds of South America*, 1936, p. 577).

[2] A shag, *Phalacrocorax albiventer* (Lesson). Solander, p. 15; Parkinson I, pl. 29. Dr Falla has identified this pencil sketch as one of a sub-mature individual of the species.

[3] Diego Ramirez, lat. 56° 30′ S, long. 68° 43′ W. It is really a small group of islets and rocks stretching about 5 miles north and south, the northernmost rock 56 miles south-east of Cape Horn.

[4] The Light-mantled Sooty Albatross, *Phoebetria palpebrata* (Forst.). Parkinson's drawing of this bird was made on this date (I, pl. 26).

[5] This MS name of Banks's appears to have been used for the bird he referred to also as *P. lugens*, which we have identified as *Pterodroma inexpectata* (Forster). Parkinson's drawing, dated 1 February 1769, (I, pl. 21), of what is probably this species, has *Procellaria antarctica* written on the back, but *antarctica* is crossed through and *lugens* written above it. Banks's actual note on *P. lugens* is doubtfully applicable to *P. inexpectata*, inasmuch as that species does not fly heavily; on the other hand Murphy has shown (*American Museum Novitates*, 1580, 1952, p. 6) that the underwing pattern of the species could be interpreted in the way Banks described.

[6] Parkinson's unfinished, dated drawing (I, pl. 15) of this specimen probably represents the Slender-billed Whale bird, *Pachyptila belcheri* (Mathews). Flocks of countless thousands of these and other whale birds are one of the most remarkable sights to be seen in those areas of the southern oceans that are rich in the plankton on which the birds feed. In this group of petrels there is a series of lamellae within the bill which acts in rather the same way as the baleen within the mouth of a whale and enables them to skim the organisms on which they live from the surface layers of the sea—hence their popular name.

distinguishd by his flight which is heavy, and two fascia or streaks of white under his wings which are very conspicuous when he flies. *Procellaria turtur* Mother Careys dove is of the peteril kind about the size of a barbary dove, of a light silvery blue upon the back which shines beautifully as he flies which he does very swiftly keeping generaly near the surface of the water; more or less of these birds have been seen very often since we left the lat. of Fauklands Island where in a gale of wind we saw immense quantities of them.

2. This morn calm and Foggy much like the weather on the Banks of Newfoundland; after dinner went in the boat and shot *Procellaria fuliginosa*,[1] *Turtur*, *gigantea*[2] and *Fregata*.[3] I saw also a small bird not larger than a blackbird who flew quick flapping his wings like a partridge, but was not able to get a shot at him, probably he was of the *alca* tribe.[4]

3. Calm again: went out and shoot *Diomedæa Exulans* Albatross or Alcatrace, differing from those seen to the Northward of Streights of La Maire in being much larger and often quite white on the back between the wings, tho certainly the same species;[5] *Diomedæa antarctica* Lesser black billd Albatross;[6] *diomedæa profuga* Lesser Albatross with a party coloured bill, differing from the last in few things except the bill the upper and under sides of which were yellow and between them black;[7] and *Procellaria vagabunda*.[8] Therm. 41.

4. Blew brisk today, made some northing and westing; we now began to account ourselves certainly past the cape and the Captain (as in his orders was recommended) resolvd to stand as far to the westward as the winds will allow him to do. Two crabs were taken today in the cloaths that hang overboard to tow.[9]

---

[1] *Procellaria aequinoctialis* Linn., the Cape Hen; Solander's description (p. 77) and Parkinson's drawing (I, pl. 19) of this species bear this date. Cf. 26 December 1768.

[2] *Macronectes gigantea* (Gm.), the Giant Petrel; cf. 22 December 1768.

[3] *Fregetta grallaria* (Vieill.), the White-bellied Storm Petrel; cf. 22 December 1768.

[4] This would have been a diving-petrel; cf. 10 January 1769.

[5] This Wandering Albatross was described by Solander, p. 5, and although its wingspan was 10 ft 1 in. he shows clearly that it was an immature bird; Banks's remark about there being larger and whiter specimens here seems to be a generalization.

[6] The Light-mantled Sooty Albatross; cf. 27 January 1769.

[7] *Diomedea chrysostoma* Forster, the Grey-headed Albatross. The details of Parkinson's sketch of this bird (I, pl. 27) and of Solander's account (pp. 11-12) suggest that this was an immature bird: it was identified by Sharpe (*History of the Collections*, II, p. 176, 1906) as *D. chlororhynchos*, but that species has not been recorded from the west coast of South America nor from the Eastern Pacific. Banks's MS is not quite clear here: it seems that his remark about a 'Lesser Albatross differing from the last in but few things except the bill', may concern a second specimen which, according to his note on the colour of the bill, was a mature bird. Solander, however, described only immature specimens, including one captured twelve days later which Banks does not record.

[8] The White-headed Petrel, *Pterodroma lessonii* (Garnot). Solander, p. 95.

[9] These crabs are unidentifiable; no drawings or descriptions seem to relate to them.

I had been unwell these three or four days and today was obligd to keep the Cabbin with a bilious attack, which tho quite slight alarmd me a good deal, as Cap^tn Wallis had in the Streights of Magellan such an attack which he never got the better of throughout the whole voyage.

5. All but calm today: myself a little better than yesterday, well enough to eat part of the Albatrosses shot on the third, which were so good that every body commended and Eat heartily of them tho there was fresh pork upon the table. The way of dressing them is thus: Skin them over night and soak their carcases in Salt water till morn, then parboil them and throw away the water, then stew them well with very little water and when sufficiently tender serve them up with Savoury sauce.

6. Foul wind, myself something better.

7. Myself better again, in the evening ship made a little westing.

8. Fair wind, blew fresh.

9. Blew fresh all last night which has given us a good deal of westing. This morn some sea weed floated past the ship and my servant declares that he saw a large beetle fly over her: I do not beleive he would deceive me and he certainly knows what a beetle is, as he has these 3 years been often employd in taking them for me.[1]

10. During all last night the ship has pitchd very much so that there has been no sleeping for land men. Today misty with little wind.

11. Fair wind, stand to the westward.

12. Foul wind, but prodigious fine weather and smooth water makes amends to us at least.

13. Wind still Foul and blew fresh, at night a little mended.

14. Wind South, water soon became smooth, at night little wind.

15. Calm this morn: went in the boat and killd *Procellaria velox*,[2]

[1] Presumably Banks here refers to Peter Briscoe, who was with him in Newfoundland, rather than the younger James Roberts.

[2] One of the small grey and white gadfly petrels of the subgenus *Cookilaria* (cf. Falla, *Emu*, 1942, p. 111) since this is the only group of the genus *Pterodroma* (*Bulweria*) characterized by the blue feet mentioned as a diagnostic character by Solander. His notes suggest (p. 68) that he may have examined and classified together under this name specimens of up to eight of the members of this group, but the specimen under consideration, which was figured by Parkinson, I, pl. 16, must belong to one of the two species exploiting this zone of surface water, *Pterodroma cookii* or *P. longirostris*, and very probably to one of the two races nesting nearby at Juan Fernandez, *P. cookii defilippiana* (Gigl. and Salvad.) or *P. longirostris longirostris* (Stejneger). The drawing shows the short bill typical of *longirostris* so that the name *Procellaria velox*, which was restricted by Mathews to this specimen (*Birds of Australia*, 1912, p. 170) must be regarded as a synonym of *Aestralata longirostris*, Stejneger 1893. (Dr W. R. P. Bourne, personal communication.)

Nectris munda[1] and *fuliginosa*,[2] which two last are a new genus between Procellaria and Diomedea: this we reckon a great acquisition to our bird collection. My stay out today was much shortned by a breeze of wind which brought me aboard by 11 o clock and before night blew very fresh.

16. All last night and this morn it has blown very fresh, wind South, so that we have 3 reefs in the topsails for the first time since we left the streights of La Maire.

17. Blew fresh yet and wind stood, so we went well to the westward. In the evening more moderate; I ventur'd upon deck for the first time and saw several porpoises without any pinna dorsalis, black on the backs, under the belly and on the noses white;[3] also a kind of Albatross different from any I have seen, he being black all over except the head and bill which were white.[4]

18. Fair weather, ship stood NW.

19. Went very slowly through the water tho pleasan[t]ly for the ship had scarcely any motion.

20. Wind still foul but very moderate and the ship almost without motion.

21. Still no swell from the west tho the ship had fresh way through the water. A bird not seen before attended the ship about the size of a pidgeon, black above and light coloured underneath, darting swiftly along the surface of the water in the same manner as I have observd the Nectris to do of which genus he is probably a species.[5]

22. This morn settled rain and scarce any wind, the whole evening small puffs of wind and rain and calms succeeded each other.

23. Calm: went out in the boat, shott *Procellaria velox*,[6] *fuliginosa*[7]

---

[1] *Puffinus assimilis* (Gould), the Little or Allied Shearwater. Parkinson I, pl. 24, Solander, pp. 115-16. This bird has been much discussed and notes on variation in the southern races are given by Bourne, *Emu*, 1959, p. 212.

[2] *Puffinus griseus* (Gm.), the Sooty Shearwater or New Zealand Mutton-bird. Parkinson I, pl. 23, Solander, pp. 111-12. Both these drawings of '*Nectris*' spp. are dated. Solander was the first to recognize the distinctive character of the shearwater bill, which for long was used to separate these birds from the other petrels.

[3] The Right Whale Dolphin, *Lissodelphis peroni* (Lacépède).

[4] Perhaps the Giant Petrel, *Macronectes giganteus*, in which there are various colour phases. The Galapagos Albatross, *Diomedea irrorata* Salvin, has a whitish head and is otherwise dusky but it is unlikely to have been so far south.

[5] A number of small petrels occur hereabouts; this note is not sufficient to identify the one Banks observed.

[6] *Pterodroma* sp., one of the gadfly petrels. See 15 February 1769.

[7] *Procellaria aequinoctialis*, the Cape Hen. Solander, p. 77. See also 2 February 1769.

and *velificans*.[1] At night wind came to the east tho very little of it, it was however a matter of comfort to have any as we have not had the name of East in the wind since 31st of Jan^ry.

24. At 12 last night the wind settled at NE; this morn found studding Sails set and the ship going at the rate of 7 knots, no very usual thing with Mrs Endeavour.

25. Almost calm so that we trembled for the continuance of our east wind and soon after noon it left us; at night Rain and dirty weather wind N.

26. Blew fresh, before dinner handed[2] all topsails. Albatrosses began to be much less plentifull than they have been. Lat. 41.8'.

27. Moderate and fine, the weather began to feel soft and comfortable like the spring in England.

28. Weather fine with a pleasant breeze. In the evening a great many Porpoises of a very large size came about the ship; they differ'd from any I have seen before in being very much larger, in having their back fins a great deall higher in proportion, and in every one having a white spot on each side of his face as large as the crown of a hat but of an oval shape.[3]

MARCH 1769

1. Fine weather and very pleasant, began the new month by pulling off an under waistcoat.

2. Rather squally this morn and had been so all night: it did not however blow up to a gale tho the ship had a good deal of motion, indeed I began to hope that we were now so near the peacefull part of the Pacifick ocean that we may almost cease to fear any more gales.[4]

3. Calm: went in the boat and killd *Procellaria velox*, 2 *velificans*, 3

[1] Dr W. R. P. Bourne in a personal communication has pointed out that Solander's description (pp. 93-4) of *P. velificans* agrees well with *Pterodroma externa externa* (Salvin), the White-necked Petrel, and that his suggestion that his specimen was like a large *Procellaria mollis* (from which it differs in the white underwing noted by him) is clearly diagnostic.

[2] Furled. Cook is rather stronger in his language than Banks: 'very strong gales and Squally with Showers of rain which at length brought us under our two courses and close reef'd Main topsail'.—I, p. 61.

[3] *Orcinus orca*, the Killer Whale.

[4] This remark may have some connection with Banks's entry for 11 March, pp. 237-8 below, on which see the note. Cook records for the morning 'a strong fresh gale and pretty clear weather'; his definition of a gale was probably more technical than Banks's. His noon position for this day was lat. 37° 19' S, long. 112° 5' W.

sordida,[1] 4 *melanopus*,[2] 5 *lugens*,[3] *agilis*[4] and *Diomedæa exulans*.[5] The Albatross very brown exactly the same as the first I killd, which if I mistake not was nearly in the same latitude on the other side of the continent. Caught *Holothuria obtusata*,[6] *Phillodoce velella*[7] exactly the same as those taken on the other side of the continent except in size, which in these did not exceed that of an English sixpence. Also *Dagysa vitrea* the same as that taken off Rio de Janeiro; now however we had an opportunity of seeing its ext[r]ordinary manner of breeding which is better to be understood from the drawing than any description I can give; suffice it therefore to say that the whole progeny 15 or 20 in number hung in a chain from one end of the mother, the oldest only or the largest adhering to her and the rest to each other.[8]

While in the boat among a large quantity of birds I had killd, 69 in all, caught 2 *Hippoboscas* forest flies, both of one species different from any described.[9] More than probably these belongd to the birds and came off with them from the land. I found also this day a large *Sepia* cuttle fish laying on the water just dead but so pulld to peices by the birds that his Species could not be determind; only this I know that of him was made one of the best soups I ever eat. He was very large, differd from the Europæans in that his arms instead of being (like them) furnished with suckers were armd with a double row of very sharp talons, resembling in shape those of a cat and like them retractable into a sheath of skin from whence they might be thrust at pleasure.[10]

[1] *P. sordida*: ? the Kermadec Petrel, *Pterodroma neglecta neglecta* (Schlegel). According to Solander, p. 83, another specimen was taken on the 21st of this month; although his account of the dorsal plumage is not altogether satisfactory for *P. neglecta*, his notes on the undersurface of the wing agree closely with the description and figure of this species given by Murphy and Pennoyer, *Amer. Mus. Novit.* 1580, 1952, and it seems probable that he had some light phase birds of this polymorphic species.

[2] *P. melanopus*: another Kermadec Petrel, *Pterodroma neglecta* (Schl.). Solander's description, p. 85, is quite close to that given by Murphy and Pennoyer (op. cit.) for birds in the dark phase of this species, and he placed *sordida* next to *melanopus* both in MS Z4 and in his interleaved edition of the *Systema Naturae*. Gould states that he examined a drawing in Banks's collection with *melanopus* written on it in Solander's hand (*Ann. Mag. Nat. Hist.* 13, p. 363, 1844) but unfortunately no trace of it can be found now. *P. melanopus* Gm. was a different bird, taken from Latham's account, and only 13 inches long. Solander's birds were 15 inches long with a wing span of 39 inches; they weighed 14 oz.

[3] *P. lugens*: Peale's Petrel, *Pterodroma inexpectata* Forster. See 1 February above.

[4] *P. agilis*: the Sunday Island Petrel, *Pterodroma externa cervicalis* (Salvin). Solander's careful description, p. 69, giving details of the head, neck and back as well as the under-wing pattern, clearly points to this identification.

[5] An immature Wandering Albatross.

[6] A small specimen of the Portuguese Man-of-war of which there is an unfinished dated sketch (III, p. 41) by Parkinson.   [7] *Velella velella* (Linn.).

[8] Parkinson's labelled drawings (III, pls. 31, 32) of this animal show a nectophore of the siphonophore *Diphyes dispar*, but Banks's account of the reproductive chain refers to a salp.   [9] Unidentifiable in the absence of a description or drawing.

[10] One of the Onychoteuthidae, a family of cephalopods, with retractile claws.

The weather is now become pleasan[t]ly warm and the Barnacles upon the ships bottom seemd to be regenerate, very few only of the old ones remaining alive but young ones without number scarce bigger than Lentils.

4. Fine weather, the ship goes 5 knotts without rowling or pitching which she has not done this great while; this we attribute to the empty water cask[s] in the fore hold having been filld with salt water yesterday.

There were several bonitos about the ship or at least fish something like them.[1]

5. Fine weather but foul wind, it now begins to be very hot. Therm. 70 and damp, with prodigious dews at night greater than any I have felt, this renews our uncomfortably damp situation, every thing beginning to mould as it did about the æquinoctial line in the Atlantick.

6. Weather wind and heat continued, dew to night as strong as ever.

7. Wind weather heat and dew as yesterday. No Albatrosses have been seen since the 4th, and for some days before that we had only now and then a single one in sight so conclude we have parted with them for good and all.[2]

8. Rains today with uncommonly large and heavy drops, accompanied with calms and small puffs of wind all round the Compass; in the Evening a SE wind took the ship aback and before night blew brisk.

9. Fine weather wind right aft. A tropick bird[3] was seen by some of the people but myself did not see him.

10. Fine weather continued, wind aft and very pleasant.

11. Wind and weather much the same as yesterday. Tho it had blown a steady breeze of wind these three days no sea at all was up, from whence we began to conclude that we had pass'd the Line drawn between the Great South Sea and the Pacifick ocean by

[1] Possibly *Euthynnus pelamis*.
[2] The albatrosses of the southern oceans are commonly found between latitudes 30° and 60° S, but sometimes further north when there are currents of cool water. There is one species, *Diomedea irrorata* Salvin, which breeds in the Galapagos islands. Three other species are confined to the north Pacific. It would seem that albatrosses in general keep to cooler waters on account of the richer food supply there.
[3] Tropic birds are widely distributed in low latitudes. Races of both the Red-tailed Tropic Bird, *Phaethon rubricauda* Boddaert, and the White-tailed, *P. lepturus* Daudin, occur almost throughout the south-west Pacific (for distribution map of tropic birds and albatrosses in the south Pacific see Fleming, *Emu*, 49, 1950, p. 183).

the Council of the Royal Society,[1] notwithstanding we are not yet within the tropicks.

12. Wind continued fair but in the even flaggd a little; we began to imagine that it must be the trade, at least if it continues we resolv'd [to] call it so.

13. Almost calm to day tho not quite enough for going out in the boat. I saw a tropick bird for the first time hovering over the ship but flying very high; if my eyes did not deceive me it differd from that describd by Linnæus, *Phaeton æthereus*, in having the long feathers of his tail red and his crissum black.[2]

Towards even set the servants to work with a dipping net who took *Mimus volutator*[3] and *Phyllodoce velella*, both exactly the same as those we have seen in the Atlantick ocean. Lat. 30.45, Long. 126.23.45.

14. Very light winds today shifting from South to East: at noon an alarm of Land being seen which proved at night to be no more than a fog bank tho it certainly remain many hours without any change in its appearance.

The tropick birds this Evening made a noise as they flew over the ship not unlike some gulls.

15. All but calm all this day: many tropick birds were about the ship. The sea today was remarkably quiet so that the ship had little or no motion.

This night happend an occultation of Saturn by the moon, which M[r] Green observ'd but was unlucky in having the weather so cloudy that the observation was good for little or nothing.[4]

[1] I am quite at a loss to explain when or where this line was drawn. By courtesy of the President, Council and Fellows of the Royal Society, I was enabled to consult the Council Minutes, but have found no reference to the matter in the eighteenth century up to 1768. When Balboa first named the sea he saw in 1513, looking south from the Gulf of San Miguel, he called it the *Mar del Zur*, the South Sea. It was Magellan who conferred the name Pacific. Dampier, writing of his passage from Juan Fernandez to the Galapagos in 1684, remarks, 'Our passage lay now along the Pacifick-Sea, properly so called. For tho' it be usual with our Map-makers to give that Name to this whole Ocean calling it Mare Australe, Mar del Zur, or Mare Pacificum; yet, in my opinion, the Name of the Pacifick-Sea ought not to be extended from South to North farther than from 30 to about 4 deg. South Latitude, and from the American shore Westward indefinitely, with respect to my observation. . . . Nor are there in this Sea any Winds but the Trade-wind, no Tempests, no Tornadoes or Hurricanes (tho' north of the Equator, they are met with as well in this Ocean as in the Atlantick. . .)'.—*New Voyage* (*Voyages*, ed. Masefield, I. pp. 120-1). The eighteenth century cartographers seem to have placed the names according to individual fancy.

[2] *Phaethon rubricauda*, the Red-tailed Tropic Bird. The crissum, i.e. the feathers immediately posterior to the vent, is not black: see Banks's note for 21 March. See Pl. 6.

[3] A nudibranch, *Glaucus atlanticus*; see 4 October 1768.

[4] Cook mentions the observation, but leaves blank the times of immersion and emersion; so evidently Banks was right, and the details were not worth noting.

16. Calm almost, but the ship stole through this remarkably smooth water so that I do not think it worth while to have a boat hoisted out; by observation to day they find that she has gone these two days much faster than the log which they tell me is very often the case in light winds when the ship goes before them.

Our water which was taken aboard at Terra del Fuego has remaind till this time perfectly good without the least change, an instance which I am told is very rare, especialy as in our case when water is brought from a cold climate into a hot one. This however has stood it without any damage and now drinks as brisk and pleasant as when first taken on board, or better, for the red colour it had at first is subsided and it is now as clear as any English spring water.

17. Most of this day as yesterday almost calm, at night a small breeze came on from ENE so that the ship went 4 knotts.

18. Squally weather all night with heavy rain: this morn much the same, the rain so heavy that the Cabbin was twice baild of more than a bucket full at a time, all which came in at the crevises of the weather quarter window,[1] for there was no leak of any consequence in any other part of the cabbin. The Wind was at N and brought with it a hot damp air which affected (I may safely say) every man in the ship more or less; towards even however it shifted towards the west and was much dryer.

19. Pleasant breeze, ship went N by W. Some flying fish were seen this morn and several procellarias cheifly of the brown sorts as *sordida*.

20. Very fine as yesterday: many tropick birds were about the ship, as indeed there has been every day since I first mentiond them but still more of them as the weather was finer. Lat. today . Long.   .[2] When I look on the charts of these Seas and see our course, which has been Near a streight one at NW since we left Cape Horne, I cannot help wondering that we have not yet seen land.[3] It is however some pleasure to be able to disprove that which does not exist but in the opinions of Theoretical writers, of which sort most are who have wrote any thing about

---

[1] The 'quarter window' was one of the windows next the ship's stern, the 'weather quarter window' that one exposed to the wind. The winds this day as noted by Cook were north-east and north, and the ship's course was N 60° 45′ W, so it was the window on the starboard side that took in the rain.

[2] In Cook, lat. 25° 44′ S, long. 129° 28′ W. The ship was now approaching the Tuamotus, within which it would in a fortnight make its first landfall, but the closest land was Pitcairn, a little farther north and west—lat. 25° 04′ S, long. 130° 05′ W.

[3] i.e. the Southern Continent.

these seas without having themselves been in them. They have generaly supposd that every foot of sea which they beleivd no ship had passd over to be land, tho they had little or nothing to support that opinion but vague reports, many of them mentiond only as such by the very authors who first publishd them, as for instance the *Orange Tree* one of the Nassau fleet who being separated from her Companions and drove to the westward reported on her joining them again that she had twice seen the Southern continent;[1] both which places are laid down by Mr Dalrymple[2] many degrees to the eastward of our track, tho it is probable that he has put them down as far to the westward as he thought it possible that she could go.

To streng[t]hen these weak arguments another Theory has been started which says that it is Nescessary that so much of the South sea as the authors of it call land should be so, otherwise this wor[l]d would not be properly bal[a]nc'd as the quantity of Earth known to be situated in the Northern hemisphere would not have a counterpoise in this. The number of square degrees of their land which we have already chang'd into water sufficiently disproves this, and teaches me at least that till we know how this globe is fixd in that place which has been since its creation assignd to it in the general system, we need not be anxious to give reasons how any one part of it counterbalances the rest.

21. Calm this morn: went out in the boat and shot Tropick bird *Phaeton erubescens*,[3] and *Procellaria atrata*,[4] *velox*[5] and *sordida*. Took *Turbo fluitans*[6] floating upon the water in the same manner as *Helix Janthina*, *Medusa Porpita* exactly like those taken on the other side of the continent,[7] and a small *Cimex*? which also was taken before

---

[1] The Nassau fleet, so called after its patron the Prince of Nassau, was the Dutch fleet that set out in 1623 under Jacob le Hermite and Hugo Schapenham to raid Peru. The raid was a failure, but geographers were excited by the news that one of the ships, the *Orange*, separated from the fleet by bad weather, rejoined it at Juan Fernandez in April 1624 after sighting the Southern Continent twice, in lat. 50° and 41°.

[2] In the chart included in his *Account of the Discoveries made in the South Pacifick Ocean, Previous to 1764* (London 1769). It will be remembered that Dalrymple presented Banks with a copy of this pamphlet, previous to the *Endeavour*'s departure. On the chart the Dutch 'discoveries' of 1624 are indicated about 91° W, so that on this reckoning the *Endeavour* had already sailed more than 38 degrees of longitude into the continent.

[3] The Red-tailed Tropic Bird. There is a painting by Parkinson, I, pl. 31, of one of these birds in flight, dated 1769. Solander's description bears this date but he does not refer to a painting. see pl. 6.

[4] Perhaps one of the Herald Petrels, *Pterodroma arminjoniana heraldica* (Salvin); Solander's description, p. 81, is suggestive of one of these birds in the dark phase.

[5] One of the gadfly petrels recorded by Solander; cf. 15 February above.

[6] ? *Janthina* sp. There seem to be no drawings or descriptions of this gastropod, which can only doubtfully be assigned to this genus.

[7] *Porpita porpita*. See 20 September 1768.

but appears to be a larva, if so probably of some animal that lives under water, as I saw many but none that appeard perfect tho they were enough so to propagate their species or copulate at least.[1] In examining the Phaetons found that what appeard to me a black crissus as they flew was no other than their black feet; on them was plenty of a very curious kind of *acarus Phaetintis*[2] which either was or appeard to be viviparous.

Besides what was shot today there were seen Man of war birds *pelecanus aquilus*,[3] and a small bird of the Sterna? kind calld by the seamen egg birds, which were white with red beaks about the size of *sterna hirundo*.[4] Of these I saw several just at night fall who flew very high and followd one another all standing towards the NNW; probably there is land on that point as we were now not far from the Lat and Longitude in which Quiros saw his southermost Islands Incarnation and St J^no Baptist.[5]

22. Fresh breeze of wind today, the ship layd no better than west so we were forcd to give over our hopes on the NNW point.[6] Many man of war birds were about the ship today and some egg birds, I shot 3 of the first but none of them fell onboard the ship. All today the weather very hot and damp, Thermometer 80, which it never was at sea before except in the calms under the line.

23. Most troublesome weather, calms and squalls with very heavy rain but the wind will not stirr. Many Egg birds seen today and some few Tropick.

24. Blew fresh still, wind as foul as ever. The officer of the watch reported that in the middle watch the water from being roughish became on a sudden as smooth as a mill pond, so that the ship from going only 4 knots at once increasd to six, tho there was little or no more wind than before this, and a log of wood which

---

[1] Probably *Halobates* sp. Cf. 7 October 1768.

[2] *sic*; Sol. MS *Phaetontis. Alloptes phaetontis* (Fabr.), a mite. See Parkinson III, pl. 3, and Solander, p. 291.

[3] Man-of-war or Frigate Birds belong to the genus *Fregata*, and have distinctive forked tails.

[4] The terns may have been the Roseate Tern, *Sterna dougalli* Montagu, which is said to occur in this region. Egg Bird is a name generally applied by sailors to terns, and particularly to the Wideawake or Sooty Tern, *Sterna fuscata*.

[5] Quiros came on these islands when outward bound in January 1606. His La Encarnacion, now called Ducie island, lies in lat. 24° 40′ S, long. 124° 48′ W; his San Juan Batista, or Henderson, in lat. 24° 22′ S, long. 128° 18′ W—about 190 miles westward of Ducie. Dalrymple, from whom Banks probably worked, in his *Account of the Discoveries*, pp. 20-1, gives the position of La Encarnacion as 25° S, 146° 9′ W, and of San Juan Batista as two days' sail to the westward of it. Cook's position for this day was lat. 25° 21′ S, long. 129° 28′ W.

[6] i.e. of sighting the land which the flight of birds the previous evening had indicated. The birds were no doubt flying to one of the eastern Tuamotus.

was seen to pass by the ship by several people made them beleive that there was land to windward.[1]

At 8 when I came on deck the signs were all gone, I saw however two birds which seemed to be of the sterna? kind both very small, one quite white and another quite black[2] who from their appearance probably could not venture far from Land.

Today by our reckoning we crossed the tropick.[3]

25. Wind continued much the same but more moderate, few or no birds were about the ship but some sea weed was seen by some of the people, only one bed.

This even one of our marines threw himself overboard and was not miss'd till it was much too late even to attempt to recover him. He was a very young man scarce 21 years of age, remarkably quiet and industrious, and to make his exit the more melancholy was drove to the rash resolution by an accident so trifling that it must appear incredible to every body who is not well accquainted with the powerfull effects that shame can work upon young minds.

This day at noon he was sentry at the Cabbin door and while he was on that duty one of the Capts servants being calld away in a hurry left a peice of seal skin in his charge, which it seems he was going to cut up to make tobacco pouches some of which he had promisd to several of the men; the poor young fellow it seems had several times askd him for one, and when refus'd had told him that since he refusd him so trifling a thing he would if he could steal one from him, this he put in practise as soon as the skin was given into his charge and was of course found out immediately as the other returnd, who was angry and took the peice he had cut off from him but declard he would not complain to the officers for so trifling a cause.

In the mean time the fact came to the ears of his fellow soldiers, who stood up for the honour of their Core 13 in number so highly that before night, for this hapned at noon, they drove the young fellow almost mad by representing his crime in the blackest coulours as a breach of trust of the worst consequence: a theft committed

---

[1] Cook notes his feelings at this indication of land, which he did not see himself (it passed, or was thought to pass, the ship, about 3 AM) in his own journal for 24 March: he did not think himself at liberty to search for land he was not sure to find. On this point, and Dalrymple's criticism, see my note, Cook I, p. 66, n. 3.

[2] The former was possibly the White Tern, *Gygis alba* Sparrman, or perhaps the Marquesan White Tern, a small race of the same species. There are no very small black terns; the White-capped Noddy, *Anous minutus* (Boie) is 13-14 inches long and breeds in the Tuamotus. See also Banks's note about terns on 4 April 1769.

[3] The Tropic of Capricorn. Cook gives his latitude for March 24 as 23° 23' S, and for March 25 as 22° 11' S.

by a sentry upon duty they made him think an inexcusable crime, especialy when the thing stole was given into his charge: the Sargeant particularly declard that if the person acgreivd would not complain he would, for people should not suffer scandal from the ill behaviour of one. This affected the young fellow much, he went to his hammock, soon after the Sargeant went to him calld him and told him to follow him upon deck. He got up and slipping the Sargeant went forward, it was dusk and the people thought he was gone to the head and were not convincd that he was gone over till half an hour after it hapned.[1]

26. This whole day calms succeeded by hard squalls with much rain, which weather the seamen call trolly lollys; the wind went more than once round the Compass which made us hope that we were near the trade at least. Few or no birds and no tropick birds.

27. Weather much like yesterday, no birds, at night a little more setled.

28. Calm today: one tropick bird was seen this morn. After dinner a Shark came the first we had seen in these seas, he greedily took the bait but the line being old broke, very soon he however returnd with the hook and chain hanging out of his mouth but would not take the second bait.

29. Calm again. Bent a new shark line in the even a shark alongside took the bait but broke the new line just as we were going to hoist him in, I am told by the people that common fishing line will never last above a year if ever so much care is taken of it.

30. Some birds and bonitos seen this morn but none after I came upon deck.

31. Pleasant breeze of wind which is the trade: some few tropick birds seen this morn. Myself not quite well a little inflammation in my throat and swelling of the glands.

APRIL 1769

1. Something better today. As my complaint has something in it that at least putts me in mind of the scurvy I took up the lemon Juice put up by Dr Hulmes direction[2] and found that which was

---

[1] This unfortunate young man was William Greenslade.

[2] See Hulme's letter to Banks, Appendix, II, p. 301 below. Nathaniel Hulme (1732-1807) joined the navy as a surgeon's mate in 1755, and his observations and reflections on the common ill of seamen, scurvy, provided the groundwork for his thesis for his Edinburgh M.D. (1765), *De Scorbuto*. He expanded this in a Latin essay of 1768 on scurvy, which had an appendix in English on the benefits of lime—i.e. lemon—juice on long voyages,

concentrated by evaporating 6 Gall[s] into less than 2 has kept as well as any thing could do. The small Cagg in which was lemon juice with one fifth of brandy was also very good tho large part of it had leak'd out by some fault in the Cagg; this therefore I began to make use of immediately drinking very weak punch made with it for my common liquor.

2. Many birds today about noon passd by the ship making a noise something like gulls, they were black upon the back and white under the belly probably of the sterna kind;[1] in company with them were 20 or 30 Men of war birds soaring over the flock, probably the whole were in pursuit of a shoal of fish.

3. Several of the same kinds of birds seen today as were seen yesterday, also many Egg-birds; the trade continued to blow fresh with very pleasant weather.

4. At 10 this morn my servant Peter Briscoe saw the Land which we had almost passd by, we stood towards it and found it to be a small Island (Lagoon Island)[2] about 1½ or 2 miles in lengh. Those who were upon the topmast head distinguishd it to be nearly circular and to have a Lagoon or pool of water in the middle which occupied much the largest part of the Island. About noon we were Close to it within a mile or thereabouts and distinctly saw inhabitants upon it of whoom we counted 24. They appeard to us through our glasses to be tall and to have very large heads or possibly much hair upon them, 11 of them walkd along the beach abreast of the ship with each a pole or pike as long again as himself in his hand and every one of them stark naked and appearing of a brown copper colour; as soon however as the ship had fairly pass'd the Island they retird higher up on the beach and seemd to put on some cloaths or at least cover themselves with something which made them appear of a light colour.

The Island was coverd with trees of many very different verdures; the Palms or Cocoa nut trees we could plainly distinguish particularly two that were amazingly taller than their fellows and at a distance bore a great resemblance to a flag. The land seemd all very low

showing that this had been familiar to the English since the sixteenth century. Nevertheless lime juice proper, as later used, did not become a common precaution on ships till the nineteenth century. Cook set more store on wort of malt and on fresh food generally. Hulme held important medical posts and was elected F.R.S. in 1794.

[1] Probably a flock of Wideawake or Sooty Terns, *Sterna fuscata*. This is confirmed by Cook's remarks on these birds '—a large flock of Birds, they had brown backs and white bellies they fly and make a noise like Stearings [an old name for the Arctic Tern] and are shaped like them only something larger'.—Cook I, p. 68.

[2] The ship was passing through the Tuamotus. The land bore south, says Cook, distant three or four leagues; its native name is Vahitahi.

Pl. III. *Berberis ilicifolia*

Tierra del Fuego

tho at a distance several parts of it appeard high yet when we came near them they provd to be clumps of Palms. Under the shade of these were the houses of the natives in places cleard of all underwood so that pleasanter groves can not be imagind, at least so they appeard to us whose eyes had so long been unus'd to any other objects than water and sky.

After dinner land was again seen which we came up with at sunset; it provd a small Island not more than ¾ of a mile in lengh but almost round,¹ we ran within less than a mile of it but saw no signs of inhabitants nor any Cocoa nut trees, or indeed any that bore the least resemblance to Palms tho there were many sorts of trees or at least many varieties of verdure.

In the neighbourhood of both this and the other Island were many birds, man of war birds and a small black sort of *sterna?* with a white spot on his head which the seamen calld Noddies² but said that they were much smaller than the West Indian Noddies.

While we were near the Island a large fish was taken with a towing line baited with a peice of Pork rind cut like a swallows tail ⟋ the seamen calld it a King fish *Scomber lanceolatus*.³

5. Less wind this morn than yesterday with some showers of rain. While we were at dinner word was brought down that there was land in sight from the mast head, and found it a low Island but of much greater extent than either of those seen yesterday being from 10 to 15 leagues in circumference. Myself remaind at the mast head the whole evening admiring its extrordinary structure: in shape it appeard to be like a bow the wood and string of which was land⁴ and the parts within occupied by a large lake of water, which bore about the same proportion to the land as the void space within the bow does to the string and wood. The string of the bow was a flat beach without any signs of vegetation on it but heaps of sea weed laying in ridges as higher or lower tides had left them; this was 3 or 4 Leagues long and appeard not more than

¹ Banks notes the name in his margin, 'Thrum cap'. It was Aki Aki. The name Thrum Cap was conferred by Cook because of its shape and the shaggy appearance it was given by palms and bushes. Thrums were the end-pieces sticking out in rough weaving; to thrum, in nautical speech, was to fasten bunches of rope yarn over a sail or mat, for the purpose, e.g., of stopping a leak.
² The White-capped Noddy, *Anous minutus*.
³ *Acanthocybium solandri* (Cuv. and Val.). Cuvier and Valenciennes in their *Hist. Nat. Poiss.* 8, p. 192, founded the species on the description of this fish by Solander, pp. 267-8; they make no reference to Parkinson's painting of it (II, pl. 87).
⁴ Marginal note 'Bow Island'; Hao. It was seen first by Bougainville, who called it *La Harpe*.

200 yards wide in any part tho doubtless as flat objects foreshorten themselves so much it might be much more. The Horns or angles of the bow were two large tufts of Cocoa nut trees and much the largest part of its arch was filld up likewise with trees of different hights and appearances, a small part of it however was in my opinion low and like the string. Here some thought there was an opening into the Pool in the center and myself cannot say there was not, indeed it was at so great a distance that all must be conjecture.[1]

Along the low beach or bowstring we saild within less than a league of the shore till sunsett when we judg'd ourselves about half way between the two horns, we then brought too and sounded, 130 fathom of line out and no ground; night which came on here almost instantly after sunset made us lose sight of the land before the line was well hauld in. We then steerd by the sound of the breakers which were very distinctly heard in the ship till we were clear of all.

That this land was inhabited appeard clearly by three smoaks in different parts of the Island which we saw repeated several different times, probably as signals from one to the other of our aproach. Our 2nd Lieutenant affirmed that he saw from the deck many inhabitants in the first clump of Trees, that they were walking to and fro as if on their ordinary business without taking the least notice of the ship, he saw also many houses and Canoes hauld up under the trees. To this I only say that I did not see them or know that any one else had till the ship had passd the place ½ an hour.

6. Pleasant breeze, at ½ past 11 land in sight again, at 3 came up with it, proved to be two distinct Islands with many small ones near them Joining by reefs under water.[2]

The Islands themselves were long thin strips of land ranging in all directions sometime ten or more miles in lengh but never more than a quarter of a mile broad; upon them were many Cocoa nut and other trees and many inhabitants several of whoom came out in Canoes as far as the reefs but would not come without them; 6 particularly who for some time walkd along shore abreast of the ship, on our passing the end of the Island launchd two Canoes with great quickness and dexterity and 3 getting into each the[y] put off as we thought intending to come to us. The ship was brought

---

[1] The conjecture that there was an opening through the northern reef was right: it is the Kaki pass, very narrow, and certainly hardly to be seen distinctly from the ship.

[2] Marginal note, 'the groups'. Called by Cook the Two Groups: Marokau to the north, Ravahere to the south. Banks's description which follows is much longer and more circumstantial than Cook's.

to and we waited some time but they like their fellows came no farther than the reef, where they stoppd and waited for two messengers who we saw dispatchd from the great canoes wading and swimming towards them along the reef, they met and after a council I suppose resolvd not to come off. The ship after waiting some time stood off and when 2 or 3 miles from the shore was followd by a canoe with a sail, but not thinking it worth while to bring too for her she soon gave over the chase and returnd to the reef.

The people seemd as well as we could judge (who were a good ½ mile from the shore) to be about our size and well made, of a dark brown complexion, stark naked, wearing their hair tied back with a fillet which passd round their head and kept it sticking out behind like a bush. The greatest number of them carried in their hands two weapons, one a slender pole from 10 to 14 feet in lengh at one end of which was a small knob or point not unlike the point of a spear, the other not above 4 feet long made much like a paddle as possibly it was intended, for their canoes were very different in size. The two which we saw them launch seemd not intended to carry more than barely the 3 men who got into each of them, others there were which had 6 and some 7 men; one of these hoisted a sail which did not seem to reach above 6 feet high above the boat, this (as soon as they came to the reef and stoppd their boat) they took down and converted into a shed to shelter them from a small shower of rain which then fell. The Canoe which followd us to sea hoisted a sail not unlike an English lugsail and near as lofty as an English boat of the same size would have carried.

The people on the shore made many signals but whether they meant to frighten us away or invite us ashore is dificult to tell: they wavd with their hands and seemd to beckon us to them but they were assembld together with clubs and staves as they would have done had they meant to oppose us. Their signs we answerd by waving our hats and shouting which they answerd by shouting again. Our situation made it very improper to try them farther, we wanted nothing, the Island was too trifling to be an object worth taking possession of; had we therefore out of mere curiosity hoisted out a boat and the natives by attacking us oblige us to destroy some of them the only reason we could give for it would be the desire of satisfying a useless curiosity. We shall soon by our connections with the inhabitants of Georges Island (who already know our strengh and if they do not love at least fear us) gain some knowledge of the customs of these savages; or possibly persuade one of them to come with us who may serve as an interpreter, and give us an opportunity hereafter of landing where ever we please without running the risk of being obligd to commit the cruelties which the Spaniards and most others who have been in these seas have often brought themselves under the dreadfull nescessity of being guilty of, for guilty I must call it.

7. This morn at day break Land in sight again, by 8 O'Clock came up with an Island made up like the last of narrow slips of land and reefs of rocks, the greatest part of the land lookd green and pleasant but it was without cocoa nut trees or any sign of inhabitants.[1]

I purposely omit to mention the size of these Islands as it is almost impossible to guess at, and very dificult to give an idea of the contents of narrow strips of land which run one within another as a ribband thrown carelessly down would do. If you measure the lengh of it, it 4 or 5 times exceeds the space of sea that it occupies, if the circumference, such land of 100 Leagues in circumference would scarce contain 100 square miles; if the Space of sea that they occupy you err as much, for of that 20, 40, nay sometimes 100 parts are sea for one of land, tho that sea is so shut in by banks and reefs that no ship can get into it.

8. Pleasant breeze but we have as yet found the trade hardly so strong as it was in the Atlantick. At 2 O'Clock Land was seen from the masthead, the ship stands for it and about sunset came abreast of it distant 2 leagues. It prove'd an Island larger than any we had seen as it extended 6 or 7 leagues, it was every where coverd with plenty of large trees probably Cocoa nuts and it is also inhabited as[2] we judge from a smoak rising from among the trees; in everything it appeard exactly of the same nature with the rest which we have seen.[3] We could plainly distinguish it in some places broken off into reefs behind which we saw distant land and thence judg'd that there was a lagoon within it; the land however appeard to be broader than any we had seen before.

9. Fine weather and pleasant breeze. It is now almost night and time for me to wind up the clue[4] of my this days lucubrations, so as we have found no Island I shall employ the time and paper which I had allotted to describe one in a work which I am sure will be more usefull at,[5] if not more entertaining to all future

---

[1] Marginal note, 'Bird Island'. Cook notes, 'there is some wood upon it but no Inhabitants but birds and for this reason is call'd *Bird Island*'.—I, p. 72. It was Reitoru.

[2] I substitute this *as* for Banks's &. SP read &.

[3] Marginal note, 'Chain Island'. Anaa.

[4] i.e. clew, a ball of thread or yarn.

[5] *sic*; perhaps a slip for *to*. S *at* P *at*.

navigators, by describing the method which we took to cure Cabbage in England; which Cabbage we have eat every day since we left Cape Horne and have now good store of, remaining as good at least to our palates and full as green and pleasing to the eye as if it was bought fresh every morning at Covent Garden market. Our Steward has given me the receipt which I shall copy exactly false spelling exceptd.[1]

Take a strong Iron bound cask for no weak or wooden bound one should ever be trusted in a long voyage, take out the head and when the whole is well cleand cover the bottom with salt. Then take the Cabbage and stripping off the outside leaves take the rest leaf by leaf till you come to the heart which cut into four; these leaves and heart lay upon the Salt about 2 or 3 inches thick and sprinkle Salt pretty thick over them and lay cabbage upon the salt stratum super thick till the cask is full. Then lay on the head of the cask with a weight which in 5 or 6 days will have pressd the cabbage into a much smaller compass. After this fill up the cask with more cabbage as before directed and Head it up. N.B. the Cabbage should be gatherd in dry weather some time after sun rise that the dew may not be upon it. Halves of cabbages are better for keeping than single leaves.

10. Last night a halo was observ'd round the moon which was followd by a very disagreable night, the wind being all round the compass and sometimes blowing very fresh with severe thunder and lightning and very heavy rain.

This morning the wind from N to NW, the weather very hazey and thick. About 9 it cleard up a little and showd us Osnabrug Island[2] discoverd by the Dolphin in her last voyage, it was distant about 6 leagues and appeard like a very short cone. Very light winds NW. About one land was seen ahead in the direction of Georges Land, it was however so faint that very few could see it. Soon after it was seen off the deck in the same faint manner but appearing high. Our distance when it was first seen was 25 leagues. At sun set the ship was nearly abreast Osnabrug Island 2 or 3 leagues from it, it appeard to have many trees upon it but in some parts the rocks were quite bare.

At this time it remaind in dispute whether what had been so long seen to the Westward was realy land or only vapours; myself

---

[1] This pickled cabbage is not to be confused with the *sauerkraut* on which Cook set such store as a preservative of health.

[2] Spelt *Osnabrugh* in the margin, and by Cook Osnaburg. The name was given by Wallis, who discovered it in 1767; Bougainville called it *Le Boudoir*. Mehetia or Maitea.

went to the Masthead but the sunset was cloudy and we could see nothing of it.

As soon as I came down a shark att the stern attackd the net in which tomorrows dinner was towing to freshen, we hookd and took him just as it became dark.

11. Up at 5 this morn to examine the shark who proves to be A blew Shark *Squalus glaucus*,[1] while we were doing it 3 more came under the Stern of which we soon caught 2 which were common grey Sharks *Squalus Carcharias*,[2] on one of whom were some sucking fish *Echinus remora*.[3] The seamen tell us that the blew shark is worst of all sharks to eat, indeed his smell is abominably strong so as we had two of the better sort he was hove overboard.

Little wind and variable with Squalls from all points of the Compass bringing heavy rain. Georges Island in sight appearing very high in the same direction as the land was seen last night, so I found the fault was in our eyes yesterday tho the non-seers were much more numerous in the ship than the seers.

Today and yesterday many birds were about the ship among which a bird which I took to be the common tropick bird *Phaeton æthereus* was one, he was about the size of our tropick bird but differd from him in having black barrs upon his back and the long feathers in his tail white,[4] so much I say[5] but the weather was so uncertain that I could not go out to shoot one.

Calm this even, at sunset Georges Land appeard plain tho we had not neard it much: since the clouds went from the tops of the hills it appeard less high than it did tho it certainly is very high.

As I am now on the brink of going ashore after a long passage thank god in as good health as man can be I shall fill a little paper in describing the means which I have taken to prevent the scurvy in particular.

The ship was supplyd by the Admiralty with Sower crout which I eat of constantly till our salted Cabbage was opend which I preferd as a pleasant substitute. Wort[6] was servd out almost con-

---

[1] *Prionace glauca*. There are two signed and dated paintings by Parkinson, I, pls. 49, 50, of this fish.

[2] Now *Carcharodon carcharias*. This species had been taken in the Atlantic; cf. September 29, 1768.

[3] *Remora remora*.

[4] The White-tailed Tropic Bird; when immature these birds have crescentic black bars on their upper parts.

[5] The MS is a mixture of *saw* and *say*. S *say*, P *say*.

[6] This was a decoction of malt, used as a standard remedy for scurvy: 'the Sanguine and well-grounded expectations of the certain efficacy the Wort possesses to cure the Sea-scurvy and the very great probability of that distemper raging at some time or other in the course of a long voyage induced, I apprehend, the R^t Honour^{ble} the Lords

stantly, of this I drank from a pint or more every evening but all this did not so intirely check the distemper as to prevent my feeling some small effects of it. About a fortnight ago my gums swelld and some small pimples rose in the inside of my mouth which threatned to become ulcers, I then flew to the lemon Juice which had been put up for me according to Dr Hulmes method describd in his book and in his letter which is inserted here:[1] every kind of liquor which I usd was made sour with the Lemon juice N° 3 so that I took near 6 ounces a day of it. The effect of this was surprizing, in less than a week my gums became as firm as ever and at this time I am troubled with nothing but a few pimples on my face which have not deterrd me from leaving off the juice intirely.

12. Very nearly calm all last night, Georges Land was now but little nearer to us than last night, the tops of the hills were wrap'd in clouds. About 7 a small breze sprung up and we saw some Canoes coming off to us, by ten or eleven they were up with us. I forbear to say any thing about either people or canoes as I shall have so many better opportunities of observing them: we however bought their cargoes consisting of fruits and cocoa nuts which were very acceptable to us after our long passage.

Commissioners of the Admiralty to send out a quantity of Malt in the *Endeavour* . . .'.—William Perry the surgeon reporting to Cook at the end of the voyage, encl. in Cook to Stephens, 12 July 1771, P.R.O. Adm 1/1609.
    [1] Banks had Hulme's letter bound up in his journal at this point: see p. 243, n. 2 above, and Appendix, II, p. 301.

II

13. This morn early came to an anchor in Port Royal bay[1] King George the thirds Island. Before the anchor was down we were surrounded by a large number of Canoes who traded very quietly and civily, for beads cheifly, in exchange for which they gave Cocoa nuts Bread fruit both roasted and raw some small fish and apples. They had one pig with them which they refus'd to sell for nails upon any account but repeatedly offerd it for a hatchet; of these we had very few on board so thought it better to let the pig go away than to give one of them in exchange, knowing from the authority of those who had been here before that if we once did it they would never lower their price. As soon as the anchors were well down the boats were hoisted out and we all went ashore where we were met by some hundreds of the inhabitants whose faces at least gave evident signs that we were not unwelcome guests, tho they at first hardly dare aproach us, after a little time they became very familiar. The first who aproachd us came creeping almost on his hands and knees and gave us a green bough[2] the token of peace, this we receivd and immediately each gatherd a green bough and carried in our hands. They march'd with us about ½ a mile then made a general stop and scraping the ground clean from the plants that grew upon it every one of the principals threw his bough down upon the bare place and made signs that we should do the same: the marines were drawn up and marching in order dropd each a bough upon those that the Indians had laid down, we all folowd their example and thus peace was concluded. We then walkd into the woods followd by the whole train to whoom we gave beads and small presents. In this manner we walkd for 4 or 5 miles under groves of Cocoa nut and bread fruit trees loaded with a protusion of fruit and giving the most gratefull shade I have ever experienced, under these were the habitations of the people most of them without walls: in short the scene we saw was the truest picture of an arcadia of which we were going to be kings that the imagination can form.

Our pleasure in seeing this was however not a little allayd by finding in all our walk only 2 hogs and not one fowl. The Dolphins

[1] Matavai Bay. Port Royal, Royal Bay, Port Royal Bay were names bequeathed by Wallis's expedition; but Cook always used a native name if he could.
[2] A plantain or banana frond.

people who were with us told us that the people who we saw were only of the common sort and that the bettermost had certainly removd, as a proof of this they took us to the place where the Queens palace formerly stood of which there was no traces left.[1] We howev[e]r resolved not to be discouraged at this but to proceed tomorrow morning in search of the place to which these superior people had retreated, in hopes to make the same peace with them as we have done with our freinds the blackguards.[2]

14. This morn several Canoas came on board among which were two in which were people who by their dress and appearance seemd to be of a rank superior to those who we had seen yesterday. These we invited to come on board and on coming into the Cabbin each singled out his freind,[3] one took the Cap^{tn} and the other me, they took off a large part of their cloaths and each dress'd his freind with them he took off: in return for this we presented them with each a hatchet and some beads. They made many signs to us desiring us to go to the places where they livd to the SW of where we lay; the boats were hoisted out and we took them with us and immediately proceeded according to their directions.

After rowing about a league they beckon'd us in shore and shewd us a long house where they gave us to understand that they livd; here we landed and were met by some hundreds of inhabitants who conducted us into the long house.[4] Matts were spread and we were desired to set down fronting an old man[5] who we had not before seen, he immediately orderd a cock and hen to be brought which were presented to Cap^{tn} Cook and me, we accepted of the present. Then a peice of Cloth was presented to each of us perfumd after their manner not disagreably which they took great pains to make us understand. My peice of Cloth was 11 yards long and 2 wide: for this I made return by presenting him with a large lacd silk neckcloth I had on and a linnen pocket handkercheif, these he immediately put on him and seemd to be much pleasd with.

---

[1] The 'Queen's palace' was evidently the guest-house or 'arioi-house', of the Haapape district, the place of general entertainment, to which Wallis was taken on his visit to Purea on 12 July 1767. It was of course not a palace, nor did it belong to Purea, nor was she the 'Queen'.

[2] 'Blackguards' in the old sense of servants, camp-followers, the lower classes or 'common sort' generally.

[3] Friend, i.e. taio, a word used to signify an attachment formal as well as warm— almost a 'blood-brother' though without the ceremony of blood.

[4] This seems to have been the arioi-house at Point Utuhaihai (the site of the tomb of Pomare V) where the chief Tuteha had a marae.

[5] Marginal note to these words, 'Dootahah'. This note, like others, was obviously written in later, because it is not till 28 April that Banks registers the discovery of Tuteha's correct name.

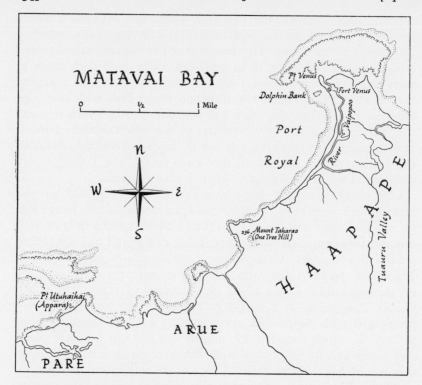

After this ceremony was over we walkd freely about several large houses attended by the ladies who shewd us all kind of civilities our situation could admit of, but as there were no places of retirement, the houses being intirely without walls, we had not an opportunity of putting their politeness to every test that maybe some of us would not have faild to have done had circumstances been more favourable; indeed we had no reason to doubt any part of their politeness, as by their frequently pointing to the matts on the ground and sometimes by force seating themselves and us upon them they plainly shewd that they were much less jealous of observation than we were.

We now took our leave of our freindly cheif and proceeded along shore for about a mile when we were met by a throng of people at the head of whoom appeard another cheif.[1] We had learn'd the ceremony we were to go through which was to receive the green bough which was always brough[t] to us at every fresh

[1] Marginal note, 'Tubourai Tamaide'. See p. 265, n. 2 below.

meeting and to ratifie the peace of which that was the emblem
by laying our hands on our breasts and saying Taio, which I
imagine signifies freind. The bough was here offerd and accepted
and in return every one of us said Taio. The cheif then made us
signs that if we chose to eat he had victuals ready: we accepted
the offer and dind heartily on fish and bread fruit with plantains
&c dressd after their way, raw fish was offerd to us which it seems
they themselves eat. The adventures of this entertainment I much
wish to record particularly, but am so much hurried by attending
the Indians ashore almost all day long that I fear I shall scarce
understand my own language when I read it again.

Our cheifs own wife[1] (ugly enough in conscience) did me the
honour with very little invitation to squat down on the mats close
by me: no sooner had she done so than I espied among the common
croud a very pretty girl with a fire in her eyes that I had not before
seen in the countrey. Unconscious of the dignity of my companion
I beckond to the other who after some intreatys came and sat
on the other side of me: I was then desirous of getting rid of my
former companion so I ceas'd to attend to her and loaded my
pretty girl with beads and every present I could think pleasing
to her: the other shewd much disgust but did not quit her place
and continued to supply me with fish and cocoa nut milk. How
this would have ended is hard to say, it was interupted by an
accident which gave us an opportunity of seeing much of the peoples
manners. D[r] Solander and another gentleman[2] who had not been
in as good company as myself found that their pockets had been
pickd, one had lost a snuff box the other an opera glass.[3] Complaint
was made to the cheif, and to give it weight I started up from
the ground and striking the but of my gun made a rattling noise
which I had before used in our walk to frigh[t]en the people and
keep them at a distance. Upon this as a signal every one of the
common sort (among whom was my pretty girl) ran like sheep
from the house leaving us with only the cheif his 3 wives and two
or three better dressd than the rest whose quality I do not yet
guess at. The cheif then took me by the hand to the other end of
the house where lay a large quantity of their cloth, this he offerd
to me peice by peice making signs that if it would make me amends
I might take any part or all. I put it back and by signs told him
that I wanted nothing but our own which his people had stole. On

---

[1] Marginal note, 'Tomio'.
[2] Cook says this other gentleman was Monkhouse, the surgeon.
[3] Cook says a spy glass, which seems more in keeping.

this he gave me into charge of my faithfull companion his wife who had never budged an inch from my elbow; with her I sat down on the mat and convers'd by signs for near $\frac{1}{2}$ an hour after which time he came back bringing the snuff box and the case of the opera glass, which with vast pleasure in his countenance he returnd to the owners, but his face soon changed when he was shewn that the case was empty which ought to have been full. He then took me by the hand and walkd along shore with great rapidity about a mile. By the way he receivd a peice of cloth from a woman which he carried in his hand. At last we came to a house in which we were receivd by a woman; to her he gave the cloth he had and told us to give her some beads. The cloth and beads were left on the floor by us and she went out, she stayd about $\frac{1}{4}$ of an hour and then returnd bringing the glass in her hand with a vast expression of joy on her countenance, for few faces have I seen which have more expression in them than those of these people. The beads were now returnd with a positive resolution of not accepting them and the Cloth was as resolutely forcd upon Dr Solander as a recompence for his loss. He then made a new present of beads to the lady and our ceremonies ended we returnd to the ship admiring a policy at least equal to any we had seen in civilizd countries, excercisd by people who have never had any advantage but meer natural instinct uninstructed by the example of any civilizd countrey.

15. This morn we landed at the watering place[1] bringing with us a small tent which we set up. In doing this we were attended by some hundreds of the natives who shewd a deference and respect to us which much amazd me. I myself drew a line before them with the butt end of my musquet and made signs to them to set down without it, they obeyd instantly and not a man attempted to set a foot within it, above two hours were spent so and not the least disorder being committed. We propos'd to walk into the woods and see if today we might not find more hoggs &c. than when we last visited them supposing it probable that a part of them at least had been drove away on our arrival: this in particular tempted us to go away, with many other circumstances, as our old man (an Indian well known to the Dolphins)[2] attempted by many signs

---

[1] This was on the bank of the Vaipopoo river, close to the end of Point Venus; the river ran parallel with the beach from about half-way along the bay.

[2] Banks has not previously mentioned this old man. Cook gives his name as Owhaa (? Faa, but he is often referred to as Hau); he appears to have been some sort of sub-chief, who was useful as an intermediary both to the *Dolphin*'s people and in the first days of the *Endeavour*'s visit.

to hinder us from going into the woods. The tent was left in charge of a Midshipman[1] with the marines 13 in number. We marchd away and were absent above 2 hours. A little while before we came back we heard several musquet shots. Our old man immediately calld us together and by waving his hand sent away every Indian who followd us except 3 every one of whoom took in their hands a green bough: on this we suspected that some mischeif had happned at the tent and hastend home with all expedition. On our return we found that an Indian had snatchd a sentrys musquet from him unawares and run off; the midshipman (may be) imprudently orderd the marines to fire, they did fire into the thickest of the flying croud some hundreds in number several shot, and pursueing the man[2] who stole the musquet killd him dead but whether any others were killd or hurt no one could tell. No Indian was now to be seen about the tent but our old man, who with us took all pains to reconcile them again; before night by his means we got together a few of them and explaining to them that the man who sufferd was guilty of a crime deserving of death (for so we were forcd to make it) we retird to the ship not well pleasd with the days expedition, guilty no doubt in some measure of the death of a man who the most severe laws of equity would not have condemnd to so severe a punishment.

16. No canoes about the ship this morning, indeed we could not expect any as it is probable that the news of our behaviour yesterday was now known every where, a circumstance which will doubtless not increase the confidence of our freinds the Indians. We were rather surprizd that the Dolphins old man who seemd yesterday so desirous of making peace was not come on board today; some few people were upon the beach but very few in proportion to what we saw yesterday. At noon went ashore the people rather shy of us as we must expect them to be till by good usage we can gain anew their confidence.

Poor Mr Buchan the young man who I brought out as lanscape and figure painter was yesterday attackd by an epileptick fit, he was today quite insensible, our surgeon gives me very little hopes of him.

17. At two this morn Mr Buchan died, about nine every thing was ready for his interment he being already so much changd

[1] Jonathan Monkhouse.

[2] In a marginal note Banks gives the man's name as 'Outou'. This may conceivably be correct; but he is rather more likely to have picked up the word *utu*, a price paid, reward, penalty—i.e. the man had paid with his life for the musket.

that it would not be practicable to keep him even till night. Dr Solander Mr Sporing Mr Parkinson and some of the officers of the ship attended his funeral.[1] I sincerely regret him as an ingenious and good young man, but his Loss to me is irretrevable, my airy dreams of entertaining my freinds in England with the scenes that I am to see here are vanishd. No account of the figures and dresses of men can be satisfactory unless illustrated with figures: had providence spard him a month longer what an advantage would it have been to my undertaking but I must submit.

Our two freinds the cheifs of the west came this morn to see us. One I shall for the future call Lycurgus from the justice he executed on his offending subjects on the 14th, the other from the large size of his body I shall call Hercules.[2] Each of these brought a hog and bread fruit ready dressd as a present for which they were presented in return with a hatchet and a nail each. Hercules's present is the largest he seems indeed to be the richest man.

In the afternoon we all went ashore to measure out the ground for the tents, which done Cap Cooke and Mr Green slept ashore in a tent erected for that purpose after having observd an eclipse of one of the satellites of Jupiter.

18. This morn at day break all hands were ashore and employd in getting up the tents and making a defence round them. The ground we have pitchd upon is very sandy which makes it nescessary to support it with wood, for the doing of this our people cut the boughs of trees and the Indians very readily assisted them in bringing them down to the place. Three sides of our fort are to be thus guarded the other is bounded by a river on the banks of which water cask[s] are to be placd.

The Indians brought down so much provision of Cocoa nuts and bread fruit today that before night we were obligd to leave off buying and acquaint them by signs that we should not want any more for 2 days; every thing was bought for beads, a bead about as large as a pea purchasing 4 or 6 breadfruits and a like number of Cocoa nutts.

My tents were got up before night and I slept ashore in them for the first time. The lines were guarded round by many Sentries but no Indian atempted to come near them during the whole night.

---

[1] It is curious that Banks does not mention the very sensible precaution he himself suggested: Cook writes, 'Mr Banks thought it not so adviseable to Enterr the Body a shore in a place where we was utter strangers to the Customs of the Natives on such Occasions, it was therefore se[n]t out to Sea and commited to that Element with all the decencey the circumstance of the place would admit of'.—I, p. 81.

[2] See below, p. 266.

19. This morn Lycurgus and his wife come to see us and bring with them all their household furniture and even houses to be erected in our neighbourhood, a circumstance which gave me great pleasure as I had spard no pains to gain the freindship of this man who seemd more sensible than any of his fellow cheifs we have seen. His behavior in this Instance makes us not doubt of having gaind his confidence at least.

Soon after his arrival he took me by the hand and led me out of the lines, signing that I should accompany him into the woods, this I made no dificulty of dooing as I was desirous of knowing how near us he realy intended to settle. I followd him about a quarter of a mile when we arrivd at a small house or rather the awning of a canoe set upon the shore, which seemd to be his occasional habitation; here he unfolded a bundle of their cloaths and cloth'd me in two garments, one red cloth[1] the other very pretty matting, after this we returnd to the tents. He eat pork and bread fruit which was brought him in a basket using salt water instead of sauce, and then retird into my bedchamber and slept about half an hour.

About dinner time Lycurgus's wife brought a hansome young man about 22 to the tents whoom they both seemd to acknowledge as their son. At night he and another chief who had also visited us went away to the westward, but Lycurgus and his wife went towards the place I was at in the morning which makes us not doubt of their staying with us for the future.

Mr Monkhouse our surgeon walkd this evening into the woods and brought back an account of having seen the body of the man who was shot on the 15th. It was placd on a kind of Bier supported by stakes and coverd by a small hut which seemd to have been built for the purpose; the body was wrappd up in cloth and near it were plac'd war instruments a hatchet some hair a cocoa nut and a cup of water. Farther he did not examine on account of the stench of the body which was intolerable. They also [saw] two more huts of the same kind in one of which they saw the bones of the person who had lain there quite dry. A custom so new as this appears to be surprized us all very much, but whether all who die are thus disposd of or it is a peculiar honour shewn to those who dye in war is to be cleard up by future observation.

20. Raind hard all this day at intervals, so much so that we could not stir at all, the people however went on briskly with the forti-

---

[1] The cloth made of the bark of trees, called *tapa*.

fication in spite of weather. Lycurgus dind with us, he imitates our manners in every instance already holding a knife and fork more handily than a Frenchman could learn to do in years. Notwistanding the rain some provisions are brought to the market which is kept just without the lines; indeed ever since we have been here we have had more breadfruit every day than both the people and hogs can eat, but in the pork way we have been so poorly supplyd that I beleive fresh pork has not been servd to the ships company above once.

21. Several of our freinds at the tents this morn, one whoom from his grim countenance we have calld Ajax[1] and at one time thought to be a great king. He had on his canoe a hog but he chose rather to sell it at the market than give it to us as a present; which we account for by his having in the morning receivd a shirt in return for a peice of cloth, which made him fear that had he given the hog it might have been taken into the bargain—a conduct very different from that of our freind Lycurgus who seems in every instance to place a most unbounded confidence in us.

22. Pleasant weather, our freinds as usual come early to visit us, Hercules with two piggs and a Dolphins ax[2] which he wishd to have repaird as it acordingly was. Lycurgus brought 2 large fish an acceptable present as that article has always been scarce with us. Trade brisk today; since our new manufacture of hatchets has been set on foot we get some hogs tho our tools are so small and bad that I only wonder how they can stand one stroke.

The flies have been so troublesome ever since we have been ashore that we can scarce get any business done for them; they eat the painters colours off the paper as fast as they can be laid on, and if a fish is to be drawn there is more trouble in keeping them off it than in the drawing itself.

Many expedients have been thought of, none succeed better than a mosquito net which covers table chair painter and drawings, but even that is not sufficent, a fly trap was nesscessary to set within this to atract the vermin from eating the colours. For that purpose yesterday tarr and molasses was mixt together but did not succeed. The plate smeard with it was left on the outside of the tent to clean: one of the Indians observing this took an opportunity when he thought that no one observd him to take some of this mixture up

---

[1] It does not seem possible to identify this person clearly. No doubt he was an *arii*; he may have been the huge chief later well known as Potatau, of Punaauia, though Potatau was generally regarded as affable rather than grim.

[2] The *Dolphin* disposed of a number of axes in trade.

Hibiscus. Abelmoschus.

Pl. IV. *Hibiscus abelmoschus*

Tahiti

into his hand, I saw and was curious to know for what use it was intended, the gentleman had a large sore upon his backside to which this clammy liniament was applyd but with what success I never took the pains to enquire.

Hercules gave us today a specimen of the musick of this countrey: 4 people performd upon flutes which they sounded with one nostril while they stopd the other with their thumbs, to these 4 more sang keeping very good time but during ½ an hour which we stayd with them they playd only one tune consisting of not more than 5 or 6 notes. More I am inclind to think they have not upon their instruments which have only two stops.

23. Mr Green and myself went today a little way upon the hills in order to see how the roads were. Lycurgus went with us but complaind much in the ascent saying that it would kill him. We found as far as we went, possibly 3 miles, exceeding good paths and at the farthest part of our walk boys bringing wood from the mountans, which we look upon to be a sure proof that journey will be easy whenever we atempt to go higher.

In our return I visited the Tomb or Bier in which was deposited the body of the man who was shot. I lifted up the cloth and saw part of the body already dropping to peices with putrefaction about him and indeed within all parts of his flesh were abundance of maggots of a species of Beetle very common here   .[1]
Such an advance of putrefaction in 8 days for it was no more since he was shot is almost past credit but what will not a hot climate and plenty of insects do.

We had this evening some conversation about an ax which was brought in the morning by Hercules, it wanting grinding. Its make was very different from that of our English ones, several gentlemen were of opinion that it was a French one, some went so far as to give it as their opinion that some other ship had been here since the Dolphin. The difficulty however appeard to me at least easily solvd by supposing axes to have been taken in the Dolphin as trade, in which case old ones might have been bought of the make of any countrey, for many such I suppose there are in every old iron shop in London.[2]

[1] Fabricius worked on Banks's insect collection but he does not, in his *Species Insectorum* (1781), describe any beetle which can be identified with this reference. Different kinds of maggots live in succession on decaying flesh as it ripens and alters.
[2] The axe under discussion must have been one of those traded by Bougainville, which had travelled from his anchorage at Hitiaa. The gentlemen who opposed Banks in the argument were right: another ship had been at Tahiti.

T

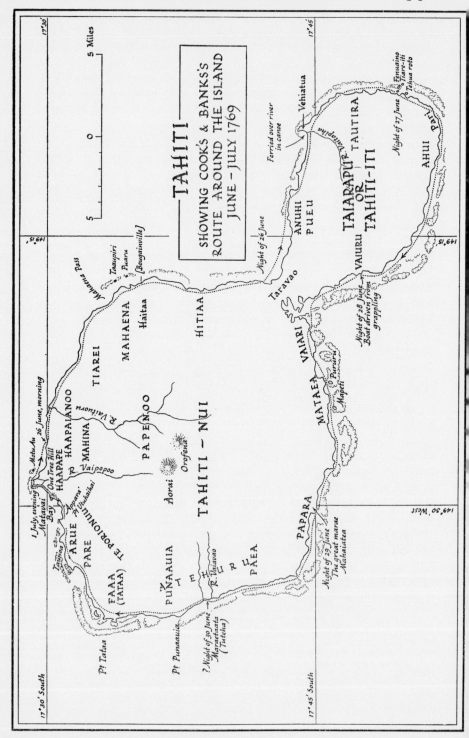

24. Dr Solander and myself went along shore to the eastward in hopes of finding something worth observation by inlarging our ground. For about 2 miles the countrey within us was flat and fertile, the hills then came very near the waters edge and soon after quite into the sea so that we were obligd to climb over them. This barren countrey continued for about 3 miles more when we came to a large flat full of good houses and wealthy looking people; here was a river much more considerable than our own, it came out of a very deep and beautifull valley and was where we crossd it near 100 yards wide tho not quite at the sea.[1] About a mile farther than this river we went when the Land became again as barren as possible, the rocks every where projecting into the sea, so we resolvd to return. Soon after this resolution one of the natives made us an offer of refreshment which we accepted. He was re-markable for being much the whitest man we had seen. On examining him more nearly his skin was dead pale without the least signs of Complexion in any part of it, some parts were lighter than others but the darkest was lighter than any of our skins, his hair and eyebrows and beard were as white as his skin, his eyes bloodshot, he apeard to be very short sighted, his whole body was scurfy and maybe disease had been the cause of his colour;[2] if not we shall see more such. In our return met Lycurgus who seem'd much rejoicd at seeing us as did all his women, to shew their regard I suppose they all cry'd most heartily.

25. I do not know by what accident I have so long omitted to mention how much these people are given to theiving. I will make up for my neglect however today by saying that great and small cheifs and common men all are firmly of opinion that if they can once get possession of any thing it immediately becomes their own. This we were convincd of the very second day we were here, the cheifs were employd in stealing what they could in the Cabbin while their dependants took every thing that was loose about the ship, even the glass ports not escaping them of which they got off with 2. Lycurgus and Hercules were the only two who had not yet been found guilty, but they stood in our opinion but upon tickilish ground as we could not well suppose them intirely free from a vice their countrey men were so much given up to.

[1] This was the Vaituoru river, flowing down the Haapaianoo (Whapaiano on Cook's chart) valley. Both the river and the valley, now known as Papenoo, were the largest on the island.

[2] This seems to have been a case of island albinoism, but the scurfy skin suggests that perhaps over-indulgence in the drink called [k]ava had something to do with it. Or it may have been what was called 'chief's leprosy', o'ovi arii.

Last night Dr Solander lent his knife to one of Lycurgus's women who forgot to return it, this morn mine was missing. I could give no account of it so resolvd to go to Lycurgus and ask him whether or not he had stole it trusting that if he had he would return it.

I went and taxd him with it. He denyd knowing any thing concerning it, I told him I was resolvd to have it returnd. On this a man present produc'd a rag in which was tied up 3 knives, one was Dr Solanders the other a table knife the other no one laid claim to. With these he marchd to the tents to make restitution while I remaind with the women who much feard that he would be hurt; when come there he restord the two knives to their proper owners and began immediately to search for mine in all the places where he had ever seen it lay. One of my servants seeing what he was about brought it to him, he had it seems laid it by the day before and did not know of my missing it. Lycurgus then burst into tears making signs with my knife that if he was ever guilty of such an action he would submit to have his throat cut. He re- turnd immediately to me with a countenance sufficiently upbraiding me for my suspicions; the scene was immediately changd, I became the guilty and he the innocent person, his looks affected me much. A few presents and staying a little with him reconcild him intirely; his behavior has however given me an opinion of him much superior to any of his countreymen.

26. Plenty of trade this morn indeed we have always had enough of bread fruit and cocoa nuts, refreshments maybe more nescessary for the people than pork tho they certainly do not like them so well.

Our freinds as usual at the tents today but do nothing worthy record.

27. The day passd as usual. Lycurgus and a freind of his (who eats most monstrously) dind with us, we christend him Epicurus.[1] At night they took their leave and departed but Lycurgus soon returnd with fire in his eyes, seizd my arm and signd to me to follow him. I did and he soon brought me to a place where was our butcher, who he told me by signs had either threatned or atempted to cut his wives throat with a reaphook he had in his hand. I signd to him that the man should be punishd tomorrow if he would only clearly explain the offence, for he was so angry that his signs were almost unintelligible. He grew cooler and shewd

---

[1] This person seems to be unidentifiable.

me that the Butcher had taken a fancy to a stone hatchet which
lay in his house, this he offerd to purchase for a nail: His wife who
was their refus'd to part with it upon which he took it and throwing
down the nail threatnd to cut her throat if she atempted to hinder
him; in evidence of this the hatchet and nail were produc'd and
the butcher had so little to say in his defence that no one doubted
of his guilt. After this we parted and he appeard satisfied but
did not forget to put me in mind of my promise that the butcher
should tomorrow be punished.[1]

This day we found that our freinds had names and they were
not a little pleasd to discover that we had them likewise; for the
future Lycurgus will be calld *Tùboùrài tamaide* and his wife *Tòmìò*
and the three women who commonly come with him *Tèràpò*,
Tèràrù and *Omìé*.[2] As for our names they make so poor a hand of
pronouncing them that I fear we shall be obligd to take each of
us a new one for the occasion.

28. Many of our freinds were with us very early even before day,
some strangers with them. Terapo was observd to be among the
women on the outside of the gate, I went out to her and brought
her in, tears stood in her eyes which the moment she enterd the
tent began to flow plentifully. I began to enquire the cause; she
instead of answering me took from under her garment a sharks
tooth and struck it into her head with great force 6 or 7 times. a
profusion of Blood followd these strokes and alarmd me not a
little; for two or 3 minutes she bled freely more than a pint in
quantity, during that time she talkd loud in a most melancholy
tone. I was not a little movd at so singular a spectacle and holding
her in my arms did not cease to enquire what might be the cause
of so strange an action, she took no notice of me till the bleeding
ceas'd nor did any Indian in the tent take any of her, all talkd and
laugh'd as if nothing melancholy was going forward; but what
surpriz'd me most of all was that as soon as the bleeding ceas'd she
lookd up smiling and immediately began to collect peices of cloth
which during her bleeding she had thrown down to catch the blood.
These she carried away out of the tents and threw into the sea,
carefully dispersing them abroad as if desirous that no one should

---

[1] The butcher was Henry Jeffs. Cook does not mention this incident, but it is referred
to by Molyneux the master, 29 April.
[2] Tubourai tamaide: Tepau i Ahurai Tamaiti. *Tamaiti*, the son. He was the eldest
son of the *arii* Vaetua i Ahurai, chief of Faaa, and brother of Purea—an important
chief. Molyneux gives his name as Tuburi, so he was probably habitually addressed by
some shortened form. Cook Toobouratomita. Tomio, probably Tamaio; Banks later
changes his spelling to Tamio. Terapo and Teraro are probably correct. Omie, Omae?

be reminded of her action by the sight of them; she then went into the river and after washing her whole body returnd to the tents as lively and chearfull as any one in them.[1]

After breakfast M[r] Molineux came ashore and the moment he enterd the tent fixing his eyes upon a woman who was setting there declard her to be the Dolphins Queen, she also instantly acknowledg'd him to be a person who she had before seen.[2] Our attention was now intirely diverted from every other object to the examination of a personage we had heard so much spoken of in Europe: she appeard to be about 40, tall and very lusty, her skin white and her eyes full of meaning, she might have been hansome when young but now few or no traces of it were left.

As soon as her majesties quality was known to us she was invited to go on board the ship, where no presents were spard that were thought to be agreable to her in consideration of the service she had been of to the Dolphin. Among other things a childs dol was given to her of which she seemd very fond. On her landing she met Hercules who for the future I shall call by his real name *Tootahah*.[3] She shewd him her presents: he became uneasy nor was he satisfied till he had also got a doll given to him, which now he seemd to preferr to a hatchet that he had in return for presents, tho after this time the dolls were of no kind of value.[4]

The men who visited us constantly eat with us of our provisions, but the women never had been prevaild on to taste a morsel; today however they retird sometime after dinner into the servants apartment and eat there a large quantity of plantains, tho they could not be persuaded to eat with us, a mystery we find it very dificult to account for.[5]

29. My first business this morning was to see the promise I had made to Tubourai and Tomio of the butchers being punishd per-

---

[1] This was undoubtedly a mourning ceremony, which might be indulged in at any time. Blood was a potent medium of psychic influence, therefore *tapu*, and must be safely disposed of.

[2] This was of course Purea, Wallis's Oborea.

[3] S has a note: 'Tootahah, spelt here; but in many other places Dootahah; both which mean the same Person. Indeed Tootahah is rather the properest manner of spelling it, as the sound of the t is more generally expressed in their language than the d'. Tuteha.

[4] Cook gives a very amusing account of this incident in his log—though not in his journal—which perhaps casts some light on the relations between these two important *arii*, as well as on a not to be suspected side of the character of Cook. See I, pp. 525-6.

[5] Eating *tapu* was stringent, and the sexes never ate together, or shared the same food. But it is plain that the women of a lower social class who came on board the ship found it convenient to eat whatever they could get in the 'servants' apartment', as long as they were not seen, or the adventure known, by their countrymen. After all, infringement of *tapu* did not necessarily have the same result in a European environment as in a Tahitian.

formd, a promise they had not faild to remind me of yesterday
when the croud of people who were with us hinderd it from being
performd. In consequence of this I took them on board of the ship
where Capt Cooke immediately orderd the offender to be punishd;
they stood quietly and saw him stripd and fastned to the rigging
but as soon as the first blow was given interfered with many tears,
begging the punishment might cease a request which the Cap^tn
would not comply with.[1]

On my return ashore I proceeded to pay a visit to her majesty
Obôrea [as] I shall for the future call her. She I was told was still
asleep in her Canoe-awning, where I went intending to call up
her majesty but was surprizd to find her in bed with a hansome
lusty young man of about 25 whose name was *Obâdée*.[2] I however
soon understood that he was her gallant a circumstance which
she made not the least secret of.[3] Upon my arrival Her majesty
proceeded to put on her breeches[4] which done she clothd me in
fine cloth and proceeded with me to the tents.

At night I visited Tubourai as I often did by candle light and
found him and all his family in a most melancholy mood: most
of them shed tears so that I soon left them without being at all
able to find out the cause of their greif. *Ouwhá* the Dolphins old
man and another who we did not know had prophesied to some
of our people that in 4 days we should fire our guns: this was the
4th night and the circumstance of Tubourai crying over me as it was
interpreted alarmd our officers a good deal. The sentrys are therefore doubled and we sleep tonight under arms.

30. A very strict watch was kept last night as intended, at 2 in
the morn myself went round the point, found every thing so quiet
that I had no kind of doubts.

Our little fortification is now compleat, it consists of high breast-
works at each end, the front palisades and the rear guarded by
the river on the bank of which are placd full Water cask[s], at every

---

[1] This is a good example of Cook's even-handed justice. Cf. Molyneux: 'All hands
being called, and the Prisoner being brought aft, the Captain explained the nature of
his Crime in the most lively manner, and made a very Pathetick speech to the Ship's
Company during his punishment. The woman was in the greatest agonies, and strongly
interceded for him. . . .'—Cook I, p. 554.

[2] ? Pati.

[3] The marriage connection between Purea and Amo was by this time purely a matter
of form, and both as an important *arii* and as an *arioi* large liberties were in order for
her without any loss of respectability. They did not necessarily make her, as William
Wales later referred to her, 'an old demi-rep'. (Wales, *Remarks on Mr. Forster's Account
of Captain Cook's last Voyage round the World*, 1778, p. 52 n.)

[4] Breeches, one supposes, in a metaphorical sense. He probably refers to the *pareu*,
the skirt worn by both sexes, coming rather below the knees.

angle is mounted a swivel and two carraige guns pointed the two ways by which the Indians might attack us out of the woods. Our sentrys are also as well releivd as they could be in the most regular fortification.

About 10 Tomio came running to the tents, she seizd my hand and told me that Tubourai was dying and I must go instantly with her to his house. I went and Found him leaning his head against a post. He had vomited they said and he told me he should certainly dye in consequence of something our people had given him to eat, the remains of which were shewn me carefully wrapd up in a leaf. This upon examination I found to be a Chew of tobacco which he had begg'd of some of our people, and trying to imitate them in keeping it in his mouth as he saw them do had chewd it almost to powder swallowing his spittle. I was now master of his disease for which I prescribd cocoa nut milk which soon restor'd him to health.

MAY 1769

1. This morn in walking round the point I saw a canoe which I suppose to have come from a distance by her having a quantity of fresh water in her in Bamboes; in every other respect she is quite like those we have seen, her people however are absolute strangers to us. Before noon our freinds visit us as usual and the day passed without any events.

2. About 10 this morn the astronomical quadrant which had been brought ashore yesterday was miss'd, a circumstance which alarmd us all very much. It had been laid in Cap^{tn} Cook's birth where no one slept, the telescopes were in my tent safe. Every place was searchd aboard and ashore but no such thing to be found. It appeard very improbable that the Indians could have carried so large a thing out of the tents without being observd by the sentries, our people might have stole [it] as it was packd up in a deal case and might by them be suppos'd to contain nails or some kind of traffick; a large reward was therefore offerd to any one who could find it and all hands sent out to search round the fort, upon a supposition that the Indians would immediately quit a prize that could be of so little use to them. In about an hour all returnd, no news of the Quadrant. I now went into the woods to get intelligence no longer doubting but that it was in the hands of the Indians. Tubourai met me crossing the river and immediately made with 3 straws in his hand the figure of a triangle: the Indians had opend the cases. No time was now to be lost; I made signs to

him that he must instantly go with me to the place where it was, he agreed and out we set acompanied by a midshipman and Mr Green, we went to the Eastward. At every house we went past Tubourai enquird after the theif by name, the people readily told him which way he had gone and how long ago it was since he pass'd by, a circumstance which gave great hopes of coming up with him. The weather was excessive hot, the Thermometer before we left the tents up at 91 made our journey very tiresome. Sometimes we walk'd sometimes we ran when we imagind (which we sometimes did) that the chase was just before us till we arrivd at the top of a hill about 4 miles from the tents: from this place Tubourai shew'd us a point about 3 miles off and made us understand that we were not to expect the instrument till we got there. We now considerd our situation, no arms among us but a pair of pocket pistols which I always carried, going at least 7 miles from our fort where the Indians might not be quite so submissive as at home, going also to take from them a prize for which they had venturd their lives. All this considerd we thought it proper that while Mr Green and myself proceeded the midshipman should return and desire cap^{tn} Cooke to send a party of men after us, telling him at the same time that it was impossible we could return till dark night. This done we proceeded and in the very spot Tubourai had mentiond were met by one of his own people bringing part of the Quadrant in his hand. We now stop'd and many Indians gatherd about us rather rudely, the sight of one of my pistols however instantly checkd them and they behav'd with all the order imaginable, tho we quickly had some hundreds surrounding a ring we had markd out on the grass. The box was now brought to us and some of the small matters such as reading glasses &c. which in their hurry they had put into a pistol case, this I knew belongd to me, it had been stole out of the tents with a horse pistol in it which I immediately demanded and had immediately restord. Mr Green began to overlook the Instrument to see if any part or parts were wanting, several small things were, and people were sent out in search of them some of which returnd and others did not; the stand was not there but that we were informd had been left behind by the theif and we should have it on our return, an answer which coming from Tubourai satisfied us very well; nothing else was wanting but what could easily be repaird so we pack'd all up in grass as well as we could and proceeded homewards. After walking about 2 miles we met Cap^{tn} Cooke with a party of marines coming after us, all were you may imagine not a little pleasd at the event of our excursion.

The Captⁿ on leaving the Tents left orders both for the ship and shore, which were that no canoes should be suffer'd to go out of the bay but that nobodys person should be seizd or detaind, as we rightly guessd that none of our freinds had any hand in the theft. These orders were obeyd by the 1st Lieutenant who was ashore, but the second aboard seeing some canoes going along shore sent a boat to fetch them back; the boatswain commander did so and with them brought Dootahah, the rest of their crews leap'd overboard, he was sent ashore prisoner. The 1st Lieutenant of course could not do less than confine him which he did to the infinite dissatisfaction of all the Indians, this we heard from them 2 miles before we reachd the tents on our return. Tubourai, Tomaio and every Indian that we let in Joind in lamenting over Dootahah with many tears. I arrivd about a quarter of an Hour before the Captⁿ during which time this scene lasted; as soon as he came he orderd him to be instantly set at liberty which done he walkd off sulky enough tho at his departure he presented us with a pig.

3. Dr Solander and myself who have all along acted in the capacity of market men attended this morn but no kind of provisions were brought, indeed few Indians appeard except the servants of Dootahah who very early took away his Canoe. Soon after *Tubia*[1] (Obereas right hand man who was with her in the Dolphins time) came and overhauld every part of her canoe which had also been detaind, seemd satisfied with what he saw so much so that he would not take it away. About noon several fishing boats came abreast the tents, they however parted with very few fish. In the course of the whole day a small quantity of bread fruit was got cheifly in a present and 6 Cocoa nuts only were bought, a very disagreable change this from our former situation; we have now no cocoa nuts and not $\frac{1}{4}$ enough of bread fruit for the people, who have scarce ever before faild to turn away the latter from the market and purchase of the other from 3 to 400 a day.

In the course of the day I went into the woods. The Indians were civil but every where complaind of the ill usage Dootahah had met with, they said that he had been beat and pulld by the hair; I endeavour'd all I could to convince them that no violence had been offerd to them but without success, I fear the Boatswain

---

[1] Tupaia. This man, of considerable importance in the voyage, now comes into the story for the first time. He was an *arii* and priest of Raiatea, who, when driven from his possessions by invaders from Borabora, had arrived in Tahiti and become very influential with Purea—apparently her chief priest. He had survived the great defeat, and Tuteha, against whom he had actively plotted, let him alone. He was both able and knowledgeable.

has been rougher in his usage of him than he chuses to acknowledge. Tupia stayd with us all day and at night slept in Oboreas Canoe not without a bedfellow tho the gentleman cannot be less than 45.

4. No trade this morn but a little fish so we are for the first time in distress for nescessaries. I went into the woods to Tubourai and perswauded him to give me 5 long baskets of bread fruit, a very seasonable supply as they contain above 120 fruits. A very few Indians appear today before the fort, fewer than yesterday. After dinner came a messenger from Dootahah requesting a shirt and a hatchet (he had been here yesterday with the same demand) I suppose in return for the hog he gave us on his release; the Cap^{tn} sent him back telling him that he would tomorrow visit him and bring the things himself. In the Evening I went into the woods, found the Indians as usual civil but complaining much of the treatment Dootahah had met with on the 2nd.

5. This morn *Obàdée* (her majesties bedfellow) came pretty early to visit us or rather himself to take a view of her canoe. He carefully overhauld every thing in it and complaind of the Loss of some trifling thing I could not understand what; after this he brought every thing out of it and deliverd them into my charge desiring that they might be taken care of, after which he left us. A very small quantity of Bread fruit brought this morn. At breakfast time came two messengers from Dootahah to put the cap^{tn} in mind of his promise of Visiting him. Accordingly at 9 the boat set out carrying the Cap^{tn} Dr Solander and myself. We arrivd in about an hour, *Eparre*[1] his residence being about 4 miles from the tents. An immence throng of people met us on the shore crowding us very much tho they were severely beat for so doing by a tall well looking [man] who lacd about him with a long stick most unmercifully, striking all who did not get out of his way without intermission till he had cleard us a path sufficient to go to Dootahah, who was seated under a tree attended by a few grave looking old men. With him we sat down and made our presents consisting of an ax and a gown of Broad cloth made after their fashion and trimmd with tape, with these he seemd mightily satisfied. Soon after this Oborea joind us and with her I retird to a house adjacent where I could be free from the suffocating heat occasiond by so

---

[1] Cook writes it in his journal as Apparra. Pare was meant, more particularly the *marae* at Point Utuhaihai. Both Cook and Banks thus rendered wrongly the Tahitian *o*, an article prefixed to proper names (and also pronouns) when in the nominative case; cf. O Tahiti, whence the early European form of the name, Otaheite. But 'O' might be an integral part of a name.

large a crowd of people as were gatherd about us. Here was prepard for our diversion an entertainment quite new to us, a wrestling match at which the other gentlemen soon joind us. A large court yard raild round with Bamboo about 3 feet high was the scene of this diversion; at one end of this Dootahah was seated and near him was left seats for us but we rather chose to range at large among the spectators than confine ourselves to any particular spot.

The diversion began by the combatants some of them at least walking round the yard with a slow and grave pace every now and then striking their left arms very hard, by which they causd a deep and very loud noise, which it seems was a challenge to each other or any one of the company who chose to engage in the exercise. Within the house stood the old men ready to give applause to the victor and some few women who seem'd to be here out of compliment to us, as much the larger number absented themselves upon the occasion.

The general challenge was given as I before said, the particular one soon followd it by which any man singled out his antagonist, it was done by joining the finger ends of both hands even with the breast and then moving the Elbows up and down. If this was accepted the challenged immediately returnd the signal and instantly both put themselves in an attitude to engage, which they very soon did striving to seize each other by the hands hair or the cloth they had round their middles, for they had no other dress. This done they attempted to seize each other by the thigh which commonly decided the contest in the fall of him who was thus taken at disadvantage; if this was not soon done they always parted either by consent or their freinds interferd in less than a minute, in which case both began to clap their arms and seek anew for an antagonist either in each other or some one else.

When any one fell the whole amusement ceasd for a few moments, in which time the old men in the house gave their aplause in a few words which they repeated together in a kind of tune.

This lasted about 2 hours, all which time the man who we observd at our first Landing continued to beat the people who did not keep at a proper distance most unmercifully. We understood that he was some officer belonging to Dootahah and was calld his Tòmítè.[1]

---

[1] ? *Tamaiti*, son. From the context it seems that this person was probably the official called the *taumihau*, the chief's administrator—who might very well be a member of his family.

The wrestling over the gentlemen informd me that they understood that 2 hoggs and a large quantity of Bread fruit &c. was
cooking for our dinners, news which pleasd me very well as my
stomach was by this time sufficiently prepard for the repast. I
went out and saw the ovens in which they were now buried, these
the Indians readily shewd me telling me at the same time that they
would soon be ready and how good a dinner we should have.
In about half an hour all was taken up but now Dootahah began to
repent of his intended generosity; he thought I suppose that a
hog would be lookd upon as no more than a dinner and consequently
no present made in return, he therefore changd his mind and
ordering one of the pigs into the boat sent for us who soon collected
together and getting our Knives prepard to fall too, saying that
it was civil of the old gentleman to bring the provisions into the
boat where we could with ease keep the people at a proper distance,
who in the house would have crouded us almost to death. His
intention was however very different from ours for instead of asking
us to eat he ask'd to go on board of the ship, a measure we were
forcd to comply with and row 4 miles with the pig growing cold
under our noses before he would give it to us. Aboard however
we dind upon this same pig and his majesty eat very heartily with
us. After dinner we went ashore, the sight of Dootahah reconcild
to us acted like a charm upon the people and before night bread
fruit and cocoa nuts were brought to sell in tolerable plenty.

6. Plenty of bread-fruit at market this morn but few cocoa nuts.
After dinner Dootahah visited the tents bringing 5 baskets of breadfruit and some cocoa nuts; he went to the eastward and slept tonight
at the long house. Trade rather slack this morn, but we have so
much bread-fruit before hand from the trade and presents of yesterday that [it] is immaterial whether we buy any or not today.

7. After dinner Dootahah came in a double canoe, after him came
another bringing 4 hogs and one of these he orderd out of the
boat with some bread fruit. I undertook to coax him out of the
rest but had not the success I could have wishd, he would part
with only one more and for that both the Cap^{tn} and myself were
obligd to go aboard with him and give him a broad ax.

8. M^{srs} Molineux and Green went to the eastward today in the
pinnace intending to purchase hoggs. They went 20 miles, saw
many hogs and one turtle but the people would part with neither
one nor the other, they belongd they said to Dootahah and without
his leave they could not sell them. We now begin to think that

Dootahah is indeed a great king much greater than we have been usd to imagine him, indeed his influence upon the late occasion as well as today has prov'd to be so great that we can hardly doubt it. Mr Green measurd today a tree which he saw, it provd to be 60 yards in circumference. He brought home some boughs of it but they were thrown overboard before I could see them so the species of this monstrous tree remains a doubt with us.[1]

This morn I fix'd my little boat before the door of the Fort, it serves very well for a place to trade in. Trade is not now as it has been, formerly we usd to buy enough for all hands between sunrise and 8 O'Clock now attendance must be given all day or little can be done.

9. Cocoa nuts have been for some days rather scarce, we are therefore obligd for the first time to bring out our nails. Last night our smallest size about 4 inches long was offerd for 20 Cocoa nutts, accordingly this morn several came with that number so that we had plenty of them. Smaller lots as well as bread fruit sold as usual for beads.

Soon after breakfast Came Oborea, Obadee and Tupia bringing a hog and some breadfruit; they stayd with us till night then took away their canoe and promisd to return in 3 days. We had to day 350 Cocoa nuts and more bread fruit than we would buy so that we aproach our former plenty.

10. This morn Cap^tn Cooke planted divers seeds which he had brought with him in a spot of ground turnd up for the purpose. They were all bought of Gordon at Mile End and sent in bottles seald up, whether or no that method will succeed the event of this plantation will shew. Plenty of Bread fruit and cocoanuts again today. Towards evening Tubourai and Tomio returnd from the west and seemd extreemly glad to see all of us.

We have now got the Indian name of the Island, *Otahite*,[2] so therefore for the future I shall call it. As for our own names the Indians find so much dificulty in pronouncing them that we are forcd to indulge them in calling us what they please, or rather

---

[1] Since a tree circumference of 60 yards is incredible any identification here can only be conjectural. Dr A. C. Smith suggests the Polynesian fig, *Ficus prolixa* Forst.— if the combination of a mass of closely grown aerial roots together with the main trunk be admitted.

[2] O Tahiti: *O* as the nominative article. Cf. p. 271, n. 1 above. Banks's phonetic rendering (his *i* would be long, as in 'time') differs rather on paper, but perhaps not in intention, from the 'Otaheite' used by Cook and others, and perhaps no more from the classical pronunciation of the name than does the present version. There was in this older pronunciation a 'forced diphthong' or 'vowel glide' that tended to play down the intermediate *h* and assimilate somewhat the *a* of the first syllable and the *i* of the second.

what they say when they attempt to pronounce them. I give here the List: Cap^tn Cooke *Tootê*, Dr Solander *Tôrànô*, Mr Hicks *Hêtê*, Mr Gore *Tôárrô*, Mr Molineux *Bôbà* from his Christian name Robert, Mr Monkhouse *Màtô*, and myself *Tàpánê*. In this manner they have names for almost every man in the ship.

11. Cocoa nuts were brought down so plentifully this morn that by ½ past 6 I had bought 350: this made it nescessary to drop the price of them least so many being brought at once we should exhaust the countrey and want hereafter; notwistanding I had before night bought more than a thousand at the rates of 6 for an amber coulourd bead, 10 for a white one, and 20 for a fortypenny nail.[1]

12. Cocoa nuts very plentifull this morning. About breakfast time Dootahah visits us. Immediately after while I sat trading in the boat at the door of the fort a double Canoe came with several women and one man under the awning. The Indians round me made signs that I should go out and meet them, by the time I had got out of the boat they were within ten yards of me. The people made a lane from them to me. They stopd and made signs for me to do the same. The man in company with them had in his hand a large bunch of boughs; he advancd towards me bringing two, one a young plantain the other   .[2] Tupia who stood by me acted as my deputy in receiving them and laying them down in the boat: 6 times he passd backwards and forwards in the same manner and bringing the same present. Another man then came forward having in his arms a large bundle of cloth, this he opend out and spread it peice by peice on the ground between the women and me, it consisted on nine peices. Three were first laid. The foremost of the women,[3] who seemd to be the principal, then stepd upon them and quickly unveiling all her charms gave me a most convenient opportunity of admiring them by turning herself gradualy round: 3 peices more were laid and she repeated her part of the ceremony: the other three were then laid which made a treble covering of the ground between her and me, she then once more displayd her naked beauties and immediately marchd up to me, a man following her and doubling up the cloth as he came forwards which she immediately made me understand

---

[1] A 'fortypenny nail' was a nail 4½ inches long, sold at forty pence for a hundred.

[2] The MS has a space here for the name of the tree from which the second bough came, which with Banks's lack of punctuation has led to corruption in P—i.e. 'he advanced towards me bringing to one a young plantain the other' etc. S has the blank, and punctuates 'two; one a young plantain, the other' etc.

[3] A marginal note gives her name as Ourattooa: Uratua or Ura-atua?

was intended as a present for me.[1] I took her by the hand and led her to the tents acompanied by another woman her freind, to both of them I made presents but could not prevail upon them to stay more than an hour. In the evening Oborea and her favourite attendant *Othéóthéa*[2] pay us a visit, much to my satisfaction as the latter (my flame) has for some days been reported either ill or dead.

13. Our Freinds with us this morn in very good time as they generaly are, very shortly after sunrise plenty of cocoa nuts &c. at the market. After it was over, about 10 O'Clock, I walkd into the woods with my gun, as I generaly did to spend the heat of the day in the Indian houses where I could be cool from the shade of the trees which every where grow about them. In my return I met Tubourai near his house; I stopd with him, he took my gun out of my hand, cockd it and holding it up in the air drew the trigger, fortunately for him it flashd in the pan. Where he had got so much knowledge of the use of a gun I could not conceive but was sufficiently angry that he should attempt to exersise it upon mine, as I had upon all occasions taught him and the rest of the Indians that they could not offend me so much as even to touch it. I scolded him severely and even threatned to shoot him. He bore all patiently but the moment I had crossd the river he and his family bag and baggage movd of to their other house at Eparre. This step was no sooner taken than I was informd of it by the Indians about the fort. Not willing to lose the assistance of a man who had upon all occasions been particularly usefull to us I resolv'd to go this evening and bring him back, acordingly as soon as dinner was over I set out acompanied by Mr Molineux. We found him setting in the middle of a large circle of people, himself and many of the rest with most melancholy countenances some in tears; one old woman on our coming into the circle struck a sharks tooth into her head many times till it foamd with blood but her head seemd to have been so often excersisd with this expression of greif that it was become quite callous, for tho the crown of it was coverd with blood enough did not issue

---

[1] The precise meaning of this pleasant ceremony is not easy to disentangle. The formal presentation of cloth by stripping off large quantities of it from the body until the officiating young woman was almost naked was common enough practice, and the ceremony was called *taurua*. But this one has points of difference: it may have been merely an elaboration, or as the plantain had phallic significance it may (the suggestion has been made) have symbolized the generous feelings entertained by the female population of the district towards the young and attractive Banks. No such ceremony appears to have been performed for Cook or any other of the English identifiable as *arii*; and yet Cook was clearly the greatest chief of all.

[2] ? O Tahiatahia (the *tah* sound often came to the European ear as *th*); or possibly Tiatia. Parkinson writes the name Otea Tea.

from the wounds to run upon her cheeks. After some few assurances of forgiveness Tubourai agreed to return with us, in consequence of which resolution a double canoe was put off in which we all returnd to the tents before supper time, and as a token of a renewal of freindship both him and his wife slept in my tent all night.

About 11 one of the natives atempted to scale our walls intending no doubt to steal whatever he could find, but seeing himself observd he made off much faster than any of our people could follow him.

14. Our freinds Dootahah, Oborea, Otheothea &c. at the tents this morn as usual. It being Sunday Cap^tn Cooke proposd that divine service should be celebrated[1] but before the proper time of doing it most of our Indian freinds were gone home to eat. I was resolvd however that some should be present that they might see our behaviour and we might if possible explain to them (in some degree at least) the reasons of it. I went therefore over the river and brought back Tubourai and Tomio and having seated them in the tent plac'd myself between them. During the whole service they imitated my motions, standing setting or kneeling as they saw me do, and so much understood that we were about something very serious that they calld to the Indians without the fort to be silent; notwisthstanding this they did not when the service was over ask any questions nor would they attend at all to any explanation we attempted to give them. We have not yet seen the least traces of religion among these people, maybe they are intirely without it.

15. In the course of last night one of the Indians was clever enough to steal an Iron bound cask; it was indeed without the fort but so immediately under the eye of the Sentry that we could hardly beleive the possibility of such a thing having [happened][2] when we lookd at the place. The Indians however acknowledg'd it and seemd inclind to give intelligence, in consequence of which I set off in pursuit of it and tracd it to a part of the bay where they told me it had been put into a canoe. The thing was not of consequence enough to pursue with any great spirit so I returnd home where I found Oborea, Otheothea, Obadee &c. At night Tubourai made

[1] Cook had been both recommended by Lord Morton and enjoined by the Articles of War to give frequent performance to Divine Worship; he, like Banks, mentions it for this day, but from neither would one gather that it was a constant practice. Nor does Cook appear to have read the service, while Banks clearly was more interested in Polynesian theology. Other logs and journals however mention a Sunday service more frequently, and whatever part of the ship's company was not indispensably employed got a half-day off 'at their own Leisure'.

[2] MS *sic*; a slip for *hapning*? S writes *having*, and adds *happened* interlineally. P *having*, which does not make sense, though Banks may have intended *having been done*.

many signs that another cask would be stole before morning, and thinking I suppose that we did not sufficiently regard them himself his wife and family came to the place where the cask[s] lay and making their beds said that they would themselves take care that no one should steal them. On being told this I went to them and explaining to them that a Sentry was this night put over those particular casks they agreed to come and sleep in my tent, but insisted upon leaving a servant to assist the sentry in case the theif came, which he did about 12 and was seen by the Sentry who fird at him on which he retreated most expeditiously.

16. The morning wet and disagreable. We hauld the Seine in several parts of the bay without the least success; the Indians are so fond of fish and so expert in catching it, using almost every method we do in Europe, that our want of success is not at all to be wonderd at. Tonight Tubourai, Tamio, Oborea, Obadee and Otheothea slept in my tent. At midnight the water casks were again atempted and two shot fird at the theif which alarmd my bedfellows not a little, they were however soon quieted by my going out and bringing back word of the reason of the firing.

17. Fine weather. Oborea and her freinds went early to Eparre as the rest of our cheifs did yesterday in 18 double canoes, so that we are quite dull for want of company in the tents. Tubourai and Tamio slept with me as usual.

18. Fine weather and good market, the apples[1] begin now to be ripe and are brought in in large quantities very cheap so that apple pies are a standing dish with us.

19. This morning Tubourai who had slept [with] me as usual was observd by my servant to have an uncommonly large nail under his Cloaths, this I was informd of and knowing that no such had been either given or dispos'd of in trade was obligd to suspect my freind of theft. I therefore went instantly to his house and chargd him with it, he immediately confessd but atempted to keep his booty by telling me that the nail was gone to Eparre. I became much in earnest and a few threats soon produc'd the stolen goods. I was more hurt at the discovery than he was, I firmly beleive he was the only Indian I trusted and in him I had placd a most unbounded confidence, this event shews more than he could

---

[1] This may be either the fruit of the Vi or yellow apple, *Spondias dulcis*, also called the Brazilian plum (Parkinson says it was the size of a middling apple); or the Ahia, *Eugenia malaccensis*, the East Indian jambo, commonly called in Tahiti (apart from its native name) the rose-apple or mountain apple, which however has a pear-shaped fruit— I think more likely the former; cf. pp. 342-3 below, and PL. VI.

bear: 7 of these nails lay in a basket in one of the tents and on examining it 5 were missing. I thought it nesscessary after this discovery to bring the offender to the tents to receive judgement which I did. Every body there was of opinion that his fault was pardonable. I confess that upon thinking over the circumstances I blam'd myself more for leaving the nails in his way than him for stealing them. It was therefore resolvd that if he brought back the other 4 he should be forgiven and his fault forgot: this I told him and he agreed readily, but instead of performing his part he and his family movd off before night taking with them all their furniture.

20. Rain and very disagreeable weather so that we had but little trade. About 10 Oborea came to the fort and brough[t] a large present of bread fruit, she had with her Otheothea and her other maids of honour as we call them but Obadee her gentleman attendant was absent. We enquird the reason, she told us that she had dismiss'd him; about 8 however he came by torch light and going to the house in the woods where she slept slept with her.

21. Sunday, Divine service performd, at which was present Oborea, Otheothea, Obadee, &c. all behav'd very decently. After dinner Obadee who had been for some time absent returnd to the fort. Oborea desird he might not be let in, his countenance was however so melancholy that we could not but admit him. He lookd most piteously at Oborea, she most disdainfully at him; she seems to us to act in the character of a Ninon d'Enclos[1] who satiated with her lover resolves to change him at all Events, the more so as I am offerd if I please to supply his place, but I am at present otherwise engag'd; indeed was I free as air her majesties person is not the most desireable.

22. This morning showery and cool, seemingly a good opportunity of going upon the hills. I went accompanied only by Indians, indeed all of them but one soon left me, he however accompanied me during my whole walk. The paths were very open and clear till I came to the woods but afterwards very bad, so much so that I could not reach the top of the lowest of the two high hills seen from the fort, which was all I intended.[2] I was in some measure

[1] Banks's scholarship had lapses. Ninon de l'Enclos (1620-1705), the free and dazzling mistress of the most celebrated of seventeenth century salons. The passage which follows, that Banks was 'at present otherwise engag'd', does not seem to refer to Miss Blosset.

[2] It is difficult to know what Banks meant by 'the lowest of the two high hills seen from the fort'. There were a number of high hills visible: if he meant the highest, Aorai or one of the peaks of Orofena, he was making a serious miscalculation of distance and accessibility.

however recompens'd by finding several plants which I had not before seen, with which I returnd before sunset, and had Oborea, Obadee and Otheothea to sleep with me in my tent.

23. Trade very slack today, so much so that we have only Cocoa nuts for the sick, and the people are obligd to have bread servd them at dinner.

24. We had receivd repeated messages from Dootahah signifying that if we would go and visit him we should have 4 hogs for our pains; in consequence of this our first Lieutenant was sent today with orders to go to him and try if by any civilities he could shew him he could procure them. He found him removd from his old residence at Eparre to a place calld Téttaháh[1] about 5 miles farther. He was reciv'd with great cordiality, one hog was immediately producd and he was told that the others should be brough[t] somewhere from a distance if he would stay till next morning. This he did not at all scruple, the morning came however without the hogs so he was obligd to return with the one he had got over night not a little dissatisfied with Dootahahs nonperformance of his promises.

M[rs] Monkhouse and Green atempted this day to climb the same hill that I attempted on the 22nd, with much the same success; they got however higher than I did but could not reach the summit.

25. Tubourai and Tamio made their appearance at the fort for the first time since the breach of the 19th, he in particular seemd much frightned nor did my behavior to him give him much comfort. I had resolvd not to restore him either to my freindship or confidence unless he restord the nails which he seemd to have no intention of dooing; after staying a little time he went home sulky as he came.

26. M[r] Monkhouse who I think is rather too partial to Tubourai went this morn to his house intending to persuade him to come to the tents. He made many excuses, he was hungry, he must sleep, his head achd, in short he would not nor did not come. Tamio however did but took alarm at my being absent who was aboard of the ship and soon departed.

27. This day M[r] Monkhouse went to Eparre with Tubourai and Tamio. Market tolerable. M[r] Hicks in his return from Dootahah brought word that if the Capt[n] would go over the 4 piggs would

---

[1] Tataa, an old name for the district of Faaa, adjoining Pare. Point Tataa on the modern map is the seaward limit of the line separating Faaa from the Punaauia district. The harbour of the district was the present Papeete harbour.

be given to him: this producd a resolution of going tomorrow, tho we none of us much credited his promise, yet we would leave no stone unturnd to keep him in good humour. I omitted to mention on the 25th that the longboat being very leaky was hauld dry and her bottom found to be eat intirely through by the worm,[1] which surprizes us much as the Dolphins boats met with no such inconvenience: her bottom was payd with brimstone and tallow. The pinnace which has been in the water as long as her is totaly untouchd which we atribute to hers being painted with white lead and oil.

28. This morn the pinnace set out for the Eastward[2] with the Cap^{tn} Dr Solander and myself. Dootahah was removd from Tettahah where Mr Hicks saw him on the 24th to Atahourou, about 6 miles farther, a place to which the boat could not go.[3] We were resolv'd not to be disapointed so walkd afoot. It was evening before we arrivd, we found him setting under a tree with a vast croud about him as usual; we made our presents in due form consisting of a yellow stuff peticoat &c. which were graciously receivd, and a hog immediately [brought][4] with many promises of more in the morning. Night came on apace, it was nescessary to look out for lodgings; as Dootahah made no offer of any I repair to my old Freind Oborea who readily gave me a bed in her canoe much to my satisfaction. I acquainted my fellow travelers with my good fortune and wishing them as good took my leave. We went to bed early as is the custom here: I strippd myself for the greater convenience of sleeping as the night was hot. Oborea insisted that my cloths should be put into her custody, otherwise she said they would certainly be stolen. I readily submitted and laid down to sleep with all imaginable tranquility. About 11 I awakd and wanting to get up felt for my clothes in the place in which I had seen them laid at night but they were missing. I awakd Oborea, she started up and on my complaining of the Loss candles were immediately lit. Dootahah who slept in the next canoe came to us and both went in search of the theif, for such it seems it was who had stolen

---

[1] The wood-boring shipworm, *Teredo* sp.

[2] A slip for *Westward*.

[3] This may have been at Point Punaauia, where there was a great *marae*; but it may also have been at Tuteha's *marae* of Maraetaata, about two miles farther on. We do not know where the party started walking; for Tettaha as a place name is almost as vague as Atahourou. Why the boat could not go farther is unclear, unless Cook feared difficulty with the reef. He himself merely says, 'as we had left the Boat about half way behind us we were oblige'd to take up our quarters with him for the night'.

[4] *receivd, and a hog*, P *received with a hog*; S *received, & a hog immediately brought* [*brought* added interlineally].

my coat and waistcoat[1] with my pistols powder horn &c., they returnd however in about ½ an hour without any news of the stolen goods. I began to be a little alarmd, my musquet was left me, but that by my neglect the night before was not loaded; I did not know where Capt[n] Cooke or D[r] Solander had disposd of themselves, consequently could not call upon them for assistance; Tupia stood near me awakd by the Hubbub that had been raisd on account of my Loss; to him I gave my Musquet charging him to take care that the theif did not get it from him, and betook myself again to rest, telling my companions in the boat that I was well satisfied with the pains that Oborea and Dootahah had taken for the recovery of my things. Soon after I heard their musick and saw lights near me; I got up and went towards them, it was a heiva or assembly according to their custom. Here I saw Capt[n] Cooke and told my melancholy story, he was my fellow sufferer, he had lost his stockins and two young gentlemen[2] who were with him had lost each a Jacket. D[r] Solander was away we neither of us knew where: we talkd over our losses and agreed that nothing could be done toward recovering them till the morning, after which we parted and went to our respective sleeping places.

29. At day break we rose according to the custom of our companions. Tupia was the first man I saw, atending with my Musquet and the remainder of my cloaths, his faith had often been tried, on this occasion it shone very much. Oborea took care to provide me with cloth to supply the place of my lost Jacket so that I made a motley apearance, my dress being half English and half Indian. Dootahah soon after made his apearance; I pressd him to recover my Jacket but neither he nor Oborea would take the least step towards it so that I am almost inclind to beleive that they acted principals in the theft. Indeed if they did it may be said in their excuse that they knew I had in my pockets a pair of pistols, weopons to them more dreadfull than a cannon to a man marching up to its mouth: could they get possession of them they thought no doubt that they would be as usefull to them as to us; self defence and preservation therefore in this case came in opposition to the laws of hospitality, duties to which mankind usualy give the preference in all cases.

About 8 D[r] Solander returnd from a house about a mile off where he had slept: he had met with more honest companions

---

[1] Parkinson (p. 31) tells us that 'Mr. Banks lost his white jacket and waistcoat, with silver frogs'. The contrast between Banks the elegant spark and Banks the anthropological researcher will later become apparent.

[2] Cook does not refer to these 'two young gentlemen'; I take it they were two of the midshipmen.

than we had for nothing of his was missing. We spent the most of the morning in trying to persuade our freinds either to restore our cloaths or give us some hogs acording to promise, but neiether could we do, so we were forcd to set out for the boat with only the pig got yesterday, dissatisfied enough with our expedition.

In our return to the boat we saw the Indians amuse or excersise themselves in a manner truly surprizing. It was in a place where the shore was not guarded by a reef as is usualy the case, consequently a high surf fell upon the shore, a more dreadfull one I have not often seen: no European boat could have landed in it and I think no Europæan who had by any means got into [it] could possibly have saved his life, as the shore was coverd with pebbles and large stones. In the midst of these breakers 10 or 12 Indians were swimming who whenever a surf broke near them divd under it with infinite ease, rising up on the other side; but their cheif amusement was carried on by the stern of an old canoe, with this before them they swam out as far as the outermost breach, then one or two would get into it and opposing the blunt end to the breaking wave were hurried in with incredible swiftness. Sometimes they were carried almost ashore but generaly the wave broke over them before they were half way, in which case the[y] divd and quickly rose on the other side with the canoe in their hands, which was towd out again and the same method repeated. We stood admiring this very wonderfull scene for full half an hour, in which time no one of the actors atempted to come ashore but all seemd most highly entertaind with their strange diversion.

30. Carpenters employd today in repairing the long boat which is eat in a most wonderfull manner, every part of her bottom is like a honeycomb and some of the holes $\frac{1}{8}^{th}$ of an inch in diameter, such a progress has this destructive insect made in six weeks.

31. The day of Observation now aproaches. The weather has been for some days fine, tho in general since we have been upon the Island we have had as much cloudy as clear weather, which makes us all not a little anxious for success. In consequence of hints from Lord Morton the Cap^{tn} resolves to send a party to the eastward, and another to *Imáò*, an Island in sight of us,[1] thinking that in case of thick weather one or the other might be more successfull than the observatory. The Carpenters work very hard to finish the long boat. I resolve to go on the Imáò expedition.

[1] Cook and others generally spelt the name of the island Eimeo; it was Aimeo or Aimeho, clearly visible from Point Venus; now called Moorea.

JUNE 1769

1. The boat could not be got ready till after dinner when we set out; we rowd most of the night and came to a grapling just under the land of Imáò.

2. Soon after day break we saw an Indian canoe and upon hailing her she shewed us an inlet through the reef, into [which] we pulld and soon fixd upon a Coral rock about 150 yards from the shore as a very proper situation for our Observatory;[1] it was about 80 yards long and 60 broad and had in the middle of it a bed of white sand large enough for our tents to stand upon. The 2nd Lieutent and people therefore immediately set about it while I went upon the main Island to trade with the inhabitants for provisions, of which I soon bought a sufficient supply. Before night our observatory was in order, telescopes all set up and tried &c. and we went to rest anxious for the events of tomorrow; the evening having been very fine gave us however great hopes of success.

3. Various were the Changes observd in the weather during the course of last night, some one or other of us was up every half hour who constantly informd the rest that it was either clear or Hazey, at day break we rose and soon after had the satisfaction of seeing the sun rise as clear and bright as we could wish him. I then wishd success to the observers Msrs Gore and Monkhouse and repaird to the Island, where I could do the double service of examining the natural produce and buying provisions for my companions who were engagd in so usefull a work. About eight a large quantity of provisions were procurd when I saw two boats coming towards the place where I traded; these I was told belongd to *Tàrróa*[2] the King of the Island who was coming to pay me a visit. As soon as the boats came near the shore the people formd a lane; he landed bringing with him his sister *Nùnà*[3] and both came towards the tree under which I stood. I went out and met them and brought them very formaly into a circle I had made, into which I had before sufferd none of the natives to come. Standing is not the fashion among these people, I must provide them a seat, which I did by unwrapping a turban of Indian cloth which I wore instead of a hat and spreading it upon the ground; upon this we all sat down and the kings present was brought Consisting

---

[1] This was the islet of Irioa, just inside the reef beyond the Taotoi pass, almost at the north-west point of Moorea.

[2] Ta'aroa.

[3] This may be the correct form of the name.

of a hog, a dog and a quantity of Bread fruit Cocoa nuts &c. I
immediately sent a canoe to the Observatory to fetch my present,
an adze a shirt and some beads with which his majesty seemd well
satisfied. Tubourai and Tamio who came with us now came from
the observatory; she said that she was related to Tarroa and brought
him a present, a long nail and a shirt, which she gave to Nuna.
After the first Internal contact was over I went to my Companions
at the observatory carrying with me Tarroa, Nuna and some of
their cheif atendants; to them we shewd the planet upon the sun
and made them understand that we came on purpose to see it.
After this they went back and myself with them. I spent the rest
of the day in examining the produce &c. of the Island and found it
very nearly similar to that of Otahite, the people exactly the same,
indeed we saw many of the Identical same people as we had often
seen at Otahite, and every one knew well every kind of trade we
had and the value it bore in that Island. The hills in general came
nearer to the water and flats were consequently less, and less
Fertile, than at Otahite—the low point near which we lay was
composd intirely of sand and coral. Here neither Breadfruit nor
any usefull vegetables would grow; it was coverd over with *Pandanus
tectorius*[1] and with these grew several plants we had not seen at
Otahite, among them Iberis   ,[2] which Mr Gore tells
me is the plant calld by the voyagers scurvy grass which grows
plentifully upon all the low Islands.

At sunset I came off having purchasd another hog from the
King. Soon after my arrival at the tent 3 hansome girls came off
in a canoe to see us, they had been at the tent in the morning with
Tarroa, they chatted with us very freely and with very little perswasion agreed to send away their carriage and sleep in [the] tent,
a proof of confidence which I have not before met with upon so
short an acquaintance.

4. We prepard ourselves to depart, in spite of the intreaties of our
fair companions who persuaded us much to stay. What with
presents and trade our stock of Provisions was so large that we were
obligd to give away a large quantity. This done we put off and
before night arrivd at the tents, where we had the great satisfaction
that the observation there had been attended with as much success
as Mr Green and the Cap^tn could wish, the day having been

---

[1] There are many varieties of Fara or pandanus, growing both on high and on low
ground; Banks is probably referring to the common Fara-iri, much used in the islands
for mats.

[2] *Lepidium bidentatum* Montin (*L. piscidium* Forst. <JDH>). Parkinson's drawing is
labelled 'Ulhietea [i.e. Raiatea] 1769'. Thellung refers this sp. to *L. hyssopifolium*.

perfectly clear not so much as a cloud interveining. We also heard the melancholy news that a large part of our stock of Nails had been purloind by some of the ships company during the time of the Observation, when every body was ashore who had any degree of command. One of the theives was detected but only 7 nails were found upon him out of 100 W^t and he bore his punishment without impeaching any of his acomplices. This loss is of a very serious nature as these nails if circulated by the people among the Indians will much lessen the value of Iron, our staple commodity.

5. During our absence at Imao an old woman of some consequence, a relation of Tamio, was dead and was plac'd not far from the fort to rot above ground as is the custom of the Island. I went this morn to see her. A small square was neatly raild in with Bamboe and in the midst of it a Canoe awning set up upon two posts, in this the body was laid coverd with fine cloth. Near this was laid fish &c. meat for the gods not for the deceasd, but to satisfie the hunger of the deitys least they shoud eat the body, which Tubourai told us they would certainly do if this ceremony was neglected. In the front of the square was a kind of stile or place lower than the rest, where the relations of the deceasd stood when they cry'd or bled themselves, and under the awning were numberless rags containing the blood and tears they had shed. Within a few yards were two occasional houses; in one of them some of the relations constantly remaind generaly a good many; in the other the cheif male mourner resided and kept a very remarkable Dress in which he performd a ceremony, both which I shall describe when I have an opportunity of seeing it in perfection which Tubourai promises me I shall soon have.

This day we kept the Kings birthday which had been delayd on account of the absence of the two observing parties; several of the Indians dind with us and drank his majesties health by the name of Kihiargo, for we could not teach them to pronounce a word more like King George. Tupia however to shew his Loyalty got most enormously drunk.

6. In walking into the woods yesterday I saw in the hands of an Indian an Iron tool made in the shape of the Indian adzes, very different I was sure from any thing that had been carried out or made either by the Dolphin or this ship. This excited my curiosity, much the more so when I was told that it did not come out of either of those ships but from two others which came here together. This was a discovery not to be neglected. With much dificulty and labour

I at last got the following account of them, viz. that in their month
of *Pépéré* which answers to our January 1768[1] 2 Spanish ships came
here commanded by a man whoom they calld *To Otterah*;[2] that they
lay 8 days in a bay calld *Hidea*,[3] some leagues to the eastward of
Matavie where the ship now lies; that during their stay they sent
tents ashore and some slept in them; that they were cheifly connected
with a cheif whose name was *Oréttè*,[4] whose younger brother[5]
they carried away with them promising to return in nine months;
that they had on board their ships a woman;[6] and that on their
departure they stood to the westward as long as they were seen from
the Island. I was very particular in these inquiries as the Knowledge
got by them may be of some consequence. The methods I took
to gain this account would be much too tedious to mention: one
of my greatest dificulties was to determine of what nation they were
which was done thus, I pointed to our colours and ask'd whether
the ships had such or not. No, was the answer when the question
was thouroughly understood. I opend a large sheet of Flaggs and
askd which of them they had: Tubourai lookd stedfastly over them
and at last pitchd upon the Spanish[7] ensign and to that he adhered
tho we tryd him over and over.

7. We were this morn visited by several of Dootahahs relations
women especialy, probably to sound us upon the score of our
usage at Atahourou. We had resolvd at that place rather to
put up with our losses than to mattow[8] or frighten the Indians,
the consequence of which we knew to be scarcity of provisions;

[1] The lunar month *Pipiri*, generally taken to include parts of February and March.
The MS is amended; Banks first had February 1767, then changed the year to 1768
and the month (apparently) to May, and finally deletes all this for January 1768. But
it was in the first half of April 1768 that Bougainville paid his visit.
[2] This name is generally given as Toottera, as in Cook. It may be a rendering of Duclos,
Bougainville's second in command; he himself was known as Putaveri.
[3] Hitiaa was the district, but Haitaa is in the immediate vicinity of Bougainville's
anchorage, and Hidea may signify this latter name.
[4] Reti, Ereti, Oreti—there is some slight doubt about the chief's name.
[5] The name Outorrou is given marginally: Ahutoru.
[6] This was true—and a fact which astonished the French themselves. It was Jeanne
Baré or Baret, whom, dressed as a man, the naturalist Philibert Commerson said he engaged
in good faith as his valet on the quay-side at Brest. Her deceit was suspected, but not
admitted, until the arrival in Tahiti, when a glance from the natives served to dispel it.
Unfortunately for Commerson, he was a man of the most elevated and tedious sentiments
on the subject of morality and refinement of taste, at the expense of his shipmates. The
ribald laughter in which these shipmates then indulged may well have seemed to poor
Commerson one of the corruptions of civilization with which he compared the primitive
virtues of the Isle of Cythera, in his famous letter published in the *Mercure de France*,
November 1769.
[7] Bougainville disclaimed ever having flown the Spanish ensign.
[8] *matau*, to fear; to frighten would be *faa-matau*. There is a note here in S: 'Mattow
in their Language signifies to frighten, or affront. Indeed the general consequence of
frightening them, was their being affronted'.

we therefore treated these people very well, making them presents to tempt them to come again and bring Dootahah, king of the hogs as we calld him and certainly have always found him.

8. Fresh proofs of the Spanish ships every day in thing[s] of theirs which have been left here, among the rest a course shirt and a woolen jacket both of manufacture different from any English.

9. Yesterday and today the *Heiva no Meduah*[1] or funeral ceremony walkd. My curiosity was raisd by his most singular dress. I was desirous of knowing what he did during his walk; I askd Tubourai, at the same time desird leave to atend him tomorrow which upon my consenting to perform a character was readily granted. Tomorrow therefore I am to be smutted from head to foot and to do whatever they desire me to do. Bread fruit has for some time been scarce with us; about 10 days ago the trees were thinnd all at once from their being a great shew of fruit; every one was employd in making *Mahie*[2] for about a week. Where the breadfruit we now have comes from we cannot tell, but we have more than the woods in our neighbourhood can supply us with. Probably our consumption has thinnd the trees in this neighbourhood, as the Dolphins who came here about this time saw great plenty all the time they stayd; if this is the case what we now get may be brought from some neig[h]bouring place where the trees are not yet exhausted.

10. This evening according to my yesterdays engagement I went to the place where the *medua* lay, where I found Tubourai, Tamio, Hoona[3] the *Meduas* daughter and a young Indian prepard to receve me. Tubourai was the *Heiva*, the three others and myself were to *Nineveh*.[4] He put on his dress, most Fantastical tho not unbecoming, the figure annexd will explain it far better than

---

[1] *Heiva no metua*; *metua*, a parent, of either sex. As we see from the next entry and that for 26 June below, it was a ceremony of mourning for the mother of a young woman called Hoona or Huna.

[2] *mahi*, the 'sour-paste' made from breadfruit. See pp. 344-5 below.

[3] Huna?

[4] *neneva* means fool or foolish, giddy; and *nevaneva*, mad, distracted (Davies, 1851). Some confusion of words is not unlikely. Cf. *Journal of James Morrison*, p. 233: 'This Ceremony is also Calld Tyehaa [*taihaa*; *tai*, to weep or grieve] or Mourning, the Performers are Called Naynevva, Madmen Hevva tyehaa—Mourning Spirits, Gosts, or Spectres'. It is clear from Banks's description, the earliest we have, as well as from later ones, that the near-naked assistants were to act in as thoroughly terrifying a manner as possible, as if they were violently out of their minds with grief. There is no figure annexed in the MS to explain the dress of the *Heiva* (which was properly the ceremony itself, not the principal figure in it); but there is a drawing in B.M. Add. MS 15508, f. 9, entitled 'Chief Mourner', on which is founded the presentment in Plate V in Hawkesworth, II. There is also a pencil drawing by Spöring, entitled 'Dress of the Chief Mourner', B.M. Add. MS 23921.32. Henry (*Ancient Tahiti*, p. 293) says the ceremony was called *heva-tupapau*, mourning for the corpse; the principal, a priest, seems to have represented the ghost of the deceased. See pl. 15.

words can.[1] I was next prepard by stripping off my European
cloths and putting me on a small strip of cloth round my waist,
the only garment I was allowd to have, but I had no pretensions
to be ashamd of my nakedness for neither of the women were a
bit more coverd than myself. They then began to smut me and
themselves with charcoal and water, the Indian boy was compleatly
black, the women and myself as low as our shoulders. We then set
out. Tubourai began by praying twice, once near the Corps again
near his own house. We then proceeded towards the fort: it was
nesscessary it seems that the procession should visit that place
but they dare not to do it without the sanction of some of us, indeed
it was not till many assurances of our consent that they venturd to
perform any part of their ceremonies. To the fort then we went
to the surprize of our freinds and affright of the Indians who were
there, for they every where fly before the *Heiva* like sheep before a
wolf. We soon left it and proceeded along shore towards a place
where above 100 Indians were collected together. We the *Ninevehs*
had orders from the *Heiva* to disperse them, we ran towards them but
before we cam[e] within 100 yards of them they dispers'd every
way, running to the first shelter, hiding themselves under grass
or whatever else would conceal them. We now crossd the river
into the woods and passd several houses, all were deserted, not
another Indian did we see for about $\frac{1}{2}$ an hour that we spent in
walking about. We the *Ninevehs* then came to the *Heiva* and said
imatata,[2] there are no people; after which we repaird home, the
Heiva undressd and we went into the river and scrubbd one another
till it was dark before the blacking would come off.

11. This Evening Tubourai came to the tents bringing a bow
and arrows, in consequence of a challenge M[r] Gore had given
him sometime ago to shoot. This challenge was however misunderstood, Tubourai meant to try who could shoot the farthest,[3]
M[r] Gore to shoot at a mark and neither was at all practisd in what
the other valued himself upon. Tubourai to please us shot in his

---

[1] S footnotes this as follows: 'Alluding to a drawing of the Heiva note tatta Matte
Dress ['tatta Matte' is presumably *taata mate*, dead man]. Besides the Nineveh going
before, by way of giving notice of the approach of the Heiva; he (the Heiva) carries
in one hand Shells of Mother of Pearl; which by his knoucking together, gives farther
notice of his approach: and, should any Indian not get out of his way, he would beat him
unmercifully with a Staff he carries: the top of which has many small, jagged points'.
The British Museum has in its ethnological collection a specimen of the 'Heiva's' dress,
together with the shell 'clackers' and a very dangerous-looking staff.

[2] *aima taata.*

[3] Archery was an aristocratic sport in Tahiti, confined to the *arii* and generally held
with great ceremony from sacred platforms; shooting was always for distance. The best
description is in Ellis, *Polynesian Researches*, I, pp. 217-19.

way; he knelt down and drew the bow and as soon as he let slip the string droppd the bow from his hand, the arrow however went 274 yards.

12. In my mornings walk today I met a company of traveling musicians;[1] they told me where they should be at night so after supper we all repaird to the place. There was a large concourse of people round this band, which consisted of 2 flutes and three drums, the drummers acompanying their musick with their voices; they sung many songs generaly in praise of us, for these gentlemen like Homer of old must be poets as well as musicians. The Indians seeing us entertaind with their musick, askd us to sing them an English song, which we most readily agreed to and receivd much applause, so much so that one of the musicians became desirous of going to England to learn to sing. These people by what we can learn go about from house to house, the master of the house and the audience paying them for their musick in cloth, meat, beads or any thing else which the one wants and the other can spare.

13. Mr Monkhouse our surgeon met to day with an insult from an Indian, the first that has been met with by any of us. He was pulling a flower from a tree which grew on a burying ground and consequently was I suppose sacred,[2] when an Indian came behind him and struck him; he seiz'd hold of him and attempted to beat him, but was prevented by two more who coming up seizd hold of his hair and rescued their companion after which they all ran away.

14. I lay in the woods last night as I very often did. At day break I was calld up by Mr Gore and went with him shooting, from which party we did not return till night when we saw a large number of Canoes in the river behind the tents, of which we had this account. Last night an Indian was clever enough to steal a Coal rake out of the fort without being perceivd. In the Morning it was missing and Cap^tn Cooke being resolvd to recover it, as also to discourage such atempts for the future, went out with a party of men and seizd 25 of their large sailing Canoes which were just come in from *Tethuroa*,[3] a neighbouring Island, with a supply of fish for the inhabitants of this. The Coal rake was upon this soon brought back but Cap^tn Cooke thought he had now in his hands an opportunity of recovering all the things which had been stolen: he therefore

---

[1] A company of *arioi*.

[2] By 'burying-ground' Banks means a *marae*, which would certainly be *tapu*.

[3] The atoll Tetiaroa, a group of five small islets within one reef, about 26 miles north-west of Moorea; it belonged to the *arii* of Pare, to whom it served as a sort of country-seat. Teturoa was an older name.

proclaimd to every one that till all the things which had been stolen from us were brought back the boats should not stir, a list of these was immediately drawn up and read several times to the Indians, who readily promisd that every thing should be brought back. Great application was made to me in my return that some of these might be releasd. I did not till I got to the fort understand the reason of their being detaind, and when I did nothing apeard so plain as that no one of them should on any account be let go from favour, but the whole kept till the things were [returnd] if ever they were, which I much doubted as the Canoes pretty certainly did not belong to the people who had stolen the things. I confess had I taken a step so violent I would have seizd either the persons of the people who had stolen from us, most of whoom we either knew or shrewdly suspected, or their goods at least instead of those of people who are intirely unconcernd in the affair and have not probably interest enough with their superiors (to whom all valuable things are carried) to procure the restoration demanded.

15. Some few presents today but no trade at all. We found ourselves today involvd in an unexpected dificulty with regard to the boats: they were loaded with provisions which their owners must live upon or starve, in consequence of which they ask leave to go and take them out and are allowd to do so as much as they can eat. We are not able however to distinguish the true owners, so many avail themselves of this indulgence by stealing their neighbours which we cannot prevent, indeed in a few days more the whole consisting cheifly of fish (curd to keep about that time) will be spoild.

16. Some presents today but no trade. Several petitions for canoes backd by our principal freinds but none complied with. In the afternoon the body of the old woman which lay near us was removd, but to what place or on what account we could not learn.

17. This morn Mr Gore and myself went to Oparre[1] to shoot Ducks,[2] little thinking what the consequence of our expedition would be; for before we had half filld our baggs we had frigh[t]ned away Dootahah and all his household and furniture, a matter of no small diversion to us to find his majesty so much more fearfull than his ducks.

[1] Pare; Banks has merely prefixed O instead of his earlier E, perhaps showing his increasing acquaintance with the language.
[2] It seems probable that these were the common duck of the South Sea islands, the Australian Gray Duck, *Anas superciliosa* Gm.

18. This morn the boat was sent to get Ballast for the ship; the officer sent in her not finding stones convenient began to pull down a burying ground.[1] To this the Indians objected much and [a] messenger came to the tents saying that they would not suffer it. I went with the 2nd Lieutenant to the place. They had desird them to desist from destroying the burying ground they had began upon, but shewd them another. The officer however though[t] it best not to molest any thing of the kind and sent the people to the river where they gatherd stones very Easily without a possibility of offending anybody.

19. The fish in the Canoes stink most immoderately so as in some winds to render our situation in the tents rather disagreable. This evening Oborea, Otheothea and Tuarua[2] came to visit us for the first time since the affair of the Jacket; they were very desirous of sleeping in the fort but my Marque[e] was full of Indians and no one else chose to entertain them, so they were obligd to repair to their Canoes to sleep there rather out of humour.[3]

20. This morn early Oborea and Co came to the tents bringing a large quantity of provisions as a present, among the rest a very fat dog. We had lately learnt that these animals were eat by the Indians and esteemd more delicate food than Pork, now therefore was our oportunity of trying the experiment. He was immediately given over to Tupia who finding that it was a food that we were not acustomd to undertook to stand butcher and cook both. He killd him by stopping his breath, holding his hands fast over his mouth and nose, an operation which took up above a quarter of an hour; he then proceeded to dress him much in the same manner as we

---

[1] A 'burying ground' undoubtedly here means a *marae*. If men serving under Cook could be so almost criminally thoughtless, one can hardly be surprised that the history of race-contacts in the Pacific includes more than one incident of bloodshed.

[2] 'Tuarua' has not previously come into the journal; the name as it stands may be correct.

[3] There seems to have been more behind this brief account than meets the eye. Cook is also brief, expressing surprise that Purea should appear without restoring stolen property, and noting her excuse that 'her gallant' was responsible and that 'she had beat him and turn'd him away'; but Parkinson (p. 32) tells a story which is inherently far from improbable. According to him, two of the girls 'were very assiduous in getting themselves husbands'; Monkhouse the surgeon took one, and one of the lieutenants the other; all went well 'till bed-time, and then they determined to lie in Mr. Banks's tent, which they did accordingly; but one of the engaged coming out, the surgeon insisted that she should not sleep there, and thrust her out, and the rest followed her, except Otea Tea, who whined and cried for a considerable time, till Mr. Banks led her out also. Mr. Monkhouse and Mr. Banks came to an eclaircissement some time after; had very high words, and I expected they would have decided it by a duel, which, however, they prudently avoided'.—Clearly Mr Banks experienced the penalties as well as the delights of popularity. It was very agreeable to have the charming Tiatia in his tent—'my flame'—when she did not whine and cry; but it was difficult when everybody wanted to sleep there.

Pl. V. *Barringtonia speciosa*

Tahiti

would do a pig, singing him over the fire which was lighted to
roast him and scraping him clean with a shell. He then opend him
with the same instrument and taking out his entrails pluck &c.
sent them to the sea where they were most carefully washd, and
then put into Cocoa nut shells with what blood he had found in
him. The stones were now laid and the dog well coverd with leaves
laid upon them. In about two hours he was dressd and in another
quarter of an hour compleatly eat. A most excellent dish he made
for us who were not much prejudicd against any species of food;
I cannot however promise that an European dog would eat as well,
as these scarce in their lives touch animal food, Cocoa nut kernel,
Bread fruit, yams &c, being what their masters can best afford
to give them and what indeed from custom I suppose they preferr
to any kind of food.

21. This Morning came *Oámò*,[1] a cheif we had not before seen;
with him came a boy and a young woman to whoom all the people
present shewd a most uncommon respect, every one taking their
garments from their shoulders and wrapping them round their
breasts. We were upon this very desirous of shewing them all the
respect we could as well as learning who they were: we could not
however prevail upon the woman to come into the tents tho she
seemd very desirous of it, the people all joind in preventing her
by their advice at some times almost using force; the boy was in
the same manner kept without. Dr Solander met him by accident
close by the gate and laying hold of his hand he followd him in
before the people were aware; those in the tents however very soon
sent him out again. Upon inquiry we find that this boy is son to
Oamo and Oborea who are husband and wife, but have long ago
been parted by a mutual consent which gives both leave to enjoy
the pleasures of this life without controul from their former engage-
ments. The girl about 16 is intended for his wife but he being not
more than 8 years old they have not yet cohabited together.[2]

22. Our visiters returnd early this morn, Oborea, Otheothea,

[1] Amo.
[2] This was the famous appearance of Temarii or Teriirere, the *arii rahi* or *arii nui*
of Teva-i-uta, who had his great *marae* in the Papara district. His person was sacred,
hence the removal of the upper garments. The young woman was Te arii na vaho roa,
the sister of Tu of Pare. Both being of such exalted rank, their presence in the tents would
under Tahitian custom have made them *tapu*, and hence unusable by commoners.
Cook notes that Teriirere was carried on a man's back—which was again due to his
sacredness, lest his feet should render the ground he trod on *tapu*. Cook thought the
boy was about 7 and the young woman 18 or 20 and that she was his sister, but this last
assumption was a natural consequence of the Tahitian language. She was duly married
to Teriirere, but died childless.

V

Oamo &c. &c. The latter begins to shew himself a very sensible man by the shrewd questions he asks about England its manners and customs &c. Much interest is made to procure the release of the boats, indeed Cap^tn Cooke is now tird of keeping them as he finds that not the least motion is made towards returning any of the stol'n goods; four of them are therefore set at liberty.

23. Our Freinds with us as usual. One of our seamen a Portugese[1] was last night missing; as there was no news of him this Morning we concluded that he was run away and meant to stay among the Indians. Cap^tn Cooke therefore offerd a hatchet to any man who would bring him back, one soon offerd and returnd with him at night. He said that two Indians seizd him and stopping his mouth forcd him away, but as he was out of the fort after a woman this account apeard improbable, the man was however not punishd.

24. Our freinds all went to the westward last night; nothing material happend during our solitude. The market has been totaly stoppd ever since the boats were seizd, nothing being offerd to sale but a few apples; our freinds however are liberal in presents so that we make a shift to live without expending our bread, which and spirits are the most valuable articles to us. Late in the evening Tubourai and Tamio returnd from Eparre bringing with them several presents, among the rest a large peice of thick cloth[2] which they desird that I would carry home to my Sister *Opia*,[3] and for which they would take no kind of return. They are often very inquisitive about our families and remember any thing that is told them very well.

Tapa

25. Prayers today it being sunday, soon after *Potattow* and *Polotheara*[4] came to see us.

26. At 3 O'clock this morn Cap^tn Cooke and myself set out to the

---

[1] Emanuel Pereira, who volunteered into the ship at Rio.

[2] This was evidently *tapa* of the very best quality, such as was appropriated to chiefly wear.

[3] Sophia.

[4] Potatau, an Atehuru *arii*, and Poro-tahiara. Corney, III, p. 266 gives her name as Purutifara. They have not been previously mentioned, though they appear to have been prominent people, who made their presence felt both at this time and later. George Forster, on Cook's second voyage, picked up a curious story which does not appear elsewhere: 'Polatehera, his [Potatow's] former wife, was so like him in stature and bulk, that we unanimously looked upon her as the most extraordinary woman we had ever seen. Her appearance and her conduct were masculine in the highest degree, and strongly conveyed the idea of superiority and command. When the Endeavour bark lay here, she had distinguished herself by the name of captain Cook's sister, (*tuaheine no* Toote;) and one day, being denied admittance into the fort on Point Venus, had knocked down the sentry who opposed her, and complained to her adopted brother of the indignity which had been offered to her'.—*Voyage round the World* (1777), I, p. 361. It is odd that the story is not otherwise known, but it is not impossibly true.

eastward in the pinnace, intending if it was convenient to go round
the Island, the weather calm and pleasant. We rowd till 8 and
then went ashore in a district calld *Ohiânâ*[1] governd by a cheif
calld *Ahiô*,[2] who favour us with his company to breakfast. Here
we saw our old acquaintances *Titùbôâlô*[3] and *Hoona*,[4] who carried
me immediately to their House near which was placd the body
of the old woman which was removd from Matavie on the 16th.
This it seems was the estate which descended to Hoona by inheritance from her and it was on that account nescessary that she
should be brought here. From hence we proceeded on foot, the
boat atending within call, till we came to *Ahidea*[5] the place where
the Spanyards were said to lay. We met with the cheif their freind
Oréttė, whose brother *Outorrou* went with them. Our inquiries here
were very particular and we had the account I have before given
confirmd; they shewd us also the place where the ships lay, which
is situate on the west side of the great bay under the shelter of a
small Island calld *Boooúrou*[6] near which is another calld *Taawirry*.[7]
The breach in the reef was here very large but the shelter for ships
indifferent. We saw also the place where their tents were pitchd:
they pointed out the hole in which each pole stood and shewd one
corner in which they set up a cross I had made for them, and said
Turu turu which in their language signifies the knees.[8] In searching
about upon this spot I found a small peice of potsheard or tile,
a sure proof tho a small one that in place at least the indians had
not deceivd me.

Soon after this we took boat and askd Tituboaro to go with us.
He refusd and advisd us not to go: on the other side of the bay
he said livd people who were not subjects to Dootahah and who
would kill him and us.[9] On seeing us put balls into our musquets

[1] Haapaianoo, which Banks had before reached on his walk with Solander on 24 April.
[2] ?Ahaio.
[3] ?Te aitu-poaro.
[4] This, it will be remembered, was the young woman who was Banks's fellow 'nineveh'
on 10 June.
[5] Haitaa, or Hitiaa. One is not always finally certain what sounds Banks's vowels
are intended to carry. Cf. p. 274, n. 2 above.
[6] Puaru or Puuru.
[7] Taaupiri.
[8] *Turi* is the word for knee. *Turu* or *turuturu* means side-posts of a house, and the late
Mr J. Frank Stimson suggested that the word may have once by metaphor signified the
two knees as well; or the shape of the cross may simply have reminded the Tahitians of
side-posts. Or if *turi* was the word they used, possibly they simply meant that the
'Spaniards' had fallen on their knees before a cross similar to the one Banks made.
[9] It is difficult to know what is meant by this. The other side of the bay was the northern
coast of Taiarapu, and its people were certainly not subject to Tuteha (nor were the
people of Hitiaa); but we have no record of enmity at this time. Indeed Tuteha and the
high chief of Taiarapu had recently been allies against Purea and Amo. Certainly a
few years later, 1772-3, Tuteha attacked Taiarapu, with disaster to himself.

he however consented to go with us. We rowd till dark at which
time we arrivd at the bottom of the deep bay; we were not yet
among our enemies, we might go ashore and sleep with safety.
We did so but found few houses, here were however some double
canoes whose owners were known to us; they provided us with
supper and lodgins, for my share of which I was indebted to
Ourattooa a Lady remarkable among us for the ceremonies she
performd on the 12th of May last.

27. At day break we turnd out to see a little of the countrey about
us which we did not arrive at last night till dark. We found the
traces of Canoes having been hauld inland and the people told
us that the Island was in this place very narrow and that they
draggd their canoes quite across cheifly over soft boggs.[1]—We now
prepard to set out for the other Kingdom for so we are told it is,
Calld *Tiarreboo* and governd by *Waheatua*,[2] as ours is called *Oboreonoo*
and governd by *Dootahah*.[3] Tituboalo is in better spirits now than
yesterday, they will not kill us he says but they have got no meat.
Indeed we had not since we came out seen a bit of breadfruit;
we thought that we might have exhausted it in this part of the
Island but hop'd to find plenty in the other, the people of which if
enemies had certainly not traded with us. After a few miles rowing
we landed in a District calld *Anniúhé*,[4] the Name of the cheif of
which was *Màràitátá*[5] (the burying place of men) and his father
Pàhàirèdò[6] (the stealer of boats) names which did not a little confirm
Tituboalos relation. These gentlemen however notwithstanding
their terrible titles receivd us with all manner of civility, gave us
provisions and after some delay sold us a very large hog for a
hatchet. We saw among the crowd only two people whose faces
we knew and not one bead or ornament which came out of our
ship, tho there were several European ones; in one of the houses
lay 2 12 pound shot one of which was markd with the English
broad arrow, these they said had been given them by *Toottero*
the Spanish commander.—We now walkd forward on foot till

---

[1] This was the isthmus of Taravao, about 1½ miles across.

[2] Taiarapu or Tahiti-iti (Little Tahiti), as a political division called Teva-i-tai or
Seaward Teva; its high chief bore the traditional title of Vehiatua.

[3] Oboreonoo=Porionuu or Te Porionuu; Cook and Banks, having picked up the
name in the country close to Matavai Bay, gave it a far wider significance than it really
had, applying it to the whole of Tahiti-nui, or Great Tahiti. But it included only the
two small districts of Pare and Arue, and did not even extend to Matavai Bay. Nor
was it all governed by Tuteha, whose importance came from his personality and not
his rank, nor by any other one man.

[4] Anuhi, the name then used for the present Pueu.

[5] Maraetaata; burial place was not necessarily the main significance of *marae* here.

[6] ?Pahi-riro; *pahi*, a canoe, *riro*, lost or missing.

we came to the district which particularly belongd to Waheatua,
it was situate on the westernmost point of the large bay before
mentiond, a large and most fertile flat.¹ On it was a river so large
that we were obligd to ferry over in a canoe² and our Indian train
to swim, which they did with as much facility as a pack of hounds
taking the water much in the same manner. Here were no houses but
ruind remains of very large ones. We proceeded along shore and
found at last Waheatua setting near some pretty Canoe awnings
which seemd to be intended to furnish him with lodgins, he was a
thin old man with very white hair and beard; with him was a well
looking woman of about 25 year old whose name was *Toudidde*,³
we had heard her name mentiond very often and by what the
people told she was a woman of much consequence in this part
of the Island, answering in some measure to what Oborea is in the
other. From this place *Tearre*⁴ son to Waheatua acompanied us
after having sold us a hog. The countrey we went through was more
cultivated than any thing we have seen in the Island; the brooks
were every where bankd into narrow channels with stone and the
very sea was confind by a wall of stone also. The houses were not
very large or very numerous but the large canoes which were hauld
up every where along shore almost innumerable; they were of a
different built from those which we have seen at Oboreonoo,
longer and their heads and sterns higher. Upon these were kind
of crotches which we suppos'd were to support large images many
of which we saw hanging up in their houses; their awnings also
were supported on pillars. At almost every point was a *morai* or
burying place and many within land. They were like those of
Oboreonoo raisd into the form of the roof of a house, but these
were cleaner and better kept and also ornamented with many
carvd boards set upright, on the tops of which were various figures of
birds and men; on one particularly a figure of a cock painted red
and yellow in imitation of the feathers of that bird. In some of them
were figures of men standing on each others heads which they
told me was the particular ornament of Burying grounds.⁵—But

¹ This is the peninsula of Tautira (then called Fatutira) where Vehiatua had his
residence; 'westernmost' is an obvious slip for 'easternmost'.
² The Vaitepiha river.
³ Tautiti. Cf. Corney, *Quest and Occupation of Tahiti*, II, pp. xxiv-xxv.
⁴ i.e. *Te arii*, the chief; Banks spells the name *Tearee* below, which looks like *Terii*,
short for *Te arii* (cf. Teriirere, the son of Purea and Amo). His more personal name was
Taata-uraura.
⁵ In this description of the *marae* Banks describes a part as the whole. It was the *ahu*,
the principal feature of the *marae*, a stone platform at the end of the *marae* court, that was
'raisd into the form of the roof of a house'. The 'carvd boards set upright' were called
unu; they were erected in honour of departed chiefs whose bones were deposited at the

fertile as this countrey was we did no[t] get or even see a single
breadfruit, the trees were intirely bared, the people seemd to live
intirely on *Ahee Fagifera*[1] which were plentifull here.

After tiring ourselves with walking we calld up the boat but
both our Indians were missing, they had it seems staid behind at
Waheatuas, depending upon a promise we had made to the old
man of returning and sleeping with him (a promise we were often
forcd to make without any intention of performing it). Tearee
and another went with us. We rowd till we came abreast a small
Island calld *Tuarrite*[2] when it became dark and our Indians piloted
us ashore to a place where they said that we might sleep; it was a
deserted house and near it was a very snug cove for the boat to
lay, so we wanted nothing but Victuals of which article we had met
with very little since morning. I went into the woods, it was quite
dark so that neither people nor victuals could I find except one
house where I was furnishd with fire, a breadfruit and a half and
a few *ahees*, with which and a duck[3] or 2 and a few curlews[4] we
were forcd to go to sleep, which I did in the awning of a Canoe
that followd us belonging to Tearee.

28. This morn at day break we rose and agreed to stay here an
hour or two in hopes to get some provision: salt beef we had with us
but nothing of the bread kind, for that we depended on the natives
who had on all former occasions been both able and willing to supply
us with any quantity of Breadfruit. I went out meaning to go among
the houses; in my way I went through several burying grounds
(*Marai*) on the pavements of which I saw several vertebræ and
sculls of men laying about as if no care was taken to bury them,
in every thing else they were quite like what we had seen before.
In my excursion I could not procure the least supply of provision
so we were forcd to set out in hopes of meeting some countrey
where provision was less scarce. We walkd and the boat followd

marae. The figures of men, carved in flat relief, were called *tii*; they were symbolical and
not representational, and in no sense 'idols'. Birds were believed to be 'shadows', or
symbols, or temporary dwelling-places, of the gods. What Banks took to be a cock was
perhaps the *manu ura* or sacred bird; red and yellow were sacred colours (cf. the *maro-ura*
and *maro-tea*, the sacred red and yellow feather girdles with which *arii rahi* were invested);
but it may also possibly have been a cock, sacred to Ruaifaatoa, a god of warriors and
strength whose diversion was cock-fighting.

[1] *ihi*, the fruit of the *mape* or Tahitian chestnut (*Inocarpus edulis*). 'Fagifera' is added in
pencil in a blank left for the purpose.

[2] Cook spells this name on his chart Otooareite. It is probably the islet now called
Tiere, one of a cluster of three; its former name was Tiare-iti, and from the spellings
given perhaps also Tuarae-iti.

[3] Probably *Anas superciliosa* Gm., the Australian Gray Duck.

[4] Probably the Bristle-thighed Curlew, *Numenius tahitiensis* (Gm.). Non-breeding birds of
this species sometimes winter in Polynesia.

us. In about 3 miles we arrivd at a place where were several large
canoes and a number of people with them; we were not a little
surprizd to find that these people were our intimate acquaintance,
several at least, who we had often seen at the tents and other places,
Tòwià[1] who we were told was brother to *Towdidde*, *Ròudèrò*[2] &c.
Here we thought ourselves sure o getting a supply of provisions
and apply'd to our freinds accordingly. They told us we should
have some if we would wait, we did till we were out of patience;
we then desird them to get us some cocoa nuts the kernels of which
make a substitute for bread, they said yes but nobody went up the
trees. We were resolvd to [have] them at least so calling for a hatchet
we threatned to cut down the trees if our demands were not complied with; nobody objected to our doing so if we chose it, nor
did any body atempt to climb the trees to supply us. Just now
however we luckily saw two men busy in stripping a parcel o them,
these we obligd to sell their stock consisting of 16, with these we
embarkd taking with us *Tùàhów*[3] one of our Indians who had
returnd to us last night long after dark. When we in the boat
talkd over this behaviour of our freinds we were inclind to beleive
that they were strangers here, and consequently had not the disposal
of the provisions; indeed we never had before met with any dificulty
in getting from them any provisions of which they had enough.

The reef here was irregular and the ground very foul so that
the boat was continualy surroundd with breakers. We followd
a canoe which led us to a passage where by waiting for a slatch[4]
of still water we got out, tho not without danger, for the sea broke
quite across almost as soon as the boat was clear. We were now off
the SW end of the Island. The land apeard very barren, no ree
to shelter the coast and the hills every where butting out to the sea
without any flatts;[5] here were however some houses and inhabitants,
and on ledges of the hills here and there a little breadfruit and
higher up large quantities o *Fàé*.[6] This lasted for about a League
when we again saw the ree and a flat on which we went ashore by
the recomendation of our Indian guide, who told us that the
countrey was rich and good. The name of this district or whennua[7]
was *Ahowe*:[8] the cheif *Màthìàbò*[9] soon came down to us, he seemd

---

[1] ?Tohaia.   [2] Roudero *sic*.   [3] Tuahou or Tuahau.
[4] A nautical term for a brief spell or interval.   [5] This was Pari (*pari*=the cliffs).
[6] Fei, mountain plantains.
[7] *fenua*.
[8] Ahui, the old name for a sub-district called Vai-ao-tea, now included in the district
of Teahupoo. It is not to be confused with another sub-district of the same name on the
northern coast of Tahiti-iti.
[9] Matahiapo—i.e. the 'first-born' of a great *arii* family.

a total stranger both to us and our trade. His subjects brought down plenty of Cocoa nuts and about 20 breadfruits, which latter we bought at a very dear rate, while his majesty sold us a pig for a glass bottle preferring that to any thing we could give him. We saw here an English goose and a turkey cock which they told us had been left by the Dolphin, both of them immensely fat and as tame as possible, following the Indians every where who seemd immensely fond of them.[1] In a long house in this neighbourhood I saw a sight quite new to me: 15 underjaw bones of men were fastned to a semicircular peice of board and hung up at one end of it, they appeard quite fresh, not one at all damagd even by the Loss of a tooth. I askd many questions about them but the people would not attend at all to me and either did not or would not understand either words or signs upon that subject.[2] On our departure from hence Mathiabo desird leave to acompany us which was granted, he provd a good pilot but persuaded us to land often, 5 or 6 times in as many miles. In all these districts we saw nothing remarkable; the general face of the countrey was greener than on our side of the Island and the hills were coverd with wood almost down to the waters edge, the flats in general small but fertile enough. At last we opend a large bay, which being opposite to as large a one on the other side almost intersects the Island at the place over which they drag their canoes; about 2 thirds down this bay we resolvd to lodge at a large house which we saw and which Mathiabo informd us belongd to a freind of his. From this place many Canoes came off to meet us and in them some very hansome women who by their behaviour seemd to be sent out to entice us to come ashore, which we most readily did, and were receivd in a very freindly manner by *Wiverou*[3] who was cheif of the district which was calld *Owiourou*.[4] He orderd his people to assist us in dressing our provisions, of which we had now got a tolerable stock about 30 breadfruit some plantains and fish, enough to last us two days. I stuck close to the women hoping to get a snug lodging by that means as I had often done; they were very kind, too much so for they promisd more than I ask'd, but when they saw that we were resolvd to stay they dropd off one by one and at last left me jilted 5 or 6 times and obligd to seek out for a

[1] These were trophies of war; they had come from Matavai Bay to Papara, and been snatched away with other trophies when Amo and Purea were defeated.
[2] These were also trophies of war; they were the jawbones of the Papara men.
[3] Corney, *Discovery of Tahiti*, III, Descriptive Index, gives his name as Tuivirau or Tuivivirau—which last he says is incorrect; but it tallies better with the name picked up by Banks and Cook.
[4] Vaiuru, the old name for the district of Vairaao.

lodging myself. Supper was by this time ready and we repaird
to that part of the house where Wiverou was to eat it; he sent for
his at the same time and Mathiabo supping with us we made a
snug party. As soon as we had done we began to think of sleeping
and askd for a bed. We were shown a part of the house where we
might lay; we then sent for our cloaks and began to prepare
ourselves, myself as my constant custom was by stripping myself
and sending my cloaths into the boat, covering myself only with a
peice of Indian cloth after their fashion which I have done ever
ever since I had my Jacket &c. stolen at Atahourou. Mathiabo
complaind of cold and a cloak was sent for for him also, Cap^{tn}
Cooke and myself agreed that he had behavd so well to us that
there was not the least doubt of his honesty. We laid down, Mathiabo
did not come, I imagin'd that he was gone to wash as the Indians
always do in the evening. I was almost asleep when an Indian who
was a stranger to me came and told me that he was gone off with the
Cloak, I did not beleive him but laid down again. Tuahow our
Indian then came and confirmd the report; I then found it was high
time to give chase so I leapd up and declard my case to the company,
shewing one of my pocket pistols which I always kept with me. They
took the alarm and began to walk of, I seizd however the best
looking man I could see and told him that if he did not find out where
Mathiabo was I would shoot him in his stead. The threat had the
desird effect: he offerd to accompany me in the chase: the Cap^{tn}
myself and him set out as hard as we could run and in about ten
minutes met a man bringing back the cloak; but our freind Mathiabo
was fled and by that means escapd a severe thrashing which we had
decreed to be a proper reward for his breach of trust. When we
returnd every body was gone from the house; we quickly however
made them sensible that our anger was intirely confind to Mathiabo
and they all returnd, Wiverou and his wife taking up their lodging
within 10 feet of us.

29. About 5 O'Clock our sentry awakd us with the alarming
intelligence of the boat being missing, he had he said seen her
about $\frac{1}{2}$ an hour before at her grapling which was about 50 yards
from the shore, but that on hearing the noise of Oars he lookd
out again and could see nothing of her. We started up and made
all possible haste to the waterside, the morn was fine and starlight
but no boat in sight. Our situation was now sufficiently disagreable:
the Indians had probably attackd her first and finding the people
asleep easily carried her, in which case they would not fail to attack

us very soon, who were 4 in number armd with one musquet and cartouch box and two pocket pistols without a spare ball or charge of powder for them. In about a quarter of an hour however we had the satisfaction to see the boat return, which had drove from her grapling by some effect of the tide probably as it was perfectly calm.

As soon as the boat returnd we got our breakfast and set out. The first district on which we landed was the last in Tiarreboo, it was governd by *Omóê*.[1] He was employd in building a house for which purpose he wanted a hatchet very much and was inclind to offer any price for it but our stock was quite spent; after some conversation we found that he would not deal for nails and put off the boat. He and his wife *Whánnóoudá*[2] followd in a canoe; we took them into the boat and after rowing about a league they desird we would put ashore, which we did and found his people who had brought a very large hog. We had much chafering about the price of it, it was worth any ax we had in the ship but we had no ax at all in the boat. We therefore told Omoe that if he would come to Matavie with his hog he should have a large ax and a nail into the bargain for his trouble; which he after having consulted his wife readily agreed to, and gave us a large peice of cloth as a pledge of his intention to perform this agreement.

At this place we saw a singular curiosity, a figure of a man made of Basket work, roughly but not ill designd; it was 7 feet high and two bulky in proportion to its hight; the whole was neatly coverd with feathers, white to represent skin and black to represent hair and *tattow*;[3] on the head were three protuberances which we should have calld horns but the Indians calld them *tata ete*,[4] little men. The image was calld by them *Máúwé*; they said it was the only one of the kind in Otahite and readily atempted to explain its use, but their language was totaly unintelligible and seemed to referr to some customs to which we are perfect strangers.[5]—After this we got into the boat and rowd several miles before we went ashore. When we did we saw nothing remarkable but a burying ground whose pavement was unusualy neat; it was ornamented by a pyramid about 5 feet high coverd intirely with the fruits of

---

[1] Moe. Cook writes Omae.
[2] ?Fanau-tua (cf. p. 328, n. 2 below).
[3] *tatau*, the tattooing of the skin.　　　[4] *taata iti*.
[5] This is rather mysterious. The image apparently represented the great Polynesian culture-hero Maui; but I do not know of any other reference to it, besides that in Cook on this same occasion, nor what the three *taata iti*—'little men'—were. Cook writes (pp. 111-12) that it was 'said by the Natives to be used in their Heiva's or publick entertainments, probably as punch is in a Puppet Show'; he says there were 'four nobs resembling stumps of horns', three in front and one behind. This was at what Cook calls 'the first Whennua in *Opooreonoo*'—Vaiari, now Papeari.

Pandanus [*tectorius*] and *Cratæva* [*gynandra*].[1] In the middle of all near the Pyramid was a small image of stone very roughly workd, the first instance of carving in stone I have seen among these people, and this they seemd to value as it was coverd from the weather with a kind of shed built purposely over it; near it were three sculls of men laid in order, very white and clean and quite perfect. From hence we proceeded to *Pápárrá*,[2] the district of our freinds Oamo and Oborea, where we proposd to sleep tonight; we came there an hour before night and found that they were both from home, they were gone to Matavie to see us. This did not alter our resolution of sleeping here and we chose for that purpose the house of Oborea, which tho small was very neat and had nobody in it but her father who was very civil to us. After having setled our matters we took a walk towards a point on which we had from far observd trees of Etoa,[3] *Casuarina equisetifolia*, from whence we judgd that thereabouts would be some *marai*; nor were we disapointed for we no sooner arrivd there than we were struck with the sight of a most enormous pile, certainly the masterpeice of Indian architecture in this Island so all the inhabitants allowd. Its size and workmanship almost exceeds beleif, I shall set it down exactly. Its form was like that of *Marais* in general, resembling the roof of a house, not smooth at the sides but formd into 11 steps, each of these 4 feet in hight making in all 44 feet, its lengh 267 its breadth 71. Every one of these steps were formd of one course of white coral stones most neatly squard and polishd, the rest were round pebbles, but these seemd to have been workd from their uniformity of size and roundness. Some of the coral stones were very large, one I measurd was $3\frac{1}{2}$ by $2\frac{1}{2}$ feet. The foundation was of Rock stones likewise squard, one of these corner stone[s] measurd $4^{ft}:7^{in}$ by $2^{ft}:4^{in}$. The whole made a part of one side of a spatious area which was walld in with stone, the size of this which seemd to be intended for a square was 118 by 110 paces, which was intirely pavd with flat paving stones. It is almost beyond beleif that Indians could raise so large a structure without the assistance of Iron tools to shape their stones

---

[1] The two names in square brackets have been added in pencil, to supply blanks in the text, apparently in the hand of Robert Brown, the eminent botanist and Banks's later librarian. Hooker altered the former to *Pandanus odorus*, without indicating in any way what he had done. This is only one of many instances of 'mutilation' perpetrated by Hooker (cf. Warren Dawson, *Jour. Soc. Bibliog. Nat. Hist.* 2 : 218-22). No *Crataeva* coll. has been located but Parkinson's coloured drawing of 'Crataeva frondosa mscr.' dated 1769 and Solander's usual full description are preserved. Britten identifies this as *C. uliginosa* L. It is *C. religiosa* Forst. f. See Pl. 29.

[2] Papara.

[3] Toa or Aito, ironwood, *Casuarina equisetifolia*. The scientific name has not changed. As Banks had noticed, it was a characteristic tree about *marae*.

or mortar to join them, which last appears almost essential as the most of them are round; it is done tho, and almost a⁵ firmly as a European workman would have done it, tho in some things it seems to have faild. The steps for instance which range along its greatest lengh are not streight, they bend downward in the middle forming a small Segment of a circle: possibly the ground may have sunk a little under the greatest weight of such an immense pile, which if it happend regularly would have this effect. The labour of the work is prodigious: the quarry stones are but few but they must have been brought by hand from some distance at least, as we saw no signs of quarry near it tho I lookd carefully about me; the coral must have been fishd from under water, where indeed it is most plentifull but generaly coverd with 3 or 4 feet water at least and oftenest with much more. The labour of forming them when got must also have been at least as great as the getting them; they have not shewn us any way by which they could square a stone but by means of another, which must be most tedious and liable to many accidents by the breaking of tools. The stones are also polishd and as well and truly as stones of the kind could be by the best workman in Europe, in that particular they excell owing to the great plenty of a sharp coral sand which is admirably adapted to that purpose and is found everywhere upon the seashore in this neighbourhood.[1] About 100 yards to the west of this building was another court or pavd area[2] in which were several *ewhattas*,[3] a kind of altars raisd on wooden pillars about 7 feet high, on these they offer meat of all kinds to the gods; we have seen large Hogs offerd and here were the Sculls of above 50 of them besides those of dogs, which the preist who accompanied us assurd us were only a small part of what had been here sacrafisd. This *marai* and aparatus for sacrafice belongd we were told to Oborea and Oamo. The greatest pride of an inhabitant of Otahite is to have a grand *Marai*, in this particular our freinds far exceed any one in the Island, and in the Dolphins time the first of them exceeded every one else in riches

---

[1] Thus Banks describes the great *marae* called *Mahaiatea*, built 1766-8, the greatest work of architecture in all the islands, the symbol of Purea's pride and of her pride in her son. Banks's measurements differ in some details from Cook's: Cook over-estimates the size of the enclosure. The squared 'Rock stones' of the foundation were volcanic. The remains of the *ahu*, that great edifice, once about 45 or 50 feet high, can still be seen at Mahaiatea, a melancholy witness to the passage of time and the destructive stupidity of man. The early accounts have been collated, and careful diagrams drawn, by Kenneth P. Emory, in his *Stone Remains in the Society Islands* (Bernice P. Bishop Mus. Bull. 116, Honolulu 1933) pp. 30, 72-4.

[2] This was the ancient *marae* of Tetooarai.

[3] *e fata*, an altar. These are described by Emory, op. cit., p. 15, as 'small tables (*fata* 'ai 'ai) set up on the court', for sacrificial offerings of food.

and respect as much. The reason of the difference of her present apearance from that I found by an accident which I now relate: in going too and coming home from the *Marai* our road lay by the the sea side, and every where under our feet were numberless human bones cheifly ribbs and vertebræ. So singular a sight surprizd me much; I enquird the reason and was told that in the month calld by them *Owiráhêw*[1] last, which answers to our December 1768, the people of Tiarreboo made a descent here and killd a large number of people whose bones we now saw; that upon this Occasion Oborea and Oamo were obligd to fly for shelter to the mountains, that the Conquerors burnt all the houses which were very large and took away all the hoggs &c., that the turkey and goose which we had seen with Mathiabo were part of the spoils, as were the jaw bones which we saw hung up in his house; they had been carried away as trophies and are usd by the Indians here in exactly the same manner as the North Americans do scalps.

30. After having slept last night without the least interuption we proceeded forwards but during the whole day saw little or nothing worth observation. We bought a little bread fruit which article has been equaly scarce all round the Island, more so even than it is at Matavie. At night we came to Atahourou, the very place at which we were on the 28th of May: here we were among our intimate freinds, who expressd the pleasure they had in entertaining us by giving us a good supper and good beds, in which we slept the better for being sure of reaching Matavie tomorrow night at the farthest. Here we learnd that the bread fruit (a little of which we saw just sprouting upon the trees) would not be fit to use in less than 3 months.

JULY 1769

1. Proceed homewards without meeting any thing new, the countrey we pass'd by and over being the same as we had gone over on the 28th of last month. The day turnd out rainy and bad, the only bad weather we have had since we left the ship, in which instance we are certainly fortunate as we had neither of us a change of Cloaths with us, so little did either of us expect to go round the Island when we set out from Matavie.

2. All our freinds crouded this morn to See us and tell us that they were rejoicd at our return, nor were they empty handed,

---

[1] *Varehu*, the lunar month December-January. Banks seems first to have written 'Owo-' and altered it to 'Owi-'.

most of them brought something or other. The Canoes were still in the river: Cap[tn] Cooke finding that there was no likelihood now of any of the stolen goods being restord resolvd to let them go as soon as he could. His freind Potattow sollicited for one which was immediately [granted?] as it was imagind the favour was askd for some of his freinds, but no sooner did he begin to move the boat than the real owners and a number of Indians opposd him, telling him and his people very clamorously that it did not belong to them. He answerd that he had bought it of the Cap[tn] and given a pig for it. The people were by this declaration satisfied and had we not luckily overheard it he would have taken away this and probably soon after have sollicited for more. On being detected he became so sulky and ashamd that for the rest of the day neither he or his wife would open their mouths or look streight at any of us.

3. This morn very early M[r] Monkhouse[1] and myself set out, resolving to follow the cour[s]e of the valley down which our river comes[2] in order to see how far up it was inhabited &c. &c. When we had got about 2 miles up it we met several of our neighbours coming down with loads of breadfruit upon their backs. We had often wonderd from whence the small supplys of breadfruit we had came, as there was none to be seen upon the flats, but they soon explaind the mystery, shewing us breadfruit trees planted on the sides of the hills and telling us at the same time that when the fruit in the flats faild this became ready for use, which had been by them planted upon the hills to preserve the succession. The quantity was they informd us much less than was in the low land and not sufficient by any means to supply all the interval of scarcity; when this was exhausted they must live upon *ahee* nuts, Plantains, and *Vae*,[3] a wild plantain which grows very high up in the mountains. How the Dolphins who were here much about this time came to find so great plenty of Breadfruit upon the trees is to me a mystery, unless perhaps the seasons of this fruit alter;[4] as for their having met with a much larger supply of hoggs fowls &c. than we have done I

---

[1] If this was the surgeon, presumably Banks and he were reconciled after their 'eclaircissement' and high words of 19 June. It may have been Jonathan Monkhouse the midshipman.

[2] The Vaipopoo river flows down the Tuauru valley.

[3] The Fei was a different sort from the lowland plantain or Meia. But perhaps Banks refers here to the mountain banana with erect spikes, *Musa troglodytarum* (cf. Merrill, p. 343.)

[4] The breadfruit has three crops, in March-April (the largest), late July, and November; but different varieties of trees fruit at different times. It must be remembered that the *Dolphin* made a shorter stay than the *Endeavour*, and did not cause the same strain on food-supplies.

can most readily account for that, as we have found by constant experience that these people may be frightned into any thing. They have often describd to us the terrour which the Dolphins guns put them into and when we ask how many people were killd they number names upon their fingers, some ten some twenty some thirty, and then say *worrow worow*[1] the same word as is usd for a flock of birds or a shoal of fish; the Journals[2] also serve to confirm this opinion. 'When' say they 'towards the latter end of our time provisions were scarce a party of men were sent towards Eparre to get hoggs &c. an office which they had not the smallest dificulty in performing, for the people as they went along the shore drove out their hoggs to meet them and would not allow them to pay any thing for them.'

We proceeded about 4 miles farther and had houses pretty plentifully on each side the river, the vally being all this way 3 or 400 yards across. We were now shewn a house which we were told would be the last we should see, the master offerd us Cocoa nutts and we refreshd ourselves. Beyond this we went maybe 6 miles (it is dificult to guess distances when roads are bad as this was, we being generaly obligd to travel along the course of the river) we passd by several hollow places under stones where they told us that people who were benighted slept. At lengh we arrivd at a place where the river was bankd on each side with steep rocks, and a caskade which fell from them made a pool so deep that the Indians said we could not go beyond it, they never did, their business lay upon the rocks on each side on the plains above which grew plenty of *Vae*. The avenues to these were truly dreadfull, the rocks were nearly perpendicular, one near 100 feet in hight, the face of it constantly wet and slippery with the water of numberless springs; directly up the face even of this was a road, or rather a succession of long peices of the bark of *Hibiscus tiliaceus*[3] which servd them as a rope to take hold of and scramble up from ledge to ledge, tho upon those very ledges none but a goat or an Indian could have stood. One of these ropes was near 30 feet in lengh.[4] Our

---

[1] No such word was used for a flock of birds or a shoal of fish in the early nineteenth century, when John Davies was compiling his dictionary—at least collectively. Banks was probably rendering *ua rau, ua rau,* 'hundreds and hundreds'.

[2] i.e. the journals of the *Dolphin*'s officers.

[3] This hibiscus, Tahitian Fau, is widespread through Polynesia, and often called Purau; its bark has a strong bast fibre.

[4] It seems to be on this experience that Banks bases a draft passage in Grey MS 48, which he does not later use: 'The surface of the Island is very uneven near the shore in most but not all places are flats of different breadths never exceeding a mile & half here much the largest part of their fruits &c grow and all the natives live except a few who are up valleys where rivers are from these the ridges run up into mountains high

guides offerd to help us up this pass but rather recomended one lower down a few hundred yards which was much less dangerous, tho we did not chuse to venture, as the sight which was to reward our hazard was nothing but a grove of *Vae* trees which we had often seen before.

In the whole course of this walk the rocks were almost constantly bare to the view, so that I had a most excellent opportunity of searching for any apearance of minerals but saw not the smallest. The stones every where shewd manifest signs of having been at some time or other burnd; indeed I have not seen a specimen of stone yet in the Island that has not the visible marks of fire upon it, small peices indeed of the hatchet stone may be without them but I have peices of the same species burnd almost to a pumice, the very clay upon the hills gives manifest signs of fire. Possibly the Island owes its original to a volcano which now no longer burns;[1] or Theoreticaly speaking, for the sake of those authors who balance this globe by a proper weight of continent placed near about these latitudes, that so nesscessary continent may have been sunk by Dreadfull earthquakes and Volcanos 2 or 300 fathoms under the sea, the tops of the highest mountains only still remain[in]g above water in the shape of Islands: an undoubted proof that such a thing now exists to the great emolument of their theory, which was it not for this proof would have been already totaly demolishd by the Course our ship made from Cape Horn to this Island.

4. Very little company today. I employd myself in planting a large quantity of the seeds of Water melons, Oranges, Lemons, limes &c. which I had brought from Rio de Janeiro; they were planted on both sides of the fort in as many varieties of soil as I could chuse.[2] I have very little Doubt of the former especialy coming to perfection as I have given away large quantities among the natives and planted also in the woods; they now continualy ask me for seeds and have already shewd me melon plants of their raising which look perfectly well. The seeds that Capt^tn Cooke sewd have provd so bad that no one has come up except mustard, even the Cucumbers and melons have faild, owing probably to the

enough to be seen at 20 leagues distant which produce several kinds of fruits of [which] the natives make use particularly Wild plantains Whei [?] for which as well as birds they climb almost inaccessible rocks & have paths up them with ropes tied by which they climb'.

[1] Banks's suggestion here is quite valid: Tahiti, like the other 'high islands' near it, is volcanic in origin.

[2] A significant statement in light of the subsequent spread (and interpretation of origins) of Polynesian cultivars and weeds (cf. Merrill. *The Botany of Cook's Voyages*, Waltham, Mass., 1954, p. 216).

Pl. VI. *Spondias dulcis* Vi or Vi-apple

Tahiti

method of their being packd which was in small bottles seald down with rosin.

5. This morn I saw the operation of *Tattowing* the buttocks performd upon a girl of about 12 years old, it provd as I have always suspected a most painfull one. It was done with a large instrument about 2 inches long containing about 30 teeth,[1] every stroke of this hundreds of which were made in a minute drew blood. The patient bore this for about ¼ of an hour with most stoical resolution; by that time however the pain began to operate too stron[g]ly to be peacably endurd, she began to complain and soon burst out into loud lamentations and would fain have persuaded the operator to cease; she was however held down by two women who sometimes scolded, sometimes beat, and at others coaxd her. I was setting in the adjacent house with Tomio for an hour, all which time it lasted and was not finishd when I went away tho very near. This was one side only of her buttocks for the other had been done some time before. The arches upon the loins upon which they value themselves much were not yet done, the doing of which they told causd more pain than what I had seen. About dinner time many of our freinds came, Oamo, Otheothea, Tuarua &c.

6. We begin now to prepare in earnest for our departure, the sails were today carried on board and bent, the guns also were taken on board. Our freinds begin now to beleive that we are realy preparing for our departure, a circumstance which they have of late much doubted. This evening we had a second visit from *Tearee derry*[2] and *Toimata*,[3] the people again paying them the same respect as on the 21st of June: poor Toimata was again baulkd in her desire of seeing the fort, Oamo insisting that she should not come in. Soon after these had left us some of our freinds came to inform us that *Monaamia* the man who stole the Quadrant was landed and meant this night to make an atempt upon us; all were ready to assist us and several, *Tuanne Matte* especialy, very desirous of sleeping in the Fort, which probably was the reason why this arch theif did not this night exercise his abilities.

7. The carpenters were this morn employd in taking down the gates and palisades of our little fortification to make us firewood for the ship, when one of the Indians without made shift to steal the staple and hook of the great gate. We were immediately

---

[1] This was called the *ta*; see below, p. 336.

[2] *Te arii-rere*: Banks seems to be spelling out the more formal version of Teriirere.

[3] This name is used for the first time of Teriirere's betrothed. It was taken from the name of a goddess.

W

app[r]ised of the theft to the great affright of our visiters of whoom the bell tent was full; their fears were however presently quieted and I (as usual) set out on my ordinary occupation of theif catching. The Indians most readily joind me and away we set full cry much like a pack of fox hounds, we ran and walkd and walkd and ran for I beleive 6 miles with as little delay as possible, when we learnt that we had very early in the chase passd our game who was washing in a brook, saw us a coming and hid himself in the rushes. We returnd to the place and by some intelligence which some of our people had got found a scraper which had been stole from the ship and was hid in those very rushes; with this we returnd and soon after our return Tubourai brought the staple.

8. Our freinds with us as usual, the fort more and more dismantled. Our freinds seem resolvd to stay till we go tho the greatest part of them are absolutely without victuals; we have been for some days obligd to spare them every little assistance that we can and the best of them are most thankfull for a single basket of apples. Notwithstanding this we had 4 small pigs brought today from Oborea and Polotheara.

9. Our freinds with us early in the morning as usual, some I beleive realy sorry at the aproach of our departu[r]e others desirous to make as much as they can of our stay. Several of the people were this evening out on liberty. Two foreign seamen were together and one had his knife stolen; he atempted to recover it, may be roughly, for the Indians attackd him and wounded him greivously with a stone over his eye, the other was also slightly wounded in the head; the people who had done this immediately fled to the mountains. — Two of our marines left the fort some time last night or this morn without leave.[1] Their doing this at a time when our departure is so near makes us suspect them of an intention of staying among these people; nothing however has been said about them today in hopes of their returning which they have not yet done.

10. We are told by the Indians this morn that our people do not intend to return; they are they say gone up into the mountains where our people cannot get at them and one is already married and become an inhabitant of Otahite. After some deliberation however *Tuanne matte* and *Patea*[2] undertook to carry our people to the place where they were; they were known to have no arms so two were thought sufficient for the service, a midshipman and

[1] Their names were Clement Webb and Samuel Gibson.
[2] ?Patia.

a marine,[1] who set off without loss of time. We were now quite ready for the sea so no time was to be lost in recovering the deserters. The Indians gave us but little hopes of our people bringing them back: one certain method remaind however in our power, the seizing of some of their principal people and detaining them, which was immediately resolvd upon. Oborea, Potattow, Polotheara, Tubourai, Tamio, Tuarua, Otheothea and Tetuahitea and Nuna were in the fort and were told that they would not be permitted to go from it till our people returnd. At first they were not at all alarmd, they hardly beleivd us in earnest till they saw the Pinnace come ashore and soon after go away to the westward, the[y] immediately suspected what was the case, that she was gone to fetch Dootahah. They were now alarmd but depending on our having usd them well on all occasions shewd but little signs of either discontent or fear, but assurd us that the people should be brought back as soon as possible. In the evening Dootahah was brought on board, Lieutenant Hickes who had been sent on the service found him at Tettahah and easily took him or rather stole him from the people. Night came on, it was thought unsafe to let the prisoners remain in the fort, which was totaly dismantled; Oborea, Potattow and Tubourai were orderd to the ship; in going into the boat they expressd much fear and shed many tears. The Cap[tn] staid on board with them, I slept ashore and the rest of the prisoners in my tent. About 8 our Indians came back with the two deserters but brought the disagreable news of one of the people who had been sent after them being seizd by the Indians, who declard that they would not release them[2] till Dootahah had his liberty. The news was sent aboard and a boat came off immediately for Nuna and Tuanne matte. They were sent to the ship, a boat armd went immediately in search of the people and in her the latter and Tupia who was our voluntary prisoner.

11. The night was spent tolerably well, the women cryd a little at first but were soon quieted by asurances that at all events they should not be hurt. At day break a large number of people gatherd about the fort many of them with weapons; we were intirely without defences so I made the best I could of it by going out among them.

---

[1] Monkhouse was the midshipman. Cook says 'a Petty Officer and the Corporal of Marines'. Midshipmen were at that period petty officers; the corporal was John Truslove.

[2] *sic*; it should be *him*, but Banks, who has first written 'our two people', alters this to 'one of the people', and forgets to make the consequential alteration. S and P follow the MS. But Cook, whose account must be taken as correct, says that Webb was first brought back, and that Monkhouse and Truslove had been disarmed and detained with Gibson. He then sent Hicks away in the longboat with a strong party to recover the men.

They wer[e] very civil and shewd much fear as they have done of me upon all occasions, probably because I never shewd the least of them but have upon all our quarrels gone immediately into the thickest of them. They told me that our people would soon return. Acordingly about 8 they did safe and sound, we saw them through our glasses go up the side and immediately dischargd our prisoners, making each such a present as we though[t] would please them with which some were well content. The prisoners from the ship were by this time coming ashore. They were receivd with much joy by the multitude; I met them from the boat but no sign of forgiveness could I see in their faces, they lookd sulky and affronted. I walkd with Oborea along the beach: 4 hoggs were soon offerd me, two from her and as many from Dootahah, I refusd them however positively unless they would sell them which they refusd to do. The rest of the morning was employd in getting the tents aboard, which was done by dinner time and we dind on board. The small bower[1] had been got up and the stock found to be so much worm eaten that we are obligd to make a new one, and as we have no hopes of the best bower being in better repair it is probable that we shall not get to sea this day or two.

12. This morn Tupia came on board, he had renewd his resolves of going with us to England, a circumstance which gives me much satisfaction. He is certainly a most proper man, well born, cheif *Tahowa*[2] or preist of this Island, consequently skilld in the mysteries of their religion; but what makes him more than any thing else desireable is his experience in the navigation of these people and knowledge of the Islands in these seas; he has told us the names of above 70, the most of which he has himself been at.[3] The Cap[tn] refuses to take him on his own account, in my opinion sensibly enough, the goverment will never in all human probability take any notice of him; I therefore have resolvd to take him. Thank heaven I have a sufficiency and I do not know why I may not keep him as a curiosity, as well as some of my neighbours do lions and

[1] The anchor from the port side of the bow.

[2] *Tahua* (cf. Maori *tohunga*, and other Polynesian variants).

[3] This is rather an overstatement. Cook, in the list of islands which he gives (I, pp. 291-3) from Tupaia's information, marks no more than twelve that Tupaia said he had himself visited, and one of those was Raiatea, his native place. Cook writes, 'This man had been with us the most part of the time we had been upon the Island which gave us an oppertunity to know some thing of him: we found him to be a very intelligent person and to know more of the Geography of the Islands situated in these seas, their produce and the religion laws and customs of the inhabitants then any one we had met with and was the likeliest person to answer our purpose; for these reasons and at the request of M[r] Banks I received him on board together with a young boy his servant'.—p. 117. Tupaia came of a family well-known for its skill in navigation.

tygers at a larger expence than he will probably ever put me to; the amusement I shall have in his future conversation and the benefit he will be of to this ship, as well as what he may be if another should be sent into these seas, will I think fully repay me. As soon as he had made his mind known he said that he would go ashore and return in the evening, when he would make a signal for a boat to be sent off for him; he took with him a miniature picture of mine to shew his freinds and several little things to give them as parting presents. After dinner we went ashore to the *Marai no Dootahah* of which I was desirous to have a drawing made and had not yet done it.[1] We no sooner landed than several of our freinds, those who were not totaly afronted at the imprisonment of the day before yesterday, came to meet us; we proceeded with them to Dootahahs house where was Oborea &c. They were glad to see us and a perfect reconciliation ensued, in consequence of which they promisd to visit us tomorrow morning to take their leave of us, as we told them that we should sail before noon. With them was Tupia who most willingly returnd in the boat with us aboard the ship where he took up his lodgins for the first time.

13. About 10 this morn saild From Otahite leaving our freinds Some of them at least I realy beleive personaly sorry for our departure, notwisthstanding the confinement of the day before yesterday had frigh[t]ned and affronted them as much as possible, yet our nearest freinds came on board at this Critical time except only Tubourai and Tamio. We had Oborea, Otheothea, Tayoa,[2] Nuna, Tuanna Matte, Potattou, Polotheara &c. on board when the anchor was weighd; they took their leaves tenderly enough, not without plenty of tears tho intirely without that clamourous weeping made use of by the other Indians, several boats of whoom were about the ship shouting out their lamentations, as vyeing with each other not who should cry most but who should cry loudest — a custom we had often condemnd in conversation with our particular freinds as savouring more of affected than real greif.

Tupia who after all his struggles stood firm at last in his resolution of acompanying us parted with a few heartfelt tears, so I judge them to have been by the Efforts I saw him make use of to hide

---

[1] If they simply went ashore after dinner to visit the *marae no Tuteha*, Tuteha's *marae*, it must have been at Point Utuhaihai; it can hardly have been that more usually known as his, Maraetaata. No drawing of the *marae* as such seems to have survived, though in B.M. Add. MS 15508 there is a very rough sketch-plan.

[2] It is curious that Banks has not mentioned this 'nearest friend' before.—? Te-oa or Taioa.

them. He sent by Otheothea his last present, a shirt to *Potamai*,[1] Dootahah's favourite mistress. He and I went then to the topmast head where we stood a long time waving to the Canoes as they went off, after which he came down and shewd no farther signs of seriousness or concern.

In the Evening Tethuroa in sight; before night it appears clearly to be a very low Island and but small, which with Tupias declaring that there were no fixd inhabitants upon it only the people of Otahite who went there for a few days to fish, determind us to content ourselves with what we had seen and stand on in search of *Urietea*,[2] which he describd to be a well peopled Island as large as Otahite.[3]

14. Before Noon today two Islands are in sight which Tupia calls *Huahine* and *Ulhietea*, both of them make high and large.

15. Calm all last night, this morn hazey so that no land is seen; light breezes and calms succeeding each other all morn. Our Indian often prayd to *Tane*[4] for a wind and as often boasted to me of the success of his prayers, which I plainly saw he never began till he saw a breeze so near the ship that it generaly reachd her before his prayer was finishd. At sunset a pleasant breeze. Owahine[5] and Ulhietea very plainly seen.

16. This morn we were very near the Island; some Canoes very soon came off but appeard very much frightned, one however came to us bringing a cheif and his wife, who on Tupia's assurances of Freindship from us came on board. They were like the Otahite people in Language, dress, tattow, in short in Every thing. Tupia has always said that the people of this Island and Urietea will not steal, in which they indeed differ much from our late freinds if they only keep up to their Character.

Soon after dinner we came to an anchor in a very fine bay calld by the natives *Owalla*[6] and immediately went ashore. As soon as

---

[1] The name may be correct: or Potomai?

[2] It is difficult to know precisely what name Banks was representing here. The fact that he heard an *r* in the word, which he follows with *ie*, suggests Raiatea. But then why the initial *U*?—which, one gathers from other spellings (e.g. Parkinson, Yoolee-Eteah) represents the English *Yoo* or *you*. It does not help matters that in his next entry he goes over to 'Ulhietea'. The *r/l* sound in that part of the ocean was very indeterminate, and came to most early voyagers as *l*. Parkinson's 'Yoolee-Eteah', and hence the other variants, seems clearly derived from the island's older name, Ioretea; and presumably Banks's *ie* is not to be given its full value as in the English *lie*.

[3] Raiatea is considerably smaller than Tahiti.

[4] Tane was one of the great members of the Polynesian pantheon, a god of beauty, peace, and growing things: Tupaia here prays to him as also the god of fine weather.

[5] Huahine.

[6] Cook writes it Owharhe—another example of the indeterminate *r/l*. The harbour was Fare, on the west side of the island.

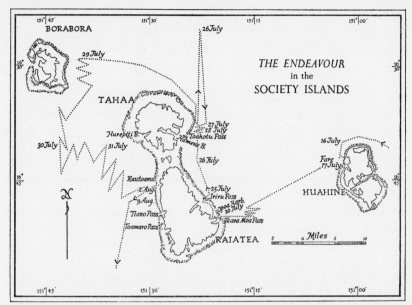

THE ENDEAVOUR
in the
SOCIETY ISLANDS

we landed Tupia squatted down on the ground and ranging us on one side and the Indians on the other began to pray, our cheif who stood opposite to him answering him in kind of responses. This lasted about a quarter of an hour in which time he sent at different intervals two hankercheifs and some beads he had prepard for the purpose as presents to *Eatua*;[1] these were sent among many messages which pass'd backwards and forwards with plantains, malapoides[2] &c. In return for this present to the gods which it seems was very acceptable we had a hog given for our *Eatua*, which in this case will certainly be our bellys.

17. Went ashore this morn and walkd up the hills; found the productions here almost exactly similar to those of Otahite; upon the hills the rocks and clay were burnt if any thing more than they were in that Island. The people also were almost exactly like our late [friends] but rather more stupid and lazy, in proof of which I need only say that we should have gone much higher up the hills than we did if we could have perswauded them to accompany us, whose only excuse was the fear of being killd by the fatigue. Their houses are very neat and their boathouses particularly very large, one of those I measurd 50 long paces in lengh 10 broad

---

[1] *e atua*, a god; *atua* was the word for any god.
[2] S has here the note, 'Young Plantains, and Malapoides, are plants used in Sacred Ceremonies'.

and 24 f^t high: the Gothick arch of which it consisted was supported on one side by 26, on the other by 30 pillars or rather clumsey thick posts of about 2 f^t high and one thick. Most of these were carvd with heads of men, boys or other devices, as the rough fancy and more rough workmanship of these stone hatchet furnishd gentrey suggested and executed. The flats were filld with very fine breadfruit trees and an infinite number of Cocoa nuts, upon which latter the inhabitants seemd to depend much more than those of Otahite; we saw however large spaces occupied by lagoons and salt swamps upon which neither breadfruit nor Cocoa nuts would thrive.

18. This morning went to take a farther view of a building which we had seen yesterday and admird a good deal, taking with us Tupias boy *Tayeto*[1] for himself was too much engagd with his freinds to have time to accompany us. The boy told us that it was calld *Ewharre no Eatua*[2] or the house of the god but could not explain at all the use of it. It consisted of a chest whose lid was nicely sewd on and thatched over very neatly with palm nut leaves, the whole was fixd upon two poles by little arches of carvd wood very neat; these poles seemd to be usd in carrying it from place to place tho when we saw it it was supported upon two posts. One end of the

chest was open with a round hole within a square one, this

was yesterday stopd up with a peice of cloth which least I should offend the people I left untouchd, but to day the cloth and probably the contents of the chest were removd as there was nothing at all in it.

Trade today does not go on with any spirit, the people when any thing is offerd will not take it on their own judgement, but take the opinion of 20 or 30 people about them which takes up much time; we however got 11 piggs.

19. This morn trade rather better: got 3 very large hogs and some piggs by producing hatchets, which had not been before given and we hop'd to have had no occasion for in an Island which had not before been seen by Europæans.[3] In the afternoon go to Sea.

---

[1] The name of this rather pathetic figure in history cannot be given with confidence. Banks Tayeto (?Te-ito or Taiato); Cook Tiata (?Taiata); Parkinson Taiyota (?Taiota).

[2] *fare no atua.*

[3] Cook also gave to 'Oree' the chief 'a small plate on which was stamp'd the following Inscription viz. *His Britannick Maj. Ship Endeavour, Lieut^t Cook Commander 16th July 1769. Huaheine,*' with some medals or counters and other presents, which Oree promised never to part with; 'this we thought would prove as lasting a Testimony of our having first discover'd this Island as any we could leave behind'.—Cook I, p. 143.

The Island of Huahine differs scarce at all from that of Otahite either in its productions or in the customs of the people. In all our searches here we have not found above 10 or 12 new plants, a few insects indeed and a species of scorpions which we did not see at Otahite.[1] This Island seems however this year at least to be a month forwarder than the other, as the ripeness of the Cocoa nuts now full of kernel and the new breadfruit, some of which is fitt to Eat, fully evinces. Of the Cocoa nut kernels they make a food which they call *Poe*[2] by scraping them fine and mixing them with yams also scrapd; these are put into a wooden trough and hot stones laid among them, by which means a kind of Oily hasty pudding is made which our people relishd very well especialy fryd.

The men here are large made and stout, one we measurd was 6ft 3 high and well made; the women very Fair, more so than at Otahite tho we saw none so hansome. Both Sexes seem'd to be less timid as well as less curious, the firing of a gun frightned them but they did not fall down as our Otahite freinds at first generaly did. On one of their people being taken in the fact of stealing and seizd upon by the hair they did not run away, but coming round inquird into the cause and seemingly at least approving of the Justice recomended a beating for the offender which was immediately put in practise.

When they first came on board the ship they seemd struck with a sight so new and wonderd at every thing that was shewn to them, but did not seem to search and inquire for matters of curiosity even so much as the Otahite people did, tho they had before seen almost every thing we had to shew them.

20. At noon today come to an anchor at *Ulhietea* in a bay Calld by the natives *Oapoa*,[3] the entrance of which is very near a small Islet Calld *Owhattera*.[4] Some Indians soon came on board expressing signs of fear, they were two Canoes each of which brought a woman, I suppose as a mark of confidence, and a pig as a present. To each of these ladies was given a spike nail and some beads with which they seemd much pleasd. Tupia who has always expressd much fear of the men of *Bola Bola*[5] says that they have conquerd this

---

[1] *Hormurus australasiae* Fabr. Fabricius described this from a specimen in Banks's museum and it is still in the British Museum (Natural History).

[2] This spelling is also the orthodox spelling.

[3] Opoa.

[4] Oatara.

[5] Porapora (more properly) or Borabora (as spelt today). See p. 314, n. 2 above. Borabora was a much smaller island, but its men were determined fighters.

Island and will tomorrow come down and fight with us, we therefore
lose no time in going ashore as we are to have today to ourselves.
On landing Tupia repeated the ceremony of praying as at Huahine
after which an English Jack was set up on shore and Captⁿ Cooke
took possession of this and the other three Islands in sight viz.
Huahine Otahah[1] and *Bola Bola* for the use of his Britannick majesty.
After this we walk together to a great *Marai* calld *Tapodeboatea*
whatever that may signifie;[2] it is different from those of Otahite
being no more than walls about 8 feet high of Coral Stones (some
of an immense size) filld up with smaller ones, the whole ornamented
with many planks set upon their ends and carvd their whole lengh.
In the neighbourhood of this we found the altar or *ewhatta*[3] upon
which lay the last sacrafice, a hog of about 80 pounds weight which
had been put up there whole and very nicely roasted. Here were
also 4 or 5 *Ewharre no Eatua* or god houses which were made to be
carried on poles. One of these I examind by putting my hand
into it: within was a parsel about 5 feet long and one thick wrappd
up in matts, these I tore with my fingers till I came to a covering of
mat made of platted Cocoa nut fibres which it was impossible to
get through so I was obligd to desist, especialy as what I had
already done gave much offence to our new freinds.[4] From hence
we went to an adjoining long house where among several things
such as rolls of cloth &c. was standing a model of a Canoe about
3 feet long upon which were tied 8 under jaw bones of men. Tupia
told us that it was the custom of these Islanders to cut off the Jaw
bones of those who they had killd in war; these were he said the
jaw bones of Ulhietea people but how they came here or why
tied thus to a canoe we could not understand, we were therefore
contented to conjecture that they were plac'd there as a trophy

---

[1] Tahaa. Raiatea and Tahaa are enclosed by the same reef.

[2] Taputapu-atea. Banks's spelling shows the ambiguity between the Tahitian *t* and
d sounds. S has the note, 'Tapodeboatea. Signifies in their Language, Head of the white
Hog'. This is an unhappy bloomer on Banks's part; perhaps he gets it out of *Te upoo*
(the human head) + *te puaa* (the hog) + *tea* (white). Henry (*Ancient Tahiti*, p. 95)
gives its meaning as 'Sacrifices from abroad'. *Taputapu* was a sacrifice, generally human,
to the god Oro; one of the meanings of *atea* was 'distant, far off'. Davies defines the word
as 'the name of a public and principal heiva, where the human sacrifices were made to
Oro'. Such sacrifices were made at other *marae* in Tahiti named after this one. It was
the most famous of all *marae*, and of international significance, as the most important
marae of Raiatea, the centre from which the Society Islands and Tahiti were populated,
and the homeland to which the Maori people trace back their historic origin. Emory
(op.cit., pp. 145-8) has a full discussion of the *marae*, with drawings.

[3] *fata*; Banks again includes the verbal *e*, it is.

[4] Not surprisingly; and it is a tribute to Raiatean tolerance that they remained the
young man's friends after this calm piece of sacrilege. The object which Banks was
trying to get at was a sennit representation of an ancestral god, perhaps the great god
Oro, to whom the *marae* was sacred.

won back from the men of Bola Bola their mortal enemies. Night
now came on apace but Dr Solander and myself walkd along shore
a little way and saw an *Ewharre no Eatua*, the under part of which
was lind with a row of Jaw bones which we were also told were
those of Ulhietea men. We saw also Cocoa nut trees the stemms
of which were hung round with nutts so that no part of them could
be seen, these we were told were put there that they might dry a
little and be prepard for making *poe*; we saw also a tree of *Ficus
prolixa* in great perfection, the trunck or rather congeries of roots
of which was 42 paces in circumference.[1]

21. Dr Solander and myself walkd out this morn and saw many
large Boathouses like that describd at Huahine page 303 and 401.[2]
On these the inhabitants were at work making and repairing
the large Canoes calld by them *Pahee*,[3] at which business they workd
with incredible cleverness tho their tools certainly were as bad as
possible. I will first give the dimensions and description of one of
their boats and then their method of building. Its extreme lenght
from stem to stern not reckoning the bending up of both those
parts 51 feet; breadth in the clear at the top forward 14 inches,
midships 18, aft 15; in the bilge forward 32 inches, midships 35,
aft 33; depth midships 3 f^t 4; hight from the ground she stood on
3 f^t 6; her head raisd without the figure 4 f^t 4 from the ground, the
figure 11 inches; her stern 8 f^t 9, the figure 2 feet. Alongside of her
was lashd another like her in all parts but less in proportion being
only 33 feet in her extreme lengh. The form of these Canoes is
better to be expressd by a drawing than by any description.

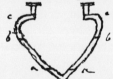
This annexd may serve to give some
Idea of a section: *aa* is the first seam,
bb the second, *cc* the third. The first
stage or keel under *aa* is made of
trees hollowd out like a trough for
which purpose they chuse the longest trees they can get,[4] so that 2
or three make the bottom of their largest boats (some of which

---

[1] *Ficus prolixa* Forst., called Aoa by the Tahitians, was a sacred tree planted about
temples, its 'congeries of roots' like a banyan; its bark was used in making *tapa* cloth.
Solander provided a full description both of this and of *F. tinctoria* (*Prim. Fl. Insul. Oceani
Pac.* pp. 352-3 MS) but Forster in true form purloined Solander's names for his *Prodromus*
(cf. Merrill, p. 352).
[2] i.e. pp. 316 above, and 368 below.
[3] *pahi*. The people of Raiatea were the great canoe-builders of the Society group.
The description which Banks proceeds to give is more detailed than anything in Cook.
[4] The timbers used for canoe-building were mainly Faifai (*Serianthes myriadenia*) a
large valley-growing tree, a favourite for *pahi*; the Uru or breadfruit, and the Hutu
(*Barringtonia speciosa*)—for which last see Pl. V.

are much larger than that describd here as I make a rule to describe every thing of this kind from the common size); the next stage under *bb* is formd of streght plank about 4 feet long and 15 inches broad and 2 inches thick; the next stage under *cc* is made like the bottom of trunks of trees hollowd into its bilging form; the last or that above *cc* is formd also out of trunks of trees so that the moulding is of one peice with the plank. This work dificult as it would be to an Europæan with his Iron tools they perform without Iron and with amazing dexterity; they hollow with their stone axes as fast at least as our Carpenters could do and dubb tho slowly with prodigious nicety; I have seen them take off a skin of an angular plank without missing a stroke, the skin itself scarce $\frac{1}{16}$ part of an inch in thickness. Boring the holes throug[h] which their sewing is to pass seems to be their greatest dificulty. Their tools are made of the bones of men, generaly the thin bone of the upper arm; these they grind very sharp and fix to a handle of wood, making the instrument serve the purpose of a gouge by striking it with a mallet made of a hard black wood,[1] and with them would do as much work as with Iron tools was it not that the brittle Edge of the tool is very liable to be broke.

When they have prepard their planks &c. the keel is layd on blocks and the whole Canoe put together much in the same manner as we do a ship, the sides being supported by stantions and all the seams wedg'd together before the last sewing is put on, so that they become tolerably tight considering that they are without calking.[2]

With these boats they venture themselves out of sight of land; we saw several of them at Otahite which had come from Ulhietea and Tupia has told us that they go voyages of twenty days, whether true or false I do not affirm. They keep them very carefully under such boathouses as are describd p.　,[3] one of which we measurd today 60 yards by 11.

22. Weather worse than yesterday, in the course of last night it blew very fresh, this morn rainy. Walk out but meet little worth observation. Saw a double *pahie* such as that describd yesterday but much larger, she had upon her an awning supported by pillars which held the floor of it 4 feet at least above the deck or upper surface of the boat; also a trough for making *Poe poe* or sour paste

---

[1] Toa or ironwood.

[2] This is evidently a mistake. Caulking was done with fine coconut fibre and the adhesive sap of the breadfruit used as pitch; but Banks probably did not see the process.

[3] p. 316 above.

carvd out of hard black stone such as their hatchets are made of,[1] it was 2 f^t 7 long and 1 f^t 4 broad, very thick and substantial and supported by 4 short feet, the whole neatly finishd and perfectly polishd tho quite without ornaments. Today as well as yesterday every one of us who walkd out saw many Jaw bones fix'd up in houses as well as out of doors, a confirmation of their taking them instead of scalps.

23. Weather mended a little. Dr Solander and myself go upon the hills in hopes of finding new plants but ill rewarded; return home at night having seen nothing worth mentioning.

24. Foul wind. The Captn attempts to go out of the reef at another passage situate between the two Islets of *Opourourou* and *Taumou*.[2] The ship turning to windward within the reef in doing which she narrowly escapes going ashore, the Quartermaster in the chains calld out 2 fathom; the ship drawing at least 14 feet made it impossible that such a shoal could be under her Keel, so either the man was mistaken or she went along the edge of a coral rock many of which are here as steep as a wall.

Soon after this we came to an anchor and I went ashore but saw nothing but a small *marai* ornamented with 2 sticks about 5 feet long, each hung with Jaw bones as thick as possible and one having a skull stuck on its top.

25. This morn get to sea and turn to windward all day. Find that the two Islands Ulhietea and Otahah are inclosed by one reef: Tupia says that there is a large passage throug[h] it between them and a harbour within it, also another fronting a large bay on the Eastermost end of Otahah.

26. Foul wind Continues last night, the ship has faln much to leward. Before night however we have gaind our loss and something more, as we discover a low Island ahead which Tupia tells us is calld by the natives *Tupi*;[3] he says that it is low without a harbour and yields nothing but Cocoa nuts and fish.

27. Turn to leward all night and all day again, so much that at night Tupi is not in sight.

28. Wind still baffles us as much as ever. This morn hoisted out a boat and sent ashore on the Island of Otahah in which Dr Solander

---

[1] Probably dolerite from the island of Maurua, now Maupiti. Corney, III, pl. 2 is a picture of a larger example.
[2] On the chart in Hawkesworth as Opururu and Tamou. They have changed their names to Iriru and Tipaemau.
[3] Tubai in Cook; now Motu-iti.

and myself took a passage. We went through a large breach in the reef situate between two Islands calld *Toahattu* and *Whennuaia*[1] within which we found very spatious harbours, particularly in one bay which was at least 3 miles deep.[2] The inhabitants as usual so that long before night we had purchasd 3 hoggs, 21 fowls and as many yams and plantains as the boat would hold. Indeed of these last we might have had any quantity and a more useful refreshment they are to us in my opinion even than the pork; they have been for this week past boild and servd instead of bread; every man in the ship is fond of them and with us in the Cabbin they agree much better than the Bread fruit did which sometimes gripd us. But what makes any refreshments of this kind the more acceptable is that our bread is at present so full of vermin that notwistanding all possible care I have sometimes had 20 at a time in my mouth, every one of which tasted as hot as mustard.

The Island itself seemd more barren than Ulhietea tho much like it in produce, bread fruit being less plentyfull than Plantains and Cocoa nuts. The people perfectly the same, so much so that I did not observe one new custom or any thing Else among them worth mention; they were not very numerous but flockd from all Quarters to the boat wherever she went bringing with them what-ever they had to sell. Here as well as in the rest of the Islands they paid us the same Compliment they are used to pay to their own Kings, uncovering their shoulders and lapping their Garments round their breasts; here particularly they were so scrupulously observant of it that a man was sent with us who calld out to every one we met telling him what we were and what he was to do.

29. The wind last night has favourd us a little so that we are this morn close under the Island of Bola Bola, whose high craggy peak seems on this side at least totaly inaccessible to men; round it is a large quantity of low land which seems very barren. Tupia tells us that between the shore and the mountain is a large salt lagoon, a certain sign of barrenness in this climate; he however tells us that there are upon the Island plenty of Hogs and fowls as well as the vegetables we have generaly met with.

We see but few people on the shore, Tupia tells us that they are gone to Ulhietea where we shall find them. He says also that there is no breach in the reef on this side the Island but on the other there is one large enough for the ship to go in and a good harbour within it.

[1] Toahatu and ?Fenu-aia; the latter is now called Mahea. The breach in the reef is the Toahatu pass.　　　[2] Haamene or Hamene.

30. This morn wind right on end. See a new Island calld by Tupia *Maurua*,[1] he says it is fertile and yeilds plentifully all kinds of provision, but that there is no breach in the reef large enough for the ship to go into.

31. Still turning to windward with the wind right in our teeth, towards evening however it mends and gives us hopes that we may tomorrow morn come to an anchor in Ulhietea. Tupia today shewes us a large breach in the reef of Otahah through which the ship migh[t] conveniently pass into a large bay, where he says there is good anchorage.[2] We have now a very good opinion of Tupias pilotage, especialy since we observd him at Huahine send a man to dive down to the heel of the ships rudder; this the man did several times and reported to him the depth of water the ship drew, after which he has never sufferd her to go in less than 5 fathom water without being much alarmd.

AUGUST 1769

1. The wind right off the land of Ulhietea mak[in]g it dificult to get in tho we see a good inlet; after turning to windward till afternoon we however at last get hold of anchorage in the mouth of it.[3] Many canoes came immediately about the ship bringing all sorts of trade so that before night we have purchas'd several piggs and fowls and a large quantity of Plantains and Cocoa nutts.

On attempting to warp the ship in this even the anchor was found to be fast in a rock; at least no attempts could stir it till night when the tide (which runs strong through the inlet) turnd, the ship then going over the anchor tripd it herself.

2. Dr Solander and myself have spent this day ashore and been very agreably entertaind by the reception we have met with from the people, tho we were not fortunate enough to meet with one new plant. Everybody seemd to fear and respect us but nobody to mistrust us in the smallest degree, men women and children came crouding after us but no one shewd us the least incivility, on the contrary wherever there was dirt or water to pass over they strove who should carry us on their backs. When we came to the houses of the principal people we were receivd with a form quite new to us. The people who generaly followd us rushd into them before us leaving however a lane sufficiently wide for us to pass;

[1] Now Maupiti.
[2] The Paipai pass into the bay called by Cook 'Oherurua', now Hurepiti.
[3] It was the harbour of Rautoanui.

when we came in we found them rangd on each side a long mat
spread upon the ground, at the farther end of which sat one or
more very young women or children neatly dressd, who without
stirring expected us to come up to them and make them presents,
which we did with no small pleasure for prettier children or better
dressd we had no where seen. One of these *Tettuas*[1] as they were
calld was about 6 years old, her *ahou*[2] or gown was red and round
her head was wound a large quantity of *Tamou*[3] (plaited hair)
an ornament they value more than any thing they have. She
sat at the farther end of a mat 30 feet long on which no one of the
spectators presumd to set a foot notwistanding the crowd, leaning
upon the arm of a well looking well dressd woman about 30, possibly
her nurse. We walkd up to her, as soon as we aproachd she stretchd
out her hand to receive the beads we were to give, but had she been a
princess royal of England giving her hand to be kissd no instruction
could have taught her to have done it with a better grace. So much
is untaught nature superior to art that I have seen no sight of the
kind that has struck me half so much.

Gratefull possibly for the presents we had made to these girls
the people in our return tryd every method to Oblige us; particularly
in one house the master orderd one of his people to dance for our
amusement which he did thus:

He put upon his head a large cylindrical basket about 4 feet
long and 8 inches in diameter, on the front of which was fastned
a facing of feathers bending forwards at the top and edged round
with sharks teeth and the tail feathers of tropick birds: with this
on he dancd moving slowly and often turning his head round,
sometimes swiftly throwing the end of his headdress or *whow*[4] so
near the faces of the spectators as to make them start back, which
was a joke that seldom faild of making every body laugh especialy
if it happned to one of us.

We had also an opportunity of seeing the inside of the *Ewharre
no eatua* so often mentiond. There were 3 of them much ornamented
with jaw bones and very full of bundles lapd up with their cloth;
these the people opned with some perswasion and in them we
found complete skulls with their lower jaw bones in their proper
places. Perhaps these were the skulls of those of the victorious

[1] *tetua*, in general a girl or young woman, but more particularly a title given to the daughter of an *arii* family—'a young noblewoman'. S has the note, 'Tettua, or Gentlewoman. A person who we (in England) should in speaking to say, Madam'.

[2] *ahu*, a sort of cloak, a piece of *tapa* thrown over the shoulders and fastened round the waist.

[3] *taamu*. The knowledge of how this plaiting was done has perished.

[4] It is possible Banks mistook the meaning of this word—? *faeo*, a children's game.

party who died in battle and the jaw bones fastnd on the outside were those of the conquerd, but for this conjecture I had no authority from the Indians who seemd to avoid as much as possible any questions upon the subject.

3. This day went along shore in the opposite direction to that we took yesterday, intending to spend most of our time in purchasing stock, which we have always found the people readyer to part with at their houses and selling cheaper than at the market. In the course of our walk we met a set of stroling dancers Calld by the Indians *Heiva*[1] who detain us 2 hours and during all that time entertaind us highly indeed. They consisted of 3 drums, 2 women dancers and 6 men; these Tupia tells us go round the Island as we have seen the little *Heivas* do at Otahite, but differ from those in that most of the people here are principal people, of which assertion we had in the case of one of the women an undoubted proof.

I shall first describe their dresses and then their dances. The women had on their heads a quantity of *tamou* or plaited hair which was rolled and between the interstices of it flowers of Gardenia[2] were stuck making a head dress truly Elegant. Their shoulders arms and breasts as low as their arms[3] were bare, below this they were coverd with black cloth and under each shoulder was placd a bunch of black feathers much as our ladies nosegays or Bouquets. On their hips rested a quantity of cloth pleated very full which reachd almost up to their arms and fell down below into long peticoats reaching below their feet, which they managd with as much dexterity as our opera dancers could have done; these pleats were brown and white alternately but the peticoats were all white.

In this dress they advancd sideways keeping excellent time to the drums which beat brisk and loud; they soon began to shake their hips giving the folds of cloth that lay upon them a very quick motion which was continued during the whole dance, they sometimes standing, sometimes sitting and sometimes resting on their knees and elbows and generaly moving their fingers with a quickness scarce to be imagind. The chief entertainment of the spectators

[1] A group of *arioi*; their performance was the *heiva*.

[2] *Gardenia taitensis* DC., of which a beautiful coloured drawing by Parkinson, labelled 'Gardenia florida', and a specimen in the Pocket Book survive. See pl. 30.

[3] The expression 'as low as their arms' is rather baffling: the breasts were covered, the arms were bare. One gets a rough idea of the dress Banks describes from the central dancing figure in Hawkesworth's pl. IX, which is apparently founded on a crude drawing in Add. MS 15508, f.9. (There are much better representations in Webber's drawings for Cook's Third Voyage, pls. XXVIII, XXIX.) The elegantly formed young female bare to the waist in Hawkesworth appears to be an innovation by Cipriani. See pl. 12.

X

seemd however to arise from the Lascivious motions they often made use of which were highly so, more indeed than I shall atempt to describe.

One of these girls had in her ear 3 pearls, one of them very large but so foul that it was worth scarce any thing, the other two were as large as a midling pea and of a good and clear water as well as shape. For these I offerd at different times any price the owner would have but she would not hear of parting with them; I offerd once the price of 4 hogs down and any thing she would ask beside, but she would not hear of it. Indeed they have always set a value upon their pearls, if tolerably good, almost equal to our valuation supposing them as they always are spoild by the drilling.[1]

Between the dances of the women (for they sometimes rested) the men acted a kind of interlude in which they spoke as well as dancd. We were not however sufficiently vers'd in their language to be able to give an account of the Drama.

4. We had often heard Tubia speak of Lands belonging to him which had been taken away by the Bola Bola men: these he tells us now are situate in the very bay where the ship lies. On going ashore this morning the inhabitants confirmd What he has told us and shewd us several different *whennuas* which they all acknowledged belong of right to him. The largest number of the people here are it seems the so much feard Bola Bola men, and we are told that tomorrow *Opoony*[2] the King of that Island will come to visit us. We are much inclind to receive him civilly as we have met with so civil a reception from his subjects.

D[r] Solander and myself go upon the hills accompanied by several Indians, who carried us by excellent paths so high that we plainly saw the other side of the Island and the passage through which the ship went out of the reef between the Islets of *Opoorooroo* and *Tamou*. Our walk did not turn out very profitable as we found only two plants that we had not seen before.

In coming down again we saw the game that the Indians call *Erowhaw*,[3] which is no more than pitching a kind of light lances headed with hard wood at a mark: of this amusement they seem to be very fond but none that we saw now excelld in doing it,

---

[1] In his Tahitian vocabulary, p. 373 below, Banks gives the phrase 'Poe Matawewwe' as the name for a pearl. This seems to be the fruit of enquiry upon the present occasion, and to be his recording of *mata viivii*: *mata*, the face or eye, and *viivii*, corrupt, impure— probably referring to the large but 'foul' pearl.

[2] Puni.

[3] The game is elsewhere noted as *patia fa* (*patia*, spear; *fa*, the target); or, in Ellis, *Polynesian Researches*. I, p. 294, as *vero patia*, 'throw a spear'. It may be suggested that Banks's 'erowhaw' is a combination of *vero* with *fa*—i.e. to throw a spear at a target.

not above one in 12 striking the mark which was the bole of a plantain tree about 20 yards distant.

5. Went in the boat to the Southward with the Captn &c. Saw two inlets in the reef and good harbours within them; they were both situate close to Islets, one having one on each side of it[1] (indeed in general I have seen Breaches in Reefs almost wherever there are Islands upon them). The people all along shore were very poor, so much so that after all our days work we did not procure either hog or fowl nor indeed did we see either.

6. Yesterday Opoony the King of Bola Bola sent his Compt^s and a present of hogs and Fowls to the King of the ship, sending word also that he would in person wait upon him today. We therefore all hands staid at home in hopes of the honour of his excellencys visit. We were disapointed in our expectations not disagreably for instead of his majesty came 3 hansome lively girls who staid with us the morning and took off all regret for the want of his majesties company.

In the evening we all went to see the great king and thank him for his civilities particularly of this morning. The King of the *Tata toas*[2] or Club men who have conquerd this and are the terror of all other Islands we expected to see young lively hansome &c &c. but how were we disapointed when we were led to an old decrepid half blind man who seemd to have scarce reason enough left to send hogs, much less galantry enough to send ladies.

7. We learnd from Opoony yesterday that his cheif residence was at Otahah, to this place he proposd to acompany us. As today Captn Cooke and Dr Solander went upon the expedition myself staid at home. They proceeded with Opoony and all his train, many Canoes, to a bay in Otahah calld *Obooto-booto*,[3] his majesties cheif residence; here the houses were very large and good and the Canoes also finer than any the gentlemen had before seen. Such a prelude made them expect much from the owners of so fine houses, a boat load of hogs was the least they thought of, especialy as they had plenty of Spartan money[4] to pay for them; but alas, the Gentlemen who had fatigued themselves with building the houses, chose to refresh themselves with eating the hogs; so

[1] The 'inlets' were (1) the Tiano pass, flanked by the two islets Horea and Tiano, and leading into Tetoroa bay; and (2) the Toamaro pass, with the islet Toamaro on its northern edge, leading into Vaiaeho bay. The latter bay or harbour is called Maarahai on the chart in Hawkesworth.
[2] *taata toa*, warriors.
[3] Hawkesworth chart Apotopoto Bay, now Hurepiti; a deep inlet giving excellent shelter.
[4] i.e. iron. No doubt the nails used reminded Banks of the iron 'spits' of the Spartans.

that after the whole day was spent a small number only were pro-curd in proportion to what were expected.

Myself staid at home this morning and traded for some provisions and curiosities; in the afternoon took Mr Parkinson to the *Heiva* that he might scetch the dresses. The dancing was exactly the same as I had seen it before except that another woman was added to the two I saw before. The interludes of the men were varied, they gave us 5 or 6 which resembled much the Drama of an English stage dance. Most of my Freinds were constan[t]ly at the *Heiva*. Their names I set down and relationships as they are cheifly one family (1) *Tiarree no Horoa*[1] a King or cheif; (2) *Whannooutooa*[2] wife to 1; (3) *Otoobooi*[3] sister to 2; (4) *Orai*[4] Elder brother to 2; (5) *Tettuanue*[5] younger brother to 2; (6) *Otehammena*[6] dancing girl; (7) *Ouratooa*[7] D^o; (8) *Mattehea*[8] father to 1; (9) *Opipi*[9] mother to 1.

8. Dr Solander and self went along shore to gather plants, buy hogs or any thing else that might occurr. We took our course towards the *Heiva* and at last came up to it; it has gradualy moved from very near us till now it is 2 Leagues off, Tupia tells us that it will in this manner move gradualy round the Island. Our Freinds receivd us as usual with all manner of civility, dancing and giving us after the amusement a very good dinner as well as offering us a quantity of their Cloth by way of present, which we should have accepted had we not been full stockd with it before. We now understood a little more of the interludes than we had formerly done. I shall describe one as well as I can. The men dancers were divided into two parties differing in the colour of their clothes, one brown the other white. The cheif of the brown ones gave a basket of meat to the rest his servants that they might take care of it; the white represented theives who atempted to steal it several times, dancing all the time. Several different expedients they make use of without success till at last they found the watchmen asleep; they then gently went up to them and lifting them off from the basket, which for security sake they had placd in the middle of them, they went off with their prize. The others woke and danced but seem'd to shew little regret for their loss or indeed hardly to miss the basket at all.

9. This morn spent in trading with the Canoes for whatever they would bring, resolving to sail as soon as they left off to bring pro-

---

[1] *Te arii* (the chief) Nohoroa?　　　[2] ?Fanau-tua (born at sea).　　　[3] Tupuai.
[4] This may be right; or Rai?　　　[5] ?Tetua-nui?　　　[6] ?Te Hamena.
[7] ?Ouratua or Uratua; the same name as that borne by the young woman of 12 May.
[8] ?Matihia or Matehea.　　　[9] Pipi.

vision, which about noon they did and we again Launchd out into the Ocean in search of what chance and Tupia might direct us to.

10. Myself sick all day.

11. Tupia talks of an Island which he calls *Mànnúá*,[1] he says that we shall see it tomorrow morning but points out its place upon our weather bow so we shall probably go to leward of it.

12. Get rid of sea sickness today. Tupias Island not in sight, he tells us that it is *étópà*[2] (we are past it) for the same word is usd by them for the setting of the sun and the leaving behind of an Island. He says however that tomorrow or next day we shall see another which he calls *Ohétéróá*.

13. At noon today high land in sight which proved to be Tupias Island of Ohétéróa.[3] At night we were close in with it. He sayd that there were many other Islands from south to south west of us most of their names beginning with *Ohete*,[4] none however were in sight.

Many Albecores have been about the ship all the evening, Tupia took one and had not his rod broke would probably have taken many.[5] He usd an Indian fish hook made of mother of pearl so that it servd at the same time both for hook and bait.

14. Close under the land: a boat was sent from the ship in which Dr Solander and myself took a passage, she rowd right in for the land on which several natives appeard armd with long lances. The boat standing along shore not intending to land till she got round the next point made them (I beleive) think that we were afraid of them. The main body about 60 sat down upon the shore and sent two of their number forwards, who after walking sometime abreast of us leap'd into the water intending to swim to us but were soon left behind; two more then atempted the same thing and were in like manner left behind; a single man then ran forwards and taking good start of the boat fetchd her easily, but when he was alongside I could not persuade the officer of the boat[6] to take

---

[1] The existence of this island is dubious and perhaps mythical; according to Cook, Tupaia placed it three days' sail NE of 'Oheteroa' or Rurutu. It has been discussed a number of times: e.g. George Forster, *Voyage*, II, p. 151; J. R. Forster, *Observations*, pp. 327, 515; Corney, *Quest and Occupation of Tahiti*, II, pp. xxii, 190 n. If this was the mythical Mannua, it was inhabited by ferocious and man-eating demons.

[2] *e topa*; a better translation would be, 'it has fallen behind'.

[3] Hiti-roa, now Rurutu.

[4] *hiti*, edge, border, borderland, with the implication of distance.

[5] Apparently *Neothunnus macropterus* (Schlegel). See the dated drawing by Parkinson, II, pl. 100, and Solander's notes, pp. 265-6.

[6] Gore.

him, notwisthstanding it was so fair an opportunity of making freinds with a people who certainly lookd upon us as their enemies. He was therefore left behind as was another who followd his example.

We now came round a point where all our followers left us. We had opend a large bay[1] at the bottom of which we saw another body of men armd like the former; here we hopd to land and pushd towards the place. The natives had pushd off a canoe which came out to meet us. As soon as it aproachd us we lay upon our oars and calld to them that we were freinds and would give them nails if they would come to us; they after a very little hesitation came up to the boats stern and took the nails that were given them, seemingly with great satisfaction, but in less than a minute seemd to have formd a design of boarding our boat and taking her, in pursuance of which 3 leapd almost in an instant into our boat and the others brought up the canoe which had flown off a little in-tending probably to follow their countrey mens example. The first who came in the boat was close to me, he instantly snatchd my powder horn out of my pocket which I immediately laid hold of and wrenchd out of his hand, not without some dificulty; I then laid my hand on his breast and attempted to shove him over-board but he was two strong for me and kept his place. The officer orderd a musquet to be fir'd over their heads his own having mis'd fire, two were immediately fird and they all instantly leapd into the water; one of our people however inconsiderately leveld a 3^d at one of them who was swimming and the ball gras'd his forehead but I beleive did him no material harm, as he recoverd his boat and stood up in her as active as ever. The canoe now stood for the shore where were a large number of people collected I beleive 200; our boat also pulld in but found the land guarded all round with a shoal upon which the sea broke much, so was obligd to go along shore in hopes of finding a more convenient landing place. We saw the canoe go ashore where the people were assembled who came down to her seemingly very eager to enquire into our behavior to them; soon after a single man came along shore armd with a long lance, he came abreast of the boat and then began to dance and shake his weapon calling out in a very shrill voice, which we understood from Tupia was a defiance sent from the people. We rowd along shore and he attended us sometime, we

---

[1] This seems from what Cook says, and from the description given by Banks later, to have been Avera bay, about the middle of the west coast, though Cook notes having made the circuit of the island.

found it however impracticable to land and as for the gen lemans
tricks we gave ourselves very little concern about them: we therefore
resolvd to return to the bay and try if it would be practicable to
land where the Canoe did, hoping that if we should not the people
would at least come and make peace either on the shoal or in their
Canoes of which we saw only two in the Island, which was one
more than Tupia allowd them who said they had but one.

As we rowd gently along shore our defying champion was joind
by another likewise armd with a lance and dressd with a large
cap of the tail feathers of tropick birds and his body coverd, as
indeed many of them were, with stripes of different coulourd
cloths, yellow red and brown; he (who we now calld Harlequin)
danc'd as the other had done only with much more nimbleness and
dexterity. These two were soon after Joind by an older looking
man likewise armd who came gravely down to the beach and
hailing us askd from whence we came, Tupia answerd him from
Otahite. The three then went peaceably along shore till the boat
came to a shoal upon which a few people were collected; they
talkd together and soon after began to póoràh[1] or pray very loud
to which Tupia made his responses but continued to tell us that they
were not our freinds. We after this enterd into a parley with them,
telling them that if they would lay by their arms which were lances
and clubbs we would come ashore and truck with them for whatever they would bring; they agreed but upon condition that we
should lay down our musquets, an article which we did not think
fit to comply with, so our negotiation dropt for the present at least.
After a little time however they took courage and came nearer to
the boat, near enough to begin to trade which they did very fairly
for a smal quantity of cloth and some of their weapons, but as
they gave us no hopes of provisions or indeed any thing else unless
we would venture through a narrow channel to the shore we put
off the boat and left them.

In this expedition we labourd under many disadvantages: we
left the ship in a hurry taking with us no kind of arms but our
musquets, which without bayonets would have made but a poor
resistance against these peoples weapons all meant to fight hand to
hand; but what was worst of all was the dificulty of landing which
we could not do without wetting ourselves and arms unless we had
venturd through the passage I have spoke of, which was so small
that tho the weather was perfectly fine the sea often broke right
across it, so that had we gone in and the least surf rose we could

[1] *pure.*

never have got out again but must have remaind the night in shoal water, liab[l]e to any stratagems that our enemies might devise, ill furnishd as we were to oppose their boarding us by swimming to which we were always liable.

The Island to all apearance that we saw was more barren than any thing we have seen in these seas, the cheif produce seeming to be *Etóá* (the wood of which make their weapons); indeed every where along shore where we saw plantations they were coverd by trees of this kind planted between them and the sea. It is without a reef[1] and the ground in the bay we were in so foul and corally that tho a ship might come almost close to the shore she could not possibly anchor. The water was clearer than I ever saw it, I saw distinctly the ground at 25 fathoms depth.

The people seemd strong lusty and well made but were rather browner than those we have left behind; they were not tattowd on their backsides, but instead of that had black marks about as broad as my hand under their armpits the sides of which were deeply indented, 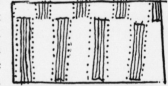 they had also circles of smaller ones round their arms and 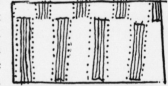 legs. Their dress was indeed most singular as well as the cloth with which they were dressd which I shall first describe. It was made of the same materials as the inhabitants of the other Islands make use of and generaly died of a very bright and deep yellow. Upon this was on some sorts spread a composition which coverd it like oil colour or varnish, it was either red or of a dark lead colour; upon this again was painted stripes in many different patterns with infinite regularity much in the same way as some lute string silks in England are wove, all the streight lines upon them drawn with such accuracy that we were almost in doubt whether or not they were stampd on with some kind of press. The red cloth was painted in this manner with black, the lead coulord with white. Of this cloth, generaly the lead coulourd, they had on a short jacket that reachd about their Knees made of one peice with a hole through which they put their heads, the sides of which hole was contrary to any thing I have seen before stichd with long stitches. This was confind to their bodies by a peice of Yellow cloth which pass'd behind their necks and came across their breasts in two broad stripes crossing each other, it was then collected

---

[1] i.e. there is no barrier reef, of the sort Banks was familiar with in the islands he had come from; but the coast has a coral fringe all round.

round their waists in the form of a belt, under which was another of the red cloth so that the whole made a very gay and warlike apearance. Some had on their heads caps as before describd made of the tails of tropick birds, but they did not become them so well as a peice of white or lead colourd cloth which the most of them had wound on like a small turban.

Their arms consisted of long lances made of the *etoa* or hard wood well polishd and sharp[nd] at one end; of these there were some near 20 feet long and scarce so thick as three fingers; they had also clubs or pikes of the same wood about 7 feet long, well polishd and sharpned at one end into a broad point. How expert they may be in the use of these weapons we cannot tell but the weapons themselves seem more intended for shew than use, as the lance was not pointed with the stings of Sting rays, and the clubs or pikes which must do more execution by their weight than their sharpness were not more than half so heavy as the smallest I have seen in the other Islands. Defensive weapons I saw none, they however guarded themselves against such weapons as their own by matts folded and laid upon their breasts and bellys under their other cloths.

Of the few things we saw among these people every one was ornamented infinitely superior to any thing we had before seen: their cloth was better coulourd as well as nicely painted, their clubs were better cut out and polishd, the Canoe which we saw tho a very small and very narrow one was nevertheless carvd and ornamented very highly. One thing particularly in her seemd to be calculated rather for the ornaments of a thing that was never intended to go into the water than a boat, which was two lines of small white feathers that were placd on the outside of the canoe which were when we saw them totaly wet with the water.

After leaving these unhospitable people we Stood to the Southward as usual and had in the evening a great dew which wetted every thing.

Manners & customs of S. Sea Islands

We have now seen 17 Islands in these Seas and been ashore upon 5 of the most principal ones. Of these the Language manners and customs have agreed almost exactly, I should therefore be tempted to conclude that those of the Islands we have not seen differ not materialy at least from them. The account I shall give of them is taken cheifly from Otahite where I was well acquainted with their most interior policy, as I found them to be a people so free from deceit that I trusted myself among them almost as freely as I could do in my own countrey, sleeping continualy in their houses in the woods with not so much as a single companion. Whither or not I am right in judging their manners and customs to be general throughout these seas any one who gives himself the trouble of reading this Journal through will be as good a Judge as myself.

All the Islands I have seen are very populous all along the sea coast, where are generaly large flats coverd with a vast many breadfruit and Cocoa nut trees. Here are houses almost every 50 yards with their little plantations of Plantains, the tree that makes their cloth[1] &c. but the inland parts are totaly uninhabited except in the vallies where are rivers and even there are but a small propo[r]tion of people to what live upon the flats.[2] They are of the larger size of Europæans, all excellently made, and some handsome both men and women, the only bad feature they have is their noses which are in general flat, but to balance this their teeth are almost without exception even and white to perfection, and the eyes of the women especialy are full of expression and fire. In Colour they differ very much: those of inferior rank who are obligd in the excersise of their professions, fishing especialy, to be much exposd to the sun and air are of a dark brown; the superiors again who spend most of their time in their houses under shelter are seldom browner (the women especialy) than that kind of Brunette which many in Europe preferr to the finest red and white. Complexion[3] indeed they seldom have tho some I have seen shew a Blush very manifestly; this is perhaps owing to the thickness of their skins, but that fault is in my opinion well compensated by their infinite smoothness much superior to any thing I have met with in Europe.

The men as I have before said are rather large, I have measurd one 6 feet 3½; the superior women are also as large as Europæans but the inferior sort generaly small, some very small owing possibly to their early amours which they are much more addicted to than their superiors. Their hair is almost universaly black and rather coarse: this the women wear always cropt short round their ears, the men on the other hand wear it in many various ways, sometimes

[1] He does not mean that cloth was made from the plantain; he is mentioning separate trees.

[2] The population question, which Banks disposes of so briefly, is difficult. He may have had reliable information, but he saw very little of the interior even of Tahiti, and nothing of it at all on the other islands. Archaeological remains suggest more population inland than he thought, but its extent is extraordinarily difficult to estimate. It was certainly a *manahune*, lower class, and not an *arii* or chiefly, population. See Cook I, pp. clxxiv-clxxvii.

[3] In the sense of colour. He is thinking of the complexion of the English lady.

cropping it short, sometimes letting [it] grow very long and tying it at the top of their heads or letting it hang loose on their shoulders &c. Their beards they also wear in many different fashions always however plucking out a large part of them and keeping that that is left very clean and neat. Both sexes eradicate every hair from under their armpits and they look upon it as a great mark of uncleanliness in us that we did not do the same.

During our stay in these Islands I saw some not more than 5 or 6 who were a total exception to all I have said before. They were whiter even than us but of a dead Colour like that of the nose of a white horse; their eyes hair eyebrows and beards were also white; they were universaly short sighted and lookd always unwholesome, their skins scurfy and scaly and eyes often full of Rheum. As they had no two of them any connextions with one another I conclude that the difference of colour &c. was totaly accidental and did not at all run in families.[1]

So much for their persons. I shall now mention their method of Painting their bodies or *Tattow* as it is calld in their language. This they do by inlaying the colour of Black under their skins in such a manner as to be indelible; every one is markd thus in different parts of his body according may be to his humour or different circumstances of his life. Some have ill designd figures of men, birds or dogs, but they more generaly have this figure Z eitheir simply, as the women are generaly markd with it, on every Joint of their fingers and toes and often round the outside of their feet, or in different figures of it as square, circles, crescents &c. which both sexes have on their arms and leggs; in short they have an infinite diversity of figures in which they place this mark and some of them we were told had significations but this we never learnt to our satisfaction. Their faces are in general left without any marks, I did not see more than one instance to the contrary. Some few old men had the greatest part of their bodies coverd with large patches of black which ended in deep indentations like coarse imitations of flame, these we were told were not natives of Otahite but came there from a low Island called *Noouoora*.[2]

[1] Cf. p. 263, n. 2 above. Morrison in his *Journal* (p. 230) describes something of the same sort, which may be *o'ovi arii* or 'chief's leprosy': 'They Have also a kind of leprosy which changes the Body to a Dead Wite in some parts while the natural Collour is heightened to Black; this Change of Collour extends to the Hair on the head & body some of which is white as snow, while the rest is Jet Black, which gives them a very odd appearance. Some are Changed all over but this does not effect their Health or Strength'. Davies, in his dictionary (1851), defines *o'ovi* as 'a certain scrophulous disorder'; Andrews (1944) as 'a disease like leprosy indigenous to the islands'.

[2] Probably Au-ura, one of the Tuamotus; I suspect Banks was given some such information as that they were *taata no Au-ura*, people of or from that island.

Tho they are so various in the application of the figures I have mentiond that both the quantity and situation of them seems to depend intirely upon the humour of each individual, yet all the Islanders I have seen (except those of Ohiteroa) agree in having all their buttocks coverd with a deep black; over this most have arches drawn one over another as high as their short ribbs, which are often ¼ of an inch broad and neatly workd on their edges with indentations &c. These arches are their great pride: both men and women shew them with great pleasure whether as a beauty or a proof of their perseverance and resolution in bearing pain I can not tell, as the pain of doing this is almost intolerable especialy the arches upon the loins which are so much more susceptible of pain than the fleshy buttocks.

Their method of doing it I will now describe. The colour they use is lamp black wich they prepare from the smoak of a kind of oily nutts usd by them instead of candles;[1] this is kept in cocoa nut shells and mixt with water occasionaly for use. Their instruments for pricking this under the skin are made of Bone or shell, flat, the lower part of this is cut into sharp teeth from 3 to 20 according to the purposes it is to be usd for and the upper fastned to a handle.[2] These teeth are dippd into the black liquor and then drove by quick sharp blows struck upon the handle with a stick for that purpose into the skin so deep that every stroke is followd by a small quantity of Blood, or serum at least, and the part so markd remains sore for many days before it heals.

I saw this operation performd on the 5th of July on the buttocks of a girl about 14 years of age; for some time she bore it with great resolution but afterwards began to complain and in a little time grew so outrageous that all the threats and force her freinds could use could hardly oblige her [to] indure it. I had occasion to remain in an adjoining house an hour at least after this operation began and yet went away before it was finished, tho this was the blacking of only one side of her buttocks the other having been done some weeks before.

It is done between the ages of 14 and 18 and so essential it is that I have never seen one single person of years of maturity without it. What can be a sufficient inducement to suffer so much pain is difficult to say; not one Indian (tho I have askd hundreds) would ever give me the least reason for it; possibly superstition may have something to do with it, nothing else in my opinion could be a

---

[1] The Tiari, Tutui or Candlenut, *Aleurites moluccana.*
[2] This instrument was called the *ta*; *ta* is also to strike.

sufficient cause for so apparently absurd a custom. As for the smaller marks on the fingers, arms &c they may be intended only for beauty; Our European ladies have found the Convenience of patches, and something of that kind is more usefull here, where the best complexions are much inferior to theirs, and yet whiteness is esteemd the first Essential in beauty.[1]

They are certainly as cleanly a people as any under the sun except in their lousyness, every one of them wash their whole bodies in the running water as soon as they rise in the morn, at noon, and before they sleep at night; and if they have not such water near their houses as often happens, they will go a good way to it; as for their lice had they the means only they would certainly be as free from them as any inhabitants of so warm a climate could be. Those to whoom combs were given provd this, for those who I was best acquainted with kept themselves very clear while we staid by the use of them; as for their eating lice it is a custom which none but children and those of the inferior people can be chargd with. Their cloths also as well as their persons are kept almost without spot or stain; the superiour people spend much of their time in repairing, dying, &c the cloth, which seems to be a genteel amusement for the ladies here as it is in Europe.

Their Clothes are either of a kind of cloth made of the Bark of a tree, or matts of several different sorts. Of all these and their manner of making them I shall speak in another place, here I shall only mention their method of covering and adorning their Persons, which is of course most various as they never form dresses, or sew any two things together. It must be a peice of cloth which is generaly 2 yards wide and 11 long, is sufficient Clothing for any one, and this they put on in a thousand different ways, often very genteel. Their dress of form however is, in the women, a kind of Peticoat (*Parou*)[2] wrappd round their hipps, and reaching about the middle of their leggs; 1, 2 or 3 peices of thick cloth about $2\frac{1}{2}$ yards long and one wide (*Te buta*)[3] through a hole in the middle of which they put their heads, and suffer the sides of it to hang before and behind them, the open edges serving to give their arms liberty of moving; round the ends of this, about as high as their wastes, are tied 2 or 3 large peices of thin Cloth, and sometimes another

---

[1] The punctuation in this paragraph and the following five is almost entirely by Banks; an indication that he did know the use of punctuation marks, though generally so erratic in their application.

[2] *pareu.*

[3] *tiputa*, in origin a more aristocratic garment than the *ahu*, which was merely thrown over the shoulders.

or two thrown over their shoulders loosely, for the rich seem to
shew their greatest pride in wearing a large quantity of cloth.
The dress of the men differs but little from this; their bodys are
rather more bare, and instead of the petticoat they have a peice of
Cloth passed between their leggs and round their waists (*Maro*)
which keeps up the strictest rules of decency, and at the same time
gives them rather more liberty to use their limbs than the womens
dress will allow.[1] Thus much of the richer people, the poorer sort
have only a small allowance of cloth given them from the tribes
or families to which they belong, and must use that to the best
advantage.

It is reckond no shame for any part of the body to be exposd
to view except those which all mankind hide; it was no uncommon
thing for the richest of the men to come to see us with a large
quantity of cloth rolld round their loins, and all the rest of their
bodies naked, tho the cloth wrappd round them was sufficient
to have clothd a doz[n] people. The women at sun set always bard
their bodys down to the navel, which seemd to be a kind of easy
undress to them as to our ladies to pull off any finery that has
been usd during the course of the day, and change it for a loose
gown and capachin.[2]

Both sexes shade their faces from the sun with little bonnets of
cocoa nut leaves which they make occasionaly in a very few minutes,
some have these made of fine matting but that is less common. Of
matting they have several sorts, some very fine, which is usd in
exactly the same manner as Cloth for their dresses, cheifly in
rainy weather, as their cloth will not bear the least wett.[3]

Ornaments they have very few, they are very fond of earings
but wear them only in one ear. When we came they had them of
their own, made of Shell, stone, berries, red pease,[4] and some small
pearls which they wore 3 tied together; but our beads very quickly
supplyd their place; they also are very fond of flowers, especialy of
the Cape Jasmine[5] of which they have great plenty planted near
their houses; these they stick into the holes of their ears, and into
their hair, if they have enough of them which is but seldom. The
men wear feathers often the tails of tropick birds stuck upright

---

[1] But the *pareu* was also worn by men (and still is). The *maro* was an older Polynesian
dress, characteristic of the lower social order—a 'working dress'.

[2] The capuchin, a female garment favoured in the eighteenth century, was a cloak
and hood imitating the dress of Capuchin friars.

[3] Mats of varying degrees of fineness were made from the different sorts of pandanus.

[4] Probably he is thinking of the peas of the Pitipitio, *Abrus precatorius*, a prickly vine;
they were much used for ornament.

[5] The sweet-scented Tiare, *Gardenia taitensis*.

in their hair, they have also a kind of wiggs made upon one string of the hair of men, dogs, or Cocoa nut strings, which they tie under their hair upon the back of their heads; I have seen them also wear whimsical garlands made of a variety of flowers stuck into a peice of the rind of plaintain, or of scarlet pease stuck upon a peice of wood with gum, but these are not common. Their great pride of Dress seems to be centerd almost in what they call *Tamou*, which is human hair platted, scarce thicker than common thread, of this I may easily affirm that I have peices above a mile in lenght worked upon an end without a single Knot, and I have seen 5 or 6 of such peices wound round the head of one woman, the effect of which if done with taste was most becoming.[1] Thus much of their common dresses, their dancing dresses I have describd in the Island of Ulhietea and that of the *Heiva* I shall when I come to their mourning ceremonies. They have also several more suited to particular ceremonies which I had not an opportunity of seeing, tho I was very desirous, as the singular taste of those promise much novelty at least if not something worth imitation in whatever they take pains with.

I had almost forgot the Oil with which they anoint their heads, *monoe*[2] it is calld in their language, a custom more disagreable to Europeans than any other among them. This is made of Cocoa nut oil in which some sweet woods or flowers are infusd;[3] the oil is most commonly very rancid and consequently the wearers of it smell most disagreably, at first we found it so but very little use reconcild me at least very compleatly to it. These people are free from all smells of mortality and surely rancid as their oil is it must be preferrd to the odoriferous perfume of toes and armpits so frequent in Europe.

The houses or rather dwellings of these people are admirably calculated for the continual warmth of their climate. They do not build them in villages or towns but seperate each from the other according to the size of the estate the owner of the house possesses; they are always in the woods and no more ground is cleard away for each house than is Just sufficient to hinder the Dropping of the branches from rotting the thatch with which they are coverd, so that you step from the house immediately under shade and that

[1] *taamu.* It is not now known how this plaiting was done. A marginal note in the MS, not in Banks's hand, runs, 'Jany. 21. 1772 measurd one 6144 feet another 7294 feet'.

[2] *monoi.*

[3] Grated sandalwood (Ahi) was much used, and the resulting *monoi-ahi* was thought of highly as a liniment as well as a hair-dressing.

the most beautifull imaginable. No countrey can boast such delight-
full walks as this, the whole plains where the people live are coverd
with groves of Breadfruit and cocoa nut trees without underwood;
these are intersected in all directions by the paths which go from
one house to the other, so the whole countrey is a shade than which
nothing can be more gratefull in a climate where the sun has so
powerfull an influence. They are built without walls so that the
air coold by the shade of the trees has free access in whatever
direction it happens to blow. I shall describe one of the middle
size which will give an Idea of all the rest as they differ scarce at
all in fashion.

Its lengh was 24 feet, breadth 11, extreem high[t] $8\frac{1}{2}$, hight
of the eaves $3\frac{1}{2}$; it consisted of nothing more than a thatchd roof[1]
of the same form as in England supported by 3 rows of posts or
pillars, one on each side and one in the middle; the floor was
coverd some inches deep with soft hay upon which here and there
were laid matts for the convenience of setting down; this is almost
the only furniture as few houses have more than one stool which is
the property of the master of the family and constantly usd by
him, and most are intirely without. These houses serve them cheifly
to sleep in and make their cloth &c., they generaly Eat in the open
air under the shade of the next tree if the weather is not rainy.
The matts which serve them to set upon in the day time are also
their beds at night; the Cloth which they wear in the day serves
for covering, and a little wooden stool, block of wood or a bundle
of cloth for a pillow. Their order is generaly this, near the middle
lay the master of the house and his wife and with them the rest
of the married people, next to them the unmarried women, next
to them at some small distance the unmarried men; the Servants,
Toutous[2] as they are calld, generaly lay in the open air or if it rains
come just within shelter. Thus all privacy is banishd even from
those actions which the decency of Europæans keep most secret:
this no doubt is the reason why both sexes express the most indecent
ideas in conversation without the least emotion; in this their language
is very copious and they delight in such conversation beyond any
other. Chastity indeed is but little valued especialy among the
midling people;[3] if a wife is found guilty of a breach of it her only
punishment is a beating from her husband. Notwithstanding this

---

[1] The leaves of the coconut and the pandanus made a very secure thatched roof.
[2] *teuteu.*
[3] Banks here over-states; and he does indeed make a modification in his next sentence.
The 'midling people' appear on the whole to have been quite as virtuous as Banks and
his fellows, allowing for the difference between Polynesian and European convention,

some of the *Eares* or cheifs are I beleive perfectly virtuous. They indeed tho they have no decency in conversation have privacy; most or all of them have small houses which when they move are tied upon their Canoes; these have walls made of Cocoa nut leaves &c. in them they constantly sleep, man and wife, generaly lifting them off from their canoes and placing them on the ground in any situation they think proper.

Besides these there are another kind of houses much larger. One in our neighbourhood measurd length 162 feet, breadth 28½, high[t] of one of the middle row of pillars 18. These we conjecturd to be common to all the inhabitants of a district and raisd and kept up by their joint labour, of use maybe for any meetings or consultations, for the reception of any visitants of consequence, &c; such we have also seen usd as dwelling houses by the very principal people, some of them much larger than this which I have here describd.[1]

In the article of food these happy people may almost be said to be exempt from the curse of our forefather; scarcely can it be said that they earn their bread with the sweat of their brow when their cheifest sustenance Bread fruit[2] is procurd with no more trouble than that of climbing a tree and pulling it down. Not that the trees grow here spontaneously but if a man should in the course of his life time plant 10 such trees, which if well done might take the labour of an hour or thereabouts, he would as compleatly fulfull his duty to his own as well as future generations as we natives of less temperate climates can do by toiling in the cold of winter to sew and in the heat of summer to reap the annual produce of our soil, which when once gatherd into the barn must be again resowd and re-reapd as often as the Colds of winter or the heats of Summer return to make such labour disagreable.

and a good deal more chaste than some of them. Banks and Cook (as Cook afterwards realized) were observing a society—or portion of a society—undergoing the upheaval caused by the arrival of a strange ship and the availability of the marvellous material, iron, for which 'virtue' was no very high payment. Nor were the young women who rushed the ship the leading representatives of Tahitian respectability, though one can hardly blame Banks for not immediately realizing that. Eighteenth century visitors were bound to talk nonsense on this subject. James Morrison, who made the first considerable stay in Tahiti, is a witness all the other way.—See his *Journal*, pp. 225, 235-7. I have discussed the matter at rather more length in my Note on Polynesian History, in the introduction to Cook I, pp. clxxxvi-viii. Cook himself found more to say on his second voyage.—II, pp. 238-9.

[1] Henry calls these *arioi* houses, *fare-arioi;* they seem to have been structures used for general entertainment (though much entertainment was carried on in the open air) and also as guest-houses, *fare-manihini.*

[2] Known as Uru (*Artocarpus* spp.). There are about forty varieties, and a great breadfruit tree is a noble sight. See Wilder, *The Breadfruit of Tahiti* (B. P. Bishop Mus. Bull. 50, Honolulu 1928). See pl. 32.

Y

O fortunati nimium sua si bona norint[1]

may most truly be applied to these people; benevolent nature
has not only supplyd them with nescessaries but with abundance
of superfluities. The Sea about them in the neighbourhood of
which they always live supplys them with vast variety of fish better
than what is generaly met with between the tropicks, but these they
get not without some trouble; every one desires to have them and
there is not enough for all, tho while we remain in these seas we
saw above   [2] species more perhaps than our own Island
can boast of. I speak now only of what is more properly calld Fish;
but almost every thing which comes out of the sea is eat and esteemd
by these people, Shellfish, lobsters, Crabbs, even Sea insects and
what the seamen call blubbers[3] of many kinds conduce to their
support. Some of the last indeed that are of a tough nature are
prepard by suffering them to stink; custom will make almost any
meat palatable and the women especialy are very fond of this,
tho after they had eat it I confess I was not extreemly fond of their
company.

Besides the Bread fruit the earth almost spontaneously produces
Cocoa nuts, Bananas of 13 sorts the best I have ever eat, Plantains
but indiffer[e]nt,[4] a fruit not unlike an apple which when ripe is
very pleasant,[5] Sweet potatoes,[6] Yamms,[7] Cocos,[8] another kind of
Arum known in the East Indies by the name of Arum   ,[9]

[1] A reminder that to be an eighteenth century gentleman with a university education
was not necessarily to be secure in the classics. If Banks had given more time to Virgil
and less to botany he would have written 'O fortunatos. . . .'—'Oh greatly happy,
if they but knew their own happiness!'

[2] Blank space in the MS.

[3] Blubbers: a term generally used by seamen to denote medusae or 'jellyfish'. Some
medusae are still used for food in China; they are preserved in salt or alum, or with the
leaves of an oak, then soaked in water for half an hour, cut up and flavoured. They are
said to be tender and palatable after such treatment. 'Sea-insects' is too vague a term
for identification to be possible.

[4] There were, and are, many sorts of bananas and lowland plantains, called Meia
(Henry lists thirty-four native ones that are cultivated) and mountain plantains (of
which she lists eighteen). They differ in colour of leaves, bark and sap. The plantains
used to be cooked before eating, which is perhaps why Banks found them but indifferent;
his bananas were probably the cultivated ones.

[5] The Vi (*Spondias dulcis*), known by a variety of English names, among them the
'yellow apple'. See Pl. VI.

[6] Umara (*Ipomoea batatas*). It was spread all over Polynesia and found in South
America.

[7] Uhi (*Dioscorea alata*); there was another yam, wild, called Patara (*Dioscorea penta-
phylla*).

[8] Taro (*Colocasia esculenta*).

[9] Blank in MS, with an almost illegible word supplied, possibly Arum. P blank, S
illegible. Banks seems to refer to another variety of Taro (between thirty and forty
varieties, cultivated and wild, are known); probably to *Alocasia macrorrhiza*, the 'E ape' of
Parkinson's account, for which a leaf drawing labelled 'Arum costatum' was made in
1769, and of which a small example is preserved in the Pocket Book. Hooker misprinted
this phrase with a resulting altered meaning.

a fruit known there by the name of [Eug mallacc][1] and reckond most delicious, Sugar cane which the inhabitants eat raw, a root of the Salop kind Calld by the inhabitants *Pea*,[2] the root also of a plant calld *Ethee*[3] and a fruit in a Pod like a large Hull of a Kidney bean, which when roasted eats much like Chestnuts and is call[d] *Ahee*;[4] besides a fruit of a tree which they call *wharra*[5] in appearance like a pine apple, the fruit of a tree calld by them *Nono*,[6] the roots and perhaps leaves of a fern[7] and the roots of a plant calld *Theve*[8] which 4 are eat only by the poorer sort of people in times of scarcity.

For tame animals they have Hogs, fowls and doggs, which latter we learn'd to eat from them and few were there of the nicest of us but allowd that a S-Sea dog was next to an English lamb; this indeed must be said in their favour that they live intirely upon vegetables, probably our dogs in England would not eat half as well. Their pork is certainly most excellent tho sometimes too fat, their fowls are not a bit better rather worse maybe than ours at home, often very tough.

Tho they seem to esteem flesh very highly yet in all the Islands I have seen the quantity they have of it is very unequal to the number of their people, it is therefore seldom usd among them. Even their most principal people have it not every day or even week, tho some

---

[1] In the MS the words 'Eug mallacc' are written in pencil in a blank, and are but faintly decipherable. They caused some trouble: P blank. S *Eug mallec*, and the marginal note, referring both to this and to Arum (?), 'I fear I have not spelt these names right'. Cook, in copying from Banks, was misled, and wrote 'Eag melloa', which as a contribution to botany is not very helpful. In making the copy of the journal on which Hooker worked, Miss Turner or the clerk also was deceived, and wrote 'eng mallow', which inveigled the great botanist into a footnote suggesting '*Hibiscus esculentus*, Linn?' (the hibiscus is a mallow). But Banks was referring to the Jambo or *Eugenia malaccensis*, sometimes called the Malay Apple, a well-known and well-spread tropical fruit, in Tahiti the Ahia. Hooker could have saved himself by a reading of Hawkesworth (II, p. 186), 'a fruit known here by the name of *Jambu* and reckoned most delicious'.

[2] Pia, *Tacca leontopetaloides* (L.) O. Ktze (*T. pinnatifida* Forst. <JDH>), from the rhizome of which was obtained a starchy meal called by the same name, something like arrowroot. (Molyneux the master: 'Peea a strong white Jelly'.) Salop or saloop was also a starchy meal, from which was made one of the popular eighteenth century drinks; there are numerous references to it in the literature of the time. See pl. 35.

[3] Probably Ti (*Cordyline terminalis*), a sort of 'cabbage-tree', some varieties of which had a succulent root. Parkinson lists 'E tee' as 'a large root . . . counted very good'.

[4] Ihi, the Tahitian chestnut, the fruit of the Mape or—its older name—Rata (*Inocarpus edulis*). Parkinson calls it the 'E hee or E ratta'—which confuses indefinite article and first syllable.

[5] Fara, pandanus or screw-pine, an immensely valuable tree for a number of island purposes.

[6] Nono, called by the English the Sour Apple and sometimes known as the Indian mulberry (*Morinda citrifolia*); its leaves were much used in cookery, to wrap fish. It has a seedy, insipid fruit. See pl. 34b.

[7] Nahe (*Angiopteris evecta*), a small tree-fern, with a large insipid tuberous root.

[8] Teve (*Amorphophallus campanulatus* or *Dracontium polyphyllum*), a plant resembling the Pia in appearance, which has a bitter tuber, edible when cooked and mashed and strained through water. A small leaf is preserved in the Pocket Book.

of them had piggs that we saw quarterd upon different Estates as we send Cocks to walk's in England; when any of these kill a hog it seems to be divided almost equaly among all his dependands himself taking little more than the rest. Vegetables are their cheif food and of these they eat a large quantity. Cookery seems to have been little studied here: they have only two methods of applying fire, broiling, or baking as we calld it which is done thus. A hole is dug in depth and size according to what is to be prepard seldom exceeding a foot in depth, in this a heap is made of wood and stones alternately laid; fire is then put to it which by the time it has consumd the wood has heated the stones sufficiently just enough to discolour any thing which touches them. The heap is then divided; half is left in the hole the bottom of which is pavd with them, on them any kind of provisions are laid always neatly wrappd up in leaves, the whole is then coverd with leaves on which are laid the remaining hot stones then leaves again 3 or 4 inches thick and over them any ashes rubbish or dirt that lays at hand. In this situation it remains about 2 hours in which time I have seen a midling hog very well done, Indeed I am of opinion that victuals dressd this way are more juicy if not more Equably done than by any of our European methods, large fish more especialy. Bread fruit cookd in this manner becomes soft and something like a boild potatoe, tho not quite so farinaceous as a good one yet more so than the midling sort. Of this 2 or 3 dishes are made by beating it with a stone pestil till it make a paste, mixing water or Cocoa nut liquor with it and adding ripe plantains, bananas, sour paste &c.

As I have mentiond Sour paste I will proceed to de[s]cribe what it is. Bread fruit by what I can find remains in season only 9 or 10 of their 13 months so that a reserve of food must be made for those months when they are without it. To do this the fruit is gatherd when just upon the point of ripening and laid in heaps where it undergoes a fermentation and becomes disagreably sweet; the core is then taken out which is easily done as a small pull at the stalk draws it out intire, and the rest of the fruit thrown into a hole dug for that purpose generaly in their houses; the sides and bottom of which are neatly lind with grass; the whole is coverd with leaves and heavy stones laid upon them. Here it undergoes a second fermentation and becomes sourish in which condition it will keep as they told me many months. Custom has I suppose made this agreable to their palates tho we dislikd it extreemly, we seldom saw them make a meal without some [of] it in some shape or other.

As the whole making of this *Mahai*[1] as they call it depends upon fermentation I suppose it does not always succeed. It is done at least always by the old women who make a kind of superstitious mystery of it. No one except the people employd by them is allowd to come even into that part of the house where it is; I myself spoild a large heap of it only by inadvertenly touching some leaves that lay upon it as I walkd by the outside of the house where it was. The old directress of it told me that from that circumstance it most certainly would fail and immediately pulld it down before my face, who did less regret the mischeif I had done as it gave me an opportunity of se[e]ing the preparation which perhaps I should not otherwise have been allowd to do.[2]

To this plain diet prepard with so much simplicity salt water is the universal sauce; those who live at the greatest distance from the sea are never without it keeping it in large bamboes set up against the sides of their houses. When they eat a cocanut shell full of it always stands near them, into which they dip every morsel especialy of fish and often leave the whole soaking in it, drinking at intervals large supps of it out of their hands, so that a man may use $\frac{1}{2}$ a pint of it at a meal. They have also a sauce made of the Kernels of cocoa nutts fermented till they dissolve into a buttery paste and beat up with salt water; the taste of this is very strong and at first was to me most abominably nauseous, a very little use however reconcild me intirely to it so much that I should almost preferr it to our own sauces with fish. It is not common among them, possibly it is thought ill management among them to use cocoa nuts so lavis[h]ly, or we were on the Islands at the time when they were scarce ripe enough for this purpose.

Small fish they often eat raw and sometimes large ones. I myself by being much with them learnt to do the same insomuch that I have made meals often of raw fish and bread fruit, by which I learnt that with my stomach at least it agreed as well as dressd and if any thing was still easier of digestion, howsoever contrary this may appear to the common opinion of the people at home.

Drink they have none but water and cocoa nut Juice, nor do they

---

[1] *mahi*.
[2] Morrison casts a little more light on this incident: 'The Men and Weomen having each their own trees have also their own Mahee and should a Man who is not the Servant of a Woman toutch even the Covering of the Womans Mahee it is rendered unfit for Her Use, which at once accounts for Sir Joseph Banks's having spoild a quantity which belongd to a Woman by his being desirous to see the nature of the Process of making it and examining the Contents of the pit—which was not only rendered of no use to the Woman but the place in which it was underwent the same fate and no woman Could ever use it afterwards'.—*Journal*, p. 215.

seem to have any method of Intoxication among them. Some there
were who drank pretty freely of our liquors and in a few instances
became very drunk but seemd far from pleasd with their intoxication,
the individuals afterwards shunning a repitition of it instead of
greedily desiring it as most Indians are said to do.

Their tables or at least apparatus for Eating are set out with
great neatness tho the small quantity of their furniture will not
admit of much Elegance. I will describe the manner in which one
of their principal people is servd; they commonly eat alone unless
some stranger makes a second in their mess.

He setts commonly under the shade of the next tree or on the
shady side of the house; a large quantity of leaves either of Bread
fruit or Banana are neatly spread before him which serves instead of
a table cloth, a basket is then set by him which contains his provisions and two cocoa nut shells, one full of fresh water the other
of salt. He begins by washing his hands and mouth thoroughly
with the fresh water which he repeats almost continualy throughout
the whole meal. He then takes part of his provision from the basket.
Supose (as it often did) it consisted of 2 or 3 bread fruits, 1 or 2
small fish about as big as a perch in England, 14 or 15 ripe bananas
or half as many apples: he takes half a breadfruit, peels of the rind
and takes out the core with his nails; he then cramms his mouth
as full with it as it can possibly hold, and while he chews that
unlapps the fish from the leaves in which they remain tied up since
they were dressd and breaks one of them into the salt water; the
rest as well as the remains of the bread fruit lay before him upon the
leaves. He generaly gives a fish or part of one to some one of his
dependants, many of whoom set round him, and then takes up
a very small peice of that that he has broke into the salt water in
the ends of all the fingers of one hand and sucks it into his mouth
to get with it as much salt water as possible, every now and then
taking a small sup of it either out of the palm of his hand or the
cocoa nut shell. In the mean time one of the standers by has prepard
a young cocoa nut by peeling of the outer rind with his teeth (an
operation which at first appears very surprizing to Europeans
but depends so much upon a sl[e]ight that before we left the Islands
many of us were ourselves able to do it, even myself who can scarce
crack a nut) which when he chuses to drink he takes from him
and boring a hole through the shell with his finger or breaking
the nut with a stone drinks or sucks out the water. When he has
eat his bread fruit and fish he begins with his plantains, one of
which makes no more than a mouthful if they are as big as black

puddings; if he has apples a shell is nescessary to peel them, one is pickd of the ground where they are always plenty and tossd to him, with this he scrapes or cutts off the skin rather awkwardly as he wastes almost half the apple in doing it. If he has any tough kind of meat instead of fish he must have a knife, for which purpose a peice of Bamboo is tossd him of which he in a moment makes one by splitting it transversly with his nail, with which he can cut tough meat or tendons at least as readily as we can with a common knife. All this time one of his people has been employd with a stone pestle and a block of wood beating breadfruit which by much beating and sprinkling with water he Reduces to the consistence of soft paste; he then takes a vessel made like a butchers tray and in it he lays his paste mixing it with either bananas sour paste or making it up alone according to the taste of his master; to this he adds water pouring it on by degrees and squeezing it often through his hand till it comes to the consistence of thick custard; a large cocoa nut shell full of this he then sets before his master who supps it down as we would do a custard if we had not a spoon to eat it with; and his dinner is then finishd by washing his hands and mouth, cleaning the cocoa nut shells and putting any thing that may be left into the basket again.

It may be thought that I have given rather too large a quantity of provision to my eater when I say he has eat 3 bread fruits each bigger than two fists, 2 or 3 fish and 14 or 15 plantains or Bananas, each if they are large 6 or 7 inches long and 4 or 5 round, and conclude his dinner with about a quart of a food as substantial as the thickest unbaked custard; but this I do affirm that it is but few of the many of them I was acquainted with that eat less and many a great deal more. But I shall not insist that any man who may read this should beleive it as an article of faith; I shall be content if politeness makes him think as Joe Millers[1] freind said, 'Well Sir as you say so I beleive it but by g—d had I seen it myself I should have doubted it excedingly'.

I have said that they seldom eat together the better sort hardly ever, even two brothers or sisters have each their respective baskets one of which contains victuals the other cocoa nut shells &c. for furniture of their seperate tables. These were brought every day to our tents to those of our freinds who having come from a distance chose to spend the whole day or sometimes 2 or 3 in our company; these two relations would go out and setting down upon the ground

[1] Joe Miller (1684-1738), a celebrated comedian whose name was given to a popular jest-book published after his death, and was in time linked to any quip, stale or fresh.

within a few yards of each other turn their faces different ways and make their meals without saying a word to each other.

The women carefully abstain from eating with the men or even any of the victuals that have been prepard for them. All their victuals are prepard seperately by boys[1] and kept in a shed by themselves where they are lookd after by the same boys who attend them at their meals; notwithstanding this when we visited them at their houses the women with whoom we had any particular acquaintance or freindship would constantly ask us to partake of their meals, which we often did, eating out of the same basket and drinking out of the same cup.[2] The old women however would by no means allow the same liberty but would esteem their victuals polluted if we touchd them; in some instances I have seen them throw them away when we had inadvertently defil'd them by handling the vessels which containd them.

What can be the motive for so unsocial a custom I cannot in any shape guess, especialy as they are a people in every other instance fond of society and very much so of their women. I have often askd the reason of them but they have as often evaded the question or given me no other answer but that they did it because it was right, and expressd much disgust when I told them that in England men and women eat together and the same victuals; they however constantly affirm that it does not proceed from any superstitious motive, *Eatua* they say has nothing to do with it. But whatever the motive may be it certainly affects their outward manners more than their principles: in the tents for instance we never saw an instance of the women partaking of our victuals at our table, but we have several [times] seen them go 5 or 6 together into the servants apartment and there eat very heartily of whatever they could find, nor were they at all disturbd if we came in while they were doing [it] tho we had before usd all the intreatys we were masters of to invite them to partake with us. When a woman was alone she would often eat even in our company, but always took care to extort a strong promise that we should not let her countrey people know what she had done.[3]

---

[1] *by boys* is substituted for the words *indifferently I beleive by either men or women*; and *the same boys* a little farther on from *little boys*. But even the corrected statement is a puzzling one: women prepared their own food.

[2] Cf. p. 266, n. 5 above. This seems to be another proof that Tahitian restrictions were held not to apply to the visitors.

[3] A full discussion of 'eating tapu' would occupy a good deal of space. The core of it has been succinctly stated by Handy thus: 'What is known as the "eating tapu", a custom peculiar to Polynesia, furnishes one of the clearest and simplest illustrations of the working of the system based upon the theory of dualism in nature. This tapu required that men and women and persons of different degrees of sacredness eat part. Since food

After their meals and in the heat of the day they often sleep, middle ag'd people especialy, the better sort of whoom seem to spend most of their time in eating or sleeping. The young boys and girls are uncommonly lively and active and the old people generaly more so than the middle ag'd ones, which perhaps is owing to the excessive venery which the heat of the climate and their dissolute manners tempt them to. Diversions they have but few: shooting with the bow is the cheif one I have seen at Otahite which is confind almost intirely to the cheifs; the[y] shoot for distance only with arrows unfledgd, kneeling upon one knee and dropping the bow from their hands at the instant of the arrows parting from it. I measurd a shot that Tubourai Tamite made, 274 yards, yet he complaind that as the bow and arrows were bad he could not shoot so far as he ought to have done. At Ulhietea bows were less common, but the people amusd themselves by throwing a kind of Javelin 8 or 9 feet long at a mark which they did with a good deal of force and dexterity, often striking the body of a plantain tree their mark in the very center,[1] but I could never observe that either these or the Otahite people stakd any thing but seemd to contend merely for the honour of victory.

Musick is very little known to them which is the more wonderfull as they are very fond of it. They have only two instruments the flute and the drum. The former is made of a hollow bamboo about a foot long in which is 3 holes; into one of these they blow with one nostril stopping the other with the thumb of the left hand, the other two they stop and unstop with the fore finger of the left and middle finger of the right hand; by this means they produce 4 notes and no more of which they have made one tune that serves them for all occasions, to which they sing a number of songs *pehay*[2] as they call them generaly consisting of two lines affecting a coarse metre and generaly in Rhime. May be they would appear more musical if we well understood the accent of their language but are as downright prose as can be wrote. I shall give two or 3 specimens of songs made upon our arrival:

Te de pahai de parow-a
Ha maru no mina.

was capable of acting as a medium to carry psychic influences into the body, it was considered safer for men not to eat in company with women, not to have their food prepared by them, or to employ the same fire or the same utensils. . . . Since food and womankind were thought to be the two chief mediums through which evil influences could enter and take possession of man, when it was especially desirable to guard against psychic risk, it was necessary to take unusual precautions in the matter of eating'.— *Polynesian Religion* (B. P. Bishop Mus. Bull. 34, Honolulu 1927), pp. 49, 54.

[1] MS note: 'Compare with the Acc^t referred to p 321 & 322'—i.e. 326-7 above.   [2] *pehe*.

E pahah Tayo malama tai ya
No Tabane tonatou whannomiya.

E Turai eattu terara patee whennua toai
Ino o maio Pretane to whennuaia no Tute.[1]

At any time of the day when they are lazy they amuse themselves
by singing these couplets but especialy after dark. Their candles
are then lighted which are made of the kernel of a nut abounding
much in oil; many of these are stuck upon a skewer of wood one
below the other and give a very tolerable light which they often
keep burning an hour after dark and if they have many strangers
in the house it is sometimes kept up all night—a kind of guard
maybe upon the chastity of the ladies who upon such occasions
are very shy of receiving any mark of regard from their lovers.

Their Drumms they manage rather better: they are made of a
hollow block of wood coverd with sharks skin, with these they
make out 5 or 6 tunes[2] and accompany the flute not disagreably;
they know also how to tune two drums of Different notes into con-
cord which they do nicely enough. They also tune their flutes if
two play upon flutes which are not in unison, the short one is
leng[t]hned by adding a small roll of leaf which is tied round the
end of it and movd up and down till their ears (which are certainly
very nice) are satisfied. The drumms are usd cheifly in their *heivas*
which are at Otahiti no more than a set of musicians,[3] 2 drums
for instance two flutes and two singers, who go about from house
to house and play; they are alway receivd and rewarded by the
master of the family who gives them a peice of cloth or whatever

---

[1] It appears impossible to convert these couplets into intelligible and translatable
Tahitian, which would at the same time fit into the historical situation of 'songs made
upon our arrival'. It is certainly easy enough to render certain words and phrases—e.g.
'no Tabane', 'of [or perhaps 'for the sake of'] Banks'; while 'Pretane to Whennuaia no
Tute' seems to be *Pretane* (or *Paretane*) *to fenua ia no Tute*, 'Britain, your country, the
country of Cook'. The trouble is, as J. R. Forster acutely put it a few years later, in his
Observations (p. 402), 'The numerous vowels require a variation of diphthongs and accents,
to produce a multiplicity of sounds, and a nicety of ear to observe all these little
distinctions, which often occasioned a material alteration of the sense. . . .' This 'variation
of diphthongs and accents' Banks most unfortunately does not give us, and probably
could not. Forster goes on to remark (p. 469) that 'Their verses seem to be regularly
divided into feet, and they observe the quantity and express it in singing . . . . we observed
that many words occurred in their poems which were not used in common conversation'.
On the same page he himself makes an attempt to mark the quantities of Banks's second
pehe (which he had not heard), and by way of translation provides an heroic couplet
which shows great invention, but must be taken with so much reserve that it is not given
here.

[2] By this he must mean rhythms.

[3] Once again Banks is using the word *heiva* rather indiscriminately; it was not the
performers but the performance—any sort of diversion or *divertissement* from a dance
by a single performer to a massed 'ballet' or a 'grand Dramatick *heiva*', an elaborate
piece of miming; or a ceremony bound up with a formal occasion, like the *heiva no metua*
in which Banks himself had taken part.

else he can best spare and while they stay, 3 or 4 hours maybe, receives all his neighbours who croud his house full. This diversion the people are extravagantly fond of most likely because like concerts assemblys &c. in Europe they serve to bring the Sexes easily together at a time when the very thoughts of meeting has opend the heart and made way for pleasing Ideas. The grand Dramatick *heiva* which we saw at Ulhietea is I beleive occasionaly performd in all the Islands but that I have so fully Describd in the Journal of that Island Aug^st ye 3^d 7th and 8th that I need say no more about it.

Besides this they dance especialy the young girls whenever they can collect 8 or 10 together, singing most indecent words using most indecent actions and setting their mouths askew in a most extrordinary manner, in the practise of which they are brought up from their earlyest childhood; in doing this they keep time to a surprizing nicety, I might almost say as true as any dancers I have seen in Europe tho their time is certainly much more simple. This excercise is however left off as soon as they arrive at Years of maturity for as soon as ever they have formd a connection with a man they are expected to leave of Dancing *Timorodee*[1] as it is calld.

One amusement more I must mention tho I confess I hardly dare touch upon it as it is founded upon a custom so devilish, inhuman, and contrary to the first principles of human nature that tho the natives have repeatedly told it to me, far from concealing it rather looking upon it as a branch of freedom upon which they valued themselves, I can hardly bring myself to beleive it much less expect that any body Else shall. It is this that more than half of the better sort of the inhabitants of the Island have like Comus in Milton enterd into a resolution of enjoying free liberty in love without a possibility of being troubled or disturbd by its consequences; these mix together with the utmost freedom seldom cohabiting together more than one or two days by which means they have fewer children than they would otherwise have, but those who are so unfortunate as to be thus begot are smotherd at the moment of their birth. Some of these people have been pointed out to me by name and on being askd have not denyd the fact, who have contracted intimacies and livd together for years and even now continue to do so, in the course of which 2, 3 or more children have been born and destroyd.

They are calld *Arreoy* and have meetings among themselves

---

[1] There appears to be no single word corresponding to this. Obviously the dance was a matter of light-hearted erotic amusement. The phrases *te ai moro-iti* or *ti moro-iti* would mean copulation or a sort of pseudo-copulation. Parkinson, p. 61, gives the meaning of 'Taimòradee' as 'To reel to and fro'.

where the men amuse themselves with wrestling &c. and the women with dancing the indecent dances before mentiond, in the course of which they give full liberty to their desires but I beleive keep strictly up to the appearances of decency. I never was admitted to see them, one of our gentlemen saw part of one but I beleive very little of their real behavior tho he saw enough to make him give credit to what we had been told.

This custom as indeed it is natural to suppose Owes as we were told its existence cheifly to the men. A Woman howsoever fond she may be of the name of Arreoy and the liberty attending it before she conceives, generaly desires much to forfeit that title for the preservation of her child: in this she has not the smallest influence; if she cannot find a man who will own it she must of course destroy it; and if she can, with him alone it lies whether or not it shall be preserv'd: sometimes it is, but in that case both the man and woman forfeit their title of Arreoy and the privelege annext thereunto, and must for the future be known by the term *Whannownow*,[1] or bearer of children: a title as disgracefull among these people as it ought to be honourable in every good and well governd society. In this case the man and woman generaly live together as man and wife for the remainder of their lives.[2]

The great facility with which these people have always procurd the nescessaries of life may very reasonably be thought to have originaly sunk them into a kind of indolence which has as it were benumbnd their inventions, and prevented their producing such a variety of Arts as might reasonably be expected from the aproaches they have made in their manners to the politeness of the Europeans. To this may also be added a fault which is too frequent even among the politest nations, I mean an invincible attachment to the Customs which they have learnt from their forefathers which these people

---

[1] *fanaunau*, degraded.

[2] Banks's account of the *arioi*, that famous society, is true as far as it goes, but naturally enough it does not go very far. About the best account is in Williamson, *Essays in Polynesian Ethnology*, pp. 113-35; see also, for its perception into the religious significance of the cult, Moerenhout, *Voyages aux Iles du Grand Océan* (Paris 1837), I, 499 ff. I have discussed them briefly in my Note on Polynesian History already referred to. They were a society fairly widely-spread in Polynesia, though founded too late to be brought to New Zealand; with functions both secular and religious—if the two can be really separated, in a social system so thoroughly interpenetrated with religion. They were the great actors of ritual, and for the islands the opera, drama and dance rolled into one. The infanticide which was so widely practised seems to have been both an aid to what might be called celibacy, so advantageous to public performers, constantly on the move, and a measure of population-control; for in an island economy increase always brought considerable problems. It was natural therefore that the *arioi* should have divine origin and sanctions, and elaborate gradations and ceremonial observances of their own. Obviously they represented the erotic side of life, but as we have seen, their functions were much wider than that. Purea, Amo, Tupaia (to take only three examples) were all *arioi*.

are indeed in this degree excusable for: they derive their original not from Creation but from the womb of an inferior divinity who was herself with those of equal rank descended from the God Causer of Earthquakes;[1] they therefore look upon it as a Kind of Sacriledge to attempt to amend Customs which they suppose to have had their original either from their deities or their first ancestors, who they hold as little inferior to the divin[i]ties themselves.

The thing in which they shew the most ingenuity is the making and dying of their Cloth: in the description of these especialy the latter I shall be rather diffuse, as I am not without hopes that my countrey men may receive some advantage either from the things themselves or at least by hints derivd from them.

The Material of which it is made is the interior bark or liber of 3 sorts of trees, the Chinese paper mulberry *Morus Papyrifeta*,[2] the Breadfruit tree *Sitodium altile*,[3] and a tree much resembling the wild fig tree of the west Indians *Ficus prolixa*.[4] Of the first which is calld by them *Äouta*[5] the finest and whitest cloth is made which is worn cheifly by the principal people, it is likewise the properest for dying especialy with the Colour of red; of the second which is calld by them *ooroo*[6] is made a cloth inferior to the former in whiteness and softness, worn cheifly by people of inferior degree; of the third which is much the most rare is made a coarse harsh Cloth of the colour of the deepest brown paper,[7] which is the only one they have that at all resists water. It is much valued, the greatest quantity of it is perfumd and usd by the most principal people as a Morning dress.

These three trees are cultivated with much care especialy the former which covers the largest part of their cultivated land. Young plants of them only are us'd of 1 or 2 years growth, whose great

[1] See below, p. 380.
[2] *Broussonetia papyrifera* (L.) Vent.
[3] *Artocarpus altilis* (Sol.) Fosberg. Hooker and others took *utile* as the intended specific name; for the problem in nomenclature cf. Merrill, p. 359. See Pl. 32.
[4] *Ficus prolixa*, the Ora or Aoa; it has little purple figs. That Banks used this and other names when the Journal was written is clear enough; the decision on nomenclature was certainly reached during the progress of the voyage. It is equally clear that Forster pirated this and other names from the Solander MSS.
[5] Aute. But Banks is wrong in thinking the 'finest and whitest cloth' was made from this; it was what might be called the 'standard' raw material, and gave a strong brown cloth.
[6] Uru. It was a variety of this, the *pu'upu'u*, that gave the finest and choicest white cloth; the underbark of the young branches was used.
[7] This cloth does not seem to be elsewhere described as coarse and harsh. It was greatly esteemed as a bed-covering. In legend the tree was propagated on the earth from the moon; and so it came to pass, says Henry (p. 49) 'that ora cloth on earth became the preferred wrapping of the great idols of the marae; it was especially chosen for the god Oro'.

merit is to be thin, streight, and tall, without branches; to prevent the growth of which they pluck off with great care all the lower leaves and their Gemms, as often as there is any appearance of a tendency to produce branches.

Their Method of manufacturing the Bark is the same in all the sorts: one description of it will therefore be Sufficient: first then, the thin cloth they begin to make thus. When the trees are arrivd at a sufficient size they are drawn up and the roots and topps cut of and strippd of their leaves; the best of the *Aouta* are in this state about 3 or 4 feet long and as thick as a mans finger but the *ooroo* are considerably larger. The bark of these rods is then slit up longitudinaly and in this manner drawn off the stick; when all are stripd the bark is carried to some brook or running water into which it is laid to soak with stones upon it and in this situation it remains some days. When sufficiently soakd the women servants go down to the river, and stripping themselves set down in the water and scrape the peices of bark, holding them against a flat smooth board, with the shell calld by the English shell merchants Tygers tongue *Tellina Gargadia*,[1] dipping it Continualy in Water untill all the outer green bark is rubbd and washd away and nothing remains but the very fine fibres of the inner bark. This work is generaly finishd in the afternoon; in the evening these peices are spread out upon Plantain leaves. In doing this I suppose there is some dificulty as the mistress of the family generaly presides, all that I could observe was that they laid them 2 or 3 layers thick, and seemd very carefull to make them every where of equal thickness; so that if any part of a peice of Bark was scrapd thinner than it ought, another peice of the same thin quality was laid over it, in order to render it of the same thickness as the next.[2] When laid out in this manner the size of a peice of cloth [is] 11 or 12 yards long and not more than a foot broad, for as the longitudinal fibres are all laid lenghwise they do not expect it to stretch in that direction tho they well know how considerably it will in the other. In this state they suffer it to remain till morning, by which time a large proportion of the water with which when laid out it is thouroughly soakd is either draind off or evaporated and the fibres begin to adhere together, so that the whole may be lifted from the ground without dropping in peices. It is then taken away by the women servants who beat it in the following manner: they lay it upon a long peice of wood one side

---

[1] The name *Tellina gargadia* Linn. remains unchanged.

[2] The MS has here a marginal note, 'just contrary to that purpose'. It is not in Banks's hand, and is clearly wrong-headed.

of which is very Even and flat, which side is put under the Cloth; as many women then as they can muster or as can work at the board begin; each is furnishd with a battoon made of a very hard wood calld by the natives *Etoa (Casuarina equisetifolia)* these are about a foot long and square with a handle; on each of the 4 faces of the square are many small furrows of as many different fineness, in the first or coarsest not more than [15] in the finest one [56][1] which cover the whole face of the side. With the coarsest then they begin, keeping time with their strokes in the same manner as smiths or Anchor smiths, and continue until the Cloth which extends itself very fast under these strokes shews by the too great thinness of the Grooves which are made in it that a finer side of the beater is requisite; in the same manner they proceed to the finest side with which they finish, unless the Cloth is to be of that very fine sort which they call *Hoboo*[2] which is almost as thin as muslin. For the making of this they double the peice several times and beat it out again and afterwards bleach it in the sun and air which in these Climates cause whiteness in a very short time, but I beleive that the finest of their *Hoboo* does not come to either its whiteness or softness untill it has been worn some time, then washd and beat over again with the very finest beaters. Of this thin cloth they have as many different sorts almost as we have of Linnen, distinguishing it into different finenesses and the different materials of which it is made. Each peice is from 9 to 15 yards in lengh and about 2 and a half broad and serves them for Cloths in the day and bedding at night. When by use it is sufficiently worn and become dirty it is carried to the river and washd, cheifly by letting it soak in a gentle stream fasned to the bottom by a stone, or if very dirty wringing it and squeesing it gently; several of the peices of Cloth so washd are then laid on each other and being beat with the coarsest side of the beater adhere together and become a cloth as thick as coarse broad cloth, than which nothing can be more soft or delicious to the feel. This however is not the case with it immediately after being beat: it is then stiff as if newly starchd and some parts not adhering together as well as others it looks ragged, and is also of various thicknesses wherever any faults were in the Cloth from whence it was made; to remedy this is the business of the mistress of the family and principal women of it, who in this, and dying, seem to amuse themselves as our English women do in making Caps, ruffles,

[1] These figures are supplied from S. Plate 9 in the second volume of Hawkesworth includes a diagrammatic representation of the furrows on the four faces as numbering 11, 23, 43 and 56.
[2] *hopua.*

&c; and in this they spend the greatest part of their time. They are furnishd with each a k[n]ife made of a peice of Bamboo cane, to which they make, by splitting it diagonaly with their nails, an edge which with great ease cuts any kind of cloth or soft substance; and a certain quantity of a Paste made of the root of a Plant which serves them also for food, and is calld by them *Pea* (*Chaitæa Tacca*)[1]: with the former they cut off any ragged edges or ends which may not have been sufficiently fixd down by the Beating; and with the Paste they fasten down others which are less ragged, and also put on patches upon any part which may be thinner than the rest, generaly finishing their work, if intended for the best, by pasting a compleat covering of the finest thin Cloth or *Hoboo* over the whole. They make the thick Cloth also sometimes of thin, only half worn, and which having been worn by cleanly people is not soild enough to require washing; of this it is sufficient to paste the Edges together, which is done with the same paste. This thick cloth, made in either of these ways, is usd either for the garment calld *Maro*, which is a long peice passd between the legs and round the waste that serves instead of breeches; or the *Tebuta*[2] as it is calld, a garment usd equally by both sexes instead of a Coat or gown, which exactly resembles that worn by the inhabitants of Peru and Chili that is calld by the Spanyards Poncho.

The cloth itself both thick and thin resembles most the finest cottons in softness especialy in which article it even exceeds them. Its tenderness (for it tears by the smallest accident) makes it very impossible that it can ever be usd in Europe; indeed it is properly adapted to a hot climate; I usd it to sleep in very often in the Islands and always found it far cooler than any English cloth, and that it much prevented perspiration or else, by drying it up immediately, the disagreable sensation of it.

Having thus describd their manner of making the Cloth I shall proceed to their method of dying it. They have principaly two Colours in which they excell, Red and Yellow; the first of these is most beautifull, I might almost venture to say a more delicate colour than any we have in Europe, aproaching however nearest to Scarlet; the second is a good bright colour but of no particular excellence. They also upon some occasions dye brown and black but so seldom that I had not an opportunity during my stay to see the methods or learn the materials which they make use of; I shall therefore say no more of these Colours than that they were so

---

[1] Pia.
[2] *tiputa*.

a.

b.

c.

Pl. VII *a. Zebrasoma flavescens* *b. Zanclus cornutus* Moorish Idol
c. Rhinecanthus aculeatus Trigger Fish

Tahiti

indifferent in their qualities that they did not much raise my curiosity to enquire concerning them.[1]

To begin then with the red, in favour of which I shall premise that I beleive no Voyager has past these seas but he has said something in praise of this colour, the brightness and elegance of which is so great that it cannot avoid being taken notice of by the slightest observer. This colour is made by the admixture of the Juices of two vegetables neither of which in their seperate state have the least tendency to the colour of Red, nor have any Parts of them that I have at least been able to observe any circumstance relating to them from whence any one should be led to conclude that the colour of red was at all latent in them. They are *Ficus tinctoria* which is calld by them *Matte*[2] the same name as the colour and *Cordia Sebestena orientalis* calld *Etou*;[3] of these the fruits of the first and the leaves of the second are usd in the following manner.

The fruits which are about as large as a rounceval pea or very small Gooseberry, produce upon breaking off the stalk close to them each one drop of a milky liquor resembling the Juice of a fig tree in Europe, for indeed the tree itself is a kind of wild fig tree. This liquor the women collect, breaking off the footstalk and shaking the drop which hangs to the little fig into a small quantity of cocoa nut water: to sufficiently prepare a gill of Cocoanut water will require 3 or 4 quarts of the little figs, tho I never could observe that they had any rule in Proportioning the quantity except observing the Cocoa nut water, which was to be of a Whey colour when a sufficient quantity of the Juice of the little figs was mixd among it. When this liquor is prepard the leaves of the *Etou* are brought which are well wetted in it, they are then laid upon a Plantain leaf and the Women begin first gently to turn and shake them about; afterwards as they grow more and more flaccid by this operation to squeese them a little, increasing the pressure gradualy, all which is done merely to prevent the leaves from breaking; still as they become more flaccid and spongy they supply them with more of the juice. In about 5 minutes the Colour begins to appear on the Veins of the leaves of the *Etou* and in 10 or a little

---

[1] Brown came from a sort of tanning with the bark of more than one kind of tree, especially *toa* or ironwood; for black the sap of the *fei*, or mountain plantain, was used, or the cloth was seeped repeatedly in swampy ground beneath the roots of a coconut.

[2] Mati. The juice of the berries is yellow. The scientific name, *Ficus tinctoria* Forst., was certainly founded on its use in dyeing. A Banks and Solander coll., Solander's MS description, and Parkinson's coloured drawing establish this name. See Pl. 33*a*.

[3] Tou, *Cordia subcordata* Lam. Banks alluded to the difference between the Tahitian plant and the American *C. sebestena* by his trinomial (which Hooker altered), whereas Parkinson's coloured drawing was labelled simply 'Cordia sebestena'. See Pl. 33*b*.

Z

more all is finishd and ready for straining, at which time they press and squeese the leaves as hard as they possibly can. The method of straining is this: they have for the purpose a large quantity of the fibres of a kind of Cyperus Grass (*Cyperus stupeus*) calld by them *Mooo*,[1] which the boys prepare very nimbly by Drawing the stalks of it through their teeth or between two little sticks untill all the green bark and the branny substance which lays between them is gone. In a covering of these fibres then they invelop the leaves, and squeesing or wringing them strongly express the dye which turns out very little more in quantity than the liquor employd; this operation they repeat several times, soaking as often the leaves in the dye and squeesing them dry again until they have sufficiently extracted all their virtue, when they throw away the remaining leaves keeping however the *Mööo* which serves them instead of a brush to lay the colour upon the Cloth. The receptacle usd for the liquid dye is constantly a Plantain leaf, whether from any property it may have agreable to the colour, or the great ease with which they are always got and the facility of dividing one and making of it many small cups in which the dye may be distributed to every one in company I do not know. Their method of laying it on the Cloth is this: they take it up in the fibres of the *Mööo* and rubbing that gently over the Cloth spread the outside of it with a thin coat of dye. This of the thick cloth, the thin they very seldom dye more than the edges of; some indeed I have seen dyed through as if it had been soakd in the dye, but had not near so elegant a colour as that on which a thin coat only was laid on the outside.

Though the *Etou* leaf is the most generaly usd and I beleive produces the finest colour, yet there are several more which being mixd with the Juice of the little figs produce a red colour, as *Tournefortia Sericea* which they call *Taheinoo*;[2] *Convolvulus brasilienis, Pohue* the *Eurhe*;[3] *Solanum latifolium, Ebooa*.[4] From the use of these different

---

[1] Mou or *mou-taviri-haari*, sword-grass; *Cyperus javanensis* Houtt. (*C. pennatus* Lam.) • Hooker published the original Banksian specific name as 'stupeus' (and I think this is what Banks wrote), evidently interpreting the choice as 'woolly'; but the word has also been read as 'strepens', to signify 'rustling' from the sound made by the rubbing of the culms. S *stupeus*, P *stupens*. *Strepens* is certainly a misreading. For the taxonomy of the sp. cf. Seemann, *Fl. Vit.* 319.

[2] Tahinu, *Tournefortia argentea* L. f.

[3] Pohue, the strand-creeping and precipice-festooning vine, *Ipomoea pes-caprae*. This identification is supported by the Banks and Solander coll. What Banks means by '*the Eurhe*' is not quite certain, but from what he goes on to say about dyeing cloth, he probably refers to this use of the plant: *uri* means dark-coloured or black, and his word signifies *e* [indefinite article] *uri*. I fancy he underlined *the* by mistake; it is not underlined in S, though it is in P.

[4] Pua, *Solanum repandum* Forst. f., a shrub. There is another Pua, *Fagraea berteriana*, a tree sacred to the god Tane, but it was the shrub that Banks meant: Parkinson has a coloured plate labelled with Banks's name and marked 'Otaheite'.

plants or from different proportions of materials many varieties of the colour are observable among their cloths, some of which are very conspicuously superior to others.

When the women have been employd in dying cloth they industriously preserve the colour upon their fingers and nails upon which it shews with its greatest beauty. They look upon this as no small ornament and I have been sometimes inclind to beleive that they even borrow the dye of each other merely for the purpose of dying their fingers; whether it is esteemd as a beauty, a mark of their housewifry in being able to dye, or their riches in having cloth to dye I know not.

Of what use this preparation may be of to my Countreymen either in itself or in any hints which may be drawn from an admixture of vegetable substances so totaly different from any thing of the kind that is practis'd in Europe, I am not enough vers'd in Chymistry to be able to guess, I must however hope that it will be of some. The latent qualities of vegetables have already furnishd our most valuable dyes; no one from an inspection of the Plants could guess that any coulour was hid under the herbs of Indigo, Woad, Dyers weed, or indeed the most of the Plants whose leaves are usd in dying, and yet those latent qualifications have when discoverd produc'd Colours without which our dyers could hardly go on with their Trades.

The Painter whoom I have with me tells me that the nearest imitation of the colour that he could mak[e] would be by mixing together vermilion and Carmine, but even that would not equal the delicacy of it tho a body colour, and the Indian only a stain in the way that the Indians use it. I can not say much for its standing: they commonly keep their cloth white till the very time when it is to be us'd and then dye it as if conscious that it would soon fade. I have however usd Cloth dy'd with it myself for a fortnight or three weeks, in which time it has very little alterd itself and by that time the Cloth was pretty well wore. Of it I have also some now in chests which a month ago when I lookd into them had very little alterd their colour; the admixture of fixing drugs would however certainly not a little conduce to its standing.

So much for their Red: their yellow though a good colour has certainly no particular excellence to recomend it in which it is superior to our known Yellows: it is made of the bark of the Root of a shrub calld by them *Nono* (*Morinda umbellata*)[1] this they scrape

---

[1] Nono, *Morinda citrifolia*. Banks confused *M. citrifolia*, the source of the dye, with a quite different sp. (now properly distinguished as *M. forsteri* Seem.). Both were illustrated in colour by Parkinson. See Pl. 34*b*.

into water and after it has soakd there a sufficient time strain the
water and dip the cloth into it. The wood of the root is no doubt
furnishd in some degree with the same property as the Bark but
not having any vessels in which they can boil it it is useless to the
inhabitants. The genus of Morinda seems worthy of being examind
as to its propertys in dying; *Browne* in his hist of Jamaica[1] mentions
3 species whose roots he says are usd to dye a brown colour, and
Rumphius says of his *Bancudus angustifolia*, which is very nearly
allied to our *Nono*, that it is usd by the inhabitants of the East
Indian Islands as a fixing drug for the colour of red with which
he says it particularly agrees.

They also dye Yellow with the fruits of a tree calld by them
Tamanu (*Calophyllum Inophyllum*)[2] but their method I never had the
fortune to see; it seems however to be cheifly esteemed by them
for the smell which it gives to the cloth, a smell that is more agreable
to an Indian than a Europæan nose.

Besides their cloth the women make several kinds of matting
which serves them to sleep upon, and the finest for cloths: with
the last they take much pains, especialy with that sort which is
made of the Bark of the Tree calld by them *Poorou*, *Hibiscus tiliaceus*,[3]
of which I have seen matting almost as fine as coarse cloth. But
the most beautifull sort, calld by them *Vanne*,[4] which is white
and extreemly glossy and shining is made of the leaves of a sort o
Pandanus calld by them *Wharra*, of which we had not an opportunity
of seing either flowers or fruit.[5] The rest of their *Möeäs*[6] as they
call them which serve to set down or sleep upon are made of a
variety of sorts of Rushes, grass &c: these they are extreemly nimble

[1] Patrick Browne (1720?-90), an Irish physician and student of natural history, and
a correspondent of Linnaeus, lived much in the West Indies from 1745; he published
his folio *Civil and Natural History of Jamaica* in 1756. He also compiled catalogues, published
and unpublished, of the birds, fishes, and plants, of Ireland and the West Indies. His
herbarium, of more than 1000 rare plants, was bought by Linnaeus for eight guineas.

[2] Tamanu, *Calophyllum inophyllum* L. The seed-kernel contains an oil much-esteemed
also as a liniment and for perfuming coconut oil. Seemann, who describes the use of the
oil, remarks that the round fruits are one of the four kinds most often encountered on the
sandy beaches in Polynesia. Guppy (*Naturalist in the Pacific* 2 : 434. 1906) treats of this
and other spp. comprising beach-drift in tropical latitudes. It is notable that many of
the Polynesian economic plants are members of the strand-flora: *Hibiscus tiliaceus*, *Calophyllum
inophyllum*, *Thespesia populnea*, etc. Natural factors in their biology, seed structure
and the like, supplement their dispersal. See Pl. 34*a*.

[3] Purau, *Hibiscus tiliaceus*. The bark was soaked, scraped and bleached.

[4] *vane*; they were fine mats, sometimes interwoven with a pattern and fringed, worn
by the *arii* at festivals or offered to the gods.

[5] The Fara-paeore, which had long leaves without the thorns characteristic of the
other Fara. It has neither flower nor fruit. Banks must have seen other varieties, because
he refers above (p. 343) to the 'fruit of a tree which they call *wharra* in appearance like a
pineapple'.

[6] *moea.*

in making and indeed every thing which is platted, baskets of a thousand different patterns, some very neat &c. As for occasional Baskets or Paniers made of a Cocoa nut leaf, or the little Bonnets which they wear to shade the eyes from the sun of the same material, every one knows how to make them at once; as soon as the sun was pretty high the women who had been with us since morning sent generaly out for cocoa nut leaves of which they made such bonnets in a few minutes, which they threw away as soon as the sun became again low in the afternoon. These however serve merely for a shade, coverings to their heads they have none except their hair for these bonnets or shades only fit round their heads not upon them.

Besides these things they make netts for fishing in the same manner as we do, Ropes of about an inch, and lines, of the *Poorou*; threads with which they sew together their canoes, and also belts, of the fibres of the Cocoa nut, platted either round or flat very neatly; all their twisting work they do upon their thighs in a manner very dificult to describe and indeed unnecessary, as no European can want to learn how to do an operation which his instruments will do for him so much faster than it possibly can be done by hand.[1] But of all the strings that they make none are so excellent as the fishing lines &c. which are made of the bark of a kind of frutescent nettle calld by them *Erowa (Urtica argentea)*[2] which grows in the mountains and is consequently rather scarce; of this they make the lines which are employd to take the briskest and most active fish as bonetos, Albecores[3] &c. As I never made experiments with it I can only ascertain its strengh by saying that it was infinitely stronger than silk lines which I had on board made by the best fishing shops in London, tho not so thick by almost half.

In every expedient for taking fish they are vastly ingenious. Their Seines, netts for fish to mesh themselves in &c. are exactly like ours: they strike fish with harpoons made of Cane and pointed with hard wood in a more dextrous[4] manner than we can do with ours that are headed with Iron, for we who fasten lines to ours need only lodge them in the fish to secure it, while they on the other

[1] Any European who nevertheless cares to learn how to do the operation may consult Willowdean C. Handy, *Handcrafts of the Society Islands* (Bernice P. Bishop Mus. Bull., 42, Honolulu 1927), p. 108.

[2] Roa, *Pipturus argenteus* (Forst.) Wedd. It is represented by both an herbarium coll. and Parkinson's coloured drawing; Banks's name appears in an unfinished unsigned pencil sketch and in Solander's MS. The thread was enormously strong. (Cf. C. Skottsberg, 'Remarks on Pipturus argenteus and P. incanus of Weddell', Meddel. Fran Göteborg Trad. 7: 43-63. 1932.)

[3] Possibly he means *Euthynnus pelamis* and *Neothunnus macropterus*.

[4] Banks here has an unusual search for a word; he first writes *cleverer*, which he discards for *better*, and in turn discards this.

hand throwing theirs quite from them must either mortaly wound
the fish or loose him. Their hooks indeed as they are not made of
Iron must be very different from ours in construction. They [are]
of two sorts, first that calld by them *Witte witte*[1] which is usd for
towing, of which fig 1 is the profile and fig 2 the view of the bottom

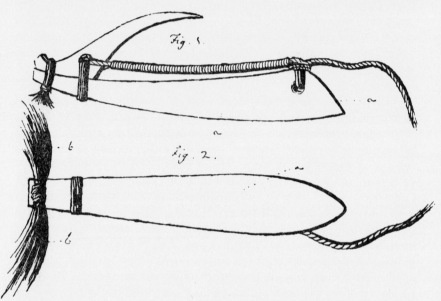

part. The shank (a) is made of mother of Pearl the most glossy
that can be got, the inside or naturaly bright side of which is put
undermost as in fig 2; (b) is a tuft of white dogs or hogs hair which
serves may be to imitate the tail of a fish. These hooks require
no bait. They are usd with a fishing rod of Bamboo; the people
who go out with them having found by the flights of birds which
constantly attend shoals of Bonetos where they are, Paddle their
Canoes as swift as they can across them and seldom fail to take some.
This Indian invention seems far to exceed any thing of the kind
which I have seen among Europæans, and is certainly more successful
than any artificial flying fish or other thing which is generaly usd
for the taking of Bonitos, so far it deserves imitation at any time
when the taking of Bonitos is at all desirable.

The other sort of hooks which they have are made likewise of
mother of Pearl or some hard shell, and as they can not make them
bearded as our hooks they supply that fault by making the points

---

[1] Not the name of a hook; probably a rendering of *vitiviti*, clever, neat, well-finished

turn much inwards as in the annexd figure; they
have them of ₁all sizes and catch with them all
kinds of fish very successfully I beleive. The manner
of making them is very simple, every fisherman
makes them for himself. The shell is first cut by the edge of another
shell into square peices; these are formd with files of Coral which
work in a manner surprizing to any one who does not know how
sharp Corals are; a hole is then bord in the middle by a drill which
is no more than any stone that may have a sharp corner in it tied
to a hand[l]e of cane, which is turnd in the hand like a Chocolate
mill untill the hole is made; the file then comes into the hole and
compleats the hook which is done in such a one as the figure shews
in less than a quarter of an hour.

In their carpenters, joiners and stone cutters work &c. they are
almost as little obligd to the use of tools as in making these hooks:
an axe of Stone in the shape of an adze, a chisel or gouge made
of a human bone, a file or rasp of Coral, skin of Sting rays, and
coral sand to polish with, are a sufficient set of tools for building a
house and furnishing it with boats, as well as for quarrying and
squaring stones for the pavement of any thing which may require
it in the neighbourhood. Their stone axes are made of a black
stone not very hard but tolerably tough;[1] they are of different
sizes, some that are intended for felling weigh 3 or 4 Pounds,
others which are usd only for carving not so many ounces.
Whatever these tools want in goodness is made up by the industry
of the people who use them. Felling a tree is their greatest labour, a
large one requires many hands to assist and some days before it
can be finishd, but when once it is down they manage it with far
greater dexterity than is credible to an Europæan. If it is to be made
into boards they put wedges into it, and drive them with such
dexterity (as they have told me — for I never saw it) that they
divide it into slabs of 3 or 4 inches in thickness, seldom meeting
with an accident if the tree is good.　These slabs they very soon
dubb down with their axes to any given thinness; in this work
they certainly excell; indeed their tools are better adaptd for it
than any other performance; I have seen them dubb of the first
rough coat of a plank at least as fast as one of our carpenters could
have done it; and in hollowing, where they have liberty to raise
large floors of the wood, they certainly work quicker, owing to

---

[1] These adzes (and other stone tools very often) were made from a black dolerite
ound on the island of Maurua (modern Maupiti) 24 miles west of Borabora, where there
was a sort of quarry which supplied the whole of the Society Islands with the valued
material.

the weight of their tools: those who are masters of this business, will take of a surprizing thin coat from a whole plank, without missing a stroke; they can also work upon a peice of wood of any shape as well as they can upon a flat one, for in making their canoes every peice is formd first into its proper shape, bilging or flat: for as they never bend a Plank all the bilging peices must be shap'd by hand which is done intirely with axes. They have small axes for carving also but all their carvd work was so bad and in so very mean a taste that it scarce deservd that name. Yet they love much to have carvd work and figures stuck about their canoes, the great ones especialy, which generaly have a figure of a man at the head and another at the stern of them. Their *marai's* also are ornamented with different kinds of figures, one sort of which represent many men standing on Each others heads; they have also the figures of animals, and Planks whose faces are carvd in patterns of squares and circles &c. but every part of their carving is in an equaly bad taste. All their work however acquires a certain neatness in the finishing for they polish every thing, even the side of a canoe or a Post of a house, with Coral sand rubbd on in the outer husk of a Cocoa nut and rays skin, which makes them very smooth and neat.

Their Boats all at least that I have seen of them may be divided into two general classes. The first which are calld by the natives *Ivahah*[1] are the only sort which are usd at Otahite; they serve for fishing, and for short trips to sea but do not at all seem calculated for long ones. The others again which are calld *Pahei*[2] and are usd by the inhabitants of the Societies Isles viz. Ulhietea, Bola Bola, Huaheine &c. are rather too clumsey for fishing, for which reason the inhabitants of those Isles have also *Ivahas* but are much better adapted for long voyages than the others. The figure below gives a section of both the kinds of which fig. 1 is the *Ivahah* and fig. II the *Pahei*. To begin then with the *Ivahah* these boats differ very

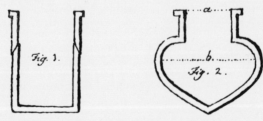

---

[1] *vaa*. Presumably then Banks's 'Iv' is sounded as in *give*, and the initial I represents the Tahitian particle *e*.
[2] *pahi*.

much in lengh, I have measurd them from 10 f^t to 72, but by no means proportionaly in breadth, for that of 10 feet was about 1 in breadth and that of 72 scarce 2, nor is their hight increasd in a much greater proportion. They may be subdivided into three sorts, the fighting *ivahah*, the common sailing or fishing *ivahah*, and the traveling *ivahah*. The fighting *Ivahah* is by far the largest; the head and stern of these boats are considerably raisd above the body of them in a semicircular form, the latter especialy which is 17 or 18 feet in hight when the body of the boat is scarcely 3. These boats never go to sea singly: two are always fastned together side by side at the distance of about 2 feet by strong poles of wood [which] go across them, and upon them is built a stage in the fore part, about 10 or 12 feet long and a little broader than the two boats; this is supported by pillars about 6 feet high and upon it stand the people who fight with slings, spears &c; below are the rowers who are much less engagd in the battle on account of their confind situation but who receive the wounded from the stage and furnish fresh men to ascend in their room. This much from description for I never saw any of their battles. The Sailing and fishing *Ivahahs* vary in size from about 40 feet in lengh to the smallest I have mentiond, but those which are under 25 feet in lengh seldom or never carry sail; their Sterns only are raisd and those not above 4 or 5 feet; their heads are quite flat and have a flat board projecting forwards beyond them about 4 feet. Those which I have calld traveling *Ivahas* differ from these in nothing but their being constantly joind 2 and 2 together in the same manner as the fighting ones, and having a small neat house 5 or 6 feet broad and 7 or 8 long fastned upon the fore part of them, in which the principal people, who use them very much, set when they are carried from place to place. The sailing *Ivahas* have also sometimes this house upon them when they are joind two and two together, which is but seldom however; indeed the difference between these two consists almost intirely in the rigging, and I have divided them into two more because they are generaly seen employd in very different occupations than from any real difference in their built. All *Ivahas* however agree in that they are built wall sided and with flat bottoms, in which they differ from the *Pahie* fig. II: whose sides are built rounding out, or bilging as it is calld, and her bottom sharp which answers in some measure instead of a Keel.

These *Pahies* differ very much in size. I have seen them from 60 to 30 feet in lenght but like the *Ivahas* they are very narrow in proportion to their lengh: one that I measurd was 51 feet in lengh, in breadth at the top (a) only 1½ f^t and in the bilge (b) 3 feet, which is about the general proportion; their round sides however make them capable of carrying much greater burthens and being much more safe sea boats, in consequence of which they are usd merely for fighting and making long voyages; for the purposes of fishing and traveling along shore the natives of the Islands where these are cheifly usd have *Ivahas*. The fighting *Pahies* which are the largest are fitted in the same manner as the fighting *Ivahas*, only as they carry far greater burthens the stages are proportionaly larger. The Sailing ones are most generaly fastned two and two together: for this purpose the middling sizd ones are said to be the best and least liable to accidents in stormy weather; in these if we may credit the reports of the inhabitants they make very long voyages, often remaining out from home several months, visiting in that time many different Islands of which they repeated to us the names of near a hundred. They cannot however remain at sea above a fortnight or 20 days tho they live as sparingly as possible, for want of proper provisions and places to put them in safe, as well as water of which however they carry a tolerable stock in hollow Bamboes.

All these imbarkations which indeed are all that I saw us'd in any of the Islands are disproportionaly narrow in respect to their lengh, Which causes them to be so very Easily overset that not even the Indians dare venture in them till they are fitted with a contrivance to prevent this inconvenience; which is done either by fastening two together side by side as has been before describd, in which case one supports the other and they become the most steady Veh[i]cle that can be imagind, or if one of them is to go out single a log of wood fas[t]ned to two poles which are tied across the boat serves to balance it tolerably, tho not so securely but that I have seen the Indians overset them very often. This is upon the same principles as that usd in the flying Proa of the Ladrone Isles describd in Ld Ansons voyage, where it is calld an out-rigger; indeed the vessels themselves enough resemble the flying Proa to make it appear at least possible that either that is a very art-full improvement of these or these a very aukward imitation of that.[1]

These boats are paddled along with large paddles which have a long handle and a flat blade resembling more than any thing I recollect a Bakers peel;[2] of these generaly every one in the boat

---

[1] Walter, in his account of Anson's voyage, spends some pages (339-43 and plan) on what he calls the 'flying proa'. It differed from the canoes Banks is describing in having a head and stern of identical shape; what was intended to be its lee side was flat, while the windward side was rounded in the ordinary manner.

[2] The shovel used to place bread in the oven and withdraw it.

has one except those who set under the houses and with these they push themselves on pretty fast through the water. They are so leaky however that one person at least is employd almost constantly in throwing out the water. The only thing in which they excell is landing in a surf, for by reason of their great lengh and high sterns they would land dry in a surf when our boats could scarcely land at all, and in the same manner put off from the shore as I have often experienc'd.

When fitted for sailing they have either one or two Masts fitted to a frame which is above the canoe; they are made of a single stick; in one that I measurd of 32 feet in lengh the mast was 25 ft high which seems to me to be about the common proportion. To this is fastned a sail of about one third longer but narrow, of a triangular shape, pointed at the top and the outside curvd; it is borderd all round with a frame of wood and has no contrivance either for reefing or furling, so that in case of bad weather it must be intirely cut away, but I fancy in these moderate climates they are seldom brought to this necessity; the material of which it is made is universaly Matting. With these sails their Canoes go at a very good rate and lay very near the wind, probably on account of their sail being borderd with wood which makes them stand better than any bowlines could possible do. On the top of this sail they carry an ornament which in taste resembles much our Pennants, it is made of feathers and reaches down to the very water so that when blown out by the wind it makes no inconsiderable shew. They are indeed fond of ornaments in all parts of their boats; they commonly in the good ones have a figure at the stern; in the *Paheis* which rise rounding both at the head and stern they have a figure at both, and the smaller *ivahas* have commonly a small carvd pillar standing upon their stern.

Considering these people as intirely destitute of Iron they build these Canoes very well. Of the *Ivahas* the foundation is always the trunks of one or more trees, hollowd out; the ends of these are Slopd off, and sewd together with the fibres of the Husk of the cocoanut; the sides of them are then raisd with plank, sewd together in the same manner. The *Paheis* as they are much better embarkations so they are built in a more ingenious manner. Like the others they are laid upon a long keel which however is not above 4 or 5 inches deep; upon this they raise with two ranges of Plank each of which is about 18 inches high and about 4 feet in lengh. Such a number of peices must necessarily be framd and fitted together before they are sewd and this they do very dexterously, supporting the Keel by ropes made fast to the top of the house under which they work and then each plank by a stantion: so that the canoe is compleatly put together before any one part of her is fastned to that which is next to it, and in this manner supported till the sewing is compleated. This however soon rotts in the salt water: it must be renewd once a year at least, in doing which the canoe is intirely taken to peices and every plank examind, by which means they are always in good repair. The best of them are however very leaky for as they use no calking the water must run in at every hole through which the sewing is past; this however is no great inconvenience to them who live in a climate where the water is always warm, and go barefoot.

For the convenience of keeping these *Paheis* dry we saw in the Islands where they are usd a peculiar sort of houses which were built on purpose for their reception, and put to no use but that; they are built of Poles stuck upright in the ground and tied together at the top so that they make a kind of Gothick arch; the sides of these are compleatly coverd with Thatch down to the ground but the ends are left open. One of these I measurd, 50 paces in lengh, 10 in breadth and 24 feet high, and this was of the midling size.

The people excell much in predicting the weather, a circumstance of great use to them in their short voyages from Island to Island. They have many various ways of doing this but one only that I know of which I never heard of being practisd by Europæans, that is foretelling the quarter of the heavens from whence the wind shall blow by observing the Milky Way, which is generaly bent in an arch either one way or the other: this arch they conceive as already acted upon by the wind, which is the cause of its curving, and say that if the same curve continues a whole night the wind predicted by it seldom fails to come some time in the next day; and in this as well as their other predictions we found them indeed not infallible but far more clever than Europæans.

In their longer Voyages they steer in the day by the Sun and in the night by the Stars. Of these they know a very large part by their Names and the clever ones among them will tell in what part of the heavens they are to be seen in any month when they are above their horizon; they know also the time of their annual appearing and disapearing to a great nicety, far greater than would be easily beleivd by an Europæan astronomer.

For their Method of dividing time I was not able to get a compleat Idea of it, I shall however set down what little I know. In speaking of Time either past or to come they never use any term but Moons, of which they count 13 and then begin again: this of itself sufficiently shews that they have an Idea of the Solar year but how they manage to make their 13 months agree with it I never could find out: that they do however I beleive because in mentioning the names of months they very frequently told us the fruits that would be in season in each of them, the sort of weather that was usual in them &c. They have also a name for the 13 months collectively but they never use it in speaking of time, they use it only in explaining the mysteries of their religion: in their metaphorical way they say that the Year *Tettowmatatayo* was the daughter of their cheif Divinity *Taroataihetoomoo* and that she in process of time brought forth the months, who in their turn produc'd the days,[1] of which they count 29 in every month including one on which the moon is invisible. Every one of these has its respective name and is again subdivided into 12 parts containing about 2 hours each, 6 for the day and 6 for the night, each of which has likewise its respective name; in the day time they guess the divisions of these parts very well, but in the night tho they have the same number of divisions as in the day seem very little able to tell at any time which of them it then is, except the cleverer among them who know the stars.

In counting they proceed from 1 to 10, having a different name for each number; from thence they say one more, 2 more &c. till the number 20, which after being calld in the general count 10 more acquires a new name, as we say a score; by these scores they count till they have got 10 of them, which again acquires a new name, 200; these again are counted till they get 10 of them, 2000; which is the largest denomination I have ever heard them make use of and I suppose is as large as they can ever have occasion for, as they can count 10 of these 20,000 without any new term.

In measures of space they are very poor, indeed one fathom and ten fathoms are the only terms I have heard among them; by these they convey the size of any thing as a house, a boat, depth of the sea &c; but when they speak of distances from one place to

---

[1] In the first part of this statement Banks, through his inadequate knowledge of the language, is unintentionally misleading. We may elucidate as follows: (1) 'a name for the 13 months collectively', or year, 'in speaking of time', did exist: it was *matahiti*. (2) Omitting this, he plunges us straight into the depths of cosmogony. His 'Tettomatatayo' seems to be equivalent to *te tau mata a Te A-Io*. Te A-Io is a personified notion of 're-productive power mingled with procreative urge'; *te tau mata*, 'the period beginning', or 'the period in-the-beginning'. Hence the whole phrase signifies the time of the first origin of things, as a creative act. (3) His 'Taroataihetoomoo' is *Ta'aroa-tahi-tumu*, 'Ta-aroa the one (i.e. unique) source'—or, esoterically, 'the Unknowable Maker, the Cause'. What we have, therefore, is a First Cause creating, and moving creatively in, Time, his 'daughter'—from whom, as Banks goes on to say, issue the months and the days.

another they have no way but time of making themselves understood, but by the number of days it takes them in their canoes to go the distance.

Their Language appeard to me to be very soft and tuneable, it abounds much with vowels and was very easily pronounc'd by us when ours was to them absolutely impracticable. I shall instance particularly my own name which I took much pains to teach them and they to learn: after three days fruitless trials I was forc'd to select from their many attempts the word *Tabáne*, the only one I had been able to get from them that had the least similitude to it. Again Spanish or Italian words they pronouncd with ease provided they ended with a vowel, for few or none of theirs end with a consonant.

I cannot say that I am enough acquainted with it to pronounce whether or not it is copious. In one respect however it is beyond measure inferior to all European languages, which is its almost total want of inflexion both of Nouns and verbs, few or none of the former having more than one Case or the latter one tense. Notwithstanding this want however we found it very easy to make ourselves understood in matters of common necessaries, howsoever paradoxical that may appear to an European.

The[y] have certain Suffixa and make very frequent use of them, which puzzled us at first very much tho they are but few in number. An instance or two may be necessary to make myself understood as they do not exist in any modern European language. One asks another *Harre hea*? where are you going? the other answers *Ivahinera*, to my Wives; on Which the first questioning him still farther *Ivahinera*? to your wives do you say? is answered *Ivahinereia*, Yes I am going to my wives.[1] Here the suffixa *era* and *eia*[2] save several words to both parties.

From the vocabularies given in Le Mair's voyage[3] (See *Histoire des navigations aux Terres australes* Tom 1. p.410) it appears clearly that the Languages given there as those of the Isles of Solomon and the Isle of Cocos are radicaly the identical same languages as those we met with, the greatest number of words differing in little but the greater number of consonants. The languages of New Guinea and Moyse Isle have also many words Radicaly

---

[1] Properly *E haere i hea*?, 'Where are you going?'—*I a'u [va]hine ra*, 'To my wives over there'.—*I a'u hine ra*?—*I a'u hine ra ia*, 'To my wives over there aforesaid'.

[2] Properly *ra* and *ia*.

[3] Willem Cornelisz Schouten and Jacob le Maire crossed the Pacific from Cape Horn to Batavia, February-October 1616. The history of the voyage was abstracted by de Brosses in the great work Banks refers to, one of the literary foundations of Pacific exploration in the eighteenth century. Cf. p.230, n. 2 above.

the same, particularly their Numbers, tho they are so obscurd by a multitude of consonants that it is scarce possible that they should be found out by any but one in some measure acquainted with one of the Languages; for instance

New Guinea *Hissou* fish, is found to be the same as the Otahite *Eia* by the medium of *Ica* of the Isles of Solomon; *Talingan* ears, in Otahite *Terrea*; *Limang* a hand, *Lima* or *Rima*; *Paring* cheeks *Paparea*; Isle of Moyse *Sou Sou* Breasts, *Eu*; *Mattanga* Eyes, *Mata*. They calld us says the author *Tata*, which in Otahite signifies men in general; besides several more.[1]

That the people who inhabit this numerous range of Isles should have originaly come from one and the same place and brought with the[m] the same numbers and Language, which latter especialy have remaind to this time not materialy alterd, is in my opinion not at all past beleif, but that the Numbers of the Island of Madagascar should be the same as all these is almost if not quite incredible. I shall give them from a book calld *a Collection of voyages by the Duch East India Company* Lond. 1703.[2] p. 116, where supposing the author Who speaks of ten numbers and has only nine to have lost the fifth their similarity is beyond dispute.

	Madagascar	Otahite	Cocos Isle	New Guinea
1.	Issa	Tahie	Taci	Tika
2.	Rove	Rua	Loua	Roa
3.	Tello	Torou	Tolou	Tola
4.	Effat	Hea	Fa	Fatta
6.	Enning	Whene	Houno	Wamma
7.	Fruto	Hetu	Fitou	Fita
8.	Wedo	Whearu	Walou	Walla
9.	Sidai	Heva	Ywou	Siwa
10.	Scula	Ahourou	Ongefoula	Sangafoula

It must be rememberd however that the author of this voyage during the course of it touchd at Java and several more of the East Indian Isles as well as at Madagascar, so that supposing by any misarangement of his papers that he has given the numerals of some of those Isles for those of Madagascar our wonder will be

[1] There seems little point in giving the equivalents in modern orthography either of these words or of those in the list of numerals that follows, as Banks's argument rested on the words as he knew them.

[2] *A Collection of Voyages undertaken by the Dutch East-India Company, for the improvement of trade and navigation. Containing an account of* . . . *their discoveries in the East-Indies, and the South Seas.* . . . *Translated into English.* London 1703.

much diminishd;[1] for after having tracd them from Otahite to New Guinea it should seem not very wonderfull to carry them a little farther to the East Indian Isles, which from their situation seem not unlikely to be the place from whence our Islanders originaly have come; but I shall wave saying any more on this subject till I have had an opportunity of myself seeing the customs &c of the Javans, which this Voyage will in all probab[i]lity give me an opportunity of doing.[2]

All the Isles I was upon agreed perfectly as far as I could understand them; the people of Ulietea only chang'd the t of the Otahiteans to a k, calling Tata which signifies a man or woman Kaka, a circumstance which made their Language much less soft.[3] The people of Ohiteroa as far as I could understand their words which were only shouted out to us seemd to do the same thing, and add many more consonants and harshness's which made their Language still more untuneable. I shall give a few of their words from whence an Idea may be got of their language.[4]

Eupo the Head	*Booa* a hog
Ahewh the Nose	*Moa* a fowl
Roourou the Hair	*Eurèe* a dog
Outou the mouth	*Eùre-Eùre* Iron
Nihëo the teeth	*Ooroo* Bread fruit
Arrero the Tongue	*Hearee* Cocoa nuts
Meu-eumi the Beard	*Mia* Bananes
Tiarraboa the throat	*Vaèe* wild Plantanes
Tuamo the shoulders	*Poe* Beads

[1] Confusion of papers is not necessary as an explanation. The language of Madagascar was in fact part of the Austronesian group, the geographical extent of which Banks might well be surprised at.

[2] This passage is an indication that the later course of the voyage had already been discussed.

[3] This consonantal change is no longer a feature of the Raiatean dialect, which has become one with the species of neo-Tahitian now spoken all through the islands of French Oceania.

[4] Banks's list is interesting, and if allowance is made for the rendering on paper of vowel sounds natural to an eighteenth century Englishman, and for the ambiguity to Europeans of Polynesian consonants (on which those who later reduced the language to writing had themselves to make some rather arbitrary decisions), it gives a very fair equivalent to the Tahitian words he had collected. The other things mainly to be allowed for are the incorporation of the verbal particle *e* with the noun, and sometimes a little confusion of other parts of speech. Thus Eupo, the head = [*e*] *upoo*; Eurèe, a dog = [*e*] *uri*. Ambiguity of vowel sounds is seen in Ahewh, the nose = *ihu*; Ahee, a fruit like chestnuts = *ihi*. Ambiguity of consonants is seen in Ewharre, a house = [*e*] *fare*; Whennua, a high island = *fenua*; Mala-mala, bitter = *maramara*. Ambiguity in both consonant and vowel is seen in Booa, a hog = *puaa*; Whettu-euphe, a comet = *fetuave*. With Warriddo, to steal, and Woridde, to be angry, we seem to have combinations of *ua*, a particle used in expostulation, (or perhaps, as Davies says, 'a verb of being') with *riro*, to be lost or missed, and *riri*, to be angry. With such words as Poto, short; Roa, tall; Poe, beads (pearl); Toto, blood, Banks hit on the later missionary rendering which became standard.

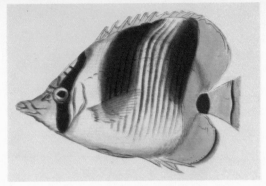

a.

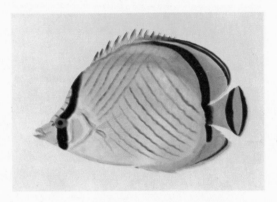

b.

c.

Pl. VIII. Butterfly-fish

a. Anisochaetodon falcula b. Anisochaetodon vagabundus

c. Megaprotodon strigangulus

Society Islands

Tuah the Back
Öoma the Breast
Eu the Nipples
Oboo the Belly
Rema the arm
Aporema the hand
Manneow the fingers
Mieu the Nails
Towhe the Buttocks
Hoowhah the thighs
Avai the legs
Tapoa the feet
Eraou a tree
Ama a Branch
Tiäle a flower
Huero fruit
Etummoo the stem
Aaa the root
Eiherre herbaceous plants
Oooopa a pidgeon
Avigne a parroquet
A-a another species
Mannu a Bird
Mora a duck
Mattow a fish hook
Toura a rope
Mow a shark
Mahimahi a Dolphin
Mattera a fishing rod
Eupea a Net
Mahanna the Sun
Malama the Moon
Whettu a star
Whettu-euphe a Comet
Erai the sky
Eatta a cloud

Poe Matawewwe Pearl
ahow a garment
Avee a fruit like apples
ahee another like Chestnuts
Ewharre a house
Whennua a high Island
Motu a low one
Toto Blood
Aeve bone
Äeo flesh
Mäe fat
Huru-huru Hair
Miti good
Eno Bad
A Yes
ima no
Paree ugly
Pororee Hungry
Pia Full
Tuhea Lean
Timahah Heavy
Mama Light
Poto short
Roa tall
Nenenne sweet
Mala-mala bitter
Whanno to go Far
Harre to go
Arrea to stay
Enoho to remain or tarry
Rohe-rohe to be tird
Maa to Eat
Inoo to Drink
Ete to understand]
Warriddo to steal
Woridde to be angry
Teparahie to beat

Among people whose dyet is so simple and plain Distempers cannot be suppos'd to be so frequent as among us Europeans, we observd but few and those cheifly cutaneous as erysipelas and scaly eruptions upon the skin. This last was almost if not quite advanc'd to Leprosy;[1] the people who were in that state were

---

[1] Possibly *oʻovi arii*, 'chief's leprosy', supposed to descend on persons who had infringed chiefly *tapu*; cf. p. 263, n. 2 above. Henry identifies *oʻovi arii* with scrofula, but that hardly matches the descriptions we have; Davies defines *oʻovi* as 'a certain scrophulous disorder'; Andrews as 'a disease like leprosy indigenous to the islands'.

AA

secluded from society, living by themselves each in a small house built in some unfrequented place where they were daily supplyd with provisions; whither these had any hopes of releif or were doom'd in this manner to languish out a life of solitude we did not learn. Some but very few had ulcers upon different parts of their bodies, most of which lookd very virulent;[1] the people who were afflicted with them did not however seem much to regard them, leaving them intirely without any application even to keep off the flies. Acute distempers no doubt they have but while we stayd upon the Island they were very uncommon, possibly in the rainy season they are more frequent.[2] Among the numerous acquaintance I had upon the Island only one was taken ill during our stay; her I visited and found her as is their custom left by every body but her three children who sat by her; her complaint was cholick which did not appear to me at all violent; I askd her what medicines she took, she told me none and that she depended intirely upon the preist who had been trying to free her from her distemper by his prayers and ceremonies, which she said he would repeat till she was well, shewing me at the same time Branches of the (*Thespesia populnea*)[3] which he had left with her. After this I left her and, whether by the ceremonies of the preist or the goodness of her constitution I know not, in three days time she came down to our tents compleatly recoverd.

I never hapned to be present when their preists performd their ceremonies for the cure of sick people, but one of our gentlemen who was informed me that it consisted in nothing but the preist repeating certain fixd sentences during which time he platted the leaves of the Cocoa nut tree into different figures, neat enough, some of which he fas[t]ned to the fingers and toes of the sick man, who [was during] the time uncoverd as in respect to the prayers, the whole ceremony almost exactly resembling their method of praying at the *Marai's* which I shall by and by describe. That they have however besides these operations of Preistcraft a knowledge of Medecine not to be despis'd we were abundantly convinc'd of by the following fact. The Spanish ship which visited this Island about 17 months before we came brought with it the Venereal

---

[1] The ulcers of yaws?

[2] Henry (op. cit., p. 289) gives the diseases of pre-European Tahiti as *o'ovi* (scrofula), *tutoo* (tuberculosis), *hotate* (asthma) and *feefee* (elephantiasis). Curiously enough, she does not mention yaws, which was endemic in the islands. 'Scrofula' was a very vague and wide medical term in the eighteenth and early nineteenth centuries. Cf. p. 375, n. 2 below.

[3] The Miro or Amae, *Thespesia populnea,* a tree regarded as highly sacred and frequently planted about *marae.*

disease and that in a most virulent degree; these people have often describd to me in most pathetick terms the shocking symptoms with which the poor wretches were afflicted who were first seizd by this filthy distemper, which in their Language they call by a name of Nearly the same but a more extensive signification than rotteness in English;[1] their hair and nails dropd off and their very flesh rotted from their bones so that they dyed miserable objects shunnd by their nearest relations, fearfull least they themselves might be tainted with the dreadfull Contagion. Yet shocking as these symptoms were they had even at the time when we came there found a method of cure and that I should suppose not of a despicable nature, as we saw no one during the whole of our stay in whoom the distemper arrivd to any hight and some who went from us for their cure returnd in a short time perfectly recover'd. When first we discoverd this distemper among these people we were much alarmd, fearing that we ourselves had notwithstanding our many precautions brought it among them; but upon strict inquiry we found that one of our people had been infected within 5 days after our arrival and when we a little better understood the Language the natives explaind the matter fully to us.[2]

That they have skillfull Chirurgeons among them we easily gatherd from the dreadfull scars of wounds which we frequently saw that had been cur'd, some of which were far greater than any I have seen any where else, and these were made by stones which these people know how to throw with slings with great dexterity and force. One man I particularly recolect whose face was almost intirely destroyd, his nose one cheek and one eye being beat in and all the bones there flatted down so that the hollow would

---

[1] One can only conjecture what Banks means here. Perhaps he was misled through the similarity of *opi*, gonorrhoea, and *o pe*, 'is [something] rotten'—hence rottenness.

[2] Venereal disease was certainly carried to Tahiti by some European ship, but by whose it is impossible to say. Wallis's surgeon declared that the *Dolphin* was quite free of it. Bougainville rebutted with horror the idea that his men were responsible, and said that signs of it were already there on his arrival. Naturally there was great willingness on all hands to shift the responsibility. Cook on his second voyage concluded that it was pre-European. Bligh on his visit in 1789 seems to have been the first to suspect something other than syphilis; his conclusion was that 'former Navigators' had 'assuredly been mistaken' and that what they thought was 'confirmed lues' was scrofula.—*Log of the Bounty* (London 1937), II, p. 60. Scrofula would give swelling of the glands; but it seems likely that Bligh himself was mistaken, in spite of his careful examination, and that the disease that misled 'former Navigators' was yaws, which was contagious, and produced raspberry-like eruptions on the skin not unlike venereal symptoms. Dr S. M. Lambert, *A Doctor in Paradise*, pp. 30-2, seems to give a clear answer to the problem: 'It is quite understandable that the early voyagers should have confused yaws and syphilis. That such confusion still persists is reasonable. . . . Yaws is not a venereal disease, nor is it hereditary. . . . The treatment for yaws is exactly the same as the treatment for syphilis— arsenical injections'.—On the other hand, it is equally clear that syphilis did come to Tahiti—but when?

receive a mans fist, yet this dreadfull wound was heald clean without any ulcer remaining. Tupia who has had several wound[s] has had one made by a spear of his countrey headed with the bone of a stingrays tail which has peircd quite through his body, entering at his back and coming out just under his breast, yet this has been so well curd that the remain[in]g scar is as smooth and as small as any I have seen from the cures of our best European surgeons.

Vulnerary herbs they have many, nor do they seem at all nice in the choice of them so they have plenty of such herbaceous plants as yeild mild juices devoid of all acridity, such as chickweed ground-sell &c. in England. With these they make fomentations which they frequently apply to the wound, taking care to cleanse it as often as possible, the patient all the time observing great abstinence; by this method if they have told us true their wounds are curd in a very short time. As for their medicines we learn'd but little concerning them; they told us indeed freely that such and such plants were good for such and such distempers, but it requird a much better knowledge of the language than we were able to obtain during our short stay to understand the method of application even of those they attempted to explain to us.

Their Manner of Disposing of their dead as well as the ceremonies relating to their mourning for them are so remarkable that they deserve a very particular description. As soon as any one is dead the House is immediately filld with their relations who bewail their Loss with Loud lamentations, especialy those who are the farthest removd in blood from or who profess the least greif for the deceasd; the nearer relations and those who are realy affected spend their time in more silent sorrow, while the rest join in Chorus's of Greif at certain intervals between which they laugh, talk and gossip as if totaly unconcernd; this lasts till day light on the Morn after their meeting, when the body being shrowded in their cloth is laid upon a kind of Bier on which it can conveniently be carried upon mens shoulders. The preists office now begins; he prays over the body, repeating his sentences, and orders it to be carried down to the sea side; here his prayers are renewd, the Corps is brought down near the waters edge and he sprinkles water towards but not upon it, it is then removd 40 or 50 yards from the sea and soon after brought back and this ceremony repeated which is done several times. In the mean time a house has been built and a small space of ground round it raild in; in the center of this house are posts set up for the supporting of the bier which as soon as the ceremonies are finishd is brought here and set upon them, where the Corps is to remain and putrifie in state to the no small disgust of every one whose business requires them to pass near it.

These houses of corruption, *Tu papow*[1] as they are calld here, are of a size proportionate to the rank of the Person containd in them; if he is poor they merely cover the bier and these generaly have no railing round them, the largest I ever saw was 11 yards in lengh. They are ornamented according to the abilities and inclinations of the surviving relations, who never fail to lay a profusion of Good Cloth about the body and often almost cover the outside of the house; the two ends which are open are also hung with kind of garlands of the Fruits of the Palm nut (*Pandanus*) Cocoa nut leaves knotted by the Preists in kind of Mystick knots, and a plant calld by them *Ethee no ta Marai (terminalia)*[2] which is particularly consecrated to funerals. Near the House is also laid fish, fruits and cocoa nut or Common water or such provisions as can well be spard, not that they suppose the dead any way capable of eating this provision, but think that if any of their gods should descend upon that place and being hungry find that these preparations had been neglected he would infalibly satisfy his appetite with the flesh of the dead corps.

No sooner is the corps fixd up within the House or *ewhatta*[3] as they call it than the ceremony of mourning begins again. The women (for the men seem to think lamentations below their dignity) assemble Led on by the nearest relation, who walking up to the door of the House swimming almost in tears strikes a sharks tooth several times into the crown of her head, on which a large effusion of blood flows, which is carefully caught in their linnen and thrown under the Bier. Her example is imitated by the rest of the women and this ceremony is repeated at the interval of 2 or 3 days as long as the women chuse or can keep it up, the nearest relation thinking it her duty to Continue it longer than any one else. Besides the blood which they beleive to be an acceptable present to the deceasd, whose soule they beleive to exist and hover about the place where the body lays observing the actions of the survivors, they throw in Cloths wet with tears, of which all that are shed are carefully preservd for that purpose, and the younger people cut

---

[1] *tupapau* was the corpse. The 'house of corruption' was *fare-tupapau*. See Pl. 14.

[2] *e ti no te marae*, a variety of Ti (*Cordyline terminalis*) known as *ti-uti*, a sacred tree planted in *marae* courtyards for the uses of religion.

[3] Banks seems to have got his words mixed here: *fare*, a house; *fata*, an 'altar'. The *fata* would be the bier, already mentioned by Banks, within the temporary house erected for the purpose.

off their hair either all or in part and throw that also under the Bier.[1]

When these ceremonies have been performd for two or three days the men, who till now seemd to be intirely insensible of their loss, begin their part which the Nearest relations take in turns. They dress themselves in a dress so extrordinary that I question whether words can give a tolerable Idea of it, I therefore refer intirely to the annexd figure. In this dress they patrole the woods early in the morn and late at night, preceeded by 2 or 3 boys who have nothing upon them but a small peice of Cloth round their wrists and are smutted all over with Charcoal; these sable emissaries run about their principal in all directions as if in pursuit of people on whoom he may vent the rage inspird by his sorrow, which he does most unmercifully if he catches any body, cutting them with his stick the edge of which is set with sharks teeth, but this rarely or never happens for no sooner does this figure appear than every one who see either him or his emissaries fly inspird with a sort of religious awe, fly with the utmost speed, hiding wherever they think themselves the most safe but by all means quitting their Houses if they lie even near the path of this dreadfull apparition.[2]

These ceremonies continue for 5 moons decreasing however in frequency very much towards the latter part of that time. The body is then taken down from the *ewhatta*, the bones washd and scrapd very clean, and buried according to the rank of the person either within or without some one of their *Marais* or places of publick worship; and if it is one of their *Earees* or cheifs his Scull is preservd and being wrappd up in fine Cloth is plac'd in a kind of case made for that purpose which stands in the *marai*. The mourning then ceases unless some of the women who find themselves more than commonly afflicted by the Loss repeat the ceremony of *Poopooing*[3] or bleeding themselves in the head, which they do at any time or in any place where they happen to be when the whim takes them.

The ceremonies however are far from Ceasing at this time.

---

[1] This shedding of blood may have been propitiatory; but, says Handy (*Polynesian Religion*, pp. 191, 255) it was also a means of strengthening the bond of blood between the mourners and the deceased; possibly both aspects come into Banks's phrase, 'an acceptable present'. At the same time one may perhaps suggest that the ceremony was a formalization, and the theory a 'rationalization', of one of the oldest and most instinctive ways of expressing grief, in some sort of self-mutilation. Cutting the body was a well-spread Polynesian custom; as we shall see, in New Zealand it was not confined to the head.

[2] Cf. Banks's description of the *heiva-tupapau* above.

[3] Perhaps from *pupu*, shells, because of the instrument often used (not always a shark tooth). The word *tāpū*, to cut, comes from the same root.

Frequent prayers are to be said by the preist and frequent offerings made for the benefit of the deceasd, or more properly for that of the Preists who are well paid for their prayers by the surviving relations. During this ceremony Emblematical devices are made use of: a young plantain tree signifies the Deceasd and a bunch of feathers the Deity invokd; opposite to this the preist places himself often attended by relations of the deceasd and always furnish'd with a small offering of some kind of Eatables intended for the God; he begins by adressing the God by a set form of sentences and during the time he repeats them employs himself in weaving Cocoa nut leaves into different forms, all which he disposes upon the Grave where the bones have been deposited; the Deity is then adressed by a shrill scritch usd only on that occasion and the offering presented to his representative, the little tuft of feathers, which after this is removd and every thing else left in statu quo, to the no small Emolument of the Rats who quickly devour the offering.

Religion has been in ages, is still in all Countreys Cloak'd in mysteries unexplicable to human understanding. In the South Sea Islands it has still another disadvantage to present to any one who has a desire to investigate it—the Language in which it is conveyd, at least many words of it, are different from those usd in common conversation,[1] so that tho Tupia often shewd the greatest desire to instruct us in it he found it almost impossible; in short it is only needfull to remember how dificult it would be to reconcile the apparent inconsistencies of our own religion to the faith of an infidel, and to recolect how many excellent discourses are daily read to instruct even us in the faith which we profess, as articles of excuse in my favour when I declare that I know less of the religion of these people than of any other part of their policy. What I do know however I shall here write down wishing that inconsistencies may not appear to the eye of the candid reader as absurdities.

This Universe and its marvelous parts must strike the most stupid with a desire of knowing from whence themselves and it were producd. Their Preists however have not Ideas sufficiently enlarg'd to adopt that of Creation: that this world should have been originaly created from nothing far surpasses their comprehension.

[1] i.e. the invocations were traditional, and their meanings partly esoteric, so that even the ordinary Tahitian kept a respectful and compulsory distance when religious ceremony was in progress; at the same time cosmogony was wrapped up with theology, and esoteric, and the esoteric was *tapu*. Hence what might be called, mildly, certain differences of opinion among modern scholars of the subject.

They observd however that every animal and every plant producd new ones by procreation and adopted the Idea; hence it is necessary to suppose two original beings one of whom they call *Ettoomoo* and the other which they say was a rock *Tepapa*;[1] these at some very remote period of time, and by the common means allowd to us males and females their children, begat all that is seen or known of by us; some things however they imagine have increasd among themselves, as the Stars, the different species of plants, and even the different divisions of Time; the Years say they producd the Months who intermingling with each other produc'd the days.

The First man say they was the Issue of a Connection between two of their inferior deities or *Eatuas* who at that time inhabited the Earth. He was when first born round like a ball but his mother with great care drew out each Limb and formd him as we now are, after which he was Calld *Eothe*[2] which signifies finishd. When he arrivd at maturity the Stings of nature made him very desirous of Excersising those faculties with which the males of all animals are indued; his mother was the only female he could find and consequently the Object of his attempts; ignorant however what part of her he was in search of he made several unsuccessfull efforts, at Last however chance leading him right he begat a daughter whoom also he compressd and begat another, nor could for several generations have one son; at last however he had one who by the asistance of his many Sisters peopled this world and is the ancestor of us all.

Their Gods are numerous; they are divided into two Classes, the Greater and the Lesser Gods and of each Class are some of Both Sexes. The cheif of all is *Tarroati'ettoomoo*[3] the procreator of all things whoom they emphaticaly stile the Causer of Earthquakes; his Son *Tane*[4] was however much more generaly calld upon as supposd to be the more active deity. The Men worshipd the male Gods and the Women the Females,[5] the Men however supply the office of Preist for both sexes.

---

[1] *E*, more properly *Te Tumu*, the Source or Cause, the male parent of the gods; and *Te Papa*, the 'Earth foundation', their female parent.

[2] *e oti*; *oti* to be done or finished. At the same time Banks may have incorporated in this the name *Ti'i*, the first man. But according to what appears to be the orthodox Tahitian account, it was Taaroa, the original Creator or First Cause (Taaroa-ta'ahi-tumu) who created man, from Te Papa, or the Earth. One story gives him the aid of Tu, 'the great artisan', whom he had himself created to help him in his work. But in Banks's story there appears to be an ingredient from the creation of the god Tane, who was moulded into shape by his mother Atea or Space (or the Sky).

[3] Taaroa-ta'ahi-tumu, who figures in all the versions of Polynesian theology with appropriate consonantal changes—Tangahoa, Tangaroa, Kanaloa.

[4] Tane, the god of craftsmanship, forests and all growing things, of beauty and—as Tupaia illustrated—favourable weather.

[5] This statement is in error; there was no such division.

They beleive in a heaven and a hell, the first they call *Tairua l'orai*[1] the other *Tiahoboo*.[2] Heaven they describe as a place of Great happines and hell is only a place enjoying less of the luxuries of life; to this they say that the souls of the interior people go after death and those of the cheifs and rich men to the other. This is one of the strongest instances to shew that their religion is totaly independent of Morality: no actions regarding their neighbours are supposd to come at all under the Cognizance of the Deity, a humble regard only is to be shewn him and his assistance askd on all occasions with much Ceremony and some sacrafice, from whence are derivd the Perquisites of the Preists.

The *Tahowa*[3] or Preist is here a hereditary Character. They are numerous and all ranks of People have preists among them, the cheif is generaly however the younger brother of some very Good Family and is respected in a degree next to their kings. All ranks of preists are commonly more learned than the laity; their learning consists cheifly in knowing well the names and ranks of the different *Eatuas* or divinities, the origin of the universe and all its parts &c; these things have been handed down to them in set sentences of which those who are clever can repeat an almost infinite number, in doing which few words occur the same as those usd in common conversation, which greatly increasd the dificulty we found in Gaining a knowledge of their Theology.

Besides religion the Practise of Physick and the knowledge of Navigation and Astronomy is in the Possession of the Preists. The name indeed of preist, *Tahowa*, signifies a Man of Knowledge, so that even here the Preists Monopolize the greatest part of the learning of the Countrey in much the same manner as they formerly did in Europe; the practise of which gains them profit as well as respect each in his particular order, for each order has preists of its own nor will the preists of the *Manahounies*[4] do any thing for a *Toutou*[5] who is below them in rank.

Marriage is [in] these Islands no more than an agreement between

1 Interpretation here is made difficult by uncertainty over what precisely Banks meant to write: it may have been 'Tavirua t'orai', the *l* being a large uncrossed *t*. In either case, a meaning is hard to extract. Davies (1851) gives *airaua* as one of the names of the *po* or 'hades', but doubt has been cast on his correctness. *Te rai* is the sky or heaven: *orai* is meaningless. Banks may possibly have joined two separate expressions together.

2 Possibly *te aia o Po*, the homeland of the goddess of the *po* or world of darkness—darkness here personified as the great goddess *Po-nui*.

3 *tahua*; in general a mechanic or artificer, i.e. someone skilled, and with special knowledge. A priest was properly a *tahua-pure*, one skilled in prayer; a high priest, *tahua-nui* or *ahua-rahi*.

4 *manahune*.

5 *teuteu*. Banks makes an error here; the *teuteu*, the hereditary servants of *arii*, were themselves of *manahune* families.

the man and the woman totaly independent of the preist,[1] it is in general I beleive pretty well kept unless they agree to seperate, which is done with as little trouble as they came together. Few people however enter this state but rather chuse freedom in their Amours,[2] tho bought at the inhuman expence of murthering their children, whose fate is in that case intirely dependant on the father; who if he does not chuse to acknowledge both them and the woman and engage to contribute his part towards their support, orders them to be strangled which is instantly put in execution.[3]

If our preists have excelld theirs in persuading us that the Sexes can not come lawfully together without having bought their benediction, they have done it by intermingling it so far with religion that the fear of punishment from above secures their power over us; but these untaught parsons have securd to themselves the profit of two operations without being driven to the necessity of so severe a penalty on the refusal, viz. *Tattowing* or painting their bodies and Circumsizing. Neither of these can be done by any but preists,[4] and as the highest degree of shame follows the wanting either the people are as much necessitated to make use of them as if bound by the highest ties of Religion, of which both customs are totaly independent. For the first they give no reason but that their ancestors did the same, for the other Cleanliness in hot climates always will be a sufficient reason. For both these operations they are paid by every one according to his abilities in the same manner as weddings Christnings &c &c. are paid for in Europe.

Their places of publick worship, which they call *Marai*, are square enclosures of very different sizes, from 10 to 100 yards in diameter; at one end of these is a heap or built up pile of stones near which the bones of the principal people are interrd, those of their dependants

[1] It might be, but with *arii* families there was considerable ceremony and feasting; see e.g. Henry, pp. 281-4.

[2] This is an overstatement, which seems to be due both to what Banks had heard of the *arioi*, and to his imperfect acquaintance with the elements of stability in Tahitian society.

[3] This again is over-simplification. If Banks's understanding of the situation had been right, there would have been no, or very few, children in Tahiti and the Society Islands, whereas there were plenty. But it is true that infanticide was widespread, and not confined to the *arioi*. Engaging 'to contribute his part to their support' was an idea brought from England and its social code rather than one found in Polynesia, where family relationships sat more easily on the people. In cases of infanticide a mother might be quite as code-bound as a father, as the early missionaries found. But even the code had its modifications—e.g. if a child on delivery was seen by the mother, or heard to cry, it might be spared; and it seems that Teriirere may have owed his existence to the fact that, though Purea and Amo were both *arioi*, he was delivered by Purea herself. An article by Paul I. Nordmann, 'Contribution à l'étude de l'infanticide à Tahiti', in *Bulletin de la Société d'Etudes Océaniennes*, VI, pp. 337-54, is useful.

[4] Both operations called for skill, and tattooing for skill of a high degree. *Tatau* or 'tapping' was carried out by the *tatatau* or *tahua tatau—tatau* artist or priest; circumcision or *tehe* by the *tahua tehe*.

laying all round on the outside of the wall. Near or in these enclosures are often placd planks carvd into different figures and very frequently images of many men standing on each others heads; these however are in no degree the objects of adoration, every prayer and sacrafise being here offerd to the Invisible deities.

Near or even within the *Marai* are one or more large altars raisd upon high posts 10 or 12 feet above the ground which are calld *Whatterow*:[1] on these are laid the offerings, Hogs, dogs, fowls, fruits or what ever else the piety or superfluity of the owner thinks proper to dedicate to the gods.

Both these places are reverencd in the highest degree, no man aproaches them without taking his Cloths from off his shoulders and no woman is on any account permitted to enter them. The women however have *Marais* of their own where they worship and sacrifice to their Godesses.[2]

Of these *Marais* each family of consequence has one which serves him and his dependants; as each family values itself upon its antiquity so are these esteemd. In the Society Isles especialy Ulhietea were some of great antiquity particularly that of Tapodeboatea; the building of these is rough and coarse but the stones of which they are composd immensely large. At Otahite again where either from frequent wars or other accidents many of the most ancient families are extinct they have tried to make them as elegant and expensive as possible, of which sort is that of Oamo describd in the Journal of going round the Island.[3]

Besides their Gods each Island has a Bird to which the Title of *Eatua* or God is given, for instance Ulietea has the Heron[4] and Bola Bola a kind of Kingfisher;[5] these birds are held in high respect

---

[1] *fata-rau.*

[2] This is a mis-statement. Women had places of their own on the family *marae*. Banks could not become encyclopaedic in the time he had, and he was unable to discriminate (except so far as he goes in his next paragraph) between the public *marae*, of international or national, or general local importance, on the one hand, and the family or ancestral *marae*, let alone those devoted to particular callings, on the other. 'Doctors', for example, had their own *marae* and women could be doctors.

[3] For an illuminating discussion of the place occupied by the *marae* in old Polynesian life, see Henry, pp. 119 ff., and for their construction Kenneth P. Emory, *Stone Remains in the Society Islands* (B. P. Bishop Mus. Bull. 116, Honolulu 1933). Banks was thinking as an Englishman. Elegance and expense had nothing to do with the extinction of ancient families, everything to do with the rivalry of existing families—whence the magnificence of Mahaiatea as a glorification of Teriirere as the head of a family, and the consequent family downfall. The worked stone facings of the Tahitian *marae* were a later development than the architecture of the Leeward Islands (e.g. Taputapuatea at Raiatea), but the Leeward Islands stuck to their own style. Here the built-up *marae* were faced with great slabs of limestone set on end; and when it was felt necessary to keep up the architectural prestige of Taputapuatea, a new facing was simply added, of still greater slabs. See Emory, pp. 145 ff.   [4] The Reef Heron, *Demigretta sacra* (Gm.).

[5] *Halcyon tuta* (Gm.). Solander, Z1, calls it *Alcedo superstitiosa*, with the island name 'Erurho'—i.e. *ruro.*

and by no means killd or molested. They are thought to be givers of Good or Bad fortune but no kind of Worship is offerd to them.[1]

Tho I dare not assert that these people, to whoom the art of writing and consequently of Recording Laws &c. is totaly unknown, live under a regular form of Goverment, Yet the Subordination which takes place among them very much resembles the early state of the feudal laws by which our Ancestors were so long Governd, a System evidently formd to secure the Licentious Liberty of a few while the Greater part of the Society are unalterably immersd in the most abject Slavery.

Their Orders are *Earee ra hie* which answers to King; *Earee*, Baron; *Manahouni*, Vassel; and *Toutou*, Villain.[2] The *Earee ra hie* is always the head of the Best family in the countrey; to him great respect is paid by all ranks but in Power he seemd to us inferior to several of the Principal *Earees*, nor indeed did he once appear in the transacting of any part of our business.[3] Next to him in Rank are the *Earees*, each of whoom hold one or more of the Districts into which the Island is divided (in Otahite there may be about 100 such districts);[4] which are by the *Earees* parceld out to the *Manahounies*, who cultivate each his part and for the use of it owe their Cheif service when calld upon and provisions, especialy when he travels, which he often does accompanied by many of his freinds and their families often amounting to near 100 principals besides their attendants. Inferiour to the *Manahounes* are the *toutous* who are upon almost the same footing as the Slaves in the East

---

[1] Birds were *ata*, 'reflections' or 'shadows' of the gods, and might even be temporarily their incarnations. Thus the heron represented Ti'i, the first man, who became a secondary god. An added reason for the sacredness of kingfishers would be their frequenting of *marae*, where the flies and small lizards on which they feed were abundant. But they are sacred birds all over the Pacific.

[2] Banks's inadequate study and his feudal analogy combine to mislead him here, nor is it just to write as he does in his previous paragraph of 'licentious liberty' and 'most abject slavery'. There were three classes in the Tahitian (and Society Islands) social order: (1) the *arii* or *hui arii*, the chiefly 'family' or group, (2) the *raatira*, landed proprietors not of 'noble' or chiefly blood, (3) *manahune* or commoners. Among this third group the *teuteu* were the hereditary retainers of the *arii*, not villeins or slaves. *Earee ra hie = e arii rahi*, a high chief; *Earee = e arii*, an *arii*.

[3] There were three *arii rahi*, not one—Teriirere of Papara, Vehiatua of Taiarapu, and Tu of Pare. (This summary statement ignores the complicated question of larger political divisions and interests apart from Taiarapu). There was no one 'Best family'. Banks is thinking of Tu, a far from impressive figure, in spite of his rank, who was much under the influence of Tuteha, his great-uncle, the powerful personality to whom Banks has referred so often above. It was only after Tuteha's death that Tu came into any prominence in island politics and began to show the family ambition that resulted in the installation of 'kings' in Tahiti.

[4] It is difficult to know what Banks means by 'districts'; there were nineteen main districts in Tahiti, but many 'sub-districts'; within them were many more *mataeinaa*, or people-district groupings, and within them again ancestral sub-divisions under the *raatira*. No doubt his 100 was merely a rough round-figure equivalent for a large number.

indian Islands,[1] only that they never appeard to us transferrable
from one to the other; these do all kinds of Laborious work, till
the land, fetch wood and water, dress the victuals, under the direction
however of the Mistris of the family, catch fish &c. Besides these
are the two classes of *Erate* and *Towha*[2] which seem to answer to
Yeoman and Gentleman as they came between *Earee* and *Manahouni*; but as I was not acquainted with the existence of these classes
during our stay on the Island I know little of their real situation.[3]

Each of the *Earees* kept a kind of Court and hade a large attendance
cheifly of the Younger brothers of their own family and of other
Earees; among these were different officers of the Court, as *Heewa
no t'Earee Whanno no t'Earee*,[4] who were sometimes sent to us upon
business. Of all these Courts Dootahah's was the most splendid, indeed
we were almost inclind to believe that he acted as Locum tenens
for *Otou* the *Earee rahie*, his nephew, as he livd upon an estate belonging to him and we never could hear that he had any other publick
place of residence.[5]

The *Earees* or rather the districts which they Possess are obligd
in time of a general attack to furnish each their Quota of soldiers
for the service of the Publick. Those of the Principal districts which
Tupia recolected when added together amounted to 6680 men
to which army it is probable that the small Quotas of the rest would
not make any great addition.[6]

[1] See p. 384, n. 2 above.
[2] 'Erate' is dubious: I think Banks must have made a slip in writing 'Eratera' or
raatira. 'Towha': *toofa*, a chief ranking next to an *arii*.
[3] i.e. he learnt of their existence from Tupaia in shipboard conversation, this part
of his journal being written up on the voyage south from the islands.
[4] S has here a linguistic note: 'Heowa no t'Earee, or Perspiration of the Earee. A
name given to a sort of flying Messenger, who is trusted with messages that require
care; and kind of Embassies. Whanno no t'Earee, or Bow of the Earee. Another kind of
flying Messenger, who is to go quick with common Messages: not so honourable a Post
as the former.

Otaheite Language	English D°	
Heowa	Perspiration	So called from their Employments
Whanno	Bow	obliging them to use great Expedition'.

Houa, to be in a state of perspiration; *fana*, bow: *houa/fana no te arii*.
[5] Great-nephew. Tuteha's elder brother was the father of Teu, the father of Tu. The
arii rahi became head of his family immediately on his birth, but pending his arrival
at an age to rule effectively, his father or some other great *arii* nearly related acted as
'regent'. There appears to have been no conventional 'age of majority'. Hence Tu,
though he seems to have been about 25 at this time, still lived under the shadow of
Tuteha—which indicates the timidity of his character. Tuteha evidently took up
residence where he liked; his own *marae* was Maraetaata in the Paea district, which
Banks calls Atahourou, and where Banks and Cook had visited him on 28 May, so that
Banks's last remark is hard to reconcile with what has gone before.
[6] A stray note by Banks, B.M. Add. MS 27889, f. 71, seems to list the 'Principal districts
which Tupia recolected' (14 in number) and their 'quotas'. It is headed, however,
'Forces of Otahite 6780'; while careful addition makes the sum no more than 6280.

Besides these publick wars, which are to be headed by the *Earee ra hie*, any private difference between two *Earees* is decided by their own people without at all disturbing the tranquility of the Publick. Their weapons are Slings which they use with great dexterity, pikes headed with the stings of sting Rays, and Clubbs of 6 or 7 feet long made of a very heavy and hard wood.[1] With these they fight by their own account very obstinately, which appears the more probable as the Conquerors give no Quarter to Man Woman or Child who is unfortunate enough to fall into their hands during or for some hours after the Battle, that is till their Passion is subsided.

Otahite at the time of Our being there was divided into two Kingdoms, Oporeonoo the larger and Tiarrebo the smaller. Each had its seperate king &c. &c. who were at Peace; the king of Oporeonoo however Calld himself king of both in just the Same manner as most European Monarchs usurp the Title of king over kingdoms over which they have not the least influence.[2]

It is not to be expected that in a Goverment of this kind Justice can be strictly administerd, we saw indeed no signs of Punishments during our stay. Tupia however always insisted upon it that Theft was punishd with death and smaller crimes in proportion: in cases of Adultery the offenders were in the power of the offended party who if he takes them in the fact frequently kills them both. All punishments however were the business of the injurd party, who if superior to him who committs the crime easily executes them by means of his more numerous attendants; equals seldom chuse to molest each other unless countenancd by their superior who assists them to defend their unjust acquisitions. The cheifs however to whoom in reality all kinds of Property belong punish their dependants for crimes committed against each other, and the dependants of others if caught doing wrong within their districts.[3]

---

[1] Toa or Aito, ironwood.

[2] There is misapprehension here. The two primary geographical divisions of Tahiti were Tahiti-nui or Great Tahiti, and Taiarapu or Tahiti-iti, Little Tahiti. Oporeonoo is the English rendering of Porionuu (or Te Porionuu), the district where Tu was the *arii rahi*. The English habitually looked for a king wherever they went, but neither Tu nor Vehiatua of Taiarapu, a much greater man, was a king. What Tu called himself must have been unknown to Banks, as Banks never met him; but there may have been some vain boasting on the part of someone else—quite vain, and quite misleading. All English visitors, from this time on, gave Tu much more attention than was his due, to the natural disgust of the other leading chiefs of the island. Banks was making a shrewd observation that Cook (and others) would have done well to heed.

[3] The first volume of the MS Journal ends here.

III

15. Crossd the tropick this morn, wind North and weather very pleasant; at night wind rather variable.

16. Soon after we rose this morn we were told that land was in sight; it provd to be a cloud but at first sight was so like land that it deceivd every man in the ship, even Tupia gave it a name. The ship bore down towards it but in about 3 hours all hands were convincd that it was but a cloud.

17. A heavy swell from the SW all day so we are not yet under the Lee of the continent:[1] in the Even no wind. Our *Taros* (roots of the Yam kind calld in the W. Indies *Cocos*) faild us today, many of them were rotten; they would probably have kept longer had we had either time or opportunity of drying them well, but I beleive that at the best they are very much inferior to either Yamms or potatoes for keeping.

18. SE swell continues today with little wind at N.

19. Weather and swell much as yesterday; some of our people tell me that they have seen Albatrosses both yesterday and the day before.

20. A Large Albatross about the ship most of the day.[2] Little wind, the swell less than yesterday but still troublesome, at night a heavy Dew.

21. A fine breeze at NW. Some Pintado birds (*Proc. capensis*)[3] about the ship. This day our Plantains faild us, they were all eat, not one ever was rotten. Indeed since we left Ulhietea the Hogs have almost intirely subsisted upon them, of which we have no small number who I fear will feel the loss of them most sensibly as not one I beleive has yet eat the smallest proportion of English food.

22. Fresh breeze of wind but little sea. Several Albatrosses and Pintado birds about the ship today.

23. Light breeze. Our hogs and fowls begin to die apace, of the latter a great many, want of proper food and cold which now begins

[1] The great Pacific swell, to those who had experienced it, was a continual incitement to scepticism about the southern continent; but Banks's phrasing implies his belief that the continent existed.

[2] Probably the Wandering Albatross (see Fleming, *Emu*, 49, 1950, p. 182).

[3] The Cape Pigeon, *Daption capensis*.

to pinch even us is I suppose the cause. Afternoon calm, many Albatrosses and Pintado birds about the ship.

24. The morning was calm. About 9 it began to blow fresh with rain which came on without the least warning, at the same time a water spout was seen to leward; it appeard to me so inconsiderable that had I not been shewd it I should not have particularly notic'd the apearance; it resembled a line of thick mist, as thick as a midling tree, which reachd not in a strait line almost to the waters edge and in a few minutes totaly disapeard; its distance I suppose made it appear so trifling, as the Seamen judg'd it not less than 2 or 3 miles from us. Many Birds about the ship, Pintado, Common and Southern Albatross.[1]

25. Less wind today but the swell occasiond by yesterdays wind still troublesome. Birds today about the ship Pintado, Common and Southern Albatross and a shearwater in size and shape like the common, but grey or whitish on the head and back.[2] It was this day a twelvemonth since we left England, in consequence of which a peice of cheshire cheese was taken from a locker where it had been reservd for this occasion and a cask of Porter tappd which provd excellently good, so that we livd like English men and drank the hea[l]ths of our freinds in England.

26. Few birds today cheifly Albatrosses, few pintados. In the evening several grampuses[3] about the ship.

27. Pleasant breeze: birds today as plentifull as ever, Albatrosses of both kinds, Pintados and grey shearwaters.

28. Birds as yesterday with the addition of a kind of shearwater, quite black, the same as was seen and shot on the 21st of March last in our passage to the westward (*p. atrata*).[4] Tupia not well today, he complains of a pain in his stomach; his distemper probably proceeds from cold of which we have for some days past had more than from our latitude we shoud have expected. One of the seamen Rayden by name was this morn found so drunk that he had scarce any signs of life and in about an hour he expird.[5] Where he could

---

[1] It is difficult to discover what Banks regarded as the Southern Albatross.

[2] Probably the White-headed Petrel, *Pterodroma lessonii* (Garnot). See 19 September 1769 below.

[3] Possibly the Killer Whale, *Orcinus orca*.

[4] *Procellaria atrata*: the Herald Petrel was taken on 21 March 1769, and this was probably the same species (see Murphy and Pennoyer, *Amer. Mus. Novit.*, 1580, 1952, p. 39).

[5] The man's name (variously spelt) was John Reardon; he was the boatswain's mate. Hicks records that 'his death was occasioned by His drinking three half pints of Rum' (Turnbull MS); given him by the boatswain, says Cook, 'out of mere good nature', so that the unfortunate toper at least got his liquor fairly.

have got his liquor is a mystery which however nobody seems to enquire into, probably not fairly. I have more than once had occasion to congratulate myself on my prudence in not taking wine on board at Madera, as I beleive I may safely say that there is not a cask on board the ship that has not been tap'd to the great dissatisfaction of the owners, who in general have had the comfort to find the gentlemen honest enough not to have filld up with salt water; in some cases however this was not a Consideration of much comfort as many of the casks were ⅔ empty and some quite.

29. Very moderate and pleasant, scarce any motion; few or no birds about the ship. In the course of last night a phenomenon was seen in the heavens which Mr Green says is either a comet or a Nebulus he does not know which, the Seamen have observd it these 3 nights.[1]

30. Our Comet is this morn acknowledged and proves a very large one but very faint. Tupia as soon as he saw it declard that the people of Bola bola would upon the sight of it kill the people of Ulhietea who would as many as could fly into the mountains. More sea today than yesterday heaving in from WSW. Several birds, Pintados, Albatross's of both kinds, the little silver backd bird which we saw off Faukland Isles and Cape Horn, *Pr. velox*[2] and grey shearwater.[3] Peter saw a green bird about the size of a dove, the colour makes us hope that it is a land bird,[4] it took however not the least notice of the ship. Some sea weed was also seen to pass by the ship but as it was a very small peice our hopes are not very sanguine on that head. The thermometer today 52 which pinches us much who are so lately come from a countrey where it was seldom less than 80. A swell from SW.

31. Blows fresh this morn with a good deal of sea; about 7 in the morn a heap of sea weed passd the ship. An immense quantity of birds are about her today: Albatrosses of both kinds which are

---

[1] For this 'Comet of 1769', which created much contemporary excitement, cf. Cook I, p. 160, n. 2.

[2] According to Banks's entries for 31 August and 19 September (pp. 390 and 392 below), it is clear that he used Solander's MS name (pp. 67-8) of *Procellaria velox* for a species of *Pachyptila* or *Halobaena*, whereas it clearly applies to a gadfly petrel (cf. 15 February 1769); one of these was taken on 19 September. Solander gave a clear description of *Pachyptila vittata* Forst. on 2 October (p. 61), saying that it was blue-grey above with a conspicuous oblique dark streak.

[3] This particular bird is unidentifiable. There are no drawings or descriptions of a grey shearwater of this date.

[4] Unidentifiable; there are no green sea-birds, but it is possible that this was a Golden Plover going southward on migration. Dr D. L. Serventy states that at sea the plumage of these birds sometimes appears to have a greenish gloss.

easily distinguishd one from the other by their beaks, which in one is white in the other black;[1] also large black shearwaters and a smaller sort with grey backs,[2] Pintados; but above all many millions I may safely say of the small bird mentiond yesterday about as large as a dove, greyish on the back, some with a dark colourd mark going in a crooked direction on that and its wings.[3] I try'd today to catch some of these numerous attendants with a hook but after the whole morning spent in the atempt caught only one Pintado which provd to be *Procellaria capensis* of Linnæus.

SEPTEMBER 1769

1. Blows very fresh with a heavy sea; the ship was very troublesome all last night and is not less so today. Many birds are about but not so many as yesterday, there are however all the sorts.

2. Wind still fresher, ship lays too. Bird[s] of all the sorts before mentiond in great numbers round her. In the evening the weather moderates and the sea falls fast. At night the comet was seen brighter than when last observd but the tail was something shorter, which when last seen measurd 42 degrees in lengh. Great sea from WSW. At 4 lat. 40°.

3. Sea quite down, a pleasant breeze. Few birds today about the ship, cheifly Pintado birds and black beakd Albatrosses.

4. Almost calm, few birds as yesterday. In the Evening a light breeze springs up and the sun sets among many dark black clouds edg'd with fiery red, which is lookd upon by some seamen as a sure sign of a gale of wind.

5. In the morn a pleasant breeze which increasd gradualy till about 4 when it blew fresh; about 6 hard rain came on which made both sea and wind fall in a very short time. Many birds were seen today, all of the 2nd and two that had not been seen before, probably varieties of the common albatross; one at a distance appeard snow white but nearer was easily seen to be thickly powderd

---

[1] 'Albatrosses of both kinds': Wandering Albatrosses have pale bills throughout life; immatures of *Diomedea melanophris* Temminck, the Black-browed Albatross, and of *D. chrysostoma* Forster, the Grey-headed Albatross, have very dark bills, and both occur in these seas. According to Fleming (*Emu*, 49, 1950, p. 183) *D. melanophris* is the albatross most commonly seen in the area.

[2] Several dark shearwaters occur here. The smaller bird with a grey back may have been *Pterodroma lessonii* (Garnot), to which Solander gave the name of *Procellaria vagabunda*. See 19 September below.

[3] A flock of whale birds; *Pachyptila vittata* is common here.

over with small grey spotts,[1] the other milk white except the tipps of the wings which were black as in Gannetts.[2] Saw a peice of rock weed.

6. Moderate all day: few individuals of Birds but all the sorts of yesterday.

7. Blows fresh: many birds, all the sorts of yesterday and one added to the number, a shearwater of the common size (of a sea gull) black above and white underneath except his chin and neck which were black.[3] A seal seen.

8. Little wind in the morn, at noon calm with rain; few birds seen all of the common sorts. Great swell from SW.

9. Fair wind, light breeze and very pleasant weather: a small peice of sea weed was seen; few birds only the Pintado and small shearwater.

10. This morn a fog bank was seen upon our quarter which much resembled land, we bore after it but were soon convincd of our mistake. More birds than yesterday: Pintado birds, both the albatrosses, the small grey backd bird like a dove (Mother Careys dove), the grey backd shearwater of the 31st, and a small kind of Mother Careys chicken black above and white underneath.[4]

11. Fine weather and few birds.

12. Moderate. Saw another of the small bird of the 20th[5] which are the only two that have yet been observd. Swell from SSW.

13. Almost calm all last night; weather today very uncertain, breezes succeeding calms. Few birds are about the ship, two were however seen swimming in the water that were perfectly white and appeard larger than Albatrosses.[6]

[1] No white albatross has grey spots. This bird was perhaps a Giant Petrel, *Macronectes giganteus*, which is rather smaller than a Wandering Albatross. It has two colour phases, a grey and a white—the latter less common and mostly found in the southern part of the bird's range, the Antarctic continent. It wanders as far north as the tropics. Old-time sailors called it Stinker; the modern vernacular name is Nellie.

[2] Cook compared these birds with some seen off Tahiti which were almost certainly the Blue-faced Booby, *Sula dactylatra* Lesson; these observed by Banks were probably the same species.

[3] This shearwater may have been the Tahitian Petrel, *Pterodroma rostrata* Peale.

[4] One of these storm petrels was shot on 19 September; Solander described it (p. 59) and called it *Procellaria passerina*; it was closely allied to *Pelagodroma marina* (Latham). Murphy considers that it differs markedly, however, from the known Pacific races (*Amer. Mus. Novit.* 1506, 1951, p. 16) and is 'identifiable only as a representative of the species *Marina* but of unknown source as regards nesting station'.

[5] This must be a slip—perhaps for the 30th?—as the only bird seen on 20 August was an albatross.

[6] Probably old male Wandering Albatrosses.

14. Weather much as yesterday; swell from SSW.

15. Fresh breeze of wind but fair abundance of birds are again about the ship, both the Albatrosses, Pintados, grey backd shear-water, black backd d⁰ of the 7ᵗʰ, Dove. In the even it blew hard, myself far from well, complaint much like sea sickness.

16. Weather rather more moderate but still blows fresh. My self rather better but still very sick at the stomach which continualy supplys a thin acid liquor which I discharge by vomit. Birds as yesterday.

17. Moderate, few birds; myself quite well.

18. Moderate this morn, several pintados and albatrosses; in the evening quite calm.

19. Quite calm today go out in the boat and shoot *Procellaria velox*[1] (the dove of the 31ˢᵗ), *vagabunda*[2] (the grey backd shearwater of the same day), *Passerina*[3] (the small mother Careys chicken of the 10ᵗʰ). Took with the dipping net *Medusa vitrea*,[4] *Phillodoce velella*[5] to one specimen of which stuck *Lepas anatifera*,[6] *Doris complanata*,[7] *Helix violacea*,[8] *Cancer*. . . .[9] Very few birds were to be seen, there were however some Albatrosses and a kind of Shearwater quite black which I was not fortunate enough to shoot. A large hollow swell from the South.

20. Uncertain weather, Calms and light breezes often succeeding each other; few birds about the ship.

21. Pleasant breeze: some birds about us, Albatrosses and black and grey shearwaters.

22. Moderate. Few birds cheifly Albatrosses and Pintados; towards night a large flock of Black shearwaters are seen that do not change their place but keep hovering as if some prey was under them;[10] two whales were also seen. Southerly swell still continued.

---

[1] *Pterodroma* sp., one of the gadfly petrels recorded by Solander.
[2] *Pterodroma lessonii* (Garnot), the White-headed Petrel; Solander, pp. 95-6.
[3] See note 10 September on *Pelagodroma marina* Latham.
[4] Solander remarks (p. 459) that this was close to *Medusa radiata* and *M. fimbriata*; these are MS names for *Aequorea forskalia* Péron and Lesueur, so it is likely that *M. vitrea*, no figure of which is known, is an *Aequorea* sp.
[5] *Velella velella*; cf. 7 October 1768.
[6] The Goose Barnacle; cf. 9 October 1768.
[7] A planarian, *Planocera* sp., probably *gaimardi* Blainville 1828, which is synonymous with *pellucida* (Martens) 1832. See Parkinson III, pl. 24, painted on this very day. Solander, p. 409.
[8] *Janthina globosa* Swainson; cf. 7 October 1768.
[9] Unidentified.
[10] Probably Sooty Shearwaters.

23. Moderate today. Several birds are about the ship cheifly Pintados and Albatrosses; in the evening another flock of Black shearwaters passd the ship and soon after two whales were seen.

Dr Solander has been unwell for some days so today I opend Dr Hulme's Essence of Lemon Juice, Mr Monkhouse having prescribd it for him, which provd perfectly good, little if at all inferior in taste to fresh lemon juice. We also today made a pye of the North American apples which Dr Fothergill[1] gave me, which provd very good, if not quite equal to the apple pyes which our freinds in England are now eating, good enough to please us who have been so long deprivd of the fruits of our native Countrey. In the main however we are very well off for refreshments and provisions of most species: our ships *beef* and *Pork* are excellent as are the *peas*; the *flour* and *oatmeal* which have at some times faild us are at present and have in general been very good. Our *water* is as sweet and has rather more spirit than it had when drank out of the river at Otahite. Our *bread* indeed is but indifferent, occasiond by the quantity of Vermin that are in it, I have often seen hundreds nay thousands shaken out of a single bisket. We in the Cabbin have however an easy remedy for this by baking it in an oven, not too hot, which makes them all walk off, but this cannot be allowd to the private people who must find the taste of these animals very disagreable, as they every one taste as strong as mustard or rather spirits of hartshorn. They are of 5 kinds, 3 *Tenebrios*, 1 *Ptinus* and the *Phalangium cancroides*;[2] this last is however scarce in the common bread but was vastly plentyfull in white Deal bisket as long as we had any left.

Wheat was allowd to the ships company which has been boild for their breakfasts 2 or 3 times a week in the same manner as firmity[3] is made; this has I beleive been a very usefull refreshment to them as well as an agreable food, which myself and most of the officers in the ship have constantly breakfasted upon in the cold

[1] For Fothergill see p. 58 above. It is quite possible that the apples Banks refers to were sent from Pennsylvania by the notable American naturalist John Bartram, who shipped seeds, plants, live bull-frogs, bird skins, etc. to both Fothergill and Collinson, who in turn distributed the produce to their friends. But we have no documentary confirmation of this hypothesis.

[2] Some tenebrionid beetles are practically cosmopolitan and all stages occur in flour and other stored products. Beetles of the family Ptinidae are similarly destructive pests. *Phalangium cancroides* is the pseudoscorpion, *Chelifer cancroides*, which is a scavenger and would have been feeding not on biscuit but on the eggs etc. of the other pests.

[3] Firmity (furmety or frumenty): 'A dish made of hulled wheat boiled in milk, and seasoned with cinnamon, sugar, etc.'—O.E.D. The *Endeavour* variety must have been simplified, as one ship's goat could not possibly have kept up with the demand for milk. Cook had anything boiled with the wheat that seemed useful—raisins, wort, portable soup, greens.

weather; the grain was originaly of a good quality and has kept without the least damage. This however cannot be said of the *Malt* of which we have plainly had two kinds, one very good but that has been some time ago us'd; that that is at present in use is good for nothing at all, it has been originaly of a bad light grain and so little care has been taken in the making of it that the tails are left in with innumerable other kinds of Dirt; add to all this that it has been damp'd on board the ship so that with all the care that can be usd it will scarce give a tincture to water. *Portable Soup* is very good, it has now and then requird an airing which has hinderd it from moulding. *Sour Crout* is as good as ever and I have not the least doubt of its remaining so.

So much for the Ships Company. We ourselves are hardly as well of as them; our live stock consists of 17 Sheep, 4 or 5 fowls, as many S. Sea hogs, 4 or 5 Muscovy ducks, an English boar and sow with a litter of piggs; in the use of these we are rather sparing as the time of our Getting a supply is rather precarious. Salt Stock we have nothing worth mentioning except a kind of Salt Beef which was put up by one *Mellish* a butcher at New Crane Stairs, which is by much the best salt meat I have ever tasted, and Our Salted Cabbage, see p. 210[1] which is now as good as it was then.

Our Malt liquors have answerd extreemly well: we have now both small beer and Porter upon tap as good as I ever drank them, especialy the latter which was bought of *Sam. & Jno. Curtiss* at Wapping New Stairs. The Small beer had some art usd to make it keep, it was bought of *Bruff & Taylor* in Hog Lane near St Giles's. Our wine I cannot say much for tho I beleive it to be good in its nature, we have not a glass fine these many months I beleive cheifly owing to the Carelessness or ignorance of the Steward.

24. Weather very moderate: some birds seen, in the morning a flock. A peice of sea weed and a peice of wood or something that lookd like it and was coverd with Barnacles were seen from the ship.

25. Fine weather and fair wind: several birds seen of most of the usual sorts.

26. Blows fresh today: fewer birds in sight than usual in such weather. Several large leaves of sea weed have been seen to go by the Ship today but no heaps of it.

---

[1] i.e. p. 249 above.

27. Blows fresh still. A good deal of sea weed has been seen this morn some in heaps as much together as would fill a large wheel-barrow; after dinner a Seal is seen asleep upon the water which gives new life to our hopes. In the evening a shoal of Porpoises black upon the back, white under the belly and upon the nose, with either no back fin or one placd very far behind.[1] Few birds today, but some of almost all the kinds we have usualy seen.

28. Blows fresh all day: some but not many birds seen, several heaps of sea weed pass by the ship.

29. Pleasant weather: birds more plentiful than usual in such weather; about noon saw one like a snipe but less and with a short bill which I judge to be a land bird.[2] Mr Gore saw a bird which he calls a Port Egmont hen which he describes to be brown on the back, like a gull in size and shape, but flyes like a crow flapping its wings.[3] Some large heaps of sea weed have been seen; some of the gentlemen upon deck think that the colour of the water is chang'd consequently we are in soundings.

30. Pleasant weather: several small peices of weed go by the ship; one was taken with the hoave or dipping net, it seemd not to have been long at sea as it was not much broken or rubbd.

OCTOBER 1769

1. Very little wind and yet vast quantities of small birds are about the ship which has been to us a very uncommon sight in such fine weather; a Seal seen from the ship. Several peices of sea weed are taken and among them a peice of wood quite overgrown with *sertularias*;[4] it must have been a long time at Sea yet more hopes are drawn from this than the sea weed, as we now have in our possession a part of the produce of our Land of Promise. Among the weed are many sea insects which are put into spirits weed wood and all, so we shall at least have this to shew. Several whales have been seen today.

2. Calm: I go in the boat and take up *Dagysa rostrata*,[5] *Serena*,[6]

---

[1] Probably the Right Whale Dolphin, *Lissodelphis peroni* (Lacépède); this has no dorsal fin.

[2] Unidentified. There are various migratory waders which pass through this area.

[3] A southern form of the Great Skua, *Catharacta skua* Brünnich; another race is common at Port Egmont in the Falkland Islands, hence the popular name.

[4] *Sertularia*, a common hydroid.

[5] *Thetys vagina*: cf. 6 September 1768.

[6] *Dagysa serena*: *Thalia democratica*; see 2-4 September 1768.

polyedra,[1] *Beroe incrassata*,[2] *coarctata*,[3] *medusa vitrea*,[4] *Phyllodoce velella*, with several other things which are all put in spirits. See a seal but cannot come near him to shoot. Shoot *Diomedea exulans*,[5] *Procellaria velox*,[6] *pallipes*,[7] *Latirostris*,[8] *longipes*[9] and *Nectris fuliginosa*.[10]

3. Calm almost this morn. About 5 a sudden squall came on with such violence that the officer of the watch was obligd to settle the topsails, it did not however last above 5 minutes; this we look upon as a sure sign of land as such squalls are rarely (if ever) met with at any considerable distance from it. I go in the boat and kill *Procellaria capensis, longipes* and *latirostris*. In the course of the day several peices of sea weed are taken up of species very new and one peice of wood coverd with Striated Barnacles *Lepas Anserina*?[11]

Now do I wish that our freinds in England could by the assistance of some magical spying glass take a peep at our situation: Dr Solander setts at the Cabbin table describing, myself at my Bureau Journalizing, between us hangs a large bunch of sea weed, upon the table lays the wood and barnacles; they would see that notwisthstanding our different occupations our lips move very often, and without being conjurors might guess that we were talking about what we should see upon the land which there is now no doubt we shall see very soon.

4. Several small peices of sea weed are seen today but no heaps;

[1] *D. polyedra*: a nectophore of a siphonophore, probably *Stephanomia rubra* (Vogt), or perhaps *Agalma elegans* (Sars). See Parkinson III, pl. 36a. Solander, p. 511, gives only this record.

[2] Probably *Beroe ovata*; see 12 January 1769.

[3] *B. coarctata*: possibly a species of *Lampetia*. See Parkinson III, pl. 60b, for a drawing made on this day, and Solander, p. 433, for a description.

[4] Probably *Aequorea* sp.; see 19 September 1769.

[5] Parkinson in his Journal (p. 85), and Solander, p. 7, both give the wing span of this albatross as 10 ft 7 in., and Solander records its weight as 28 lb. Murphy discusses weights in this species and quotes a maximum of 20 lb (*Oceanic Birds of South America*, 1936, p. 543), from which it would appear that a slip has occurred in Solander's MS. His other weights for *exulans* are only 12 and 16 lb.

[6] The gadfly petrels taken on 2 and 7 October were possibly distinct, since Solander remarks that they were somewhat larger and heavier than his other specimens of '*P. velox*' (see 15 February 1769).

[7] *P. pallipes*: the Grey Petrel or Pediunker, *Adamastor cinereus* (Gm.), which was described by Solander, p. 71.

[8] *P. latirostris*: the Broad-billed Whale Bird, *Pachyptila vittata* Forster. See Solander, pp. 61-2, who gives only this record of the species.

[9] *P. longipes*: the Grey-backed Storm Petrel, *Garrodia nereis* (Gould). There is no painting by Parkinson of this species although it was taken on four occasions; Solander described one specimen as *P. saltatrix*, p. 49, and four others as *P. longipes*, p. 63.

[10] *Puffinus griseus* (Gm.), the Sooty Shearwater or Mutton-bird. Solander records this specimen; see 15 February 1769.

[11] This was probably *Lepas anserifera*, which is a striped barnacle and which was recorded by Solander, p. 389, on 23 October; a slip has occurred over this date, as Solander gives the ship's position as 37° S and 171° 30′ W, which is close to Cook's figure for 3 October but differs considerably from the position given by Cook on 23 and 24 October.

weather pleasant, breeze rather of the gentlest. Towards evening
we were entertaind by a large shoal of Porpoises like those of the
30[th] of last month;[1] they came up to the ship in prodigious circl[in]g
action leaping out of the water sometimes 2 or 3 feet high as nimbly
as Bonetos; immediately after them came a number of a larger
sort quite black who movd very heavy in the water;[2] both these
troops kept their course by the ship without taking much notice
of her probably in pursuit of some prey.

5. Our old enemy Cape fly away entertaind us for three hours
this morn all which time there were many opinions in the ship,
some said it was land and others Clouds which at last however
plainly appeard. 2 Seals passd the ship asleep and 3 of the birds
which M[r] Gore calls Port Egmont hens, *Larus Catarrhactes*,[3] and says
are a sure sign of our being near land. They are something larger
than a crow, in flight much like one, flapping their wings often
with a slow motion; their bodies and wings of a dark chocolate
or soot colour, under each wing a small broadish bar of dirty white
which makes them so remarkable that it is hardly possible to
mistake them. They are seen as he says all along the Coast of
America and in Faulklands Isles; I myself remember to have seen
them at Terra del Fuego but by some accident did not note them
down. Just before sun set we were much entertaind by a shoal of
Porpoises like those seen yesterday; they kept in sight of the ship for
near an hour, all that while as if in hot pursuit of some prey, leaping
out of the water almost over each other; they might be very justly
compard to a pack of hounds in full cry only their numbers which
were some thousands made them a much more considerable object;
sometimes they formd a line near $\frac{1}{4}$ of a mile in lengh, sometimes
contracted them selves into a much smaller compass, keeping the
water wherever they went in a foam so that when they were so
far from the ship that their bodys could not be distinguishd any
man would have taken them for breakers.

6. This morn a Port Egmont hen and a seal were seen pretty early.
At $\frac{1}{2}$ past one a small boy who was at the mast head[4] Calld out Land.

---

[1] There seems to be some slip here, as neither Banks nor Cook recorded porpoises
on either 30 September or 30 August.

[2] Possibly Pilot Whale, *Globicephala* sp. Since Cook was keeping nautical time, we sometimes find that the dates given by him and by Banks for the same observations do not
agree. It is probable that Cook's note for 5 October, in which he gives a brief description
of *Lissodelphis peroni*, the Right Whale Dolphin, and mentions the presence of a larger
species, covers this entry by Banks.

[3] The southern form of the Great Skua. See 29 September.

[4] This was Nicholas Young, on whom see Cook I, pp. ccxxxv, 173, 589.

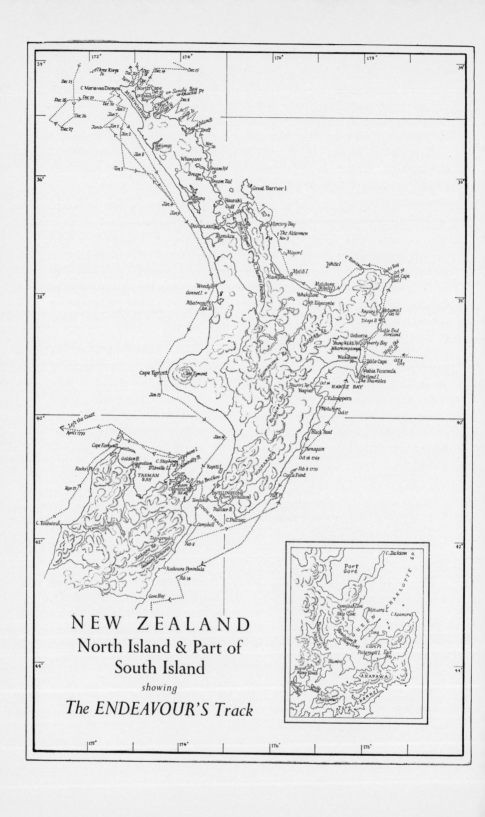

NEW ZEALAND
North Island & Part of
South Island

showing

The ENDEAVOUR'S Track

I was luckyly upon deck and well I was entertaind, within a few minutes the cry circulated and up came all hands, this land could not then be seen even from the tops yet few were there who did not plainly see it from the deck till it appeard that they had lookd at least 5 points wrong.

Weather most moderate. We came up with it very slowly; at sun set myself was at the masthead, land appeard much like an Island or Islands but seemd to be large. Just before a small shark was seen who had a very piked nose something like our dog fish in England.[1]

7. This morn the Land plainly seen from the deck appears to be very large; about 11 a large smoak was seen and soon after several more, sure sign of inhabitants. After dinner dropd calm: myself in little boat shot *Nectris munda*[2] and *Procellaria velox*,[3] took with the dipping net *Dagysa gemma*[4] and a good deal of *Fucus*,[5] *sertularia*[6] &c, the examination of which is postpond till we shall have more time than we are likely to have at present.

In the Evening a pleasant breeze. At sunset all hands at the mast head; Land still distant 7 or 8 leagues, appears larger than ever, in many parts 3, 4 and 5 ranges of hills are seen one over the other and a chain of Mountains over all, some of which appear enormously high.[7] Much difference of opinion and many conjectures about Islands, rivers, inlets &c, but all hands seem to agree that this is certainly the Continent we are in search of.[8]

8. This morn the land very near us makes in many white cliffs like chalk; the hills are in general clothd with trees, in the valleys some appear to be very large; the whole of the appearance not so fruitfull as we could wish. Stood in for a large bay in hopes of finding a harbour; before we are well within the heads saw several Canoes standing across the bay, who after a little time returnd to the place they came from not appearing to take the least notice of us. Some houses were also seen which appeard low but neat, near one a good many people were collected who sat down on the beach seemingly

---

[1] Unidentifiable.

[2] The Little or Allied Shearwater, *Puffinus assimilis*; or perhaps the Fluttering Shearwater, *Puffinus gavia* (Forster). See 15 February 1769 and 16 October below. This specimen was not recorded by Solander.

[3] See 15 February and 30 August 1769. This was recorded by Solander.

[4] *Thalia democratica*. See 2 October 1768.

[5] Fucus is seaweed generally, or was in Banks's time.

[6] Some form of polyzoan.

[7] Probably this was the Huiarau range, which rises to 4500 feet at its highest point.

[8] Several of the early charts of New Zealand by Pickersgill are entitled 'A Chart of Part of the Southern Continent' etc.

observing us, possibly the same as we saw in the canoes as they landed somewhere near that place. On a small peninsula at the NE head we could plainly see a regular paling, pretty high, inclosing the top of a hill, for what purpose many conjectures were made: most are of opinion or say at least that it must or shall be either [a] park of Deer or a feild of oxen and sheep.[1] By 4 oclock came to an anchor near 2 miles from the shore. The bay appears to be quite open without the least shelter: the two sides of it make in high white Cliffs, the middle is low land with hills gradualy rising behind one another to the chain of high mountains inland. Here we saw many great smoaks, some near the beach others between the hills, some very far within land, which we lookd upon as great indications of a populous countrey.

In the evening went ashore with the marines &c. March from the boats in hopes of finding water &c. Saw a few of the natives who ran away immediately on seeing us; while we were absent 4 of them attackd our small boat in which were only 4 boys, they got off from the shore in a river, the people followd them and threatned with long lances; the pinnace soon came to their assistance, fird upon them and killd the cheif. The other three draggd the body about 100 yards and left it. At the report of the musquets we drew together and went to the place where the body was left; he was shot through the heart. He was a middle sizd man tattowd in the face on one cheek only in spiral lines very regularly formd; he was coverd with a fine cloth of a manufacture totaly new to us, it was tied on exactly as represented in M[r] Dalrymples book[2] p. 63; his hair was also tied in a knot on the top of his head but no feather stuck in it; his complexion brown but not very dark.

Soon after we came on board we heard the people ashore very distinctly talking very loud no doubt, as they were not less than two miles distant from us, consulting probably what is to be done tomorrow.

9. We could see with our glasses but few people on the beach; they walkd with a quick pace towards the river where we landed yesterday, most of these without arms, 3 or 4 with long Pikes in their hands. The capt[n] orderd three boats to be mannd with seamen and marines intending to land and try to establish a communication with them. A high surf ran on the shore. The Indians about 50

---

[1] The 'paling' was the stockading of a *pa* or fortified village.

[2] This was the engraved 'View of Murderers Bay in New Zeland', in Dalrymple's *Account of the Discoveries made in the South Pacifick Ocean, Previous to 1764*, which he got from Valentyn's *Oudt en Nieuw Oost-Indien*.

remaind on the farther side of the river; we lookd upon that as a sign of fear, so landing with the little boat only the Cap^tn Dr Solander, Tupia and myself went to the river side to speak to them. As soon almost as we appeard they rose up and every man producd either a long pike[1] or a small weapon of well polishd stone about a foot long and thick enough to weigh 4 or 5 pounds,[2] with these they threatned us and signd to us to depart. A musquet was then fird wide of them the ball of which struck the water, they saw the effect and immediately ceasd their threats. We though[t] that it was prudent to retreat till the marines were landed and drawn up to intimidate them and support us in case of nesscessity. They landed and marchd with a Jack[3] carried before them to a little bank about 50 yards from the river, which might be about 40 broad; here they were drawn up in order and we again advancd to the river side with Tupia, who now found that the language of the people was so like his own that he could tolerably well understand them and they him. He immediately began to tell them that we wanted provisions and water for which we would give them Iron in exchange: they agreed to the proposal but would by no means lay by their arms which he desird them do: this he lookd upon as a sign of treachery and continualy told us to be upon our guard for they were not our freinds. Many words passd the cheif purport of which was that each side desird the other to come over to them; at last however an Indian stripd himself and swam over without arms, he was followd by two more and soon after by most of the rest who brought with them their arms. We gave them Iron and beads, they seemd to set little value upon either but especialy upon the iron the use of which they certainly were totaly ignorant of. They caught at whatever was offerd them but would part with nothing but a few feathers: their arms indeed they offerd to exchange for ours which they made several atempts to snatch from us; we were upon our guard so much that their atempts faild and they were made to understand that we must kill them if they snatchd any thing from us. After some time Mr Green in turning himself about exposd his hanger, one of them immediately snatchd it, set up a cry of exultation and waving it round his head retreated gently. It now appeard nescessary for our safeties that so daring an act should be instantly punishd,

[1] This must have been the ordinary Maori fighting spear or *tao*, six to nine feet long.
[2] No doubt the *mere*, one of the *patu* class of weapons. Cook and his men (and Banks himself later) generally referred to them as 'Pattoo Pattoos'.
[3] i.e. the small-sized ship's flag of the period, the 'Union Jack' incorporating the crosses of St George and St Andrew.

this I pronouncd aloud as my opinion, the Cap[tn] and the rest Joind
me on which I fird my musquet which was loaded with small
shot, leveling it between his shoulders who was not 15 yards from
me. On the shot striking him he ceasd his cry but instead of
quitting his prize continued to wave it over his head retreating
as gently as before; the surgeon who was nearer him, seeing this
fird a ball at him at which he dropd. Two more who were near him
returnd instantly, one seizd his weapon of Green talk,[1] the other
attempted to recover the hanger which the surgeon had scarce
time to prevent. The main body of them were now upon a rock[2]
a little way in the river. They took the water returning towards us,
on which the other three, for we were only 5 in number, fird on
them. They then retird and swam again across the river. On their
landing we saw that 3 were wounded, one seemingly a good deal
hurt: we may hope however that neither of them were killd as
one of the musquets only was loaded with ball, which I think
I saw strike the water without taking effect, and Tupias gun which
was the last that was fird I clearly saw strike two men low down
upon their legs, who probably would be so lame as to walk with
difficulty when they landed.

The Indians retird gently carrying with them their wounded
and we reembarkd in our boats intending to row round the bay,
see if there might be any shelter for the ship on the other side,
and attempt to land there where the countrey appeard to be much
more fruitfull than where we now were. The bottom of the bay
provd to be a low sandy beach on which the sea broke most
prodigiously so that we could not come near it; within was flat,
a long way inland over this water might be seen from the mast
head probably a lagoon but in the boat we could see no entrance
into it.[3] We had almost arrivd at the farthest part of the bay when
a fresh breze came in from the seaward and we saw a Canoe sailing
in standing right towards [us], soon after another padling. The
Cap[tn] now resolvd to take one of these which in all probability
might be done without the least resistance as we had three boats
full of men and the canoes seemd to be fishermen, who probably
were without arms. The boats were drawn up in such a manner
that they could not well escape us: the padling canoe first saw us

---

[1] i.e. talc—nephrite or greenstone, sometimes referred to by Cook as jade.
[2] Called Te Toka a Taiau—the rock of Taiau. It no longer exists, having been blasted
out in the course of harbour works.
[3] There is no lagoon there now; but the meandering course pursued by the Waipaoa
river on that flat land could easily have produced one as the result of rain or the overflowing
of an oxbow bend. There was a lagoon in the 1860's—but whether Banks's lagoon (if he
indeed saw one) or not we do not know.

and made immediately for the nearest land, the other saild on
till she was in the midst of us before she saw us, as soon as she did
she struck her sail and began to paddle so briskly that she outran
our boat; on a musquet being fird over her she however immediately
ceasd padling and the people in her, 7 in all, made all possible
haste to strip as we thought to leap into the water, but no sooner
did our boat come up with her than they began with stones, paddles
&c. to make so brisk a resistance that we were obligd to fire into
her by which 4 were killd. The other three who were boys leapd
overboard, one of them swam with great agility and when taken
made every effort in his power to prevent being taken into the
boat, the other two were more easily prevaild upon. As soon as they
were in they squatted down expecting no doubt instant death, but
on finding themselves well usd and that Cloaths were given them
they recoverd their spirits in a very short time and before we got
to the ship appeard almost totaly insensible of the loss of their
fellows. As soon as they came onboard we offerd them bread to
eat of which they almost devourd a large quantity, in the mean
time they had Cloaths given them; this good usage had such an
effect that they seemd to have intirely forgot every thing that had
happned, put on chearfull and lively countenances and askd and
answerd questions with a great deal of curiosity. Our dinner came,
they expressd a curiosity to taste whatever they saw us eat, and did;
salt pork seemd to please them better than any thing else, of this
they eat a good deal. At sunset they eat again an enormous quantity
of Bread and drank above a quart of water each; we then made
them beds upon the lockers and they laid down to sleep with all
seeming content imaginable. After dark loud voices were heard
ashore as last night. Thus ended the most disagreable day My
life has yet seen, black be the mark for it and heaven send that
such may never return to embitter future reflection.[1] I forgot to
mention in its proper place that we pickd up a large pumice stone
floating in the bay in returning to the ship today, a sure sign that
there either is or has been a Volcano in this neighbourhood.[2]

10. In the middle of last night one of our boys seemd to shew more
reflection than he had before done sighing often and loud; Tupia
who was always upon the watch to comfort them got up and soon
made them easy. They then sung a song of their own, it was not

[1] Cf. Cook's entry for this date (or rather for 10 October, p.m.), I, p. 171, and the drafts,
which show his troubled conscience.
[2] The nearest volcano inland was Ngauruhoe, in the centre of the island, which could
hardly have been the origin of this pumice. It may have been carried round by the
current from White Island, in the Bay of Plenty.

without some taste, like a Psalm tune and containd many notes
and semitones; they sung it in parts which gives us no indifferent
Idea of their taste as well as skill in musick. The oldest of them is
about 18, the middlemos[t] 15, the youngest 10; the midlemost
especialy has a most open countenance and agreable manner;
their names are *Tadhourange, Koikerange,* and *Maragooete,*[1] the
two first brothers. In the morning they were all very chearfull
and eat an enormous quantity, after that they were dressd and
ornamented with bracelets, ancklets and necklaces after their
own fashion. The boats were then hoisted out and we all got into
them: the boys express'd much joy at this till they saw that we
were going to land at our old Landing place near the river, they
beggd very much that they might not be set ashore at that place
where they said were Enemies of theirs who would kill and eat
them. The Cap^tn resolvd to go ashore at that place and if the boys
did not chuse to go from us, in the evening to send a boat with them
to the part of the bay to which they pointed and calld their home.
Accordingly we went ashore and crossd the river. The boys at first
would not leave us. No method was usd to persuade them; it was
even resolvd to return and carry them home when on a sudden
they seemd to resolve to go and with tears in their eyes took leave.
We then went along a swamp intending to shoot some ducks of
which there was great plenty;[2] the countrey was quite flat; the
Sergeant and 4 marines attended us walking upon a bank abreast
of us which overlookd the countrey. We proceeded about a mile
when they Calld out that a large body of Indians was marching
towards us, we drew together and resolvd to retreat; before we
had put this in execution the 3 boys rose out of a bush in which
they were hid and put themselves again under our protection.
We went upon the beach as the clearest place and walkd briskly
towards the boats. The Indians were in two parties, one marchd
along the bank before spoke of, the other came round by the morass
where we could not see them; on seing us draw together they
ceasd to run as they had done and walkd but gently on, a circumstance most fortunate for us, for when we came to our boats the
pinnace was a mile at least from her station, (sent their by the
officer ashore to pick up a bird he had shot); the small boat only

---

[1] Te Hourangi or Haurangi, Ikirangi (*Ko* = it is), and Marukauiti.

[2] There are several species of ducks in New Zealand, and nowadays the Gray Duck
Anas superciliosa Gm. is the most common. Parkinson comments (*Journal*, p. 87), 'Shot
some wild ducks of a very large size': as the Gray Duck is the largest New Zealand
species, being almost as large as a mallard, and as it is common wherever there is water,
even in intertidal inlets and estuaries, it is likely that this was the species taken.

remaind, which was carried over the river, and without the midshipman who was left to attend her: the consequence of this was
that we were obligd to make 3 trips before we were all over to the
rest of the party. As soon as we were well drawn up on the other
side the Indians came down, not in a body as we expected, but
2 and 3 at a time, all armd and soon increasd to a considerable
number; we now despaird of making peace with men who were not
to be frightned with our small arms. As the ship lay so far from the
shore that [she] could not throw a shot there, we resolvd to reembark
as our stay would most likley be the cause of killing still more
people: we were begining to go towards the boats when on a sudden
one of the boys calld out that the people there were their freinds
and desird us to stay and talk with them, we did and much conversation past but neither would the boys swim over to them
nor they to the boys. The bodys both of the man who was killd
yesterday, and he who was killd the day before, were left upon
the beach. The first lay very near us, to it the boys went and coverd
it with part of the cloths we had given them; soon after a single
man unarmd swam over to us (the uncle of Maracouete, the younger
boy), he brought in his hand a green bough, probably emblem of
peace; we made him many presents after having receivd his bough
which he presented to Tupia our interpr[e]ter. We askd him to
go onboard of the ship but he refusd so we left him, but all the
3 boys chose rather to return with us than stay with him.

As soon as we had retird and left him to himself he went and
gatherd a green bough; with this in his hand he aproachd the body
with great ceremony, walking sideways, he then threw the bough
towards it and returnd to his companions who immediately sat
down round him and remaind above an hour, hearing probably
what he said without taking the least notice of us, who soon returnd
to the ship. From thence we could see with our glasses 3 men cross
the river in a kind of Catamaran[1] and take away the body which
was carried off upon a pole by 4 men.

After dinner the Cap^tn desird Tupia to ask the boys if they had
now any objection to going ashore at the same place, as taking
away the body was probably a ratification of our peace. They
said they had not and went most nimbly into the boat in which
two midshipmen were sent; they went ashore willingly but soon
returnd to the rocks, wading into the water and begging hard
to be taken in again; the orders were positive to leave them so they

---

[1] By this Banks probably means a *moki* or *mokihi*, a raft generally made of bundles of
flax stalks, often used in the absence of a canoe, though its life was short.

CC

were left. We observd from the ship a man in a catamaran go over
the river and fetch them to a place where 40 or 50 were assembled:
they sat till near sunset without stirring. They rose then and the
3 boys appeard who had till now been conceald by being surrounded
with people, they left the party came down upon the beach and
3 times wavd their hands towards the ship, then nimbly ran and
joind the party who walkd leisurely away towards the place
where the boys live. We therefore hope that no harm will happen
to them especialy as they had still the cloaths which we gave them
on. After sunset loud voices were heard as usual in the bottom of
the bay.

11. This morn We took our leave of Poverty bay[1] with not above
40 species of Plants in our boxes, which is not to be wonderd at
as we were so little ashore and always upon the same spot; the only
time we wanderd about a mile from the boats was upon a swamp
where not more than 3 species of Plants were found.

Weather this day was most moderate: several Canoes put off
from shore and came towards us within less than a quarter of a
mile but could not be persuaded to come nearer, tho Tupia exerted
himself very much shouting out and promising that they should
not be hurt. At last one was seen coming from Poverty bay or near
it, she had only 4 people in her, one who I well rememberd to
have seen at our first interview on the rock: these never stopd to
look at any thing but came at once alongside of the ship and with
very little persuasion cam[e] on board; their example was quickly
followd by the rest 7 Canoes in all and 50 men. They had many
presents given to them notwithstanding which they very quickly
sold almost every thing that they had with them, even their Cloaths
from their backs and the paddles out of their boats; arms they
had none except 2 men, one of whom sold his *patoo patoo* as he calld
it, a short weapon of green talk of this shape intended doubtless
for fighting hand to hand and certainly well contrivd
for splitting sculls as it weigh[s] not less than 4 or 5
pounds and has sharp edges excellently polishd.

We were very anxious to know what was become of our poor
boys, therefore as soon as the people began to lose their first impressions of fear that we saw at first disturbd them a good deal we
askd after them. The man who first came on board immediately

---

[1] Cook: '*Poverty Bay* because it afforded us no one thing we wanted'. Banks heads
his pages with the native name Taoneroa, which he takes for the name of the bay (cf.
II, p. 3 below). *Te one roa* = the long beach (*one*, beach or shore); Te Oneroa was the
beach stretching westward from the Turanganui river.

answerd that they were at home and unhurt and that the reason
of his coming on board the ship with so little fear was the account
they had given him of the usage they had met with among us.

The people were in general of a midling size tho there was one
who measurd more than 6 feet, their colour dark brown. Their
lips were staind with something put under the skin (as in the
Otahite tattow) and their faces markd with deeply engravd furrows
Colourd also black and formd in regular spirals; of these the oldest
people had much the greatest quantity and deepest channeld,
in some not less than $\frac{1}{16}$ part of an inch.[1] Their hair always black
was tied on the tops of their heads in a little knot, in which was
stuck feathers of various birds in different tastes according to the
humour of the wearer, generaly stuck into the knot, sometimes
one on each side the temples pointing forwards which made a most
disagreable apearance; in their Ears they generaly wore a large
bunch of the down of some bird milk white. The faces of some
were painted with a red colour in oil[2] some all over, others in parts
only, in their hair was much oil that had very little smell, more
lice than ever I saw before! and in most of them a small comb
neatly enough made, sometimes of wood sometimes of bone, which
they seemd to prize much. Some few had on their faces or arms
regular scars as if made with a sharp instrument: such I have seen
on the faces of negroes. The inferior sort were clothd in something
that very much resembled hemp;[3] the loose strings of this were
fastned together at the top and hung down about 2 feet long like a
petticoat; of these garments they wore 2, one round their shoulders
the other about their wastes. The richer had garments probably
of a finer sort of the same stuff, most beatifully made in exactly
the same manner as the S. American Indians at this day, as fine
or finer than one of them which I have by me that I bough[t] at
Rio de Janeiro for 36 shillings and was esteemd uncommonly

[1] Maori tattooing was incised, and not pricked as in the islands. Buck (*The Coming
of the Maori*, p. 298) explains the affinity with wood-carving, in design and technique:
'the main lines of the designs are deep or sunk below the surface so that the spaces between
parallel lines appear as ridges, to some extent similar to the designs on wood. . . . the
Maori tattooing artists took a further cue from the carving experts and ground down
or sharpened some of their bone blades like an adze with a plain edge witnout teeth . . . .
the toothed implements were used for filling in and for subsidiary motifs'. Cf. p. 495
below.
[2] This was an ochre commonly obtained from streams or swamps in the form of mud
coloured by oxide of iron: the mud was collected on fern fronds, moulded into balls
and dried at a fire. But any red earth might be used. The oil was generally a vegetable
oil, got from the berries of the tree called Titoki.
[3] Probably *Phormium tenax*, the so-called New Zealand Flax, so important in the
Maori textile crafts; but the leaves of the Kiekie, a sort of *Freycinetia*, and of the Ti (more
than one variety of the Cordyline) were also used.

cheap at that price. Their boats were not large but well made, something in the form of our whale boats but longer; their bottom was the trunk of a tree hollowd and very thin, this was raisd by a board on each side sewd on, with a strip of wood sewd over the seam to make it tight; on the head of every one was carvd the head of a man with an enormous tongue reaching out of his mouth. These grotesque figures were some at least very well executed, some had eyes inlaid of something that shone very much;[1] the whole servd to give us an Idea of their taste as well as ingenuity in execution, much superior to any thing we have yet seen.

Their behavior while on board shewd every sign of freindship, they invited us very cordialy to come back to our old bay or to a small cove which they shewd us nearer to it.[2] I could not help wishing that we had done so, but the capt[tn] chose rather to stand on in search of a better harbour than any we have yet seen. God send that we may not there have the same tragedy to act over again as we so lately perpetrated: the countrey is certainly divided into many small principalities[3] so we cannot hope that an account of our weapons and management of them can be conveyd as far as we in all probability[4] must go and this I am well convincd of, that till these warlike people have severly felt our superiority in the art of war they will never behave to us in a freindly manner.

About an hour before sunset the canoes left us, and with us three of their people who were very desirous to have gone with them but were not permitted to return to the Canoes. What their reason for so doing is we can only guess, possibly they may think that their being on board will induce us to remain here till tomorrow when they will return and renew the traffick by which they find themselves so great gainers. The people were tolerably chearfull, entertaind us with dancing and singing after their custom, eat their suppers and went to bed very quietly.

12. During last night the ship saild some leagues which as soon as the 3 men saw they began to lament and weep very much, Tupia with dificulty could comfort them. About 7, 2 Canoes apeard; they left no sign unmade which might induce them to come to the ship. One at last venturd, out of her came an old man who seemd to be a cheif from the finenes of his garment and weapon, *patoo*

---

[1] The shell of the Paua, *Haliotis* sp.

[2] Probably the 'small cove' called Whareongaonga.

[3] This was a good guess, though somewhat modified by Banks later when he comes to talk of a 'king'; and 'tribal areas' would be a phrase more familiar to the New Zealander than the word 'principalities'.

[4] MS *probabley*; S P *probability*.

patoo, which was made of Bone (he said of a whale); he staid but a short time on board but when he went took with him our 3 guests much to our as well as their satisfaction.

In sailing along shore we could clearly see several spots of land cultivated, some fresh turnd up and laying in furrows like ploughd land, others with plants growing upon them some younger and some older; we also saw in two places high rails upon the Ridges of hills, but could only guess that they belong to some superstition as they were in lines not inclosing any thing.[1] Before noon another Canoe appeard carrying 4 people; she came within about ¼ of a mile of us and there (I beleive) performd several ceremonies, the man in the bow of her sometimes seeming to ask and offer peace, at others seeming to threaten with a weapon he held in his hand, sometimes dancing sometimes singing. Tupia talkd much to him but could not persuade him to come to the ship. About this time very distant land was seen to the Southward forming a very large bay.[2]

About dinner time the ship was hauling round an Island calld by the inhabitants *Teahoa*,[3] by us Portland, the ship on a sudden came into very broken ground which alarmd us all a good deal;[4] the officers all behavd with great steadyness and in a very short time we were clear of all dangers; we never had less than 7 fathom but the soundings hardly ever were twice the same jumping from 11 to 7, which made us very glad once more to get deep water under us. The Island lay within a mile of us making in white cliffs, a long spit of low land running from it towards the main. On the sides of these cliffs sat a vast quantity of people looking at us, these probably observd some confusion in the manoev^re of the ship for 5 Canoes almost immediately put off from the shore full of armd people; they came so near us shouting and threatning that at last we were in some pain least they [should seize][5] our small boat which had been lowerd down to sound and now towd along side. A musquet was therefore fird over them: the Effect of this was rather to encourage them than otherwise so a great gun was orderd to be prepard and fird wide of them loaded with grape, on this they

---

[1] If this observation was correct, probably in each case what was seen was the stockading of a disused *pa*.

[2] Which Cook called Hawke's Bay.

[3] See entry for the following day.

[4] This broken ground was called the Shambles. Curiously enough Cook gives the name neither in his journal nor on his charts, but it is attested by both Molyneux and Pickersgill, and was used on the second voyage and thereafter. No doubt the Shambles off the English Bill of Portland was in mind.

[5] *should seize* omitted in the MS and supplied from P, where the words have been inserted in a blank left for the purpose by the copyist. S *should take* added interlinearly.

all rose in their boats and shouted but instead of continuing the chase drew all together and after a short consultation went quietly away.

About half an hour after this we hawld in with the land again and two more canoes came off, one armd the other a small fishing boat with only 4 men in her; they came tolerably near and answerd all the questions Tupia askd them very civily; we could not persuade them to come on board but they came near enough to receive several presents which we hove over board to them, with these they seem'd very much pleasd and went away. At night the ship came to an anchor; many fires were kept up on shore possibly to shew us that our freinds there were too much upon their guard to be surprizd.

13. Brisk breeze of wind: 9 Canoes came after the ship this morn, whether with war or peace we cannot tell for we soon left them behind. We found that the land within *Teahoura*[1] or Portland Isle makes another Island or peninsula, both sides of this the natives have calld *Teracaco*[2] so that is in all likelyhood the name of it. Before noon we were almost surrounded with land; that nearest us made in green hills without the white Clifts which we have generaly seen, the appearance more fertil tho we can not distinguish any cultivation as we did yesterday; on the tops of the hills were several palings like those seen yesterday. Towards evening stood in for a place that had the appearance of an opening which provd no harbour so stood off again with a pleasant breeze. A very large canoe soon put off carrying 18 or 20 men armd who tho they could not get within a mile of us shouted and threatned most prodigiously; after this the white cliffs and more barren land began again to appear. At night pleasant light breeze, stood along shore.

14. This morn high mountains inland were in sight on the tops of which the snow was not yet melted,[3] the countrey near the shore low and unfavourable; in one place was a patch of something yellow that bore much resemblance to a corn feild, probably some kind of flaggs decayd as is common in swampy places, at a distance some detachd groves of trees upon the flat that appeard very high and tapering.[4] Several canoes had put off from shore in the morning

---

[1] Te Houra.   [2] Terakako. It was what is now called the Mahia peninsula.

[3] It was probably the Kaimanawa and Ruahine ranges that were thus seen.

[4] Banks seems here to be reporting the appearance of some part of the district afterwards called the Heretaunga plains, which were very swampy. The 'flaggs' were possibly the long rushes called Toetoe (*Arundo conspicua*) with their yellow feathery heads. The trees seem to have been Kahikatea or White Pine (*Podocarpus dacrydioides*), which grow well in swampy country; possibly they were the trees known to old Hawke's Bay settlers as the White Pine Bush, the last remains of which were still visible at Mangateretere in the early years of this century. The Kahikatea grows as high as 80 feet.

and came towards us, about 10 O'Clock 5 were together seemingly holding a consultation after which they pulld towards the ship in a body as if resolvd to attack her, 4 more were coming after them from the shore. This manoevre was not to be disregarded: the canoes were large, we judgd that they could not contain less than 150 people, every one armd with a sharp pike of hard wood and their little hand instrument calld *patoopatoo*; were they to attempt any thing daring there could not fail to be a dreadfull slaughter among such a croud of naked men were we nesscesitated to fire among them; it was therefore though[t] proper to fire a gun over their heads as the effect of that would probably prevent any designs they might have formd from being put into execution. They were by this time within 100 yards of the ship singing their war song and threatning with their pikes; the gun was levelld a little before their first boat and had the desird effect, for no sooner had they seen the grape which scatterd very far upon the water than they paddled away in great haste. We all calld out that we were freinds if they would only lay down their arms. They did so and returnd to the ship; one boat came close under the quarter and taking off his Jacket offerd it to sale, but before any body had time to bid for it she dropd astern as did the rest, refusing to come to the ship again because they were afraid that we should kill them, so easily were these warriors convincd of our superiority.

Before noon we plainly saw that there was a small river ashore[1] but no signs of shelter near it. About this time 6 more armd canoes came off from the land, they got together about ½ a mile from the ship and threatned most furiously with their lances paddles &c. After they had done this for some time they came nearer and Tupia talkd with them from the stern; they came into better temper and answerd his questions relating to the names of the countreys kings &c. very civily; he desird them to sing and dance and they did so. He often told them that if they would come to the ship without their arms we should be freinds with them; at last one boat venturd and soon after 3 or 4 more, they put all their arms into one boat which stayd at a distance while the others came to the ship and receivd presents, after which they went away. One of these men had hanging round his neck a peice of Green stone seemingly semitransparent, some of our people imagind it to be a Jewel, myself thought it no more than the green stone of which most of their tools and ornaments are made.

In the evening the countrey flat: upon it were 3 or 4 prodigiously

[1] The Wairoa.

pretty groves of tall trees; near one of them was a square inclosure made with close and very high rails, what was within it we could not guess. Some thunder and lightning this even, weather otherwise vastly moderate. Many shoals of small fish about the ship.

15. Snow was still to be seen upon the mountains inland. In the morn we were abreast of the Southermost Cape of a large bay, the northermost of which is Portland Isle; the bay itself was calld Hawks bay. From this point several canoes came of with netts and other fishing implements in them; they came along side with a little invitation and offerd to trade, we gave them Otahite cloth for their fish which they were excessively fond of, often snatching it from one another.[1] With us they dealt tolerably fairly tho they sometimes cheated us by bargaining for one thing and sending up another when they had got their prise; after they had sold all their fish they began to put the stones with which they sink their netts into baskets and sell them but this was soon stoppd as we were not in want of such commodities. About this time an armd boat came alongside and offerd to trade for their Jackets. One of them had on one made of furr,[2] this the Capt^tn wanted to buy and bargaind for it offering a peice of Red baize; the bargain was struck and the baize sent down but no sooner had the man got hold of it than he began with amazing coolness to pack up both it and his furr jacket in a basket, intirely deaf to the Capt^ns Demands, and the canoe immediately dropd astern. A small consultation now ensued among the boats after which they all returnd alon[g]side and the fishermen again offerd fish to sale which was accepted and trade renewd. The little Tayeto, Tupias boy, was employd with several more to stand over the side and reach up what was bought: while he was doing this one of the men in a canoe seizd him and draggd him down, 2 then held him in the fore part of the Canoe and three more in her paddled off as did all the other boats. The marines were in arms upon deck, they were orderd to fire into the Canoe which they did; at lengh one man dropd, the others on seeing this loosd the boy who immediately leapd into the water and swam towards the ship; the large boat on this returnd towards him but on some musquets and a great gun being fird at them left off the chase. Our boat was lowerd down and took up the

---

[1] It was the cloth, not the fish, they were excessively fond of. The Aute or paper mulberry of the warmer islands had been brought to New Zealand by the Maori, but was cultivated only with great difficulty, so that *tapa* made from it was rare and consequently highly prized.
[2] It was a *topuni*, or dog-skin cloak, a valuable article.

boy frigh[t]ned enough but not at all hurt. What number were killd in the boats we cannot tell, probably not many as the people who fird at the boat in which the boy was were obligd to fire wide of her least they should strike him, and the other boats had only a few shots fird at them; when they attempted to return some of the gentlemen who lookd through glasses said however that they saw three carried up the beach when the boats landed who were either dead or much wounded.[1] From this daring attempt the point was calld Cape Kidnappers.[2]

As soon as Tayeto was a little recoverd from his fright he brought a fish in to Tupia and told him that he intended it as an offering to his Eatua or god in gratitude for his escape. Tupia approvd it and orderd him to throw it into the sea which he did.

In the evening pleasant breeze. The land to the southward of Cape Kidnappers made in bare white cliffs barren enough to appearance.

16. Mountains coverd with snow were in sight again this morn[3] so that there is probably a chain of them runs within the countrey. Land makes in smooth hills like downs with little or no wood in sight; after breakfast white cliffs again look as barren as ever. Vast shoals of fish were about the ship, pursued by as large flocks of brownish birds a little bigger than a pigeon *Nectris munda*.[4] Their method of fishing was amusing enough, a whole flock of birds would follow the fish who swam fast along: they continualy plungd themselves under water and soon after rose again in another place, so that the whole flock vanishd sometimes, at others a large part of it and rose again often where you did not expect them, and in less than a minutes time they were down again and so alternately as long as we saw them. Before dinner we were abreast of another cape which made in a bluff rock, the upper part of a reddish coulourd stone or clay the lower white; beyond this the Countrey appeard pleasant with little smooth hills like downs. The Cap*tn thought it not nescessary to proceed any farther on this side of the coast so the ships head was again turnd to the northward and the cape

---

[1] This incident was much described by the voyagers, and its memory lasted long in Maori tradition—in which however the number killed varied. See e.g. A. G. Bagnall and G. C. Petersen, *William Colenso* (Wellington 1948), p. 462.

[2] In Grey MS 51 Banks gives the native name for the cape as 'Mataruwhow'. This however is wrong: Mataruahou was the name of 'Scinde Island', the site of the present Napier; the cape was called Matau a Maui, the fish-hook of Maui.

[3] This was certainly the Ruahine range.

[4] Mr Graham Turbott has suggested (personal communication) that this type of behaviour is not typical of *Puffinus assimilis* (see 15 February), but that the petrels seen were perhaps the Fluttering Shearwater, *Puffinus gavia*.

from thence call Cape Turnagain.[1] At night we were off Hawks bay and saw two monstrous fires inland on the hills: we are now inclind to think that these and most if not all the great smoaks and fires that we have seen are made for the convenience of clearing land for tillage, but for whatever purposes intended they are a certain indication that where they are the countrey is inhabited.

17. Foul wind, ship turning to windward off Hawks bay. A seal was seen floating on the water asleep. At night calm.

18. Fair wind: a whale was seen this morn. In the evening a small boat with 5 people in her came off from Teracaco, the peninsula within Portland Isle; they with much difficulty overtook the ship; 2 of them who seemd to be the cheif people came on board with very little invitation and orderd the other three their servants to stay in the boat. They soon expressd satisfaction at their treatment and came down into the cabbin where they very soon informd us that they would sleep with us and not think of going ashore that night. We remonstrated much against this telling them that tomorrow morn the ship might be at a great distance from where she now was; they were however resolvd and we were obligd to let them sleep in the ship, into which they consented to have their canoe hoisted which was accordingly done. The countenance of one of these men was the most open I have ever seen, I was prejudicd much in their favour and surely such confidence could not be found in the breasts of designing people. They expressd great curiosity and surprize, attending to any thing that was shewn to them and thankfully accepted the presents which were made them but would not eat with us;[2] their servants however were not at all scrupolous on that head for they eat most enormously almost every thing they could get.

19. Pleasant breeze all last night so that in the morn we were off Table cape.[3] Our guests expressd some surprize at finding themselves so far from home but had their boat hoisted out and went

[1] Cook writes (I, p. 179), 'Seeing no likelyhood of meeting with a harbour and the face of the Country Vissibly altering for the worse I thought that the standing farther to the South would not be attended with any Valuable discovery, but would be loosing of time which might be better employ'd and with a greater probabillity of Success in examining the Coast to the Northward'; which Banks in Grey MS 51 renders, 'it was resolved to stand back to the Northward where a warmer climate promised more valuable discoveries'. This is somewhat poetic licence.

[2] There was evidently an 'eating *tapu*' at work here: the chiefs might have hesitated to eat with Banks and his friends for some reason, but they certainly could not eat with their own slaves, who appear to have been fed at the same time.

[3] Banks has not mentioned this cape before in his text; the ship was abreast of it when 'our 3 guests' took their departure on the morning of the 12th. It had been so named because of its flat top.

ashore abreast of the ship. We saild very briskly, soon passd Poverty
bay; the countrey beyond it seemd to be fertile with few or no
cliffs. About noon we passd by a remarkable white Cliff of a
triangular shape not unlike the Gable End of a farm house; this
same cliff we had seen from the sea when first we made the land
and from its triangular shape had compard it to a latteen sail,
it was now calld Gable End Foreland. Just here 3 Canoes came off,
one man from them venturd on board but soon went back and the
boats dropd astern. In the evening many shoals of very small brown
shrimps passd by the ship that coulurd the water as if dirt had
been thrown into it.[1]

20. During last night it once blew very fresh: in the morn the
weather was pleasant tho we felt ourselves rather cold, the Therm
50°. Several canoes followd us and seemd very peaceably inclind,
inviting us to go into a bay[2] they pointed to where they said that
there was plenty of fresh water; we followd them in and by 11
came to an anchor. We then invited two who seemd by their dress
&c. to be cheifs to come on board, they immediately accepted
our invitation; in the mean time those who remaind in the canoes
traded with our people for whatever they had in their boats most
fairly. The cheifs who were two old men, the one Dressd in a Jacket
ornamented after their manner with dogs skin, the other in one
coverd almost intirely with small tufts of red feathers,[3] receivd
our presents and staid with us till we had dind. When we went
into the boat to go ashore they accompanied us. The evening
was rainy with heavy squalls of wind, we rowd almost round the
bay but found so much surf every where that we were forcd to
return; at last we told this resolution to our cheifs who calld to the
people ashore telling them to bring off a canoe for them which
was immediately done, and they went ashore in her promising
to return the next morn and bring of fish and sweet potatoes &c.
We returnd on board but in the course of the evening it became
fair and we went ashore. We were receivd with great freindship
by the natives in general who seemd carefull of giving us umbrage
by collecting in too great bodies: each family or the inhabitants
of 2 or 3 houses which generaly stood together were collected in a
body, 15 or 20 men women and children, these sat on the ground

---

[1] In the absence of a specimen or a more precise description it seems impossible to
identify this shrimp.

[2] The name of this bay is Anaura.

[3] Evidently a *kahukura*, a very distinguished garment, in which the crimson feathers
from under the wings of the Kaka parrot, (*Nestor meridionalis*(Gm.), were woven into the
phormium base.

never walking towards us but inviting us to them by beckoning with one hand movd towards the breast. We made them small presents, walkd round the bay, and found a place for watering where the people are to land tomorrow and fill some at least of our empty cask.

21. This morn at day break the waterers went ashore and soon after Dr Solander and myself; there was a good deal of Surf upon the beach but we landed without much difficulty. The natives sat by our people but did not intermix with them; they traded however for cloth cheifly, giving whatever they had tho they seemd pleasd with observing our people as well as with the gain they got by trading with them. Yet they did not neglect their ordinary occupations: in the morn several boats went out fishing, at dinner time every one went to their respective homes and after a certain time returnd. Such fair appearances made Dr Solander and myself almost trust them. We rangd all about the bay and were well repaid by finding many plants and shooting some most beautifull birds;[1] in doing this we visited several houses and saw a little of their customs, for they were not at all shy of shewing us any thing we desird to see, nor did they on our account interrupt their meals the only employment we saw them engagd in.

Their food at this time of the year consisted of Fish with which instead of bread they eat the roots of a kind of Fern *Pteris crenulata*,[2] very like that which grows upon our commons in England. These were a little roasted on the fire and then beat with a stick which took off the bark and dry outside, what remaind had a sweetish clammyness in it not disagreable to the taste; it might be esteemd a tolerable food was it not for the quantity of strings and fibres in it which in quantity 3 or 4 times exceeded the soft part; these were swallowd by some but the greater number of people spit them out for which purpose they had a basket standing under them to receive their chewd morsels, in shape and colour not unlike Chaws of Tobacco.

---

[1] It is curious that amongst the numerous natural history paintings of New Zealand and Australian plants and animals made by Parkinson, and to some extent by Spöring on this voyage, there is only one sketch of a land bird, the Banksian Cockatoo—which was made at Endeavour River. We know from Parkinson's journal, as well as from Banks, that many others were collected and that he noted the colours of the soft parts of some of them, which he would scarcely have done had he not already made the outline drawings according to his usual practice. It would appear that a folio of sketches of birds was mislaid on the voyage, and this is understandable, since his death and that of Spöring took place so close together (in February 1771), and there may easily have been some confusion over their belongings, especially at that time when so many other men on the *Endeavour* were sick.

[2] The common New Zealand bracken fern, *Pteridium aquilinum* var. *esculentum* (Forst.) Kuhn.

Tho at this time of the year this most homely fare was their principal diet yet in the proper seasons they certainly have plenty of excellent vegetables, tho we have seen no sign of tame animals among them except doggs, very small and ugly. Their plantations were now hardly finishd but so well was the ground tilld that I have seldom seen even in the gardens of curious[1] people land better broke down. In them were planted sweet potatoes, cocos[2] and some one of the cucumber kind,[3] as we judgd from the seed leaves which just appeard above ground; the first of these were planted in small hills, some rangd in rows other in quincunx[4] all laid by a line most regularly, the Cocos were planted on flat land and not yet appeard above ground, the Cucumbers were set in small hollows or dishes much as we do in England. These plantations were from 1 or 2 to 8 or 10 acres each, in the bay might be 150 or 200 acres in cultivation tho we did not see 100 people in all. Each distinct patch was fencd in generaly with reeds placd close one by another so that scarce a mouse could creep through.

When we went to their houses Men women and children receivd us, no one shewd the least signs of fear. The women were plain and made themselves more so by painting their faces with red ocre and oil which generaly was fresh and wet upon their cheeks and foreheads, easily transferrable to the noses of any one who should attempt to kiss them; not that they seemd to have any objection to such familiarities as the noses of several of our people evidently shewd, but they were as great coquetts as any Europæans could be and the young ones as skittish as unbroke fillies. One part of their dress I cannot omit to mention: besides their cloth which was very decently rolld round them each wore round the lower part of her waist a string made of the leaves of a highly perfumd grass, to this was fastned a small bunch of the leaves of some fragrant plant which servd as the innermost veil of their modesty.[5] Tho the men did not so frequently use paint upon their faces yet they often did: one especialy I observd whose whole body and garments were rubbd over with dry Ocre, of this he constantly kept a peice in his hand and generaly rubbd it on some part or other of him.

[1] This is eighteenth century usage. Johnson gives as his fifth definition of the word, 'Difficult to please; solicitous of perfection; not negligent; full of care'; and as his sixth, 'Exact; nice; subtle'.

[2] Yams.

[3] These must have been Taro; the 'small hollows or dishes' which Banks goes on to mention were characteristic of Taro cultivation.

[4] S has a note: 'quincunx: the way of planting to lose the least ground, in the following form'—followed by a diagram.

[5] The grass was called Karetu (*Hierochloe redolens* R. Br.); there were various leaves that might be used. A drying bunch of Karetu smells rather like vanilla.

One peice of cleanliness in these people I cannot omit as I beleive it is almost unexamp[l]ed among Indians. Every house or small knot of 3 or 4 has a regular nescessary house where every one repairs and consequently the neighbourhood is kept clean which was by no means the case at Otahite. They have also a regular dunghil upon which all their offalls of food &c. are heapd up and which probably they use for manure.[1]

In the evening all the boats being employd in carrying on board water we were likely to be left ashore till after dark; the loss of so much time in sorting and putting in order our specimens was what we did not like so we applied to our freinds the Indians for a passage in one of their Canoes. They readily launchd one for us, but we in number 8 not being usd to so ticklish a convenience overset her in the surf and were very well sousd; 4 then were obligd to remain and Dr Solander, Tupia, Tayeto and myself embarkd again and came without accident to the ship well pleasd with the behaviour of our Indian freinds who would the second time undertake to carry off such Clumsy fellows.

22. The surf being so great on the shore that water was got with great difficulty made the Cap^tn resolve to leave the bay this morn, which he did tho the wind was foul so the whole day was spent in turning to windward.

23. This morn found ourselves gone backwards, Tegadu[2] bay which we left yesterday was now to windward of us. Several canoes came alon[g]side and told us that there was a small bay to leward of us where we might anchor in safety and land in the boats without a surf where there was fresh water; we followd their directions and they soon brought us into a bay calld Tolaga[3] where at 1 we anchord. Many Canoes came from the shore and all traded for fish, curiosities &c. very honestly. After dinner we went ashore and found as they had told us a small cove where the boat might land without the least surf, and water near it, so the Cap^tn resolvd to wood and water here.[4]

24. This morn Dr Solander and myself went ashore botan[i]zing

---

[1] No, they did not.

[2] The origin of this name for Anaura has been more than once discussed. J. A. Mackay, *Historic Poverty Bay* (Gisborne 1949), p. 50, suggests *Te ngaru*, the heavy breakers of surf encountered there. Parkinson's version *Te karu* is all too Maori to be more than accidental: it would literally mean 'the eye'.

[3] The correct name was Uawa. 'Tolaga' (which has persisted) is perhaps a rendering of *tauranga*, anchorage (elsewhere found as a place-name); the dubiety about *r* and *l* being parallel with that in the Society Islands. Cf. Samoan *taulaga*.

[4] Cook's Cove, a little within the south point of the bay.

and found many new plants. The people behavd perfectly well, not mixing with or at all interrupting our people in what they were about but on the contrary selling them whatever they had for Otahite cloth and Glass bottles, of which they were uncommonly fond.

In our walks we met with many houses in the vallies that seemd to be quite deserted, the people livd on the ridges of hills in very slight built houses or rather shedds. For what reason they have left the vallies we can only guess, maybe for air, but if so they purchase that convenience at a dear rate as all their fishing tackle and lobster potts of which they have many must be brought up with no small labour.

We saw also as extrordinary natural curiosity. In pursuing a valley bounded on each side by steep hills we on a sudden saw a most noble arch or Cavern through the face of a rock leading directly to the sea, so that through it we had not only a view of the bay and hills on the other side but an opportunity of imagining a ship or any other grand object opposite to it. It was certainly the most magnificent surprize I have ever met with, so much is pure nature superior to art in these cases: I have seen such places made by art where from an appearance totaly inland you was led through an arch 6 feet wide and 7 high to a prospect of the sea, but here was an arch 25 yards in lengh, 9 in breadth and at least 15 in hight.[1] In the evening we returnd to the watering place in order to go on board with our treasure of plants, birds &c. but were prevented by an old man who detaind us some time in shewing the excercise of this countrey, arms, lance and *patopato* as they are calld. The lance is made of hard wood from 10 to 14 feet long very sharp at the ends,[2] the *patopatoo* is made of stone or bone about a foot long shapd   . A stick was given him for an enemy, to this he   advancd with most furious aspect brandishing his lance which he held with vast firmness; after some time he ran at the stick and supposing it a man run through the body he immediately fell upon the upper end of it, laying on most unmercifull blows with his *patopatoo* any one of which would probably have split most sculls; from hence I should be led to conclude that they give no quarter.

[1] The enthusiasm raised by this archway (which still exists) provides an interesting annotation on the eighteenth century taste for romantic prospects; no doubt certain connoisseurs would have made some reference to the Gothick, but Banks was architecturally uneducated. It is illustrated both in Hawkesworth and in Parkinson. See II, Pl. 1.

[2] This is a rather puzzling weapon: the *koikoi*, or spear pointed at both ends, was normally six to eight feet long, but the old man may have had an exceptionally long specimen.

25. Went ashore this morn and renewd our searches for plants &c. with great success. In the mean time Tupia who staid with the waterers had much conversation with one of their preists; they seemd to agree very well in their notions of religion only Tupia was much more learned than the other and all his discourse was heard with much attention. He askd them in the course of his conversation with them many questions, among the rest whether or no they realy eat men which he was very loth to beleive; they answerd in the affirmative saying that they eat the bodys only of those of their enemies who were killd in war.

26. All this day it raind without intermission so hard that notwisthstanding our wishing neither Dr Solander or myself could go ashore. In the course of the day very few canoes came on board and not more than 8 or 10 Indians came down to the waterers.

27. Several Canoes came on board at day break and traded as usual. Dr Solander went with the Cap^tn to examine the bottom of the bay, myself went ashore at the watering place to collect Plants. He saw many people who behavd very civily to the boats crew shewing them every thing they wanted to See; among other nicknacks he bought of a boys top shap'd like what boys play with in England which they made signs was to be whippd in the same manner;[1] he found also several new plants. Myself found some plants and went to the top of the hill above the watering place to see a fence of poles which we had Observd from the ship: it was on a hill almost inaccessible by wood and steepness, we however climbd it and found several deserted houses near the rails which only consisted of Poles of 14 or 16 feet high set in two rows, each pole 10 feet from the next; the 2 rows were about 6 feet distant joind on the topps by a few sticks laid across sloping like the roof of a house; this rail work with a ditch which was paralel to it went about 100 yards down the hill in a kind of curve, but for what purpose it had been intended I could not at all guess. The people of the watering place at our desire sung their war song in which both men and women joind, they distorted their faces most hideously roling their eyes and putting out their tongues but kept very good time often heaving most loud and deep sighs.

28. This morn we went ashore in an Island on the left hand as you come into the bay calld by the natives *Tubolai*.[2] Here we saw

---

[1] Best has an illustration of these *potaka* or tops, *The Maori*, II, p. 124.

[2] In Grey MS 51 *Tuboulai*; S *Tubolui*; P *Tubolai*. This is a word Maori scholars find it hard to account for. The only known name is Pourewa.

Pl. IX. *Clianthus puniceus* Kaka Beak

New Zealand

the largest canoe we had met with: her lengh was 68½ feet, her breadth 5, hight 3:6: she was built with a sharp bottom made in 3 peices of trunks of trees hollowd, the middlemost of which was much longer than either of the other two; Her gunnel planks were in one peice 62 f^t 2 in lengh carvd prettily enough in bass releif, the head was also richly carvd in their fashion. We saw also a house larger than any we had seen tho not more than 30 feet long, it seemd as if it had never been finishd being full of chipps. The woodwork of it was squard so even and smooth that we could not doubt of their having among them very sharp tools; all the side posts were carvd in a masterly stile of their whimsical taste which seems confind to the making of spirals and distorted human faces. All these had clearly been removd from some other place so probably such work bears a value among them.

While Mr Sporing was drawing on the Island he saw a most strange bird fly over his head; he describd it about as large as a kite and brown like one, his tail however was of so enormous a [length]¹ that he at first took it for a flock of small birds flying after him. He who is a grave thinking man and is not at all given to telling wonderfull stories says he judg'd it to be at least   yards in lengh.²

29. Our water having been compleat the day before yesterday and nothing done yesterday but getting on board a small quantity of wood and a large supply of excellent Celary,³ with which this countrey abounds, we this morn saild tho the wind was foul. We turnd to windward all day and at night according to custom found ourselves to leward of the place we had left in the morning.

30. Fine breeze: some canoes followd the ship in the morn but could not come up with her. Before noon we passd by a Cape which the Cap^tn judgd to be the eastermost point of the countrey and therefore calld it East Cape, at least till another is found which better deserves that name.

31. Breeze continued fair: Countrey very pleasant to appearance. Several canoes came off and threatnd us at a distance which gave us much uneasiness, as we hop'd that an account of us and what we could and had done had spread farther than this; we had now our

---

¹ Word omitted both in MS and P. S *length*, added interlinearly.
² The New Zealand naturalist can cast no light on this bird, and Mr Spöring's vision must somehow have deceived him. We should at least have liked to know how many yards long the tail was. Cook named the island on his chart Sporing's Island, no doubt to celebrate the event.
³ Wild Celery, *Apium prostratum* and *A. filifolium*.

work to begin over again and heartily joind in wishing that it might be attended with less bloodshed than our late unfortunate Rencounters. After a little time one of the canoes came almost close to the ship and soon after we saw an immense large canoe coming from the shore crowded full of People, all armd with long lances. They came near and receivd signals from the boat that was near us: we Judgd there could not be less than 60 people in her, 16 padlers of a side, besides some who did not paddle and a long row of people in the middle from stem to stern crowded as close as possible. On a signal from the small canoe the[y] pulld briskily up towards the ship as if to attack. It was judgd right to let them see what we could do, least should they come to extremities we might be obligd to fire at them in which case numbers must be killd out of such a croud: a gun loaded with grape was therefore fird ahead of them: they stop'd padling but did not retreat: a round shot was then fird over them: they saw it fall and immediately took to their paddles rowing ashore with more haste than I ever saw men, without so much as stopping to breathe till they got out of sight.[1] The countrey from whence they came and indeed all round about appeard to be well wooded and pleasant; several small clusters of houses were seen interspersd with trees appearing very pleasant, some had a fence of pails round them others were to appearance quite open. Towards evening 3 or 4 Canoes came off unarmd but would scarce venture within musquet shot of us.[2]

NOVEMBER 1769

1. Calm in the morn: at sun rise we counted 45 Canoes who were coming towards us from different parts of the shore; 7 soon came up with us and after some conversation with Tupia began to sell Muscles and lobsters[3] of which they had great plenty. In the beginning they dealt fair but soon began to cheat, taking what we gave them without making any return; one who had done so on being threatned began to defy us and laugh, on which a musquet was fird over the boat which instan[t]ly brough[t] him back and made trade very regular for some time. At lengh the cabbin and gun room having got as much as they wanted the men were allowd

[1] This was off Cape Runaway, so called by Cook from the incident.

[2] On this and the following page of the MS Banks has the running-head 'off White Island'. The ship was now in the Bay of Plenty.

[3] Lobsters: the common New Zealand Crayfish, *Jasus lalandi*; mussels, no doubt *Mytilus canaliculus*. Pickersgill adds that the latter making some of the men sick when eaten they were suspected of being poisonous, 'but this I do not believe as I eat very hearty of them and felt no bad effect'. We may suspect overeating and not poison. A pencil sketch of a small specimen of the crayfish is on the back of pl. 12 in Parkinson II.

to come to the gangway and trade for themselves, and I must say that there was not the same care taken to prevent their being cheated as had been before, by which neglect the Indians soon began to cheat with impunity and to despise our threats; the consequence of which was that as soon as they had sold all they had got one of the boats pulld forward and seeing some linnen which was hanging overboard a man in her untied it without ceremony and put it into his bundle. He was calld to but instead of returning it let his boat drop astern and laughd at us. A musquet was fird over him which did not at all spoil his mirth, small shot was then fird at him which struck him upon the back; heated I suppose he was, for he regarded it less than most men would do a stripe, just shrinking his body without ceasing to bundle up the very linnen he had stole which he was at that moment employd about. The boats dropd astern about 100 yards and several musquet balls were fird near them but they continued their song of Defiance till the ship had left them 3 or 400 yards; a round shot was then fird which went over them and struck the water 3 or 4 times at a large distance beyond them. This effectualy shewd them that they could not easily get out of our reach for they immediately began to paddle and proceeded quite ashore without stopping to look behind them.

Just at night fall we were under a small Island[1] from whence came off a large double canoe,[2] or rather 2 canoes lash'd together at the distance of about a foot which was coverd with boards so as to make a kind of deck; she came pretty near the ship and the people in her talkd with Tupia with much seeming freindship, but when it was just dark they ran their canoe close to the ship and threw in 3 or 4 stones after which they padled ashore.

2. Pass this morn between an Island[3] and the main which appeard low and sandy with a remarkable hill inland, flat and smooth as a mole hill tho very high and large.[4] Many canoes and people were seen along shore: some followd us but could not overtake us. A Sailing canoe that had chasd us ever since day break came up with us and provd the same double canoe as pelted us last night which made us prepare for another volley of their ammunition, dangerous to nothing on board but our windows. The event provd as we expected for after having saild with us an hour they threw

---

[1] Motuhora or Whale Island: running head 'of Moutohora'.
[2] The voyagers were used to double canoes in the islands, but not very many were seen in New Zealand seas.
[3] Motiti or Flat Island.
[4] Called by Cook Mount Edgcumbe—with some variety of spelling.

their stones again; a musquet was fird over them and they
dropd astern not I beleive at all frightned by the musquet but
content with having shewd their courage by twice insulting us.
We now begin to know these people and are much less afraid of
any daring attempt from them than we were. At 12 the countrey
appeard low with small clifts near the shore but seemingly very
fertile inland. We saw plainly with our glasses villages larger than
any we had before seen situated on the topps of cliffs in places
almost inaccessible, besides which they were guarded by a deep fosse
and a high paling within it, so that probably these people are much
given to war. In the evening the countrey low as before: many
towns were in sight larger than those at noon, always situated like
them on the topps of cliffs and fenc'd in the same manner; under
them upon the beach were many very large canoes, some hundreds
I may safely say, some of which either had or appeard to have
awnings but not one of them were put off. From all these circumstances we judgd the countrey to be much better peopled hereabouts
and inhabited by richer people than we had before seen,[1] may be
it was the residence of some of their princes. As far as we have
yet gone along the coast from Cape Turnagain to this place the
people have acknowledgd only one cheif, *Teratu*: if his dominion
is realy so large he may have princes or governors under him capable
of Drawing together a vast many people: for himself he is always
said to live far inland.[2]

3. Continent appeard this morn barren and rocky but many
Islands were in sight, cheifly inhabited with such towns upon
them as we saw yesterday; 2 Canoes put off from one but could
not overtake us. At breakfast a cluster of Islands and rocks were
in sight which made an uncommon appearance from the number
of perpendicular rocks or needles (as the seamen call them) which
were in sight at once: these we calld the Court of Aldermen in
respect to that worthy body and entertaind ourselves some time
with giving names to each of them from their resemblance, thick
and squat or lank and tall, to some one or other of those respectable
citizens. Soon after this we passd an Island[3] on which were houses

---

[1] Hence the name given, Bay of Plenty.

[2] I have written at some length on the problem presented by this 'chief', of territorial
dominion so much greater than that of any otherwise known Maori historical figure,
in my introduction to Cook I, pp. cli-iii. The conclusion there drawn, as at least a reasonable conjecture, is that Banks (among others) confused a personal name and a direction:
the name of a minor chief—or of two minor chiefs, indeed—in the Poverty Bay district,
Te Ratu, with the phrase *te ra to*, the westward (lit. the setting sun). It is difficult to
see any other way in which Cook and Banks could have constructed the great king or
prince of whom they write.   [3] Castle Rock.

built on the steep sides of cliffs inaccessible I had almost said to birds, how their inhabitants could ever have got to them much surpassd my comprehension; at present however we saw none so that these situations are probably no more than places to retire to in case of Danger which are totaly evacuated in peaceable times. At 12 the Continent appeard still rocky and barren, few houses were seen, they were not built in towns but stood seperate. About dinner time 3 Canoes came alongside of much the most simple construction of any we have seen, being no more than the trunks of trees hollowd out by fire without the least carving or even the addition of a washboard[1] on their gunnels; the people in them were almost naked and blacker than any we had seen only 21 in all, yet these few despicable gentry sang their song of defiance and promisd us as heartily as the most respectable of their countrey men that they would kill us all. They remaind some time out of stones throw but at last venturd close to the ship; one of our people gave them a rope from the side to save them the trouble of Padling, this they accepted and rewarded the man who gave it by thrusting at him with a pike which however took no effect; they then went a few yards from the ship and threw a lance into her which struck nobody; a musquet was fird over them on which they all went off.

Late in the evening the ship came into a bay which appeard well shelterd by Islands[2] and gave hopes for the morn. Several Canoes with people like the last came about the ship and talkd very civily to us. A bird was shot from the ship in their sight as it swam on the water, this they took up and tied to a fishing line that was towing astern for which they were rewarded with a peice of cloth. Notwisthstanding all this they became very saucy Just at night singing their song of Defiance and attempting to tow away the buoy of the anchor; 2 or 3 musquets were fird over them which had not the least effect, they threatned hard and promisd that tomorrow they would return with more force and kill us all and dispatchd a boat who told us that he was going to another part of the bay for assistance.

4. Our freinds meant to be still better than their word for they visited us twice in the night intending I suppose to wake us if we should be asleep, but as they found us not so they went away as they came without saying a single word. In the morn they returnd

---

[1] S has the note, 'Washboard, a kind of additional edge or board to hinder the Sea from washing in so immediately as it otherwise would'.

[2] This is the cluster of islands off and within the south-eastern point of Mercury Bay— Mahurangi, Motueka (properly Motu Iki), Motukorure or Middle Island, and their attendant quite small islets.

with the earlyest day break, about 150 men in 10 or 12 Canoes
all armd with pikes lances and stones. We all got up to see the
event. An hour and a half was spent in conversation sometimes
civil sometimes otherwise: our resolution was that as we had in
vain shewd them the power of musquets by firing near them and
killing the bird yesterday we would on the first provacation they
gave us fire at them with small shot, the last resource we had to
shew them our superiority without taking away their lives. They
at lengh offerd to trade for their arms and sold two weapons very
fairly, but took a price for the third and refusd to send it up but
offerd it for a second; the second was sent down but a third was
requird instead of the weapon being parted with; this was a convenient time for the execution of our project as the man who had
thus cheated us swaggerd prodigiously, having paddled the boat
a few yards from the ship. Accordingly a musquet ball was fird
through the bottom of the boat and small shot at the offender
which struck him and another who sat next him, on which the
canoe was immediately paddled off and remaind about 100 yards
from the ship; but what was truly surprizing was that tho the men
who were shot bled a good deal not one of the other boats went
near them or enquird at all how much or in what manner they were
hurt. They returnd to the ship and renewd trade for their arms,
a large quantity of which they sold without attempting to play
any tricks; at last however one gentleman padled off with two
different peices of cloth which had been given for one weapon, he
got about 100 yards from the ship and thought himself safe. A
musquet was fird after him which fortunately struck the boat Just
at the waters edge and consequently made 2 holes in her; the people
in her and the rest of the Canoes padled hard, as a finishing stroke
to convince them of our superiority a round shot was fird over
them and not a boat stoppd till they got ashore. Soon after this the
Captn went in the boats to seek a place for the ship to stay that
she might observe the transit of Mercury; it raind and as we were
sure of staying 5 days Dr Solander and myself stayd on board.
The Indians ashore were neither freinds nor foes, they shewd
however much fear whenever our boats approachd them. After
dinner the ship removd to the place he had found[1] where were
great plenty of birds, much Celery and good hopes of fish.

5. This morn some canoes came off but brought nothing to sell.

[1] The anchorage is exactly known from the extant charts, in Hawkesworth and elsewhere—a mile offshore from the mouth of the Purangi or Oyster river, almost at the
eastern end of the beach of Cook Bay.

One old man whose name was *Torava*[1] came on board; he seemd to be the cheif both today and yesterday but in all the transactions of yesterday he was observd to behave sensibly and well, laying in a small canoe always near the ship and at all times speaking civily to those on board. With some persuasion he venturd down into the cabbin and had presents, Cloth, Iron &c. given him; he told us that the Indians were now very much afraid of us, we promisd freindship if they would supply us with provision at their own price.

After breakfast we went ashore on the banks of a river.[2] The Indians who were on one side made all the signs of freindship imaginable, beckoning to us to land among them; it suited our convenience for hawling the sein and shooting Birds of which there were great numbers to land on the other side and it was not without much persuasion that they about noon venturd over to us.

The Sein was hawld with no success but several Birds were shot, like sea pies but Black with red bills and feet,[3] the trawl and drudge were also today employd and caught nothing but a few shells. The people who stayd by the boats saw two Indians fight on some quarrel of their own: they began with Lances which were soon taken from them by the old men but they were allowd to continue their battle, which they did like Englishmen with their fists for sometime after which all of them retird behind a little hill so that our people did not see the event of the combat.

6. Went ashore: Indians as yesterday very tame. Their habitations certainly were at a distance as they had no houses but slept under the bushes. The bay may be a place to which parties of them often resort for the sake of shell fish which are here very plentifull; indeed where ever we went, on hills or in valleys in woods or plains, we continualy met with vast heaps of shells often many waggon loads together, some appearing to be very old; where ever these were it is more than probable that Parties of Indians had at some time or other taken up their residence, as our Indians had made much such a pile about them. The countrey in general was very barren but the topps of the hills were coverd with very large Fern, the roots of which they had got together in large quantities as they said to carry away with them.[4] We did not see any kind of cultivation.

[1] Toiawa.

[2] The Purangi—from which was derived the name Opooragee, and its variants, used as a name for the whole bay in many of the logs and journals.

[3] Probably the Black Oyster-catcher, *Haematopus unicolor* Forster, the descendants of which are found in the district still.

[4] Again *aruhe*, the roots of *Pteridium aquilinum*.

In the evening I walkd up the river which at the mouth looks very fine and broad, it in 2 miles or less shoald to nothing. The countrey inland was still more barren than that near the sea side.

7. Rain and most disagreable weather all day kept us on board as well as the Indians from coming off to us.

8. Fine weather: many Canoes came off, in them our freind Torava. While he was along side he saw 2 Canoes coming from the opposite side of the bay on which he immediately went ashore with all the canoes, telling us that he was afraid; he however soon returnd finding I suppose that the canoes had not in them the people he expected. In the two boats came an amazing number of fish of the macarel kind[1] which the people sold for little or nothing, so that all hands had today fish enough.

We went ashore and botanizd with our usual good success which could not be doubted in a countrey so totaly new. In the evening we went to our freinds the Indians that we might see the method in which they slept: it was as they had told us on the bare ground without more shelter than a few shrubs over their heads, the women and children were placd innermost or farthest from the sea, the men lay in a kind of half-circle round them and on the trees close by them were rangd their arms in order, so no doubt they are afraid of an attack from some enemy not far off. They do not acknowledge any superior king which all we have before seen have done, so possibly these are a set of outlaws from Teratu's kingdom; their having no cultivation or houses makes it clear at least that it is either so or this is not their real habitation.[2] They say however that they have houses and a fort somewhere at a distance but do not say that even there is any cultivation.

9. At day break this morn a vast number of boats were on board almost loaded with macarel of 2 sorts, one exactly the same as is caught in England.[3] We concluded that they had caught a large shoal and sold us the overplus what they could not consume, as they set very little value upon them. It was however a fortunate circumstance for us as by 8 O'clock the ship had more fish on board than all hands could eat in 2 or 3 days, and before night so many that every mess who could raise salt cornd as many as will last them this month or more. After an early breakfast the astronomer went on shore to Observe the transit of Mercury which he did without the

---

[1] See n. 3 on this page.

[2] It seems clear that they were at that particular beach for the fishing.

[3] The Southern Mackerel, *Pneumatophorus colias* (Gm.), is rather similar to the English species. The other sort was perhaps *Trachurus novae-zelandicae* Richardson; cf. II, p. 6.

smallest cloud intervening to Obstruct him,[1] a fortunate circumstance as except yesterday and today we have not had a clear day for some time.

About noon we were alarmd by the report of a great gun fird from the ship, the occasion of which was this: two canoes came to the ship very large and full of people, they shewd by their behaviour that they were quite strangers or at least so much so as not to be at all afraid; they soon enterd into trade and almost immediately cheated by taking the Cloth which was given to them without returning that which was bargaind for. On this they immediately began to sing their war song as if to defy any revenge those on board might chuse to take, this enragd the 2nd lieutenant so much that he leveld a musquet at the man who had still got the cloth in his hand and shot him dead. The canoes went off to some distance but did not go quite away. It was nescessary to send a boat ashore, so least they might atempt to revenge his death upon the boat A round shot was fird over them which had the desird Effect of putting them to flight immediately. The news of this event was immediately brought on shore to our Indians who were at first a little alarmd and retreated from us in a body; in a little time however they returnd on their own accords and acknowledgd that the dead man deservd his punishment — unaskd by us, who thought his fate severe knowing as we did that small shot would have had almost or quite as good an effect with little danger to his life, which tho forfeited to the laws of England we could not but wish to spare if it could be done without subjecting ourselves to the derision and consequently to the attacks of these people; which we have now learnt to fear not least they should kill us, but least we should be reducd to the nescessity of killing a number of them which must be the case should they ever in reality attack us.[2]

A little before sunset we went home with the Indians to see them eat their supper. It consisted of fish, shell fish, lobsters and birds: these were dressd either by broiling them upon a skewer which was stuck into the ground leaning over the fire, or in ovens as we calld them at Otahite which were holes in the ground filld with

---

[1] Cook and Hicks shared in these observations, though Green was rather scornful of their efforts.

[2] Cf. the sober Cook, after giving his brief account: 'I have here inserted the account of this affair just as I had it from Mr Gore but I must own that it did not meet with my approbation because I thought the punishment a little too severe for the Crime, and we had now been long enough acquainted with these People to know how to chastise trifling faults like this without taking away their lives'.—I, p. 196. Gore was in charge of the ship while Cook and Hicks were on shore.

provision and hot stones and coverd over with leaves and Earth. Here we saw a woman who mournd after their fashion for a dead relation. She sat on the ground near the rest who (except one) seemd not at all to regard her: the tears constantly trickled down her cheeks; she repeated in a low but very mournfull voice words which we did not at all understand, still at every sentence cutting her arms, face or breast with a shell she held in her hand, so that she was almost coverd with blood, a most affecting spectacle. The cutts she made however were so managd as seldom to draw blood and when they did to peirce a very small way into the flesh; but this is not always the case with them, for many we have seen and some were among these very people who had shocking large scarrs on their arms, thighs, breasts, cheaks &c. which they told us had been done in this manner and upon this occasion; may be they proportion the depth of their cutts to the regard they have for the deceasd.

10. This day was employd in an excursion to view the large river at the bottom of the bay which lay at some distance from it. The mouth of it provd to be a good harbour with water sufficient for our ship but scarce for a larger, the stream in many places very wide with large flats of mangroves which at low water are coverd.[1] We went up about a league where it was still wider than at the mouth and divided itself into innumerable channels seperated by mangrove flatts, the whole several miles in breadth, the water shoal, so we agreed to stop our disquisition here and go ashore to dine. A tree in the neighbourhood on which were many shaggs nests and old shaggs setting by them[2] confirmd our resolution; an attack was consequently made on the Shaggs and about 20 soon killd and as soon broild and eat, every one declaring that they were excellent food as indeed I think they were. Hunger is certainly most excellent sauce, but since our fowls and ducks have been gone we find ourselves able to eat any kind of Birds (for indeed we throw away none) without even that kind of seasoning. Fresh provision to a seaman must always be most acceptable if he can get over the small prejudices which once affected several in this ship, most or all of whoom are now by vertue of good example compleatly curd. Our repast ended we proceeded down the river again. At the mouth of it was a small Indian village where we landed and were most civily receivd by the inhabitants who treated us

---

[1] Called by Cook the River of Mangroves. The mangroves were *Avicennia resinifera*.
[2] Several species of New Zealand shags nest in trees, and there is nothing to identify the victims of this feast.

with hot cockles, at least a small flat shell fish, most delicious food, *Tellina*   .[1] Near the village was the ruins of an old Indian *Eppah*[2] or Fort which we went to see. It was situate on the point of a peninsula[3] inaccessible on three sides from the steepness of the cliffs; the fourth was guarded by a ditch the bank of which nearest the fort could not be less than 20 feet high, there had also been pallisades both on the Inside and outside of he ditch but of these nothing was left but thick posts almost rotten. Was any ship to winter or stay any time here this would be a most excellent place to set up tents as it is sufficiently spatious.

11. Rain and blowing weather all this day so that no canoes came off nor did we go ashore. An oyster bank had been found at the river by the wooding place, about ½ a mile up on the starboard hand Just above a small Island which is coverd at high water; here the longboat was sent and soon returnd deep loaded with I sincerely beleive as good oysters as ever came from Colchester and about the same size.[4] They were laid down under the booms and employd the ships company very well who I verily think did nothing but Eat from the time they came on board till night, by which time a large part were expended, but that gave us no kind of uneasiness as we well knew that not the boat only but the ship might be easily loaded in one tide almost, as they are dry at half Ebb.

12. Two canoes came early this morn who appeard to be strangers who had heard of us by the caution and fear they shewd in approaching the ship; two of them were however persuaded to come on board and the rest traded for what they had very fairly. A small canoe also came from the other side of the bay and sold some large fish which had been taken the day before yesterday, as yesterday it blew too [hard][5] for any Canoes to go to Sea. After breakfast we all went ashore to see an Indian Fort or *Eppah* in the neighbourhood, uncertain however what kind of reception we should meet with as they might be Jealous of letting us into it, where probably all their valuable effects were lodgd. We went

---

[1] Probably the Pipi, *Amphidesma australe*—perennially esteemed; as Banks has it, 'most delicious food'.

[2] *E* or *he* (the indefinite article) *pa*.

[3] Pa Point.

[4] Possibly, as the phrase 'an oyster bank' is used, they were *Ostrea sinuata*, which occurs throughout New Zealand, but in the largest beds in Foveaux Strait—whence its popular name of Stewart Island Oyster. But they may have been 'Auckland Rock' oysters, *Ostrea glomerata* Gould, an admirably delicate species.

[5] Supplied from S. P *fresh*.

to a bay where were two,[1] we landed first near a small one the most beautifuly romantick thing I ever saw. It was built on a small rock detachd from the main and surroundd at high water, the top of this was fencd round with rails after their manner but was not large enough to contain above 5 or 6 houses; the whole appeard totaly inaccessible to any animal who was not furnishd with wings, indeed it was only aproachable by one very narrow and steep path, but what made it most truly romantick was that much the largest part of it was hollowd out into an arch which penetrated quite through it and was in hight not less than 20 yards perpendicular above the water which ran through it.[2] The inhabitants on our aproach came down and invited us to go in but we refusd intending to visit a much larger and more perfect one about a mile off, we spent however some little time in making presents to their women. In the mean time we saw the inhabitants of the other come down from it, men women and children about 100 in number, and march towards us; as soon as they came near enough they wav'd and calld *horomai*[3] and set down in the bushes near the beach (a sure mark of their good intentions). We went to them and made a few presents and askd leave to go up to their heppah which they with joy invited us to do and immediately accompanied us to it. It was calld *Wharretoowa*[4] and was situate on the end of a hill where it Jutted out into the sea which washd two sides of it, these were sufficiently steep but not absolutely inaccessible; up one of the land sides which was also steep went the road, the other was flat and open to the side of the hill. The whole was inclosd by a pallisade about 10 feet high made of strong pales bound together with withs; the weak side next the hill had also a ditch the face of which next the pallisade we measurd to be 20½ feet in depth. Besides this over the pallisade was built a fighting stage which the[y] call *Porāvā*,[5] which is a

---

[1] That is, they rowed across to the other side of the bay. Banks has here rather telescoped his impressions: the two *pa* he now describes were not in the same 'bay', but at the ends of different, though adjacent, stretches of beach.

[2] This rock and *pa* were called Te Puta o Paretauhinau (*puta*, hole). When the *pa* next described was taken by the enemies of the Ngatihei people of Mercury Bay, in 1800, a small remnant escaped to safety on this impregnable rock. It is now much worn away.

[3] *haere mai*, 'welcome', lit. 'come hither'.

[4] Whare-taewa. The words *calld Wharretoowa* are an interlineation, and the name is rather difficult to read; it is possibly *Wharretoawa*. I have printed it wrongly in Cook I, p. 198, n. 2, as 'Wharretouwe'. There are certain discrepancies between Banks's and Cook's accounts of this great fortification, the remains of which are still visible in the grass-grown ditches on the bluff above the north-east end of Buffalo Beach. It has been made the subject of detailed study by Mr Leslie G. Kelly, 'Whare-taewa Pa, Mercury Bay, 1952' in *Journal of the Polynesian Society*, Vol. 64 (1953), pp. 384-90, with interesting photographs. Best, op. cit., II, p. 315 has a diagram, but mistakenly calls the *pa* Wharekaho, the name of a village on the beach below.

[5] *puwhara* or *pourewa*.

flat stage coverd with boughs of trees upon which they stand to throw darts or stones at their assailants out of danger of their weapons. The dimensions of it were thus: the hight from the ground 20½ feet, breadth 6 f^t 6, the lengh 43 feet. Upon it were laid bundles of darts and heaps of stones ready in case of an attack. One of the Young men at our desire went up to shew their method of fighting and another went to the outside of the ditch to act assailant; they both sung their war song and dancd with the same frigh[t]full gesticulations as we have often seen them, threatning each other with their weapons; this I suppose they do in their attacks to work themselves to a sufficient fury of courage, for what we call calm resolution is I beleive found in few uncivilizd people. The side next the road was also defended by a stage like this but much lower, the other two were by their steepness and the pallisade thought sufficiently secure. The inside was divided into I beleive 20 larger and smaller divisions, some of which contain not more than 1 or 2 houses others 12 or 14; every one of these were enclosd by its own pallisade tho not so high and strong as the general one. In these were vast heaps of Dryd fish and fern roots pild up in heaps, so much that had they had water I should have though[t] them well prepard for a siege but that must be fetchd from a brook below, so probably they do not use to beseige a town as we do in Europe.[1] Without the fence were many houses and large netts which I suppose were brought in upon any alarm; there was also about ½ an acre of Gourds[2] and sweet potatoes planted, the only Cultivation we have seen in the bay.

13. Rainy and blowing weather today so we did not go ashore, indeed there was little temptation for we hade got by much the greatest number or perhaps all the plants that the season afforded.

14. But midling weather. As we were resolvd to stay no longer here we all went ashore,[3] the boats to get as much Celery and Oysters as possible, Dr Solander and myself to get as many green plants as possible of sea stock for finishing scetches[4] &c, so an enormous

---

[1] They did, and lack of water was often the cause of the downfall of a great *pa* such as this, which fell precisely because the besiegers in 1800 cut off the supply.

[2] The hard rind of the gourd, Hue or *Lagenaria siceraria*, was much used as a container. It probably came to New Zealand with the Maoris.

[3] Cook mentions landing on one of the islands off the south head of the bay on the evening of the 15th (Banks's 14th). Banks, who had collected names, writes in Grey MS 51, 'the Island on which he landed is calld by the natives *Poegaig* [Poikeke] near it were two more called Motueike [Motu Iki, charted as Motueka] & Motucara [Motukorure] the rock like a castle seen in coming in is called Teruamahow [? Te rua mahau] and a remarkable steep clift spiring up like a Pillar Komutoro [*Ko* (it is) *Moturoa*]'—which illustrates his thirst for all available knowledge.

[4] i.e. for Parkinson to draw on board. There are many of these drawings extant.

number of all these articles came on board. Dr Solander who was today in a cove different from that I was in saw the natives catch many lobsters in a most simple manner: they walkd among the rocks at low water about middle deep in water and still felt about with their feet till they felt one, on which they divd down and constantly brought him up. I do not know whether I have before mentiond these lobsters but we have had them in tolerable plenty in almost every place we have been in and they are certainly the largest and best I have ever eat.[1]

15. Little wind and that foul, sail however. Several canoes were on board and in one of them Torava who sayd that as soon as ever we are gone he must go to his heppah or fort, for the freinds of the man who was killd on the 9th threatend to revenge themselves upon him as being a freind to us.

16. Wind foul as yesterday. Many Islands were seen but neither the main or them appeard at all Fertile or well inhabited; only one town was seen all day and no people, indeed we were rather too far off.

17. Foul wind and blowing fresh, so that we did not come near enough to the land to make many observations.

18. Fine weather and Fair wind today repayd us for yesterdays Tossing. The countrey appeard pleasant and well wooded. At 7 we were abreast of a remarkable bare point jutting far into the sea;[2] on it stood many people who seemd to take but little notice of us but talkd together with much earnestness. In about ½ an hour we saw canoes put off almost at the same time from several different places and come towards us, on which these people also put off a small Canoe they had with them and came likwise towards us, she soon came up with us and had in her 20 people and soon after another with 35. They sung the song of Defiance as usual which we took very little notice of, in about ½ an hour they threw 3 or 4 stones on board and then departed towards the shore; we though[t] we were quite clear of them but they soon returnd as if inclind (which I beleive is the common policy of these people) to provoke us to shew them whether we had or not arms superior to theirs. Tupia who I beleive guessd that they were coming to attack us immediately went upon the poop and talkd to them a good deal,

---

[1] They were *Jasus lalandi*, the same as the lobsters bought in the Bay of Plenty, p. 420 above. Parkinson (*Journal*, p. 99) says that some of the crayfish caught at Tolaga Bay weighed eleven pounds.

[2] Grey MS 51, 'it was calld cape Colvil' or Colville.

telling them what if they provokd us we should do and how easily
we could in a moment destroy them all. They answerd him in
their usual cant 'come ashore only and we will kill you all'. Well,
said Tupia, but while we are at sea you have no manner of Business
with us, the Sea is our property as much as yours. Such reasoning
from an Indian who had not had the smallest hint from any of us
surprizd me much and the more as these were sentiments I never
had before heard him give a hint about in his own case. All his
preaching however had little effect for they soon renewd their
stone attack, on which a musquet ball was fird through one of their
boats on which they dropd astern and left us. At night the ship
was in a place which some people conjecturd to be a channel
betwixt an Island and the main, others a deep bay,[1] where she came
to an anchor.

19. This morn two Canoes came from the land who said they knew
Torava and calld Tupia by his name. We took some of them onboard who behavd very well. Afterwards canoes came from the
other side of the bay who likewise mentiond Toravas name and
sent a young man into the ship Who told us that he was the old
mans grandson: we never suspected him to have had so much
influence. In the evening it came on thick and misty so we came
to an anchor not a little pleasd to find our selves at least in a peaceable countrey.

20. Weather still thick and hazey. We had yesterday resolvd to
employ this day in examining the bay so at day break we set out
in the boats. A fresh breeze of wind soon carried us to the bottom
of the bay, where we found a very fine river broad as the Thames
at Greenwich tho not quite so deep, there was however water
enough for vessels of more than a midling size and a bottom of
mud so soft that nothing could possibly take damage by running
ashore. About a mile up this was an Indian town built upon a
small bank of Dry sand but totaly surrounded by Deep mud, so
much so that I beleive they meant it a defence. The people came
out in flocks upon the banks inviting us in, they had heard of us
from our good freind Torava; we landed and while we stayd they
were most perfectly civil, as indeed they have always been where we
were known but never where we were not. After this visit we
proceeded and soon met with another town with but few inhabitants.
Above this the banks of the river were compleatly cloathd with

[1] It was towards the bottom of the Hauraki Gulf: running-head 'Ooohoorage or
River Thames'.

the finest timber my Eyes ever beheld, of a tree we had before
seen but only at a distance in Poverty bay and Hawks bay; thick
woods of it were every where upon the Banks, every tree as streight
as a pine and of immense size: still the higher we came the more
numerous they were. About 2 leagues from the mouth we stopd
and went ashore. Our first business was to measure one of these
trees: the woods were swampy so we could not range far, we found
one however by no means the largest we had seen which was
　　feet in circumference and　　in hight without a branch;[1] but
what was most remarkable was that it, as well as many more that
we saw, carried its thickness so truely up to the very top that I dare
venture to affirm that the top where the lowest branch took its rise
was not a foot less in diameter than where we measurd, which was
about 8 feet from the ground. We cut down a young one of these
trees; the wood provd heavy and solid, too much so for mast but
would make the finest Plank in the world, and might possibly by
some art be made light enough for mast as the pitch pine in America
(to which our Carpenter likened this timber) is said to be lightned
by tapping.[2]

As far as this the river had kept its depth and very little decreasd
even in breadth; the Captn was so much pleasd with it that he
resolvd to call it the Thames.[3] It was now time for us to return,
the tide turning downwards gave us warning so away we went
and got out of it into the bay before it was dark. We rowd for the
ship as fast as we could but nigh[t] overtook us before we could

[1] Cook gives the circumference of this tree six feet above the ground as 19 feet 8 inches,
and the height, taken with a quadrant, from the root to the first branch as 89 feet; 'it
was as streight as an arrow and taper'd but very little in proportion to its length, so that
I judged that there was 356 solid feet of timber in this tree clear of the branches'.—
Cook I, p. 206. Cook and Banks were in the great forest of Kahikatea or *Podocarpus
dacrydioides* that then covered the valley of the Waihou or Thames river for about 25
miles—now alas! completely vanished. Mr Leslie G. Kelly tells me that their activities
were watched by Maoris close by, and the tree remembered in tradition which in due
course was passed on to Europeans. It was felled for milling a little before 1900, but
abandoned as the trunk was hollow. Measurements taken by Mr Courtenay Kenny,
surveyor, of Paeroa, and his brother, tallied with Cook's. The site of the tree is given by
Mr Kenny as almost due west of the present Hikutaia railway station, on the west side
of the river and close to the Cook Road. So close to, as well as so far from, the eighteenth
century are we.

[2] The description here given argues that the tree cut down was not one of 'these' trees
at all, if 'these' were Kahikatea, but a Matai, *Podocarpus spicatus*. As a standing tree this
would look much like the other. The timber of the Kahikatea is light. Furthermore
the description of the leaf and berries given below, II, p. 10, pretty obviously refers to the
Matai; see II, Pl. 12. I owe this piece of discrimination to Professor W. P. Morrell's *Sir
Joseph Banks in New Zealand* (Wellington 1958), p. 80, n. 1.

[3] '. . . on account of its bearing some resemblence to that river in england'.—Cook.
He was thinking of the lower reaches of the Thames—'broad as the Thames at Green-
wich', as Banks says above; and apparently of its estuary, for he extended the name in
New Zealand to cover the whole of the Hauraki gulf.

Pl. X. *Fuchsia excorticata* Kotukutuku or Tree Fuchsia

Anaura Bay

get w[i]th[i]n some miles of it. It blew fresh with showers of rain, in this situation we rowd till near 12 and then gave over and running under the land came to a grapling and all went to sleep as well as we could.

21. Before daybreak we set out again. It still blew fresh with mizling rain and fog so that it was an hour after day before we got a sight of the ship. However we made shift to get on board by 7 tird enough, and lucky it was for us that we did, for before 9 it blew a fresh gale so that our boat could not have rowd ahead so that had we been out we must have either gone ashore or shelterd ourselves under it. Before evening however it moderated so that we got under way with the Ebb tide but did little or nothing.

22. This morn we weighd with the Ebb but breeze was so light that the Cap^{tn} went into the boat and d^{r} Solander with him. There were many Canoes about the ship with which I traded for their clothes, arms &c. of which I had got few so I stayd on board, they sold cheifly for paper. In the course of this commerce one young man who was upon Deck stole a half minute glass[1] which was in the Binnacle and was catchd attempting to go off with it. The first Lieutenant took it into his head to flogg him for his crime. He was accordingly seezd but when they atempted to tie him to the shrowds the Indians on board made much resistance: I heard it and came upon deck: they then began to call for their arms which were handed them out of the boats and one canoe atempted to come up the ships side. Just then Tupia came upon deck, they ran to him immediately, he assurd them that their freind would not be killd he would only be whippd, on which they were well satisfied. He endurd the discipline and as soon as he was let go an old man who perhaps was his father beat him very soundly and sent him down into the canoes, into which they all went and dropd astern, saying that they were afraid to come any more near us. They venturd however at last but stayd a very short time promising however at their departure to return with fish which they never performd.

---

[1] The half-minute glass, on the hour-glass principle, was used with a rope or 'log-line' knotted every fifty feet (at least in theory) and attached to a floating piece of wood to find the rate at which the ship was going. One half-minute was one 120th part of an hour; 50 feet was one 120th part of a nautical mile of 2000 feet. 'Heaving the log' consisted in flinging it overboard and noting how many knots ran off the reel while the sand in the glass ran, thus giving the ship's speed in nautical miles per hour—i.e. so many 'knots'. In practice there were modifications both of the length of the line and of the 'half-minute' measured by the glass; but Cook always speaks of an unmodified 50 feet and half-minute. See Cook I, p. 57 for the effect of too much error in the division of the line. It was not for a light-fingered Maori to make free with half-minute glasses.

23. Very light breezes: we have got but little as yet by Tideing.[1] In the morn 2 small canoes came off and promisd to return at night with fish but did not.

24. Strong breeze off the land so we soon got clear of the bay. Land in the morn appeard unfruitfull, few or no houses were seen; in the Evening large sands which extended some way into the countrey in little hills as I have seen in England. At night we came to an anchor in a small open bay;[2] our fishing lines were tried and we soon caught a large number of fish which were calld by the seamen Sea bream,[3] as many as I beleive the ships company could eat in 2 days.

25. The countrey had a tolerably good appearance. In the morn some stragling houses and 3 or 4 fortified towns were in sight, near which was a large quantity of Cultivation; in the Evening 7 large canoes came off carrying about 200 Indians. Two of them who said they had heard of us came on board and receivd our presents: this did not however hinder some of their companions from cheating as usual by offering to trade and keeping what they had got without sending up what they had offerd. Our usual punishment was inflicted, small shot, which made the offender immediately relinqu[i]sh his prize (an old pair of Black breches) which he threw into the water on seeing a second musquet presented. His companions however as soon as they thought themselves out of our reach began as usual to defy us which made us think it nescessary to shew them what we could do, a conduct surely most right when it can be done without hurting them: musquets were fird near them which made them draw a little farther off, a round shot was then fird over their heads on which they all set off for the shore most stoutly.

26. Two small canoes came off early in the morn and told us that they had heard of yesterdays adventure, they came on board and traded queitly for whatever they had: soon after two larger ones came from a distance, they calld the others to them and then All came up together to the ship. The strangers were numerous and appeard rich: their Canoes were well carvd and ornamented and they had with them many weapons of *patoo patoos*[4] of stone and

---

[1] 'by Tideing'—i.e. by drifting with the outgoing tide and anchoring when it turned, in the attempt to make some progress in spite of the absence of real wind.

[2] Bream Bay. But the two outer points of the bay, Bream Head and Bream Tail, were estimated by Cook to be five leagues apart.

[3] This haul was not of Snapper as has been suggested (Cook I, p. 210) but of Tarakihi, *Dactylopagrus macropterus* (Bloch and Schneider), a common and good food fish of New Zealand waters which was described by Solander as *Sciaena abdominalis* (*Pisc. Aust.* pp. 29-30) under this date. Solander refers to a painting which cannot now be found.

[4] 'Weapons of *patoo patoos*': S reads 'weapons, as *patoo patoos*', which makes better sense. P follows the MS.

whales bones which they value much; they had also ribbs of whales of which we had often seen imitations in wood carvd and ornamented with tufts of Dogs hair.[1] The people themselves were browner than to the Southward as indeed they have been ever since we came to Opoorage, and they had a much larger quantity of *Amoco*[2] or black stains upon their bodys and faces; almost universaly they had a broad spiral on each buttock and many had their thighs almost intirely black, small lines only being left untouchd so that they lookd like stripd breeches. In this particular, I mean *Amoco*, almost every different tribe seem to vary their customs:[3] we have some days seen Canoes where every man has been almost coverd with it, and at the same time others where scarce a man has had a spot except his lipps black'd, which seems to be always Essential.

These people would not part with any of their arms &c. for any price we could offer; at last however one producd an axe of Talk and offerd it for Cloth, it was given and the Canoe immediately put off with it. A musquet ball was fird over their heads on which they immediately came back and returnd the cloth but soon after put off and went ashore.

In the afternoon other Canoes came off and from some inattention of the officers were sufferd to cheat unpunishd and unfrightned. This put one of the Midshipmen who had sufferd upon a droll tho rather mischeivous revenge. He got a fishing line and when the Canoe was close to the ship hove the lead at the man who had cheated, with so good success that he fastned the hook into his backside, on which he pulld with all his might and the Indian kept back, so the hook soon broke in the shank leaving its beard in his backside, no very agreable legacy.[4]

27. Light breeze. Several canoes came off and traded for fish but were most abominably saucy, continualy threatning us, at last they began to heave stone[s] with more courage than any boats we had seen. This made it nescessary to punish them: the Cap^tn went upon the Poop where they immediately threw at him, he leveld a gun loaded with small shot at the man who held a stone in his hand in the very action of throwing and struck him. He sunk down so immediately into the Canoe that we suspected he was

---

[1] The 'ribbs of whales' were probably *hoeroa*, objects which have been generally taken to be weapons, but are now regarded as rather a sort of chiefly staff. The 'imitations in wood' were more likely to have been *taiaha*, a favourite two-handed striking-weapon, 5 to 6 feet long. For more detailed discussion, see II, p. 28, n. 2 below.

[2] *moko*.

[3] Variety was individual, not tribal.

[4] These visits, and the midshipman's prank, were off Cape Brett.

materialy hurt; this however did not prevent another Canoe from coming up with stones in their hands who met another load of small shot at about 50 yards distant which struck several of them and at once stopd their speed. The two canoes which had been fird at went immediately for the shore, the others dropd astern and we left them behind. The land appeard rocky and full of Islands, the Continent behind them rose in a gradual slope and seemd fertile; some cultivation was in sight. In the even foul wind.

28. Foul wind continued and this morn the ship was 2 leagues at least to leward of yesterday. The Continent rose in gentle hills but did not appear so fertile when near it as it did at a distance; several large heppas were in sight one the largest we have seen, to appearance far inland.

29. Wind as foul as ever and the ship moved more to leward, so we res[o]lvd to bear away for a bay which we had Passd. We did so and by 10 came to an anchor in a most spatious and well shelterd harbour or rather collection of harbours almost innumerable formd by Islands.[1]

Canoes crowded upon us from all quarters so that we soon had 37 large and small about us; the people in them traded very fairly for what they had and shewd much fear of us, especialy if they saw any thing like a gun which they were well acquainted with. They became however soon a little more bold and while we were at dinner one of them went to the Buoy which they atempted to tow away: a musquet was fird over them without effect [and?] small shot at them but they were too far off for that to take effect. A ball was then fird at them which was thought to strike one of them as they immediately threw out the Buoy which by this time they had got into their Canoe; a round shot was then fird over them which struck the water and then went ashore; 2 or 3 canoes landed immediately and the men ran about on the beach as if in search of it. After this we calld to them and in a little time they all returnd to the ship.

By this time she was properly moor'd and the Boats out, so we set out for the shore.[2] At our parting from the ship not a canoe stirrd which we Judgd a good sign, but no sooner had we set a foot on the shore about ¾ of a mile from the ship but every Canoe put off in a moment and pulld towards us. We were in a sandy cove

---

[1] The Bay of Islands.
[2] The ship was moored off the south-west end of the island called Motu Arohia, and it was on this island that the landing was made.

behind the two heads of which the most of them landed, one or 2
only in sight; out of these they came running with every man his
arms, others appeard on the tops of the hills and numbers from
behind each head of the Cove so that we were in a moment surrounded by (the gentlemen in the ship say) 5 or 600 men tho we
I beleive never saw more than 200 of them. We now every man
expected to be attackd but did not chuse to begin hostilities so
the Cap^{tn} and myself marchd up to meet them. They crouded a
good deal but did not offer to meddle with us, tho every man had
his arms almost lifted up to strike. We brought them towards the
party and made a line signing to them that they were not to pass it:
they did not at first but by this time a party from the other side
had come up and mixd with our people. They now began to sing
their war song but committed no hostility till 3 steppd to each of
our boats and attempted to draw them ashore. It was now time to
fire, we whose Guns were loaded with small shot did so which
drove them back. One man attempted to Rally them; he who was
not 20 yards from us came down towards us waving his *Patoo patoo*
and calling to his companions; Dr Solander whose gun was not
dischargd fird at him on which he too ran. They now got upon
rising ground about us from whence we dislogd them by firing
musquet balls, none of which took effect farther than frightning
them. In this way we were about $\frac{1}{4}$ of an hour, resolving to maintain
our ground, when the ship had brought her broadside to bear
and fird at the Indians who were on the topps of the hills.[1] The balls
went quite over them notwithstanding which they went off and at
last left us our cove quite to ourselves, so that the musquets were
laid down upon the ground and all hands employd in gathering
Cellery which was here very plentifull. An Old Indian now appeard
who had been on board in the morn with two more, they came
immediately to us and provd to be his wife and brother. He said
that another brother of his was struck with the small shot and
askd whether he would dye: we told him no and gave him a musquet
ball with some small shot telling him that it was the latter with
which he was struck, but that if they again attackd us we would
shoot them with the former which would infallibly kill them.
After this we went into the boats and rowd to another Cove in
the same Island near which was a high hill from whence we might
have a good view of the bay. We climbd up it and from thence saw

---

[1] Hicks, left in command of the ship, and somewhat alarmed by the crowding of the
natives on shore, had immediately manoeuvred her to bring her broadside to bear—a
fortunate circumstance.

that the bay we were in was indeed a most surprizing place: it was full of an innumerable quantity of Islands forming as many harbours, which must be as smooth as mill pools as they Landlock one another numberless times. Every where round us we could see large Indian towns, houses and cultivations: we had certainly seen no place near so populous as this one was very near us, from whence several Indians came to us taking however great pains to shew us that they were unarmd. They acompanied us down to the boat. Night coming on we went onboard carrying much Celery, the only plant of any use even to us, for of all the places I have landed in this was the only one which did not produce one new vegetable.

30. Several canoes came off to the ship very Early but sold little or nothing, indeed no merchandice that we can shew them seems to take with them. Our Island cloth which usd to be so much esteemd has now intirely lost its value: they have for some days told us that they have of it ashore and shewd us small peices in their Ears which they said was of their own manufacture, this at once accounts for their having been once so fond of it and now setting so little value upon it.[1] Towards noon however they sold a little dryd fish for paper cheifly or very white Island Cloth. Among other things they told us that the man who was shot at with small shot on the [2]7th was dead, 3 shot they said struck his Eye and I suppose found there an easy passage to his brain.

In the Even we went ashore upon the Continent:[2] the people receivd us very civily and as tame as we could wish. One general observation I here set down, that they Always after one nights consideration have acknowledgd our superiority but hardly before: I have often seen a man whose next neighbour was wounded or killd by our shot not give himself the trouble to enquire how or by what means he was hurt, so that at the time of their attacks they I beleive work themselves up into a kind of artificial Courage which does not allow them time to think much.

DECEMBER 1769

1. Several Canoes were on board by Day break and sold some things cheifly for Indian Cloth and quart bottles. The day misty and stewy: the boats were on shore on the Island which we searchd on the

---

[1] Cf. p. 412, n. 1 above, and II, p. 9 below.
[2] Banks, as we shall see, was letting the continental theory go hard. Cf. Cook, p. 216: 'At 3 PM the Boats having returnd from sounding, I went with them over to the south side of the Harbour and landed upon the Main, accompanied by Mr Banks and Dr Solander'.

29th with so little success that we did not think it worth while to go ashore.

It is now a long time since I have mentiond their custom of Eating human flesh, as I was loth a long time to beleive that any human beings could have among them so brutal a custom. I am now however convincd and shall here give a short account of what we have heard from the Indians concerning it. At *Taoneroa* the first place we landed in on the Continent the boys who we had on board mentiond it of their own accords, asking whether the meat they eat was not human flesh, as they had no Idea of any animal but a man so large till they saw our sheep: they however seemd ashamd of the custom, saying that the tribe to which they belongd did not use it but that another very near did. Since that we have never faild wherever we went ashore and often when we convers'd with canoes to ask the question; we have without one exception been answerd in the affirmative, and several times as at Tolaga and today the people have put themselves into a heat by defending the Custom, which Tubia who had never before heard of such a thing takes every Occasion to speak ill of, exhorting them often to leave it off. They however as universaly agree that they eat none but the bodies of those of their enemies who are killd in war, all others are buried.

2. Boats went ashore on the Island again. I do not know what tempted Dr Solander and myself to go there where we almost knew nothing was to be got but wet skins, which we had very sufficiently for it raind all the time we were ashore as hard as I ever saw it.

3. Many Canoes were on board in the morn, one very large which carried 82 people. After breakfast Dr Solander and myself went ashore on the Continent; we found few plants and saw but few people but they were most perfectly civil; we went by their invitation to their little town which was situated in the bottom of a cove without the least defence. One of the old men here shewd us the instruments with which they stain their bodies which was exactly | Tattoo like those usd at Otahite. We saw also here the man who was shot at on the 29th in atempting to steal the Buoy; the ball had gone through the fleshy part of his arm and grazd his breast; the wound was open to the air without the smallest application upon it yet it had as good an appearance and seemd to give him as little pain as if he had had the best dressings to it. We gave him a musquet ball and with a little talking to he seemd very fully sensible of the escape he had had.

In the Even we went ashore on another Island[1] where were many more people than we had seen in the morn, who livd in the same peacable stile and had very large plantations of sweet potatoes, yamms &c. all about their village. They receivd us much as our freinds in the morning had done and like them shewd much satisfaction at the little presents of necklaces &c. which were given to them.

4. Our Old man came on board and brought with him his brother who had been shot with small shot on the 29th; it had slanted along his thigh which I suppose had not less than 100 shotts in it. This wound was likewise without any application and seemd to give him little or no pain but was crusted over with a hard crust, natures plaister, equal maybe when she chuses to apply it to any that art has contrivd.

After breakfast we went ashore at a large Indian fort or heppah;[2] a great number of people immediately crouded about us and sold almost a boat load of fish in a very short time. They then went and shewd us their plantations which were very large of Yamms, Cocos, and sweet potatoes; and after having a little laught at our seine, which was a common kings seine,[3] shewd us one of theirs which was 5 fathom deep and its lengh we could only guess, as it was not stretchd out, but it could not from its bulk be less than 4 or 500 fathom. Fishing seems to be the cheif business of this part of the countrey; about all their towns are abundance of netts laid upon small heaps like hay cocks and thatchd over and almost every house you go into has netts in it making.

After this they shewd us a great rarity 6 plants of what they calld *Aouta* from whence they made cloth like the Otahite cloth; the plant provd exactly the same, as the name is the same, as is usd in the Islands, *Morus papyrifera* Linn., the same plant as is usd by the Chinese to make paper. Whether the Climate does not well agree with it I do not know, but they seemd to value it very much and that it was very scarce among them I am inclind to beleive, as we have not yet seen among them peices large enough for any use but sticking into the holes of their Ears.

In the afternoon we went to a very distant part of the bay, the people here were very few. All but one old man ran away from us; he accompanied us where ever we went and seemd much pleasd

---

[1] According to Maori tradition, this island was Moturua.
[2] This, as we learn from Cook, was again on the mainland, but the particular *pa* seems impossible to identify.
[3] i.e. the seine net commonly used in the navy.

with the little presents we made him. Near where we landed was a little fort built upon a small rock, surrounded by the sea at high water and accessible only by a ladder. We expressd a desire to go there; he said there was his wife but if we would promise to practice no indecencies towards her he would accompany us; this we most readily did and he was as good as his word. The ascent was so difficult that tho there were stepps and a pole we found it dangerous enough. When we came up there were in it 3 women who on our first coming cried, but presents soon put them into better humour. There were in all only 3 houses, but the situation as I have before describd was so steep that the inhabitants of them might easily defend themselves against almost any force that could be brought against them.

5. A small spirt of fair wind before day break made us heave up the anchor in a great hurry, but before we were well underway it was as foul as ever so we were obligd to atempt turning out. Many canoes came from all parts of the bay which is by far the most populous place we have been in. In the middle of the day we were becalmd and caught many fish with hooks. About 10 at night as we were going through the outer heads on a sudden we wer[e] becalmd so that the ship would neither wear nor stay: in a moment an eddy tide took hold of us and hustled us so fast towards the land that before the Officers resolvd what was best to be done the ship was within a Cables lengh of the breakers, we had 13 fathom water but the ground so foul that they dar'd not drop an anchor. The eddy now took another turn and set her along shore opening another bay but we were too near the rocks to trust to that: the pinnace was orderd to be hoisted out in an instant to take the ship in tow, Every man in her was I beleive sensible of the Danger we were in so no one spard to do his best to get her out fast. The event however shewd how liable such situations must be to Confusion: they lowerd down too soon and she stuck upon a gun: from this she must be thrust by main force, in doing which they had almost ove[r]set her which would have tumbled out her oars: no man thought of running in the gun: at last that was done and she was afloat, her crew was soon in her and she went to her duty.[1] A faint

[1] This difficulty with the gun is mentioned in none of the seamen's journals—perhaps from professional pride; though Pickersgill the master's mate does not lose the opportunity to be dramatic: 'all this Time the Indians on Shore Making a great Noise and Rejoiceing at our Missfortune Exspecting us to be a Pray for them'. The laconic Cook merely remarks, 'At this time the tide or Curent seting the Ship near one of the Islands, where we was very near being a shore but by the help of our boat and a light air from the southward we got clear'.—I, p. 219.

breeze of wind now sprung up off the land and with that and towing she to our great Joy got head way again, at a time when she was so near the shore that Tupia who was not sensible of our danger was conversing with the Indians ashore, who made themselves very distinctly heard notwithstanding the roaring of the breakers.

We were all happy in our breeze and fine clear moonlight; myself went down to bed and sat upon my cott undressing myself when I felt the ship strike upon a rock, before I could get upon my leggs she struck again.[1] I ran upon deck but before I could get there the danger was over; fortunately the rock was to wind ward of us so she went off without the least damage and we got into the proper channel, where the officers who had examind the bay declard there to be no hidden dangers—much to our satisfaction as the almost certainty of being eat as soon as you come ashore adds not a little to the terrors of shipwreck.

6. In the morn we were clear of all our dangers and at sea to our no small satisfaction notwithstanding the wind was as foul as possible.

7. Wind not much better than yesterday.

8. Very light breeze: we have ran off so far from the land that we can distinguish nothing upon it. In the evening fair wind.

9. Fair wind tho but little of it. Many Canoes came off who shewd much fear of us and after some time said that they had heard of our Guns.[2] Tupia at last persuaded them to come under the stern and after having bought of them some of their cloths, which they sold very fairly, began to enquire about the countrey. They told him that at the distance of three days rowing in their canoes, at a place calld *Moorewhennua*,[3] the land would take a short turn to the southward and from thence extend no more to the West. This place we concluded must be Cape Maria Van Diemen,[4] and finding these people so intelligent desird him to enquire if they knew of any Countries besides this or ever went to any. They said no but that their ancestors had told them to the NW by N or NNW was a large countrey to which some people had saild in a very large canoe, which passage took them up a month: from this expedition

---

[1] This was on Whale Rock—'which we took for a whale as the Sea broak over it seldom and [had] much the Appairance of one', to quote a seaman's log, now in the Public Record Office, Adm 51/4547/153.

[2] This was off the Cavalli Islands.

[3] Muriwhenua, the Maori name for the northernmost part of the North Island of New Zealand: *whenua*, district; *muri*, the hind part or end.

[4] So called by Tasman, after the wife of the governor-general of the Dutch East Indies, in January 1643.

a part only returnd who told their countreymen that they had seen a countrey where the people eat hogs, for which animal they usd the same name (*Booah*) as is usd in the Islands.[1] And have you no hoggs among you? said Tupia. — No. — And did your ancestors bring none back with them? — No. — You must be a parcel of Liars then, said he, and your story a great lye for your ancestors would never have been such fools as to come back without them. Thus much as a specimen of Indian reasoning. After much conversation our freinds left us but promisd to return at night and bring with them fish, which they did and sold it very reasonably.

10. This morn we were near the land which was as barren as it is possible to conceive: hills within hills and ridges even far inland were coverd with white sand on which no kind of vegetable was to be seen, it was conjecturd by some that the wind blow[s] the sand quite across it.[2] Some Indian forts or Heppah's were seen and from them some canoes put off but did not overtake us.

11. Wind as heard hearted as ever: we turnd[3] all day without loosing any thing, much to the credit of our old Collier, who we never fail to praise if she turns as well as this.

12. Wind &c. as yesterday.

13. Wind as foul as ever and rather overblows so that in this days turning we lost all we had [gaind?][4] last week.

14. Blows almost as fresh as it did yesterday but rather more fair; a heavy swell from the west made us almost conclude that there was no land to the Northward of us.[5]

15. More moderate but not more fair: we begin to think this Cape our Ne plus ultra.

16. We stood out to sea yesterday and last night so that we could

---

[1] One does not know quite what to make of this story. The direction is that of New Caledonia. *Puaa* was the general Polynesian word for a pig.

[2] The land here was about six miles wide. The appearance of the country, says Cook, 'occasioned Mr Banks to give it the name of *Sandy bay*'; though in the Mitchell MS of his journal he has deleted 'Mr Banks' and substituted 'me'. The name was changed in the nineteenth century, rather fatuously, to Great Exhibition Bay.

[3] Tacked.

[4] This verb is omitted in the MS, which is followed by all the copies. Something however seems needed.

[5] Banks's running-head to this page of his journal is 'Mount Camel'. But this hill, standing in from the shore of Sandy Bay, had been noted by Cook on the 10th. Although the wind was 'rather more fair' this day, the 14th, the long period of bad and contrary weather had begun that made the weathering of the North Cape and the fixing of the positions so difficult; and during which (on the afternoon of Banks's 15 December) Surville in the *St Jean Baptiste* doubled the Cape, coming from west to east, and quite out of sight of the *Endeavour*.

in the morn only Just see the land from the mast head: stood in for it and at night made it plain.

17. This morn we were in with the land which trends[1] a little to the Southward so we hoped that our troubles are nearly at an end; during the days turning however we contrivd to lose near a leag[u]e, no great comfort to us.

18. Still more to leeward this morn and in the even still more. On a rock pretty near us an Indian fort was seen through our glasses which we all thought was encircled with a mud wall;[2] if so tis the only one of the kind we have seen.

19. Stood out to sea last night: tonight were in with the land and found we had gaind something as we did also the last time we stood far off, which made the seamen conclude that some small current along shore must be the reason why we could never get any thing by our short trips.[3]

20. Some hopes of a fair wind in the morn but they soon left us and it began to blow hard with violent claps of thunder, on which we again stood out to sea.

21. Wind not quite so bad as yesterday but a great swell from the West hinderd the ship much.

22. Swell as yesterday but the wind has come more to the Southward so that we cannot come in with the land at all.

23. Little wind more favourable than yesterday so that at night the land was seen from the Mast head.

24. Land in sight, an Island or rather several small ones most probably 3 Kings,[4] so that it was conjecturd that we had Passd the Cape which had so long troubled us. Calm most of the Day: myself in a boat shooting in which I had good success, killing cheifly several Gannets or Solan Geese so like Europæan ones that

---

[1] S has the note, 'Trends when the Land goes off a different shape from what it was before'.

[2] At 7 p.m. this day Cook reckoned the North Cape to be distant four or five miles NWbN. Of the 'Indian fort' he merely remarks, 'We saw a Heppa or Village upon the Cape and some few inhabitants'. What Banks calls a rock may have been the 'appearance' referred to by Cook in his description of the cape (p. 225) as follows: 'It [the cape] appears still more remarkable when to the southward of it by the appearance of a high round Island at the SE point of the Cape, but this is likewise a deception being a round hill join'd to the Cape by a low narrow neck of land'. A 'mud wall' is quite un-Maori; but it may have been the outside wall of a defensive ditch somehow built up.

[3] This conclusion was correct: there is a strong north-easterly current here which changes direction down the eastern side of New Zealand.

[4] So called by Tasman, who discovered them on Twelfth Night 1643; they lie a few miles north-west of his Cape Maria van Diemen.

they are hardly distinguishable from them.[1] As it was the humour of the ship to keep Christmas in the old fashiond way it was resolvd of them to make a Goose pye for tomorrows dinner.

25. Christmas day: Our Goose pye was eat with great approbation and in the Evening all hands were as Drunk as our forefathers usd to be upon the like occasion.[2]

26. This morn all heads achd with yesterdays debauch. Wind has been Easterly these 3 or 4 days so we have not got at all nearer the Island than we were.

27. Blows very hard a[t] SE so that we were again drove off the Land, not much displeasd as we all rejoicd much that it was not an on shore wind.

28. Wind now SW right on shore but thank god we have so good an offing that we are in not the least danger. All our sea people said that they never before were in so hard a summers Gale.

29. Wind more moderate but still blows prodigiously fresh with a monstrous sea. No such summer Gales as this to the Norward sayd our Capt[n].

30. Blew very fresh still tho the heart of the Gale seemd to be broke: we have been driven much to the Northward so that today we once more passd in sight of Cape Maria and the 3 Kings.

31. Wind as yesterday, sea something abated: stood in for the Land which we had not now seen for some time: dared not venture very near as the wind was right on shore, it appeard very sandy and barren.

JANUARY 1770

1. The new year began with more moderate weather than the old one ended with, but wind as foul as ever. We venturd to go a little nearer the land which appeard on this side the cape much as it had done on the other, almost intirely occupied by vast sands: our Surveyors suppose the Cape shapd like a shoulder of mutton with the Knuckle placd inwards, where they say the land cannot be above 2 or 3 miles over and that here most probably in high winds the sea washes quite over the sands which in that place are low.[3]

---

[1] *Sula bassana serrator* Gray, the New Zealand Gannet.

[2] Cook is too busy with nautical detail to mention this Christmas Party.

[3] Precisely what Banks means by this sentence, after the colon, I do not know—unless he is making some reference, when he writes 'the Cape' to the shape of the whole stretch of the land north of 35°. A few miles north of that parallel, on the east side of the island, on December 10, Cook had named Knuckle Point, but with no thought of Cape Maria

2. Weather not yet setled: in the morn we stood S and soon lost sight of the land which we saw no more all day.

3. Stood in for the land with weather more moderate than it has been for some days past: it appeard high but the sides of the hills often interspersd with long tracts of sand even high up, their bottoms were every where coverd with it. Many Albatrosses were about the ship today swimming upon the water in small companies 10 or 20 together.

4. Stood rather nearer the land than yesterday but not near enough to see whether or not it was inhabited: indeed we were obligd to hawl off rather in a hurry for the wind freshning a little we found ourselves in a bay which it was a moot point whether or not we could get out of: indeed I beleive most people thought that we should not till a lucky change in the wind at once allowd us to weather every thing, to our no small Joy who had so lately been in so severe and long a Gale of wind blowing right upon the shore which we had now just weatherd.[1]

5. Blew fresh and we stood out all day maybe rather too sensible of the danger we had escapd yesterday.

6. Calm today: myself in the Boat shot *Procellaria longipes*,[2] *velox*[3] and *Diomedæa exulans* (the Albatross).[4] I had an opportunity to see this last setting upon the water and as it is commonly said by seamen that they cannot in a calm rise upon the wing I tryd the experiment. There were two of them, one I shot dead, the other who was near

van Diemen in mind. That Banks is making this reference seems probable from Cook's entry for 1 January 1770, 7 p.m. (p. 228).—'At this time Mount Camel bore N 83° E and the northermost land or Cape Maria van Diemen NBW. . . . Note, Mount Camel doth not appear to lay little more than a Mile from the sea on this side and about the same distance on the other, so that the land here cannot be above 2 or 3 Miles broad from sea to sea, which is what I conjecter'd when we were in Sandy bay on the other side of the coast'. Knuckle Point separated Doubtless Bay and Sandy Bay. Cook underestimated the width of the land, but the shore is very low here, and such underestimation was natural enough from nine to ten miles out at sea; he does not however anywhere suggest that the sea might wash right over the land.

[1] This seems to be a heightened account of Cook's approach to the entrance of Kaipara Harbour, which had the appearance of a bay or inlet. 'In order to see more of this place we kept on our Course until 11 oClock when we were not above 3 Leagues from it and then found that it was neither a Bay nor inlet but low land bounded on each side by higher lands which caused the deception.' Cook called it False Bay. There was a good harbour across the bar. Nobody else registers the alarm expressed by Banks; but Cook, remarking on this part of the coast in general, regards it as very dangerous: 'this I am so fully sencible of that was we once clear of it I am determined not to come so near again if I can possible avoide it unless we have a very favourable wind indeed'.—p. 230.

[2] The Grey-backed Storm Petrel, *Garrodia nereis*. See 2 October 1769, p. 396 above.

[3] Probably *Pterodroma longirostris* (Stejneger) or *P. cookii* (G. R. Gray). See 15 February and 30 August 1769 for a note on other gadfly petrels taken on this voyage.

[4] This Wandering Albatross was classed by Solander with one caught on 2 October 1769, q.v., and another taken 11 April 1770.

him swam off near as fast as my small boat could row; we gave chase and came up a little; he attempted to fly by taking the moment of a waves falling but did not succeed. I who was so far off that I knew I could not hurt him fird at him to make his attempts more vigourous, which had the effect for the third effort he got upon the wing, tho I beleive had it not been for a little swell upon the water he could not have done it.

7. Calm again: Myself shooting killd *Procellaria longipes* and *melanopus*[1] and saw a turtle Just before sunset who being awake divd immediately. What wind there was was fair tho scarce a breath of it, yet even that made us hope for better times.

8. Our fair wind continued but still so little of it that was there any plenty of Birds or hopes of new ones I could outrow the ship in much. More Land just in sight.[2]

9. Much as yesterday, Land in sight but so faintly seen that a Landsman would scarce distinguish it from Clouds.

10. In the morn a breeze of fair wind put us all into high spirits. The countrey we passd by appeard fertile, more so I think than any part of this countrey I have seen, rising in gentle slopes not over wooded but what trees there were well grown. Few signs of inhabitants were seen, a fire and a very few houses.

About noon we passd between the main and a small Island or rock[3] which seemd almost totaly coverd with birds probably Gannets; towards evening a very high hill was in sight but very distant.

11. Calm this morn, some fish were caught: in the even foul wind. Our high hill has been sometimes seen and sometimes wrappd up in clouds, some of our people think it is as high as the Pike of Teneriffe; tho I cannot be of half that opinion yet it is certainly in appearance very like it.

12. This morn we were abreast of the great hill but it was wrappd up in clouds and remaind so the whole day; it is probably very high as a part of its side which was for a moment seen was coverd

---

[1] Mathews (1912, p. 145) considered that Solander's description of this species perhaps referred both to the Kermadec Petrel, *Pterodroma neglecta* Schlegel, and to the Great-winged Petrel, *P. macroptera* Smith, but the revision of the former species by Murphy and Pennoyer suggests that birds in the dark phase described by them may be identical with those discussed by Solander. Gould states that he examined a drawing in Banks's collection with *melanopus* written on it in Solander's hand (*Ann. Mag. Nat. Hist.* 13, p. 363, 1844) but unfortunately no trace can be found of it now. *Procellaria melanopus* Gm., taken from Latham's account, was a different bird and only 13 inches long. Solander's birds (p. 85) were 15 inches long, with a wing span of 39 inches and a weight of 14 oz.

[2] This seems to have been the high land about Hokianga harbour.

[3] Called Gannet Island.

with snow.[1] The countrey beyond it appeard very pleasant and fertile, the sides of the hills sloping gradualy; with our glasses we could distinguish many white lumps in companies of 50 or 60 together which probably were either stones or tufts of grass but bore much the resemblance of flocks of sheep.[2] At night a small fire which burnd about ½ an hour made us sure that there were inhabitants of whoom we had seen no signs since the 10th.

13. This morn soon after day break we had a momentary view of our great hill the top of which was thick coverd with snow, tho this month answers to July in England. How high it may be I do not take upon me to judge, but it is certainly the noblest hill I have ever seen and it appears to the utmost advantage rising from the sea without another hill in its neighbourhood one 4th part of its hight. At sun set the top appeard again for a few minutes but the whole day it was coverd with clouds.

14. In a large bay calld in the Draughts Murderers bay.[3] We stood across it all day: at night had the appearance of a harbour just ahead of us on the shore of which the natives made a fire: resolvd to stand off and on all night and in the morn go in.[4]

15. In the course of the last night we were drove to the Eastward more than we had any reason to expect, so much that we found ourselves in the morn past the harbour we intended to go into. Another however was in sight into which we went: the land on both sides appeard most miserably barren till we got pretty deep in when it began to mend by gradual degrees. Here we saw some canoes who instead of coming towards us went to an Indian town or fort built upon an Island nearly in the middle of the passage,[5] which appeard crowded with people as if they had flockd to it from all parts; as the ship aproachd it they wavd to us as if to invite us to come to them but the moment we had passd by they

---

[1] Cook called it Mount Egmont, after the 2nd earl of that name, who had been First Lord of the Admiralty, 1763-6. It is 8260 feet in height, and dominates the whole provincial district of Taranaki, as well as being a notable landmark from the sea.

[2] Hooker's identification of these 'white lumps' as *Raoulia mammillaris*, the 'Vegetable Sheep' known only from the South Island, is certainly an error. Lucy B. Moore writes, 'there is a great deal of moss above the forest on the western side of Mt. Egmont, and the conspicuous large white cushions are formed by one which, in the latest treatment of New Zealand mosses (G. O. K. Sainsbury, *Handbook of the New Zealand Mosses*, 1955) is referred to as *Rhacomitrium lanuginosum* (Hedw.) Brid. var. *pruinosum* H.f. and W. I think it would be generally agreed that the whitish lumps seen by Banks would be most likely to be this plant.' But they *may* have been stones or boulders.

[3] Banks's running-head here is more accurate—'Mouth of Cooks Streights'. The 'Draughts' were those maps founded on Tasman's rough chart, with his name Murderers' Bay (the present Golden Bay) given a much wider significance.

[4] It is impossible to say what harbour this was: there are several eligible openings, with good harbours behind them.   [5] Motuara.

set up a loud shout and every man brandishd his weapons which none of them were without. The countrey about us was now very fertile to appearance and well wooded so we came to an anchor[1] about long cannon shot from the fort, from whence 4 Canoes were immediately dispatchd to reconoitre I suppose and in case they were able to take us, as they were all well armd. The men in these boats were dressd much as they are represented in Tasmans figure,[2] that is 2 corners of the cloth they wore were passd over their shoulders and fastned to the rest of it just below their breast, but few or none had feathers in their hair. They rowd round and round the ship defying and threatning us as usual and at last hove some stones aboard which we all expected to be a prelude of some behaviour which would oblige us to fire upon them; but just at this time a very old man in one of the boats express'd a desire of coming on board, which we immediately encouraged, and threw a rope into his canoe by which she was immediately hawld up along side and the old man (contrary to the opinion of all the other Indians who went so far as to hold him fast for some time) came on board, where he was receivd in as freindly a manner as we possibly could and had many presents given to him, with which he returnd to the canoes who immediately joind in a war dance — whether to shew their freindship or enmity it is impossible to say, we have so often seen them do it upon both those occasions. After this they retird to their town and we went ashore abreast of the ship where we found good wood and water and caught more fish in the Seine than all our people could possibly destroy,[3] besides shooting a

---

[1] Cook: 'A 2 oClock we Anchor'd in a very snug Cove which is on the NW side of the Bay faceing the S West end of the Island'—Ship Cove.

[2] This was the 'View of Murderers Bay' referred to on p. 400, n. 2 above.

[3] Parkinson lists the fish etc. taken here in his *Journal*, p. 114: (1) Cuttle-fish, probably a squid since true cuttle-fish do not occur in New Zealand seas. (2) Large breams, perhaps Snapper, *Pagrosomus auratus* (Forster). See Parkinson II, pl. 72, and Solander's description of *Sciaena lata* (*Pisc. Aust.* pp. 25-6). Small grey breams, probably Tarakihi. See 24 November 1769. (3) Barracoutas, *Thyrsites atun* (Euphrasen). (4) Flying Gurnards, *Chelidonichthys kumu* (Lesson and Garnet). This was the *Trigla papilionacea* of Parkinson II, pl. 104, and of Solander's MS description in *Pisc. Aust.*, p. 24 where he gives Tolaga, Opuragi etc. as localities. (5) Colefish, *Parapercis colias* (Bloch and Schneider). See Parkinson II, pl. 54, *Labrus macrocephalus*, an MS name used by Solander (*Pisc. Aust.*, p. 27) for this species, the famous Blue Cod; he adds 'Colefish nostratibus'. (6) Horse-mackerel, *Trachurus novae-zelandicae* Richardson; probably the *Scomber clupeoides* of Solander (*Pisc. Aust.*, p. 37) from Motuaro. (7) Dogfish, probably the Smooth Hound Dogfish, *Emissola antarctica*. (8) Soles and dabs. There are several New Zealand species of flat fishes. (9) Mullets: probably Grey Mullet, *Mugil cephalus*. This may be Solander's MS species *Mugil lavaretoides* (*Pisc. Aust.*, p. 15). (10) Drums, a name usually applied to members of the Sciaenidae on account of their sound-producing capacities. (11) Scorpaenas, *Helicolenus percoides* (Richardson). This species was the *Scorpaena percoides* of Solander (*Pisc. Aust.*, p. 3); there is an unfinished painting of it (Parkinson II, pl. 16). (12) Chimera: Elephant fish, *Callorhinchus callorhynchus*. Solander listed it as *Chimaera callorynchus* Linn. (*Pisc. Aust.*, p. 43). Cf. II, p. 7 below.

multitude of Shaggs. The countrey however did not answer so well to Dr Solander and myself as to the ship, we finding only 2 new plants in the whole even.

16. At day break this morn 3 Canoes and about 100 Indians came to the ship bringing their women with them, a sign tho not a sure one of peacable inclinations. Soon after our longboat put off from the ship with Cask in her, they atempted to follow her on which a musquet loaded with small shot was fird at them which made them immediately return, tho as they were full 100 yards from the ship it is improbable that blood was drawn from any of them. They had in their canoes some fish which they offerd to sell and we to buy, so a man in a small boat was dispatchd among them to trade; he bought several bundles which they sold very fairly when one Indian seeing his opportunity snatchd at the trade which he had in his hand, but missing immediately put himself in a posture of defence flourishing his *patoo-patoo* as if he meant to strike. A musquet load of small shot was fird at him[1] a few of which struck his knee, the rest missd him, on which they all left of to trade but paddled peaceably enough round the ship and at last came under the stern to Tupia and discoursd with him about their antiquity and Legends of their ancestors.

The women in these canoes and some of the men had a peice of Dress which we had not before seen — a bunch of black feathers made round and tied upon the top of their heads which it intirely coverd, making them look twice as large as they realy were.[2] On seeing this my Judgement paid an involuntary compliment to my fair English countrey women; for led astray by this head dress which in some measure resembles their high foretops I was forward to declare it as my opinion that these were much the hansomest women we had seen upon the coast, but upon their nearer aproach I was convincd that nothing but the head dress had misled me as I saw not one who was even tolerably hansome.

After dinner we went in the boat towards a cove about a mile from the ship.[3] As we rowd along something was seen floating

---

[1] It was Cook who fired; cf. Cook I, p. 235 and n. 3 on that page.

[2] This peculiar head-dress, which Sir Peter Buck thought was 'a form of mourning cap' (*The Coming of the Maori*, p. 284), is portrayed in the drawing by Parkinson called 'New Zealanders Fishing', B.M. Add MS 23920.44, reproduced in Cook I, fig. 41. The mourning cap, *potae-taua*, was more generally worn by widows to demonstrate great grief; it was woven of rushes dyed black, and decorated with feathers. Augustus Hamilton, *Maori Art* (Wellington 1901), p. 297, figures a very elaborate specimen, but his pl. xxxix, fig. 6, shows a cap very much more like those in Parkinson's drawing.

[3] Probably the one called Cannibal Cove. S has a note: 'Cove. A little Harbour of which there are often many within a larger one, for any Vessells'. Cannibal Cove, like Ship Cove its neighbour, was within Queen Charlotte's Sound.

upon the water which we took to be a dead seal; we rowd up to it and it provd to our great surprize to be the body of a Woman who seemd to have been dead some time. We left it and proceeded to our cove where we found a small family of Indians who were a little afraid of us as they all ran away but one; they soon however returnd except an old man and a child who staid in the woods but not out of sight of us; of these people we inquird about the body we had seen. They told Tupia that the woman was a relation of theirs and that instead of Burying their dead their custom was to tie a stone to them and throw them into the sea, which stone they supposd to have been unloosd by some accident.

The family were employd when we came ashore in dressing their provisions, which were a dog who was at that time buried in their oven and near it were many provision baskets. Looking carelessly upon one of these we by accident observd 2 bones, pretty clean pickd, which as apeard upon examination were undoubtedly human bones. Tho we had from the first of our arrival upon the coast constantly heard the Indians acknowledge the custom of eating their enemies we had never before had a proof of it, but this amounted almost to demonstration: the bones were clearly human, upon them were evident marks of their having been dressd on the fire, the meat was not intirely pickd off from them and on the grisly ends which were gnawd were evident marks of teeth, and these were accidentaly found in a provision basket. On asking the people what bones are these? they answerd, The bones of a man. — And have you eat the flesh? — Yes. — Have you none of it left? — No. — Why did not you eat the woman who we saw today in the water? — She was our relation. — Who then is it that you do eat? — Those who are killd in war. — And who was the man whose bones these are? — 5 days ago a boat of our enemies came into this bay and of them we killd 7, of whoom the owner of these bones was one. — The horrour that apeard in the countenances of the seamen on hearing this discourse which was immediately translated for the good of the company is better conceivd than describd.[1] For ourselves and myself in particular we were before too well convincd of the existence of such a custom to be surprizd, tho we were pleasd at having so strong a proof of a custom which human nature holds in too great abhorrence to give easy credit to.

17. This morn I was awakd by the singing of the birds ashore from whence we are distant not a quarter of a mile, the numbers

---

[1] This horror was reflected in their logs and journals, where, apart from what they write about this incident, Queen Charlotte Sound is generally referred to as Cannibal Bay.

of them were certainly very great who seemd to strain their throats with emulation perhaps; their voices were certainly the most melodious wild musick I have ever heard, almost imitating small bells but with the most tuneable silver sound imaginable to which maybe the distance was no small addition. On enquiring of our people I was told that they had observd them ever since we have been here, and that they begin to sing at about 1 or 2 in the morn and continue till sunrise, after which they are silent all day like our nightingales.[1]

A small canoe came this morn from the Indian town: as soon as they came along side Tupia began to enquire into the truth of what we had heard yesterday and was told over again the same story. But where are the sculls, sayd Tupia, do you eat them? Bring them and we shall then be convinced that these are men whose bones we have seen.— We do not eat the heads, answerd the old man who had first come on board the ship, but we do the brains and tomorrow I will bring one and shew you. — Much of this kind of conversation passd after which the old man went home.

18. Among other things that the Indians told us yesterday one was that they expected their enemies to come and revenge the death of the 7 men, and some of our people thought they said that they had intelligence that they were to come as today; which made us observe the Indians town where we thought the people more quiet than usual and seemingly not atending their usual occupations of fishing &c. and no one canoe atempted to come near the ship. After breakfast we went in the pinnace to explore some parts of the bay which we had not seen, as it was immensely large or rather consisted of numberless small Harbours, coves &c; we found the countrey on our side of the Bay very well wooded every where but on the opposite side very bare. In turning a point today we saw a man in a small canoe fishing who to our surprize shewd not the least fear of us. We went to him and quite alongside his Canoe, he all the while following his occupation. On our desiring him he took up his netts and shewd us his machine, which was a circular net about 7 or 8 feet in diameter extended by 2 hoops; the top of this was open and to the bottom was tied sea Ears[2] &c.

---

[1] This was the bird called by the Maori Korimako or Makomako and by the European the Bell-bird (*Anthornis melanura*). The reason for the European name has never been better put than by Banks. But alas! that chorus of melodious wild music is no longer heard where he heard it.

[2] The shell-fish called Paua, *Haliotis* sp., related to the Abalone of the United States and the Ormer of the Channel Islands.

as bait; this he let down upon the ground and when he thought that fish enough were asembled over it he lifted it up by very gentle and even motion, so that the fish were hardly sensible of being lifted till they were almost out of the water. By this simple method he had caught abundance of fish and I beleive it is the general way of Fishing all over this coast, as many such netts have been seen at almost every place we have been in. In this bay indeed fish were so plenty that it is hardly possible not to catch abundance whatever way is made use of.

In the course of this days excursion we shot many shaggs from their nests in the trees and on the rocks. These birds we roast or stew and think not bad provisions, so between shaggs and fish this is the place of the greatest plenty of any we have seen.

19. Indians came this morn from another part of the bay where they said was a town which we had not seen: they brought plenty of fish which they sold for nails of which they hade by this time learnt the value.

20. Our old man came this morn according to his promise, with the heads of 4 people which were preservd with the flesh and hair on and kept I suppose as trophies, as posibly scalps were by the North Americans before the Europæans came among them; the brains were however taken out as we had been told, maybe they are a delicacy here. The flesh and skin upon these heads were soft but they were somehow preservd so as not to stink at all.[1]

We made another excursion today. The bay every where where we have yet been is very hilly, we have hardly seen a flat large enough for a potatoe garden. Our freinds here do not seem to feel the want of such places as we have not yet seen the least apearance of cultivation, I suppose they live intirely upon fish dogs and Enemies.

21. Dr Solander and myself were fishing today with hook and line and caught an immence number of fish every where upon the rocks in 4 or 5 fathom water. We have indeed immence plenty, the Seine is hawld every night and seldom fails to furnish us with as much fish as we can possibly destroy.

22. Made an excursion today in the pinnace in order to see more of the Bay. While Dr Solander and Myself were botanizing the cap^tn went to the top of a hill and in about an hour returnd in high spirits, having seen the Eastern sea and satisfied himself of the existence of a streight communicating with it, the Idea of

[1] See II, p. 31, n. 1 below.

which had Occurd to us all from Tasmans as well as our own observations.[1]

23. Disagreable day squally with rain so we all staid at home. M[r] Monkhouse told me today that the day before yesterday he was ashore in a place where were many Indian houses deserted: here he saw several things tied up to the branches of trees, particularly hair of a man which he brought away with him, enough to have made a sizeable wig. This inducd him to think the place he had seen was a place consecrated to religious purposes.[2] Possibly it was as they certainly have such places among them tho I have not yet been lucky enough to meet with them.

24. Went today to the *Heppah* or Town to see our freinds the Indians, who receivd us with much confidence and civility and shewd us every part of their habitations which were neat enough. The town was situated upon a small Island or rock divided from the main by a breach in a rock so small that a man might almost Jump over it; the sides were every where so steep as to render fortifications even in their way almost totaly useless, accordingly there was nothing but a slight Palisade and one small fighting stage at one end where the rock was most accessible. The people brought us several Bones of men the flesh of which they had eat, which are now become a kind of article of trade among our people who constantly ask for and purchase them for whatever trifles they have. In one part we observd a kind of wooden Cross ornamented with feathers made exactly in the form of a Crucifix cross. This engagd our attention and we were told that it was a monument for a dead man, maybe a Cenotaph as the body was not there: thus much they told us but would not let us know where it was.[3]

All the while we were among the Indians they kept still talking something about gunns and shooting people which we could not

---

[1] Cook and a seaman climbed the hill called Kaitapeha on the south-east side of the sound. His high spirits were justified, for he had solved a problem left unsolved by Tasman; his own journal remarks that 'I was abundantly recompenced for the trouble I had in assending the hill'.

[2] It seems probable that Monkhouse had been in some *tapu* place, and was perhaps lucky to have got away with his booty unobserved by the Maori. Hair was very *tapu*, and cut hair, which might be used in sorcery, was usually burnt or concealed. Sometimes the hair of the whole head was cut as a sign of mourning, and it may have been this that accounted for Monkhouse's discovery.

[3] This is the only record we have of such a memorial, though there is no reason for doubting the truth of the story Banks picked up. The Maori was accustomed to raise 'cenotaphs' or memorials of one sort or another, sometimes exactly like the Tahitian *ti'i* noted by Banks (in Maori, *tiki*). A plain or carved post, a stone, half a canoe set on end, were common forms of such observance; the cross with its feathers may have been some individual invention. The refusal to reveal the whereabouts of the body was characteristic and proper.

at all understand. They did it however so much that it engagd us all so much that we talkd about it in our return, but the more we thought the more dark was the subject till we came on board, when on mentioning [it] I was told that on the 21st one of our officers who went out on pretence of fishing came to the *heppah* intending at a distance to look at the people: but 2 or 3 canoes coming off towards his boat he imagind that they meant to attack him and in consequence thereof fird 3 musquets, one with shot and 2 with ball, at them on which they very precipitately retird, as well they might who probably came out with freindly intentions (so at least their behaviour both before and since seems to shew) and little expected so rough usage from people who had always acted in a freindly manner to them, and whoom they were not at all conscious of having offended.

25. Dr Solander and myself (who have now nearly exhausted all the Plants in our neighbourhood) went today to search for Mosses[1] and small things, in which we had great success gathering several very remarkable ones. In the evening we went out in the Pinnace and fell in with a large family of Indians, who have now begun to disperse themselves as I beleive is their custom into the different creeks and coves where fish is most plenty, a few only remaining in the *Heppah* or town to which they all fly in times of danger. These people came a good way to meet us at a place where we were shooting shags and invited us to the place where the rest of them were, 20 or 30 in number, men, women, children, Dogs &c. We went and were receivd with all possible demonstrations of freindship, if the numberless huggs and kisses we got from both sexes old and young in return for our ribbands and beads may be accounted such: they also sold and gave us a good many fish with which we went home well pleasd with our new acquaintance.

26. Went today to take an other view of our new streights the Westermost end of which the Captn was not quite sure of; we found however a hill in a tolerably convenient situation upon which we got and saw the Streight quite open and 4 or 5 leagues wide.[2] We then erected a small monument of stone such a[s] 5 stout men could do in half an hour and laid in it musquet balls beads shot &c. that if perchance any Europeans should find and pull it down they will

---

[1] The MS 'Catalogue of the plants of Cook's First Voyage in the order in which they were loosely placed in the drying books in which they were brought home' lists 33 bryophytes for Tierra del Fuego but none for New Zealand.

[2] This was out towards Cape Koamaru, the eastern point of the entrance to the sound, but the hill cannot be certainly identified. The hills there rise to over 1400 feet.

be sure it is not Indian workmanship. This done we returnd to
our dinners of Shags and fish which we had shot and caught in
coming and were dressd by the boats crew. In the place we had
apointed to dine in was a family of Indians who as usual behavd
with much freindship and civility to us, shewing us water &c.
from whence we went to the town from whence Indians came on
the 19th which was in this arm of the bay. Here we were receivd
as usual, every body seemd glad to see us and conducted us through
the whole works. The town was much like the other, situated upon
an Island or rock[1] so steep in all parts that it was almost in danger
of our necks that we climbd up to it; like the other it had also only
one fighting stage; it containd maybe from 80 to 100 houses about
as many as the other. Just as we were going away our freinds took
so great a fancey to our merchandise that they filld our boat full
of Dryd fish for which they took nails, ribbands, Paper &c.

27. Indians came aboard in the morn and traded a little, afterwards
the D[r] and myself went ashore but could find no plants at all.
We have I beleive got all that are in our neighbourhood, tho the
immense thickness of the woods which are almost renderd impassable
by climbing plants intangling every way has not a little retarded
us.

28. This morn at day break it Raind very hard but not enough to
disturb the concert of our little musical [neighbours][2] which we
every morning attend to with the greatest pleasure, they sung
their time till the sun disturbd them as usual; the rain however
continued the whole day.

29. This morn Our Old Man (*Topaa* by name, he that came first
on board the ship) came with 3 more Indians in a canoe and unfolded the story of the 19th, saying that 2 Indians were struck with
the balls one of whoom was dead, this causd a good deal of conversation in the ship and totaly unfolded the whole affair which
had till now been kept a secret from most people. After breakfast
the Cap[tn] and D[r] Solander went out in the Pinnace, myself went
ashore to air plants &c. &c. In the even when we all returnd Tupia
who had been with some of our people and seen the Indians Told
us that what we heard in the morn was absolutely false, that so
far from dead nobody was even hurt by the shot. Our Freind Topāa
is he says given too much to Lying.

---

[1] Evidently a rock lying off either Blumine or Pickersgill island.
[2] Omitted in MS, supplied from P, where it has been inserted in a blank left for the
purpose. S *band*, added interlineally.

30. Bad weather today rainy: myself out gathering Shells in which I had some success.[1]

31. Day but indifferent so of course but little could be done. Dr Solander and myself fishd a little in the Evening and had good sport.[2]

FEBRUARY 1770

1. Raind this morn very hard, as hard I think as it possibly could; our poor little wild musicians were totaly disturbd by it. In the Even it came on to blow very hard, so much so that the ship drove and for the first time in the Voyage we had 3 anchors down.

2. Still rainy so little could be done today, indeed little remain to be done.

3. Fine weather: the ship began to prepare for sailing so the D^r and myself employd ourselves in getting together our last specimens of seeds, shells &c. I stayd at the watering place, he went with the Cap^tn to the farther *Heppah* who wanted to buy Dry fish for sea stock, and did buy so much that at last the Old men fairly told him that he must go away or he would leave them without provisions, which they enforcd by some threats; matters were however so well conducted that they parted peacably.

One of our gentlemen came home to day abusing the natives most heartily whoom he said he had found to be given to the detestable Vice of Sodomy. He, he said, had been with a family of Indians and paid a price for leave to make his adresses to any one young woman they should pitch upon for him; one was chose as he thought who willingly retird with him but on examination provd to be a boy; that on his returning and complaining of this another was sent who turnd out to be a boy likewise; that on his second complaint he could get no redress but was laught at by the Indians. Far be it from me to attempt saying that that Vice is not practisd here, this however I must say that in my humble opinion this story proves no more than that our gentleman was fairly trickd out of his cloth, which none of the young ladies chose to accept of on his terms, and the master of the family did not chuse to part with.

[1] There are only eight species of New Zealand shells in the Banksian collection reported on by Wilkins, *A Catalogue and Historical Account of the Banks Shell Collection*, 1955.
[2] The journal here is quite closely confined to Banks's own observations. It was on the morning of this day that Cook with Surgeon Monkhouse and Tupaia crossed over to the island Motuara, set up a post with an inscription and the Union flag on it, and formally took possession of 'Queen Charlottes Sound . . . and the adjacent lands in the name and for the use of his Majesty'—not forgetting to drink Her Majesty's health in a bottle of wine. He also picked up some geographical information and place-names.

4. Prevented from sailing by our hay which had been so thoroughly soked by the late rains that it was too wet to put on board. Some conversation passd today concerning a report we heard yesterday. Two of our boats went out different ways and returnd at different times; the people of one said that they had met a double canoe who told them that they had a few days ago lost a female child who they suspected had been stole and eat by some of their neighbours; the other said that they had also met a double canoe whose people told them that they had yesterday eat a child, some of whose bones they sold them. From hence many of our gentlemen were led to conclude that thefts of this kind are frequent among these Indians. This story in my opinion throws very little light upon the subject as I am inclind to beleive that our two boats who went out at very different times in the morn both in the same direction, one only farther than the other, saw one and the same canoe and only differently interpreted the conversation of the people, as they know only a few words of the language, and eating people is now always the uppermost Idea in their heads. This however I must say, that when such families have come off to the ship even with an intention to fight with us they have very often brought Women and young children in arms as if they were afraid to leave them behind.

5. Ship employd in Warping herself into a better berth for sailing, When after the anchor was carried out a fortunate eddy wind blew her into it. Our Old Man Topaa was on board, of whoom Tupia askd many questions concerning the Land &c. His answers were nearly as follows: 'that the streights which we had seen from the hills were realy a passage into the Eastern sea; that the Land to the South consisted of 2 Islands or several which might be saild round in 3 or 4 days in their canoes;[1] that he knew of no other great land than that we had been upon, *Aehia no Mauwe*,[2] of which *Terawhitte*[3] was the southern part; that he beleivd his ancestors

---

[1] This is certainly garbled. Both Cook and Pickersgill refer to two islands, one of which could be circumnavigated in four days. This must have been Arapawa, which formed a large part of the eastern side of Queen Charlotte Sound, and was cut off from the rest by the narrow Tory Channel. See Cook I, p. 243.

[2] This is a different form from the name picked up by Cook, 'Aeheino mouwe', but equally puzzling. The conventional name was *Te Ika no Maui*, 'the fish of Maui'. The suggestion made to me by Mr J. M. McEwen, that the words heard were *He hi no Maui*, 'a thing fished up by Maui', is persuasive for Cook's version. Banks's *i* in his versions of native words is generally long, as in *fine*; but if in this case it was the Italian *i* one could argue that his informant had smothered the Maori *k* of *ika* and that what he heard was *e i'a no Maui*, 'a fish of Maui'. See also Cook I, p. 243, n.3.

[3] Terawhiti or Tarawhiti. The latter was the Maori name for the south-west corner of the North Island of New Zealand. *Te rawhiti*, the east, or land to the east—which was the direction in which it lay when the conversation took place.

were not born there but came originaly from *Heawyê*[1] (the place
from whence Tupia and the Islanders also derive their origin)
which lay to the Northward where were many lands; that neither
himself his father or his grandfather ever heard of ships as large
as this being here before, but that [they] have a tradition of 2
large vessels, much larger than theirs, which some time or other
came here and were totaly destroyd by the inhabitants and all
the people belonging to them killd'. This Tupia says is a very old
tradition, much older than his great grandfather, and relates to
two large canoes which came from *Olimaroa*, one of the Islands
he has mentiond to us. Whether he is right, or whether this is a
tradition of Tasmans ships whose size in comparison to their own
they could not from relation conceive a sufficient Idea of, and
whoom their Warlike ancestors had told them they had destroyd,
is dificult to say.[2] Tupia all along warnd us not to beleive too much
any thing these people told us; For says he they are given to lying,
they told you that one of their people was killd by a musquet and
buried Which was absolutely false.

Myself and the D[r] went ashore today to wind up our bottoms[3]
and fell in by accident with the most agreable Indian family we
had seen upon the coast, indeed the only one in which we have
observd any order or subordination. It consisted of 17 people;
the head of it was a pretty child of about 10 years old who they
told us was the owner of the land about where we wooded, the

---

[1] *Hawaiki* (there is certainly a *k* elided in Banks's version of this word), the semi-mythological homeland of all the Polynesian people; cf. Tahitian *Havaii*. The name turns up with dialectal differences from one end of Polynesia to the other.[6]

[2] This story has caused a great deal of difficulty, and what the old man meant is far from clear. Two large canoes might quite well have come from one of the Polynesian islands some time after the principal Maori migration in the Fleet, and their crews being taken for enemies, have met disaster. According to Cook's version (p. 245) a small vessel came, and four men were killed, which would tally, up to a point, with Tasman's visit—if the small vessel was Tasman's cockboat. But according to Cook again, the old man's information was that this small vessel came from the north, and Tasman did not arrive at New Zealand from the north. To the old man, certainly, one direction might have been as good as another. We do not get much help from the name 'Olimaroa'; it is not on the map now, and it is not in the list of names of islands which Cook got from Tupaia (pp. 291-3). But the map which Tupaia drew has the names 'Oremaroa', roughly north-east of Tahiti, and 'Olemateroa', north-west of Tahiti. Oremaroa has no island attached to it. J. R. Forster picked up the name 'O-Rima-Roa' somehow on the second voyage (*Observations*, p. 519) and says it 'coincides nearly with the situation of the *Isles of Disappointment*, seen by Admiral Byron in 1765'. These, Napuka and Tepoto, form part of the north-eastern fringe of the Tuamotus. The name seems otherwise unknown. After it appeared in Hawkesworth, one or two fanciful geographers and novelists applied it to Australia, which is absurd. Curiously enough, this happened particularly in Sweden: see Gösta Langenfelt, 'Ulimaroa', in *Särtryck ur Festskrift Tillägnad Elias Wessén* (Lund 1954).

[3] 'Wind up our bottoms': this idiom has now vanished from the language; to wind up one's bottom was to bring one's business or tempoɪary occupation to a close, or to 'clean up a job'.

only instance of property we have met with among these people. He and his mother (who mournd for her husband tears of blood according to their custom) sat upon matts, the rest sat round them; houses they had none, nor did they attempt to make for themselves any shelter against the inclemencies of the weather which I suppose they by custom very easily endure. Their whole behaviour was so affable, obliging and unsuspicious that I should certainly have accepted their invitation of staying the night with them had not the ship been to sail in the morn. Most unlucky I shall always esteem it that we did not sooner get acquainted with these people, from whoom we might have learnt more in a day of their manners and dispositions than from all that we have yet seen.

6. Foul wind continued but we contrivd to turn out and get into the streights, which are to be calld Cooks streights.[1] Here we were becalmd and almost imperceptibly drawn by the tide near the land. The lead was dropd and gave 70 fathom; soon after saw an apearance like breakers towards which we drove fast. It was now sunset and night came on apace. The ship drove into this which provd to be a strong tide which set her directly upon a rock to which she aproachd very near,[2] when the anchor was dropd which brought her up about a Cables lengh from it; now we were sensible of the force of the tide which roard like a mill stream and ran at 4 knots at least when it came in its strongest pushes, for it varied much. It ran in this manner till 12 O'Clock, when with the slack water we got up the anchor with great dificulty which lay in 70 fathom, and a light breeze from the Northward cleard very soon from our dangers.

7. Sensible again of the Violence of the tides here which past us in great ripples, even in the middle of the streights, tho they were judgd to be 5 leagues over in the narrowest part. A large hill was seen with much snow upon it on the SW side: at noon we were almost abreast of it and clear of the streights, it provd to be so far inland that we could hardly trace its outline so probably it is very high indeed.[3] The land between us and it was flat for a large extent but seemd barren and swampy Land, after this barren and sandy and rounded away fast to the Southward; a small smoak upon it in the Even was the only sign of inhabitants that we saw.

---

[1] Who conferred this name we do not know, but may suspect Banks himself. Cook gives no mention to it in his journal, though it appears on the charts. In Grey MS 51 Banks merely writes, 'the Strait itself was calld Cooks Straight the name of the Capt.'.

[2] The rock was off one of the islands Cook called The Brothers.

[3] Cook calls this 'large hill' a 'prodegious high mountain'. It was Tapuaenuku, the highest peak of the Kaikoura range, 9460 feet.

8. As some of the officers declard last night that they[1] though[t] it probable that the land we have been round might communicate by an Isthmus[2] situate somewhere between where we now are and Cape Turnagain (tho the Whole distance is estimated at no more than 90 miles) the capt[n] resolv'd to stand to the Northward till he should see that cape, which was accordingly done in the morning the wind being fair tho but a light breeze. As soon as we were in with the land it appeard more fertile than any we had seen for some time, and the flatts larger,[3] but the weather was so hazey that we could not make use of our glasses. About this time 3 Canoes put off from the shore and followd us and had patience to do so till 3 O'Clock, when they overtook us and immediately with very little invitation came on board. They appeard richer and more cleanly than any people we have seen since we were in the Bay of Islands, and their canoes were also ornamented in the same manner as those we had formerly seen on the N and this side of the Island, but have not now seen since the river Thames if even there; they were also more civil in their behavior and on having presents made them immediately made presents to us in return (an instance we have not before met with in this Island). All these things inclind me to beleive that we were again come into the Dominions of Teratu but on asking them they said no he was not their King.

9. Weather rather more clear than Yesterday. On the land white chalky cliffs appeard such as we us'd to see; by 11 O'Clock Cape Turnagain was in sight which convincd every body that the land was realy an Island on which we once more turnd our heads to the southward.

10. Stood along shore nearer the land than when we passd it before: it made in low hills which seemd pretty well clothd with trees but at the bottom of them was lowish land making in tables,[4] the topps of which were coverd with white sand that through the glass had much the appearance of ripe corn; between these were a few vallies in which were wood and in one of these we saw a few houses. In the Evening the countrey rather mended upon us I

---

[1] MS *he*: I have altered this to *they* to match the preceding *they*, as Cook says (p. 249) 'a notion which some of the officers had just started'.

[2] That is, might be the expansion of an isthmus which joined it to the southern continent. The officers, says Cook, founded their opinion 'on a suppotision that the land might extend away to the SE from between Cape Turn-again and Cape Pallisser', though Cook himself was convinced that Aeheinomouwe was an island. One cannot resist a faint suspicion that some of the officers were taking a rise out of Cook.

[3] Banks must have been looking up to the Wairarapa plains. Running head 'off Cape Palliser'.

[4] S has the note, 'Land made in Tables. When the Hills were flat at top'.

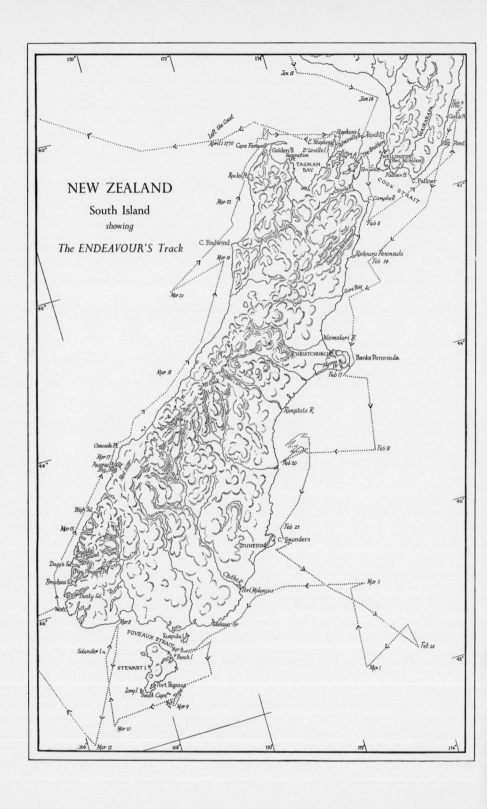

NEW ZEALAND

South Island

showing

The ENDEAVOUR'S Track

suppose, as many fires were seen by which I suppose it to be better inhabited.

11. Calm this morn: 2 Canoes came off and sold us a few fish and some of their fishing hooks made upon a peice of wood, which I beleive serves instead of bait in towing as the mother of Pearl does on the Islanders towing hooks.[1] Light breeze: the land did not look to so much advantage as when we passd it in our passage to the Northward.

12. This morn the seamen all imagind that we had passd the mouth of the streights when to our surprize the great snowy hill which we had seen on the 7th appeard right ahead. At nigh[t] however we were abreast of the streights which was it not for the hill might be dificult to find in Cloudy weather.

13. Calm which gave me an opportunity of going out in the boat and shooting some Albatrosses. The air today was so hazey that we could scarce see the least traces of land and yet the snow on the top of the mountain was very visible.

14. Shooting again, killd *Nectris munda*[2] and *Procellaria saltatrix*.[3] While I was out 4 Canoes came off from the shore which I had not the least suspicion of, as we were farther from the shore than ever canoes had come before. Signals were made but as the ship was right in the wake of the sun none of them were seen by us till we saw the canoes themselves, when we immedi[a]tely pulld for the ship and got aboard I beleive without the Indians ever seing us so much was their attention taken up with looking at the ship; indeed if they had no bad consequence could have ensued as they were so timourous that they hardly dard venture within call of the ship.[4] They stayd but a little while and then went away, not time enough to get ashore before it was dark, for at sunset we saw them not more than half way between us and the shore. I had two or three oppertunities this even of seeing Albatrosses raise from the

---

[1] This was off the point called on the chart Castle Point. The hooks mentioned seem to have been those called by the Maori *pa kahawai*, used for trolling for the Kahawai (*Arripis trutta*). The wood was lined with the iridescent *paua* shell, as a substitute for the mother-of-pearl which Banks had seen in Tahiti.—See Best, *The Maori*, II, p. 424; Buck, pp. 224-5.

[2] The Little or Allied Shearwater, *Puffinus assimilis*; cf. 15 February 1769. Solander does not record this specimen, but mentions one taken on 6 January 1770, which was not recorded by Banks.

[3] The Grey-backed Storm Petrel, *Garrodia nereis*; cf. 2 October 1769.

[4] This was off the small projection of the Kaikoura peninsula, which Cook called 'Lookers on' from the concentrated gaze which these Maoris gave the ship. The name has now been transferred to the mountains behind. Banks's running-head is 'off Cape Campbell'.

Water which they did with great ease; maybe when they are not able to do so (which I have seen) is when they are Gorgd with food.

15. Calm again: at Noon I went out and shot in less than an hour 6 Albatrosses: had the calm continued I beleive I might have shot 60, but a fair breeze of wind came which made me not much regret the Loss of the rest.

16. Land this morn lookd fertile enough. We had now enterd upon a new Island on which few signs of inhabitants were seen: a fire however made us certain that howsoever thin they might be it was not totaly destitute of them. All day the Weather was very clear. In the morn early Mr Gore imagind that he saw land to the S. Eastward.

17. This morn we were close onboard of the land which made in ridges not unlike the South Sea Islands (between the tropicks); the tops of these were bare but in the Valleys was plenty of wood.[1] On the SE part was an opening which had all possible appearance of an excellent harbour;[2] near this on the top of a hill we saw two people setting. Mr Gore notwi[th]standing Yesterdays run was of opinion that what he saw yesterday morning might be land, so he declard on the Quarter deck: on which the Captn who resolvd that nobody should say he had left land behind unsought for orderd the ship to be steerd SE.

18. All yesterday, last night and this morn we stood for Mr Gore's land but not seing any and at noon today finding ourselves in Lat. 45..17 Every body in the ship was convincd, except possibly Mr Gore, that it was impossible to have on the 17th seen as far as where we were now, so we again stood to the Westward. At night it was Haizey and a large shoal of Bottle nosd Porpoises[3] were about the ship, soon after which it began to blow brisk but fair.

19. Last night about one the officer of the watch came down to the captn with the disagreable news of land right ahead and very near, which the wind which blew strong blew directly upon; we were soon however set at ease by the Captn comeing down and telling us that it was only a white cloud. In the morn it blew hard and before noon (to our great surprize) land was indeed in sight very high and far off. Many conjectures were made whether or

---

[1] Banks Peninsula, which Cook called Banks's Island, a fact our modest journal-keeper does not mention. The peninsula is an ancient dead volcano: hence the 'ridges not unlike the South Sea Islands (between the tropicks)'—the 'high islands' which were also volcanic in origin.

[2] Akaroa.

[3] Possibly *Tursiops* sp.

not it was part of the land we had left but that can only be determind by future observations. We had most of us put great confidence in the intelligence we had got of the Indians in the last anchoring place, notwithstanding Tupia had even then warnd us much not to depend upon the people who he said he was sure were liars. We had been told however at different times by the inhabitants of both the towns that the streights realy joind the two seas and that the land to the Southward might be saild round in three or four days: the first we had found to be true and from thence there appeard the highest probability that the other was so likewise, nor could we devise any reason the Indians could have in wishing to deceive us, especialy as we had ask'd the question of two different societies who we had reason to think had not had any intercourse in the intermediate time, which had made us rather stretch the bounds of probability in allowing the practicability of a canoe sailing round the first part of the land we had seen in the time given. There was however between the farthest part of both the lands a space which we had not seen of more than 20 leagues in lengh: supposing that to be a streight the Indians certainly could not see over it, and the countrey they inhabited being very thinly peopled they might at this time be ignorant that there was land beyond it. This much for conjectures, but be it remembred that they are merely such and upon a subject that future observations will most probably clear up.[1]

Tho we saw the land by noon and at that time we had a fresh breeze of Wind, yet it dropping nearly calm soon after we were at night very distant from it. We had however soundings a great way off and the land appeard very high, so that we once more cherishd strong hopes that we had at last compleated our wishes and that this was absolutely a part of the Southern continent; especialy as we had seen a hint thrown out in some books that the Duch, not contented with Tasmans discoveries, had afterwards sent other ships who took the land upon the same lat. as he made it in and followd it to the Southward as high as Lat 64°S.[2]

[1] This paragraph must be read with n. 1 of p. 462, on Topaa's information, in mind. The 'Indians' of Queen Charlotte Sound did not say that the South Island could be circumnavigated in three or four days, but that Arapawa could, which was true enough; and Tupaia's opinion that they were liars may be attributed to a certain unjustified measure of intellectual scorn (after all he was an *arii* and a priest, and the people of the Sound were not high in the economic or educational scale). The space of land unseen was part of the Canterbury coast.

[2] It is true that the Dutch were not content with Tasman's discoveries, but what the origin of the rest of this story was I do not know. I suspect some garbling. We do know there was a copy of de Brosses on board the *Endeavour*, and in de Brosses, I, p. 434 there is the passage: 'Tasman ne fit que reconnaître cette terre sans y descendre. M. l'abbé *Prévot*

20. This morn we were close in with the land which appeard flat, sandy and very barren near the shore but rising into high hills inland. We stood in pretty near to it but saw no signs of inhabitants. W[ind] Southerly all day blowing fresh.

21. Weather rather more moderate but still foul so that we saw again today the same part of the coast as yesterday.

22. Still more moderate but will not let us proceed at all to the southward.

23. At noon today calm which gives us hopes that we may have a fair wind. As we have now been 4 days upon nearly the same part of the coast without seing any signs of inhabitants I think there is no doubt that this part at least is without inhabitants.

24. Fresh breeze of wind and fair so we went along shore briskly but kept so far off from it that no observations could be made: we can only say that we did not see any fires, other signs of people we could not have seen by reason of our distance had they been ever so numerous or conspicuous. In the evening the land ahead inclind a good deal to the West. We were now on board of two parties, one who wishd that the land in sight might, the other that it might not be a continent: myself have always been most firm for the former, tho sorry I am to say that in the ship my party is so small that I firmly beleive that there are no more heartily of it than myself and one poor midshipman, the rest begin to sigh for roast beef.

25. Wind whiffling all round the compass, at night settled at SW and blew hard.[1]

26. Still Blew hard, in some squalls very much so. Thermometer today at noon was 48 which pinchd us a little.

27. Weather a little more moderate but no standing upon legs without the assistance of hands as yet: hope however that the heart of this long-winded gale is broke according to the sea phraze.

rapporte que les Hollandois l'ont depuis visitée en 1654, sans nous apprendre le nom du navigateur, ni les remarques qu'on peut y avoir faites: au reste il ne faut pas s'arrêter â ce qu'il dit au même lieu que cette terre s'étend depuis le 44° jusqu'au 64° degré de latitude, c'est-à-dire presque jusques sous le cercle polaire.' The reference is apparently to the Abbé Prévost's *Histoire Générale des Voyages* (Paris 1746-70), XI, p. 201. The abbé was more important as a novelist than as a historian. The latitude 64° is no doubt founded on the record of Dirk Gerrards or Gerritsz, who was carried south of Tierra del Fuego by tempest in 1599, possibly to the South Shetland Islands, where 'the country was mountainous and covered with snow, looking like Norway and seemed to extend towards the Islands of Salomon'. Banks would find that in Dalrymple's *Account*, p. 2. The South Shetlands, the Solomon Islands and New Zealand *might* all have been part of the same continent, though de Brosses does not think so.

[1] On the 24th and 25th the ship was off Cape Saunders, which Banks mentions in his running-head.

28. Weather a little more moderate so that we got a little respite and our different occupations went on as usual. Opend today a Cask of Cabbage put up by the receipt p. 210 of this Journal[1] which provd most excellently good, scarce at all worse for keeping in my opinion.

MARCH 1770

1. Wind variable and weather sufficiently troublesome.

2. More moderate but a heavy swell from SW made the ship very troublesome.

3. More moderate but SW swell almost as high as ever which gave great spirits to the no Continent party.

4. Pleasant weather and fair wind so that we ran in towards the land. In the morn 1 or 2 Penguins were about us that swam as fast as the ship saild making a noise something like the shreiking of a goose; the[y] seemd to be like *Diomedæa demersa* but whether they were or not I cannot be certain.[2] In the evening ran along shore but kept so far of that little could be seen; a large smoak was however, which at night shewd itself in an immence fire on the side of a hill which we supposd to be set on fire by the natives; for tho this is the only sign of people we have seen yet I think it must be an indisputable proof that there are inhabitants, tho probably very thinly scatterd over the face of this very large countrey.

5. Thick misty weather, the smoak of last nights fire still in sight. A point of land seen this morn[3] which inclind much to the Westward was supposd by the no Continents the end of the land; towards even however it cleard up and we Continents had the pleasure to see more land to the Southward.

6. Very moderate and exceedingly clear. Land seen as far as South so our unbeleivers are almost inclind to think that Continental measures will at last prevail.

---

[1] p. 249 above.

[2] The noise made by these penguins in the water 'something like the shreiking of a goose', seems to identify them as *Megadyptes antipodes*, the Yellow-eyed Penguin. This breeds at Cape Saunders. Another candidate, the Little Blue Penguin, *Eudyptula minor minor*, is less likely to call when swimming on the surface, and the noise it makes is not a loud one. Any of the New Zealand crested penguins, which squawk loudly, might have been seen off the Otago coast. It may therefore be safer not to risk identification. The species mentioned by Banks, now known as the Jackass Penguin, *Spheniscus demersus*, is common on the coast of South Africa, but does not occur in New Zealand waters.

[3] There was no 'point' seen on this day, in the sense of a cape. Cook says, 'At 7 oClock the extremes of the land bore from N38°E to West 6° South. . . . The land appears of a moderate height and not hilly'. The coast of the South Island was turning towards Foveaux Strait.

7. Almost calm so we remaind in the same place nearly all day, to[o] far from the land to see any thing of it at least to depend upon our observations.

8. Little wind and fair, which carried us to the Southward far enough to ascertain that the appearance seen to the Southward in the eve of the 6th was nothing but clouds, tho from its fixd and steady appearance nobody at that time doubted in the least its being land.

9. At the first dawn of day a ledge of rocks were discoverd right to leward and very near us,[1] so we had much reason to be thankfull that the wind in the night had been very gentle otherwise we must in all human probability have ran right among them, at least we could have had no chance of escaping them but by hearing them as there was no moon. The land appeard barren and seemd to end in a point[2] to which the hills gradualy declind — much to the regret of us Continent mongers who could not help thinking this, a great swell from SW and the broken ground without it a pretty sure mark of some remarkable Cape being here. By noon we were pretty near the land which was uncommonly barren; the few flat places we saw seemingly produc'd little or nothing and the rest was all bare rocks, which were amazingly full of Large Veins and patches of some mineral that shone as if it had been polishd or rather lookd as if they were realy pavd with glass; what it was I could not at all guess but it certainly was some mineral and seemd to argue by its immense abundance a countrey abounding in minerals, where if one may judge from the corresponding latitudes of South America in all human probability something very valuable might be found.[3]

10. Blew fresh all day but carried us round the Point to the total demolition of our aerial fabrick calld continent.

11. Fresh gales still and wind that will not let us get to the northward. We stood in with the shore which provd very high and had a most romantick appearance from the immence steepness of the hills, many of which were conical and most had their heads coverd with snow, on their sides and bottoms was however a good deal of wood,

---

[1] The Traps—so called by Cook.
[2] Presumably by this he means South Cape.
[3] According to Cook the ship was four or five leagues off the land, and it seems that what raised Banks's excitement was the granite of the Fraser peaks, rising as high as 1400 feet above the south arm of Port Pegasus, and shining in the morning sun. His deduction of 'a country abounding in minerals', and his reasoning from South America, were not highly scientific.

so much we could see and no more and the wind baulking us would not let us stand nearer the shore than two leagues.

12. Blew hard all day: immense quantities of Albatrosses and other sea birds were seen which we had been without for some time.

13. Wind fair but still blew fresh with very unsetled weather. In the evening we saw a harbour, stood in towards it and found it to have all the appearances of a good one but it was too late to stand near.[1] The countrey about it was high inland tho not so much so as that seen on the 11th as there was no snow on any part of it. Here were veins in the rocks, very large, filld with a whiteish appearance different from what we saw on the 9th.[2] The sides of the hills appeard to be well wooded and the countrey in general as fertile as in so hilly a countrey could be expected, but not the least signs of inhabitants.

14. Stood along shore with a fair breeze and passed 3 or 4 places that had much the appearance of harbours, much to my regret who wishd to examine the mineral appearances from which I had formd great hopes.[3] The countrey rose immediately from the sea side in steep hills which however were tolerably coverd with wood; behind these were another ridge of hills coverd in many places with snow, which from its pure whiteness and smoothness in the morn and the many cracks and intervals that appeard among it at night we conjecturd to be newly falln.

15. Little wind in the morn, towards Even a brisk breeze. The countrey today appeard coverd with steep hills, whose sides were but ill wooded but on their tops was large quantities of snow especialy on the sides that lookd towards the South. We imagind

---

[1] Called by Cook, because of the approach of night, 'duskey Bay', by Banks in his running-head 'duskey Harbour', and now known as Dusky Sound.

[2] Probably this refers to the limestone of the district.

[3] They passed the entrances to Breaksea Sound, Dagg's Sound and Doubtful Sound. Banks, as we can see, was most anxious to get ashore, and in days to come he was to nourish a little grudge against Cook; contrasting him to his discredit with Flinders. But in Cook's day, he wrote to Robert Brown in 1803, natural history was not the 'favourite pursuit' it had since become. 'Cook might have met with reproof for sacrificing a day's fair wind to the accommodation of the Naturalists. Captain Flinders will meet with thanks and praise. . . .'—Smith, *Life of Sir Joseph Banks*, pp. 234-5. Cook, however, was responsible for the voyage, and of Doubtful Sound he remarks (pp. 265-6), 'The Land on each side of the entrance of this harbour riseth almost perpendicular from the Sea to a very considerable height and this was the reason why I did not attempt to go in with the Ship because I saw clearly that no winds could blow there but what was either right in or right out. This is Westerly or Easterly, and it certainly would have been highly imprudent in me to have put into a place where we could not have got out but with a wind that we have lately found does not blow one day in a month: I mention this because there were some on board who wanted me to harbour at any rate without in the least considering either the present or future concequences'. He, rather than Banks, must have our approbation.

that about noon we passd by some considerable river as the sea was almost coverd with leaves, small twigs and blades of Grass.[1] Many Albatrosses about the ship today, we have not been absolutely without them since we came on this side the land.

16. Much snow on the ridges of the high hills, two were however seen on which was little or none: whatever the cause of it might be I could not guess, they were quite bare of trees or any kind of Vegetables and seemd to consist of a mouldering soft stone of the colour of Brick or light red ocre.[2] About noon the countrey near the sea changd much for the better, appearing in broad Valleys clothd with prodigious fine woods out of which came many fine streams of water,[3] but notwithstanding the fineness of the countrey there was not the smallest signs of inhabitants, nor indeed have we seen any since we made this land except the fire on the 4th.

17. Passd today by several large flatts which seemd low. The day in general was foggy so that little could be seen.

18. Immense quantities of snow on the hills new falln which by noon was plainly seen to begin to melt. The countrey near the shore was to appearance fertile and pleasant enough.

19. Hazey weather and foul wind put us all out of spirits.

20. Blew fresh all day with much rain and hazey weather; at night however wind came fair.

21. Hazey: the land was wrap'd in a cloak of fog all day Above which the tops of some hills appeard. At night saw a Phænomenon which I have but seldom seen, at sun set the flying clouds were of almost all colours among which was green very conspicuous tho rather faint colourd.

22. Cloudey mistey and calm all day. Once we were very near the shore on which we saw that there was a most dreadfull surf, occasiond by the S and SW swell which has reignd without intermission ever since we have been upon this side of the land.

23. Fine weather and light breezes.

[1] Cook gives the noon latitude for this day as 44° 47', so that they were about off Bligh Sound. There was no 'considerable' river here, but the debris could quite easily have drifted down the coast from a number of rivers—e.g. the Awarua—with the southerly current.

[2] This must have been the Red Hills range.

[3] The fringe of low land widens out between Awarua Point and Cascade Point and does run into the foothills in valleys; there is one considerable river, the Hope, just south of Cascade Point, and it must have been this, and the streams which made Cook give Cascade Point its name, that so impressed Banks.

24. Just turnd the Westernmost point[1] and stood into the mouth of the streights intending to anchor in the first harbour we could find when an Easterly wind met us right in the teeth, to our no small dissatisfaction as I beleive there has been no other part of the time since we have left Cape Turnagain the first time when such a wind would have been disagreable.

25. Light breezes but wind still at East. The sea is certainly an excellent school for patience.

26. Light breezes and wind fair to our no small comfort. Afternoon we saw a ripple near an Island[2] which had something the appearance of Breakers, but differd from them in the small waves breaking only without any swell or large ones. Our boat sounded upon it but could get no ground; we suppos'd it to be the effect of a strong tide such as we felt in the streights a[s] we passd them. At night came to an anchor in a Bay in some part of which it is probable that Tasman anchord.[3]

27. Went ashore this morn:[4] the countrey hilly but not very high, little or no flats were however to be seen. In the place where we waterd were the remains of two or three Indian houses which clearly had not been inhabited this year at least, but no signs that people had been here since that time. While D[r] Solander and self botanizd Tupia and his boy caught almost a boat load of fish by angling in 2 or 3 fathom water.

28. Raind and blew so hard all today that going ashore was scarce practicable, at least when we had so little hopes of success as our yesterdays search had given us in which we found not one new plant.

29. Raind and blew as hard as yesterday. Myself ill with sickness at stomack and most violent headach, a complaint which in some of our people has been succeeded by a fever. During the day many fish were taken in the ship 90 out of the Cabbin windows alone.

30. Myself quite recoverd except a little soreness at my stomack occasiond I suppose by reaching yesterday. The weather being fair

[1] He means Cape Farewell.
[2] Stephens Island.
[3] This was in Admiralty Bay, off D'Urville Island; but it was nowhere near Tasman's first anchorage, which was in Golden Bay to the west. Rain and haze and the darkness of night left Cook ignorant of the line of the coast between Cape Farewell and Cape Stephens, the northern tip of D'Urville Island, and to the whole wide opening which contains both Golden Bay and Tasman Bay he gave the name of Blind Bay. But Tasman did lie at anchor for four days, 21-25 December 1642, apparently in the shelter formed by Stephens Island, D'Urville Island, and the Rangitoto Islands, which he called *Abel Tasmans Reede* (roadstead). The *Endeavour* was not far from this, but was right inside Admiralty Bay.
[4] i.e. on D'Urville Island.

I resolvd to climb some hill in hopes of meeting some plants in the upper regions as none had been found in the lower. I did with great dificulty, walking for more than a mile in fern higher than my head; success however answerd my wishes and I got 3 plants which we had not before seen.

After coming down I examind the stones which lay on the beach. They shewd evident signs of mineral tendency being full of Veins but I had not the fortune to discover any ore of metal (at least that I knew to be so) in them. As the place we lay in had no bare rocks in its neighbourhood this was the only method I had of even Conjecturing.

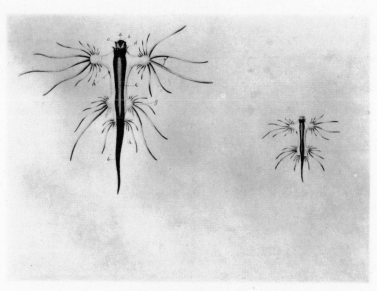

Pl. 1 *a. Munida gregaria* Lobster Krill
b. Glaucus atlanticus
Atlantic Ocean

Pl. 2. *Motacilla flava* Yellow Wagtail

North coast of Africa

Loxia nitens.

Sydney Parkinson pinx ad vivum 1768

Brasil

Pl. 3. *Volatinia jacarina* Blue-black Grassquit

Coast of Brazil

A VIEW in the *ENDEAVOURS* Watering-place in the Bay of *GOOD SUCCESS*

Pl. 4. A View of the *Endeavour's* Watering Place in the Bay of Good Success

Alexander Buchan

Pl. 5. An Indian Town at Terra del Fuego

Alexander Buchan

Pl. 6. *Phaethon rubricauda* Red-tailed Tropic Bird

Pacific Ocean

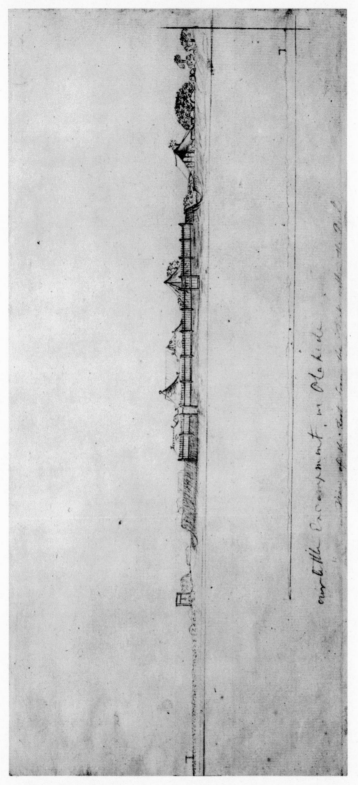

Pl. 7. View of the Fort from the Rock within the Reef

Tahiti

Pl. 8. View of the Coast and Reef in the district of Papavia
Tahiti

Pl. 9 *a*. [Tahiti. A Group of Musicians]
b. [Tahitian Scene]

Anonymous artist

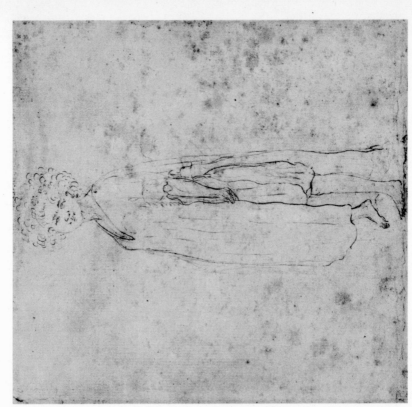

Pl. 10 *a.* Men's Dress *b.* Women's Dress

Tahiti

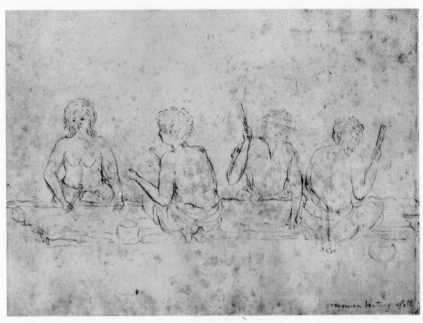

Pl. 11. [Making Tapa]

a. Woman scraping bark   *b*. Women beating cloth

Pl. 12. Sketches of Dancing Girls

Tahiti

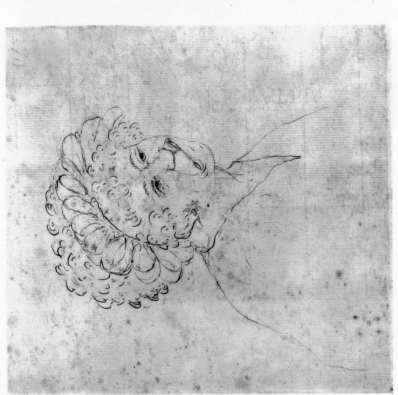

Pl. 13. Distortions of the Mouth used in Dancing

Tahiti

14. A Tupapow in the Island of Otaheite

Tahiti

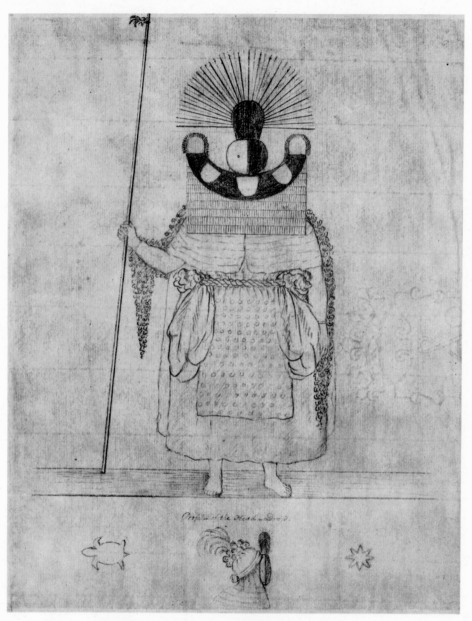

Pl. 15. Dress of the Chief Mourner

Tahiti

A platform for supporting the offerings made to the Dead

Pl. 16. A platform for supporting the offerings made to the Dead
Tahiti

Pl. 17. View in Ulietea

Raiatea

Canoe of Ulietea

Pl. 18. Canoe of Ulietea

Raiatea

Views of the Island of Otaha

Pl. 19. Vessels of the Island of Otaha

Tahaa

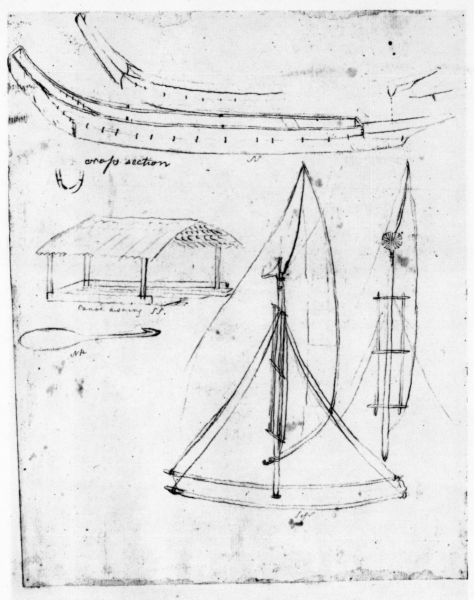

cross section

Canoe awning

Construction of Canoes

Pl. 20. Construction of Canoes

Society Islands

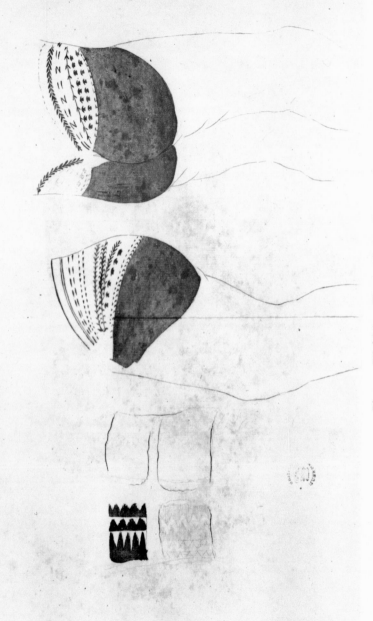

Pl. 21. [Tahitian Tattoo-designs]

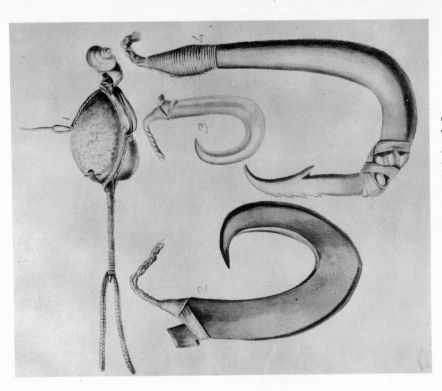

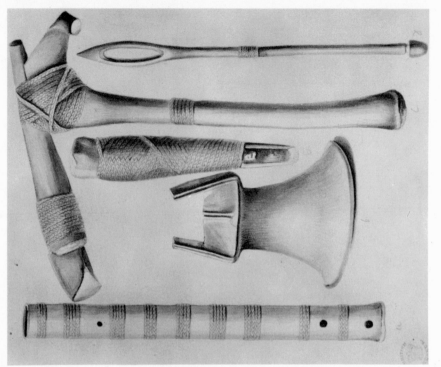

b. [South Sea Artifacts]

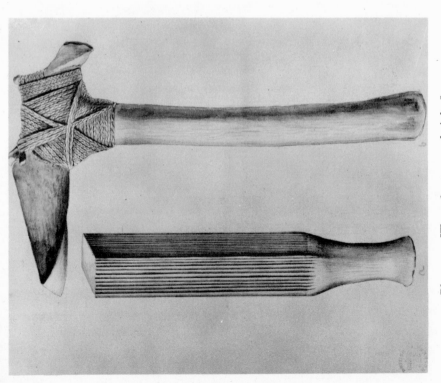

Pl. 23 a. [Tapa-beater and Adze]

Diospyres. lotus. Linn.

Pl. 24. *Diospyros lotus*

Madeira

Clusia dodecapetala.

Sydney Parkinson del. 1767

Pl. 25. *Pereskia* sp.

Brazil

Tillandsia stricta

Sydney Parkinson pinx 1769.

Pl. 26. *Tillandsia stricta*

Brazil

b. Drimys winteri

Tierra del Fuego

Pl. 27 *a. Apium prostratum*

Tierra del Fuego

Arbutus rigida.

Sydney Parkinson pinx 1769.

Pl. 28. *Pernettya mucronata*

Tierra del Fuego

Pl. 29. *Crataeva religiosa*

Tahiti

Gardenia, florida.

Pl. 30. *Gardenia taitensis* Tiare

Tahiti

Jasminum didymum.

Sydney Parkinson pinx.t 769.

Pl. 31. *Jasminum didymum* Tafifi

Tahiti

Pl. 32. *Artocarpus communis*   Uru or Breadfruit

Tahiti

b. *Cordia subcordata* Tou

Tahiti

Pl. 33 *a. Ficus tinctoria* Mati

Tahiti

b. *Morinda citrifolia* Nono
Huahine

Pl. 34 a. *Calophyllum inophyllum* Tamanu
Tahiti

Chailea Sacra.

Pl. 35. *Tacca leontopetaloides* Pia

Raiatea

Piper. inebrians.
Ulhietea

Sydney Parkinson pins 769

Pl. 36. *Piper methysticum* Ava

Raiatea

Convolvulus peltatus.

Pl. 37. *Merremia peltata*

Raiatea

Pl. 38. *Cyanoramphus zealandicus* Red-rumped Parrot
Tahiti

Pl. 39. *Vini peruviana* Vini or Tahitian Blue Lory

Tahiti

Pl. 40 *a. Acanthocybium solandri*

b. Plectorhincus orientalis Tairifa

Tahiti